Cuba

CUBA
Between Reform and Revolution

Louis A. Pérez, Jr. *1943-*

New York   Oxford
Oxford University Press
1988

972.91
p438

A-1

Oxford University Press

Oxford   New York   Toronto
Delhi   Bombay   Calcutta   Madras   Karachi
Petaling Jaya   Singapore   Hong Kong   Tokyo
Nairobi   Dar es Salaam   Cape Town
Melbourne   Auckland
and associated companies in
Berlin   Ibadan

Library of Congress Cataloging-in-Publication Data
Pérez, Louis A., 1943–
Cuba: between reform and revolution / Louis A. Pérez, Jr.
p. cm.   Bibliography: p.   Includes index.
ISBN 0-19-504586-6
ISBN 0-19-504587-4
1. Cuba—History. 2. Nationalism—Cuba—History. I. Title.
F1776.P46   1988   972.91—dc19   87-34892   CIP

9 8 7 6 5 4 3 2 1

Printed in the United States of America
on acid-free paper

To the friends who gather at Café Don José:
For all the years of Friday afternoons

Preface and Acknowledgments

I

It happened quite suddenly, and so quickly, all quite improbably: a revolution overthrew a repressive regime, to the general approval and acclaim of all. Within the space of twenty-four months, Cuba had been transformed into the first Marxist-Leninist state in the Western Hemisphere and the first New World nation to align itself totally and unabashedly with the Soviet Union—all this occurring ninety miles from the United States, in a region traditionally secure as a North American sphere of influence, in a country historically secure as a North American client state.

And the question arose immediately, and persisted subsequently: why? "It is yet too early to say with finality," wrote Russell H. Fitzgibbon in 1961, "just why a revolution of the nature and extent of that in Cuba should have come to that country rather than to any of half a dozen others in Latin America." Stanislav Andreski formulated the question in two parts: "Why did Castro's rebellion break out and why did it succeed?" Ramón E. Ruiz concluded that "no one can say precisely why a radical upheaval engulfed the island in 1959." John Fagg asked rhetorically: "How had such a dismaying situation come about?" Robert Freeman Smith asked: "What happened in Cuba?" In similar terms, Frank Tannenbaum mused in 1969: "Just why this profound tragedy has come to afflict the Cuban people . . . will always remain a matter of dispute."

The developments that transformed Cuba into a singular New World phenomenon were without precedent, without parallel. But they were not without an internal logic, the most salient elements of which served to confirm the essential historicity of the Cuban revolutionary experience. The proposition of revolution was not new. Its antecedents reached deep and ran wide through the Cuban past, back to the very sources of Cuban nationality. Whether in the name of liberty, or equality, or justice, Cubans of diverse origins—men and women, people of color, poor whites, rich whites—on one occasion or another, often in concert but just as often in conflict, mobilized to challenge the premise and practice of iniquitous authority. These themes dominate Cuban history, and recur with remarkable regularity, slightly modified from time to time, to be sure, with different emphases here and there. In the main, however, the basic issues shaping the course of Cuban history have remained fundamentally fixed and firm.

Constant too has been the ideological duality that has characterized competing versions of *cubanidad*—between, on one hand, liberal constructs of *patria* and, on the other, radical formulations of nationality. This dualism has been one of the principal sources of tension in Cuban history, for it has served to give content and context to rival versions of liberty, and equality, and justice. In its principal derivative embodiments, the dichotomy determined the form and function of Cuban mobilization—between politics and arms, class and mass, reform and revolution.

This dualism, in turn, was itself acted upon and acted out within a larger context of successive dependent relations with more powerful patron states—where indeed the very terms of those relationships were often at the source of the conflict. The ideal of self-determination, in all its historic manifestations—autonomy, self-government, independence, and sovereignty—has loomed large over the national experience. Indeed, much of Cuban history was shaped by the circumstances under which the island was integrated into hegemonial relationships, the means by which it adjusted to dependent relations, and its efforts to revise the terms of dependency.

These circumstances, further, served to impede the development of autonomous political structures, and in turn reduced considerably the range of responses available to Cubans to resolve internal differences. Rarely were political disputes settled wholly among Cubans, entirely on their own terms, completely according to their own needs. Political elites were typically linked to and dependent upon the support of outside powers, in whose behalf they often functioned and upon whose patronage they frequently depended. A political challenge to local powerholders represented at one and the same time a challenge to the foreign powers that backed them. The affirmation of self-government was potentially no less an act of self-determination. The issue of nationalism, hence, became inseparable from the quesiton of political change. Under certain circumstances, nationalism in Cuba could serve as a social value of irresistible appeal, unifying disparate and otherwise incompatible class interests and into which was subsumed the expectation of increased opportunity for social mobility, improved economic status, and greater political participation. Nationalism could serve as an agent of political change, as well as be its effect. In either case, Cuban nationalism emerged out of the dissident sectors of the body politic, who in the pursuit of political change were often also obliged to confront the question of nationality in a larger context of shifting international relations. This reality defined the character of the political exchange and the context of social change. It influenced the way Cubans looked at themselves and at the world, who was seen as a possible adversary or as perceived as a potential ally.

Cuba passed successively from colonial status under Spain to a client role with the United States to dependency under the Soviet Union. These relationships, each at its own turn, each in its own way, penetrated Cuban society deeply. Each relied on and underwrote the ascendancy of quite different dominant classes; each produced a profound realignment in the internal balance of social forces. All exercised a decisive influence on Cuban economic policy, political institutions, state structures, and international relations.

But these influences, however pervasive, were not total. Cubans learned to exploit the limits of hegemony to their advantage and with considerable skill and success. They revealed consistently a particular genius and vast resourcefulness in creating spheres of autonomy within the constraints of hegemonial relationships and through which they pursued interests that were singularly and substantively Cuban.

The influence of sugar, on the other hand, was pervasive and total. It summoned into existence a plantation economy and the attending banes of monoculture, chattel slavery, and large-scale production for export. The social composition of the Cuban population was permanently changed. Sugar shaped property relations, class structures, land tenure forms, labor systems, the process of capital accumulation, the pattern of investment, the priorities of domestic policies, the course and content of Cuban trade and commerce, and the conduct of Cuban foreign relations. In the end, sugar shaped the national character.

But if the history of Cuba is, as Fernando Ortiz was fond of saying, the history of sugar, it is also a chronicle of a people locked in relentless struggle against the by-products of their history: against slavery and racism, against inequality and injustice, against uncertainty and insecurity. Against, above all, the conditions that made Cuba peculiarly vulnerable to the dictates of the market and the metropolis and out of which was forged Cuban nationality. These elements have served as fixed correlates of the Cuban national experience, past and present.

II

In the course of completing this study, I have drawn heavily on the knowledge, talents, and wisdom of others. Over nearly two decades of research on Cuban history, I have benefited from the courtesy and attention of the professional staffs of a number of libraries and archives, including the Library of Congress, the Biblioteca Nacional "José Martí," the New York Public Library, the University of Florida Library, the Center for Cuban Studies, the National Archives in Washington, and the Archivo Nacional in Havana. Most of all, I am grateful to the staff and personnel of the University of South Florida Library for years of support and assistance. If it be not invidious to limit this acknowledgement, the staff of one department in particular should be mentioned. The personnel in the inter-library loan office, including Jana S. Futch, Marykay Hartung, Cheryl D. Ruppert, Monica Metz-Wiseman, and Gale V. Vaccaro, provided indispensable assistance through the course of the research and writing of this book.

It is necessary also to acknowledge the enormity of my debt to Cecile L. Pulin. From the first draft of the first chapter, and for weeks and months thereafter, without stop, she presided over the preparation of the manuscript. I do not dare to think at what stage this study would be were it not for the constancy of her support.

I owe a great deal also to Sylvia E. Wood, who assisted with proofreading, reviewed the tables, and otherwise tied up all loose ends associated with the final preparation of the completed draft. In this regard, I am also grateful to Nita C. Desai for her assistance with the completion of early drafts of the manuscript. Whatever else was required during the preparation and completion of manuscript was done by Peggy Cornett. She has been an indefatigable collaborator over the years, resolving crises as they occurred and, more important, preventing many more from occurring at all.

I owe an enormous debt of gratitude to colleagues who gave of their time to read the manuscript in the course of its writing. They are mainly friends, too, for upon whom else would one inflict the unremunerated task of reading an unfinished manuscript, at various stages of writing, and sometimes more than once? Nancy M. White read an early version of the first chapter and guided me in my efforts to understand something of pre-Columbian Cuba. She made many helpful suggestions, about both the text and my assumptions, and as a result the former was modified immediately and the latter changed permanently. Jules R. Benjamin provided thoughtful comments on the material dealing with post-revolutionary Cuba. I have benefited greatly from his own research and very much appreciate his critical perspectives on mine. Jorge I. Domínguez read the final draft of the later chapters and responded with helpful and constructive comments, for which I am most appreciative. I am grateful also to Thomas P. Dilkes, whose observations were helpful in the completion of the last several chapters. To Rebecca J. Scott my appreciation for her efforts in my behalf is heartfelt. Her willingness to respond so openly, so fully, and in such detail, with enthusiasm, to the formulations that follow has left me deeply in her debt. This has been an exhilarating collaboration, demonstrating, among other things, that divergent styles and interests are indeed more than compatible. I am only too conscious of the inadequacy of an acknowledgement of a friend who gave unstintingly to this project, and in the process influenced much of what follows. The manuscript also benefited from a critical and sympathetic reading by Nancy A. Hewitt. She made detailed comments on the text and raised thoughtful questions about the interpretations. As a non-specialist in Cuban history she was in a unique position to concentrate almost entirely on the internal logic of the narrative and the assumptions upon which it rested. In this instance, as so often in the past, I am grateful for the constancy of her collaboration and companionship. Marifeli Pérez-Stable read the chapters dealing with the twentieth century, and suggested improvements throughout the text. But the value of her contribution to the completion of this book goes beyond the comments and criticisms written along the margins of the typescript. Through hours of conversation, over weeks and months, on matters substantive and anecdotal, personal and professional, she has given me new understanding of the meaning of the Cuban revolution. What has made her insights so compelling is that her commitment is not uncritical and her understanding of what is desirable is tempered by an appreciation of what is possible. Going up and down in elevators and over more than one *café con leche,* my appreciation of the value of her friendship has deepened. Finally, a special acknowledgment of appreciation to Stephanie Sakson-Ford at Oxford University Press, who made innumerable suggestions, and as many queries, all of which helped to improve the narrative and sharpen the analysis.

It becomes necessary at this point to acknowledge that as hard as friends and colleagues tried to eliminate propositions with which they did not agree, and for reasons that I understood, I did not heed their counsel every time. I want to assure them, however, that their suggestions were indeed considered each time. We simply disagreed, but that disagreement has helped to give this book the form it has taken. I can only hope that they will find the final product worthy of the assistance they so generously provided. It is understood that their sustained efforts in my behalf free them of any responsibility for particular statements and arguments that I have stubbornly refused to modify. And, of course, their generosity does not make them in any way responsible for whatever errors persist on the following pages.

This book is dedicated to a special group of friends who, over many years, and through many ups and downs, has been at the center of what has made the Department of History at the University of South Florida so special to me. I am especially mindful of the largest debt of all, that which accrues from receiving the unconditional affection and constant support of friends. And for this, I am enormously grateful to Thomas P. Dilkes, Nancy A. Hewitt, Robert and Joèle Ingalls, Georg and Esther Kleine, Steven F. Lawson, Brenda and G. Kelly Tipps.

And a final word to my daughters, Amara and Maya, as they move through these years of their adolescence: they should know that they have become everything that I could have hoped for—and more.

Tampa, Florida   L.A.P.
January 1988

Contents

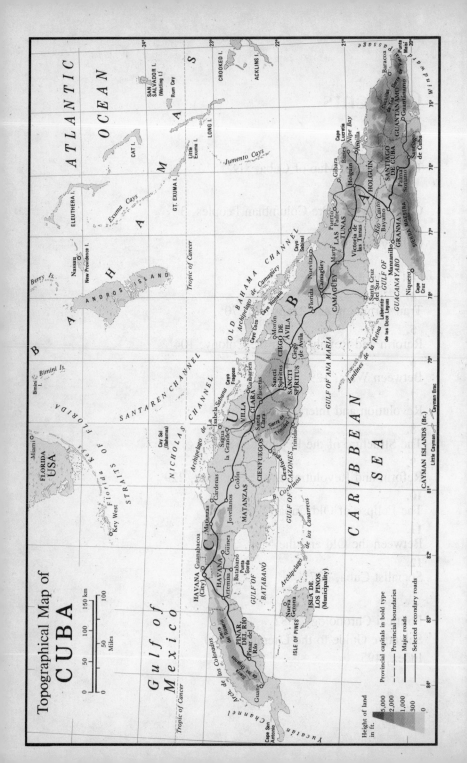

Cuba

Que tenga sabor a Cuba,
Que tenga sabor a son.

—Orquesta Aragón

Geography and
Pre-Columbian Peoples

1

I

Cuba is the largest and western-most island of the Antillean archipelago, extending at a slight northwest-southeast bearing between 74° to 85° west longitude and 19°40' to 23°30' north latitude. The coordinates establish more than the island's location—they establish too the context of its history. Geographic considerations and strategic calculations converged in fateful fashion. Cuba is situated at the key approaches to the Atlantic Ocean, the Gulf of Mexico, and the Caribbean Sea—90 miles south of the Florida Keys, 130 miles east of the Yucatán Peninsula, and 40 miles west of Haiti: the point at which the vital sea lanes of the Spanish New World empire intersected. The island dominated the maritime approaches into the Gulf from the Atlantic through the Florida Straits to the north and from the Caribbean through the Yucatán Channel to the west. Its position west of the Windward Passage placed the island along one of the principal maritime passages in and out of the Caribbean. Spain was not slow to recognize the implications of Cuba's location, and thus officially designated the island as "Fortress of the Indies" and "Key to the New World." One of the political imperatives in the New World balance of power was established early and endured long: control of Cuba was vital for the control of the New World.

II

Cuba extends 750 miles in length, from Punta del Quemado in the east to Cabo San Antonio in the west. The island rests upon a submarine platform considerably larger than the surface area itself. Over this platform the waters are comparatively shallow and coral growth is extensive. What appears as the largest island in the West Indian chain is, in fact, an

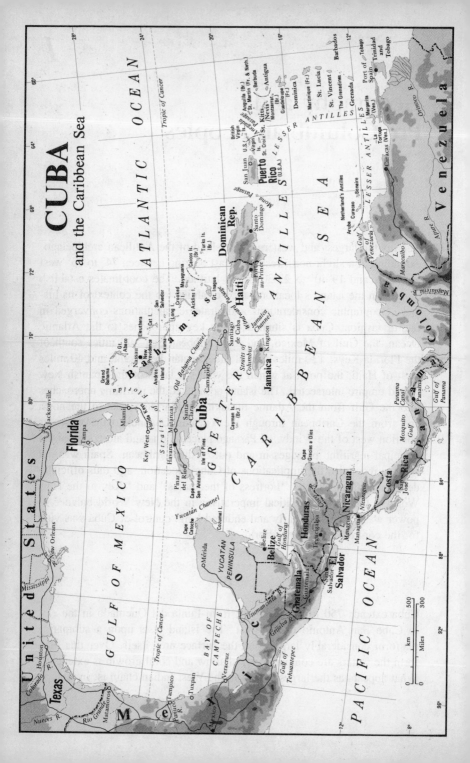

archipelago system unto itself. The main island is surrounded by more than 1600 coastal keys and islets, almost all of which are distributed in four offshore archipelago groupings. The Archipelago de los Colorados, the smallest chain with an estimated 70 keys, is located off the north coast of Pinar del Río province. The Archipelago de Sabana-Camagüey extends a distance of nearly 250 miles in length, parallel to the north coast of the provinces of Matanzas, Las Villas, and Camagüey, and includes more than 400 keys and islets. The Archipelago de los Canarreos lies along the south coast of Pinar del Río, Havana, and Matanzas, and numbers 350 isles, the largest of which is the Isle of Pines (Isle of Youth). The Archipelago de los Jardines de la Reina, accounting for an estimated 400 small islands, stretches along the south coast of Las Villas and Camagüey.

The total land mass of the Cuban archipelago measures more than 46,000 square miles. The coastline of the main island extends approximately 2500 miles in length. At its widest point, the island measures 124 miles; at its narrowest point, it barely reaches 22 miles.

Significant differences characterize each coast. The south coast between Cabo Cruz and Cabo Maisí in the east is ringed with mountains that rise abruptly from the water to altitudes of thousands of feet. Much of the southern shoreline in the west consists of a band of low marshland, broken up into hundreds of coral keys and mangrove islands, and widening west of Cienfuegos into the vast Zapata swamp, an expanse of 1800 square miles of marshland. The north coast consists of a highland belt of mountains and foothills. In the west the coast is generally low, with bluffs reaching 100 feet in Pinar del Río and rising gradually eastward.

The island is abundantly endowed with natural harbors. More than 200 harbors, bays, and inlets indent the shoreline. The larger ones are of the bottleneck variety with narrow entrances that expand into spacious, sheltered, deepwater anchorages. Most are located in the north, and include the harbors of Bahía Honda, Cabañas, Mariel, Havana, Nuevitas, Manatí, Puerto Padre, Gibara, Banes, and Antilla. Southern pouch-shaped ports include Guantánamo, Santiago de Cuba, and Cienfuegos. The two largest open ports are Matanzas and Cárdenas on the north coast.

III

The island topography is characterized by diversity. Approximately 35 percent of the total land mass is made up of three extensive mountain systems: the Sierra Maestra, the Guamuhaya (Escambray), and the Guaniguanico. The Sierra Maestra in southeast Oriente is the loftiest, maximum elevation at Pico Turquino (6500 feet) and stretching along the southeast coast for a distance of nearly 150 miles between Cabo Cruz and Guantánamo. East of Guantánamo, a subsidiary mountain network forms a maze of peaks and sharp ridges *(cuchillas),* deeply dissected by streams, and rising from the water's edge like steps along the south coast to Maisí and north to Baracoa. The system is made up of several parallel chains: the Gran Piedra, the Sierra de Boniato, the Sierra de Puerto Pelado, and the Sierra de Santa María de Loreto. With the exception of the horseshoe-shaped district of the Guantánamo valley, the eastern half of Oriente province is dominated by lesser mountain ranges, including the Sierra de Nipe (3700 feet), the Sierra del Cristal (4050 feet), the Sierra del Purial (3300 feet), and the Sierra de Imías (3900 feet).

The Guamuhaya mountain group extends along the south-central coast in Las Villas province. The chain consists of two smaller systems divided by the Agabama river: the Sierra de Trinidad (3800 feet) in the west and the Sierra de Sancti Spíritus (2800 feet) to the east.

The western-most mountain system is the Guaniguanico group, located in Pinar del Río province. This range is made up of the Sierra del Rosario (2300 feet) and the Sierra de los Organos (2000 feet), originating in western Havana province and continuing westward through the center of Pinar del Río to the western end of the island.

The three mountain ranges are set off from each other by two extensive plains that account for 65 percent of the entire island surface area and nearly 95 percent of the total population. The soil is rich and varied, allowing for diverse land usage. The more than one hundred different types of Cuban soils are categorized into five larger groupings. The productive and extensive clay soils are found across the island. Classified into scores of subdivisions according to texture, color, consistency, chemical features, drainage, and origin of material, the ubiquitous Cuban clay soils are highly prized for crop production and durability under cultivation. The fertile clay soils are characterized by good drainage and resistance to erosion and exhaustion. These soils are widely distributed through the plains of Matanzas and Camagüey, the undulating tableland in north-western Oriente, the Las Villas plains, the Trinidad plateau, and the Pinar del Río coastal plains. The savannah terrain consists of dry soils of relatively shallow depths. The flat undulating lands support vast stretches of grassland broken up by intermittent shrubbery, sparsely scattered trees, and grasses, ideal for grazing, and are found most extensively in northern Camagüey, southeast Holguín, south of Alto Cedro, the Trinidad plains, and the Manzanillo-Cabo Cruz coastal plain. Forest zones are located on slopes of the principal mountain systems of the island. Extensive pine forests, once extending across fully the western half of the island, today cover less than 5 percent of the national territory. Swamp soils are found along the low coastal zones and offshore keys, mainly water-soaked clay covered with mangrove, sawgrass, and palms. The swamp regions have served as the site of limited grazing, some charcoal production, and marginal agriculture.

The island fluvial network is determined by the relief corresponding to the three mountain regions. Almost all of the two hundred rivers originate in the interior. Due to its elongated narrow shape, the island has two principal watersheds—north and south. Water levels rise significantly during the summer rainy season, and seasonal flooding is not uncommon. Rivers are generally short, narrow, and shallow; few inland waterways are navigable for any great distances. Some have extensive estuaries that facilitate limited inland navigation. Rivers are most numerous in Oriente province and are fewest in Havana. The longest and most navigable rivers are the Cauto in Oriente, flowing parallel to the Sierra Maestra on the north into the Gulf of Guacanayabo, and Sagua la Grande, out of the Sierra del Escambray flowing north into the port of La Isabela. Seven subterranean river basins serve as the source of numerous surface waterways. Drainage in many areas is carried off through these subterranean networks, contributing to the development of extensive cave systems. Rivers often flow at the surface, disappear underground, and re-emerge at another point. Lakes are few and small.

Climate varies only slightly in Cuba, the principal distinctions being found between east and west and coastal and inland. The combination of prevailing trade winds (northeast in the summer and southeast in the winter), the warm waters of the Gulf Stream, and the resulting sea breezes serve to provide Cuba with a moderate and stable climate. That the long axis of the island extends east and west, and not north and south, also contributes to uniformity of temperature. Annual average temperature varies by ten degrees; the average winter low is 70°F and the summer high is almost 81°F. Few parts of Cuba are deficient in moisture. The rainy season, between May and October, is the period in which Cuba receives three-quarters of its total annual precipitation. Maximum rainfall is registered in April and June. Precipitation during the rainy season averages 55 to 60 inches annually; during the dry season 16 to 20 inches. Rainfall varies greatly according to locality. Cuba's annual rainfall (54 inches) is slightly less on the north coast than on the south, greater in the interior than along the coasts, and more in the west than in the east. The region of highest precipitation is the Sierra de los Organos in Pinar del Río (more than 70 inches), the lowest is Guantánamo (less than 29 inches). The distribution and quantity of precipitation between May and October is also influenced by the equatorial low-pressure zone, producing during the rainy season heavy and often severe thunderstorms *(turbonadas)*.

Cuba's bountiful agricultural resources are derived from the fertility and expanse of arable land, which makes up more than half of the island. Other areas are used for coffee, cocoa, and plantain cultivation. Much of the nonarable land is suitable for grazing.

The principal limitations on Cuban resources derive from topography and climate. That virtually all the island's arable land is at sea level and, further, that it extends west to east, means that the island lacks the climate necessary to produce non-tropical crops. This obliges Cuba to import temperate-zone products.

The island is subject to the ravages of two recurring natural phenomena: hurricanes and earthquakes. Hurricanes in particular have played a decisive role in shaping the course of Cuban history. Since 1498, when the first recorded storm almost destroyed the Columbus fleet, Cuba has experienced more than 150 hurricanes. A storm in 1768 all but leveled Havana. In 1791, hurricane flooding destroyed the entire cattle stock in Havana. Cienfuegos was almost destroyed by a storm in 1825. A succession of hurricanes in 1841, 1844, and 1846 contributed to the eventual collapse of Cuban coffee production. A storm in 1882 destroyed Pinar del Río; in 1932 one destroyed the town of Santa Cruz del Sur on the south coast of Camagüey and caused the death of more than three thousand residents. It was during the inspection of hurricane damage in September 1933 that President Carlos Manuel de Céspedes was ousted from office by an army coup. The winds of hurricane "Flora" in 1963 lashed eastern Cuba at more than 110 miles per hour, causing the loss of 4200 lives, the destruction of 30,000 dwellings, and an estimated $500 million of property damage. In 1985, hurricane "Kate" inflicted extensive damage on the sugar crop.

The island experiences occasional seismic activity, most frequently and most severely along the south coast of Oriente province. More than two hundred tremors have been recorded since the sixteenth century. The most serious earthquakes occurred in 1551, 1675, 1678, 1693, 1766, 1852, and 1932, all in southeastern Oriente and all causing extensive damage.

IV

The island can be divided into four major geographical sub-regions, differentiated by distinctive features and corresponding generally to the historic provincial organization of the island: Occidente, Las Villas, Camagüey, and Oriente. Boundaries are delineated variously by mountains, rivers, and plains, which in turn serve further to define the relationship between the inhabitants and the land in the form of demographic patterns, economic activity, and social organization.

First among the four regions is the Occidente, the largest single sub-region of Cuba, and arguably the most diverse if not the most developed. It includes the provinces of Pinar del Río, Havana, and Matanzas, as well as the capital of Havana, and accounts for nearly 30 percent of the national territory and more than 40 percent of the total population. The sub-region stretches from Pinar del Río (Cabo San Antonio) in the west to Las Villas (Santa Clara) in the east and encompasses the Guaniguanico mountain system and the vast stretches of plains that run parallel to both coasts. Principal economic activities include agriculture, largely sugar and tobacco, and industry, manufacture, and commerce based in Havana.

The sub-region of Las Villas extends east from the city of Santa Clara to Morón on the north through Júcaro in the south and includes almost all of the province of Las Villas and portions of western Camagüey. The sub-region accounts for approximately one-fifth of the island area and the same proportion of the total population. Las Villas is dominated by the Guamuhaya mountain system along the southern coastal region, and the tableland along the north. A vast network of extensive valleys and gentle plateau slopes allow for a diversity of agricultural activity, including sugar, coffee, tobacco, and ranching.

The third sub-region of Camagüey is contained almost entirely within the boundaries of the province and into northwestern Oriente through

Nipe Bay. It represents approximately 25 percent of the national territory and almost 20 percent of the total population, and is given principally to sugar production and ranching.

The fourth geographic sub-region is Oriente. It includes about one-quarter of the national territory and approximately one-fifth of the total population. The region is about equally divided between mountains and relatively low country. The most mountainous region of the island, Oriente also has the most diversified economy, ranging from sugar production to coffee cultivation, cattle ranching, mining, and lesser agricultural activity, including cacao, bananas, and citrus.

Each region has developed as a distinct historico-economic entity as a result of the interplay of unique elements of local topography, fluvial systems, access to port facilities, and in response to internal expansion and world market forces. Tobacco production flourished in the intermontane valleys of the west, along the network of rivers, and in proximity to the principal export outlet of Havana. Small tobacco farmers (*vegueros*) dominated the region, contributing to the development of a robust local economy based on small-scale commercial agriculture, organized around an independent class of farmers, largely white, based principally on wage and/or family labor. Sugar production, on the other hand, took hold on the Havana-Matanzas plains along the north coast and the plateau regions of Cienfuegos/Sancti Spíritus/Trinidad in the south, giving rise to large-scale agricultural production based on a plantation economy dependent on vast capital resources and slave labor. The flatness of the rich sugar regions allowed for the rapid and comparatively easy expansion of railroads, which in turn facilitated the expansion of cultivation and the modernization of production. The extensive undulating plains stretching across Camagüey and into Tunas, Holguín, and the Cauto valley in Oriente provided the open savannahs for large-scale cattle ranching. Further south, along the eastern labyrinthine valleys, ravines, and the network of mountains and foothills, diversified agriculture developed, based on small-scale farming of coffee, citrus, cacao, and bananas, and large-scale sugar production, ranching, and mining.

Geographic factors have served as important correlates of Cuban economic history. The elongated shape of the island provided partial compensation for the lack of many navigable rivers. Few parts of the interior were distant from adequate port facilities. The expansion of sugar production from west to east was in large measure made possible by the availability of spacious and protected harbor facilities near new agricultural zones in the interior. The existence of so many harbors across the island meant that no sugar estate was more than fifty miles from a port. Cuba possessed harbor facilities sufficient to accommodate the continued expansion of sugar production, thereby preventing port congestion that could have otherwise impeded the development of an export economy. By the early twentieth century, no less than twenty ports were in the service of sugar exports. These developments, in turn, fostered the growth of urban centers in response to the needs of the expanding export economy. Indeed, many of Cuba's principal population centers, including Havana, Santiago de Cuba, Matanzas, and Cienfuegos, developed around natural harbors. As a result of these circumstances, overland routes of travel tended to lead from the interior outward to the nearest or most accessible port, to the relative neglect of transportation connections between interior population centers.

Coastal geography influenced Cuban development in other ways. Hundreds of miles of unguarded and indented coastal lines, more than 1600 uninhabited offshore keys and islets, and areas of impenetrable coastal swamps created ideal conditions for a flourishing contraband economy during much of the colonial period. "No country in the world," observed Robert Francis Jameson during his visit to Cuba in 1820, "has coasts so well calculated for smuggling as the island of Cuba." This state of affairs was especially pronounced in the east, where the offshore archipelago maze and the multitude of remote coastal inlets in the south together with distance from authorities in Havana and inadequate supplies from the metropolis created both opportunity and necessity for smuggling and illicit trade. Southeastern Cuba operated in an economic universe separate and distinct from the rest of the island, where the local economy was integrated into and organized around illicit production for illegal trade with Jamaica and St. Domingue.

East and west were differentiated in other ways. The barriers of vast mountain chains, together with prevailing winds and ocean currents and distance from the trans-Atlantic maritime routes, served to isolate and insulate the east from the rest of the island. Oriente appeared too remote, the terrain too inhospitable, to justify large-scale settlement and extensive commercial exploitation. Eastern Cuba remained underpopulated and undeveloped. Oriente was Cuba's frontier: broken land, irregular, tranversed and intersected by countless intermontane valleys. It was also fertile land, bountiful for anyone willing to work at making it productive. Most of all, it was available land, and long after the sugar *hacienda* had appropriated most of the land in the west, land remained available in the east. The impenetrable mountain fastness of Oriente provided haven and sanctuary to untold numbers of runaway African slaves *(cimarrones)* and encouraged the rise of scores of free Afro-Cuban communities. The province attracted outcasts and outsiders of all types, the downtrodden and underdogs, fugitives and slaves, who lost themselves deep in the vast and varied expanses of forests, mountains, and valleys of the eastern interior, there to form the basis of communities of small independent peasants. The terrain held little appeal to most immigrants, however, who settled the more felicitous and economically promising zones of the west. Thus it was that Oriente developed as perhaps the most Cuban region of all of Cuba, less susceptible to outside influences, more committed to ways local and traditional. These factors contributed to making Oriente the source and site of recurring revolutionary stirrings. It was distant from authority, its communities were often inaccessible to authorities, and its residents were typically scornful of authority. It was in Oriente that Cuba's principal revolutionary struggles originated, beginning with the wars for independence in the nineteenth century through the rebellion led by Fidel Castro in the 1950s.

The island at large was neither isolated nor insulated. Cuba's geographic location at the crossroads of the New World shipping lanes subjected the island to repeated attack by rival world powers. The struggle for mastery over the Caribbean was first and foremost a struggle for control of Cuba, and over the centuries the island bore the brunt of successive international conflicts. The island was invaded, its cities attacked and plundered, its coastal settlements raided, and maritime traffic harassed. The French seized towns and sacked coastal villages in the sixteenth century. Dutch depredations followed in the seventeenth century. The English occupied Havana in the eighteenth century. The United States invaded and occupied the island in 1898. After the Cuban revolution in 1959, the island was subjected to a new round of invasion, depredations, and harassment.

Cuban insularity has influenced the course of national history in a number of important ways. It contributed to the survival of Spanish rule at the time of the mainland wars for independence. It spared Cuba from the border disputes and national wars that afflicted other Latin American countries in the nineteenth and twentieth century. Not for unrelated reasons, insularity also played an important part in the consolidation of the Cuban revolution after 1959. That Cuba did not share a common border with another country meant that counter-revolutionary forces could not launch military attacks behind the security of international boundaries. Operations were limited to the more hazardous sea and air missions that were, in turn, increasingly vulnerable to improved Cuban coastal and air defense systems.

Insularity was not, however, sufficient to shield Cuba from the effects of proximity to the United States. The strategic factors that made Cuba important to Spain in the sixteenth century also made Cuba important to the United States in the nineteenth. The acquisition of Louisiana (1803) and Florida (1819) gave a new commercial and strategic value to the Gulf shipping lanes. The opening of the Panama Canal nearly one hundred years later increased the strategic importance of the Caribbean. The defense of both was understood to require the control of Cuba. Indeed, for the better part of the nineteenth and well into the twentieth century, North American policy was based on the proposition that the island was the advance point in the defense of the southern flank of the United States.

Cuba's geographic nearness to the United States also had important economic consequences. The United States offered a ready market for Cuban exports and, increasingly through the nineteenth century, the only market capable of absorbing Cuba's expanding sugar production. For Cuban producers and consumers alike, nearness to the United States meant low transportation costs over short distances, reasonably fast delivery, and readily available supplies—all of which translated into comparatively cheaper prices. The commercial logic of geography was inexorable, and in the nineteenth and twentieth centuries the economic ties between the two countries drew closer. North American investments in Cuba rose from $50 million at the end of the nineteenth century to $1.3 billion during the 1920s. By the mid-twentieth century, Cuba operated almost entirely within the framework of the economic system of the United States.

This economic nexus was accompanied by comparable cultural ties, and over time Cubans passed under the growing influence of things and trends North American. As early as June 1931, U.S. Ambassador Harry F. Guggenheim could report:

> There is, first of all, the English language which has spread to such an extent in Cuba that most Cuban businessmen of standing have learned to speak it; the American press exercises a very great influence on the Cuban press—two press associations, the United Press and the Associated Press, supply the Cuban papers with a large part of their foreign news; American movies, American sports, particularly baseball, Amer-

ican dance music, American victrola records and last, but by no means
least, American radio and broadcasting programs have made a very definite impression on the Cuban mind.

These influences expanded in the following decades, if only because
telecommunications improved, travel increased, and trade expanded. Indeed, even after nearly thirty years of socialism, and some very determined efforts, and Cuban government has not succeeded in eliminating
the appeal of North American cultural forms. This was central to Cuban
efforts to construct socialism, an enterprise based on a system of rationing in an economy of scarcity, in the face of North American capitalism,
based on unlimited consumption, only ninety miles away.

Not all influences have been one-way. The geo-historic connection has
been at the center of the vast Cuban migration to the United States after
1959. More than one million Cubans, approximately one-tenth of the
total Cuban population, reside in the United States. That a disproportionate number are Cubans of means—propertied, educated, and professional—served to give this émigré community an influence greater than
numbers alone would suggest. A Cuban presence on this scale and of this
type has already served to reshape the cultural, economic, and political
character of scores of communities in the United States. The Cuban émigré
influence on U.S. foreign policy, particularly with respect to relations
with Cuba, has been significant. Cubans have made their presence felt in
government service, in the armed forces, and on university faculties in
ways disproportionate to their total numbers.

VI

Of the pre-Columbian past in Cuba, little is known either with certainty
or precision. The island's geographic location in the Caribbean made Cuba
a point of convergence for the aboriginal peoples of the middle latitudes
of the New World. Successive waves of migration populated the island,
variously from the west across the Yucatán Channel, from the north across
the Florida Straits, and from the south by way of the Antillean archipelago.

The Ciboney Indians were among the earliest known inhabitants of the
island. They arrived in Cuba in two distinct migrations, over the course
of two thousand years, and all but disappeared without leaving conclusive

evidence of their origins. One view is that the Ciboney entered the West Indies from Florida into the Bahamas and thereupon to Cuba and the other islands of the Greater Antilles. A second theory posits Ciboney origins from the Caribbean coasts of Honduras and Nicaragua, expanding first to Jamaica and subsequently into Cuba, Española, and Puerto Rico. A third possibility was a Ciboney migration to Cuba as part of a larger South American diaspora, originating in lower Orinoco River and subsequently expanding across the arc of the Lesser Antilles to the larger islands. What is known for certain, however, is that by the end of the fifteenth century, the Ciboney were limited largely to the Greater Antilles adjacent to the Florida peninsula. No conclusive archaeological traces of the Ciboney have been located outside the western Antilles.

The Ciboney-Guayabo Blanco arrived first, in approximately 1000 B.C., and occupied the central and western coastal zones of Las Villas, Matanzas, Havana, Pinar del Río, and the Isle of Pines. The Ciboney-Cayo Redondo migrated to Cuba almost two thousand years later, and settled along the south coast of Camagüey and the estuarial regions of the Cauto River in Oriente.

The Ciboney tended to favor the Caribbean coastal regions, principally bays and estuaries, swamps and marshes, and offshore islets and keys. Archaeological sites along the south coast suggest the prevalence of two types of settlements. One was established in open coastal areas, consisting of simple thatched dwellings. Villages were small and assumed the appearance more of camps than of permanent settlements. The second type of Ciboney habitat was established among ravines, along cliffs, and in caves. The name "Ciboney" appears derived from the Arawak words *siba,* meaning cave, and *eyeri,* man. The use of rock shelters and cave mouths along the coast was more characteristic of the Ciboney in eastern Cuba, during the height of their settlement. Open-air villages were located in the west and are associated with the later Ciboney period.

The economy of the Ciboney was relatively simple, organized entirely around wild resources and food supplies readily available from the land and sea. Their settlements in the marshy swamplands and coastal beaches all but precluded agriculture. They hunted mammals and reptiles and trapped game in deadfalls or in spring snares. They gathered wild fruits, nuts, tubers, and roots. Most of all, however, the Ciboney lived off the sea. They gathered mollusks and crustaceans, they hunted manatees and sea turtles, and they fished.

Judging from the archaeological remains of Ciboney culture, they apparently were semi-nomadic. Social life was structured around small family clusters probably organized as mobile, independent clans. Ciboney settlements were comparatively small, with larger communities rarely surpassing a hundred residents. Property was shared. Fire was apparently used irregularly; little evidence of ashes has been found. As an island people dependent on fishing, the Ciboney probably used some type of boat, such as a dugout canoe, although no remains have yet been discovered. On land they traveled on foot, lacking beasts of burden.

Few artifacts have survived. Most are of shell, stone, or wood. Ciboney artifacts that have survived are simple, fashioned principally with the shell gouge, pitted hammerstone, and stone mortar. No traces of pottery or basketry have been discovered. Sites have yielded crude beads and pendants of shell and stone, with which the Ciboney probably adorned themselves. Little is known of their religion and almost nothing about their language.

The size of the Ciboney population at the time of Spanish conquest is unknown. By the end of the fifteenth century, their numbers had dwindled considerably, reduced to scattered settlements and dispersed into isolated and inaccessible regions of western Cuba.

The Ciboney were dislodged, apparently without resistence, from the eastern two-thirds of the island by successive waves of Arawak Indians. In the course of the Arawak occupation of Cuba, the Ciboney were either enslaved or expelled to the western extremities of the island. The Arawak originated in South America and migrated northward along the West Indian archipelago, settling the Greater Antilles, the Bahamas, and possibly making occasional forays into Florida. Two Arawak groups occupied Cuba after the Ciboney. The first Arawak migration was the Sub-Taíno, entering Cuba from Española during the ninth century. In the course of the following hundred years, the Sub-Taíno dispersed westward, expanding into Camagüey, Las Villas, and Matanzas. Although the Arawak originally established settlements throughout the western and central inland regions, they favored the north coast of eastern Cuba. Of the nearly hundred known Sub-Taíno archaeological sites in Cuba, the majority are located in Oriente province, and of these half were found along the north coast.

The Sub-Taíno established settlements on the fertile uplands and high ground away from the coast, near readily available supplies of fresh water. Dwellings consisted of cone-shaped palm-thatched huts *(bohíos)*, organized in villages of multifamily dwellings. The typical village consisted of approximately one thousand to two thousand inhabitants, living in twenty to fifty multifamily houses with each village under a local chief *(cacique)*. Houses were organized in a random and loose cluster, preserving in the center a rectangular open space in which the house of the *cacique* fronted. The open area *(batey)* was reserved for assemblies and festivities. Caves were rarely used for permanent dwellings, and only during periods of migration. Otherwise, caves served principally as sites for religious ceremonies, concealment of valuables, and interment. Like the Ciboney, the Sub-Taíno employed canoes on rivers and at sea and traveled by foot on land. Also like the Ciboney, the Sub-Taíno collected roots and fruits, gathered mollusks and crustaceans, hunted land and marine animals, and fished. Unlike their predecessors, however, the Sub-Taíno cultivated a variety of crops on small plots of land.

The difference in climate between the coastal zones and the interior influenced the distribution of the native population. The dry coastal zones were occupied by the simpler Ciboney cave dwellers who subsisted principally on marine life. The interior highland, more suitable for agriculture because of greater rainfall, was chosen by the Sub-Taíno. Land was worked collectively. Farming activity was organized principally around the cultivation of such diverse products as maize, sweet potatoes, yucca, tomatoes, pineapples, and a variety of fruits and berries. Chili and annatto were cultivated both as condiments and as a source of dye. The Sub-Taíno also undertook extensive cultivation of tobacco, used principally for smoking, in religious ceremonies, and for medicinal purposes. While the Sub-Taíno did not domesticate animals, they did learn to guarantee themselves a dependable source of food by keeping wild animals alive in captivity. Captured turtles were kept in corrals constructed in the shallow offshore waters. In the area of Cienfuegos, the Arawak maintained extensive pens of live mullet.

The Sub-Taínos were also skilled at crafts, most notably woodwork, bone carving, ceramics, and textile production. Using wild cotton, palm fibers, and other plants, the Sub-Taíno assembled an array of products, including hammocks, fishing lines, nets, ropes, cord, mats, and mattresses. Typical ornaments included ear-plugs, pendants of conch and mother-of-pearl, amulets in the form of small figurines of shell, and beads.

The second Arawak migration into Cuba, that of the Taíno, also originated from Española and began during the mid-fifteenth century. The new Arawak influx was short-lived, however. Taíno migration into the island had not advanced very much, and dispersion westward across the island had not expanded very far, when the Spanish occupation of the

Antilles began. As a result, the distribution of the Taíno in Cuba was restricted largely to the eastern portion of the island, a triangular region encompassed by Baracoa, Guantánamo, and Maisí. Few remains of Taíno settlements in Cuba have survived. The nearly thirty known Taíno sites reveal distinctive changes toward greater complexity in ceramics, stone crafts, and shell artifacts. They shared with the Sub-Taíno a common diet, similar swellings, and much the same social organization.

Archaeologists in Cuba have recently established the existence of a third cultural group—the Mayarí. Located in north-central Oriente, the Mayarí appear to have settled in the region at about the time of the late Ciboney-Cayo Redondo period and early Sub-Taíno presence, between approximately the ninth and eleventh centuries. The two Mayarí sites (Arroyo del Palo and Mejía) excavated during the 1960s revealed ceramics and artifacts previously unknown in Cuban archaeology. Both sites are inland and near rivers. Remains suggest settlements dependent more upon the hunting of mammals and reptiles and the gathering of wild fruits and roots than maritime activity associated with either the Ciboney or the Arawak. Fishing and the collection of mollusks and crustaceans was organized around the many freshwater rivers of the region. The Mayarí appeared to have practiced a rudimentary form of cultivation, principally caring for the local edible plants and fruits trees. At some point during the eleventh century, the Mayarí were overrun or their culture was absorbed by the Sub-Taíno migration.

VII

The Indians first encountered by Spanish upon their arrival in Cuba were the Arawak. Indeed, much of what is known about the Sub-Taíno and Taíno originates from Spanish accounts of Arawak settlements at the time of discovery and conquest. Columbus described the dwellings of north coastal villages as "the most lovely" he had seen, "very large, and they looked like tents in a camp, with no regular streets, but one here and another there. Inside, they were well swept and clean, and their furnishing very well arranged; all were made of very beautiful palm branches." Elsewhere the Admiral wrote of larger villages, some of fifty dwellings, "all very large and built of wood with thatched roofs. These houses were round and tent-shaped. There must have been some thousands of inhabitants since in each house lived all the members of a family." And at another village: "I saw a beautiful house, not very large, and with two entrances, for so have they all, and I entered it, and I saw a wonderful arrangement like rooms, made in a certain manner that I know not how to describe, and hanging from the ceiling of it were shells and other things." He commented on Arawak social organization in which "all men are content with one woman, and to their chief or king they give as many as twenty. It appears to me that the women work more than do the men. I have not been able to learn if they hold private property; it seemed to me that all took a share in whatever anyone had, especially of eatable things." Columbus described Arawak agricultural plots as "very fertile land and all cultivated." At one point he ascended a mountain and "found its top all level and sown with pumpkins and other products of the land, so that it was glorious to behold, and in the middle of it there was a large village." He observed the "great abundance of cotton spun into balls, so much that a single house contained more than 12,500 pounds of yarn." He was struck too by Arawak use of cotton: "Strangely enough, none of the Indians make use of this cotton for clothing, but only for making their nets and beds—which they call hammocks—and for weaving the little skirts or cloths which the women wore to cover their private parts."

Several years later, as the Spanish expanded westward along the south-coast to Cienfuegos, Bartolomé de Las Casas commented on Arawak fish farming. "There were so many fish in this part," he later recalled, "especially mullet, that the Indians had made pens of canes sunk into the sea itself. Within these pens, twenty, thirty, or fifty thousand mullet were enclosed and partitioned off so that none could get out. The Indians would take as many as they wanted from the pens with their nets and leave the others, just as if they were in a reservoir or tank." And at another point: "Just as we said that they had pens for mullet, so also, between those islets, they had pens of 500 or 1,000 turtles, so that not one was able to escape from these enclosures, consisting of a fence of canes."

The Spanish also came into contact with the surviving population of the Ciboney at the western end of the island, to whom they gave the name Guanahacabibes. "The life of these people is of the manner of savages," wrote Diego Velásquez, "for they have neither houses nor village quarters, nor fields, nor do they eat anything else than the flesh they take in the mountains and turtles and fish." Las Casas also wrote of the western Indians "who are like savages, have no relation whatever with others of the island, nor do they have houses, but they live in caves, except when they go out to fish."

TABLE 1.   Sub-Taíno Population Estimates (ca. 1510)

Region	Population
Eastern Cuba	
Banes	18,000
Baracoa-Baitiquirí	9,000
Cauto Valley	9,000
North coast (Gibara-Nuevitas)	6,000
South coast (Cape Cruz-Baitiquirí)	8,000
Cape Cruz-Manzanillo	4,000
Central Cuba	
North coast (Nuevitas-Matanzas)	17,000
Jatibonico-Cienfuegos	12,000
South coast (Cauto River-Cienfuegos)	9,000

Source: Adapted from Ernesto E. Tabio and Estrella Rey, *Prehistoria de Cuba* (Havana, 1966), and Juan Pérez de la Riva, "Desaparición de la población indígena cubana," *Universidad de La Habana,* nums. 196–197 (1972), 61–84.

VIII

Estimates of the size of the Indian population of Cuba at the end of the fifteenth century have varied widely over time—from as few as 16,000 to as many as 600,000. The most current calculations estimate the pre-Columbian population of the island at approximately 112,000, with the Arawak making up more than 90 percent of the total. The Sub-Taíno numbered approximately 92,000, followed by the Taíno at 10,000, and the Ciboney also at 10,000.

The Sub-Taíno majority is believed to have been distributed across the island in the numbers shown in Table 1. The total population was not evenly distributed across the island. Oriente alone accounted for 54 percent of the total number of inhabitants (61,000), followed by Camagüey (23,000), and Las Villas (18,000). The remaining 9 percent (10,000) of the population was dispersed in the western half of the island, and most in Pinar del Río. By the end of the fifteenth century, the preponderance of the Indian population was located in the eastern part of Cuba, the precise point at which the Spanish were preparing to enter the island.

2

Colony and Society

I

"Everything is green as in Andalucia in April and May," Columbus
wrote with unabashed astonishment on October 28, 1492. A driving rain-
storm had forced the Admiral to remain anchored through the previous
night in uncharted waters along an unknown coast. Landfall was made
the following morning, and all that is certain about that historic disembarkation is that it occurred on the north coast of Cuba somewhere between Gibara and Lucrecia Bay. Once ashore, Columbus's astonishment
gave way to awe. He had "never seen anything so beautiful"; the land
was the "most lovely that eyes have ever seen," the "air all night was
scented and sweet, and neither cold nor hot." "Everything I saw," Columbus continued, "was so lovely that my eyes could not weary of be-
holding such beauty, nor could I weary of the songs of the birds large
and small." The "singing of small birds is such that it seems as if one
would never desire to depart. Flocks of parrots darken the sun. There are
trees of a thousand species, each has its particular fruit, and all of marvelous flavor." For five weeks more, Columbus sailed eastward along
the indented northern shoreline, occasionally going ashore to explore the
coastal interior. He could hardly contain his wonderment at the "November air . . . soft and healthy, tempered like the month of May." The
wonders increased. At Tánamo Bay he marveled at the offshore islands,
so many that they "could not be counted, all of a good size and very
high lands, full of various trees of a thousand kinds and an infinity of
palms," mountains "higher than any in the world, and more lovely and
clear, with no cloud or snow, and very great depth of water at their feet."
At Punta Cabagán all the land had "very high mountains, very lovely,
and not dry or rocky, but all accessible, and very beautiful valleys. The
valleys, as well as the mountains, were full of lofty and leafy trees, so
that it was bliss to see them, and it seemed that there were many pines."
At Punta Plata the prose assumed lyrical tones: "wonders of the beauty
of the land and of the woods, where there are pines and palms, and a

great plain, which, although not entirely flat and stretches away to the south-southeast, undulates with smooth and low elevations, the most lovely thing in the world.''

But there was more, and it did not take the Admiral long to discern one last attribute of the new land: "It is certain that where there is such marvelous scenery, there must be much from which profit can be made.'' He took note of more than New World natural wonders; he also took inventory of New World net worth. All along the north coast of Cuba, Columbus contemplated the prospects and calculated the potential profits of the new land, and the possibilities seemed unlimited. Of the "trees of many kinds, each with its own fruit and marvelous scent,'' he wrote: "I am quite certain that they are all valuable.'' Of the lofty mountains: "I believe that in them are very great riches and precious stones and spices.'' Of the possibilities further inland: "there must be great centers of population and innumerable people and things of great value, so that I declare that here . . . all Christendom will find trade.'' It was incalculable: "How great will be the benefit which can be derived from this land, I cannot tell.''

The entrepreneur cum explorer duly recorded all possible opportunities. Columbus met Indians wearing what appeared to be silver ornaments, evidence "that there was silver in this land.'' He tapped for resin, and in one district alone discovered "enough to collect a thousand quintals every year.'' He commented on the "very great amount of cotton,'' and concluded that "it would market very well.'' The pine forests—"so tall and wonderful that [I cannot] overstate their height and straightness, like spindles, thick and slender''—offered vast resources for shipbuilding. In an Indian village Columbus came upon a cake of wax, from which he concluded that "where there is wax, there must also be a thousand other good things.'' He hoped to discover pearls in offshore waters, gold in the streams, silver in the mountains, and spices in the forests.

Columbus completed his first voyage of discovery in early December with a landfall on the north coast of Española. He established the settlement of La Navidad and forthwith returned to Spain with news of his travels. He returned to the Caribbean in November 1493 and found La Navidad in ruins, a casualty of disease, famine, and, finally, Indian rebellion. A second settlement, Isabela, was established further east on the Española north coast, whereupon Columbus resumed his explorations to the west. He returned to Cuban waters, this time along the south coast, certain that he had discovered the headland of the Asian continent.

During his second reconnaissance of Cuba, Columbus came upon the magnificent harbors of the south coast and the hundreds of islands, islets, and keys to which collectively he gave the name of Jardines de la Reina. He sailed as far west as the Gulf of Batabanó, the point at which the Cuban coast bends southward. Columbus sighted the Isle of Pines, on which he made landfall in June 1494. The expedition had been in Cuban waters for three months, in search of gold, but without success. With supplies dwindling and the health and morale of the crew declining, Columbus made the decision to return to Española. Before sailing eastward, however, Columbus ordered the preparation of a notarized affidavit, to which senior members of his crew subscribed, certifying that Cuba was a peninsula of the Asian mainland. He would see Cuba on only one other occasion, nearly a decade later in 1503, from a distance, en route to Spain after his disastrous fourth voyage.

II

Even as the exploration of new lands continued, preparation for the administration of those already discovered commenced. The Catholic Kings moved early to consolidate royal authority over the Caribbean islands. Spanish settlements expanded rapidly. From Isabela on the Atlantic coast of Española, Spaniards moved inland toward the Cibao, lured southward by the prospects of gold and the promise of Indian grants *(encomiendas)*. En route, they established interior settlements at Magdalena, Esperanza, Santo Tomás, and Concepción de la Vega. Rumors of gold fields further to the south resulted in renewed expansion toward the Caribbean coast. In August 1496, construction of the port town of Santo Domingo began.

The timing was propitious, and the site fortuitous. Spanish maritime activities had already turned southward toward the South American mainland and the Central American isthmus. The settlement of Santo Domingo was ideally suited to the new Spanish purpose. The approach from Spain by way of the Dominica Passage to the east was shortened and downwind all the way. More important, Santo Domingo offered an excellent point of departure from which to reach the islands to the west and the mainland to the south.

Spanish successes were not without problems, however. Settlements had been organized haphazardly, with little official attention to coordination and less to control. Colonists feuded with royal officials, fell out among themselves, and forced Indians into rebellion. Even before the end of the first decade, the Crown faced the intolerable situation of colonists in revolt against royal authority and Indians in rebellion against colonists.

The Crown moved quickly to re-establish control over the Indies. In 1499 the court appointed Francisco de Bobadilla as governor of Española, a move calculated to consolidate colonial administation and centralize political authority. Bobadilla arrived at Santo Domingo in August 1500 and immediately set about the task of expanding royal authority. Feuding settlements were subdued; rival officials were retired and returned to Spain. Minerals were declared a state monopoly, thereby providing for the licensing and taxing of mining. The collection of revenues improved.

A second governor arrived in 1502 with a new mission. The appointment of Nicolás de Ovando signified a change in the purpose of the Spanish presence in Española. To the 300 colonists already on the island were added another 2500 settlers. But it was not only that more people had arrived in Española. Significant too was the character of the new population. The newcomers included soldiers, civil servants, priests, artisans, and farmers, a multitude that included a total of seventy-three families: husbands with wives, parents with children, more as colonists than *conquistadores,* more as immigrants than invaders. They arrived with blueprints for towns, building materials, and, most important, agricultural stock—tools, seeds, and animals. They came to stay, to settle the colonies with a permanent resident population in an effort that was already known in official circles as the "Enterprise of the Indies."

The new official purpose in Española after 1502 was more than consolidation. It was also expansion. Ovando undertook a ruthless pacification of Indian *villas,* slaying Indians who resisted and enslaving those who did not. Through alternate use first of the *encomienda* and later through forced labor assignments *(repartimiento),* Indians were distributed among Spanish colonists, and henceforth required to render service in the form of tribute and/or labor to the *conquistadores.* The number of Spanish settlements increased during these years. Seven new towns were established in the west, two in the southeast, one in the north—the location of each determined by one or more of three considerations: the availability of Indians, the presence of gold, and access to safe port.

These were years too of renewed Spanish interest in the surrounding islands in the western Caribbean. In 1505, Vicente Yáñez Pinzón claimed possession of Puerto Rico. Jamaica was occupied. Reconnaissance of the Bahama Islands and surrounding waters was completed.

In 1508 attention shifted to Cuba. Interest in Cuba had waned after initial explorations had failed to produce evidence of gold on the island. Conditions had changed during the intervening fifteen years, however. Not that Spaniards abandoned completely the hope of discovering gold in Cuba. On the contrary, it was precisely the recurring rumors of gold that served to revive official interest in the island. But other forces were also at work. The population of Spanish settlers in Española had increased significantly. Competition for shrinking resources intensified. The decline of the Indian population of Española, moreover, reducing the number of natives available for *encomienda* grants, served to exacerbate these conditions. Cuba offered new opportunities at a time when many Spaniards were prepared and predisposed to seek their fortunes in other lands. Proximity and opportunity combined to make the island the logical if not inevitable territory for new expansion. In 1508, Ovando dispatched Sebastián de Ocampo to reconnoiter Cuban coasts. The eight-month-long circumnavigation expedition established definitively Cuban insularity. No less important, the voyage collected detailed data about the island terrain, coastline, and harbors—all vital information preliminary to the Spanish occupation of the island. Ocampo returned to Santo Domingo with more than promising topographical information, however. He also brought back fresh reports about the existence of gold.

III

Preparations for the occupation of Cuba began in 1511 under the direction of Diego Velásquez, a wealthy landowner in western Española who had distinguished himself in previous campaigns against the Indians. The conquest of Cuba proceeded in two waves. One expeditionary force of three hundred Spaniards under Velásquez departed from Salvatierra on the southwestern peninsula of Española across the Windward Passage to the mountainous region of Maisí at the eastern end of Cuba. From Maisí, Velásquez moved quickly to establish the first permanent settlement and capital at Baracoa on the north coast. A second, smaller force originated from Jamaica under the command of Pánfilo de Narváez and occupied the southern coast around the Gulf of Guacanayabo.

The conquest of the eastern zones proceeded swiftly and ruthlessly. The Indians of the east were neither unfamiliar with Spanish motives nor unprepared for Spanish methods. Many were victims of previous Spanish pacification campaigns in Española and, as last resort, had fled across the Windward Passage to Cuba for safety and sanctuary. They did not mistake the meaning of the Spanish presence in Cuba. The Indians resisted with tenacity, the Spanish attacked with ferocity. Massacre became the means of conquest, terror the method of control. Opposition collapsed within four months, and the bands that remained dispersed in disarray.

The conquest of the east set the stage for the colonization of the west. Velásquez and Narváez reorganized their combined forces into three contingents in preparation for the advance westward and a scheduled rendezvous at Carenas Bay (Havana). One group sailed along the north coast, maintaining contact with a second infantry-cavalry unit under Narváez, who marched westward inland. The third contingent under Velásquez sailed west along the south coast.

Both coastal expeditions arrived at Carenas Bay as scheduled, without incident. The overland march, however, was an odyssey of pillage and plunder, of death and destruction, culminating in an unprovoked massacre at Caonao in northern Camagüey. The carnage at Caonao was not random violence—its purpose was as much to overcome the Indian wherewithal to resist as it was to undermine the Indian will to resist. The strategy was not without effect. Word of Caonao spread quickly, and organized resistance to Narváez henceforth all but ceased. Indians either submitted unconditionally or fled beyond the reach of Spaniards. These events made a powerful impression on Bartolomé de Las Casas who served in the Narváez expedition, causing the first doubts about the morality of the Spanish conquest. "I do not remember," he later wrote of the Narváez march, "with how much spilling of human blood he marked that road."

The early phase of Spanish expansion resulted in the establishment of seven settlements: Baracoa (1512), Bayamo (1513), Trinidad (1514), Sancti Spíritus (1514), Havana (1514), Puerto Príncipe (1514), and Santiago de Cuba (1515). With the exception of Sancti Spíritus, all were approachable by water. The original site of Bayamo had access to a navigable channel. Santiago de Cuba, Bayamo, Trinidad, and Havana faced on the Caribbean, and hence were expected to play an important support role in Spanish expansion into Central and South America. North-coast settlements included the Puerto Príncipe and Baracoa. The selection of Trinidad was influenced by the proximity of Indian settlements and the presence of gold deposits. The location of gold placers in the northern interior led to the founding of Sancti Spíritus. Puerto Príncipe provided access to the Indians *villas* of Camagüey, reported by contemporary accounts as a site of one of the largest native populations on the island. The original towns of Puerto Príncipe and Havana were subsequently relocated: Havana from its original site on the Gulf of Batabanó to its present location on the north coast in 1519 and Puerto Príncipe from its original location on Nuevitas Bay to an Indian *villa* inland known as Camagüey in 1528. In addition to the original seven towns, small Spanish settlements were established in Matanzas, La Sabana (Remedios), Jagua (Cienfuegos), Mariel, and Carenas (Havana).

IV

The establishment of the seven settlements completed the early colonization of the island. In 1515 Velásquez relocated the administrative center of the island to Santiago de Cuba, establishing the capital on the southeast coast of Cuba. At the time it seemed a wholly appropriate, even advantageous, site for the new capital. Santiago de Cuba provided easy access into the eastern interior. It offered a large and protected harbor, strategically situated at the crossroads of Spanish maritime activity in the Caribbean. Santiago was expected to prosper through its participation in trade with Española, Jamaica, and new settlements expanding on the Central American coast and South America. In fact, however, Spanish maritime activity had already started to shift westward, toward the Yucatán Peninsula and the interior land beyond. The relocation of Havana on the northwest coast four years later was both proof and portent of the redirection of empire. The selection of Santiago de Cuba as the center of administration situated the capital along the increasingly unimportant sea lanes of the central Caribbean at a time of the rising importance of the Gulf of Mexico. Santiago de Cuba was at the remote rearward location of the island, almost 700 miles from the western end, from which land and sea communication was difficult and transportation often impossible.

Elsewhere on the island, the early settlements flourished. Gold was discovered in the extensive streams *(arroyos)* of the central highland ranges and the mountain streams of the Sierra Maestra. Placer gold abounded and accounted for the early prosperity of Trinidad, Sancti Spíritus, and Bayamo. Gold production was short-lived, however, and peaked between 1517 and 1519, producing revenues estimated at 100,000 pesos annually and declining precipitously thereafter. By the mid-1540s, gold receipts had fallen to less than 3,000 pesos yearly.

The victorious *conquistadores* distributed among themselves vast parcels of land, many incorporating the fields previously cultivated by the Indians. In so doing, the Spanish appropriated more than land; they acquired possession too of available sources of food supply. Colonists readily adopted the cultivation of indigenous crops, most notably yuca, boniato, malanga, and maize. They also introduced European crops, including wheat, rice, bananas, citrus fruits, and sugar cane. Ranching flourished. Vast areas of land were appropriated and distributed for stock raising. Cattle raising developed very early into an important livelihood, providing both a staple for the local diet and a source of commercial revenues.

The early years also witnessed the appropriation of Indian *villas* and the distribution of Indian labor in the form of *encomiendas* and *repartimientos*. Through the sixteenth century, the Indian population was relocated in new settlements *(reducciones)* near the principal Spanish towns in an effort to rationalize the supply of Indian labor and facilitate educational and evangelical activities. Many *reducciones* served subsequently as the basis of permanent Cuban settlements, including Guanabacoa, Yara, Dos Brazos, Mayarí, Yateras, La Guira, El Caney, and Jiguaní.

Indians served as the principal labor force in the early colony. They mined the quarries and panned the streams, tilled the fields and tended the flocks. They were field hands and house servants. They were pressed into service aboard the fleets as deck hands, conscripted into the expeditions to the mainland as porters and bearers, and performed generally every other form of manual labor and menial task demanded by the *conquistadores*.

From the very outset the prospects for the survival of the Indian were bleak, and they never improved. Their defeat in war all but assured their demise in peace. To the thousands of Indians who perished immediately during the conquest were tens of thousands of others who succumbed subsequently in the colony. Death came in many forms. They were regularly overworked and routinely abused. They perished as much from malnutrition as from maltreatment. Indians lost at once control of their labor and the cultivation of their land. Spain introduced a new economic purpose into the island, and nowhere did this change of purpose stand in sharper relief than the new function of land. European agriculture displaced Indian farming. In the months and years that followed the conquest, the Spanish let loose onto the land vast droves of livestock. The animals found grazing ranges rich in original vegetative covering, and with few New World predators and without Old World diseases, the herds multiplied prodigiously. As early as 1515, an estimated 30,000 pigs roamed the Cuban countryside. Cattle herds flourished and multiplied at an astonishing rate. Goats, horses, mules, donkeys, sheep, and domestic fowl thrived, and mostly at the expense of the Indian. Untold numbers became wild. They fed indiscriminately on the natural grasslands and the cultivated fields upon which the Indians depended. Vast herds of untended beasts strayed freely and without restriction on unfenced ranges, and wrought havoc on Indian agriculture. This was nothing less than the wholesale substitution of an animal population for a human one. The pre-Columbian ecological equilibrium was shattered irrevocably.

The consequences for the Indian were calamitous. Indian agriculture was plunged into disarray and dislocation. Indian communities watched their crops repeatedly destroyed by the vast herds of grazing, trampling beasts, and in the end abandoned their cultivation in despair. Food supplies dwindled, famine followed. Families were shattered. Men were relocated to labor camps, women and children were left to survive as best they could. Most could not. Infant mortality apparently reached staggering proportions, and not all from malnutrition and ill-health. Infanticide became commonplace. Fertility rates declined sharply, as Indians simply ceased reproducing themselves. And in increasing numbers, many lost the will to live altogether. Suicide became one of the most common forms of Indian protest. Individuals and entire families, and on occasion whole villages, would kill themselves, by hanging, ingesting soil, or taking poison. "There were days," one Spanish officer reported, "in which they were all found hanging, with their women and children, fifty households of the same village." Indeed, so prevalent was suicide that it must be considered one of the principal causes of the demise of the Indian in post-conquest Cuba.

Overwork, malnutrition, and melancholia set the stage for the next series of calamities to befall Indian communities. Their weakened condition made them easy prey to Old World infections and illnesses. The Spanish arrival released into the Indies microbial infectious diseases previously unknown and against which the indigenous population had little immunity. Epidemics erupted periodically and traveled quickly; they spread without obstruction and killed without obstacle. Smallpox, measles, typhoid, and dysentery ravaged Indian *villas,* and ultimately contributed to the final destruction of the native population. One epidemic in 1519 swept across Cuba and reduced the population of some Indian settlements by as much as two-thirds. Another outbreak in 1530 again ravaged the native population. The population decline was as startling as it was swift. The number of Indians dwindled from an estimated 112,000 on the eve of the conquest to 19,000 in 1519 to 7,000 in 1531. By the mid-1550s, the Indian population had shrunk to fewer than 3,000.

Not all Indians acquiesced passively to their exploitation and ultimate extinction. Many refused to submit to the *conquistadores,* preferring instead to live as fugitives in flight. Many fled inland, into the inaccessible coastal mountains and interior forests; others fled outward, into the impenetrable coastal swamps and onto the offshore islands, from which they later launched periodic raids against Spanish settlements. Indian resistance was henceforth scattered and sporadic. The conquest was followed by intermittent warfare, short-lived uprisings, and abortive revolts. Indian resistance was met by Spanish repression, rebellion was met by reprisal. A type of desultory warfare continued for decades, further contributing to the disruption of Indian communities, further hastening the demise of the native population.

V

The decline of the Indian population initially caused Spanish authorities little concern. Not that they were insensible to the long-term implications of the disappearance of the Indian. Rather, they were preoccupied with more immediate concerns. The occupation of Cuba was but one phase of a larger project of exploration and expansion. Concurrent with consolidation in Cuba, and continuing immediately thereafter, the island was transformed into the center of Spanish maritime activity, as the Spanish prepared for expansion to other lands—north to Florida; west to Central America, the Yucatán Peninsula, and into Mexico; south to Venezuela, Colombia, and eventually Peru. Its strategic location along the principal approaches to the mainland made Cuba an obvious point from which to launch new expeditions and support new expansion. These considerations shaped much of the early Spanish purpose in Cuba, influencing the selection of sites for settlements and the choice of crops for cultivation: the former with an eye on mainland exploration, the latter as a source of victuals for mainland explorers. The island provided the necessary personnel for mainland exploration, in the form both of labor from among the recently pacified Indian population and of crews and soldiers from among the growing ranks of Spanish settlers.

The Spanish population of the island increased steadily and in spurts during the first decade of occupation. The first surge of population growth occurred suddenly and immediately upon the completion of the conquest, as word of the discovery of gold in Cuba spread. Much of this initial increase came at the expense of existing Spanish settlements in the Caribbean, most notably from Jamaica, Puerto Rico, and Española. Indeed, within a decade of the conquest of Cuba, many Spanish settlements in western Española had been completely abandoned. Population growth in Cuba continued thereafter steadily if modestly from Spain. By the end of the first decade, an estimated three thousand Spaniards had migrated to the island. It was an unstable population, however, the largest part of which consisted of transient males—newly arrived and soon to leave, ever on the move in search of new and greater opportunity.

These were generally good times for Cuban settlements. For almost two decades, the island served as the principal base of Spanish mainland expeditions: Pedrarias Dávila (Central America, 1513); Francisco Hernández de Córdoba (Yucatán Peninsula, 1517); Juan de Grijalva (Mexico, 1518); Hernán Cortés (Mexico, 1519); Pánfilo Narváez (Mexico, 1520, and Florida, 1527); Hernando de Soto (Florida, 1538).

Exploration stimulated economic expansion, and Cuba prospered. The conquest of the mainland raised demands for provisions, supplies, and foodstuffs and created a boom in the local economy. Sales were brisk, as ranchers and farmers furnished the livestock and food supply for the expeditions. The establishment of Spanish settlements on the mainland created new markets. The Cuban economy flourished. Trade and commerce thrived, agricultural production increased, and stockbreeding expanded.

The success of Spanish expansion was a mixed blessing, however. The conquest of Mexico and Peru changed everything, and for Cuba most of the changes were for the worse. The "Enterprise of the Indies" suddenly assumed continental dimensions, and all at once the Crown and colonists alike turned their attention away from the islands to the mainland. The implications were immediate. So was the impact. Spanish interest in the Caribbean waned, maritime activity declined. Cuban producers lost customers. The mainland settlements quickly became self-sufficient, and suppliers in Cuba lost markets, and more: the success of mainland colonization led to the establishment of rival centers of production. Cuban exports to the mainland, principally in the form of cattle, horses, and pigs, declined and ultimately ended altogether. Sugar, citrus, and wheat took hold readily in Mexico. What colonists could not produce on the mainland, they procured directly from Spain.

Cuba also lost population. Every expedition that departed for the mainland depleted the settlements of the island. In most cases the losses were permanent. More than half of the 200 men who sailed with Hernández de Córdoba perished along the Yucatán coast. Of the 550 volunteers who accompanied Cortés to Mexico, most never returned. Narváez lost almost half his force of 1,000 in Mexico and almost as many in Florida. Two-thirds of de Soto's troops perished in Florida.

The mainland conquests set the stage for the next series of misfortunes to befall the island. The mainland conquests, Mexico and later Peru, created new opportunities: new land, new *encomiendas,* a new beginning for those who had arrived late to the island or had come up second best in the distribution of the spoils of Caribbean conquests. Not a few Spanish settlers had reason to leave Cuba. Prosperity had been short-lived. Gold production was in decline. So was the Indian population. "After spending three fruitless years in Tierra Firme and Cuba," Bernal Díaz later recalled of his decision to join the Hernández de Córdoba expedition to the Yucatán, "about 110 of us, settlers from Tierra Firme or Spaniards who had come to Cuba but received no grant of Indians, decided to make an expedition to seek new lands in which to try our fortunes and find occupation." The promise of the mainland was also underscored by Cortés's call for recruits. Bernal Díaz remembered: "He ordered a proclamation to be made to the sound of trumpets and drums . . . that anyone who wished to accompany him to the newly discovered lands, to conquer and settle, would receive a share of the gold, silver, and riches to be gained, and an *encomienda* of Indians once the country had been pacified."

The mainland beckoned, and for many the call was irresistible. In Cuba the effects were immediate and long lasting. The island fell on hard times. The economy collapsed. Cuban prosperity ended almost as quickly as it had begun, giving early form to the enduring boom-bust character of the island economy. All at once gold production declined, the labor supply diminished, and mainland markets disappeared.

Adversity begot adversity. The departure for the mainland of so many so suddenly disrupted the tenuous social equilibrium of post-conquest Cuba. The Spanish presence in Cuba was reduced to a dwindling population, dispersed throughout isolated settlements, divided against itself into quarrelsome political factions. The occasion seemed auspicious for what re-mained of the Indians to rise up against what remained of the Spanish. On two occasions, and on each for a protracted period—1524–32, after the exodus to Mexico, and 1538–44, after the migration to Peru and Florida—Indian rebellions threatened Spanish settlements with extinction. Puerto Príncipe and Bayamo were destroyed and rebuilt—and destroyed again. Baracoa was attacked repeatedly.

Spanish settlers eventually re-established control over the Indians, but not until their ranks had been thinned further. Life in Cuba was trans-formed into a dreary struggle for daily survival. Settlers found themselves in an inhospitable environment within an impoverished economy, with no way out except flight from the island altogether. And increasingly, even this option was disappearing. Spanish officials made periodic efforts to halt continued migration from Cuba. During the late 1520s and early 1530s the Council of the Indies issued a number of decrees prohibiting, upon penalty of death and confiscation of property, unauthorized depar-ture from the island. A proclamation in 1528 required traveling merchants to post bond to guarantee their return. In an effort to induce permanent family settlement, the crown withheld further distribution of *encomiendas* to single men.

These measures had little immediate effect. Flight continued undimin-ished. The promise of the mainland appeared unlimited at a time when the prospects on the island seemed uncertain. And never more so than during the 1540s and 1550s, when the great silver discoveries in Mexico and Peru offered vast new opportunities for instant riches. By the middle of the sixteenth century, depopulation became a real danger. Fields were unattended, mines were deserted, towns were abandoned. The capital of Santiago de Cuba was reduced to 30 households, with an estimated pop-ulation of 150 Spanish settlers. Baracoa was in wretched condition, ap-proaching abandonment, and without even sufficient population to fill vacancies in municipal government. Trinidad was abandoned altogether. Sancti Spíritus was reduced to 18 Spanish households, Bayamo to 30, Puerto Príncipe to 14. By mid-century, the Spanish population of Cuba had fallen to an estimated 700 settlers. Almost all new settlements during the sixteenth century were in the form of Indian *reducciones*. The only new Spanish town founded during these years was El Cobre (1558) near the copper mines in southeastern Cuba. It would be nearly another one hundred years before the establishment of another Spanish town in Cuba.

VI

By the middle of the sixteenth century, Cuba assumed the appearance of an abandoned backwater outpost of the Spanish New World empire. Revenue remittances to Spain declined, and by mid-century had all but ceased completely. The island languished in varying conditions of depression, destitution, and depopulation—all to the apparent indifference of colonial authorities.

But it happened too that the conditions that relegated Cuba to the outer Caribbean fringes of empire also transformed the Caribbean into the outer defense perimeter of empire. Spain's European adversaries were not slow to recognize the implications of colonial revenues. Indeed, the sheer magnitude of the New World treasure so profoundly threatened to alter the Old World balance of power as to make the Spanish claim of exclusivity over the Indies as impossible to countenance as it was inconceivable to contemplate. Old World conflicts quickly passed into a New World context. To overturn Spanish power in Europe it was necessary first to undermine the Spanish presence in America, and no other area offered as great an advantage as the Caribbean. A thousand miles of unprotected shipping lanes, hundreds of uninhabited islands, and a score of unguarded sea channels made the Caribbean the logical choice from which to attack Spain. Over the Caribbean waterways sailed out the vast treasure fleets that subsidized Spain in Europe and the returning cargo vessels that sustained Spain in America.

The new European presence in the Caribbean thus had as its purpose two interrelated objectives: the interdiction of the Spanish treasure fleets and the interruption of the Spanish supply system. The strategic significance of Cuba suddenly loomed large. The island commanded access to the Gulf of Mexico and the Caribbean and lay astride the three principal maritime approaches to both: the Florida Straits to the north, the Windward Passage to the east, the Yucatán Channel to the west. These were the bottlenecks of empire, the points at which Spain's vital maritime lifeline was most vulnerable to attack.

European attacks began early in the sixteenth century, and continued unabated into the seventeenth century. Cuba soon found itself in the forward position of a conflict for mastery over the Caribbean waterways and, by implication, for control of the New World treasure. The island bore the brunt of European attacks against Spain. As early as 1537, a

French fleet occupied Havana. Between 1538 and 1540, French corsairs brought maritime traffic around Santiago de Cuba to a virtual halt. In 1546, Baracoa was sacked. In 1554, a French squadron plundered Santiago. A year later, a naval force under Jacques de Sores attacked Havana, reducing the city to ashes. In 1558, the French again attacked Santiago. During the 1560s and 1570s, English interlopers arrived in the Caribbean. The Dutch arrived at the close of the sixteenth century.

Cuba was subjected to a new round of adversities, all of which added to the mounting woes of the local population. Indeed, decades of intermittent plunder of the principal Cuban settlements contributed further to the continued depopulation of the island. But it was also now clear that Spain could not acquiesce to the abandonment of the island. Cuban affairs were no longer matters of limited local consequences—they had larger, global repercussions. The defense of Cuba was essential to the defense of the empire, for the former was a means to the latter. Cuba's strategic command over the principal New World waterways could not be relinquished without making colonial defense impossible.

Through the latter decades of the sixteenth century, Spain adopted a variety of strategies designed at once to safeguard maritime traffic and secure Cuba. The Spanish early learned the ways of successful seafaring over Caribbean channels. After the 1560s, virtually all trans-Atlantic shipping sailed under the escort of an armed convoy. Under the *flota* system, Spain consolidated maritime traffic into two annual fleets to the New World: one set sail in April for Vera Cruz and the other departed in August for Nombre de Dios. The fleets entered the Caribbean from the east, at Dominica, from which point they caught the prevailing tradewinds westward. They were accompanied by the powerful and pervasive ocean currents that swept them through the Yucatán Channel and the Florida Straits, and provided the immense impetus of the Gulf Stream current for the return voyage to Spain. Cuba stood at the vital exit point, and Havana, with the expansive sheltered harbor along the Gulf Stream, emerged as the ideal site from which to make final preparations for the long return trans-Atlantic voyage. Both annual *flotas* put in at Havana, whereupon the treasure-laden merchant vessels sailed for Europe under the protection of an armed convoy of galleons.

The strategic significance of Cuba now stood in sharp relief, and the frequency with which enemy vessels had previously seized and sacked Cuban ports now took on far-reaching implications. Indeed, the apparent ease with which the French had captured Havana in 1555 had a particu-

larly sobering effect on the Council of the Indies, for it served to underscore the vulnerability of the imperial defense system at one of its most
vital points. The Spanish response was immediate. Military garrisons were
established in Havana, providing for a permanent resident armed force
whose number fluctuated between 400 and 1,000 soldiers. Fortifications
strengthened Havana's defense. La Fuerza fortress was completed in 1577.
The construction of El Morro and La Punta was completed twenty years
later.

VII

The completion of Havana fortifications late in the sixteenth century gave
palpable expression to Cuba's place in the greater imperial scheme of
things. On its defense rested the defense of the Spanish empire. Its importance was more military than commercial, its value more strategic
than economic. The administration of local affairs responded more to
Spanish foreign policy needs than to Cuban domestic requirements. Increasingly, senior positions in colonial government passed to professional
soldiers, men charged with the defense of Cuba, not its development,
and under whom government was a function of military command, and
not civilian administration. Cuba assumed fully the appearance of a military outpost, and was administered accordingly.

The inauguration of the *flota* system conferred a new importance on
the island, and none too soon. In fact, the fleet system had generally a
salutary effect on the economy of western Cuba and contributed to the
rapid ascendancy of Havana. Its population increased, well out of proportion to the rest of the island, and at the expense of the rest of the
island. Construction crews to build the forts and army garrisons to guard
them contributed to population growth. The emergence of Havana as the
port of rendezvous for the annual fleets provided a powerful boost to the
expansion of the local economy. A vast floating population, often numbering as many as four to five thousand, assembled in Havana for weeks
at a time. Many were en route from the mainland with newly-made fortunes, prepared to make the most of their last port of call before the forty-
five-day trans-Atlantic voyage home. All were transients who required
entertainment, lodging, food, and goods.

A vast array of facilities developed around the needs of crews and passengers during their stay in Cuba. Havana early acquired a tawdry appearance, and became a city teeming with merchants, vendors, gamblers, deserters, and peddlers hawking wares of all types. Many passengers arrived weighed down with fortunes made on the mainland, and relieving them of this weight engaged the resourcefulness of *habaneros* from all sectors of society. There was money to be made in Havana, by many people, in many ways. "This place is the most expensive in all the Indies," Governor General Gabriel de Luján wrote of Havana as early as 1581; "that is because of the great number of ships that pass through here, and the people traveling on them cannot refrain from spending even if they wanted to." Havana experienced its first building boom, as construction expanded to accommodate the needs of a growing population of residents and transients. Between 1573 and 1578, more than 125 housing units were completed. Almost all sectors of the population participated in the new prosperity. Public works expanded. Lodging and dining facilities increased, stimulating in turn local agricultural and livestock production. Retail trade expanded. So too did illicit trade and commercialized vice. Brothels early established something of a ubiquitous presence in Havana, employing Indian women and, increasingly, female African slaves.

The fleets also stimulated the development of ancillary service sectors in Havana. Ships required repairs and preparation for the return voyage to Spain. Havana soon developed into one of the important shipyards of the New World, creating in the process almost unlimited work for artisans of all kinds, including carpenters, caulkers, shipwrights, sailmakers, riggers, and mechanics. The demands of the city led to the development of the surrounding countryside. The vast rich hardwood forests surrounding Havana provided a convenient and seemingly inexhaustible source of timber vital for repairs and construction. Lumber production expanded. At the same time, the rebellion in the Netherlands deprived Spain of an important source of lumber, much of which was made up by supplies from Cuba. Cuban hardwoods such as mahogany, ebony, and cedar served also as important items of an expanding contraband commerce.

The effects rippled through the local economy. Merchants and vendors multiplied. Farmers prospered. So did cattle breeders, as ranchers enjoyed the double boom of expanding markets for fresh meat in Havana and an equally large demand for hides and cured meat for the fleets. Local construction and maintenance of fortifications created jobs for stonecutters and masons. Several foundries were established for the manufacture of artillery and iron works of all kinds. Industrial trades expanded: shoemakers, silversmiths, bakers, blacksmiths, and tailors established small shops and organized into trade guilds.

In the course of the sixteenth century, Havana developed into the principal settlement of the island and the center of Spanish political and military authority. In 1553, the Council of the Indies ordered the governor of the island to transfer his residence from Santiago de Cuba to Havana. In 1594 Havana was elevated from a town *(villa)* to a city *(ciudad)*. The reorganization of local administration in 1607 formally established Havana as the capital of the island and the seat of the governor and captain-general. Insular government was divided into two jurisdictions. Havana received authority over Mariel, Cabañas, Bahía Honda, and Matanzas as well as fifty leagues into the interior, coast to coast. Santiago de Cuba exercised jurisdiction over Bayamo, Baracoa, and Puerto Príncipe. In matters of political administration and war, the authority of Havana took precedence; both shared equal authority in the administration of justice. Over the long run, this division created the conditions for rivalry and regional jealousies. Repeatedly officials in Santiago complained about Havana's abuse of authority and improper intervention in local affairs. One of the lasting features of Cuban demographics was established early. By the beginning of the seventeenth century, Havana accounted for a disproportionate share of the total population. More than half of the 20,000 inhabitants of the island in 1608 resided in Havana.

VIII

The effects of the *flota* system were not limited to Havana, and were not all salutary. Indeed, many of the very conditions that contributed to the rise of Havana and the west contributed to the decline of Santiago de Cuba and the east. The formal selection of Havana as the capital in 1607 served only to fix in fact what had already been established in practice. The prominence of the west over east, to be sure, had its origins early in the sixteenth century, due in part to chance, in part to choice. Trade winds and ocean currents combined with imperial defense and maritime needs pointed to Havana as the logical point of departure from the New World. The reorganization of Spanish shipping into two annual fleets and the routing of the *flotas* through the Florida Straits all but guaranteed the prosperity of the west and the impoverishment of the east. Eastern Cuba was all but excluded from regular participation in the trans-Atlantic trade. Havana henceforth served as the sole official port of entry for all goods arriving in Cuba, to the advantage of adjacent communities, to the detriment of distant ones.

These developments had far-reaching consequences. Even before the inauguration of the fleet system, settlements in eastern Cuba were languishing in varying degrees of inattention and isolation. Maritime traffic tended to flow one way—westward. Sailing west to east was arduous and time-consuming, and often impossible. Years passed without provisions arriving form Spain. As early as 1542 Santiago de Cuba officially complained that local residents had not received supplies for more than two years. The fleet system increased the isolation of the east, and afterwards abandonment was all but complete. A precarious existence now became a problematical one. The advance of the empire had left the eastern settlements behind, beyond easy reach of the source of their supplies and without ready access to markets for their products. The interior henceforth faced the uncertain prospect of depending on shipments which were infrequent and inadequate, and which arrived irregularly. In fact, the only constant feature of this exchange was cost: supplies were always expensive.

The transfer of the capital from Santiago de Cuba to Havana exacerbated existing conditions. The decision had the net effect of reducing the official presence in the eastern districts: lower ranking officeholders, fewer government officials, smaller army garrisons. Colonial government henceforth made only occasional incursions into the eastern interior zones, which in turn were only nominally under the control of the capital. One immediate effect was to increase the vulnerability of the east to the depradations of foreign interlopers. Indeed, during the course of the seventeenth century, interior towns were routinely plundered, sacked, and razed. In 1603 the French attacked Santiago and Bayamo, and again in 1628 and 1633. In 1652 they occupied Baracoa and attacked Remedios. In 1662 the English sacked Santiago. In 1665, a French fleet destroyed Sancti Spíritus. Three years later, Henry Morgan sacked Puerto Príncipe, and in 1675 John Springer plundered Trinidad. Puerto Príncipe was attacked again four years later.

Eastern Cuba was left to its own devices, to make out as best it could—against Indian raids, against corsair attacks, and most of all against neglect and isolation. Colonists in the east learned early to rely on their own resolve and on local resources, and improvised responses for their survival. What they learned most was to survive on the fringes of the island by subsisting at the fringes of illegality.

Poorly supervised and poorly supplied, the eastern population found it both easy and necessary to participate in illicit commerce and contraband. Foreign traders found ready buyers and sellers. That they were often religious and political enemies of Spain seemed to matter not at all. Settlers in the east welcomed discreet contact with traders from other countries, for they made available goods that were otherwise in low supply at high prices. For many settlements, the contraband trade was often the difference between subsistence and extinction, between surviving precariously through improvisation and succumbing certainly through attrition.

These were not chance transactions, the result of random encounters between a would-be seller and potential buyer. On the contrary, it was commerce on a large scale, illegal to be sure, but ordered and organized. It flourished, if not with the active participation of everyone then certainly with the passive acquiescence of most: men and women, young and old, farmers, ranchers, and merchants. Civil governors, military officers, and clergymen were frequently implicated in contraband. A priest in Baracoa, complained Governor Pedro de Valdés in 1602, "was one of the greatest customers of heretics and enemies to be found in all the Indies, and all the other friars and priests of the island imitate him openly, without any attempt at concealment." So widespread was the participation in contraband and so extensive was the disregard for law that it constituted opposition to government policy on a vast scale, and what was a legal issue was fraught with political implications. Indeed, in 1602, eight persons in Bayamo implicated in contraband were charged by the government not with smuggling but with rebellion and were sentenced to death and confiscation of their property. The sentence caused widespread indignation, leading to an armed uprising of two hundred residents. This first popular uprising against colonial government resulted in the release of the prisoners. Several years later, a total of five hundred contrabandists in Puerto Príncipe and Bayamo were charged with sedition, and again officials faced armed protest. Royal officials became increasingly reluctant to travel inland to enforce the ban against contraband. Rebellion was indeed very much on the minds of government authorities. "They are the most disloyal and rebellious vassals that any king or prince in this world ever had," Governor Valdés informed the Crown in 1606, "and if your Highness were to appear among them, they would sell your Highness for three yards of Rouen silk or even for nothing, because there is nothing they detest more than the authority of the king and his ministers."

Merchant vessels from Portugal, England, France, and Holland routinely visited the remote eastern settlements to trade manufactures, textiles, wine, and slaves for hides, salted meat, tobacco, and wood. In the seventeenth century, as rival European nations secured colonial possessions of their own in the Caribbean, contraband trade with Cuba expanded in volume and frequency. Baracoa on the north coast and Bayamo, Manzanillo, and Santiago de Cuba on the south emerged centers of illicit trade and distribution. "In the port of Manzanillo," reported one Spanish eyewitness to contraband traffic in 1602, "there are nine ships of Fleming, French and English engaged in contraband. . . . The Río Cauto in Bayamo is occupied so that no ship may leave without safe-conduct from the smugglers. . . . In the port of Manzanillo these enemies have artillery ashore and maintain a guard-house, where they have shops. . . . They live with so little anxiety that they sometimes leave their ships beached while their launches are scattered at sea, fetching and carrying merchandise for hides with as much freedom and shamelessness as if they were at home."

Circumstances served to differentiate the two regions of the island early. The distinctions between the east and west would deepen with the passage of time, but already at the end of the century of conquest, both Havana and Santiago occupied sharply different places on the social continuum of colonial Cuba. From these two contrary points would emerge competing views of *cubanidad*, of what it meant to be Cuban. The west flourished as a result of the official presence, in defense of colonial policy; the east flourished as a result of the official absence, in defiance of colonial policy.

IX

Between the flourishing west and the languishing east lay vast expenses of poorly governed and sparsely populated regions. Much of central Cuba, including Trinidad, Sancti Spíritus, and Remedios, was outside the jurisdiction of both Havana and Santiago. Authority was exercised by municipal councils *(cabildos)*, made up principally of local property owners. The extensive stretches of unbroken *sabanas* and plains were devoted largely to ranching. Cattle raising was particularly well suited to expanding commercial needs and changing demographic conditions. The fleets created a new demand for food and cattle products. The production of hides for both local and foreign markets increased. Leather was a coveted all-purpose building material, used for furniture, bindings, containers, and personal armor; it served in the construction of buildings, carts, and ships. Between 1570 and 1590, Cuba exported almost 300,000 hides to Spain, a legal trade very much favored by the inauguration of the fleet system. Hides served too as a major stock in trade of the contraband traffic, a source of illicit revenue and medium of illegal trade.

Cattle raising met the needs of changing colonial demographics. It expanded originally at a time of declining Indian population and dwindling Spanish settlers. The shortage of labor was mitigated by the availability of grazing land, and together combined to make livestock raising not only logical but practical and profitable as well. Capital requirements for items other than livestock were minimal, and the ability of cattle to multiply on the Cuban *sabanas* all but eliminated the need for further investment capital. Cattle grazed at will and roamed freely and extensively, thriving in more or less a wild state. The establishment of cattle ranges was determined by proximity to markets, the availability of pasturage and water, and access to ports. In time, cattle ranchers moved further inland in search of new pasturage, thereby serving as the effective instruments for continued expansion and settlement into the interior. By the early seventeenth century, the vast open expanses of the central plains in Camagüey and the western regions at Las Villas, Matanzas, and Havana had been occupied by cattle ranchers.

X

Agriculture developed haphazardly in the seventeenth century, also as a result of demographic changes and market conditions. Farming expanded on the outskirts of towns and cities, especially around Havana, where permanent residents and the transient population combined to create the largest single market on the island. Commercial agriculture also expanded, principally in the form of sugar and tobacco. Sugar production commenced during the 1520s, expanding tentatively during the uncertain years of declining labor and diminishing population. For much of the sixteenth century, sugar production was confined largely to the production of molasses concentrate, mostly for local consumption and limited export. In the 1590s, with the support of royal subsidies and official protection, including exemptions from duties and taxes on equipment imported for the construction of new mills, commercial production expanded. By the early seventeenth century, an estimated 50 mills were producing an annual average of 50,000 *arrobas* of sugar. (One *arroba* equals 25 pounds.)

The commercial production of tobacco began almost upon the completion of the conquest. Tobacco was originally cultivated and cured for a limited domestic market. Production gradually increased to meet the growing demands created by the fleet traffic. Demand suddenly surged late in the sixteenth century, when the use of tobacco products, both for snuff and smoking, gained widespread popularity in Europe. Cuban tobacco production expanded. So did profits and so did the cupidity of the Crown. Indeed, so lucrative was the trade and so large the market that tobacco production immediately attracted the attention of the royal exchequer. By the early seventeenth century, to the deepening dismay of tobacco farmers *(vegueros)*, the production, sale, and distribution of tobacco became objects of increasing government regulation and restriction. Tobacco was arguably one of the most heavily taxed colonial commodities, adding to costs, subtracting from profits, and dividing residents from rulers.

Taxation on this scale contributed to a boon of another kind. By the end of the sixteenth century, insatiable demand and increasing prices combined to make tobacco a readily negotiable article of trade. High demand in Europe and strict control in Cuba transformed tobacco instantly into a magnificent commodity of contraband. Taxes on tobacco provided a powerful boost for illicit trade, as seller and buyer alike shared a common interest in reducing unnecessary costs and raising the margin of profits. Cuban tobacco was an ideal contraband item. Commanding high prices for small volume, it was easily transported and readily concealed. It was also easy and inexpensive to cultivate, well suited for the small farmer. There was no need for large capital, large landholdings, or a large labor force. Seeds were readily available. A single plant could easily produce a million seeds, and a mere handful was sufficient to launch a family farm.

Tobacco cultivation expanded across the island during the late sixteenth and early seventeenth century, often cultivated for illicit commerce. It served to disperse the population inland, along the fertile allu-

vial plains of the interior, to promote the development of new towns and
villages and to foster the emergence of a new class of independent small
farmers. The zones of cultivation expanded first in the immediate envi-
rons of Havana, moving inland and upriver along the banks of the Al-
mendares, Mayabeque, and Ariguanabo rivers, serving as the economic
base around which the towns of San Antonio de los Baños, Santiago de
las Vegas, and Güines were formed. East toward Matanzas *vegueros*
scattered along the banks of the Canimar river. In central Cuba tobacco
farms were established on the banks of rivers near Trinidad. Cultivation
expanded into the central zones near Sancti Spíritus and Remedios, and
in the east around Bayamo, Mayarí, and El Caney. The contraband tobacco trade also served to encourage new settlements, most notably the
ports of Cabañas and Bahía Honda along the north coast of Pinar del Río.

XI

Much had changed in Cuba during the first century of the fleets. Not that
the place of Cuba within the empire had substantially improved. It had
not. The island still stood at the edge of the empire—still an entry on the
colonial ledger that represented a greater outlay of expenditures than intake of revenues. Cuba was a fiscal liability, an economic ward of the
mainland colonies, unable to produce sufficient revenues to defray even
the cost of its own administration. The ordinary expenses of colonial
administration, including the salaries of government functionaries, were
guaranteed by subventions from the mainland. The island depended on
periodic subsidies *(situados)* from Mexico to underwrite the costs of constructing fortifications and maintaining military garrisons: 21.6 million
pesos between 1766 and 1774, 36.1 million between 1766 and 1788.

By the late seventeenth century, conditions had changed slightly for
the better. The island was no longer only a remote military outpost of the
New World empire. The economy had gradually recovered from the post-
conquest depression. The rapid development of the west contributed to
important regional differentiations in the economy. Commercial agriculture expanded in the areas around Havana—in part a response to proximity of the local demand, in part a response to the expansion of European demands, but mostly in response to market forces bringing high
profits. Cattle raising around Havana declined. Land utilized earlier for
grazing passed under commercial cultivation. Cattle pasturage underwent

progressive subdivision into farms and plantations devoted to tobacco and sugar. Tobacco farms *(vegas)* and sugar estates expanded during the seventeenth century, largely in the western zones. Tobacco and sugar were developing into export products with great potential for profits, and even greater possibilities as a source of colonial revenue.

XII

The population of the island increased slowly during the seventeenth century: from 20,000 inhabitants in 1608 to 30,000 inhabitants in 1662. Much of this growth resulted from the immigration of an estimated 3,000 settlers who relocated in Cuba after the English occupation of Jamaica in 1655. Skewed settlement patterns persisted, as population in the western regions, and especially in Havana, increased well out of proportion to growth elsewhere on the island. Settlements in the west increased in number, and enjoyed some measure of prosperity. Bahía Honda and Mariel on the north and Batabanó on the south emerged as important centers of commerce, licit and illicit. Interior settlements in the east continued to suffer the effects of neglect and isolation—slow population growth with ever slower economic development. Bayamo enjoyed modest prosperity based largely on a brisk contraband trade with foreigners. The local economy expanded, principally around livestock and lumber. By 1700, the Spanish, African, and Indian population of Bayamo had reached approximately 4,000, making it the second largest city on the island. Santiago de Cuba continued to suffer from Spanish neglect and foreign attack. The eastern capital, in effect, occupied a frontier position on the island, one of the most exposed points in the central Caribbean that by the end of the seventeenth century had very much become a hostile world. The English seizure of Jamaica (1655) to the south and the French occupation of western Española (1665) to the east resulted in Santiago facing the territories of Spanish enemies. On a clear day Santiago was within sight of both. Population growth was slow: there were about 3700 residents by 1689, engaged principally in sugar and trade with Cartagena and the South American mainland. The towns of Puerto Príncipe, Sancti Spíritus, Baracoa, and Trinidad were at the margins of government jurisdiction, theoretically subject to either Santiago or Havana but in fact too distant from both for this authority to have any real meaning. Among the more important new settlements established in the seventeenth century were Santa

Clara (1689) and Matanzas (1693). At the same time, the English presence in Jamaica impelled Spanish authorities to give greater attention to the southern frontiers of the island. New colonization projects extended Spanish settlements to the Isle of Pines and Jagua Bay (Cienfuegos). By the end of the seventeenth century, the population had reached the 50,000 mark, half of which was located in Havana and the surrounding communities.

The population was a mix of European, Indian, and African. By the seventeenth century, the Indian population had declined to less than 2,000. As the number of Indians declined, the number of African slaves increased. Slaves were employed in the mines, in urban construction, in trades, and most of all on the expanding sugar estates. Between 1550 and 1650, the African slave population increased from 1,000 to 5,000.

Cuba was still very much a colony without European women. During the early decades, Cuba was a place of few settlements and of few people. Men arrived to make their fortune, and were on the march and on the move—to Mexico, to the mainland to the north and the mainland to the south. Few arrived with women. Fewer still arrived with families. The Crown prohibited emigration of unaccompanied females, and during the early years those white women who did reach Cuba arrived mostly with ranking government officials and senior military officers—the wives, daughters, and an appropriate entourage to minister to their needs. By and large, however, comparatively few white women resided in Cuba. Through much of the sixteenth century, European women represented less than 10 percent of the total Spanish population. According to sixteenth-century chronicler Francisco López de Gómara, "there were few Spanish women about, and they were much sought after." The skewed European male-female ratio continued through the sixteenth century, itself a function of a population that lived in conditions that approached a garrison existence. During the early seventeenth century, as population achieved some stability and as the economy reorganized around agriculture, families began arriving in Cuba in larger numbers. The Council of the Indies reinforced this trend and sought to encourage family migration as a means at once of populating the island and stabilizing the Cuban settlements.

In the main, however, and through much of the sixteenth century, comparatively few white woman resided in Cuba. The sex imbalance among white settlers persisted through the seventeenth century. In fact, it was exacerbated by the thousands of the transients of the fleets and the soldiers of the garrisons. Due to this relative absence of women from Europe, women of color played an increasingly prominent role in the island's development. Through the *repartimiento,* the *conquistadores* distributed among themselves Indian women *(naborías)* as personal servants and permanent concubines. The first generation creoles were largely the offspring of European men and Indian women. African slaves also served as another principal source of female labor, particularly in Havana, where they prepared food, tended or managed taverns, and discharged a variety of domestic services. The skewed sex ratio also determined decisively the character of sexual relations in the colony. Women of color served as the female population from which white men selected sex partners. Miscegenation began with the conquest, and it never ended. Out of these relationships emerged a portion of a new and significant population of free people of color.

XIII

A condition somewhere between indulgence and indifference characterized Spanish administration in Cuba at the close of the seventeenth century. Set against the larger context of the empire, Cuba was a marginal producer of marginal products. The island had become accustomed to a state of benign neglect. Indeed, it thrived on it. The fleets had created vast opportunities for commerce and contraband. Often, the transactions occurred side by side; on occasion, they were one and the same. Periodic efforts to suppress contraband failed. Spain had neither the resources nor the resolve to keep vigil over thousands of miles of coastline and the hundreds of islets and keys along the coasts. In any case, too many settlers, and probably too many officials, had too much at stake in smuggling. Until Spain could guarantee distant settlements sufficient supplies and adequate markets—and it never could—authorities were grudgingly obliged to acquiesce to the economic realities of seventeenth-century Cuba. The only other alternative was the forceful depopulation of the Cuban interior. And, indeed, depopulation of contraband centers in eastern Cuba was periodically advocated: in 1600 colonial authorities urged the depopulation and razing of Baracoa; in 1605 they considered expelling colonists from Bayamo; a year later, thought was given to relocating Trinidad closer to Santiago de Cuba. Something similar had been attempted in the western zones of Española, with disastrous results, leading to the French seizure of abandoned areas and eventually the establishment of the French colony of St. Domingue.

The presence of a Spanish population, hence, even one unabashedly engaged in widespread contraband, was not without some value in the greater imperial scheme of things. That an independent economy of any sort established itself in Cuba was an unexpected and largely welcome development. Certainly it contributed to stabilizing resident population on the island. No less important, the island did begin to make modest contributions to the royal coffers and toward its own upkeep. A rudimentary export economy developed, one based as much on illicit transactions as on legal trade. The eastern zones maintained extended and illegal trade networks with Jamaica, St. Domingue, Curaçao, and scores of smaller European colonies in the eastern Antilles. Nor were these conditions a source of undue official preoccupation. On the contrary, they flourished more or less with the sanction of local officials. On any number of occasions, during periods of critical scarcities and dire need, especially with food supplies, local officials sanctioned illegal transactions with the neighboring colonies of Spanish rivals. In the end, revenue losses attending contraband were charged to the larger overhead requirements of maintaining an economically nonproductive military outpost.

But conditions in Cuba were also symptomatic of a larger malaise of empire. Contraband commerce had assumed massive proportions everywhere in the Spanish New World. The Hapsburg colonial bureaucracy approached a state of near collapse, an accurate reflection of the condition of the dynasty in Spain. An age was coming to an end.

3

Out from the Shadows

I

The eighteenth century began with the appearance of a French fleet in
Havana harbor—not a menacing presence; on the contrary, a reassuring
one, announcing the passing of an old age and the onset of a new one.
The Hapsburg dynasty had expired, and the French Bourbons were claiming succession to the vacant Spanish throne. The arrival of French war-
ships in Cuban waters signified a commitment to defend the Bourbon
claim to rule Spain. The French presence was also a portent of Bourbon
determination to assert metropolitan rule over the Indies.

The Bourbons inherited an empire in varying degrees of decline and
disintegration. From the vantage point of the metropolis, the colonial
economies were in depression and colonial administration was in disarray. Exports from the New World had fallen, so had consumption of
imports from the Old World. And everywhere in the Indies, royal authority was on the defensive.

Only in Spain were conditions worse, and this was perhaps the one
bright aspect of an otherwise bleak assessment of the realms of the kingdom. However wretched the conditions in the colonies, the Bourbons
correctly suspected the economy of the Indies to possess greater buoy-
ancy and more potential vitality than did the economy of Spain. The
Bourbons drew the obvious inference: economic expansion in the Indies
was possible, and more—it was necessary, for the economic recovery of
Spain depended on it. But economic revival in the Indies was only a
partial solution. No less important was the development of the means and
mechanisms through which to appropriate a greater share of the revenues
of the Indies for Spanish recovery.

The suspicion took hold, too, and not without some justification, that
the New World economies remained substantially sound; that what had
broken down was not the productive capabilities of the Indies but, rather,
Spain's ability to control the products of that capability, that not enough
of what the New World produced—either in the form of resources or

49

receipts—reached Spanish coffers. The lethargy of the colonial official-dom and the laxity of colonial officials, the Bourbons were convinced, had allowed corruption and contraband to reach unmanageable propor-tions. The Bourbon intent, hence, was to make the colonial economies work again directly for the economic development of Spain, by appro-priating and transferring to Europe production surpluses that had long remained in the Indies. Spain sought to increase and improve trade be-tween the metropolis and the colonies, reduce contraband by increasing supplies, and promote Spanish manufacturers and industry by fostering exports to the Indies. That Spain had experienced a loss of colonial rev-enues at all was attributed to a century of mismanagement and maladmin-istration under the Hapsburgs. The Bourbons ascended to the Spanish throne determined to rationalize and reorganize, but most of all to regain control of the economic resources of the Indies and reassert political con-trol over the colonies.

Bourbon strategies had direct implications for eighteenth-century Cuba. Conditions on the island had changed. So, too, had the context of those changes. The island was no longer simply a military outpost with little commercial value. The economy had developed and diversified, not a great deal, certainly, but slowly, and in unspectacular fashion. A century of fleets had lifted the island from its colonial torpor, and in its own right Cuba had become an increasingly significant source of colonial revenues. Cuba's future development, to be sure, promised more than its past per-formance had delivered, but that was exactly the point: Cuba showed great promise.

It was not only that economic conditions on the island were better. It was also that economic conditions on the mainland were worse. The dif-ference between the two—an enclave of modest prosperity in an environ-ment of relative depression—under almost any circumstances would have aroused the cupidity of the royal exchequer. That these were the condi-tions at the time of the Bourbon succession to the Spanish throne invited increased royal scrutiny of Cuban affairs.

Through the early years of the eighteenth century, Cuba enjoyed mod-est economic growth, stimulated principally by increased exports to Eu-rope, and especially by new access to French markets. A good part of this expanded trade centered on the export of tobacco products. Indeed, by the early eighteenth century tobacco was Cuba's most important source of foreign exchange. The consumption of tobacco in Europe was increas-ing, in the form of powdered tobacco for snuff, cut tobacco for pipe smoking, and leaf for cigars. Cuban production organized initially around the export of rappee in response to the rising popularity of snuff in northern Europe and the manufacture of cigars for the Spanish market. Tobacco cultivation expanded, commerce increased. A flourishing industry developed around an estimated twenty tobacco mills, almost all in Havana and Matanzas, devoted to the production of powdered tobacco for export.

But success of this type, and certainly at this time, brought Cuban tobacco production again to the attention of the always penurious royal exchequer. The results were predictable. In 1717, the crown established a royal monopoly to control the production and price of tobacco and the manufacture and marketing of snuff. The monopoly company, known as the Factoría de Tabacos, located its headquarters in Havana and established four branches in Trinidad, Sancti Spíritus, Bayamo, and Santiago de Cuba. By the terms of its charter, the Factoría was established as the sole purchasing agent of all tobacco produced in Cuba, at a fixed price, according to quality. The Factoría also assumed control of the distribution and sale of Cuban tobacco products abroad. The company was obliged to buy not the entire tobacco crop produced by every *veguero* but only the quantity it desired at the prices it determined. *Vegueros* were prohibited from selling surplus production to private merchants and exporters, an arrangement that effectively condemned farmers to the loss of whatever portion of the crop the royal monopoly refused to purchase.

The Factoría sought to achieve several objectives at once. Most immediately, the monopoly was designed to regulate the price of tobacco on terms favorable to buyers in Cuba and sellers in Spain. Related to price control was production control. Monopolists sought to lower Cuban tobacco output, thereby reducing the surplus production of tobacco that would otherwise find outlet in contraband trade and compete directly with monopoly tobacco in European markets. No less important, and part of a long-term strategy, the Factoría sought to arrest the development of tobacco manufacturing in Cuba, with the goal eventually of transferring the industry to Spain and reducing Cuba to the export of the leaf. By the terms of the 1717 decree, Spanish authorities prohibited the construction of all new tobacco mills. Three years later, a decree imposed an import duty on ground tobacco 40 percent higher than the charge assessed on the whole leaf.

The use of state-sponsored monopoly was not limited to tobacco production. A far more ambitious project was launched in 1740, one aspiring to nothing less the total control over all of the island's foreign trade. The Real Compañía de Comercio de La Habana was organized as a mixed state and private enterprise, raising nearly one million pesos from Spanish merchantile investors in Cádiz and Havana and funds contributed by the Spanish Crown. By the terms of the charter of incorporation, the Real Compañía obtained exclusive rights over all trade and commerce between Spain and Cuba. The company was expected to turn over a profit quickly and handsomely, and how it was to achieve these objectives was left to the ingenuity of its organizers.

The results were not long in coming. The Real Compañía bought cheaply and sold dearly. It depressed the prices paid for Cuban exports, principally tobacco, sugar, and hides, and inflated the prices of Spanish imports, largely textiles, manufactures, and foodstuff. A barrel of flour purchased in Spain for five pesos was resold in Havana for thirty-five. Profits on tobacco ranged between 500 and 600 percent annually. Tobacco purchased in Cuba for 400,000 pesos was sold in Europe for 4 million. By 1745, five years after its organization, the Real Compañía had doubled its initial reserve of working capital while paying stockholers an annual 30 percent return on their original investment.

Increasingly the Bourbons moved to reduce local power and limit local initiative. Whereas previously the Havana town council (cabildo) exercised governing authority in the absence of a captain general, after 1715 this responsibility was transferred to a newly created position of teniente de rey, appointed by the Crown. In 1729, the Bourbon court revoked and reclaimed the authority previously awarded to Cuban cabildos to distribute public land among local residents.

Bourbon officials also made vigorous effects to suppress the contraband trade, a way both to stem the loss of colonial revenues and to stimulate metropolitan exports. Certainly this was one objective of the Real Compañía—to reduce smuggling by improving the distribution of commodities to areas poorly serviced by traditional maritime traffic. The suppression of smuggling was entrusted to a newly organized irregular force of guarda costa, fitted out privately and paid out of the booty of captured contraband. Efforts were made also to encourage Spanish privateers to intercept the illicit maritime traffic between eastern Cuba and Jamaica and St. Domingue. In 1746 a royal decree authorized Spanish privateers to retain the capture prize shares previously claimed by the government. Spoils were exempted from all taxes and duties. Military garrisons were enlarged. At the same time, municipal administration across the island was reorganized and militarized. Loyal military officials replaced lax civilian ones. In 1733 the town of Puerto Príncipe, a thriving contraband center, was detached from the jurisdiction of Santiago de Cuba and placed directly under military rule from Havana.

II

The use of state monopolies during the eighteenth century, no less than increased state intervention in local affairs, achieved the desired effects: production was consolidated, commerce was centralized. But most of all, it improved the collection of revenues by reducing illegal trade and increasing taxes on legal commerce.

It had other effects, too, not all of which were either intended or envisaged. Certainly there was no mistaking the objective of Bourbon mercantilism: it aspired to nothing less than exclusive control over colonial resources and receipts. Bourbon policy, however, had an unsettling effect in Cuba. Most immediately, and unabashedly, it favored Spanish interests over Cuban ones. It was supposed to, and Cubans were also supposed to acquiesce to this new state of affairs. Bourbon policy increased the strength of the mercantile/commercial sector, largely Spanish, over the agricultural/ranching sector, mostly Cuban, and in so doing sharpened the distinctions between *peninsular* interests and creole ones. Furthermore, these developments served to reinforce the privileged position of Havana and the west to the detriment and at the expense of Santiago de Cuba and the east. Attempts to suppress contraband succeeded only in visiting a new round of hardships on the interior settlements and winning for the Crown the enduring enmity of local residents. In fact, smuggling continued, often at greater costs to Cubans, if only because risks were greater. Spanish authorities succeeded only in disrupting the contraband trade, without adequately meeting the ensuing increase of local demand.

The new regimen of state intervention, coming as it did after decades of more or less inattention and indifference, coming too during a period in which the Cuban economy had registered some notable gains, underscored the contradictions between interests properly Spanish and interests principally Cuban. Spanish mercantilism, to be sure, was nothing new. What was new was the speed and scope of its application in Cuba. It had long been a policy applied more to the mainland than to the island, without much direct relevance to the backwater areas of the Caribbean. The languishing island had managed to escape the sustained interest of the royal exchequer, and for good reason. It had long been an object of expense, not a source of earnings. Feeble attempts were indeed made in the late seventeenth century to exert some control over Cuba, but by then the Hapsburg dynasty was so enervated and its representatives so ineffective as to make these belated efforts at fiscal efficiency all but wholly futile. The modest economic development enjoyed by Cuba in the seventeenth century occurred in a colony situated on the periphery of empire and at the periphery of legality.

Conditions changed in the eighteenth century, and Spanish policy had jolting effects on the island. For many in Cuba, Bourbon mercantilism was palpably confiscatory, and worse, distinctly prejudicial to the long-term interests of the permanent residents of the island. The immediate effect was to arouse local attachments, as a policy designed to benefit Spanish interests was seen as a bane to Cuban interests.

But Cuban complaints were not limited to the monopoly schemes. No less irksome to local producers and consumers was the endless proliferation of new taxes and the increase of old ones. Indeed, taxation was a central feature of the Bourbon strategy for transferring revenues from the colony to the metropolis. The number of taxes increased and collection improved. Profits went down, prices went up. No sector of Cuban society was immune from taxes, in one form or another, on one product or another: the *almojarifazgo* on imports and exports, the *alcabala* on sales, the *avería* for the fleets, the ecclesiastical *diezmo* for the church and the royal *quinto* on the mines. And still other surcharges: occupational license fees; taxes on farms, cattle, slaves, warehouse storage, cockfights; special levies for public works, disembarkation duties, travelers' fees; taxes on the production of tobacco, molasses, sugar, hides, jerked beef, and lumber. They seemed to increase in number and rise in rate, endlessly.

Cubans had developed some tolerance for the caprice of the Crown. They were not unfamiliar with its ways, or even unwilling to endure its excesses—at sporadic and short-lived intervals. Bourbon policy was different. It was sustained and systematic, and it affected almost everyone. The material condition of most Cubans deteriorated. State monopolies routinely engaged in profiteering and price gouging as the normal method of doing business in Cuba. Nor did Cuban producers obtain wider distribution for their exports. On the contrary, access to markets actually diminished. The problem of inadequate provisions at inflated prices worsened. Supplies did not increase, costs did not decline. Food shortages occurred in Havana with increasing frequency, most notably in 1718, 1737, 1745, and 1753. Scarcities were particularly acute in the eastern interior regions of the island, where the new restrictive policies of the Bourbons, combined with the previous neglect of the Hapsburgs, served to exacerbate conditions of privation. "The inhabitants of Santiago de Cuba," Governor General Alejandro O'Reilly reported to Crown in 1764, "see themselves abandoned for not receiving from your Majesty's dominions what they need for their dress and sustenance, and for lacking the corresponding means of exporting the valuable products of their forests and labors. In ten years, what has arrived to Santiago de Cuba, Bayamo, Puerto Príncipe and the other settlements of the interior has been barely sufficient for consumption of ten months."

Cuban reaction to Bourbon policies was not long in coming. Some Cuban producers denounced state monopoly policy, others defied it. As the inequities of the monopoly system became more flagrant, Cubans sought alternative economic relations, in and out of the colonial context, legal and illegal. Clandestine trade enjoyed a lively revival. The contraband network expanded, linking the remote eastern settlements in Spanish Cuba to British Jamaica to the south and French St. Domingue to the east. Cuban dealings with contrabandists from the North American colonies increased. Indeed, the vast share of maritime activity along the southern coast of the eastern half of the island consisted, in one form of another, of contraband commerce. Perhaps as much as 75 percent of Cuba's total tobacco production entered the world market by way of illicit transactions. The English accounted for almost one-third as many hides as did Spain. Contemporary estimates calculated that as much as 45 percent of all Cuban products left the island in the form of contraband. Illegal transactions reached an estimated 1.4 million pesos yearly. English traders from Jamaica exchanged slaves for livestock and timber in Santiago. French vendors from St. Domingue traded clothing and foodstuff for tobacco in Mayarí and Baracoa. Many of the local economies in the east organized around the contraband trade. Puerto Príncipe and Bayamo developed extensive herds of horses and mules for export to the Jamaican market. Puerto Príncipe actually flourished and grew during the early eighteenth century, increasing from a backward town of 2,766 residents in 1701 to a small entrepôt of 12,000 in 1729.

Cuban opposition to Bourbon policies was not confined to evasion of authority. It also provoked confrontation with authority. The establishment of the Factoría in 1717 led to organized resistance and armed protest from tobacco farmers in Havana, Santiago de Cuba, El Caney, and Arimao. The *vegueros* of Arimao defied the Factoría by refusing to sell their crop to the Trinidad branch. In August 1717, more than 500 armed *vegueros* in Havana marched into the capital to protest the state monopoly. The demonstration forced the resignation of Governor General Vicente Raxa and ranking officials of the Factoría and caused the temporary suspension of the monopoly's operation. For the first time in Cuban history, a popular uprising led to the removal of a senior representative of colonial authority. Spain responded subsequently by reinforcing the Havana garrison with 1,000 additional troops, and in 1720, the Factoría resumed normal operations. *Vegueros* rebelled again in 1720, and once more three years later, almost 1,000 of them. This time the colonial government responded with military force. Militia units marched into the surrounding countryside in pursuit of protesting farmers, and in the weeks that followed, scores of *vegueros* were killed in battle or executed in the aftermath of defeat.

The *vegueros'* rebellions gave expression to the emerging conflict between local interests and imperial authority. Certainly the clash sharpened the *vegueros'* determination to defend the prerogative of disposing of their products under the most favorable conditions. In some cases, this led to an increase of contraband. Spanish repression also served to disperse tobacco growers and disrupt tobacco production from traditional zones around Havana, westward into Pinar del Río and eastward toward Oriente. After 1723, many rebellious *vegueros* had been transformed into fugitives, most of whom migrated into the interior to escape Spanish repression. Many took flight into the island extremities to start over, having suffered property and crop losses during the uprising. Settlements sprang up along the banks of the Cuyaguateje River and thus began production of the famous leaf of Vuelta Abajo. Out of this migration emerged the principal tobacco centers of Guane, Guanajay, Consolación, and Pinar del Río. The migration also led to the creation of the tobacco settlements around Bayamo, Holguín, and Mayarí. These new *veguero* settlements had one other advantage: they were distant from the center of monopolists' authority. Henceforth the best Cuban tobacco reached world markets by way of illicit trade. A new age of Cuban production had commenced.

III

The end of the state monopolies came from the most improbable and wholly unexpected source. The entry of Spain in the Seven Years' War (1756–63) between England and France transformed the Caribbean into a zone of military operations and Cuba into a key military objective. In 1762 the British struck, and after a forty-four day siege, Havana fell to the English.

The English control of Havana was brief, hardly more than ten months. But this short duration belied the larger significance of the English presence. Almost two hundred years of Spanish mercantilism had exacted their toll on Havana, and the effects were telling. By the mid-eighteenth century, Havana was closed in on itself and closed out of the world, an enclave of modest prosperity, to be sure, but its prospects of future development far greater than past growth. The British occupation of Havana was the first in a series of events to transform the Cuban economy, and with it, all of Cuba. After 1762, Cuba would never be the same.

Changes had already begun to transform the island: some economic growth, some commercial development, some agricultural diversification. It happened, however, that Cuban economic expansion was obstructed by Spanish economic restrictions. Cuban producers were chafing under the crude mercantilism of the Bourbons. It happened too that local discontent with Spanish commercial policy was rising at the same time that Cuban commercial potential was increasing and that both were peaking at the time the British arrived.

The English occupation of Havana demonstrated what was possible under optimum circumstances, and demonstrated that optimum circumstances were possible. It created opportunities that producers in Cuba previously could only have dreamed about. Cubans were both prepared and predisposed to seize the opportunity, and they would never go back. Trade taxes were abolished. The port was thrown open to free trade with Great Britain and its New World colonies. Venders and jobbers from England descended upon Havana, offering Cubans a dazzling array of coveted consumer goods, staple items, and industrial wares: linens, textiles, manufactures, and especially sugar machinery. Merchants and traders from the North American colonies flocked to the Cuban capital, selling grains, tools, and foodstuff. Also available now in Cuba on a scale hitherto unknown was the most highly coveted commodity of all: African slaves. The demand was almost insatiable. Slave traders of all nationalities converged on Havana in a scramble for a share of the newly opened Cuban market. During the ten-month occupation, an estimated 10,000 slaves were introduced to Havana—as many slaves as would have normally entered in ten years.

Producers and traders in Havana, for their part, prospered through their participation in this expanded commerce. Certainly Spanish monopolist interests suffered during the occupation, but almost all local economic sectors benefited. New markets became available for Cuban tobacco, sugar, molasses, and hides. For ten months, Havana bustled with maritime traffic and mercantile transactions: ten months in which more than 1,000 ships entered Havana harbor—a port that during the previous ten years had not seen more than fifteen vessels a year.

These were good times in Cuba, or at least in western Cuba. Outside of increased possibilities for smuggling, especially with British territories, it is not certain that the rest of the island had much opportunity to participate formally in the *prosperidad británica*. The English claimed jurisdiction from Pinar del Río to Matanzas, although effective control did not exceed much beyond the north-coast ports of Mariel and Havana to the west and Matanzas to the east. Nor was formal control necessary, for prosperity was incentive enough for local merchants and producers to collaborate with the occupation government. Wider markets, increased demands, and higher prices were a boon to the surrounding countryside, all of which served to stimulate local tobacco and sugar production, ranching, and farming.

IV

The brief English occupation ended in 1763. Spain ceded Florida in exchange for Havana, and by the middle of the year, former Bourbon rulers had returned to the capital. But too much had transpired in ten months, and it was apparent that Havana could not return to the ways of former Bourbon rule—not, at least, without provoking widespread anger among important sectors of the population. Cuba had flourished during the Spanish absence, and the moral was not lost on Bourbon authorities. Too many merchants, producers, and consumers had enjoyed the benefits of liberal trade to acquiesce submissively to the restoration of former trade restrictions.

But things had changed in Spain too. A new king occupied the Spanish throne. These were the years of the Enlightenment, and Charles III was the product of his time: the very prototype of the "enlightened despots" of eighteenth-century Europe. It was a time of reason and rationality, and in the Spanish world a time to contemplate administrative reorganization, economic change, and scientific revival.

The disposition for reform in Spain coincided with the demand for reform in Cuba. There could be no going back, and changes followed in rapid sequence. Commerce was liberalized. In 1764, monthly mail packet service was inaugurated between Havana and Coruña, Spain. A year later, the trade monopoly long held by merchants of Seville and Cádiz ended when Havana was authorized to trade directly with seven other Spanish cities, Barcelona, Alicante, Cartagena, Málaga, Coruña, Gijón, and Santander. Trade was also inaugurated with the islands of Puerto Rico, Trinidad, and Margarita. No less important, Cubans were authorized to seek additional markets with their own ships. The old tax structure was dismantled and replaced by a flat 7 percent ad valorem. The state trade monopoly was abolished. In 1774 Spain rescinded all duties on Cuban imports. Four years later, Havana's commercial pre-eminence came to an official end, as three additional ports—Santiago de Cuba, Trinidad, and Batabanó—were authorized to trade directly with Spain and with the other colonies of Spanish America. Similar trade privileges were subsequently extended to Nuevitas (1784), Matanzas (1793), Caibarién (1794), Manzanillo (1802), and Baracoa (1803). Between 1789 and 1791, Spain opened Cuban ports to unlimited free trade in slaves to all individuals and all companies of any nationality, a concession subsequently extended for another six years. In 1817, the crown suppressed the Factoría de Tabacos and provided for unlimited cultivation and unrestricted sale of tobacco.

These were years, too, in which international rivalries again intruded upon Cuba, with more or less salutary effect. The British North American colonies were in rebellion, and in search of friends and friendly ports. Spain offered both, and in 1776 opened Cuban ports to direct trade with North America. Once more, Cuban producers secured access to wider markets for their sugar and molasses and received in return flour, manufactured goods, and slaves. In 1779, following the lead of France and Holland, Spain formally entered the war against England. For the next four years, Cuba enjoyed free commerce with Spanish allies and their colonies.

Trade with the thirteen colonies was especially important, for after the rebellion against England, the former North American possessions were denied access to the markets of the British Caribbean colonies. Cuba served as an alternative and became an increasingly important source of sugar, molasses, coffee, and tobacco. North American producers also acquired alternative customers of exports who were previously directed to the English Antilles.

V

Fully twenty years after the British occupation of Havana, far-reaching changes had overtaken Cuban society. If the availability of new markets made the expansion of sugar profitable, the availability of new slaves made it possible. The slave trade flourished during the latter half of the eighteenth century. Slaves had long been a highly coveted commodity, the stock in the illicit trade that had thrived for almost two centuries. But the contraband trade as a source of slaves was neither adequate nor reliable. Vital to the Cuban strategy of expanded sugar production was not only an increased supply of slave labor but a guaranteed supply of African slaves thereafter. The British occupation followed by the Bourbon liberalization of trade provided a powerful boost to the importation of slave labor. The slave trade decree of 1789–91, further, provided additional sources of slaves. Indeed, between 1789 and 1798, no less than eleven decrees, orders, and pronouncements were enacted to facilitate the trade in slaves. During the previous 250 years of Spanish rule between 1512 and 1763, an estimated total of 60,000 slaves had been introduced into Cuba. This rate changed dramatically, and between 1764 and 1790, the number of slaves imported into Cuba surpassed the 50,000 mark, averaging approximately 2,000 slaves a year.

The number of sugar mills increased, the cultivation of cane expanded, production modernized. At the outset of the eighteenth century, one hundred sugar mills were in operation, mostly around Havana, manufacturing sugar with substantially the same inefficiency of sixteenth-century mills. Sugar production was already in a state of flux during the decades preceding the British occupation. By the end of the 1730s, Cuban output had reached a record 2,000 tons. Indeed, sugar production had overtaken existing transportation capacity, and it was precisely this shipping bottleneck that Cuban producers hoped the newly founded Real Compañía would alleviate. Nor were they disappointed. Under the auspices of the Real Compañía, which guaranteed wider markets and improved transportation, planters increased sugar production to 5500 tons by the end of the 1750s. But on the eve of the English occupation, Cuban producers had again overtaken the available markets and shipping facilities.

It was in this context that the British occupation of Havana occurred and that the Bourbon reforms were enacted. Producers now faced almost unlimited opportunities. The opportunities between 1763 and 1783 provided powerful stimulus for both the conversion of old land to sugar and the expansion of sugar onto new land. During these years too, modern sugar equipment, especially from England, became generally available to Cuban planters. After the 1760s, new mills were organized in regions where none had previously existed: from Havana southward into the western interior, and eastward along the northern coastal plains to Jaruco and past Matanzas. The new, larger mills incorporated the latest technology. The size of the average sugar plantation in 1762 was 320 acres worked by six to eight slaves. Thirty years later the average had increased to 700 acres worked by almost one hundred slaves. The acreage devoted to sugar cane increased in spectacular fashion—from 10,000 acres in 1762 to 160,000 in 1792. By the early 1800s, the total number of sugar mills had increased to almost 500: 237 in Havana, 50 near Matanzas, 60 around Santiago de Cuba and Bayamo, 50 near Puerto Príncipe, and the balance located throughout western Cuba. Sugar production rose from 10,000 tons annually during the 1770s to 12,000 tons in the 1780s and 16,000 tons in the early 1790s.

Trade and commerce expanded to keep pace with increasing export opportunities and rising import needs. Import-export revenues soared, from 2 million pesos in 1770 to 16.6 million in 1790. So did public revenues: 163,000 pesos in 1760, 532,000 in 1770, and 1.2 million in 1782. In the early 1780s, Havana experienced its first serious difficulties with harbor congestion. Nor was the increased volume of shipping confined to the capital. After 1778, all the major ports of the island participated in expanded trade and commerce.

Prosperity may have served to free Cuban producers from some of the more oppressive features of Spanish mercantilism, but it also contributed to subjecting them to a new tyranny of Spanish merchants. Rising sugar production and increasing trade gave new importance to *peninsular* traders and retailers. They served as moneylenders, collectively one of the principal sources of readily available capital on the island. They dominated the critical import-export nexus upon which Cuba was becoming increasingly dependent. Sugar production expanded rapidly during these years, in the place of other forms of agriculture, in lieu of other forms of production. It served as a powerful centripetal force in the local economy: it concentrated capital, consolidated land, consumed labor. It was inimical to diversification, and almost everything else. As Cuba moved inexorably toward monoculture in the eighteenth century, dependence on imports—foodstuff, clothing, manufactures—increased, and so too did the importance of the merchants. These developments served to accelerate and accentuate the deepening contradiction of the colonial political economy: a Cuban landed elite dependent upon Spanish merchants. It was not a felicitous relationship. Merchants aspired to nothing less than complete domination of colonial trade, a position from which to exercise control over an economy increasingly dependent on imports and exports. They tended to underpay for exports and overcharge for imports. Cuban producers demanded freedom to trade directly with foreigners. They intuitively opposed and consciously resisted the proposition that Cuban commerce functioned solely for the benefit of Spain and Spaniards. This was an uneasy relationship, troublesome in the eighteenth century, and more so in the nineteenth.

VI

The new prosperity led to new population growth. New towns were founded including Holguín, Morón, Bejucal, Santa María del Rosario, and Santiago de las Vegas. Census information tends to underscore some of the more important demographic changes transforming Cuban society. The official census of 1774 counted 171,620 residents of the island in the distribution indicated in Table 2. By 1791, the population registered significant increases in every category listed.

The population growth patterns for the period 1774–91 underscored several features of eighteenth-century Cuba. An estimated 44 percent of the total population was concentrated around the Havana metropolitian area. Indeed, by the end of the eighteenth century, Havana ranked as one of the largest cities in the New World. Women constituted approximately 43 percent of the total Cuban population. The percentage of white women in the colony increased slightly between censuses (42 to 46 percent), due largely to increased family migration from Spain. At the same time, the percentage of slave women decreased significantly between 1774 and 1791

TABLE 2. Cuban Population (1774–91)

	1774	1791
White		
Male	55,576	82,299
Female	40,864	71,260
Total	96,440	153,559
Free colored		
Male	16,152	25,211
Female	14,695	28,940
Total	30,847	54,151
Slave		
Male	28,771	47,724
Female	15,562	16,866
Total	44,333	64,590
Island total	171,620	272,300

Source: Adapted from United States War Department, *Informe sobre el censo de Cuba, 1899* (Washington, D.C., 1900).

(35 to 26 percent), reflecting the increased demand for male field laborers. By far the most notable increase was registered among the free colored women, from 48 percent to 53 percent. This increase, in turn, pointed to one of the more striking developments of colonial society. Whereas the white to colored ratio remained substantially intact between 1774 and 1791 (56 percent to 44 percent), the free population of color increased both in its percentage of the total population (from 18 to 20 percent) and the percentage of the total population of color (from 41 to 46). Put another way, the fastest growing population of Cuba was the free colored, registering a 76 percent increase between 1774 and 1791, followed by whites (59 percent), and slaves (46 percent).

In no other major Caribbean slaveholding society was the number of free colored so large or the size of the free colored population so great a percentage of the total population of color. Certainly one source for expansion of the free population of color was the relatively common practice whereby slave owners freed their illegitimate children. But slavery in eighteenth-century Cuba was different from that in most other West Indian islands. One important distinction was that sugar production had not yet taken as complete a hold over the Cuban economy as elsewhere. The development of a large free population of color was also the result of the unique legal status enjoyed by slaves in Cuba. As early as the sixteenth century, African slaves possessed specified legal rights, chief among which was the right of *coartación,* an arrangement whereby slaves were entitled to negotiate emancipation with their owners. Certainly this practice diminished somewhat during the sugar boom, but it did not altogether cease. Slaves could purchase their freedom, or the freedom of their children, by agreeing to pay an owner an initial fixed sum of money and the balance in installments, usually determined by the prevailing market value of new slaves. "In no part of the world, where slavery exists," commented Humboldt early in the nineteenth century, "is manumission so frequent as in the island of Cuba."

Coartación tended to favor the emancipation of creole slaves over new slaves. The practice also benefited urban slaves more than rural slaves, since in the cities it was possible to earn supplemental wages through the development of trades and skills as cobblers, tailors, seamstresses, cigar-workers, and musicians. The process, further, tended to flourish on its own success. The presence of a growing urban population of free colored served as promise of a status potentially available to all slaves. The free population of color tended to concentrate in the towns and cities, filling the ranks of an expanding urban proletariat and gradually entering many of the liberal professions. Achievements did not always equal aspirations, however, and tension of another kind took shape in Cuban society as a color-conscious and socially stratified colony failed to accommodate the rising demands of a growing population of free people of color. Increasingly, Afro-Cubans in growing numbers found themselves subject to racial discrimination and social humiliation. Their grievances would increase and compound.

The practice of *coartación* was neither unrestricted nor available everywhere. Slaves could not, for example, apply for *coartado* status prior to seven years of service in Cuba. In agricultural zones, further, where most newly arrived slaves were destined, isolation and distance from judicial authorities combined to limit widespread knowledge of *coartación* and restrict its implementation. Then, too, opportunities for slaves to augment earnings were comparatively fewer in the countryside than in the towns and cities.

In fact, everything was different in the agricultural zones: opportunities for legal emancipation fewer, work conditions harsher, abuse greater. These circumstances meant also that the forms of emancipation were different. So were the implications. Most commonly, slaves fled, seeking refuge in the impenetrable interior fastness of the mountain systems of south and central eastern Cuba. Permanent fortified settlements *(palenques)* of runaway slaves increased in numbers, one other palpable expression of the growing population of free people of color.

A more desperate, and more feared, response was slave rebellion. Slave uprisings occurred throughout the early colonial period, and as slave numbers increased, so did the frequency of slave rebellions. During the eighteenth century, they increased also in size and scope. Three hundred slaves rebelled on one Havana sugar plantation in 1727. Four years later, another rebellion of slaves forced the closing of the copper mines of Santiago de Cuba. Uprisings occurred in Puerto Príncipe, Guanabacoa, Mariel, and Güines. As the Cuban countryside began to fill up with newly arrived slaves late in the eighteenth century, the prospect of slave rebellion loomed as a specter over the expanding plantation economy of rural Cuba.

VII

Cuba was in a state of flux in the eighteenth century. Times were changing, quickly and with far-reaching consequences. Market forces, combined with political liberalization necessary to meet them, had set in motion Cuba's vast productive potential, the implications of which Cuban producers had only begun to contemplate late in the eighteenth century. It was perhaps inevitable that Cubans would confer on these musings intellectual force and express them in cultural forms. They were prepared, indeed, predisposed, to entertain new ideas. In their own way, they were products of the Enlightenment, at home in the marketplace of ideas if only to seek ideas for the marketplace itself. They embraced the ideas of the Enlightenment more on pragmatic grounds than on ideological ones. They were above all eminently practical, and thus the emphasis on rationality and socially useful knowledge struck a particularly responsive chord. They sought practical answers to immediate problems.

These currents assumed institutional forms in the later years of the eighteenth century. The Cuban newspaper *Papel Periódico de La Habana* commenced publication in 1791. Unlike the established periodical format of the time, devoted largely to the dissemination of official notices, the weekly *Papel Periódico* published articles of information and opinion, with particular attention to new developments in agriculture, commerce, and industry. By focusing on problems and issues related specifically to Cuba, the newspaper provided a medium for the exchange of ideas and a forum for the discussion of grievances, but most of all it served as an instrument for the defense of local interests.

Simultaneous with the founding of the *Papel Periódico,* a group of twenty-seven prominent landowners in Havana obtained official authorization to organize the Sociedad Económica de Amigos del País. In part a social club, in part a special interest group, the Sociedad Economica represented some of the most powerful property interests on the island. Recruiting much of its membership from the creole *hacendados,* the organization expanded quickly from the 27 original petitioners in 1791 to 126 in 1793 and 163 two years later. Branches *(diputaciones)* were subsequently established in Sancti Spíritus, Puerto Príncipe, and Trinidad. Under the leadership of Francisco de Arango y Parreño (1765–1839), a wealthy creole planter economist, the Sociedad Económica emerged as an organization of wide-ranging influence. It committed itself to the collection and dissemination of information on stockraising, mining, commerce, industry, and, especially, agriculture and sugar. The Sociedad Económica promoted education by subsidizing schools and funding scholarships, launched a publication program, and established a public library. In 1793, it assumed responsibility for the publication of the *Papel Periódico,* whereupon it became a daily. The Sociedad disseminated scientific information, particularly in those fields with the potential to boost agricultural production, including botany, chemistry, and agronomy. It promoted the study of mathematics, mineralogical sciences, and medicine, translated books on cane growing and sugar manufacture, reported on technological progress registered elsewhere in sugar manufacture, and studied advances in tobacco production. Through the Sociedad Económica creoles increased their participation in public affairs, advocating improved inland transportation, expanded shipping facilities, and the liberalization of trade.

Two years after the founding of the Sociedad Económica, Arango y Parreño was instrumental in establishing the Real Consulado de Agricultura y Comercio de La Habana. Made up principally of planters and merchants, the Consulado served originally as an advisory body to the captain general on matters of public policy. It eventually merged into the Junta de Fomento and enlarged the sphere of its concerns to include the defense of local interests, principally sugar production, in the form of the expansion of public work programs, including the building of canals, wharves, lighthouses, and roads; the reduction of taxes; and the improvement of educational opportunities on the island. The Consulado demanded that capital at discount rates be made available to planters, one way to free local producers from the grip of usurious rates of interest charged by merchants. Prices of slaves should be regulated and lowered, the Consulado argued, and the religious holidays on which slaves were exempted from work should be abolished.

VIII

These eighteenth-century stirrings had several features in common. First and foremost they reflected a growing preoccupation in Cuba with things Cuban. Whatever else may have differentiated the spheres of the Sociedad Económica, the *Papel Periódico,* and the Real Consulado de Agricultura y Comercio, they shared one central feature: they represented principally creole interests. They provided, too, the forum from which to articulate discontent and advance demands. Creoles had developed a sense of the singularity of their own interests, and were not at all slow to organize around the defense of those interests. This was nothing less than a change of consciousness, fundamentally a change in the way Cubans thought about themselves. This was the meaning of the *vegueros'* protests, one of the earliest armed protests in defense of local interests. These changes were themselves expressions of a growing awareness of the contradictions of empire, real and potential, and the deepening conflict between interests Spanish and interests Cuban. The needs of a creole oligarchy based on land and dependent on free trade did not always coincide with the needs of metropolis. In fact, increasingly they did not, and herein was one source of the problem. Economic growth was accompanied by social change, and social change was outpacing political change.

Nor was the defense of things local confined wholly to economic interests. It also assumed cultural forms and reflected a developing sense of identity. The demand for institutions of higher learning responded in part to the recognition of the deficiencies of colonial society, but also to the desire of elites to promote the structures of a society commensurate with their sense of past achievements and future potential. That Cuba had lacked appropriate educational institutions served as an irksome reminder of the backwardness Cubans sought to eliminate.

Cuban efforts were not without effect. Creoles used their growing economic power shrewdly, if not always successfully, exacting from the court of Madrid occasional concessions and grants. Education was a matter of growing concern for local residents, important as both an element of social status for the colony and a practical educational concern within the colony. Higher education in Cuba was an important expression of material well-being, a sign of the coming of age of the colony, evidence of cultural diversity and sophistication. Spain responded favorably to entreaties from Cuba. The University of Havana was founded in 1728. Other facilities established in the eighteenth century included the Colegio of San Francisco de Sales and the seminaries of San Basilio, San Ambrosio, and San Carlos.

This changing sense of status found other expressions. The first printing press was established in 1723. Theater arrived in Havana in the eighteenth century. Churches expanded. Construction of the Cathedral of Havana began in 1748, and Havana was established as a bishopric. A public library opened in 1793. Private residences in Havana increased in number and grandeur. Public works programs expanded. Streets were paved and lighted. The Plaza de Armas was completed in 1733, followed by the Plaza del Santo Cristo and the Plaza de San Francisco. The first promenade (paseo) of Havana, the Alameda de Paula, was constructed, and followed by the construction of the Paseo del Prado.

The exaltation of things Cuban also found literary expression in the poetry of Manuel de Zequerra and Manuel Justo de Rubalcava, and in the paintings of José Nicolás de la Escalera (1734–1804) and Vicente Escobar (1757–1834). It found expression too in the emergence of a new Cuban historiography, principally in the works of Pedro Agustín Morell de Santa Cruz (1694–1768), *Historia de la Isla y Catedral de Cuba*, José Martín Félix de Arrate (1701–65), *Llave del Nuevo Mundo, antemural de las Indias Occidentales*, and Ignacio José de Urrutia y Montoya (1735–95), *Teatro histórico, jurídico y político militar de la isla Fernandina de Cuba, principalmente de su capital La Habana*.

Cuba was in transition during the eighteenth century. The population was increasing. Old cities flourished, new ones were founded. The economy was expanding. Times were good, and improving. But prosperity had not been altogether an unmixed blessing. It resulted in greater state intervention in local affairs and, in response, growing local resentment and resistance. Cuba in the eighteenth century was a society whose transformation placed traditional social and economic structures under new strains and traditional political relationships under new scrutiny. Awareness of differences with *peninsulares* heightened a consciousness of community among creoles, nothing less than a presentiment of nationality on the eve of the Latin American wars for an independent nationality.

4

Transformation and
Transition

I

Cuba approached the end of the eighteenth century enjoying sustained but by no means spectacular economic development. Growth had been steady, but the potential of Cuban production remained substantially unfulfilled. For all their achievements, and they were by no means inconsiderable, Cuban planters lagged far behind rival Caribbean producers. Compared with the economies of other islands in the West Indies during the 1770s, Cuban accomplishments were modest indeed. Cuba had comparatively smaller estates, fewer slaves, and lower sugar production. At 46,000 square miles in size, approximately the area of all the West Indian islands combined, Cuban sugar output accounted for a mere 3.2 percent of total Caribbean production. Cuban sugar production of 10,000 tons was matched by St. Christopher (68 square miles) and Antigua (108 square miles). Jamaica (4400 square miles) had almost twice as many estates, nearly four times the number of slaves, and produced three times as much sugar. Barbados (166 square miles) and Martinique (425 square miles) each had almost as many sugar estates and more slaves.

By far the most dramatic comparison was with the French colony of St. Domingue (10,700 square miles), approximately one-quarter the size of Cuba, and in the late eighteenth century arguably the wealthiest plantation society in the New World. An estimated 800 estates produced an annual average of 71,000 tons of sugar. Nearly 3,000 coffee farms produced more than 30,000 tons of coffee, accounting for more than 60 percent of the world supply. The 800 cotton plantations produced 2,800 tons of cotton, and 3,000 indigo farms exported 415 tons of dye. Only one-third of this vast productive output was consumed in metropolitan France, the balance re-exported to world markets. Prosperity made St. Domingue one of the most important slave markets in the New World.

By the 1780s, more than 500,000 African slaves toiled on the fields of St. Domingue.

Cuban producers could not compete. They were comparative latecomers to commercial sugar production. The opportunity for expansion was limited, and by the end of the eighteenth century Cuba was approaching the limits of its expansion. Production had increased in steady but modest increments. But it was also apparent that Cuban producers lacked the means to expand and were without the markets to expand into. Costs were higher, customers were fewer, and as a result of both, the incentives to expand were less. Cuban producers operated within a restrictive trade system and a retrogressive tax structure, producing for limited markets, expanding with meager capital resources. What growth had taken place was the result largely of improvised responses to fortuitous circumstances. Continued development was contingent on finding new markets or expanding into old ones, and in the late eighteenth century the prospects for either were not good. The vast productive capacity of St. Domingue alone so determined world supply and demand, so influenced the market price and profit margin, as to make the position of French producers seemingly unassailable.

II

The opportunity for Cuban producers came unexpectedly. In August 1791, the slaves of St. Domingue rose in rebellion. For the remainder of the decade, the French colony was ravaged by civil strife in which opposing forces routinely adopted methods of scorched earth as the principal means of waging war and exacting revenge. The effects were immediate, and devastating. The plantations were destroyed, production collapsed, the planters departed. The effects reverberated across the Atlantic. The world supply of sugar declined. Demand increased, and prices followed, increasing from 12 *reales* per *arroba* in 1790 to 36 in 1795.

Cubans did not hesitate to take advantage of world conditions. Few other circumstances could have so favored the expansion of Cuban sugar production. Cuban producers inherited all at once rising prices, increasing demand, and mounting world shortages. At the same time, tens of thousands of French émigrés from St. Domingue—perhaps as many as 30,000—resettled in Cuba. Many arrived with capital and slaves, but most of all with experience and skill in the production of sugar and coffee.

Political developments in Europe also favored Cuban producers. Nearly two decades of intermittent warfare followed the St. Domingue rebellion, a period during which the needs of Spanish policy and Cuban producers converged more than once and provided planters with the opportunity to expand production and increase exports. A war between Spain and France (1793–95) enabled Cuba to receive North American imports in exchange for exports of sugar and molasses. In 1796, Spain was at war again, this time allied with France against England, and for the next five years Cuban ports were opened to the shipping of neutral nations. Foreign access to Cuban markets again favored North Americans. Trade with the United States flourished. Cuba exported sugar, molasses, rum, and coffee; the United States provided foodstuffs, clothing, furniture, manufactured goods, and slaves. In 1798, for the first time—briefly but portentously—the volume of commerce between Cuba and the United States exceeded trade between Cuba and Spain. War again between Spain and England (1804–5) opened Cuban to neutral shipping. Three years later, Spain and England were at war against France. On this occasion, Cuban trade was directed to English markets.

The benefits to Cuba of these shifting if short-lived opportunities on the world market were manifest. For almost two decades, the island enjoyed the fruits of more or less free participation in international trade. There could be no return to the policies of Bourbon mercantile exclusivism. Nor did Spain try. In February 1818, in response to growing demands from Cuba, Spain opened the island to free world trade. Spanish policy was not entirely unconditional and Spanish purpose not wholly unselfish, however. Spain devised alternative ways to exploit Cuban prosperity. Exorbitant customs tariffs discriminated against foreign imports carried aboard foreign ships. Cubans protested and Spain relented, only slightly reducing customs between 20 to 36 percent ad valorem. It was not, hence, "free" trade: Cubans paid for it.

III

The early years of the nineteenth century were boom years for the Cuban economy. Coffee cultivation expanded rapidly across the island, most notably in eastern Cuba, stimulated by increasing demand and rising prices after the Haitian revolution. The world price of coffee doubled between 1792 and 1796. Newly arrived French coffee planters settled around San-

TABLE 3.   Coffee Exports
in *"Arrobas"*
(1 *"arroba"* = 25 pounds)

Year	Arrobas
1792	7,101
1804	50,000
1808	137,148
1812	263,618
1816	370,229
1820	886,046
1826	1,773,798
1831	2,103,582
1833	2,566,359

Source: Adapted from Susan Schroeder, *Cuba:
A Handbook of Historical Statistics* (Boston,
1982), 246.

tiago de Cuba and Guantánamo, and transformed the island into a major
world supplier of coffee. The number of *cafetales* increased from 2 in
1774 to 108 in 1802, 586 in 1804, 1,315 in 1806, and 2,067 in 1827.
Between 1792 and 1804, Cuban coffee exports increased almost eight-
fold, doubling thereafter every several years (see Table 3).

The most spectacular advances, however, were registered in sugar production. Cuban sugar expanded in a frenzy, an immediate and improvised
response to soaring world prices. Old producers increased production.
New ones initiated production. The number of estates increased, the zones
of cultivation expanded. Between 1792 and 1806, the number of mills
around Havana increased from 237 to 416. The initial expansion concentrated along the northern coastal ports near Havana, between Guanajay to
the west, Matanzas on the east, and Batabanó to the south, areas from
which planters could use the water to transport their goods to the capital
for export.

Sugar production subsequently expanded inland and eastward, re-
morselessly, sweeping aside obstacles and opposition alike. Entire forests
disappeared under the onslaught of sugar. Vast forest acreage was cleared
for planting cane and building mills: an estimated 1,700 acres a year in
the late eighteenth century, increasing to about 3,500 acres annually by

the 1810s, and reaching 13,000 acres cleared per year by the 1840s. Tobacco *vegas* and grazing ranges also disappeared. Tobacco farming all but ceased in the regions around Havana, confined henceforth to the western extremities in Pinar del Río. Sugar expanded onto the Matanzas plains, penetrating into the area of Bolondrón, Unión de Reyes, and by the 1830s reaching the central plains of Colón and Sagua la Grande. In subsequent decades sugar reached Sancti Spíritus, Nuevitas, and Puerto Príncipe. Production spread also along the south coast to Cienfuegos and Trinidad. Sugar made inroads in the eastern zones, principally in the regions around Bayamo, Holguín, and Santiago de Cuba.

The expansion of sugar production was also cause and effect of other changes overtaking the island, no less far reaching and long lasting, and nowhere with greater impact than in transportation. The movement of people and products over land had long been impractical if not impossible. Highway and road construction had long languished. The few roads that did exist were hardly more than rights of way, narrow passages and trails in a constant state of disrepair and neglect and all but unusable during the rainy season. Writing of the rich sugar zones of Havana province, Humboldt observed that in "no part of the world do the roads become more impassable during the rainy season, than in that part of the island, where the soil is a decomposing limestone ill adapted to the making of wheel-roads." Visiting the same region twenty years later, Robert Francis Jameson wrote: "The roads are mere tracks or gullies worn free of soil by the rains, traversing the naked rock and partaking of all its ruggedness. Convenience has traced them out in the first instance, and use has, in some degree, worked them into form." Many roads were not sufficiently wide even to permit the use of carts, thereby requiring the transportation of sugar in wooden crates by mule trains. Poor transportation discouraged the expansion of agriculture. Cuban producers made what use they could of inland waterways, along which commerce and agriculture thrived. But rivers offered only a partial solution, for few were navigable for any length. On the whole, transportation in Cuba was slow, costly, and labor consuming.

Conditions changed little in the course of three hundred years of colonial administration. Colonists complained freely and frequently, but in vain. Not until late in the eighteenth century, during the surge of Bourbon reforms, did Cuban entreaties have effect. Among the more important roads completed during these years were those linking Havana to Matanzas, Havana to Batabanó, and Havana to Güines.

In the early nineteenth century, soaring sugar prices and rising land values combined to provide new economic incentives for the expansion of transportation facilities. Old highways and roads were improved; new ones were constructed. Railroad construction commenced, and expanded rapidly. Under the direction of the Real Junta de Fomento, the first Cuban railway line, 51 miles long, was completed in 1838, linking Havana with Güines. Railroad construction expanded quickly thereafter. Within twenty-five years another 400 miles of railway had been completed, connecting the principal sugar zones with provincial ports. Branch lines extended the Havana-Güines railway to Batabanó, San Antonio, and Guanajay in the 1840s. Other lines included Matanzas-Alacranes and Regla-Guanabacoa, built in the 1840s; Remedios-Caibarién, Puerto Príncipe-Nuevitas, Trinidad-Sancti Spíritus, Cárdenas-Júcaro, and Matanzas-Jovellanos in the 1850s; and El Cobre-El Cristo, Cienfuegos-Trinidad-Santa Clara, Casilda-Trinidad, Puerto Príncipe-Santa Cruz del Sur, Güines-Matanzas, Havana-Matanzas, and Sagua la Grande-Encrucijada-Santa Clara in the 1860s.

Old port cities grew, new ones were founded. Remedios, Mariel, Nuevitas, Caibarién, and Nuevitas along the north coast, and Cienfuegos, Guantánamo, and Manzanillo on the south prospered. Matanzas was transformed from a backward port settlement into a bustling entrepôt, whose contribution to royal revenues increased from 74 pesos in 1762 to 250,000 pesos in 1818. Rail expansion into the interior, in turn, encouraged migration into the interior, with the subsequent expansion of new towns. Between 1800 and 1840, more than fifty new towns were founded across the island, including Nueva Paz, Manicaragua, Artemisa, Cabañas, Colón, Cabarién, Gibara, Palma Soriano, and Guantánamo.

The effects of new railroad construction were immediate. The railroad served to widen the export market by linking hitherto distant sugar zones to principal ports. Rail lines made possible the opening of new zones of production. Planters could expand on both sides of public trunk lines by constructing private feeder lines, and thereby obtain direct access to regional ports. Transportation costs, long the bane of Cuban planters, declined dramatically. The Güines railroad reduced shipping costs by more than 70 percent in the first year of operation. The cost of transporting a 400-weight box of sugar from Güines to Havana dropped from $12.50 by mule train in 1830 to $1.25 by rail in 1840. It was not only cheaper to haul sugar out, it was also cheaper to bring supplies in. Machines, fuel, and foodstuffs arrived in greater quantities, over longer distances, and at lower costs.

The railroad changed other facets of production as well. Narrow-gauge tracks were introduced directly into the factory complex. Tasks previously performed by slaves were henceforth more efficiently accomplished on rails, most notably the transportation of heated cane syrup from the mill to purging houses and the movement of drained sugar to drying facilities. Rail transportation also transformed the very organization of the estates. Plantations had previously reserved as much as one-quarter of attached forest land as a source of fuel. This changed after 1840. The railroad provided planters with an alternative means of obtaining cheap wood, thereby eliminating the need to hold forest lands in reserve. At a time of rising world prices, cost-conscious planters found it more profitable to convert forest land to sugar production and obtain lumber by rail from other regions, both in and out of Cuba.

The changes in the field were accompanied by changes in the factory. Indeed, the advances in sugar manufacture during the first half of the nineteenth century were nothing less than spectacular, and served at once to improve the efficiency of old productive units and encourage the organization of new ones. Steam power was introduced in Cuban mills beginning in 1817. The conversion to steam power from oxen-driven and water-powered mills proceeded across the island. Between 1846 and 1860, the number of steam-powered mills increased from 20 percent to almost 71 percent.

Other changes followed in quick order. New and improved strains of sugar cane were introduced. Iron rollers replaced wooden ones. Vacuum boilers were introduced during the 1830s and 1840s. A decade later, the introduction of the centrifuge further improved the process of purifying sugar.

Transformed too was the very dimension of sugar production. More than ever before, sugar manufacturing required extraordinary capital resources—for machinery, for equipment, for private rail lines, for slaves, for land. To compete, planters had to expand, and to do so, they had to modernize.

IV

Sugar cultivation expanded rapidly during the first half of the nineteenth century, and its expansion heralded the transformation of all Cuba. Production increased, steadily at the close of the eighteenth century, dramatically through the nineteenth (see Table 4). No less dramatic was the

TABLE 4. Sugar Exports,
1790–1868

Year	Tons
1790	15,423
1800	28,761
1805	35,238
1815	45,396
1829	84,187
1840	161,248
1850	294,952
1860	428,769
1868	720,250

Source: Manuel Moreno Fraginals, *El in-genio: complejo económico social cubano del azúcar* (3 vols., Havana, 1978), III, 43–45.

expansion of Cuban production as a percentage of the total world supply. Between 1839 and 1868, Cuba's share of the world market almost doubled, increasing from 15.8 percent (130,200 tons out of 820,318 tons) to 29.7 percent (749,000 tons out of 2.5 million tons).

Much of the increase in Cuban output, to be sure, was the result of advances in the technology of production and improvements in agricultural methods. Cubans were simply producing greater quantities of sugar more efficiently. But a great deal of increased sugar production also came at the expense of everything else. The average output per mill increased dramatically, from 72 tons per mill in 1830 to 120 tons in 1841 and more than doubling to 316 tons by 1860. The number of sugar mills doubled from 1,000 in 1827 to almost 2,000 in 1868. Sugar displaced vast forest lands of central Cuba, and in many regions deforestation was complete and irrevocable. Cattle ranches and tobacco *vegas* were converted to cane fields. By the 1840s coffee producers had come upon hard times. A series of devastating hurricanes between 1844 and 1846 all but destroyed the coffee zones. Moreover, the rise of new competition, mainly from Brazil, and the decline of world prices added to coffee growers' woes and made them especially vulnerable to displacement by the more dynamic sugar sector. Costs increased, profits fell. Increasingly, coffee growers were

TABLE 5. Distribution and Growth of Sugar Mills (1778–1862)

Jurisdiction	1778	1792	1827	1846	1862	
Pinar del Río	1	—	—	4	5	
Mariel	—	—	—	84	—	
Bahía Honda	—	—	—	—	24	
Guanajay	—	—	—	—	11	
San Cristobal	—	—	—	—	11	
	1	—	—	88	51	
Havana	136	208	231	155	—	
Bejucal	8	6	5	23	16	
Guanabacoa	22	20	12	24	3	
Jaruco	—	—	2	3	28	
Santa María del Rosario	—	—	—	—	2	
Santiago de las Vegas	—	3	40	4	8	
Güines	—	—	47	66	87	Western Zone
San Antonio Abad	—	—	1	21	22	
	166	237	338	296	166	
Matanzas	5	8	111	152	134	
Cárdenas	—	—	—	199	147	
Colón	—	—	—	—	113	
	5	8	111	351	394	
Trinidad	41	31	56	43	49	
Remedios	11	11	17	37	71	
Sancti Spíritus	15	44	38	39	41	
Santa Clara	29	30	49	59	86	
Yaguaramas	—	—	1	—	—	
Santo Domingo	—	—	—	3	—	
Cienfuegos	—	—	—	71	104	
Sagua la Grande	—	—	—	59	125	
	96	116	161	311	476	
Puerto Príncipe	50	55	85	81	100	
Nuevitas	—	—	—	12	18	
	50	55	85	93	118	

TABLE 5. (*Continued*)

Jurisdiction	1778	1792	1827	1846	1862	
Santiago de Cuba	48	48	125	112	100	
Bayamo	57	65	55	43	26	
Holguín	1	—	92	80	63	
Baracoa	—	—	7	10	8	Eastern zone
Jiguani	—	—	26	27	20	
Manzanillo	—	—	—	20	26	
Guantánamo	—	—	—	11	23	
Tunas	—	—	—	—	2	
	106	113	305	303	268	
Island Totals	424	529	1,000	1,442	1,473	

Source: Levi Marrero, *Cuba: economía y sociedad* (12 vols., Madrid, 1973–86), X, p. 278.

unable to pay the rising costs of slaves. And increasingly, coffee growers failed. The coffee estates *(cafetales)* disappeared and coffee production declined. "The damaged plantations were not restored as coffee estates," observed Richard Henry Dana during his travels through Cuba in 1859, "but were laid down to the sugar-cane; and gradually, first in the western and northern parts, and daily extending easternly and southernly over the entire island, the exquisite cafetals have been prostrated and dismantled, the groves of shade and fruit trees cut down, the avenues and foot-paths ploughed up, and the denuded land laid down to wastes of sugar-cane." The estimated value of coffee production fell from approximately $80 million in 1829 to $40 million in 1849. The number of coffee farms *(fincas)* declined from 1,680 in 1846 to 782 in 1861. Coffee exports fell from an all-time high of 2.5 million *arrobas* in 1833 to 559,332 *arrobas* in 1845 and 154,208 in 1867.

By the mid-nineteenth century, sugar production had expanded across the full breadth of the island, but not evenly or with equal effect. Indeed, the sugar system assumed striking regional manifestations. Apart from flourishing enclaves of tobacco farming in Pinar del Río and San Cristobal, the western zones had been totally transformed by sugar. Sugar production in the west tended to concentrate in three well-defined regions. One stretched from western Pinar del Río along the north coast through Bahía Honda, Havana, and Matanzas, penetrating inland to include Gu-

TABLE 6. Sugar Mills, Land Area, and Sugar Production By Jurisdictions (1860)

Western Department	Total Units	Source of Power			Land Area in Caballerías Sugar Cane	Sugar Production Total in Tons
		Steam	Water	Oxen		
Bahía Honda	25	22	—	3	429	10,119
Bejucal	20	12	—	8	296	3,976
Cárdenas	147	135	—	12	2,773	67,405
Cienfuegos	94	48	—	46	1,403	42,469
Colón	126	121	—	5	3,436	90,443
Guanabacoa	3	3	—	—	78	1,077
Guanajay	61	57	—	4	1,386	24,760
Güines	89	78	4	8	2,058	44,609
Jaruco	31	21	—	10	599	8,002
Matanzas	128	114	1	13	2,478	53,298
Nueva Filipina	6	4	—	2	59	1,382
Sagua la Grande	119	89	—	30	1,596	50,157
San Antonio	17	16	—	1	348	5,322
San Cristobal	10	5	—	5	112	1,772
Sancti-Spíritus	41	18	—	23	426	12,407
San Juan de los Remedios	44	27	—	17	368	15,634
Santa María del Rosario	1	1	—	—	14	154
Santiago de las Vegas	6	5	—	1	118	1,454
Trinidad	44	34	—	10	875	16,328
Villaclara	53	19	—	34	399	10,843
Total	1,065	829	5	232	19,251	461,611
Eastern Department						
Baracoa	7	—	—	7	3	—
Bayamo	23	1	—	22	51	1,047
Cuba (Santiago)	89	61	—	28	689	20,937
Guantánamo	25	11	—	12	144	6,108
Jiguaní	19	—	—	19	37	198

TABLE 6. (*Continued*)

| Eastern Department | Total Units | Source of Power | | | Land Area in Caballerías | Sugar Production |
		Steam	Water	Oxen	Sugar Cane	Total in Tons
Holguín	16	5	—	11	108	1,694
Manzanillo	18	6	—	12	57	1,416
Nuevitas	19	12	—	7	120	3,568
Puerto Príncipe	83	24	—	59	294	11,621
Tunas	1	—	—	1	4	49
Total	300	120	2	178	1,507	46,638
Grand Total	1,365	949	7	410	20,758	508,249

Source: Adapted from Carlos Rebello, *Estados relativos a la producción azucarera de la Isla de Cuba, formados competentemente y con autorización de la Intendencia de Ejército y Hacienda* (Havana, 1860).

anajay, Güines, and Alacranes. The second sugar zone was located largely in the central part of the island and included the jurisdictions of Matanzas, Cárdenas, and Sagua la Grande along the north and including Jovellanos and Colón inland. The third district stretched along the south coast and included Cienfuegos and Trinidad, reaching inland to Santa Clara, Sancti Spíritus, and Camagüey.

Sugar also expanded into the east, mostly around Holguín, Bayamo, Guantánamo, and Santiago, but not on the scale or with the same impact as it had in the west. The vast majority of new mills established after 1763 were located in the west, with telling results. Between 1778 and 1846, the number of sugar mills in Cuba increased from 424 to 1,442. By 1860, of the total 1,365 mills in Cuba, 1,065 were found in the west (see Table 5).

But it was not only that there were more mills in the west. They were larger, too. Transportation costs were lower, largely because there were more railroad lines and they had been laid earlier. Profits were higher and technology had advanced further in the west. Almost 80 percent of the western mills in 1860 (829 of 1,165) were steam-powered as compared to 40 percent of the mills in the eastern zones (120 out of 300). The total land engaged in sugar production was more than twelve times greater in

TABLE 7.   Select Economic Indicators by Region (1862)

	West	East
Foreign trade	89.9 percent	9.1 percent
Tax collection	87 percent	13 percent
Railroads	87 percent	13 percent
Wealth	$236,000,000	$69,000,000
Annual per capita	$350	$165

Source: Francisco López Segrera, *Cuba: capitalismo dependiente y subdesarrollo (1510–1959)* (Havana, 1981), 111.

the west than in the east (640,000 acres as compared to 50,000). It followed naturally, too, that the production disparity between west and east would be equally striking. In fact, it was stunning: western mills produced an average annual 461,611 tons of sugar, approximately 433 tons per mill, while the eastern production averaged 46,638 tons, an average of 155 tons per mill. Put in slightly different terms, the west accounted for almost 91 percent of the total sugar production of Cuba. Even the steam-powered mills of the west out-produced the steam-driven mills in the east—the west averaging 557 tons, the east, 389 tons (see Table 6). The differences between east and west were stark and everywhere in evidence, as shown in Table 7.

V

Changes no less far-reaching were also transforming the organization and orientation of Cuban foreign trade. The rise of sugar exports signaled the decline of other sources of foreign exchange, for the expansion of the former came very much at the expense of the latter. Steadily, and inexorably, Cuba developed into an export economy dependent upon the production of one crop and, increasingly, for one market. In 1761, Cuba was still an exporter of jerked beef. By 1792, Cuba was importing it by thousands of pounds. Sugar accounted for an increasing portion of total Cuban export earnings: 60 percent in 1840 and 74 percent twenty years later, and increasingly a greater share of Cuban sugar exports was expanding into North American markets. These trading patterns were established early, at the close of the eighteenth century, as the newly independent North American colonies searched for substitute sources of sugar supplies and Cuban producers sought new markets for expanding output. The timing was fortuitous. The United States served as an ideal trading partner: it was close, with a dynamic merchant marine, a growing population, rising demand, and an expanding economy. The United States was also as important a source of Cuban imports as it was a market for Cuban exports, and it was this factor that figured prominently in Cuban production strategies.

North American traders had shrewdly and effectively pursued the Cuban market, providing slaves and manufactured goods at reasonable prices, often extending generous credit arrangements, and accepting sugar and molasses as payment. The Cuba-United States trade nexus shattered the Spanish commercial monopoly, creating for Cuban producers new prospects, but also new problems. That Cubans could expand production for export at the expense of production for consumption was both a profitable and practical strategy because they could easily remedy local shortages with foreign supplies. Indeed, it was more cost effective to rely on food imports for the local market than sacrifice sugar exports for foreign markets. That the United States could meet these needs, as well as provide Cuba with necessary industrial supplies, from a short distance, in a short period of time, and at low transportation cost, encouraged and facilitated the expansion of Cuban sugar production.

The number of North American ships arriving at Cuban ports increased from 150 in 1796 to 1,886 in 1852. Commerce flourished. Trade contacts expanded steadily. North American ships originating from Boston, New York, Philadelphia, Savannah, and New Orleans provided Cubans with box shooks, staves, caskets, barrels, hoops, nails, tar, textiles, salt, fish, corn, lard, flour, and rice. They returned loaded with sugar, tobacco, molasses, and coffee. In one of more striking ironies of Cuban economic development, even as local producers were setting their forests ablaze to make room for sugar, they were one of the principal importers of U.S. lumber. During the first two decades of the nineteenth century, Cubans spent more than one million pesos annually on North American lumber stores.

The inexorable logic of circumstances transformed the United States into Cuba's single most important trading partner. Together, the United States, England, and Spain accounted for almost 80 percent of the island's total foreign trade. In 1850, Cuban trade with the United States represented 39 percent of this total, followed by England (34 percent),

TABLE 8. Cuban Trade with the United States, England, and Spain
(Pesos)

	United States		England		Spain	
	Imports	Exports	Imports	Exports	Imports	Exports
1846–1850	$27,838	$37,426	$21,682	$35,105	$27,210	$16,957
1851–1855	35,978	61,817	31,991	42,388	44,729	17,727
1856–1859	40,308	68,339	29,406	37,294	31,042	20,974

Source: José R. Alvarez Díaz et al., A Study on Cuba (Coral Gables, 1965), 129.

and Spain (27 percent). Nine years later, the North American share rose
to 48 percent (see Table 8). In the following decades, Cuban trade patterns were even more striking. In 1865, the island exported 65 percent of
its sugar to the United States and 3 percent to Spain. By 1877, the United
States accounted for 82 percent of Cuba's total exports, followed by Spain
(6 percent) and England (4 percent).

The implications of these trends were far-reaching, and Cubans were
immediately sensible to their meaning. Cuba had previously obtained a
number of important commercial concessions, particularly in trade relationships with Spain. These were benefits of limited value and less consequence, however, for Cuban trade was no longer organized around Spain
but the United States. The importance of Spanish participation in the
Cuban economy was diminishing. Spain could neither offer Cuban producers adequate markets nor guarantee Cuban consumers sufficient supplies. The United States promised both. As a result, Cuba developed
economic needs distinct from those of Spain, and increasingly divergent.

By the mid-nineteenth century, Cubans were arriving at the conclusion
that they could not achieve the full potential of their productive capabilities within the traditional framework of empire. And, indeed, the Cuban
economy was ready to expand beyond the restrictive framework of existing colonial structures. But trade with Europe and the United States was
still subject to the constraints of Spanish policy. Spain could not supply
the goods, the shipping, and the markets demanded by Cuba, but persisted in obtruding itself between Cuba and world markets. Spain was
superfluous to the Cuban economy in every way but one: it regulated the
terms of the exchange, and increasingly this was becoming a point of
contention between Cubans and Spaniards. Official efforts to promote
Spanish exports and encourage the use of Spanish carriers cost Cuban

consumers dearly. To the growing chagrin of consumers and producers in Cuba, the island was subjected to a series of discriminatory customs duties. By the terms of the 1853 tariff law, foreign products shipped on Spanish carriers paid 21.5 to 25.5 percent ad valorem, and on foreign carriers 29.5 to 35.5 percent. *Peninsular* products carried by national shippers paid 6 percent ad valorem; carried by foreigners, the duty increased to 19.5 percent. Thus, the tax on a barrel of Spanish flour was set at $2.90 while a North American barrel was charged $9.20. So too with island exports: goods shipped by foreigners paid 7.5 percent, Spanish carriers 3 percent. Spanish objectives remained unchanged: raise revenues, increase remittances, transfer local profits, and appropriate surpluses—all for the benefit of Spain, at the expense of Cuba. Colonial authorities levied custom duties on imports, imposed taxes on exports, and assessed freight charges on foreign carriers, all of which served to lower profits for Cuban producers and raise prices for Cuban consumers.

VI

The expansion of sugar production in the nineteenth century was itself cause and effect of other changes in Cuba, and none perhaps as dramatic as the increase of the population. The vast labor requirements to meet expanded sugar production led to a new demand for African slaves. Between 1763 and 1862, an estimated 750,000 slaves were introduced into Cuba. These were also years of rapid white population growth, much of which was due to unsettled New World politics. The arrival of French émigrés to Cuba in the 1790s was followed by the migration of Spaniards and Dominicans fleeing the Haitian occupation of Santo Domingo in 1801. The sale to the United States of Louisiana in 1803 and Florida in 1819 resulted in two successive waves of immigration to Cuba. Between 1810 and 1830, lastly, the successful wars for independence on the mainland colonies produced a vast migration of Spanish soliders, bureaucrats, colonists, and their creole collaborators, many of whom settled in Cuba permanently.

The population of Cuba increased dramatically through the nineteenth century. Between the census years 1791 and 1817, the total population had more than doubled, increasing from 272,300 to 553,033. By 1862, the population had doubled again, to 1,396,470 (see Table 9).

TABLE 9. Cuban Population (1817–62)

	1817	1827	1846	1862
White				
Male	130,519	168,653	230,983	468,107
Female	109,311	142,398	194,784	325,377
Total	239,830	311,051	425,767	793,484
Free colored				
Male	58,885	51,962	72,651	113,746
Female	55,173	54,532	76,575	118,687
Total	114,058	106,494	149,226	232,433
Slave				
Male	124,324	183,290	201,011	218,722
Female	74,821	103,652	122,748	151,831
Total	199,145	286,946	323,759	370,553
Island total	553,033	704,491	898,752	1,396,470

Sources: Adapted from Ramón de la Sagra, *Historia económico-política y estadística de la isla de Cuba* (Havana, 1831); Cuba, Comisión de Estadística, *Cuadro estadístico de la siempre fiel Isla de Cuba, correspondiente al año de 1846* (Havana, 1847); Cuba, Centro de Estadística, *Noticias estadísticas de la isla de Cuba, en 1862* (Havana, 1864).

VII

The changes in the size of the population were accompanied by changes in the composition of the population. The number of slaves increased almost threefold, accounting in 1827 for more than 40 percent of the total population. The proportion of the slave population subsequently declined to 36 percent in 1846 and 28 percent in 1862, due largely to high mortality rates and the decline of the slave trade.

The number of free people of color almost doubled, although the proportion of the free colored population stabilized at 15 to 20 percent. Unlike the population of whites and slaves, whose numbers increased principally from sources outside the island, the free population of color expanded internally. Whatever increases were registered through manumission were largely offset by high mortality among recently freed slaves. Slaves were often manumitted upon the completion of a lifetime of service: the elderly, the infirm, the ill—a cost-effective method by which planters minimized expenses associated with the maintenance of unproductive slaves. The population of free people of color was, in fact, prob-

Table 10. Census of 1862 (by race, age, and sex)

	Males (Years)				Females (Years)				Total Both Sexes
	0–15	16–60	Over 60	Total	0–15	16–60	Over 60	Total	
White									
West	124,333	263,460	10,919	398,712	112,818	148,080	7,535	268,433	667,145
East	29,883	37,466	2,046	69,395	27,424	27,915	1,605	56,944	126,339
Total	154,216	300,926	12,965	468,107	140,242	175,995	9,140	325,377	793,484
Free colored									
West	26,235	40,880	3,906	71,021	25,405	45,476	4,188	75,069	146,090
East	21,483	19,320	1,982	42,785	20,172	21,614	1,832	43,618	86,403
Total	47,718	60,140	5,888	113,746	45,577	67,090	6,020	118,687	232,433
Slave									
West	46,799	133,390	11,054	191,243	41,557	80,649	5,326	127,532	318,775
East	9,275	16,567	1,637	27,479	8,652	14,736	911	24,299	51,778
Total	56,074	149,957	12,691	218,722	50,209	95,385	6,237	151,831	370,553
Total	258,008	511,083	31,544	800,635	236,028	338,470	21,397	595,895	1,396,530

Source: Cuba, Centro de Estadística, Noticias estadísticas de la isla de Cuba, en 1862 (Havana, 1864)

ably larger than recorded by census enumerators. Vast numbers of slav
had fled inland, into the impenetrable mountain ranges of central an
eastern Cuba, there forming fugitive communities of free people.

The combined population of the free people of color and slaves accounted for more than half the total number of inhabitants of the island,
reaching a high of 56 percent in 1827. The sudden minority status of the
white population became a source of concern to colonial authorities.
Throughout the first half of the nineteenth century, Spanish authorities
pursued systematic policies designed to encourage white immigration to
the island. By the time of the 1861 census, the white population had
resumed a majority status, accounting for 61 percent of the total.

Overall sex ratios remained comparatively stable through the first half
of the nineteenth century: approximately 43 percent female and 57 percent male. Several notable demographic features, however, distinguish
the white, free colored, and slave populations. By mid-century, the proportion of women in the slave population was 38 percent, the lowest of
all groups and in part explaining the low birth rate among slaves. The
skewed sex ratio was even more pronounced among rural slaves, where
the proportion of males to females was customarily 2 to 1 and often as
high as 4 to 1. Male labor was preferred for field work, and accounted
for the larger share of new slaves introduced to Cuba after the 1790s.
Among the free people of color, however, women outnumbered men,
representing 51 percent of the total colored population. Indeed, only in
the free colored population did women occupy a majority status, which
partially explains the steady population growth among this group. Fertility rates among free colored women continued to increase through the
nineteenth century. By 1862, those fifteen years of age and under accounted for more than 40 percent of the total colored population, up from
38 percent in 1846 and 36 percent in 1841, and the highest percentage of
all three population groupings in Cuba. For whites the population group
0 to 15 years comprised 37 percent and among slaves it accounted for 29
percent. Data for women of childbearing age (16 to 40 years) set these
distinctions in sharper relief. Among women of color those of childbearing age represented almost 60 percent of the total, among slave women
48 percent, and among white women 40 percent.

The proportion of women within the white population remained constant through the first half of the nineteenth century at approximately 45
percent. However, it declined to 41 percent in 1862, reflecting the surge
of white male immigration during the previous decade. The increase in

the white population also served to raise the proportion of white women on the island. Whites had previously accounted for approximately 48 percent of all females. After 1862, white women made up almost 55 percent of the total female population.

The census of 1862 also revealed several notable characteristics in the composition of the Cuban population, particularly with regard to regional distribution, age composition, and size and distribution of the population of color, both free and slave (see Table 10). The population data of 1862 served to set in relief the demographic dimensions of the growing social, economic, and political disparities between east and west. A mere 19 percent of the total population, (264,520 out of 1,396,530) lived in the east. At a time when the white population had recovered its majority status across the island, the combined number of free people of color and slaves still made up 52 percent of the total eastern population. This parity of the races was accompanied by a greater balance in male-female ratios: among slaves, 53 percent were male, 47 percent female in the east (60 and 40 percent in the west), among free colored, 50 percent each were in the east (49 percent male, 51 percent female in the west), and among eastern whites there were 55 percent males to 45 percent females (60 and 40 percent in the west). Whereas in the west almost 65 percent of the combined population of color, free and slaves, was distributed in the agricultural rural zones, in the east the total population of color was almost evenly distributed between rural zones (51 percent) and urban regions (49 percent). Almost 40 percent of the total population of free colored and 16 percent of all whites resided in the east. Nearly 90 percent of the total economically productive white population (16–60 years) lived in the west. The free population of color in the east constituted almost 63 percent of total colored population, as compared with 32 percent in the west. More than 86 percent of all slaves in Cuba were located in the west and made up almost 30 percent of the total western population; the slave population in the east represented almost 20 percent of the total. There were not only more slaves in the west but also a higher average number of slaves (see Table 11).

Vast differences had developed between the two regions of Cuba. The west accounted for most of the productive estates and most of the production. It contained the majority of the white population along with most of the slaves, and for obvious reasons was the bastion of pro-slavery sentiment. The more diverse economy of the east was poorer, with greater numbers of smaller farmers, less dependent on slave labor, and less com-

TABLE 11.   Distribution of Slaves on Sugar Estates (1862)

Jurisdiction	Estates	Slaves on Estates	Average Slaves per Estate
Pinar del Río	5	494	99
San Cristobal	9	1,032	115
Bahía Honda	24	5,195	216
Guanajay	59	10,109	171
Vueltabajo	97	16,830	174
Guanabacoa	3	493	164
Jaruco	28	4,843	173
Güines	90	14,677	163
Santiago de las Vegas	9	668	74
Bejucal	17	2,640	155
San Antonio de los Baños	22	2,527	115
Havana	169	25,848	153
Matanzas	131	20,629	157
Cárdenas	144	18,290	127
Colón	140	27,019	193
Matanzas	415	65,938	159
Sagua la Grande	137	13,841	101
Cienfuegos	107	11,546	108
Trinidad	45	5,951	132
Santa Clara	84	2,978	35
Sancti Spíritus	49	4,398	90
Remedios	70	5,392	77
Las Villas	492	44,106	90
Puerto Príncipe	95	4,271	45
Nuevitas	22	1,190	54
Puerto Príncipe	117	5,461	47
Santiago de Cuba	91	9,079	100
Guantánamo	20	2,356	118
Holguín	63	1,437	23
Bayamo	24	646	27

TABLE 11.   (*Continued*)

Jurisdiction	Estates	Slaves on Estates	Average Slaves per Estate
Manzanillo	22	638	29
Jiguaní	17	81	5
Tunas	2	13	7
Oriente	239	14,250	60
Island Total	1,529	172,433	113

Source: Levi Marrero, *Cuba, economía y sociedad* (12 vols., Madrid, 1973–86), X, 243.

mitted to the production of sugar and the defense of slavery. The majority of the population consisted of people of color, most of whom were free. This group was, in fact, larger than the official census enumeration, for the east had become home and haven to untold numbers of runaway slaves.

A society of a different type had formed in the east. The eastern planter class was smaller, poorer, and more backward. The east had remained largely impervious to the currents transforming the political economy of the west. Sugar estates in the east were primitive family enterprises, mostly what they had always been. There were exceptions, of course, but in the main they were without the capital and technological resources of the west and were incapable of participating in the modernization impulse of the nineteenth century. Eastern planters lacked ready access to credit and were beyond easy reach of foreign markets. The eastern economy was mixed, the farms were smaller, and there were more of them. With proportionally fewer slaves, and larger numbers of free people of color, the east was generally less sympathetic to slavery, less tied to sugar production, and less committed to the colonial structures upon which slavery and sugar production depended.

VIII

The expansion of sugar production in the nineteenth century resulted also in the creation of new social classes and the transformation of old class relationships, developments that in turn foretold changes in the psycho-

TABLE 12. Occupations in Cuba (1861)

Occupation	White	Colored	Total
Ecclesiastics	799	—	779
Officials (active service)	4,933	—	4,933
Officials (retired)	226	—	226
Military (active service)	22,527	—	22,527
Military (retired)	450	—	450
Proprietors	16,544	1,302	17,846
Laborers	156,051	214,457	370,508
Merchants	26,204	343	26,547
Artisans	99,688	77,705	177,393
Teachers	5,658	300	5,988
Day laborers	20,476	39,865	59,988
Paupers	1,476	851	2,327
Total	355,574	335,003	690,577

Source: United States War Department, *Informe sobre el censo de Cuba, 1899* (Washington, D.C., 1900), 732.

logical and political constraints of colonial society. The successful use of slave labor relied on more than force and violence. It rested, too, on a number of ideological formulations, all of which had as their central premise the notion of unequal social evolution. Whites proclaimed themselves innately superior to non-whites. Race not only served as a useful justification of slavery but it was used to justify both the exclusion of people of color from political participation and the imposition of barriers to social mobility. The class-color correlates of the Cuban social structure were pervasive, but not exclusive. Not all whites were property owners, and some people of color were. Cuban society was divided by class and color. The lines were crossed frequently, out of economic interest, when politically expedient, and in surreptitious sexual relations. But to say that they were crossed frequently is not to suggest that they were crossed equally freely by all parties or that such crossing challenged the premises upon which they had been constructed.

Table 12, an occupational inventory of Cuba in 1861, provides a suggestive rendering of the relationship between color and class. The social structure of the island was comparatively simple during the early nineteenth century. By virtue of skin color, whites—*peninsulares* and creoles alike—occupied positions of privilege, and when joined with property provided entrée to power. In this hierarchy, whites monopolized offices in the church, colonial government, and the military. They formed generally the ruling elites, but it was an amalgam not without strains and stress. Three distinct groups made up the ruling sectors, united by race but divided by issues of property and politics. Creole elites predominated among the nearly 18,000 proprietors and constituted a majority of sugar planters, cattle ranchers, mine owners, and tobacco farmers. They possessed wide-ranging power over the population in their domains as slave masters, as employers, as rentiers. But it was not unlimited power. Cuban property owners found themselves situated between and dependent upon the *peninsular* bureaucracy and the *peninsular* mercantile community. It was an anomalous relationship, a function as much of convenience as of necessity. They were united by an inexorable reciprocity. Creole elites depended on the *peninsular* officialdom for political order and social peace and on *peninsular* merchants to market their products, service their loans, and supply their provisions. Merchants depended on the creole landowners for the stock in trade of colonial commerce. Colonial administration depended on both for revenues in the form of sales taxes, customs duties, property taxes, tariff fees, and toll charges. They were all united in their defense of sugar and slavery, upon which rested prosperity, property, and privilege.

But the three groups were divided by a logic no less inexorable. If collective self-interest made collaboration advisable, individual self-interest made conflict inevitable. Public administration continued to be a realm dominated by *peninsulares,* a world from which creoles were systematically excluded. Spanish attitudes toward commercial relations were not very much different. *Peninsular* merchants aspired to nothing less than exclusive control over commerce, all of it all the time. The *peninsular* officialdom and the *peninsular* mercantile establishment reinforced each other, defending their respective spheres of interests, a collusion that would bode ill for creole concerns. Government policy, principally in the form of tax regulation and tariff schedules, favored *peninsular* mercantile interests. *Peninsular* merchants, for their part, reciprocated, and defended the propriety of Spanish administration and the primacy of Spanish rule.

The rift between Cuban producers and consumers and Spanish bureaucrats and merchants was widening throughout the nineteenth century. Creoles demanded free trade, *peninsulares* defended monopoly. The merchants in the capital and provincial centers made the larger share of their profits not by exporting Cuban products but by controlling imports for the consumer markets, a practice particularly galling to a society becoming daily more dependent on foreign goods. As producers, Cubans wanted to place their products directly in the world market and to secure imports at the cheapest prices. They resented Spanish determination to monopolize public administration and private trade. They demanded greater control over resources, over commerce, over public office—control, in short, over all areas vital to their interests. Creole property owners were imbued with a deep sense of class solidarity, united by a determination to win political and economic concessions from Spain without losing social control over slaves.

Humboldt observed that the requirements of sugar production served to "place the landed proprietors in a state of absolute dependence upon the merchants." Planters complained that the prices and practices of Spanish merchants despoiled them of as much as 40 percent of their profits. The merchant occupied the dual role of vendor of manufacturers and lender of money (refaccionista), both often at exorbitant rates. Loans at 30 to 40 percent interest were not uncommon. In 1852, planter Fernando Diago was obliged to pay $100,000 in interest charges; for the years 1850–53, Diago paid a total of $333,815 in interest. For the same four-year period, planter Joaquín de Ayesterán paid $284,691 to refaccionistas. As early as 1805, creole Ignacio Zarragoitia addressed an affidavit to the Real Consulado accusing merchants of impoverishing Cuban society. "The merchants' interests," he insisted, "are absolutely contrary to the state."

The clash of rival economic interests between planters and merchants served to exacerbate political tensions between the colony and the metropolis. Spanish customs duties on the foreign imports upon which Cubans were becoming increasingly dependent, foodstuffs no less than agricultural and industrial equipment, raised both the cost of living and the cost of sugar production. Creole property owners demanded not only economic policies to protect and promote their interests, they demanded too the political positions to implement the policies themselves, according to their needs. Cubans demanded freedom to promote their own interests, arrange their own taxes, regulate their own economic growth. They demanded freedom to expand, to develop resources according to their needs on their terms, to earn more by producing more. *Peninsular* commercial practices and Spanish government policies were seen as the twin obstacles to continued economic expansion, and without access to the upper reaches of public office, creoles were also without the means to change commercial policy. They needed political power to protect their economic interests.

These tensions worked their way downward through the social structure. A small but growing creole upper middle class, originating largely out of the liberal professions, salaried personnel, tobacco growers, coffee farmers, and small mill owners, also found the *peninsular* presence increasingly odious. They resented the growing Spanish population that served to reduce opportunities on the island. Immigration from Spain increased throughout the eighteenth century. Between 1780 and 1790 immigration from Spain to the New World was five times greater than that of 1710–30. Other waves followed during the early decades of the nineteenth century. Thousands of Spaniards and their loyalist allies arrived from the former colonies on the mainland. They crowded into Cuba, an embittered presence, adding a previously unknown vehemence to the presumption of *peninsular* exclusivity in colonial society.

But the disaffection of the creole petite bourgeoisie was also directed increasingly at the larger structures of the colonial system, and in this sense they were on a collision course with the creole planter class. They were particularly susceptible to the appeals of nineteenth-century liberalism, and were prepared to act as the agents of change. Their growing antipathy toward Spanish administration transferred easily enough into antagonism toward the creole elites who defended Spanish administration, and just as easily generalized into misgivings about the slave system upon which rested the privilege and property of local elites.

They were joined by growing numbers of small creole farmers throughout the countryside, as well as urban artisans, lower-level civil servants, and salaried employees. The farmers were engaged in small-scale production for export and consumption; this population was also dependent on foreign imports and Spanish merchants for wares, textiles, and equipment. On a smaller scale, but no less real, the conflict between the large creole planters and large *peninsular* commercial houses was replicated between the small Cuban farmer and the small Spanish retail vendors.

In addition to *peninsulares* and creoles was a large and rapidly expanding population of free people of color. They had more than doubled their total number in less than fifty years, from 114,058 in 1817 to 232,433 in 1861, and their aspirations kept pace with their growth. They tended to concentrate in the larger provincial cities, most notably Havana, where by 1861 the free colored population approached 40,000. Many had obtained skills through service as artisan apprentices; others had received limited formal education. By the mid-nineteenth century, free people of color were located in virtually every occupational category, in the professions and in the skilled trades. Some had acquired sizable fortunes. It was not unrestricted entry, but it was significant. Free men and women of color were especially prominent in urban trades, service sectors, and mechanical arts. Men worked as cigarmakers, carpenters, tailors, shoemakers, potters, and masons. They were ordained as priests and trained as militia officers, physicians, and attorneys. Some were writers and poets, musicians and artists. They were small merchants and manufacturers, miners, and ranchers. Women worked as seamstresses, weavers, laundresses, midwives, cigarmakers, and domestic servants. Few foreign travelers to Havana at mid-century failed to note the prominence and relative prosperity of free people of color. "Certain it is that one here sees negroes and mulattoes much more frequently engaged in trade. . . ," observed Fredrika Bremer in 1851, "and their wives are commonly very well, nay, even splendidly dressed. It is not unusual to see mulatto women, with flowers in their hair, walking with their families on the principal pomenades in a manner which denotes freedom and prosperity."

The occupational distribution of the free people of color reflected also the varieties of opportunity available to the growing ranks of the free slave and mulatto population. The 1862 census in Havana listed 22,753 free colored industrial workers (industriales), but only 2,180 small farmers (labradores). In Santiago de Cuba, the census recorded 22,936 colored farmers and only 13,069 industrial laborers. The combined population of color for both cities included 104 teachers and 239 urban property owners (propietarios). Some had joined the planter ranks. An agricultural census in Havana province in 1860 recorded 360 white and 13 black landowners (hacendados) in Guanabacoa, 1,708 whites and 13 blacks in Santiago de los Baños, 14 whites and 9 blacks in Santiago de las Vegas, and 195 white landowners and 1 black in Bejucal.

But the success of free people of color was not an unmixed blessing: it aroused suspicion and enmity. Nor could it change skin color, and it was by the color of their skin that these Cubans were judged. Certainly individuals overcame the colonial taboos and legal barriers designed to obstruct the rise of the population of color. Most, however, were subject to official discrimination that barred them from attending the University of Havana or enrolling in other institutions of higher learning, denied

them access to the ranks of the Catholic clergy, and blocked their participation in the public affairs of the colony.

Victims of systematic discrimination, free people of color were also
feared as a potential source of political disorder. They occupied a strategic place in the class-color hierarchy of the colony. Under certain conditions, they were able to articulate the circumstances and grievances of
the masses of people of color, especially slaves, and bear witness to the
persisting inequities of colonial society. They generally opposed slavery
and earned the enduring suspicion of white elites, for they were perceived
as potential instigators of slave rebellion and social unrest. Throughout
the nineteenth century, the population of free blacks and mulattoes emerged
as an increasingly important force for change by giving structure and
substance to dissent and discontent. The very presence of a large free
population of color, many of whom had attained positions of distinciton,
threatened to undermine the racial assumptions of the colonial social order. No matter how kindly slaves were treated by their masters, Robert
Francis Jameson observed in Havana in 1820, "the love of liberty soon
renders them restless. They see numbers of their colour enjoy freedom,
and the laws sanction their attempt at attaining the same immunity." The
implications were not lost on the authorities. The population of free colored was considered, in the words of Captain General Francisco Dionisio
Vives, "indirectly dangerous." "The existence of free blacks and mulattoes in the midst of the slavery of their companions," warned Vives in
1832, "is an example which will become very dangerous one day."

African slaves occupied the lower end of the island social order, numbering approximately 300,000 to 400,000 through the first half of the
nineteenth century. Almost one-quarter of all slaves were located in urban
centers, working largely as domestics, in the skilled trades, and as day
laborers rented out for their owners' gain. The vast majority of slaves
toiled in the fields of rural Cuba, on the coffee *fincas,* on the *haciendas,*
on tobacco *vegas,* but mostly on the sugar *ingenios.* Approximately one-
half the total number of rural slaves were engaged in sugar production,
as shown in Table 13. Rural slaves lived in wretched conditions and
worked under dreadful circumstances and remorseless exploitation. Corporal punishment, principally in the form of flogging and beatings, was
used to coerce and intimidate. "I have heard discussed with the greatest
coolness," Humboldt wrote, "the question whether it was better for the
proprietor not to overwork his slaves, and consequently have to replace

TABLE 13.   Distribution of Slaves (1862)

	Male	Female	Total
Urban centers	37,014	38,963	75,977
Sugar plantations	109,709	62,962	172,671
Coffee estates	14,344	11,598	26,942
Tobacco vegas	11,622	6,053	17,675
Misc. agriculture	38,978	23,606	62,584

Source: Cuba, Centro de Estadística, *Noticias estadísticas de la isla de Cuba, en 1862* (Havana, 1864).

them with less frequency, or whether he should get all he could out of them in a few years, and thus have to purchase newly imported Africans more frequently.'' Six-day work weeks, eighteen-hour work days, often for months at a time, were not uncommon. Visiting sugar estates in Havana province during the 1830s, Richard R. Madden learned from a *mayoral* in Güines that the time of sleep slaves received during the harvest ''was about four hours, a little more or less. Those who worked at night in the boiling-house worked also next day in the field. . . . The treatment of the slaves was inhuman, the sole object of the *administrador* being, to get the utmost amount of labor in a given time out of the greatest number of slaves that could be worked day and night, without reference to their health or strength, age or sex.'' From a coffee grower in Batabanó, Madden learned that slaves ''required . . . three or four hours sleep, not more; and if they had more time they would not employ it in sleep, they would go out wandering or stealing.''

The effects of these conditions were palpable. The slave population of Cuba failed to sustain itself through natural growth. Slave deaths exceeded births, necessitating the maintenance of slave numbers through new acquisitions. Appalling work conditions, the prevalence of preventable disease and epidemics, illness and malnutrition, all combined to contribute to a staggering mortality rate. Life expectancy on many plantations in the nineteenth century averaged less than seven years from the time of arrival. Death rates often reached as high as 10 to 12 percent annually.

Slaves found a variety of ways to confront their oppression and resist brutalization. Resistance took many forms. In its individual expression it involved suicide, murder, and flight. Its collective form, and the most dreaded by whites, was rebellion. Both the opportunity and occasion for slave uprisings increased markedly during the nineteenth century, largely the result of the rapid expansion of slavery across the island and the sudden surge of recently arrived adult slaves. Vast numbers of African-born slaves filled the island—intractable, undisciplined, resentful, and with a memory of their lost freedom: 385,000 slaves between 1790 and 1820; 272,000 more between 1820 and 1853; another 175,000 between 1853 and 1864. Perhaps as many as 75 percent of all slaves in Cuba were born in Africa. Most were males, many from the same cultural groups, imbued with strong military traditions—Carabalís and Lucumíes (Yorubans).

Rebellions took two forms. The most common and frequent were uprisings born of local grievances, confined to a single estate, usually brief but violent affairs characterized by widespread destruction of property, the killing of whites, and the subsequent execution of slaves. Rebellions of this type occurred often during the nineteenth century, and almost everywhere on the island: most notably in 1812 on sugar estates in Puerto Príncipe, Holguín, Bayamo, and Trinidad; in 1826 in Guira; in 1830 on coffee *fincas* in Oriente; five years later on coffee and sugar estates in Jaruco, Matanzas, Macuriges, and Havana; in 1837 in Manzanillo; in 1840 on sugar estates in Cienfuegos, Trinidad, Havana, Cárdenas, and Matanzas; in 1841 in Lagunillas and Havana.

Slave rebellion of the second type involved planning, coordination, and collaboration among slaves, free people of color, and whites. Uprisings of this type were the most feared. Possessed of ideological content and political purpose, their goal was the abolition of slavery, and therefore they threatened the very foundations of colonial political economy. As early 1811, José Antonio Aponte, a free black carpenter, organized an elaborate uprising based in Havana and involving whites, free colored, and slaves in Puerto Príncipe and Oriente. The rebellion was crushed but not before the death of overseers, whites, and slaves, and the destruction of sugar mills and coffee estates. A rebellion in Matanzas in 1825 resulted in the death of scores of slaves and whites and the destruction of twenty-five estates. In 1843, another uprising in Matanzas involved three hundred slaves from more than fifteen different sugar estates and ended only after the local squadron of Spanish lancers defeated and dispersed insurgent slaves. Later that same year, a rebellion involving two hundred slaves broke out on the "Triunvirato" estate in Matanzas and spread to neighboring plantations. Official investigators charged that the "Triunvir-

ato" uprising was, in fact, part of a far-flung conspiracy involving hundreds
of slaves and thousands of whites and free people of color. In the weeks
and months that followed, Spanish authorities made more than four thousand arrests on suspicion of plotting to overthrow the government. Authorities used the dread of slave conspiracy to justify widespread repression, and pursued suspects with uncommon ferocity: torture, floggings,
and executions in the most grisly manner. Hundreds, perhaps as many as
one thousand slaves and free people of color alike were put to death—
hung, drawn and quartered, or garroted. Dr. J. G. F. Wurdemann happened to be vacationing in Cuba that winter, and wrote: " 'Slaughter-
houses' . . . were established in Matanzas and Cardenas, where the accused were subjected to the lash to extort confessions. . . . A thousand
lashes were in many cases inflicted on a single negro; a great number
died under this continued torture, and still more from spasms, and gan-
grene of the wounds." The use of ladders to which prisoners were tied
for floggings provided the grisly inspiration that gave the conspiracy the
name of "La Escalera." Cuba was never quite the same.

IX

Slave rebellions reached ominous proportions in the mid-nineteenth century, one additional source of conflict in a society already caught up in
compounding contradictions. The old fractures deepened and new stress
lines appeared. Some of the breaks corresponded neatly to the stratifica-
tion of class and the delineation of race; others traversed vertically lines
of caste and color. Divergent economic roles pitted rural landowners against
urban merchants. Economic conflicts exacerbated the political dispute between creoles and *peninsulares*. Social differences were also emerging
among creoles, between the planter class of the west and its counterpart
in the east, between the creole landed aristocracy and the creole petite
bourgeoisie.

For all these reasons, Cuban elites remained largely impervious to the
revolutionary eddies that swirled about Latin America early in the nineteenth century. Spain's mainland colonies were in rebellion. The ideal of
independence gained momentum, transformed in the end into a surge of
irresistible proportions. Cubans were unmoved. The cause for which creole elites on the mainland had committed their fates and fortunes found
little support among creole elites on the island. On the contrary, many

Cubans were genuinely horrified by the spectacle of civil strife in other realms of the empire and could contemplate no worse fate for the island than to follow the mainland into this abyss. The scattered and short-lived separatist conspiracies that challenged Spanish rule in Cuba originated largely within the ranks of the creole petite bourgeoisie and free people of color. One ambitious plot in 1809 was organized by attorneys Román de la Luz and Joaquín Infante, who proceeded to promulgate a constitution establishing an independent republic. It was crushed within the year. A decade later, poet José María Heredia and creole army officer José Francisco de Lemus organized the "Soles y Rayos de Bolívar" conspiracy, a movement advocating the abolition of slavery and the establishment of an independent republic. The plot collapsed in 1823. A year later, creole ensign Gaspar A. Rodríguez, in collaboration with creole militia officers, small farmers, and several parish priests, organized another ill-starred separatist conspiracy. In 1826, Manuel Andrés Sánchez and Francisco de Agüero Velasco launched an armed uprising near Puerto Príncipe in the name of free Cuba. It too ended ingloriously.

In fact, separatist stirrings found little support among creole elites. On the contrary, elites viewed the prospects of independence with a mixture of apprehension and alarm. Certainly creoles in Cuba had their share of grievances against *peninsular* rule, many of which were similar to those that drove their counterparts on the mainland into rebellion. Their objections to Spanish government were real and ranging. But so were their objections to independence. Creole acquiescence to colonial rule was induced as much by preference for past order as by abhorrence of the prospects of future disorder. Cubans were enjoying the first flushes of a dazzling prosperity. Sugar production was increasing, exports were expanding, profits were on the rise: this was not the time for revolution.

Separatist stirrings also posed a direct and fundamental threat to the social order of early nineteenth-century Cuba. In no other Spanish colony was the local economy so totally dependent on slavery; in no other Spanish colony did African slaves constitute so large a part of the population; in no other Spanish colony did the total population of color constitute a majority. Creole elites presided over a plantation economy based on a vast slave labor force, a production system that engendered at least as much antagonism between whites and blacks as the political system had produced between creoles and *peninsulares*. Cubans could not reasonably challenge the assumptions of Spanish primacy without inviting slaves to challenge the premises of their subjugation. Creoles preferred security to

change and were ill-disposed to risk their positions of property and privilege for independence. Hence the anomaly of the creole position: the
very social forces required to dislodge *peninsular* elites could just as easily displace the creole ones.

Even if colonial social structures were to survive intact a transition to
nationhood, Cuban elites understood correctly that independence would
mean not only the end of Spanish sovereignty but probably the end of
African slavery. Their refusal to produce an independence movement allowed the leadership of separatist projects to pass on to downwardly mobile elites, creoles of modest social origins, and Cubans of color, at the
fringes of the colonial polity, without direct and vital stakes in slavery,
and therefore less reluctant to summon slaves in behalf of separatism.
These development had far-reaching implications. Once the momentum
for Cuban separatism passed on to the popular classes, the meaning of
independence, indeed, the promise of independence, could no longer be
restricted simply to the ending of Spanish rule. It perforce expanded, and
included political equality, social justice, and, above all, the abolition of
slavery. Creole elites had, hence, one more reason to oppose independence. Under these circumstances, planters reasoned, political independence would entail economic ruin and social chaos. The moral was clear
to Cuban elites: the defense of *peninsular* rule offered the most efficacious means through which to defend creole property.

Peninsular rule also offered the best defense against slaves. Colonial
society rested on a precarious balance of social forces, an equilibrium
that creole elites alone were incapable of maintaining. Cuban property
holders were in an impossible situation. They were committed to the
defense of slavery as essential to their prosperity but lacked the wherewithal to defend themselves against slaves. This position logically and
inevitably committed them to the defense of Spanish rule as the vital and
minimum means to the defense of their interests. Creoles lived in a state
of anxiety, under the specter of social disintegration and racial disorder.
These forebodings were intensified by dread of slave rebellion. Cubans
had created at one and the same time a labor force essential to their
existence and a social force capable of their destruction. The creole fear
of slave rebellion was a recurring theme of the nineteenth century, in
fictional literature, in personal memoirs, in official reports. The possibility of slaves rising up in arms was a brooding omnipresence in the daily
lives of the planter class, and only the security symbolized by the metropolitan military presence relieved its unremitting pressure.

The fear of slaves rebelling soon generalized into a fear of rebellion by all people of color. When the population of color expanded into a majority, the fear was transformed into horror. "The fear which the Cubans have of the Negroes," Spanish Premier José María Calatrava noted with some percipience, "is the most secure means which Spain has to guarantee her domination over this island." Nothing so preyed on creole consciousness, nothing so threatened the creole sense of security as the specter of slave rebellion and race war. The presence of tens of thousands of dispossessed and displaced French refugees from St. Domingue in their midst served as palpable reminder of the most dreaded prospect of all: a successful slave revolt. Dr. J. G. F. Wurdemann summarized creole fears in the aftermath of "La Escalera": "All the horrors of San Domingo massacres were to have been repeated. Many of the white were to have been flayed and broiled while alive, and with the exception of the young women, reserved for a worse fate, all, without discrimination of age or sex, were to have been massacred." Periodic slave rebellions during the nineteenth century confirmed creoles' worse fears, and their swift repression by the Spanish army provided creoles with comforting reassurance that their confidence in the efficacy of *peninsular* arms had not been misplaced.

The possibility of independence was further dampened by the success of the mainland revolutions for independence. The island filled with tens of thousands of embittered royalist refugees of all types, *peninsulares* and creoles alike—government officials, slave owners, merchants, and landowners, among the most reactionary elements of the former colonies— all bearers of lurid tales of devastation and desolation. They resettled in Cuba and reinforced the Cuban fear of change. At the same time, elements of the Spanish army defeated on the mainland were redeployed to the island, strengthening the *peninsular* military presence in Cuba. During the 1820s, the island assumed the appearance of an armed camp. It was an imposing presence, at one point reaching almost 50,000 troops, vigilant for the slightest sign of subversion.

By the end of the 1820s, the Spanish New World empire had returned to the form in which it had begun: insular possessions on the outer Caribbean rim. In this way, Cuba regained its former singular importance, and with it, Spanish appreciation. Henceforth Cuba was to bear the official title of the "Ever-Faithful Isle."

5

Reform and Revolution in the Colony

I

Cuban elites could not contemplate the prospects of independence without first pausing to consider the potential social consequences and economic costs of political change. They understood well the political economy of colonialism and appreciated even more their stake in that order. They understood too that the quest for political power risked the loss of privilege and property: that the colonial structures that sanctioned unequal political relationships, to which they were victim, were the same structures that underwrote unequal social and economic relationships, to which they were beneficiary. They understood their system, and acted accordingly. They chose collaboration over confrontation, they sought to change policies, not challenge premises, and in the process they forfeited their claim to leadership in the formation of Cuban nationality. Creole property owners were prisoners within structures partially of their own making. Unable to articulate the larger needs of their society, they pursued the narrow interests of their class; unwilling to lead revolution against the colonial regime, they chose to limit reaction within the colonial regime. They demanded nothing more than reforms for themselves, in which parity with *peninsulares* and the pursuit of profits were the central objectives. They sought to expand their political position and advance their economic interests at the expense of *peninsular* elites above, without having to share power or sacrifice property to rival social forces below. For the remainder of the nineteenth century, Cuban elites pursued a variety of strategies, all calculated to improve their status, all sharing one feature in common: opposition to independence.

The survival of the colonial regime into the nineteenth century did not allay all creole fears. Nor did it end all creole grievances. Cuban elites had defended *peninsular* rule more out of convenience than conviction, largely because other alternatives were either unavailable or unthinkable, or both. They were not wholly sanguine about their future under Spain, and not a few understood that their interests remained always subject to forces over which they had little control.

II

Cuban misgivings were soon confirmed. Slavery was under assault from a new source, now in the form of British policy efforts to abolish the international slave trade. Spain acquiesced to English pressure, first in 1817 for an indemnity of 10 million pesetas and again in 1835 under pressure from the Royal Navy. By the terms of the 1817 treaty, Spain agreed to prohibit the introduction of new African slaves into its dominions effective May 1820. The 1835 agreement elaborated upon enforcement procedures, including search and seizure of suspected slave ships, punishment for shipowners and crews, and disposition of captured vessels. In 1845, moreover, Spain enacted the "Law of Abolition and Repression of the Slave Trade," further detailing punishment of Spanish subjects found guilty of engaging in the illicit trade.

In fact, these measures had little direct impact on the supply of slave labor in Cuba. The treaty provisions were virtually impossible to implement, much less enforce. The influx of slaves continued, almost without interruption, in the form of a vast contraband network.

The measures were not entirely without effect, however. If the suppression of the legal slave trade did not diminish the supply of slaves, it certainly increased the price of slaves. What especially rankled Cubans was the added costs of doing business. The suppression of the slave trade drove planters from the open market to illicit trade, where risks were commensurately higher and demands on available supply correspondingly greater, and where prices were inevitably steeper. Between the early 1800s and 1820s, the price of male slaves doubled from 300 to 600 pesos, and doubled again between the 1820s and the 1860s, often reaching as high as 1,500 pesos.

The suppression of the legal slave trade added expenses to production in other ways. Access to an unlimited supply of slave labor had traditionally relieved planters of concerns and costs associated with the maintenance of the slave population. The appalling level of slave mortality had not previously concerned planters—not at least as long as slave numbers could be easily and cheaply replaced. Conditions were changing. Planters were now obliged to concern themselves with the health and treatment of slaves, as a means both to protect their investment and to encourage slave reproduction.

The apparent alacrity with which Spain acquiesced to English pressure raised questions of a different sort. Not a few Cubans detected in Spanish submission evidence of complicity. The suppression of the legal slave trade struck at the very sources of the slave system in Cuba, and presaged the end of slavery altogether. Fear increased among Cuban producers that abolition was, in fact, the larger objective. It was not only that Spain had arrayed itself against Cuban interests by enacting measures that could not be reasonably enforced. This was nuisance enough, certainly, and added new costs, of course. But these measures did not fundamentally or alone threaten the system whose survival was, in fact, one of the principle reasons creoles had opted to remain under Spanish rule. If, however, the issue was not simply the supply of slaves, but the survival of slavery itself, creoles were not at all optimistic. Alarm and apprehension spread, for few believed that Spain possessed the will or the wherewithal to resist England.

Cuban dependence on contraband slaves after May 1820 raised concerns of another sort. Certainly the 1817 agreement failed to halt the slave trade, but it did establish the legal basis with which to end slavery. By the terms of the 1817 treaty all slaves introduced into Cuba after May 1820 were enslaved illegally, and therefore entitled to their freedom. This was the position adopted and advanced by the English. Thus, in the decades that followed, Cuban planters had something else to worry about. The illegal slave trade after 1820 assumed vast proportions. Between 1821 and 1831, an estimated three hundred slave expeditions landed more than 60,000 slaves in Cuba. Between 1830 and 1850, an estimated average of 10,000 slaves arrived annually. It can be reasonably presumed that by mid-century, something approaching a majority of slaves in Cuba had arrived after May 1820. Indeed, the volume of the illegal slave trade was so vast as to make strict compliance with the treaty tantamount to an act of emancipation, immediately and without indemnification. These uncertainties preyed on the minds of the planters and cast a pall over the plantation economy. If Madrid were to succumb to English pressure, either out of cupidity for a cash settlement or timidity under the threat of arms, Cubans would be without recourse, and ruined.

These were not choices to which all Cubans were reconciled, and indeed some contemplated a third alternative to the uncertainty of independence and the unreliability of Spanish rule: annexation to the United States. It was an idea that gained proponents and enthusiasm among many important sectors of the creole elites. It offered Cubans a marvelously simple and sensible solution to many of their most pressing problems. In the short run, union with the United States promised salvation of the plantation economy. Slavery would survive intact and the slave trade would resume in full. Advocates of annexation derived comfort from the Texan experience, whereby slaveholders had seceded from Mexico in defense of slavery and eventually joined the North American union.

In the longer run, annexation promised to resolve some of the more anomalous features of the mid-century colonial political economy. Everywhere in Cuba, buyers and sellers, consumers and producers had developed a considerable stake in the North American connection. Certainly Cuban commercial relationships would be simplified. By the 1840s, almost half of Cuban trade depended directly on North American markets and manufactures. Sugar, molasses, and hides went out, vital foodstuffs, sugar machinery, and, increasingly, capital came in. Cubans found themsleves too often caught up in trade conflicts not of their making. And just as often, they were among the principal casualties. To promote metropolitan flour exports in 1848, Spain raised duties on North American flour, thereby making U.S. products more expensive. The United States responded by raising duties on Cuban coffee, thereby dealing hapless coffee growers one more blow at the worst possible moment. No less important, the ban on the slave trade had increased the participation of North American traders in the economy, upon whom Cubans were becoming increasingly dependent for their supply of illegal slaves. Annexation seemed a wholly logical political outgrowth of a deepening economic relationship. It promised also to eliminate the onerous system of Spanish taxation on foreign imports and remove North American tariffs on Cuban products, both of which would contribute to increased profits on exports and reduced prices on imports.

But it was not only self-interest that motivated Cubans. Many had developed an abiding admiration for North American institutions, where democratic ideals seemed to coexist comfortably with slave institutions. Many had sent their children to the United States for their education. Many more were frequent travelers to the north, on business trips and vacations. They had developed extensive commercial contacts and social ties in the United States. In increasing numbers, they were becoming naturalized U.S. citizens. They had come to know the United States well

and looked upon union as an important step in the direction of modernity
and progress.

III

It happened too that the 1840s were years of peaking North American
interest in the acquisition of Cuba. Indeed, the timing was not coinciden-
tal. The surge of annexation sentiment was very much the result of a
reciprocal push-pull of annexationists on both sides of the Florida Straits.
North American advocacy of the acquisition of Cuba encouraged Cuban
advocacy of annexation to the United States, and vice versa.

North American interest in Cuba had its origins early in the nineteenth
century. It assumed form around a combination of several factors. Elements partly sentimental, partly historical, and partly pragmatic were bound
up in the abiding belief that Cuba's destiny was manifest. The destinies
of both countries seemed not merely intertwined but indissoluble. So certain were North Americans about the future of the island that they conferred on a policy formulation the properties of natural law. "There are
laws of political as well as of physical gravitation," John Quincy Adams
posited in 1823, "and if an apple, severed by a tempest from its native
tree, cannot choose but fall to the ground, Cuba, forcibly disjoined from
its own unnatural connection with Spain, and incapable of self-support,
can gravitate only towards the North American Union, which, by the
same law of nature, cannot cast her off from its bosom."

Subsequently repeated and refined, the notion of "political gravitation"
served as the central and enduring feature of U.S. policy through much
of the nineteenth century. It was buttressed by a corollary principle of
"no transfer," a proposition by which North Americans refused to sanction the cession of sovereignty over Cuba to a third party. Thus, the
defense of Spanish sovereignty was the most efficacious means of acquiring eventual possession of Cuba. Until such moment as Spain proved
incapable of maintaining its authority over Cuba, at which time the United
States would claim possession over the island, Spain's declining sovereignty in Cuba would be underwritten by the United States.

As guardians of the status quo, Washington pursued a policy designed
at once to defend Spanish sovereignty and to prevent any modification of
the island's political status that did not result in the cession of Cuba to
the United States. The guarantee of Cuba's "independence against all the

world *except* Spain," Thomas Jefferson insisted in 1823, ". . . would be nearly as valuable to us as if it were our own." John Forsyth, James Monroe's minister to Spain, repeatedly assured Spanish authorities that U.S. "interest required, as there was no prospect of [Cuba] passing into our hands, that it should belong to Spain." Indeed, the United States threatened war to prevent the transfer of Cuban sovereignty. In 1823 Jefferson counseled James Monroe to "oppose, with all our means, the forcible interposition of any power, either as auxiliary, stipendiary, or under any other form or pretext, and most especially [Cuba's] transfer to any power, by conquest, cession or in any other way." Twenty years later, John Forsyth, now Martin Van Buren's Secretary of State, authorized the U.S. minister in Madrid to reassure Spanish authorities "that in case of any attempt, from whatever quarter, to wrest from her this portion of her territory, she may securely depend upon the military and naval resources of the United States to aid her in preserving or recovering it."

Nor was North American support of Spanish sovereignty limited to the defense of the status quo against external threats. Any internal attempt by Cubans to establish independence posed a threat no less menacing to the United States. The Haitian experience loomed large over U.S. policy calculations, and at another point the perceptions of Cuban planters and North American policymakers converged. The prospect of Cuban independence raised the specter of another black republic in the Caribbean. For John Adams, the thought of a free black population in Cuba, so close to North American shores, offered sufficient grounds to oppose Cuban independence. "Other considerations," Martin Van Buren warned in 1829, "connected with a certain class of our population, make it the interest of the southern section of the Union that no attempt should be made in that island to throw off the yoke of Spanish dependence, the first effect of which would be the sudden emancipation of a numerous slave population, the result of which could not but be very sensibly felt upon the adjacent shores of the United States."

The prospect of Cuban independence aroused other concerns, mostly centering on fears of Cuban incapacity for self-government. The central premise of Adams's "law of political gravitation" rested on the belief that Cubans were "not competent to a system of permanent self-dependence." Henry Clay gave explicit and enduring form to U.S. opposition to Cuban independence. "This government desires no political change of that conditon," he insisted. "The population itself of the island is incompetent at present, from its composition and amount, to maintain self-government." Indeed, should Cuba become the theater of revolution, Clay concluded in a thinly veiled warning, the "possible contingencies of such a protracted war might bring upon the government of the United States duties and obligations, the performance of which, however painful it should be, they may not be at liberty to decline."

IV

Annexationist sentiment surged and subsided, in both countries, at about the same time. In the United States, President James K. Polk pursued union by offering Spain $100 million for Cuba, without success. Six years later, in 1854, President Franklin Pierce raised the offer to $130 million, also without effect. In the same year, the U.S. ministers to Spain, France, and England, met in Ostend, Belgium, and publicly urged the United States to renew its offer to purchase Cuba. The "Ostend Manifesto" further warned that if Spain refused to sell, "then, by every law, human and divine, we shall be justified in wresting it from Spain if we possess the power."

Annexationist activity peaked in Cuba during these same years. In the 1840s disaffected creoles gave institutional form to annexationist designs with the establishment of the Club de La Habana. The membership roster of the annexationist club read like a registry of the creole particiate and included planters Cristobal Madán, Domingo del Monte, Miguel Aldama, Anacleto Bermúdez, José María Sánchez Iznaga, José Aniceto Iznaga, Francisco de Frías (Count of Pozos Dulces), José Luis Alfonso, and Gaspar Betancourt Cisneros.

Between the late 1840s and the early 1850s, the Club de La Habana served as the center of annexationist conspiracy. The ill-starred uprisings of Narciso López were the efforts of the Club de La Habana. A former officer in the Spanish army, related to two important annexationist families as nephew of José María Sánchez Iznaga and brother-in-law of Pozos Dulces, López had early fallen in with the annexationist elements in Cuba. With the financial support of creoles in Cuba and political backing from annexationists in the United States, and under the unfurled banner of a newly designed flag—a tri-colored lone star, inspired by the Texan flag— López struck three times: an uprising in Manicaragua in 1848, a filibustering expedition to Cárdenas in 1850, and an invasion of Bahía Honda in 1851. All failed. At Bahía Honda López was captured and subsequently executed.

Other annexationist risings followed, and failed, in quick succession. Joaquín de Agüero led a short-lived rebellion in 1851 near Puerto Príncipe. In the same year, another uprising was organized by planter Isidro Armenteros of Trinidad. One year later Spanish authorities uncovered another annexationist plot in Pinar del Río. In 1854, a far-flung annexationist conspiracy in Havana was discovered and dissolved.

V

Annexationist stirrings subsided around mid-century. The United States became increasingly absorbed with complicated domestic issues, many of which had direct implications for Cuba. The debate over slavery, for example, eventually foreclosed any possibility of admitting a new slave territory into the union. Within the decade, the United States was embroiled in civil war.

Conditions had changed in Cuba, too. Spain had demonstrated a new resolve in resisting British anti-slavery pressure, thereby allaying some Cuban misgivings. The illegal slave trade continued and for a brief period expanded in spectacular fashion. The Spanish officialdom effectively permitted what it could not in fact repudiate. The slave trade ban was loosely and irregularly enforced, if at all, by local authorities. Between 1856 and 1860, an estimated 90,000 slaves entered Cuba, one of the largest numbers for any five-year period in the history of the slave trade. Annexationist sentiment was also on the wane—for some it was an idea whose time had not come, for others an idea whose time had passed. Certainly the Emancipation Proclamation in the United States in 1863 had a chilling effect on planters who earlier had looked to annexation as the salvation of slavery in Cuba. Those who previously advocated annexation as the best defense of slavery, now opposed it—for the same reason.

But not all creoles disaffected with Spanish rule advocated annexation as a solution, and not all who advocated annexation as a solution endorsed rebellion as the means. For many, the potential risks of rebellion were disproportionate to the possible results. Once more the planter class faced a familiar dilemma: a strategy designed to defend slavery risked creating the conditions capable of destroying slavery. Many Cubans feared that an annexationist rebellion would generalize into an emancipation movement. Nor were creole concerns confined solely to the possibility of a slave rebellion from below. No less a source of anxiety, and more probable, was the prospect of slave emancipation from above. Creole elites could not plot to end Spanish sovereignty as a way of defending slavery without provoking Spain into ending slavery as a way to defend sovereignty. They were trapped. Colonial authorities let it be known that an annexationist challenge to Spanish rule would be met immediately with a decree of emancipation. The implications had a sobering effect on even the most ardent advocates of annexation. "Emancipation would be the ruin of the proprietors and merchants of the island," Governor General Federico Roncalí informed Madrid in 1849 in a communication that was subsequently published in the Havana press. "It would put an end to the only means of preventing the island's falling to annexationists. . . . The terrible weapon could in the last extreme, prevent the loss of the island, and if the inhabitants convince themselves that it will be used, they will tremble and renounce every illusion before bringing upon themselves such an anathema." The Spanish maneuver was ingenious. It arrayed the slave population on the side of Spain by giving slaves a stake in colonial rule: emancipated slaves would defend their new freedom under Spain against Cubans who sought to preserve slavery through annexation to the United States.

VI

Creole political activism found a new outlet during the 1860s in reformist politics. In 1865, many of the same planters who had earlier advocated annexation, including Miguel Aldama, Pozos Dulces, and José Luis Alfonso, organized the Reformist party. The party gave new political form to old creole demands for sweeping changes in the colonial regime. Through the pages of the party newspaper *El Siglo,* reformists urged adoption of a multifaceted program: separation of civil and military functions in the office of governor general, the right of petition, freedom from arbitrary arrest and illegal confiscation of property, insular representation in the Spanish parliament, an increase in white immigration, and reform of tax and tariff structures. The question of slavery loomed large in reformist political strategies. By the late 1860s, many Cubans had come to accept—and some even to welcome—the suppression of the slave trade and the eventual end of slavery altogether. Several factors contributed to the change in planters' thinking. Cubans had begun to appreciate the nature of their dilemma. Slaveowners were caught up in a relationship with their slaves and with slavery that served to narrow considerably their freedom of action. Creoles critical of Spanish rule were unwilling to risk property for political change. Spain still held the upper hand, and it was prepared to use the threat of slave emancipation to check planter plottings. Some form of controlled abolition offered one way out of the dilemma. By freeing their slaves they could free themselves of slavery, and, if necessary, of Spanish rule itself.

By the 1860s, further, the slave population had decreased both in absolute numbers and as a proportion of the total population. Whites had recovered their majority, representing 57 percent of the whole population. The 1862 census set the slave population at 370,553, the lowest number since the early nineteenth century. The decline of coffee production had eliminated one important creole sector previously committed to the defense of slavery. At the height of production during the 1820s and 1830s, the more than 2,000 *cafetales* had employed more than 50,000 slaves. By the early 1860s, the number of coffee farms had declined to less than 800, with a commensurate decline in the need of slave labor in the coffee zones. Planters striving to cut costs at a time of accelerating production changes were losing patience with the rising costs of slave labor and the diminishing returns of slave maintenance. They were losing property, too, as they plunged deeper into debt.

The panic of 1857 exacerbated the economic crisis, making scarce capital even scarcer. Interest rates soared. More than 250 commercial establishments in Havana failed. Planters across Cuba had fallen on hard times, and many never recovered. Between 1850 and 1860, almost 400 sugar estates disappeared. Many creoles lost their savings and, in increasing numbers, their property as well. They were unable to service their loans, and, inevitably, lost their property to *peninsular* creditors. By the early 1860s, many of the largest sugar mills in Cuba were no longer owned by Cubans.

The 1857 crisis had one last if not immediately apparent effect. Protectionist pressure in the United States resulted in higher tariff rates on Cuban manufactures, most notably cigars. The Cuban industry plunged into crisis, as factories failed and unemployment increased. Some of the more enterprising manufacturers penetrated North American tariff barriers by relocating their cigar factories first in Key West and later in Tampa, thereby producing cigars in the United States with the leaf and labor imported from Cuba. Over the long run it signaled the flight of Cuban industry, reducing the island to an exporter of raw material. North American tariff policies achieved in the nineteenth century what Bourbon monopolists had failed to accomplish in the eighteenth: the relocation of one of the more dynamic manufacturing sectors of the Cuban economy outside the island.

The only form of abolition most planters could contemplate was gradual emancipation with indemnification—reimbursement from Spain that would allow them to recover their investments, purchase new equipment and machinery, but most of all relieve the crushing indebtedness under which many of them operated. By 1863, an estimated 95 percent of all sugar properties were mortgaged. The previous decade had taken its toll on many planters, and the moral was not lost on the survivors. Gradual abolition with indemnification promised some relief.

The economic efficiency of slavery was also under increasing scrutiny. Larger producers were experimenting with different production techniques and new production technologies, and succeeding. Increased efficiency of machines reduced the need and number of slaves in some sectors of production. The industrialization of sugar manufacture, some Cuban producers argued, was incompatible with slave labor, requiring instead the adoption of wage labor. Some anticipated that capital improvements would lessen their dependence on and, eventually, eliminate altogether the need for slave labor.

These developments did not by any means suggest that all planters were either united or unanimous on the issue of the abolition of slavery. They were not. On the contrary, the argument for gradual and indemnified emancipation was part of a larger and more complicated strategy designed to protect and promote their property interests within the colonial political economy. And on the larger strategy as well, there was neither unity nor unanimity. Planters reacted with horror to the circumstances attending the abolition of slavery in the United States. The enormously destructive conflict, one that many Cubans attributed to slavery, persuaded them that emancipation should be undertaken from above, peacefully, gradually, and with indemnification to owners—not from below, through war, suddenly, and without compensation. After the mid-1860s, one other consideration influenced creole thinking: any hope of future annexation with the United States was now contingent on the abolition of slavery.

The vagaries of the slave trade, no less than the rising cost of slave labor and the uncertainty surrounding the future of slavery itself, was also causing havoc within the planter class. Even planters capable of paying the spiraling cost of slaves were deterred from investing new capital in slavery for fear of uncompensated emancipation. There was nothing sentimental about planters' conversion to abolition. They desired, once and for all, and on their terms, resolution of what was now called euphemistically the "social question," to settle the issue of slavery and to get on with the business of making sugar without uncertainty.

In May 1865, the Reformist party published a lengthy memorandum-petition directed to the Spanish parliament, detailing four basic demands: reform of the tariff system, Cuban political representation in the Spanish parliament, judicial equality with *peninsulares,* and the suppression of the slave trade. The petition was accompanied by a registry of 24,000 supporting signatures, representing virtually every sector of the creole elite.

The timing was propitious. A liberal ministry under Leopoldo O'Donnell, former captain general of Cuba (1843–48), ruled Spain, and was inclined to consider Cuban requests and disposed to concede colonial reforms. The O'Donnell government authorized elections in Cuba for representation in a reform commission, the Junta de Información de Ultramar, to study changes in colonial administration. The Reformist party scored a stunning victory at the polls, electing twelve of the sixteen representatives. Reformism had received its most emphatic endorsement among Cuban creoles. Expectations ran high.

VII

Planters could not have committed themselves to the suppression of the slave trade immediately, and by implication slavery eventually, without guaranteeing themselves first an adequate and alternative supply of labor. Indeed, one reason that planters were able to contemplate the prospects of abolition with a measure of equanimity was due to the growing availability of labor. Between the late 1840s and early 1870s, an estimated 125,000 Chinese contract laborers were imported to work under indenture in Cuba. They were employed principally as laborers in cane fields and in sugar mills, on the railroads and as domestics in the cities. Also during these years the influx of white immigrants increased. Those who had earlier advocated white colonization as a means of reversing the Afro-

Cuban majority now did so as a way to compensate for the anticipated loss of African slave labor. Colonization schemes promised to provide local producers with a plentiful supply of cheap white labor. The demand for increased white immigration was a central issue of the Reformist party program. And, indeed, the white population increased dramatically during the middle decades of the nineteenth century: almost 86 percent between 1846 and 1861 (425,767 to 793,484). The white male population more than doubled (230,986 to 468,107), while the number of white males of economically productive ages (16 to 60) increased even more dramatically, from 132,738 to 300,926. Of these 300,926 white males, almost 86 percent were located in the west. Indeed, the increase of white males was significant everywhere in Cuba, but especially striking in the western zones (see Table 14).

At the time of the 1862 census, white labor had increased signficantly across the island, east and west, in every key agricultural sector. A reported total of 41,661 white men and women were located on the sugar estates (ingenios), 52,042 whites were located on the ranches (potreros), 57,713 whites labored on the estancias, 75,058 worked on the tobacco vegas, 178,185 were found in the commercial farms (sitios de labor), and 29,738 on other estates (fincas and haciendas). Whites outnumbered the free population of color on the sugar estates in every jurisdiction of Oriente except Santiago de Cuba. By the following decade, the labor system was in transition as slave labor was in decline, finding gradual replacement through contract labor and wage labor (see Table 15).

The transformation of the labor system also foretold of the reorganization of the production system. Increasingly, in the effort to rationalize labor and facilitate financing, planters urged the creation of sugar cane farms, owned by small farmers and worked by wage labor, leading eventually to the separation of agriculture and manufacture. The division between field and factory made a lasting contribution to the solution of some of the more pressing problems by allowing mill owners to devote resources principally to processing while independent farmers (colonos) tended to the planting, cultivation, and harvesting of cane.

These changes did not come evenly to all sectors of the economy. Sharp distinctions existed between urban and rural, between agricultural and industrial, between sugar and non-sugar. In some sectors, white migration had immediate and far-reaching effects. Indeed, this signified nothing less than the emergence of new social classes. In the countryside, it resulted in a dramatic increase in the number of independent farmers

TABLE 14.   White Male Population (1846–62)

Jurisdiction	1846	1862
Bayamo	6,274	9,068
Bejucal	4,713	8,409
Cárdenas	11,700	19,429
Cienfuegos	9,001	17,338
Guanabacoa	5,329	9,392
Güines	7,614	18,900
Havana	61,656	91,625
Holguín	8,354	22,200
Jaruco	750	12,743
Manzanillo	2,855	7,014
Matanzas	14,810	29,504
Pinar del Río	12,073	23,910
Puerto Príncipe	12,044	23,405
Sagua la Grande	5,842	18,578
San Antonio	5,328	10,568
Sancti Spíritus	11,934	15,959
Santa Clara	10,775	19,028
Santiago de Cuba	11,549	16,506
Trinidad	5,756	10,135

Source: Cuba, Comisión de Estadística, *Cuadro estadístico de la siempre fiel isla de Cuba, correspondiente al año de 1846* (Havana, 1847); Cuba, Centro de Estadistica, *Noticias estadísticas de la isla de Cuba, en 1862* (Havana, 1864).

and peasants across the island. The total number of *fincas* on the island increased from 35,116 in 1827, to 49,368 in 1846 and 50,648 in 1862.

Similar changes were occurring in the cities. The increase of white workers augmented the ranks of the urban wage labor force, arguably one of the fastest growing sectors in Cuban society. While it is difficult to ascertain the degree to which white wage labor was displacing slave labor, if at all, it is clear that white workers were extending their control over urban jobs at the expense of free people of color. In Havana, the increase of white wage labor in the trades was striking, as can be seen in Table 16.

TABLE 15. Labor Forms (1841–77)

| | 1841 | | 1861 | | 1877 | |
| | Number Employed | Percent | Number Employed | Percent | Number Employed | Percent |
Class of Labor						
Free	105,000	22.2	316,000	48.5	511,000	71.5
Contract	—	—	35,000	5.4	44,000	6.1
Slave	369,000	77.8	301,000	46.1	160,000	22.4

Source: Victor S. Clark, "Labor Conditions in Cuba," *Bulletin of the Department of Labor,* no. 41 (July 1902), 669.

Some of the most notable workers' gains were made in the Havana cigar industry. The suppression of the tobacco monopoly in 1817 had an enormously salutary effect on all sectors of tobacco. The number of *vegas* increased from 5,534 in 1827 to 9,102 in 1846. The number of cigar factories in Havana increased from 357 factories employing a total of 3,558 workers in 1846 to 490 factories with 13,071 employees in 1862. In this sector, the proportion of white labor remained constant at 70 percent. While the number of white cigarworkers increased from 2,566 to 9,352, the ranks of colored workers expanded from 1,141 to 3,719.

During the early 1860s, however, the combined effects of North Amer-

TABLE 16. Selected Occupations—Havana (1846, 1862)

| | 1846 | | 1862 | |
Occupation	White	Colored	White	Colored
Bakers	104	77	141	79
Butchers	42	83	157	40
Carpenters	822	770	1,260	744
Carters	5	52	303	287
Day laborers	705	1,141	1,714	1,374
Leather workers	64	153	190	148
Shoemakers	438	481	746	538
Tailors	353	770	548	612

Source: Cuba, Comisión de Estadística, *Cuadro estadístico de la siempre fiel isla de Cuba, correspondiente al año de 1846* (Havana, 1847); Jacobo de la Pezuela, *Diccionario geográfico, estadístico, histórico de la isla de Cuba* (4 vols., Madrid, 1863–66).

ican protectionism and the subsequent flight of cigar manufacturers to Key West began to take their toll in Havana. Unemployment increased and wages declined. Workers responded by organizing. Cigarworker unions were mainly in the form of mutual aid societies, organized along national and racial lines, providing members accident, sickness, and death benefits. In 1865, cigarworkers established the Workers Mutual Aid Society of Havana, the Brotherhood of Santiago de las Vegas, and the Workers Society of San Antonio de los Baños. In the same year, the first proletarian newspaper in Cuba, *La Aurora,* commenced publication. Labor press expanded rapidly thereafter, including the founding of *La Razón, El Boletín Tipográfico,* and *El Obrero.*

Through the 1860s, the number of mutual aid societies increased, with the founding of new organizations in Bejucal and Puerto Príncipe. So did labor militancy. In 1866, the first trade union, the Asociación de Tabaqueros de La Habana, was founded. That same year, the cigarworkers organized a strike against the Cabañas y Carvajal factory in Havana. Official response was swift. Strikers were arrested and strike leaders deported. The government seized the occasion of the Cabañas y Carvajal strike to move against the expanding labor movement. The cigar factory reader *(lector),* who read out loud to workers from the proletarian press, was abolished. *La Aurora* was censored, and in 1868 suspended altogether.

These were not isolated policies of repression—they announced the onset of reaction. The O'Donnell ministry in Spain had fallen, conservatives were again in the ascendancy, committed to dismantling liberal programs and revoking liberal policies. Parliament was suspended, liberals were arrested, and the opposition press closed. At about this time, the Junta de Información was arriving in Madrid to present Cuban demands for colonial concessions.

Timing again was crucial, but on this occasion it was all wrong. These were not good times to be liberal, nor to be seeking reform of things traditional. Spanish conservatives were not only indisposed to consider new concessions, they were intent on canceling old ones.

The failure of the Junta de Información to obtain even minimum concessions from Spain plunged Cuban reformism into disarray. It never recovered. Reform had stalled. *El Siglo* suspended publication, followed soon thereafter by the dissolution of the Reformist party.

Cubans were prepared for some resistance to reform, but not for what followed. A wave of reaction swept across the island. Repression increased. The authority of military tribunals was augmented. The opposition press was silenced, critics were exiled, political meetings were banned. Spain chose this moment to raise colonial taxes 6 percent on net income of real and industrial property. New taxes were levied on net profits from the trades, the professions, and commerce. In March 1867, Spain imposed a new series of protectionist duties on foreign products, four times the amount charged for Spanish goods—a particularly severe burden on a population so dependent on foreign imports. But there was more, for the United States responded in kind and raised tariffs on Cuban products by 10 percent. In addition to everything else, Cuban producers now faced the prospects of diminishing foreign markets.

A new round of tax increases would have been ill-conceived at any time. On this occasion it was also ill-timed. New taxes coincided with economic dislocation. The island had hardly recovered from the 1857 crisis when it was again beset by falling prices. The economy plunged into a deep recession. Sugar prices were in rapid decline, and by 1866 had fallen to their lowest point in almost fifteen years. Sugar production was also in decline, falling from 620,000 tons in 1865 to 597,000 tons in 1867. In December 1866, the principal banks on the island suspended payments, causing a momentary halt of sugar transactions, adding further to the general climate of uncertainty.

Discontent was on the rise everywhere, but it was especially high among creole elites in the east—cattle ranchers, sugar planters, and coffee growers who shared with many of their counterparts in the west similar kinds of political complaints toward Spain, but who also had special grievances of their own. Eastern producers had not participated in the prosperity of the previous decades. They had access to fewer capital resources, and what credit they were able to obtain frequently carried usurious interest rates, as much as two and three times higher than those charged in the west. In many ways they were casualties of western sugar successes, reduced to marginal producers at the margins of the sugar system. They were distant from markets, deeper in debt, with fewer slaves and lower production. Cattle ranchers were chafing under Spanish tax policies. As much as 25 percent of all profits on each head of cattle was lost to one type of tax or another. Eastern sugar planters were struggling to stay solvent, and failing. The decline of coffee production in Oriente had created a disgruntled class of landed gentry, most of whose members tended to blame sugar producers and Spanish tariff policies for many of their misfortunes. Coffee growers were in a state of advanced crisis and moving inexorably toward final ruin. Eastern planters were victims first of failure and then of foreclosure. That they attributed their difficulties to *peninsular* policymakers made their loss of property to *peninsular* moneylenders all the more intolerable. For planters perched on the brink of economic disaster, the imposition of new colonial taxes was unreasonable and unacceptable.

Reactionary policies, retrogressive taxes, and recession, all at once, served to give dramatic form to those things that the Cubans found most objectionable about Spanish rule. The eastern creoles were especially irked by these developments. The contradictions of the colonial system had finally overtaken the weakest sector of the creole elite, with devastating consequences. The crisis of the *oriental* property owners shattered the creole consensus and drove a wedge between the two sectors of the insular partriciate. Already politically marginal, in varying degrees of economic decline, not as burdened by the weight of slavery, they had less to fear from disorder, more to gain from change. The economic problem was seen as an aspect of the political problem: if the eastern zones were poor, backward, and miserable, it was because of malfeasance and misgovernment by Spain. The only solution was a political one.

Within two years, ranking representatives of the eastern creole bourgeoisie, cattle barons from Camagüey, and sugar planters from Oriente— Carlos Manuel de Céspedes, Salvador Cisneros Betancourt, Francisco Vicente Aguilera, Bartolomé Masó, Pedro Figueredo, and Ignacio Agramonte—were deep in conspiracy against Spain. Rebellion was planned in Masonic lodges in Puerto Príncipe, Santiago de Cuba, Bayamo, Holguín, Las Tunas, and Manzanillo, and contacts made with small farmers, the creole middle class, and free people of color.

On October 10, 1868, the "Grito de Yara" proclaimed Cuban independence and the establishment of a provisional republic. The rebellion expanded quickly across Oriente, and spread westward into neighboring Camagüey, and ultimately if only briefly advanced as far as the eastern zones of Las Villas province. By the early 1870s, the separatist uprising had attracted an estimated 40,000 supporters, from all classes, white and black, free and slave, from everywhere on the island and elsewhere in the Caribbean.

That creoles changed the means of opposition from the political to the military did not signify a fundamental change in the reformist character of Cuban ends. The separatist program-manifesto gave a new form and renewed vigor to what had previously served as the central reformist ten-

ets. Separatist leaders denounced discriminatory taxation, promised free
trade and representative government, and called for universal manhood
suffrage. They defended slavery and incorporated into the separatist program the slaveowners' version of abolition. The manifesto proclaimed
support for "gradual and indemnified abolition of slavery," but insisted
upon delaying implementation of abolition until the expulsion of Spain.
Some planters had emancipated their slaves immediately upon the outbreak of the war, but not really, for they were freed from economic labor
only to be impressed into military roles as recruits in the insurgent army
to fight for their former owners. Eastern slaveowners were quick to proclaim their respect for slave property elsewhere in Cuba, justifying the
emancipation of their slaves more as a result of the exigency of war than
as an objective of war. They refused to attack slavery and announced
early that slaves owned by planters sympathetic with the rebellion would
not be admitted into insurgent ranks without consent of their owners.

The Ten Years' War was reformism by another means, something the
eastern planters wanted to convey to their counterparts in the west. Eastern planters understood that rebellion would create alarm and apprehension among creole elites across the island, whose support they believed
essential to the triumph of the Cuban arms. The separatist program hence
sought to allay the fears of western elites and provide assurances that this
was, in the end, a movement dedicated to vindicating the reformist objectives and the defense of property. Insurgent leaders were hopeful of
obtaining material and financial support from their wealthy counterparts,
and hence were reluctant to enact measures capable of antagonizing sugar
planters in the west. Any prospect of obtaining the support of western
planters required respect for their estates and their slaves. In 1869, Carlos
Manuel de Céspedes proclaimed the death penalty for any attack against
sugar estates and slave property.

The effort to win planter support in the west enjoyed limited success.
Some planters, to be sure, especially those previously most active in reformist politics, announced their support of the rebellion. The majority
did not. They feared that separatist leaders lacked the ability to control
the social forces released by the war. No amount of reformist rhetoric
could allay the planters' fear of revolution. The specter of race war continued to haunt the west, as planters feared that a separatist revolt would
expand into a slave rebellion. Nor were planters who supported gradual
indemnified emancipation convinced that a new and independent Cuban

government would have the will or the wherewithal to implement the desired abolition decree.

A strategy designed to seek consensus among creole elites created instead conflict within separatist ranks. The decision to undertake at the end of the war the abolition of slavery gradually, with indemnification, was neither unanimous nor popular. It opened deep ideological cleavages within the separatist movement and shattered its fragile cohesion. Separatist leaders in Camagüey demurred and demanded immediate abolition. Indeed, *camagüeyanos* consistently defied directives from the provisional government and emancipated slaves at every opportunity.

But even the terms of emancipation were far from simple. Not all slaves emancipated by insurgent operations obtained either freedom or equality. Many liberated slaves *(libertos)* were subsequently obliged to serve in the separatist army in menial support roles. Insurgent leaders distinguished between creole slaves and African-born ones, relegating the latter to field chores that differed only in degree from conditions of prior servitude.

The debate over slavery within separatist ranks produced more than a political schism within the leadership. It also opened a social chasm within the insurgent polity. More and more, as the war progressed, the social distinction between leaders and followers became deeper and deeper: between the provisional government under patrician creoles and the army command under men of modest social origins, between white civilians and colored soldiers. As the social base of the provisional government narrowed, the social constituency of the army expanded. The ranks of the army were filling with peasants, workers, poor whites and blacks, former slaves—a vast social amalgam for whom rebellion in pursuit of reform was becoming increasingly unacceptable. Antonio Maceo was one of the many thousands of free men of color to join the rebellion at the outset for whom the emancipation of slaves was no less important than the liberation of the island.

The debate involved more than a dispute over the social function of Cuban arms. It affected too the military conduct of the war. For ten years Cubans waged war, mostly in desultory fashion, mostly in the east, mostly without effect. A war inaugurated with national objectives failed to expand much beyond provincial boundaries. This was in part due to the success of Spanish military operations. The government understood the importance of confining the conflict to the east, away from the rich sugar zones of the west. The Spanish army increased by tens of thousands, reaching almost 100,000 in the mid-1870s. Spain constructed a fortified ditch *(trocha)* across Camagüey, extending twenty-five miles across one of the narrower widths of the island between Júcaro and Morón.

The *trocha* certainly did not make it any easier for insurgent forces to cross into the west, but neither did it pose an insurmountable obstacle. What stood between the armies of the east and the sugar fields of the west was not a fortified ditch but an ideological divide. The expansion of insurgent operations into the west, Cubans sensed correctly, promised to transform inalterably the character of the war. To cross the *trocha* was to cross the threshold between reform and revolution, between the political and the social, and thereby set the stage for a war of the incendiary torch: a campaign of destruction of property and disruption of production— which was precisely what the rebel army command wanted. For military leaders the invasion of the west was linked directly to the abolition of slavery, and both were vital for Cuban success. Army chief Máximo Gómez repeatedly advocated the expansion of the war into the west to disrupt production and destroy slavery. He believed that the incorporation of slaves in the rebellion was both militarily necessary and morally correct. The presence of insurgent armies in the west, proclaiming an end to slavery, would strike a blow against colonialism at its most vital and most vulnerable point: the economy. The incorporation of slaves into the separatist armies also promised to add numbers to insurgent columns while disruption of sugar production denied revenues to loyalist coffers. "While liberty is not given to the thousands of slaves who are groaning today in the jurisdiction of Occidente, the most populated and richest of the island," Máximo Gómez insisted, "while exportation by the enemy of the production of the great sugar plantations established there is not impeded, . . . the revolution is destined to last even much longer. Cuban resources will be drained, and lakes of blood will run unfruitfully in the fields of the island."

The debate between the patrician civilians and the populist soldiers continued through the war. Civilian leaders refused to sanction military operations in the west. No less than their western counterparts, they feared class warfare and racial strife. But they had other reasons to insist upon a limited war. In large measure, the war was being waged with attention to North American sensibilities. The expansion of the war threatened the larger diplomatic objectives of the rebellion. Once again annexationism surfaced in reformist ranks. For many the independence of Cuba from

Spain was part of a larger process by which the island would ultimately join the North American union. The annexationist character of the rebellion was fixed early. Only weeks after the "Grito de Yara," Carlos Manuel de Céspedes, Pedro Figueredo, and Bartolomé Masó, among others, petitioned Secretary of State William Seward to consider Cuban admission to the union. A year later the constituent assembly of Guáimaro explicitly proclaimed annexation as the ultimate purpose of Cuban arms. Soon thereafter, the representative assembly of the provisional republic petitioned President Ulysses Grant for recognition of belligerency as prelude to admission into the union.

For almost ten years Cubans waged limited war for limited goals, and failed on both counts. They wanted the support of western planters, and thus refused to abolish slavery and disrupt production. They wanted the support of the United States, and thus refused to destroy property and risk racial war. The strategies calculated to win the political support of the planter class and the diplomatic support of the United States failed, with calamitous consequences for the Cuban cause. The war thus remained stalled in the eastern provinces, there falling prey to internal strife, supply shortages, and declining morale. A rebellion of such long duration, patently meager in insurgent successes, turned on itself with disastrous results. After ten years of war, the final blows to the separatist effort were dealt by desertions, dissension, and depletion of morale. In 1877, Spanish General Arsenio Martínez Campos arrived in Cuba with new reinforcements and the promise of new reforms. Negotiations began in early 1878 and concluded with the Pact of Zanjón. Spain pledged itself to a wide range of administrative and political reforms. A general amnesty pardoned all insurgent Cubans and guaranteed unconditional freedom to all African slaves and Asian indentured workers registered in the insurgent army at the time of the peace settlement.

Not all separatist chieftains concurred with either the decision to make peace or the terms of the peace. Meager concessions for such mighty efforts, some Cubans protested bitterly. Indeed, the Pact of Zanjón generated as much dissension among Cubans in arms as did any other single issue in the Ten Years' War. The more intransigent separatists rejected outright any peace settlement that sanctioned the continued presence of Spanish authority in Cuba. For other *insurrecto* chieftains, a formal peace that confined emancipation to only those slaves who had enrolled in the separatist armies fell far short of satisfying a central and long-standing demand for the abolition of slavery altogether.

The military leadership denounced the Zanjón settlement. General Antonio Maceo assembled the 1500 officers and men under his command to repudiate the peace protocol. The "Protest of Baraguá," as Maceo's denunciation became known, set the stage for a renewal of the conflict. In March 1878, a new provisional government, committed to continued armed struggle, was organized around the irreconcilable elements of the separatist movement. And for ten weeks more the Ten Years' War continued.

This renewed commitment to arms after Zanjón, Cubans sensed, was more symbolic than substantive: a demarcation to set the stage for a new war, some other time. By May, weakened by deaths and desertions, and reduced wholly to scattered operations in the remote eastern interior, the armed protesters of Baraguá, too, grudgingly made their peace with Spain and left Cuba.

VIII

Much had changed in the colony during the Ten Years' War—some of it apparent, some not. The conflict announced the passing of an age. Colonialism had been shaken at its foundations, and survived—after a fashion. It was a colonial society that was measurably different ten years after the "Grito de Yara." For the million and a half inhabitants of the island, life soon returned to normal, but it would never be the same.

The war released forces that continued to alter the character of Cuban society long after the insurgent armies had abandoned the field. Slavery was doomed. Abolition was an idea whose time had arrived. The Cuban rebellion had raised the promise of emancipation after the war. In fact, the process had begun during the conflict. Vast numbers of slaves had used the conditions of war to advantage. Some obtained their freedom by fighting for the insurgent cause, some became free by fighting for Spain. Others fled into the interior wilderness, not to fight for anyone but just to farm for themselves. The war itself had destroyed the plantation economy in many regions, ending further need for slave labor. The Cuban commitment to postwar abolition, moreover, had from the beginning placed Spain on the defensive and obliged colonial authorities to deal with the question of abolition, if only as propaganda to counter separatist projects. The Spanish response was contained in the Moret Law of 1870. More symbolic than substantive, the Moret Law freed few economically productive slaves, concentrating instead on the conditional freedom to all

children of slaves born after its promulgation. Free-born blacks were subject to the tutelage *(patronato)* of their former slaveowners, for whom
they worked without wages until the age of eighteen. The Moret Law,
moreover, like its Cuban counterpart, committed Spain to consider fuller
measures of emancipation upon the end of the conflict.

Thus, whatever else divided Cuban separatists and Spanish loyalists,
they had both agreed to pursue the question of abolition after the war.
And, indeed, by 1878, the timing was right. The slave population was in
decline, diminishing from 363,300 in 1869 to 227,900 in 1878. The Moret
Law had contributed to the reduction of the number of slaves. So had the
war and slave mortality. Many planters had succumbed to the economic
crisis between 1857 and 1867. The destruction of property and the ruin
of many planters during the war, moreover, reduced further the opposition to emancipation. The demise of sugar mills was dramatic. Of the 41
mills operating around Sancti Spíritus in 1861, only three survived the
war. The 49 mills in Trinidad were reduced to sixteen. In Santa Clara,
only 39 of 86 survived. The Cienfuegos mills were reduced from 107 to
77. In Güines, almost two-thirds of the 87 mills operating before the war
had disappeared. In the east, where most of the war was fought most of
the time, the losses were particularly extensive. Separatists destroyed the
property of loyalists, Spaniards destroyed the property of separatists, and
together they destroyed most of the property. The slave economy never
recovered. Almost 500 coffee farms disappeared, and coffee production
almost ceased. Sugar fared no better. In some districts, the collapse of
sugar production was all but complete. None of the 24 mills in Bayamo
and 18 mills in Manzanillo survived the war. The 64 mills of Holguin
were reduced to four. Of the 100 *ingenios* operating in Santiago de Cuba,
only 39 resumed operations after Zanjón. In Puerto Príncipe one out of
100 survived the war. Coffee growing and sugar production had all but
collapsed in the east, making slavery virtually irrelevant to the local
economy. The defense of slavery was now confined almost entirely to
the west. But here, too, planters spoke with conflicting voices. Abolition
found support among the old reformists in Cuba, who were in turn supported by old liberals in Spain.

In 1879, a liberal government headed by Arsenio Martínez Campos,
the Spanish negotiator at Zanjón, assumed power in Spain, and turned to
the task of implementing the Moret Law. One year later, Spain enacted
a law of abolition. Like the Moret Law, the abolition decree established
the *patronato* as a means of gradual adjustment and adaptation, in this

instance a period of eight years as transition to final emancipation. Former slaves *(patroncinados)* were transformed into "apprentices" and obliged to work under their former owners for monthly wages. The *patronato* represented a compromise between abolitionists and slaveholders, more in the form of a concession to the latter who did not receive indemnity.

Pressure to abolish slavery did not originate exclusively from government officials in the metropolis or government officials in the colony. Pressure emanated too from among slaves and the *patroncinados*. The 1880 law provided a legal framework for gradual abolition, an outline of reciprocal responsibilities and obligations between former masters and former slaves. *Patroncinados* were not slow to defend their own interests. They instituted litigation over a multitude of grievances: property rights, wage scales, child labor, treatment at the hands of employers, and, in the end, the very terms of their freedom. Each *patroncinado* who obtained full freedom was free also to pursue the freedom of family members. In this manner, parents secured the freedom of young children, adult children obtained the release of elderly parents, and spouses helped to free each other. Nor were all the initiatives legal. Many slaves simply deserted, and the threat of continued mass desertion forced planters to negotiate formally the terms of labor relations with their slaves. At least in one instance, in 1879, slaves in Santiago de Cuba, organized strikes as a way to dramatize their demand for freedom.

Thus, even as Cuba moved toward scheduled legal abolition in 1888, the transition years of the decade witnessed slaves themselves instrumental in accelerating the pace and enlarging the scope of final and complete emancipation. In 1886, two years before the scheduled expiration of the *patronato,* a royal decree brought slavery to an end. At the time of this proclamation, fewer than 30,000 slaves remained in a condition of compulsory labor.

6

Between Wars

The Pact of Zanjón marked more than the end of the war—it announced the passing of an age. Property relations and production modes were in transition. Social formations were in flux. Commercial ties and political loyalties were changing. Even the way things changed was different.

The forces released by the Ten Years' War transformed the colonial political economy in ways no one could have anticipated. Planters who operated before the war on marginal profits, who lacked either the finances or the foresight to modernize their mills, were among the earliest casualties of the separatist conflict. Planters fortunate enough to survive the war succumbed to peace. Capital was scarce and credit dear. Prevailing rates of interest, often as high as 30 percent, foreclosed any possibility that local credit transactions would contribute significantly to the economic recovery of post-Zanjón Cuba.

The war and the attending decline of local sugar production set the stage for the next series of misfortunes to descend upon Cuban producers. The disruption of Cuban sugar led to a decline of local production and an increase in international output. The effects were immediate: sugar production expanded on a world-wide basis. Cuban planters emerged from war to face a new adversity, this in the form of expanded competition from new producers and expanded production from old competitors. Not since the end of the eighteenth century, when revolution in St. Domingue ended French supremacy over sugar production, did rival producers have as great an opportunity to extend their share of the world market. They did not hesitate. In the United States, new varieties of cane were introduced in the South, while beet-sugar production expanded in the West and Southwest. In 1876 cane sugar from Hawaii entered the United States duty free. Cane sugar production also expanded in Latin America, most notably in Argentina, Peru, Mexico, and the Dominican Republic. But it was in Europe that sugar production recorded its most significant advances, principally in the form of beet sugar. Beet production increased

TABLE 17.   Cuban and World Production (1868–88)

Year	Cane	Beet	Cuba	Cuban Percentage of Total
1868	1,760,880	760,025	720,250	28.6
1875	1,807,041	1,377,336	750,062	23.6
1880	1,880,675	1,857,210	618,654	16.6
1885	2,296,167	2,172,200	628,990	14.1
1888	2,359,162	3,555,900	662,758	11.2

Source: Manuel Moreno Fraginals, *El ingenio: complejo económico social cubano del azúcar* (3 vols., Havana, 1978), III, 36–37.

dramatically, and by the mid-1880s, France, Austria, and Germany had become the principal sources of sugar for the world market. Beet sugar, accounting in 1850s, for only 14 percent of the total world production of sugar, had by the 1880s come to represent more than half of the international supply. Cuba's share of the world market declined from nearly 30 percent during the late 1860s to 11 percent by the late 1880s. Indeed, by 1880 beet sugar had displaced Cuban cane sugar from the European markets, leaving the United States as the only market with the capacity to absorb Cuban production. (See Table 17.)

Even as planters prepared to resume production after Zanjón, they discovered that they faced more than new sources of competition and loss of old markets. They confronted, too, and at once, an increase in local taxes and a precipitous decline in the value of their principal product. A rise in public spending during the 1870s to finance the cost of the war and an increase in the circulation of paper money in the 1880s brought on the first in a series of devastating inflationary spirals. After Zanjón, Madrid transferred the war debt directly to producers and consumers in Cuba—a new wave of trade duties, tariff increases, sales taxes, and property taxes. At about the same time, the value of sugar collapsed. In 1884, the price of sugar plummeted, dropping from eleven cents a pound to an all-time low of eight. The decline of sugar prices and the imposition of a new series of crushing taxes occurred just as planters were adjusting to the transition from slave labor to wage labor. All at once, the Cuban planter class encountered declining prices, increased taxes, mounting debts, and shrinking markets. Sugar planters everywhere in Cuba were in crisis. "Out of the twelve or thirteen hundred planters on the island," the United

States consul in Havana reported early in 1884, "not a dozen are said to be solvent."

Many planters resumed postwar production perched on the brink of disaster, heavily in debt, and lacking the resources to renovate their mills. In the past Cubans had worried about producing large harvests as a hedge against disaster. During the 1880s, they produced good crops, but their markets had dwindled and prices had declined, and disaster struck. The combination of rising taxes, increased operating costs, falling prices, and deepening indebtedness forced many planters into bankruptcy. Property changed hands at accelerating speed as planters struggled desperately to stave off insolvency.

Crisis in sugar announced calamity for Cuba. By the mid-1880s, all of Cuba was in the throes of depression. Business houses closed and banks collapsed. Seven of the island's largest trading companies failed. Credit dear after Zanjón was almost nonexistent a decade later. In October 1883 the Bank of Santa Catalina closed. In March 1884, the Caja de Ahorros, the most important savings institution in Havana, suspended payments, ostensibly in response to the suicide of the bank's president. Two weeks later the Caja de Ahorros went into liquidation. In the same month, panic runs on the Banco Industrial and the Banco de Comercio forced both institutions to close. Two months later, the Banco Industrial went into liquidation. The Bank of Santa Catalina was linked to agricultural interests, and its failure affected principally sugar planters. The Caja de Ahorros served a much broader clientele, including workers, professionals, merchants, civil servants, and shopowners; and when it failed, small depositors of all kinds faced ruin. In the first three months of 1884, business failures totalled over $7 million.

Similar conditions prevailed in the provinces. In March 1884 the prestigious house of Rodríguez in Sagua la Grande and its correspondents in Havana, Miyares and Company, failed. In Cienfuegos, the value of rural and urban property declined by half. The once opulent city of Trinidad was in an advanced state of decay and destitution. Business houses closed and retail shops were abandoned. The vital rail link to Casilda, the port of Trinidad, ceased operation due to the disrepair of the track. In Santiago de Cuba commercial houses closed in rapid succession. Economic collapse was almost total in Matanzas. The surplus of unsold sugar mounted as prices dropped and markets declined. In 1885, the prevailing price of sugar did not suffice even to defray the cost of local production. Hundreds of estates faced imminent ruin. "Firms are going into bankruptcy every day," the U.S. vice consul in Matanzas reported in July 1884; "planters are discharging their laborers and threaten—to save themselves further disaster—to abandon their estates; gold fluctuates two and three and sometimes ten points a day; all credits are denied even to the most substantial and men are wondering how and where they will obtain the means to live; and in many cases relatives are doubling up apartment style to save expenses."

These conditions affected colonial administration as well. Government revenues diminished and public services declined. In one year alone, between 1883 and 1884, customs revenues fell by almost $500,000—from $1,433,741 to $945,386. Sanitation services were periodically suspended. Public works programs stopped. The city of Havana faced a staggering utility bill of $400,000, and a threat from an impatient Spanish-American Light and Power Company in New York to suspend gas service for city street lights unless the debt was speedily and satisfactorily settled.

But more than public services were threatened. Public administration itself was in crisis. Across the island the salaries of thousands of public officials fell hopelessly in arrears, with little prospect of relief in sight. In Havana, the capital press reported the plight of public officals obliged to pawn their furniture in a desperate effort to stave off destitution.

These were desperate times in Cuba; announcing a prelude to transformation. Everywhere in Cuba the cost of living increased, even as wages and salaries decreased. The price of food rose. Rents in Havana and its immediate suburbs increased, and with them evictions.

Conditions in post-Zanjón Cuba were especially difficult for Cuban workers. Where employment existed, it became increasingly common to pay workers in depreciated scrip. They were the lucky ones. In fact, unemployment in the cities increased as factories, shops, and business houses closed in rapid succession. In Havana alone, some 20,000 workers were without jobs. In 1885, the once thriving Havana naval yard closed, forcing hundreds of workers out of jobs. Cigar exports declined in the late 1880s and early 1890s, causing havoc in one of the major labor intensive sectors of the Cuban economy. The decline was striking, as Table 18 indicates. The repercussions were immediate, and far-reaching. Cigar production had provided employment for over 100,000 people in all phases of agriculture and manufacturing, the vast majority of whom resided in the two western provinces of Pinar del Río and Havana. The factories alone employed some 50,000 workers. As the amount of cigar exports decreased, the number of cigar factory closings increased. By the

TABLE 18.   Cigar Exports (1889–91)

Year	Total Cigar Exports	Cigar Exports to the United States
1889	250,467,000	101,698,560
1890	211,823,000	95,105,760
1891	196,644,000	52,115,600

Source: *Diario de la Marina,* Aug. 16, 1892.

early 1890s some 35,000 cigarmakers were totally without work, with the balance of workers reduced to part-time employment. Thousands of workers were forced to emigrate in search of employment in the expanding cigar centers in Key West, Tampa, Ocala, and Jacksonville.

These were years, too, of deepening distress through much of the countryside. Peasant families displaced by war became destitute during peace. The conflict had created a new population of urban indigents. Not all farmers recovered their land after the war. Property titles were lost, records destroyed. Land claims became confused and were contested. Even in those instances where ownership was clear, the destruction of crops and equipment was so often complete and the cost of beginning anew so great that all but the most determined were deterred from returning to the land. Dislodged from their homes and dispossessed of their property, the displaced families of war were deprived of their livelihood. Pauperization was immediate and widespread. An urban underclass expanded alongside the urban working class during these years, made up principally of impoverished rural migrants, in which women worked in uncertain domestic labor and prostitution and men found themselves in the status of beggars, vagrants, and criminals. By the late 1880s, unemployment reached desperate proportions. Thousands of rural workers migrated to the already overcrowded cities in search of jobs, only to join the swollen ranks of the urban unemployed. Against this generally bleak economic landscape, the abolition of slavery was completed. Tens of thousands of former slaves joined Cuban society as free wage labor at a time of rising unemployment and decreasing wages.

The disarticulation of the Cuban social structures was extensive. Hard times arrived in Cuba at the precise moment the post-Zanjón generation of creoles sought a place for themselves in the colonial economy. But there was little work. The collapse of sugar receipts reverberated across

TABLE 19. Value of Cuban Property

	Agricultural and Urban Property	Industry, Commerce, and the Professions
1862	$55,072,545	$77,384,649
1877	39,656,717	17,388,125
1882	36,386,685	12,075,467

Source: *Boletín Comercial*, April 10, 1890.

the island with devastating results. Cuba was in depression, and the economy floundered somewhere between dislocation and disintegration. Contemporary observers, concerned about the economic crisis that engulfed them, drew up estimates that showed the island to have lost two-thirds of the value of its total wealth between 1862 and 1882. (See Table 19.)

The contraction of commerce, the collapse of banks, and the closing of factories were only the most visible expressions of desperate conditions. Jobs were few and competition fierce, and unemployment was a condition without immediate prospect of remedy. The Cuban economy could not absorb the growing ranks of the creole middle class. "It is not the labourer that is to be pitied," the British consul general in Havana observed in 1889, "but the middle-class creoles, who, unfit for rough manual labor, and unskilled in handicrafts, can find no employment on a par with their physical or intellectual capacity." Countless numbers of Cuban professionals, including attorneys, physicians, engineers, educators, and writers, were forced to emigrate, a necessity that engendered in many a mixture of anguish and anger, inevitably finding expression in resentment against a colonial system that failed to accommodate the growing needs of Cubans. They were white and, by Cuban standards, privileged, and yet could not find a place for themselves in their own society. A generation of expatriate creoles became socially disenfranchised, economically displaced—and politically disgruntled.

Nor could the state bureaucracy relieve unemployment pressures. These were difficult times in Spain, too, and of political necessity, public administration in Cuba served as a source of relief for economic distress in the metropolis. These were also years of remarkable population growth in Spain, a period in which the number of Spaniards doubled, rising from 9.3 million in 1768 to 18.6 million by 1900. Spaniards arrived in Cuba in vast numbers, many still in search of renewal in the New World. Cuba in the late nineteenth century remained very much what it was in the early sixteenth century: a place for the destitute and dispossessed of Spain to start over. Public office and political appointments in Cuba were themselves little more than the colonial extensions of the patronage system in Spain. The rise of one government ministry in Spain announced the arrival of countless thousands of new office seekers and the departure of countless thousands of others, a vast turnover of positions from which Cubans were largely excluded. Even the appointments as vendors of lottery tickets were emoluments reserved for retired Spanish military pensioners.

But *peninsulares* monopolized more than public positions. They also dominated private property. Spaniards controlled trade and commerce, they presided over banking and finance, as well as industry and manufacturing. They owned the factories and many of the farms, managed the plants and the plantations, were retail shopkeepers and wholesale merchants, as well as moneylenders and land brokers. Spaniards were preponderant in the professions and trades, as artisans and apprentices, in the offices as clerks, and in the fields as day laborers. They dominated the economy, and most of all they controlled the jobs. And whether by formal contract or by informal consensus, Spaniards preferred to hire Spaniards, a private practice that coincided with public policy. Spain actively encouraged immigration to Cuba as a comparatively convenient and cost-effective method through which to reduce the size of a socially unstable population at home and increase the number of the loyalist community in a politically unreliable population in Cuba.

Shipload after shipload arrived. In the decades after Zanjón, a total of some 250,000 Spaniards emigrated to Cuba. It was not only that more Spaniards arrived in Cuba—these were also different Spaniards. The new immigrants were from the north, mostly from Galicia and Asturias, many destitute, and often desperate, but strong-willed, self-possessed, and, most of all, determined to make it. They worked hard and long, often for little and always for less. It was a labor market in which Cubans could not compete, and many did not. *Peninsular* employers extended an avuncular patronage to their countrymen—giving rise among Cubans to the derisive sobriquet of *sobrinismo,* the practice, quite literally, of uncles in Cuba employing nephews from Spain.

Times in post-Zanjón Cuba were difficult, for everyone, certainly, but for Cubans especially. There seemed to be no place for Cubans in Cuba. For the peasantry, as well as members of the professions and the proletariat, Spanish administration revealed itself incapable of discharging the central clause of the colonial social contract: the opportunity for livelihood. Cubans seemed in danger of becoming a superfluous population, unemployable and expendable, outsiders and outcasts in the society they claimed as their own. They faced both exclusion and expulsion, and ultimately expatriation. And, indeed, emigration was one dramatic expression of the crisis in colonial Cuba in the late nineteenth century. During the last third of the nineteenth century, some 100,000 Cubans of all occupations and professions, of all ages, of all classes and races, emigrated—to Europe, Latin America, and the United States.

II

No sector of Cuban society escaped the depression unaffected, and even property and privilege offered insufficient hedge against social and economic decline. Indeed, the disintegration of the Cuban social order began at the top. The war had taken a devastating toll on the eastern planter class, one from which it never recovered. The Ten Years' War witnessed the dismemberment of the creole bourgeoisie, especially that sector of the eastern planter class that had enrolled in the ill-starred separatist cause.

This was nothing less than the demise of one sector of the planter class. Planters suspected of separatist sympathies paid dearly for subversive sentiments. Where property was not destroyed, it was confiscated— a way to punish adversaries and reward allies. Through a series of punitive expropriation decrees, Spain confiscated creole property, much of which was subsequently auctioned at a fraction of its value to finance the war effort.

Sugar estates, tobacco *vegas,* coffee plantations, urban real estate, business and commercial properties, and slaves passed into the hands of *peninsulares* and their loyalist allies. In this way the eastern creole elites were despoiled of property valued at more than 16 million pesos. They failed to survive the combined effects of wartime destruction and Spanish expropriation. This was a sign of things to come, and announced the onset of collapse of the creole bourgeoisie. The Ten Years' War destroyed the planter class of the east and set the stage for the demise of the planter class of the west.

Planters who survived the crisis of the 1880s did so increasingly at the cost of traditional supremacy over production. The price of solvency was immediately displacement and ultimately dependency. Planters' efforts to recover their former primacy announced the reorganization of the production system and the restructuring of property relations. A new stage of capitalist organization was about to transform sugar production, and with it all of Cuba. It would be a recovery, too, from which planters in increasing numbers would be excluded.

Changes in organization and ownership proceeded apace during the late 1880s and early 1890s. Greater efficiency was needed to market sugar profitably under existing conditions of international competition and prevailing circumstances of world prices. Production strategies shifted largely from increasing the number of sugar mills to increasing the production capacities of existing *centrales*. New credit, fresh capital, and new ownership, originating principally in the United States, provided Cuban sugar with the resources necessary for recovery. Improved varieties of cane, innovations in manufacturing techniques, and technological and industrial advances became generally available by the 1880s and gave producers in Cuba the opportunity to respond aggressively to new world conditions.

These were fateful developments, signaling the end for many planters. The modernization of sugar production, necessary if Cuba was to remain competitive on the world market, was beyond the capital reserves and credit resources of local planters. They came out of the war in debt, impoverished, and in crisis. Conditions did not improve in peace. The cost to a mill owner of converting to new machinery alone was well over a quarter of a million dollars. Additional expenditures required the development of railway systems, the expansion of storage facilities, and the acquisition of additional land—all of which served to limit Cuban participation in the postwar reorganization.

The shift in production strategies led to sharper divisions between field and factory. Unable to meet the growing capital requirements necessary to participate in the revival of sugar production, planters in growing numbers abandoned the industrial end of production altogether and devoted themselves exclusively to agriculture.

Across the island the Cuban grip over production slipped, announcing the demise of the creole planter class. These were conditions that invited foreign capital, first by way of secured loans to planters in distress, and later in the form of direct ownership through foreclosures. Many planters survived principally as sugar farmers *(colonos),* but it was a survival that transformed the character of the creole bourgeoisie. Others did not survive at all. The displacement of the planter bourgeoisie in the area of

Cienfuegos was suggestive of the developments occurring everywhere in Cuba. In 1884 E. Atkins and Company, from Boston, foreclosed on the Juan Sarria family estate Soledad. Atkins subsequently acquired the Carlota plantation from the de la Torriente family. Events moved quickly thereafter, as Atkins secured the Caledonia estate from the heirs of Diego Julián Sánchez, the Guabairo property from Manuel Blanco, the Limones farm from the Vilá family, and the Brazo estate from the Torre family. Atkins interests purchased outright or secured long-term leases on many other estates. During these same years, the interests of Perkins and Walsh in New York acquired a controlling share of Constancia, at the time the largest sugar estate in the world. Frederick Freeman also acquired sugar properties around Trinidad and William Stewart purchased a mill near Cienfuegos. The Hormiguero estate, owned by the Ponvert family of Boston, expanded its holdings at the expense of the smaller properties of insolvent Cuban planters.

The position of the Cuban planters grew increasingly precarious, and their possession of the estates became increasingly tenuous, as foreign capital expanded control over property and production. The creole bourgeoisie survived by exchanging titles of property for ownership of stocks in United States corporations and relinquishing positions as landowners for places on corporate boards of directors. They were transformed into administrators and lived off salaries and not rents. By 1895, less than 20 percent of the owners of the mills came from the old plantation-owning families. Many planters would henceforth function as agents of North American capital, instruments of United States economic penetration of Cuba, and advocates of United States intervention in Cuba. Their well-being depended increasingly on the success of foreign capital in extending control over property and production—a pursuit that would engage the active collaboration of the newly displaced bourgeoisie.

These developments were themselves products and portents of shifting colonial relationships. In the space of one decade, the Cuban economy revived with United States capital, relied on United States imports, and reorganized around United States markets. By the late 1880s, some 94 percent of Cuban sugar exports found their way to the United States. The results were immediately anomalous, and ultimately fateful: the center of Cuban political authority was no longer the same as the source of economic security. The implications of those contradictions passed virtually unnoticed during years of peace and economic recovery.

III

The Ten Years' War also had the net effect of heightening planter demand for increased political participation. For the better part of a decade,
the island had been subjected to the ravages of two opposing armies,
neither of which inspired excessive confidence among creole elites. Not
that the planters were neutral—they were not. They viewed the separatist
cause with a mixture of dismay and dread. They opposed independence,
fearful that separation from Spain would lead to political instability and
social strife, and that both would result in economic ruin.

It was true, too, however, that the creole bourgeoisie derived less than
complete comfort from the victory of Spanish arms. Colonial administration, at least traditional colonial administration, had few defenders among
Cuban elites. They needed little reminder that it was the combined follies
and failures of Spanish policy that had plunged the island into the abyss
of civil strife in the first place. Until the Ten Years' War, Spain had
administered Cuba as an overseas colony, primarily through the *peninsular* office-holding elite, principally for the benefit of *peninsular* needs.
In Cuba there had been little significant, sustained political activity. Administration prevailed in the place of politics; attempts to resolve Cuban
questions came from above and abroad. Outside of an occasional and
short-lived armed protest, a general consensus had prevailed on both the
premises and propriety of this arrangement—until the Ten Years' War.

Between 1868 and 1878, Madrid had confronted in Cuba the longest
and most serious challenge to Spanish rule since the South American
wars for independence fifty years earlier. The Peace of Zanjón, to be
sure, ended the revolutionary challenge, but only after Madrid had agreed
to concede reforms and sanction colonial politics. The war had forced
Spain to renounce the principle of metropolitan absolutism; the Pact of
Zanjón provided the standard against which to measure the performance
of Spanish administration.

Certainly creole elites welcomed the end of the colonial insurrection in
1878. But they welcomed more the opportunity to step into the colonial
breach and assert leadership over the shattered polity. The moment was
right. The Pact of Zanjón served as a summons to the planter class and
its allies. Neither revolution nor reaction seemed capable of resolving
colonial grievances. The peace created conditions for a third and familiar
alternative—reform.

The creole bourgeoisie pursued political power methodically, as a means to promote their economic interests and protect their social status. Planters and their local allies recognized the necessity of participating in the formulation of tax policies, currency and fiscal plans, and commercial programs—all of which affected them vitally. They were historically resentful of Spanish monopolization of local administration and insular government. Spain had correctly suspected the subversive undercurrents of the creole clamor for public office. They desperately needed office to defend their interests, and for this they needed to control the government.

In this one and very important sense, the Cuban planter class had arrived at a point similar to the position of the creole petite bourgeoisie. Both demanded wider participation in local government. But more than participation, they demanded public positions and political power. The social reality of the two sectors of Cuban creoles determined the course of this pursuit. Planters in possession of the material base with which to mount a political challenge to Spanish exclusivism over local affairs chose collaboration with colonialism and reformist politics. Members of the creole petite bourgeoisie lacking the resources to compete with Spaniards chose opposition to colonialism and revolutionary politics.

Politics in Cuba after 1878 organized around the reform promises of Zanjón. Thus it was that the first political party to organize after Zanjón embodied the reformist principles long associated with the creole planter elites. Established in July 1878, the new Liberal party (Autonomist) proclaimed its commitment to actualizing the promises of Zanjón and offered advocates of reform sanctioned institutional structures within which to pursue the transformation of the colonial regime. Autonomists rejected outright the means and objectives of armed separatism. An appeal to arms was as unacceptable as independence was unthinkable. They advocated home rule, representation in the Spanish parliament, and free trade. They also endorsed the legitimacy of the colonial regime and the primacy of empire as the central and unchallenged tenets of colonial politics. For Autonomists, reforms were the best guarantee of empire, and empire was the best guarantee against revolution.

In its charter manifesto published in August 1878, the Autonomist party outlined the bases of its political, social, and economic programs. On the matter of political reform, the manifesto demanded immediate equal rights for Cubans under the Spanish constitution of 1876, the uniformity of *peninsular* laws for all the constituent components of Spain, and the separation of military and political authority in Cuba. On a long-term basis,

Autonomists advocated preserving the structure of empire, with Cuba in full possession of local institutions of self-government. On social issues, liberals supported the gradual abolition of African slavery with indemnification to the planters and the adoption of the *patronato*. The party urged an increase in the white population of the island through unrestricted family immigration and the abolition of all restrictions on white immigration to Cuba. In economic matters, Autonomists advocated far-ranging reform proposals, including the abolition of all duties on Cuban exports; tariff reforms; reduction of Spanish custom fees; and the negotiation of commercial treaties with foreign countries, principally the United States, on the basis of reciprocal tariff concessions.

The strength of the new party was in planters and their allies, Cubans anxious to steer a course between the uninspired colonial policies of the metropolis and the uncertainties associated with complete separation from Spain. These creole elites were drawn again to colonial politics as a result of separatist excesses and metropolitan abuses, in pursuit of colonial reform as a means to obviate colonial revolution. This Cuban aristocracy included many of the men who presided over Cuba's principal economic institutions such as the Círculo de Hacendados y Agricultores, Centro de Propietarios, Círculo de Abogados, and the Sociedad Económica de Amigos del País, Cubans who placed their considerable wealth and prestige at the service of post-Zanjón reformist politics.

Autonomism also attracted the conservative wing of the separatist polity, many of the creole property-holding elites who during the war had served in the provisional government. The bitter experience of the Ten Years' War persuaded many former separatists of the futility of further appeals to arms. Indeed, for these insurgent leaders the peace of 1878 signaled the bankruptcy of the armed strategy. Disillusioned separatists saw in autonomism the means to achieve peacefully—if admittedly only in modified form and on a gradual basis—the objectives that had eluded them during the Ten Years' War. For conservative separatists, principally those with origins in the creole elites, the failure of Cuban arms in 1878 offered no reasonable alternative to the pursuit of reform within the newly sanctioned arena of political competition. Many of the most prestigious leaders of the unsuccessful insurrection abandoned separatist ranks to embrace autonomism.

IV

The organization of the Autonomist party did not announce the emergence of a new colonial consensus. Nor did it signal the triumph of planter leadership. On the contrary, it served to deepen the divisions in the colony and open new political schisms. Reformism split separatist ranks, dividing the veterans of 1868 into two distinct groups. Autonomism served to fix institutionally the ill-defined division shattering the separatist consensus after Zanjón—between those veterans who, on one hand, heartened by the terms of the peace settlement, remained in Cuba to seek fulfillment of the separatist agenda within the autonomist program (legal), and those veterans who, on the other, unreconciled to the post-Zanjón order, chose expatriation to prepare for a renewal of the armed struggle (extralegal). It was in this process, too, that Cuban separatism lost its affiliation with and became permanently disassociated from the local elites, who after Zanjón found autonomism considerably more convivial to their interests.

The emergence of a liberal reformist party after Zanjón also shattered the loyalist consensus. For the better part of the Ten Years' War, Spanish sentiment in Cuba remained uncommonly united around steadfast opposition to the central tenets advanced by the separatists in arms. The inadmissibility of the separatist objectives, together with the singleness of purpose occasioned by the war, shaped the conservative community in Cuba into an uncompromising and unyielding upholder of permanent Spanish sovereignty. The emergence of a liberal party dedicated to the pursuit of comprehensive colonial change after 1878, however, aroused a mixture of rancor and resentment among the most intransigent supporters of Spanish authority in Cuba. Having defeated the insurgent armies in the field, Spaniards were ill-disposed to support a policy of reconciliation that involved granting in peace concessions opposed during war. Few were prepared to compromise in any form with representatives of the rebellious colony.

By the end of the 1870s, many resident *peninsulares* had emerged as uncompromising advocates of stronger metropolitan authority in Cuba. The conciliatory tenor of Zanjón and the subsequent organization of the Autonomist party offended the sensibilities of those *peninsulares* for whom victory over the rebellious Cubans in 1878 announced only the prelude to a harsher regimen of metropolitan authority and a rigorous reaffirmation of Spanish sovereignty. Never fully trusting Cuban creoles, Spanish conservatives viewed the new liberal party with misgiving and mistrust. The organization of the Autonomist party, joining creole reformists with former separatist leaders in the pursuit of political change, aroused fear among many conservatives that the extralegal dispute of the previous decade had found a spurious if not sinister legality in post-Zanjón Cuba. The large number of former separatist leaders enrolling in the ranks of the new party served to confirm the conservatives' worst fears. Indeed, the new party was always suspect, perceived as little more than a legal political fiction behind which lurked the malevolent force of Cuban separatism.

Peninsular reaction to autonomism was not long in coming. In late 1878, the conservative reaction to liberal reformism gave post-Zanjón Cuba its second political party—the Partido Unión Constitucional. Unabashedly pro-Spanish in its sympathies, overwhelmingly *peninsular* in its composition, the Unión Constitucional attracted to its ranks the most intransigent advocates of *Cuba española*. Into the ranks of the new party flocked conservative *peninsulares*, most notably merchants, businessmen, traders, and members of the professions, as well as government employees at the colonial, provincial, and municipal levels—all devoted totally to the defense of traditional Spanish authority over Cuba.

Whatever else may have separated the two new political parties in post-Zanjón Cuba, they shared two central and reciprocally binding premises. Representatives of both the Autonomist party and the Unión Constitucional rejected outright the means and the objectives of the insurgent separatists. An appeal to arms was unacceptable; *Cuba Libre* was unthinkable. Second, and closely related, both parties accepted the legitimacy of the Spanish colonial regime and the desirability of empire as the central and unchallenged tenets of colonial politics.

V

Excluded from the new political alignments in post-Zanjón Cuba were the irreconcilable veterans of the Ten Years' War. Indisposed to accept the implied finality of Zanjón, many insurgent Cubans chose expatriation as an alternative to submitting to continued Spanish rule. Exile attracted the most intransigent elements of the separatist polity. Much of this population consisted of members of the old insurgent army, disaffected sec-

tors of the creole petite bourgeoisie, and large numbers of workers—
Cubans of modest social origins who defended the most exalted view of
separatism. An expatriate community acquired its definitive character around
the central proposition that reconciliation with Spain on any basis other
than independence was unacceptable and that independence through any
means other than arms was unattainable. Separatist sentiment remained
intact abroad, a vigorous force immune from the compromise associated
with political affiliations in the post-Zanjón colonial regime.

The ranks of exiled separatists were held together by the vision of
Cuba Libre and a commitment to armed struggle. In émigré centers abroad,
the ideal of *Cuba Libre* endured and received its earliest institutional
expression in the form of expatriate revolutionary clubs and patriotic jun-
tas. Throughout exile communities in Latin America, Europe, and the
United States, patriotic associations nurtured the notion of a free homeland. Unrepentant, unyielding in their conviction that Zanjón represented
only a truce, expatriate separatists refused to renounce armed struggle as
the means of securing Cuba's independence from Spain. Indeed, their
very presence abroad signified a singular inconformity with the post-Zanjón
regime in Cuba and a persistent commitment to arms. No tenet was so
central to separatist sentiment after Zanjón as the belief that a new war
of liberation was both imminent and inevitable.

Nor were separatist expectations unfounded. Only months after Zanjón, separatist leaders abroad completed plans for a new war. In early
1879 veteran General Calixto García organized the Cuban Revolutionary
Committee in New York and prepared for a new uprising. Several months
later, García returned to Cuba at the head of an expeditionary force. "La
Guerra Chiquita," as the short-lived war of 1879–80 became known, fell
prey immediately to many of the mishaps and misfortunes that had frus-
trated the separatist effort a decade earlier, and ended the same way.

Few saw more clearly the prevailing disorganization settling over the
separatist movement than the young writer in exile José Martí (1853–95).
Born in Havana, the son of *peninsulares,* Martí entered separatist politics
modestly enough. Anti-Spanish statements in Cuba during the Ten Years'
War had led to his arrest and exile to Spain in 1871. During the better
part of the next decade, Martí traveled throughout Europe, Latin America, and the United States. In January 1880, he arrived in New York and
immediately volunteered his services to the Cuban Revolutionary Committee during "La Guerra Chiquita." Irresistible in his rhetoric, compelling in his prose, Martí quickly distinguished himself as the outstanding

propagandist of the ill-starred separatist war of 1879–80. Even before the conflict had come to an end, Martí had assumed interim presidency of the committee and had emerged as a central force among Cuban exiles in the United States.

Martí drew the correct lessons from the Ten Years' War and "La Guerra Chiquita." Cuban separatists were ill prepared to mount, much less sustain, a successful drive for independence. Martí was convinced that the sources of Cuban failures in the past were to be found within the separatist movement itself, most notably in the lack of political organization through which to promote the purposes of separatist arms. A "war of massive effort," Martí wrote in retrospect about the Ten Years' War, was "lost only through a lack of preparation and unity." The struggle for Cuban independence could not be based on quixotic military adventures organized around well-meaning and dedicated men and women who believed that justice and virtue were sufficient reasons to expect the triumph of Cuban arms. "The revolution," Martí insisted in 1882, "is not merely a passionate outburst of integrity, or the gratification of a need to fight or exercise power, but rather a detailed understanding dependent on advanced planning and great foresight." Cuban independence, Martí argued, was a process, not an event—a process in which final victory would proceed from patient preparation and dedicated organization.

But independence itself represented only a preliminary phase of a larger process, one in which Cubans would labor to eliminate socio-economic injustice. "In my view," Martí wrote General Antonio Maceo in 1882, "the solution to the Cuban problem is not a political but a social one." A decade later, he reiterated his conviction: "Our goal is not so much a mere political change as a good, sound, and just and equitable social system without demagogic fawning or arrogance of authority. And let us never forget that the greater the suffering the greater the right to justice, and the prejudices of men and social inequities cannot prevail over the equality which nature has created." *Cuba Libre* signified a Cuba free from racism and oppression, a republic responsive to the needs of all Cubans. "The revolution will be for the benefit of all who contribute to it," he vowed. "Through the gates we exiles open . . . ," he predicted in 1892, " . . . will enter Cubans with a radical soul of the new country."

The armed struggle was to be nothing less than a war of redemption and redistribution. Martí repeatedly invoked the concept of redemption to characterize the separatist enterprise. "The war is planned abroad," he wrote, "for the redemption and benefit of all Cubans." Martí spoke both of a "holy revolution" and of the "redemptive virtue of just wars that would join all Cubans around the burning idea of decent redemption." But social and cultural equality was impossible within a system of economic inequality. His vision of the new republic included a commitment to national economic development based on diversified agriculture. "Exclusive wealth," Martí wrote in 1878, "is unjust. . . . A nation with small landowners is rich. A country with a few rich men is not rich— only the country where everyone possesses a little of the wealth is rich. In political economy and good government, distribution is the source of prosperity." Fifteen years later, Martí again addressed himself to the issue of distribution of property. Cuba possessed vast expanses of uncultivated land and had only "to make it available to anyone desiring to work it." With an equitable system of land distribution, he predicted, "a simple matter upon the inauguration of a sovereign state, Cuba will accommodate many good men." "A counterbalance for social problems and foundation for a Republic . . . should be one of enterprise and work."

Independence as an uncompromising ideal moved into a position of central importance during the late 1880s and early 1890s, largely as the result of the efforts of José Martí. He was instrumental in defining the most exalted version of *Cuba Libre:* independence from Spain and the United States—untrammeled, unconditional, uncompromising national sovereignty. Indeed, Martí directed almost as much energy toward combating the annexation of Cuba to the United States as he did promoting support for its independence from Spain. "To change masters," Martí repeatedly insisted, "is not to be free." He was deeply troubled by the prospect of Cubans winning the battle for separation from Spain only to lose the larger struggle for independence. Years of residence in the United States had alerted him to the perils attending long-standing North American designs on the islands. As early as 1886, Martí warned his compatriots that the United States had "never looked upon Cuba as anything but an appetizing possession with no drawback other than its quarrelsome, weak, and unworthy population." Anyone who "had knowingly read what was thought and written in the United States," Martí insisted, could not entertain any illusions about North American intentions in Cuba.

Martí's repeated injunction during the 1880s and 1890s on the necessity for a correctly organized war for independence stemmed in large measure from his fear that a prolonged armed struggle, one that continued indefinitely without the immediate prospect of Cuban success, would create the conditions leading to North American intervention and ultimately annexation. As early as 1886, Martí warned of the danger that "annexation might become a fact and that perhaps it may be our fate to have a skillful neighbor let us bleed ourselves on his threshold until finally he can take whatever is left in his hostile, selfish and irreverent hands." A quick and successful war was necessary to forestall U.S. intervention. A premature war, Martí warned prophetically, a protracted war, would provide the North Americans with the pretext to intervene—"and with the credit won as a mediator and quarantor, keep [Cuba] for their own." "Once the United States is in Cuba," Martí asked rhetorically, "who will drive it out?"

Everything was different after Martí. For the better part of three decades, the idea of *Cuba Libre* had not moved much beyond an essentially undefined and wholly ambiguous sentiment. Outside a commonly if loosely shared notion that *Cuba Libre* involved minimally separation from Spain, the final structure of free Cuba remained vaguely and incompletely defined by various sectors of the separatist movement. Martí took the first tentative steps toward giving ideological substance and political form to *Cuba Libre*. More and more, he occupied himself with the social, economic, and cultural content of free Cuba. These were not, to be sure, entirely new concerns within the separatist polity. Many had been addressed before, if only haphazardly. What was different after the early 1890s was a matter of degree, and eventually the difference in degree was sufficiently great to make it a distinction in kind.

After the early 1890s, the struggle for *Cuba Libre* evolved into something considerably more than the pursuit of independence. Nationhood was only one aspect of Cuban fulfillment. José Martí's republic was as much a function of his social vision as it was a product of his political aspirations. The separatist effort joined all classes and both races in a common cause. Rich and poor, black and white were summoned to participate in the making of a new nation. Martí mobilized support from those sectors of Cuban society most susceptible to appeals for a new order. His revolutionary formula was a conglomeration of national pride, social theory, anti-imperialism, and personal intuition. He rationalized it all into a single revolutionary metaphysic and institutionalized it into a single revolutionary party. Like a master weaver, Martí pulled together all the separate threads of Cuban discontent—social, economic, political, racial, historical—and wove them into a radical movement of enormous force.

So it was that the dispossessed and disinherited on both sides of the Florida Straits responded to this summons. An expatriate proletariat, a dispossessed peasantry, blacks and whites, the landless and the poor, women and men—in large numbers they ratified Martí's vision of free Cuba—"with all and for the well-being of all" to end "the malevolent regime of the creole oligarchy." For Martí, the goal of the war of independence was "not a change in forms but a change of spirit." To this end, it was "necessary to make common cause with the oppressed, to secure the system opposed to the interests and habits of the rule of the oppressors."

Martí's efforts reached fruition in 1891. In November, Martí announced the "Resolutions" of a new political party, a statement defining the organizational basis around which separatists would pursue the liberation of the homeland. April 1892 marked the formal establishment of the Cuban Revolutionary Party (PRC). The central goal of the PRC, Martí stressed, was first and foremost to organize "common revolutionary action" in one party for one purpose: the liberation of Cuba. The PRC renewed the traditional commitment to armed struggle and summoned all Cubans to participate. It was to unite all Cubans in the common purpose of waging war for independence and to provide the moral and material support for the revolution in Cuba. The party would serve as the principal unifying agent and would provide objectives around which to organize all sectors of the independence movement—the army veterans of 1868 and the civilian separatists of the post-1868 generation, Cubans from the provinces of the east and west, Cubans who lived inside and outside Cuba, blacks and whites, women and men, Cubans of all classes—brought together in one front of national liberation. Martí would die early in the new war, but his contribution would survive. He had transformed a revolutionary movement into a revolutionary party, and by the end of 1892 the third post-Zanjón political party had taken definitive form.

Subsumed into the post-Zanjón political struggle was a conflict of a different sort: competition for power between the planter class, which was identified with reform and colonialism, and the emerging populist coalition, which consisted of petit bourgeois elements, the impoverished gentry, an expatriate proletariat, blacks, and peasants, and was identified with revolution and independence. Planters adhered to colonialism as a means of political hegemony; separatists aspired to independence as a means of political power. Which meant that two obstacles stood in the way of independence: *peninsulares* and planters.

VI

The early 1890s were not good years in which to plot revolution. Cuba was prospering, and the economy was expanding. Creole producers had obtained the long desired reciprocal trade agreement with the United States. By the terms of the Foster-Cánovas agreement (1891), Cuban products received customs benefits in exchange for Spanish tariff concessions to U.S. exports.

The results of reciprocal trade arrangements between Cuba and the United States were as dramatic as they were instant. Sugar production expanded in spectacular fashion. From some 632,000 tons in 1890, sugar production approached 976,000 tons in 1892, and reached for the first time the historic one-million-ton mark in 1894.

The long-range effects of reciprocal trade went far beyond sugar. Cuban exports to the United States increased from $54 million in 1890 to $79 million in 1893. By 1893, Cuban exports to the United States were some twelve times larger than its exports to Spain ($79 million and $6 million, respectively). By 1894, the United States received almost 90 percent of Cuba's total exports ($98 million out of $116 million) and provided 40 percent of its imports ($39 million out of $97 million). Metropolitan Spain, on the other hand, accounted for some $10 million of Cuban exports while providing the island with $34 million of its imports.

Trade statistics underscored the magnitude of Cuba's economic ties with the north. In two short years, the Cuban economy had taken a giant stride toward deepening its dependence on the capital, imports, and markets of the United States. Colonial political grievances receded quietly into the background as Spain's trade and commercial policies conformed to the demands of creole producers. Pressure on the cost of living eased as the reduction of duties lowered prices on foreign imports. The sugar system was central and strategic to all other sectors of trade and commerce; when it prospered and expanded, the entire economy responded.

But celebration of prosperity was premature. Within three years, Cuba's boom ended as quickly as it had begun, and with less warning. In 1894, the United States rescinded its tariff concession to Cuban exports. By establishing a new duty of 40 percent ad valorem on all sugar imports, the United States dismantled the cornerstone of the previous reciprocal trade arrangements between Washington and Madrid. In that same year, the Foster-Cánovas agreement expired. Spanish authorities responded swiftly

TABLE 20.   Duties on Materials from the United States

	1891–93	1894
Iron bridge material	free	$48.00 per ton
Iron or steel rails	free	20.00 per ton
Iron or steel tools	free	25.00 per ton
Machinery	free	$15.00–60.00 per ton

Source: Pulaski F. Hyatt to Secretary of State, Oct. 12, 1894, Despatches from U.S. Consuls in Santiago de Cuba, 1799–1906, General Records of the Department of State, National Archives, Washington, D.C.

to U.S. tariff legislation in 1894 and canceled duty concessions to North American imports. An impenetrable protectionist wall reappeared around the island in mid-1894, reviving memories of the worst features of Spanish commercial exclusivism.

The sudden end of Cuba's prosperous but brief trade with the United States had jolting consequences on the island. Cuba lost its privileged access to the only market with the capacity to absorb its sugar exports and insulate the island from the uncertainties of world competition. The restoration of Spanish tariffs, further, raised the specter that the United States would retaliate by banning Cuban sugar from North American markets altogether.

Profits declined immediately; production followed. Sugar exports valued at $64 million in 1893 plummeted to $45 million in 1895 and $13 million a year later. The one-million-ton sugar harvest of 1894 collapsed to 225,000 tons in 1896. No less daunting to sugar producers, after 1894 planters also faced the grim prospect of losing preferential access to the equipment, machines, and spare parts around which the sugar industry had reorganized after the mid-1880s. In Santiago de Cuba, new duties on North American materials after mid-1894 raised the prices on all imports (Table 20). The loss of preferential access to U.S. markets, moreover, was simultaneous with a sudden drop in world sugar prices. For the first time in the history of Cuban sugar production, the price of sugar dropped below two cents a pound.

Reaction in Cuba to Spain's retaliatory levies was immediate. For the second time, Cuban producers joined together against Spanish policy. In November 1894, the Círculo de Hacendados y Agricultores convened in an extraordinary session to protest Madrid's tariff policies. In the largest

TABLE 21. Prices of Select Staples
(1893–95) (per 100 kilos)

	1893–94	1894–95
Wheat	$ .30	$3.95
Flour	1.00	4.75
Corn	.25	3.95
Meal	.25	4.75

Source: Ramon O. Williams to Assistant Secretary of State, Jan. 5, 1895, Despatches from U.S. Consuls in Havana, 1783–1906, General Records of the Department of State, National Archives, Washington, D.C.

meeting of its history, the Círculo petitioned the Ministry of Colonies to rescind the duties assessed against North American products entering the island. After adjournment, the planter elite took to the streets and converged on the Governor General's palace for a public meeting that one Havana newspaper described as a "peaceful protest."

The impact of the crisis of 1894, however, went far beyond the sugar system. No facet of Cuban society was unaffected. Merchants, traders, and retailers who had replaced traditional commercial ties with Spanish suppliers in the metropolis for dealers in the United States faced ruin. Unemployment rose again, the supply of commodities decreased, and prices increased. The price of foodstuffs imported from the United States, upon which large sectors of the population had come to depend, soared. Government duties were passed directly onto consumers and prices reached unprecedented heights. The restoration of colonial custom duties meant that all Cubans would henceforth pay higher prices for vital food imports (see Table 21). Even as costs increased, the availability of the higher priced goods decreased. North American imports dropped, shipping declined. By October 1894 half the U.S. steamers serving Santiago had been withdrawn from service.

The implications of the events of late 1894 were apparent to all Cubans. The passage of a decade had not dimmed Cuban memories of the crisis of the mid-1880s. A unanimous outcry of indignation and protest rose across the island against Spain.

A growing sense of economic deprivation returned Cubans' attention to their lack of political power. As Cubans grew dependent on trade with the United States, they grew increasingly subject to the vagaries of the international marketplace and the economic policies of two metropolitan centers—one political, the other economic. The well-being of the island depended more and more on forces over which the Cubans had little control. Throughout the crisis, Cubans found themselves reduced to passive onlookers of a momentous economic drama involving the very solvency of the Cuban economy. "The residents and commercial interests here," the U.S. vice consul in Santiago reported, "are protesting loud and strong against being thus summarily cut off from their natural commercial allies, and this action on the part of the home government adds greatly to the feeling of unrest that pervades all classes."

Once again the question of Cuba's status and the nature of its relationship with Spain surfaced as a topic of political debate and public discussion. A sense of uncertainty and uneasiness settled over the island. Prosperity required the expansion of trade, and that in turn required the reduction of Spanish control over the Cuban economy. The brief cycle of prosperity between 1891 and 1894 made the prospect of returning to Spanish exclusivism seem inconceivable. Cuban producers had visited the promised land and there gazed covetously at an economic destiny in which Spain had no visible place. Spain's arbitrary and unwelcome intrusion in Cuban affairs in 1894 was a dramatic reminder of the economic liabilities attending continued political association with Madrid. Cuba had experienced the fruits of close economic collaboration with the United States in the 1890s—and the possibilities seemed infinite.

The events, further, served to set in sharp relief the meager accomplishment of reformist politics. The vaunted prospects for political reform in the 1870s became the failed promises of the 1890s. The palpably inauspicious achievements of two decades of political labor strained the faith of even the most devoted Autonomists. *Peninsulares* continued to prevail at the polls and to predominate in politics. They were preponderant in the Cuban delegation to the Spanish parliament. They were in the majority in colonial government, provincial posts, and municipal administration, as well as in the military and in the clergy. They dominated the administration of justice—they were the presidents of high courts of justice *(audiencias)*, judges and magistrates, prosecutors and solicitors, court clerks and judicial scribes. Their power in the electorate was well out of proportion to their numbers. Some 80 percent of the *peninsular* population was qualified to vote, compared to only 24 percent of the Cuban population. Electoral rolls favored *peninsulares* and discriminated against

Cubans. The town of Güines, for example, counted a population of 13,000 inhabitants, 500 of which were Spaniards. The electoral census included 400 Spaniards and 32 Cubans.

The results were predictable. The Güines municipal council did not include a single Cuban. Of the 37 *ayuntamientos* in the province of Havana, Spaniards held a majority in 31. Of the 32 aldermen in the Havana *ayuntamiento,* 29 were Spaniards. Three-quarters of all mayors across the island were *peninsulares.* After two decades of political competition and loyal opposition, the Autonomist party had failed to achieve even its minimal goal—that of becoming a power contender. Spaniards clung tenaciously to public administration and political office, and they showed no intention of relaxing their grip on positions and power. It was this intransigence that gave rise within the creole bourgeoisie first to misgivings, and later to the frightful realization that perhaps Spaniards were determined to retain control at all costs. "Cubans are driven from local administration as if they resided in a foreign land," complained the Autonomist newspaper *El País* in January 1890. "The policy of the past is the one that dominates at present—the dismal policy of intransigence and exclusivism. . . . The *peninsulares* still enjoy the irritating privileges of the old regime, as well as those obtained by the subversion of the new one. They have lost nothing; in everything they have gained. The country, on the other hand, finds itself impoverished and mocked."

The planter bid for political leadership in the colony after Zanjón had failed. Worse than this, the effort had situated the creole bourgeoisie directly in the crossfire between the contentious extremes of the colonial polity, a middle position that earned Autonomists the suspicion of the loyalists and the scorn of the separatists. It was a position that reflected accurately the anomalous social reality of the planter class, dependent upon United States markets for prosperity but relying on the Spanish military for security. It was a position, too, of immense vulnerability, one that had neither the support of the leadership of the colonial body politic nor the following of the colonial body social.

For the second time in the nineteenth century, a sector of the planter class, possessed of social status and economic resources, representing principally local, landed interests, had challenged the historic *peninsular* exclusivism. It was the post-Zanjón euphoria—the belief that autonomism would lead at once to collective economic expansion through the liberalization of trade arrangements and to individual mobility through the liberalization of colonial politics, and that both would eliminate the source of future colonial instability—that rallied the planter elite to the side of metropolitan authority.

But the prospects had been overdrawn. Planters and their creole allies had reached a new stage of alienation. Expectations had been raised by the promise of liberal reform, only to be betrayed by its failure. Autonomists had not fared well in colonial politics. Not because, they insisted, they lacked public support and popular following but, rather, as a result of official intimidation and political fraud. Manipulation of suffrage requirements, ballot stuffing, and certification frauds were only the most blatant of the abuses routinely practiced by Spanish authorities in Cuba. Autonomist leaders were harassed. The provincial Autonomist press was periodically suspended. In 1891, the party withdrew from local elections to protest official indifference to formal charges of fraud. Three years later the provincial Autonomist committee of Santiago de Cuba dissolved in protest of Spanish policy.

The failure of Autonomist politics signified fundamentally a failure of both the reformist creole bid for political ascendancy and the bourgeois bid for hegemony. The Cuban planter class had failed to develop political strength adequate either to establish itself as a power contender or guarantee the protection of local property interests. Autonomists' faith in the colonial system remained unrequited. The effects of misplaced faith did more than shake Autonomist devotion to the colonial order—an impiety that was, in any case, without immediate consequences. In the end, Autonomists could not abandon colonialism without incurring the risk of visiting enormous grief on themselves—and this they were not willing to do. The creole bourgeoisie remained true to its own interests, not to a cause, royalist or revolutionary, and in the process lost something else. By seeking to establish hegemony over the colonial polity within the framework of empire, planters lost the opportunity to pursue dominance over the larger constituency organizing around the ideal of nationhood. For Spanish loyalists, planter attempts to reform empire were evidence of subversion, and always suspect; for Cuban separatists, planter attempts to reform empire were a sign of servility, and equally suspect.

After nearly two decades, the record of Spanish concessions to Cuba remained singularly meager. The economy had begun to contract and the promised political reforms remained unfulfilled. Suffrage manipulation and election rigging favored the Unión Constitucional. The participation of creoles in the Spanish parliament and in the insular government of the island remained wholly token. Spain's allies had been estranged and its opponents emboldened. Worse still, in the mid-1890s the economy was in crisis, and discontent was everywhere on the increase. And a revolution was about to begin.

7

Revolution and
Intervention

I

The year 1895 began under the pall of despair. The economy had faltered and political discontent was increasing. These were difficult times for Autonomists. Traditional allegiances were shaken. The planter class occupied a nether world where friends and foes appeared to have exchanged identities, a condition complicated by increasingly unrealizable expectations of both protection from Spain and profits from the United States. Planters in the past loyal to Spain now questioned the assumptions of their allegiance. They questioned, too, the continued efficacy of colonialism: it was not clear if it was a beneficent Spain that lacked the vitality to control the colonial system or if it was a negligent Spain that lacked the volition to defend colonial subjects. Nor perhaps did it really matter, for whatever the source, it boded ill to the property interests and social standing of creole elites.

These were idle musings, as it turned out, for in 1895 planters were spared the agony of a painful decision. In February war broke out in Cuba, again in the name of *Cuba Libre*. At first it appeared as though the new rebellion would be short-lived. Conspiracies in Havana and Matanzas had been uncovered, and crushed. Insurgent bands in Las Villas and Camagüey were routed early and easily. Only in Oriente did the uprising seem to take hold, and last, and spread. But even as the insurgency expanded throughout the east during the early spring, government supporters still took some solace in the knowledge that the rebellion remained largely a provincial affair in a historically rebellious province.

The outbreak of the new separatist war forced the disgruntled bourgeoisie to return instinctively to the metropolitan fold. It was again time to choose sides, proclaim faith, and give testimony. Not that the planters' sudden reconciliation with the colonial regime in February 1895 signaled conformity with colonial policies. Rather, the separatist alternative was wholly unacceptable. Whatever doubts may have sapped elite morale, whatever grievances may have strained elite loyalties, planters were neither so desperate nor so reckless as to confuse the separatist cause with their own. In 1895, planters had nowhere to go but back.

They went back, but not entirely without conditions. Certainly they pronounced their adherence to Spain. In April 1895, the Autonomist party dutifully issued a manifesto to the nation denouncing the insurrection as "criminal" and urging Cubans in arms to seek a peaceful resolution of their grievances. At the same time, however, Autonomists seized the newest colonial crisis to press again for reforms. The colonial insurrection, they argued, was the unfortunate but understandable consequence of Spanish misgovernment. Spain would either have to concede reforms to end the Cuban rebellion or confront a revolution that would end Spanish rule.

And for a brief moment, it actually seemed Autonomist arguments had prevailed. The appointment of Arsenio Martínez Campos as governor general in April 1895 served to renew flagging Autonomist hopes for a negotiated political settlement. No one was committed more to reconciliation through reform than Martínez Campos. It was this well-known commitment that contributed to prolong Autonomist faith in reform as the salvation of the colony—a fateful prolongation, as it turned out, for as the war expanded, the planter class became increasingly isolated between the embattled extremes of the colonial polity, and vulnerable to attacks from both.

In the spring of 1895, however, reform still seemed a wholly plausible proposition. The rebellion remained confined to the eastern end of the island, still very much a provincial affair of local proportions. But reforms originated in Spain, and they did not come easy. In fact, they did not come at all. Spanish authorities refused to concede colonial reforms as long as Cubans remained in arms, and Cubans refused to relinquish their arms for reforms that did not end colonialism.

In the meantime, during the autumn months of 1895, the unthinkable occurred: insurgent armies marched out of the eastern mountains, across the central plains, and into the western valleys. The presence of separatist armies in the west, coincident with preparations for the 1896 harvest, stunned the loyalist community. In the course of ten months, the insurrection had dramatically outgrown its provincial dimensions and spread into regions never before disturbed by the armed stirrings of *Cuba Libre*. By early 1896 insurgent armies operated in every province of the island. The prospects for the 1896 harvest were bleak—and when it was finally completed, even the pessimists were shown to have been overconfident: from the one-million-ton crop of 1894 the harvest fell to 225,000 tons in 1896. Not since the 1840s had Cuban sugar production been so low. And in 1897, it dropped again, to 212,000 tons. The effects were disastrous everywhere. Trade and commerce declined. Retail sales collapsed, unemployment increased.

The presence of insurgent armies in the west signaled more than the failure of Spanish military policy. In a very real sense, it announced the insolvency of Autonomist politics. Many rushed to fix responsibility for Spanish reversals on those officials, principally Martínez Campos, who had subordinated military operations to the search for political solutions. But the governor general was not the only one to suffer ignominy. Upon Autonomists generally fell the full weight of metropolitan wrath and *peninsular* ire. Government setbacks confirmed among conservatives the futility if not the folly of efforts to seek reconciliation with the rebellious Cubans through concessions. The politics of reaction acquired a new appeal and a new urgency. *Peninsular* patience with colonial reform and creole reformers had expired, and now conservatives demanded a turn at ending the colonial conflict.

II

During the last quarter of the nineteenth century, uprisings in the name of *Cuba Libre* had become as commonplace as they were ill-starred. After the Ten Years' War, the call to arms was heard with more or less recurring regularity across the island. "La Guerra Chiquita" of 1879 was an armed affair of only months. Another rebellion in 1883 ended in disaster. So, too, did an uprising two years later. Another abortive effort in 1892 lasted only days. In 1893, two rebellions were launched within three months of each other, and both failed just as quickly.

But 1895 was different. Certainly one difference was planning. This was a war three years in preparation, and in 1895 Cubans were united. A broad coalition had formed under the auspices of the Cuban Revolutionary Party, a coalition sustained during times of enormous adversity by commitment to a sentiment that by the late nineteenth century had assumed fully the proportions of a revolutionary metaphysic.

But neither preparation nor organization, however vital to the success of Cuban arms, was the decisive difference in 1895. The difference, rather, was found in the ideological content of separatist thought and the social origins of separatist leadership. Cuba had changed between the "Grito de Yara" in 1868 and the "Grito de Baire" in 1895, and in the intervening years the source of Cuban grievances no longer emanated exclusively from the rule of a distant European metropolis. By the late nineteenth century, Spain was neither the principal beneficiary nor the primary benefactor of colonialism. Inequity in Cuba in 1895 had a peculiarly homegrown quality. That the sources of oppression in Cuba were more internal than external and, further, that the forms of oppression were more social than political, served as the central premises around which armed separatism took definitive shape between the 1880s and 1890s. Armed separatism was committed to more than independence. It subsumed a social imperative into its vision of a free Cuba.

Not that these notions were entirely new. On the contrary, they had always been vague elements of nineteenth-century separatist thought. What was different in 1895 was the recognition that inequity was not caused principally by Spanish political rule, for which independence was the obvious panacea, but, rather, was the effect of the Cuban social system, for which the transformation of Cuban society was the only remedy. Cubans continued to speak of independence, but now they spoke too of the war as a method of redemption and a means of social revolution. Political separatism had expanded into revolutionary populism, committed as much to ending inequitable relationships within the colony as to ending colonial connections with the metropolis. The separatist enterprise was conceived as both a rebellion against Spanish political structures and a revolution against the Cuban social system.

The political conflict between bourgeois reformism and populist separatism involved more than competiton for hegemony. It turned on the social purpose to which political power would be put. For the reformist political party, power offered the means to defend property and protect privilege; for the populist revolutionary party, power promised social justice, economic freedom, and political democracy. And it quickly became evident that vast sectors of the creole bourgeoisie were just as much an enemy of *Cuba Libre* as were *peninsular* officeholders.

The vision of *Cuba Libre* remained admittedly ambiguous and imprecise. Cubans spoke more to aspiration than action, to promise rather than program. Concerns were expressed in thematic rather than programmatic terms. The separatist leadership did not develop a program so much as it identified the problems and committed the future republic to their resolution. But these vague commitments established the ideological premises of the separatist cause, the central if ambiguous creed and articles of faith around which Cubans gathered to make history. This was not merely an effort to overthrow Spanish rule, but an endeavor to change Cuban politics fundamentally by creating new ways of mobilizing and sharing political power. The separate sources of Cuban discontent—social, economic, political, racial, historic—converged into a radical movement of enormous force. To the historic objective of national liberation was added a social imperative of national revolution, and instantly a movement dedicated to the establishment of a new nation became a force devoted to shaping a new society. Rebellion was transformed into revolution.

It was not only that separatist ideology had a different social content but the social composition of armed separatism was different. A new constituency had come together around *Cuba Libre,* Cubans for whom armed struggle offered the means through which to redress historic grievances against the colonial regime and its local defenders. Displaced professionals, impoverished planters, an expatriate proletariat, former slaves, a dispossessed peasantry, poor blacks and whites, in and out of Cuba, responded to the summons to arms. The difference between the Ten Years' War and the war of 1895, army chief Máximo Gómez proclaimed, was that the former originated from "the top down, that is why it failed; this one surges from the bottom up, that is why it will triumph."

In sharp contrast to the patrician origins of separatist leadership during the Ten Years' War, spearatist leaders in 1895 consisted principally of men of modest social origins. Many came from the ranks of the disgruntled and displaced creole petite bourgeoisie, representatives of the liberal professions, including engineers, teachers, physicians, and attorneys. Many army officers had working-class backgrounds; others originated from the burgher ranks—shopkeepers, merchants, and traders. Some officers came from the ranks of the impoverished gentry, downwardly mobile victims of the confiscations and expropriations between 1868 and 1878. Some interrupted their schooling to join the patriotic cause while others did so immediately upon completion of their studies. Many were men of color, who came to occupy senior command positions in the Liberation Army. Indeed, some 40 percent of the senior commissioned ranks of the Liberation Army was made up of men of color. Other men of color moved into key positions in the PRC and the provisional government. In sum: these were Cubans for whom the old regime was as much a social anathema as it was a political anachronism. Armed separatism offered oppressed groups—poor blacks and whites, peasants and workers, the destitute and dispossessed—the promise of social justice and economic freedom. They committed themselves to a movement that promised not only to free them from the old oppression but to give them a new place in society, a new government they would control, and a new nation to belong to.

III

The appearance of insurgent columns in the west not only expanded the theater of military operations, it also enlarged the ranks of the insurgent armies. Cubans by the thousands joined the rebellion. In Cartagena, Cuban General José Miró Argenter wrote in his campaign diary of the "great increment of the Revolution in western Las Villas," and added: "the peasant abandoned his farming, the tobacco farmer his planting, the artisan his tools, and the laborer his work: all the patriots have taken to the hills." General Antonio Maceo estimated that some 10,000 new recruits had enrolled in the army during the course of the westward march. After the invasion, the total number of insurgent army regiments increased from thirty to eighty-six.

The separatist cause obtained more than the service of new soldiers, however. It received too the support of countless tens of thousands of civilians *(pacíficos)*, mainly peasants who served the liberation effort as non-combatants in a variety of roles. Those too young or too old, those who could not leave their homes, those less likely to take up arms, mainly women, could and did provide food and supplies, cared for the wounded and tended the horses, served as messengers and couriers, but most of all, they passed back and forth across enemy lines, collecting intelligence and gathering information on the movement and maneuvers of the Spanish army everywhere in Cuba.

Until 1896, the conflict was primarily a struggle between the colony and the metropolis over competing claims of sovereignty over Cuba. After 1896, the conflict expanded into a struggle between the creole bourgeoisie and the populist coalition over competing claims of hegemony within the colony. The defeat of the politico-military power of Spain required the destruction of the socio-economic power of the bourgeoisie, the only other power contender in Cuba capable of rivaling the separatist bid for political supremacy. To take power, the social amalgam that had formed

around armed separatism used the war of liberation both to expel Spain
from Cuba and to eliminate the creole bourgeoisie in Cuba.

The invasion moved the center of the armed conflict from the remote
eastern districts to the central western zones, and immediately announced
a new phase of the war. After 1896, Cubans found themselves in the
position of toppling the colonial system, fully and irrevocably, including
both its external politico-military structures in the form of Spain and its
internal socio-economic supporters in the form of the creole planter class.
With the completion of the invasion, it was no longer necessary, or even
practical—given the weakness of insurgent logistical support—for Cubans to engage the Spanish army in battle. Instead, Cubans turned on
property and production. The war was now against the dominant social
class, the local collaborators of colonialism: a war waged against the
beneficiaries of colonialsm by the victims of colonialism. In this new
design for war, the Spanish army hardly figured into it at all. The war
was directed more against the creole bourgeoisie than against the *peninsular* bureaucracy, and the material destruction of the former was an adequate substitute for the military defeat of the latter.

This was the new purpose of Cuban arms. The sugar fields became the
battlefields, the enemy became the planter class, and the war against Spain
became a siege on Cuba. The insurrection was now "an economic war,"
Colonel Fermín Valdés Domínquez recorded in his diary, "against capital
and production." In July 1895, General Máximo Gómez proclaimed a
moratorium on all economic activity—commerce, manufacturing, agriculture, ranching, and, especially, sugar production: no planting, no harvesting, no grinding, no marketing. Any estate found in violation of the
ban, Gómez vowed, would be destroyed and its owner tried for treason.
"All sugar plantations will be destroyed, the standing cane set fire and
the factory buildings and railroads destroyed," the decree warned. "Any
worker assisting the operation of the sugar factories will be considered
an enemy of his country . . . and will be executed." Five months later,
as the Cuban army advanced westward, Gómez ordered his chiefs of
operation to enforce the July decree. "The war did not begin on February
24," he proclaimed at the outset of the invasion of the west, "the war is
about to begin now."

The most devastating weapon in the insurrectionary arsenal became *la
tea*—the torch. Across the island, fire announced the Cuban purpose.
Máximo Gómez made his point by analogy: "It is necessary to burn the
hive in order to disperse the swarm." The moral was not lost on the

Cuban insurgent command. "The invasion of the western end of the island," Antonio Maceo exulted in February 1896 from Pinar del Río, "has produced the desired result: everything has changed and the Revolution is strong; the revolutionary fire has been lit even in the most remote corners of Vuelta Abajo." And two months later, Maceo again wrote with satisfaction: "With great success . . . everything that could serve as a source of revenue and an object of support for our enemies has been ordered destroyed."

The Cuban moratorium against sugar production threatened the planter class with ruin—exactly what it was supposed to do. To ignore the insurgent ban was to risk the destruction of property, and with Cuban army units operating fully across the breadth of the island, it was not a risk to be taken lightly. Some tried, unsuccessfully, and across Cuba fields and factories went up in smoke. Larger planters managed to defy the ban, but only after first organizing private squadrons of armed guards to protect their property. Many producers, however, were obliged to observe the moratorium. "If anyone had told us four months ago," wrote one planter in early 1896, "that [Gómez] would be able to stop the crushing of cane in the Province of Havana, or even in Matanzas, we would have laughed in his face. Today not a planter disobeys his orders."

But the suspension of production did not guarantee either salvation or solvency. Indeed, the economic hardship caused by compliance with the ban was potentially no less disastrous, and often far more certain, than the military reprisal Cubans threatened for the defiance of the ban. Planters had traditionally borrowed against future crops at prevailing world prices, and years of accumulated indebtedness found the planter class operating with little margin for mishap. In those circumstances where planters tottered at the brink of bankruptcy from harvest to harvest, the loss of a single year's crop promised catastrophe. Ruin was imminent, and for many inevitable. Very early in the war, scores of planters abandoned their estates to the fortunes of war, joining Spaniards in the cities or Cubans in exile.

But there was deeper meaning to the insurgent method. The suspension of production as a device of war also set the stage for the redistribution of property as a design for peace, and both gave decisive expression to the social content of armed separatism. The question of property relations occupied a position of central importance in separtist thought. Armed separatism committed itself to the idea of a nation of small landowners, each farmer to enjoy security derived from direct and independent own-

ership of land. The war provided more than the opportunity to end colonial rule. It created the occasion to destroy one social class and create
another. In a sweeping land reform decree in July 1896, the insurgent
leadership committed the revolution to a new regimen of land ownership.
Exhorting Cuban military forces to "burn and destroy all forms of property [as] rapidly as possible everywhere in Cuba," the army command
pledged:

> All lands acquired by the Cuban Republic either by conquest or confis-
> cation, except what is employed for governmental purposes, shall be
> divided among the defenders of the Cuban Republic against Spain, and
> each shall receive a portion corresponding to the services rendered, as
> shall be provided by the first Cuban Congress, after Cuban Indepen-
> dence has been recognized by Spain, and this shall be given to each in
> addition to cash compensation for all services previously rendered, and
> as a special bounty and reward. . . . All lands, money, or property in
> any and all forms previously belonging to Spain, to its allies, abettors
> or sympathizers, or to any person or corporation acting in the interest
> of Spain or in any manner disloyal to the Cuban Republic are hereby
> confiscated, for the benefit of the Cuban Army and of all the defenders
> of the Cuban Republic.

IV

The invasion had one last effect. The completion of the westward surge
sent shock waves across the island and across the Atlantic. Cuban successes stunned Spanish authorities. Few could believe that the rebellion
had spread with such speed. No longer could the insurrection be dismissed as one more disorder in the long series of desultory provincial
disturbances that had characterized separatist stirrings in the last third of
the nineteenth century. It was now national in scope and revolutionary in
intent. And because it was both, Spain could not be anything less than
unequivocal in its response and unqualified in its results. The invasion
challenged directly the basis of the colonial consensus, the unstated but
understood sources of Spanish sovereignty in Cuba. Spain's support, indeed, its very claim on the allegiance of the planter class, historically had
rested on its ability to protect property and privilege from local revolutionary challenges. This was the tacit understanding between officials in
the metropolis and property owners in the colony, an understanding with

origins early in the nineteenth century and upon which the fidelity of the Ever Faithful Island had since depended.

The western expansion of the insurrection was no less a threat to the solvency of the colonial administration than to the social system over which it presided. Cubans intended to overthrow the former by undermining the latter. What Cubans proposed to do, simply, was to make Spain irrelevant to the Cuban social reality. And more: to make the continued Spanish presence in Cuba itself the single largest liability to existing property relationships. There would be no peace, no production, no protection of property as long as Spain continued to exercise political power over Cuba. Spanish authorities understood, too, the gravity of the crisis and, further, recognized the urgency to end it quickly. The Cubans did not have to defeat the Spanish, they had only to avoid losing. Time was on the side of the Cubans, and if Spain failed to lift the insurgent siege in the west, soon all would be lost everywhere in Cuba.

Spain reacted immediately, first by reorganizing the army command in Cuba and soon thereafter by enlarging its army in Cuba to 200,000 officers and men. Appointed to oversee the new Spanish war effort was General Valeriano Weyler. A veteran campaigner known for parsimony of language, he outlined his approach to the insurgency succinctly: "I believe that war should be answered with war."

Weyler arrived in Cuba in early 1896, bringing with him some 50,000 fresh troops. He also brought an understanding of the task at hand. Any campaign that did not first deprive the insurgents of their support in the countryside, he knew, was doomed to failure. Weyler realized that the Cuban army could not be defeated without first destroying the rural communities from which it emerged, upon which it depended, and into which it dissolved. So long as the *pacífico* population remained at liberty to move between the cities and the countryside, to transport medicine and supplies, and to relay intelligence and information across government lines, so long as peasants remained free to cultivate their crops and tend to their livestock, Spain would find itself in an impossible war against insuperable odds.

After 1896 the Spanish shifted the focus of their war effort and changed the purpose of *peninsular* arms. The peasantry now became the object of government military operations. Weyler plunged the island deeply into war—totally, without quarter. That autumn Weyler implemented the most drastic measure of his "war with war" policy: a decree ordering the rural population to evacuate the countryside and relocate to specially designated fortified towns. Spanish field commanders were ordered into the interior to enforce the reconcentration decree and escort the population out of the countryside. Military operations were now directed against the rural population, its resources, its possessions. Subsistence agriculture was banned. So was trade between the cities and the countryside. Livestock owners were ordered to drive their herds into the cities.

But the worst was yet to come. Not only was war directed against the peasant, it was declared against the peasants' land, the tools for its cultivation, and its bounty—against everything, in short, capable of sustaining life in regions beyond Spanish control. Weyler campaigned with determination and ruthlessness.

The Spanish, like the Cubans, also found fire an efficient and cost-effective method of waging war. Spanish military forces scoured the countryside in search of all signs of human activity. Villages and planted fields were burned; food reserves were set ablaze, homes were razed, and livestock was seized. Animals that could not be driven to Spanish-held zones were slaughtered. In this way, thousands of cattle, horses, pigs, and mules were destroyed. To this was added the systematic plunder of anything of value and the destruction of the meager possessions owned by peasants. Peasants were herded into the reconcentration camps, and what they could not take with them was destroyed along with their homes and villages. The human presence in the countryside became a proscribed one, and whenever located was presumed indicative of subversion. By the end of 1896, a stillness had settled over vast expanses of the Cuban countryside. The farms were untended, the fields unworked, the villages uninhabited. Entire communities had disappeared. Vast stretches of rural Cuba were reduced purposefully to a wasteland, of no possible value to anyone. Wrote one traveler to Cuba a year after the reconcentration decree:

> I travelled by rail from Havana to Matanzas. The country outside the military posts was practically depopulated. Every house had been burned, banana trees cut down, cane fields swept with fire, and everything in the shape of food destroyed. It was as fair a landscape as mortal eye ever looked upon; but I did not see a house, man, woman or child, a horse, mule, or cow, nor even a dog. I did not see a sign of life, except an occasional vulture or buzzard sailing through the air. The country was wrapped in the stillness of death and the silence of desolation.

For countless numbers of Cubans life in the interior turned into an incomprehensible nightmare. Hundreds of thousands became refugees within their own country, driven from their homes, and crowded into urban centers in confusion and fear. Reconcentration camps filled the cities with distant sounds of women wailing, children shrieking, and men praying for deliverance, or else swearing vengeance on their tormentors. An estimated 300,000 Cubans, the young and the old, men, women, and children, all non-combatants, were crowded into hastily assembled and poorly constructed resettlement camps. A policy that was ill-conceived became inevitably a program ill-implemented, with frightful consequences. Municipal authorites were not prepared to assume the responsibility of caring for the *reconcentrados*. The Spanish government refused responsibility. With only scant attention to living quarters, less to diet, and none to health, the overcrowded reconcentration centers became breeding grounds for disease and sickness. The policy led eventually to mass deaths. It was designed to. The *reconcentrados* died by the tens of thousands—of hunger, of abuse, but most of all of entirely preventable epidemics. The reconcentration policy was the method Spain chose to defeat the Cubans. It was designed to deprive the insurgents of their supporters, but also to destroy the insurgents' morale. The selection of *reconcentrados* was not an entirely random affair. Spanish authorities waged war directly on the families of combatants. The grandparents and parents, the wives and children of Cuban soldiers were arrested and interned, and it was known by all at the moment of their interment that they were doomed.

Reconcentration caused a profound disruption of life in rural Cuba. It vastly accelerated the deterioration of economic conditions in the countryside, and this abrupt break with continuity had the net effect of converting much of the peasantry from passive allies to participating combatants. Forced to abandon their land, witness to the destruction of their homes and farms, peasants by the thousands joined the swelling columns of the insurgent armies. Insurgent military chieftains across the island reported the effects. "The sending here of ferocious Weyler," General José María Rodríguez wrote from Oriente in March 1896, "has been a counterproductive measure for Spain: great numbers of Cubans who had remained pacific, in the countryside as well as in the towns, are found today swelling our ranks." From the west, Maceo wrote that Weyler's policies had redounded to the benefit of the insurrection. "The Revolution," he exulted, "does not have a better ally than Weyler himself." "The time for the definitive division has arrived," Colonel Fermín Valdés Domínguez recorded in his diary. "Those who are with the Spanish will go to the cities and our supporters will be with us in the countryside.

Weyler works for us. The *good* result of his method of directing military operations will soon be seen.'' By the end of 1896, insurgent numbers had increased to 50,000.

The war took a curious turn after 1896. Spanish troops concentrated in the cities and fortified positions, and they were almost impregnable; Cuban troops overran the countryside, and they were virtually unconquerable. A good part of the war passed in this way: the Spanish in the forts, the Cubans in the fields, each beyond the other's reach. So they both found surrogates to attack, those social classes allied by persuasion or proximity, or both, to an enemy that neither could get at, those social classes who were, above all, vulnerable and whose elimination promised an adequate alternative to the otherwise unobtainable military victory. The Spanish assaulted the peasants, the Cubans assailed the planters. Both attacked property. In the process, the destruction of the island continued unabated. The Cubans were determined to destroy the island in order to win, the Spanish were determined to destroy the island in order not to lose. By the third year of the war, the despoliation of the countryside was all but complete.

V

Weyler arrived in Cuba with two purposes: first, of course, to end the Cuban conflict by military means. Second, and no less important, to restore the colonial consensus by political methods. Weyler's appointment signaled the ascendancy of the intransigent *peninsular* element, loyalists who had never acknowledged a substantive difference between autonomism and separatism. Both political tendencies were perceived as inimical to the interests of Spain, distinguished only by the means they employed to subvert metropolitan authority.

Weyler's reputation preceded him, and news of his appointment immediately precipitated a wave of emigration. In February 1896, in the space of one month, some 1300 Cubans left for the United States. In the first two months of Weyler's government, another two thousand families emigrated to Europe.

Cuban misgivings were not unfounded. Under Weyler, Autonomists were all but formally banished from political forums on the island. The rigor with which Weyler pursued separatists in the field was surpassed only by the relentlessness with which he persecuted Autonomists in the cities. Political harassment previously sporadic and local became systematic and island-wide. Public criticism of government policies was banned. Autonomist political meetings were prohibited and party newspapers suspended. Party leaders, party functionaries, and party members were routinely arrested, beaten, and subject to house searches.

This was calculated terror, a measured program directed against the creole elites. Waves of arrests resulted in the imprisonment and deportation of thousands of Cubans suspected of insufficient ardor for Spanish rule, the majority of whom were Autonomists. Within days of Weyler's arrival, provincial authorities made some fifty arrests in Pinar del Río. By July, the United States consul general reported 720 political prisoners in Havana alone. In the small Matanzas city of Jovellanos, some 600 people fled after a wave of government arrests led to the imprisonment of forty people in two days. Hundreds of Cubans were summarily deported to Spain to serve prison terms in *peninsular* jails. Others were sent to Spain's African penal colonies in Ceuta, Chafarinas, and Fernando Poo. In December 1896, several hundred more political prisoners disembarked in Cádiz; this particular group included landowners, businessmen, lawyers, and former provincial public officials.

For decades Autonomists had struggled against the abuses of colonialism rather than the system of colonialism. By the end of 1896 they were in disarray and despair. The island's propertied elites had failed in their quest for political power. More than this, they faced political extinction at the hands of the very authorities upon which they had traditionally relied for survival.

The Cuban planter class held few illusions after 1896. Spain was losing the war, or at least not winning it. In any case, the price of Spanish redemption was slowly exceeding the cost of the Cuban revolution. On one hand, planters faced extinction as a political force from above by the policies of reaction directed by Spanish loyalists. On the other, they faced extinction as a social class from below by the program of revolution directed by Cuban separatists.

Weyler's policies initially enjoyed the unanimous endorsement of Spain's most zealous supporters in Cuba. If the appointment of Weyler united conservatives around the singleness of purpose of Spanish arms, however, it also shattered Spain's base of moderate supporters committed to a political settlement of the conflict. Weyler's policies drove Autonomists into prison and exile and banished moderates from the island's political forums—these were the exigencies of war, conservatives insisted, justified by the need to unite the island around the cause of Spanish arms. Conservatives had long viewed Autonomists with suspicion, detecting in the ranks of the reformers surrogate separatists. The repression of Autonomists and the repudiation of the policies they advocated were viewed as preliminary steps necessary to the restoration of Spanish authority.

But the new conservative consensus did not fare much better than the previous, moderate government. On the contrary, the Weyler years were disappointing ones for Spain's supporters in Cuba. Original optimism gave way first to doubt and soon to despair. By late 1897, Spanish achievements in Cuba fell woefully short of the expectations that had greeted Weyler's arrival two years earlier. Increasingly, loyalists were losing confidence in Spain's ability to end the war successfully. The fury of the insurgency continued unabated, with Spain powerless to prevent the destruction of property and incapable of restoring order. Property owners found themselves caught hopelessly between the excesses of contending armies. The insurgents prohibited the movement of livestock into the cities, the government ordered all cattle and horses out of the countryside. Gómez threatened to destroy all sugar estates engaged in the harvest *(zafra,)* Weyler threatened to destroy all sugar estates not working on the harvest. In May 1896, Weyler prohibited the export of leaf tobacco to the United States. A measure designed to weaken separatist cigar centers in Florida threatened also to precipitate the collapse of the tobacco industry in Havana. In 1896, Weyler ordered the withdrawal of Spanish troops from garrison duty on the estates, leaving property owners vulnerable to insurgent attacks. Some planters hired private guards; others could not afford to do so and were forced to suspend operations. In either case, the cost of the war passed directly to Cuban producers.

Much to the dismay of Spain's supporters in Cuba, a year of Weyler's policies had failed to improve conditions on the island. On the contrary, the military situation for Spain continued to deteriorate and the economy moved toward total collapse. Trade between the cities and the countryside ceased. The resettlement of the rural population brought agriculture to a standstill. The dispersal of the rural population into insurgent camps in the interior and reconcentration camps in the cities also signified the loss of the labor force upon which planters had traditionally depended for the *zafra*. Sugar production approached collapse. The scorched earth policies of insurgent armies in Pinar del Río and Weyler's decree banning tobacco exports to the United States crippled the *vegas* of the west. Unemployment increased, taxes went up, and prices soared. Between January and March 1897, the price of food increased by some 30 percent; by May, the price of bread, milk, and flour had doubled. Eggs sold at three for twenty cents. Yams and plantains were up five times their normal price. Skyrocketing inflation affected all sectors of the population. The government printed paper money with reckless abandon. In one month alone, the Bank of Spain printed some $20 million in paper currency. Weyler's decree mandating face value to paper currency on pain of arrest for treason strained relations between the government, on one hand, and merchants, shopkeepers, and businessmen, on the other. Resentment increased and by 1897 merchants and shopkeepers began refusing depreciated currency altogether as payment for goods and services. The result was a new wave of arrests and imprisonments; many had their shops looted and their goods expropriated under military decree.

In the provinces, Weyler's policy aggrieved Cubans in still other ways. The arrival of Spanish troops thoroughly disrupted community life, converting provincial towns and cities into armed camps and interrupting normal social and commercial activities. Martial law pre-empted locally elected governmental officials. Families were required to quarter and feed Spanish troops in their homes. The war penetrated every aspect of Cuban life and now, in 1897, even the calamity many expected to follow a Cuban victory appeared somewhat diminished by the consequences attending an indefinite postponement of a Spanish defeat.

By the end of 1897 many who only a year earlier had celebrated Weyler's arrival with enthusiasm despaired at his inability to provide a satisfactory solution of the crisis. Conservatives were initially prepared to endure the hardships of Weyler's policy as the necessary and inevitable consequences of the insurrection—as long as they believed these measures capable of ending the conflict. They expected sacrifices and hardships, but defeat was still a novelty. Weyler's failure to deliver the decisive military blow to the separatist insurrection raised doubts among even Spain's most ardent supporters that the metropolis possessed either the means or the capacity to defeat the insurgent armies. The Spanish war effort was going nowhere—and at great cost. The price of Pax Hispanica taxed even the most affluent supporter of the Spanish rule. After almost two years under the regimen of the "war with war" strategy, conservatives were suffering as much at the hands of their Spanish allies as they were from their Cuban adversaries. With no military end to the conflict in sight, and economic conditions continuing to deteriorate, the foundations of Spain's narrow political base in Cuba began to crack under the strain.

By 1897 the specter of a protracted war had become as unbearable as a separatist victory was unthinkable. Disaffection among those sectors traditionally identified with Spain mounted steadily. The inability of Weyler to end the war and restore Spanish authority over the rebellious island came as the latest in a series of blows to pro-Spanish sectors in Cuba. So much depended on Weyler's success—the very solvency, many sensed, of Spanish rule in Cuba. Those who had been public in their confidence that Weyler represented Spain's best hope for restoring order also acknowledged in private that he was Spain's last hope.

For the better part of the nineteenth century, the planter class had endured the unjustness of colonial rule as the best guarantee against the uncertainties of self-rule. Whatever liabilities attended colonialism, none, planters understood correctly, could offset the guarantees of property, prosperity, and privilege. Confirmed in this conviction by periodic disorders and uprisings during much of the nineteenth century, creole elites had seen no reasonable alternative to the prevailing political order underwritten by and dependent upon Spanish arms. The elites preferred security to change and were not disposed to risk their social predominance for the sake of independence. Many had been inspired less by loyalism than by fear of social upheaval and the collapse of law and order.

If in times of war local elites looked to Spain to uphold their privilege in the political order, in times of peace they looked to the United States to underwrite the prosperity of their economy. Under more or less normal conditions, the apparent contradiction of the Cuban political economy in the nineteenth century had posed little difficulty to the local elites, for whatever else planters may have been, they were pre-eminently pragmatic. Their impatience with Spanish economic policies in 1894 was eclipsed by their fear of Cuban social revolution in 1895. In 1895, elite disaffection at metropolitan economic policies subsided only after the shadow of civil war had passed over the island. More immediate concerns now took precedence. The necessity of having to appeal to Spain for protection against the ravages of civil strife forced property owners to subordinate outstanding economic grievances to immediate politico-military needs. The earlier clamor against Spanish economic policies was muted by the distant rumblings of colonial insurrection. Led by a sector outside the traditional elite, the revolution posed as much a threat to the economic interests of property owners as it did to the political authority of Spain. Overriding concerns for property and privilege had forced planters to retreat again into the safety of the metropolitan fold—a place where they would remain unless or until Spain defaulted on the only remaining rationale for Spanish colonialism: order and security for property and privilege.

In increasing numbers Autonomists were abandoning the island and joining separatist agencies abroad. Autonomists who advocated reforms and planters who demanded repression discovered that Spain could neither offer reforms sufficient to conciliate the insurgents nor apply repression sufficient to end the insurrection. The triumph of the invasion persuaded many previously unsympathetic to separatist goals that the insurrection could indeed succeed; the ruthlessness of Weyler's regime convinced them the insurrection had to. Continued Spanish sovereignty promised only to prolong Cuban difficulties. Indeed, metropolitan authority now represented the single largest obstacle to order and stability, making it all but impossible to bring a recurring cycle of war and rebellion to an end once and for all.

By 1897 the conservative consensus began to unravel. The inability of Martínez Campos to confine the insurrection to the east and the incapacity of Weyler to expel the insurgents from the west exposed the bankruptcy of the Spanish colonial regime. The apparent futility of Spanish arms gave rise to doubt, and this uncertainty served to undermine the prevailing *peninsular* unanimity of purpose. A sense of despair settled over the conservative community in Cuba. The crisis continued to deepen, seemingly unaffected in the slightest by the mightiest of Spain's efforts. The moral of 1897 was painfully clear: neither in peace nor in war could Spain protect the interests of Cuba's producing classes. And after 1896, they did not doubt for a moment that the revolution posed as much threat to the economic interests of property owners as it did to the political authority of Spain. Planters who had originally returned to the metropolitan fold found that they were no more welcome there than they were in the liberated zones of Cuba. Caught between political reaction from above and social revolution from below, the beleaguered bourgeoisie contemplated its impending extinction.

Within two years of Weyler's appointment, elites had abandoned all hopes of salvation from Spain. In 1897 the propertied classes faced an unprecedented situation. Their traditional source of security, upon which they had depended historically for protection against local dissidents, approached exhaustion, and, for the first time, Spain gave evidence of defaulting on its security responsibilities to the colony.

Admission of Spain's impotence in Cuba forced conservatives to confront the heartsickening prospect of a victory of Cuban arms. The very interests that obliged planters in 1895 to appeal to Madrid for military assistance made them reconsider in 1897 the efficacy of continued political ties with Spain. Indeed, growing more certain in their conviction that Spain's hold over Cuba was slipping, the insular elites were not indisposed to abandoning a doomed cause if assured of an alternative source of protection and patronage. Weyler's faltering in 1897 served as the signal to begin the search for a new political arrangement, one optimally capable of preserving local pre-eminence or minimally capable of blocking the ascendency of those new forces in Cuban society that threatened the old order. Those groups who before 1895 had powerful economic reasons to seek union with the United States had, after 1897, powerful political reasons to do so.

In the face of the apparent weakness of the political metropolis, propertied elites appealed to their economic metropolis for assistance. Only U.S. intervention, many concluded, and eventual annexation, held any promise of ending the insurrectionary challenge and redeeming the beleaguered social order. Through late 1896 and early 1897, property owners had grown increasingly predisposed to sacrifice traditional colonial relationships to preserve the local socio-economic system. As early as June 1896, nearly one hundred planters, lawyers, and industrialists petitioned President Grover Cleveland for U.S. intervention to resolve the crisis. "We cannot," the petitioners wrote, "express our opinion openly and formally, for he who should dare, whilst living in Cuba, to protest against Spain, would, undoubtedly, be made a victim, both in his person and his property, to the most ferocious persecution at the hands of the Government." Spain, the petition continued, had defaulted on even the most modest promise of reform and could offer Cuba nothing for the future except continued destruction and ruin. Nor could the petitioning property owners find much comfort at the thought of independence. If the prospect of continued Spanish rule threatened to result in ruin, independence would lead to havoc. "Can there be no intermediate solution?" the petitioners asked plaintively. Without confidence in Spain, and uncertain about the future under Cuban rule, the petitioners asked Washington to intercede in their behalf: "We would ask that the party responsible to us should be the United States. In them we have confidence, and in them only."

Conservative calls for U.S. intervention increased in number and frequency. North American consular agents reported receiving individual letters, joint petitions, and private appeals asking for intervention and annexation. In November 1897, the U.S. vice-consul in Matanzas reported that "nearly all Spaniards, businessmen, and property holders in this province wish and pray for annexation to the United States." "Property holders, without distinction of nationality, and with but few exceptions," cabled the U.S. vice-consul in Santiago, "strongly desire annexation, having but little hope of a stable government under either of the contending forces." By the end of the year sentiment for U.S. intervention had become public. In December, a meeting of property owners in Cienfuegos concluded plans to forward a petition to President William McKinley asking the United States to establish a protectorate over Cuba. In February, at a meeting of ranking members of the Unión Constitucional, conservatives established a formal commission for the purpose of securing North American assistance. "The mother country cannot protect us . . . ," one spokesman insisted. "Therefore, we want the United States to save us."

VI

With the end of 1897 and the start of 1898, all signs pointed to the imminent and inevitable dénouement: the triumph of Cuban arms. Preparations for the last desperate battles of the war had begun. Holding undisputed control over the Cuban countryside, the insurgent army command prepared for the final phase of the insurrection: the assault on the cities. In late 1897, Cubans had completed the organization of artillery units and were preparing to carry the war to urban centers. In Oriente, General Calixto García laid seige on Bayamo, a city of some 21,000 residents. In August, García mounted a stunning and successful artillery attack on Victoria de Las Tunas, a city of 18,000 people. In the succeeding six months, town after town in eastern Cuba fell to Cubans, including Guisa, Guáimaro, Jiguaní, Loma de Hierro, and Bayamo. In early 1898, Manzanillo was threatened. In April, García was engaged in final preparations for an assault against Santiago de Cuba.

Across the island, the Spanish army had ceased to fight. *Peninsular* units abandoned smaller interior towns for larger provincial cities, and then abandoned these to concentrate their defenses in provincial capitals.

"The enemy," Máximo Gómez reported from Las Villas in March 1898, "has departed, ceasing military operations and abandoning the garrisons and forts which constituted his base of operations. Days, weeks and months pass without a column of troops appearing within our radius of action." He now wrote confidently about preparation for the final assault against Spaniards in the cities. With "cannons and a great deal of dynamite," a self-assured Gómez predicted, "we can expel them by fire and steel from the towns."

January was customarily the month in which the Spanish army command launched vigorous field operations—every dry season, for the previous two years, January announced the beginning of the winter campaign. Cubans braced themselves for what many believed to be the last and, perhaps, the most desperate enemy offensive. But nothing happened. In January 1898, Máximo Gómez wrote of a "dead war." The collapse was all but complete. "The enemy is crushed," Gómez reported with some surprise from central Cuba, "and is in complete retreat from here, and the time which favored their operations passes without their doing anything." Spain's failure to mount a new winter offensive confirmed the Cuban belief that the enemy was exhausted and lacked the resources and resolve to continue the war. One more campaign, the insurgent chieftains predicted confidently, would suffice to deliver the coup de grace to the moribund Spanish army. A new optimism lifted insurgent morale to an all-time high. Never before had Cubans been as certain of victory as they were in early 1898. "This war cannot last more than a year," Gómez predicted euphorically in January 1898. "This is the first time I have ever put a limit to it."

VII

The success of Cuban arms threatened more than the propriety of colonial rule or traditional property relations in the colonial regime. It challenged, too, pretensions of colonial replacement. For the better part of the nineteenth century the United States had pursued the acquisition of Cuban with resolve, if without results. The United States had early pronounced its claim to imperial succession in the Caribbean, but this proclamation had failed to deliver the coveted island into the North American union. In attempting to end Spanish sovereignty, Cubans also endangered the United States aspiration to sovereignty. Acquisition of Cuba was envisioned by North Americans as an act of colonial continuity, formally transferred and legitimately ceded by Spain to the United States—a legal assumption of sovereignty over a territorial possession presumed incapable of a separate nationhood.

The Cuban rebellion changed all this. Cuba was lost to Spain, and if Washington did not act, it would also be lost to the United States. By early 1898, U.S. officials were acknowledging what was already evident in Cuba: the days of Spanish rule were numbered. "Spain herself has demonstrated she is powerless either to conciliate Cuba or conquer it," former U.S. minister to Spain Hannis Taylor concluded in late 1897; "her sovereignty over [Cuba] is . . . now extinct." "To-day the strength of the Cubans [is] nearly double . . . ," Assistant Secretary of State William R. Day wrote in a confidential memorandum in 1898, "and [they] occupy and control virtually all the territory outside the heavily garrisoned coast cities and a few interior towns. There are no active operations by the Spaniards. . . . The eastern provinces are admittedly 'Free Cuba.' In view of these statements alone, it is now evident that Spain's struggle in Cuba has become absolutely hopeless."

Set against the landscape created by the receding tide of Spanish sovereignty, the United States confronted what was anathema to all North American policymakers since Thomas Jefferson—Cuban independence. The implications of the "no transfer" principle were now carried to their logical conclusion. If the United States could not permit Spain to transfer sovereignty over Cuba to another power, neither could the United States permit Spain to cede sovereignty to Cubans.

So it was that in April 1898 President William McKinley requested of Congress authority to intervene militarily in Cuba. War ostensibly against Spain, but in fact against Cubans—war, in any case, as an alternative medium of political exchange, just as Clausewitz posited.

The president's war message provided the purpose of policy: no mention of Cuban independence, not a hint of sympathy with *Cuba Libre*, nowhere even an allusion to the renunciation of territorial aggrandizement—only a request for congressional authorization "to take measures to secure a full and final termination of hostilities between the Government of Spain and the people of Cuba, and to secure in the island the establishment of a stable government, capable of maintaining order and observing its international obligations." The United States presence in Cuba, McKinley explained, consisted of a "forcible intervention . . . as a neutral to stop the war." "Neutral intervention" offered a means through which to establish, by virtue of arms, United States claims of sovereignty over Cuba. "The forcible intervention of the United States . . . ," McKinley announced to Congress on April 11, "involves . . . hostile constraint upon both the parties to the contest." This meant war directed against both Spaniards and Cubans, the means to establish grounds upon which to neutralize the two competing claims of sovereignty and establish by superior force of arms a third.

McKinley's message did not pass entirely unchallenged. The Cuban cause had won a wide popular following in the United States, and congressional defenders of *Cuba Libre* made repeated attempts to secure the administration's recognition of Cuban independence. By mid-April, the president grudgingly accepted a compromise. Congress agreed to forgo recognition of independence in exchange for the president's acceptance of a disclaimer. Article IV of the congressional resolution, the Teller Amendment, specified that the United States "hereby disclaims any disposition of intention to exercise sovereignty, jurisdiction, or control over said island except for pacification thereof, and asserts its determination, when that is accomplished, to leave the government and control of the island to its people." And the United States proceeded to war.

VIII

The intervention changed everything, as it was meant to. A Cuban war of liberation was transformed into a U.S. war of conquest. It was the victory to which the United States first laid claim, and from which so much else would flow. A set of developments, articulated in successive stages, would together provide the basis upon which the United States would proceed to establish its claim of sovereignty over Cuba. The Cubans seemed to have achieved little in their own behalf, the North Americans concluded. The lack of decisive battles in the war and the apparent absence of noteworthy insurgent military achievements were attributed immediately to the deficiency of Cuban operations, if not to Cuban character. These impressions served to encourage the belief that Cubans had accomplished nothing in more than three years of war and that North American arms alone determined the outcome of the war.

There was a dark side to these pronouncements. North Americans wanted more than credit. That Cubans appeared to have vanished from the campaign altogether served immediately to minimize Cuban participation in final operations against Spain, and ultimately justified excluding Cubans from the peace negotiations with Spain. In appropriating credit for the military triumph over Spain, the United States established claim to negotiate unilaterally peace terms with Spain; in appropriating responsibility for ending Spanish colonial government, the United States claimed the right to supervise Cuban national government.

So it was that the Cuban war for national liberation was transfigured into the "Spanish-American War," nomenclature that denied Cuban participation and presaged the next series of developments. This construct served to legitimize the United States claim over Cuba as a spoil of victory. The Cuban struggle was portrayed as an effort that by 1898 had stalled, if not altogether failed. The United States completed the task the Cubans had started but were incapable of completing alone. The proposition was established early and advanced vigorously. Cubans were apprised of their indebtedness to the United States, from whose expenditure of lives, treasury, and resources Cuba had achieved independence from Spain. The denial of the Cuban success over Spain denied them more than laurels of victory—it deprived them of their claim to sovereignty.

IX

Military occupation began on January 1, 1899, and after nearly a century of covetous preoccupation with the island, the United States assumed formal possession of Cuba. It was not an unqualified possession, however. Certainly the Teller Amendment obstructed direct fulfillment of the nineteenth-century design of annexation. But the main obstacle to permanent acquisition was not the congressional resolution. A far more formidable challenge appeared in the form of *independentismo*. Three decades of revolutionary activity—spanning the years between 1868 and 1898, involving two generations of Cubans, and consecrated in three major wars—had created a nationalist movement of enormous popular vitality and political vigor. It was not a sentiment to be trifled with. The principal challenge to pretensions of U.S. rule originated within the ranks of the wartime populist coalition, and it was this central political reality that determined the purpose of the U.S. military occupation.

The proponents of *independentismo* persisted through the early period of the occupation, and the ideal never lost its appeal. A great deal of U.S. effort was devoted to discrediting both. Cuban motives for independence were suspect, as if opposition to the presence of the United States was itself evidence that self-serving if not sinister motives lurked behind separatist aspirations. Cubans were not inspired by love of liberty but by the lure of looting. "From the highest officer to the lowliest 'soldier,' " one North American wrote, "they were there for personal gain." The Cuban desire for independence, U.S. officials concluded, was motivated by a desire to plunder and exact reprisals. Cubans were possessed, one observer reported, by the "sole active desire to murder and pillage." "If we are to save Cuba," one New York journalist exhorted, "we must hold it. If we leave it to the Cubans, we give it over to a reign of terror—to the machete and the torch, to insurrection and assassination."

This was a proposition from which North Americans drew a number of inferences: first, Cubans were not prepared for self-government. Again and again the same theme came up. The ideological imperative of empire took hold early, and deeply. The censensus was striking. Admiral William T. Sampson, a member of the United States evacuation commission, insisted that Cubans had no idea of self-government—and "it will take a long time to teach them." Some United States officials believed Cubans incapable of self-government at any time. "Self-government!" General William R. Shafter protested. "Why those people are no more fit for self-government than gunpowder is for hell." General Samuel B. M. Young concluded after the war that the "insurgents are a lot of degenerates, absolutely devoid of honor or gratitude. They are no more capable of self-government than the savages of Africa." For Major Alexander Brodie the necessity for a protectorate, or outright annexation, was as self-evident as it was self-explanatory. "The Cubans are utterly irresponsible," Brodie insisted, "partly savage, and have no idea of what good government means." A similar note was struck by Major George M. Barbour, the United States sanitary commissioner in Santiago de Cuba. The Cubans, he insisted, "are stupid, given to lying and doing all things in the wrong way. . . . Under our supervision, and with firm and honest care for the future, the people of Cuba may become a useful race and a credit to the world; but to attempt to set them afloat as a nation, during this generation, would be a great mistake." General William Ludlow, military governor of Havana, concurred: "The present generation will, in my judgment, have to pass away before the Cubans can form a stable government." In mid-1899, Governor General John R. Brooke agreed: "These people cannot *now,* or I believe in the immediate future, be entrusted with their own government." "We are going ahead as fast as we can,'' Governor General Leonard Wood informed the White House in 1900, ''but we are dealing with a race that has steadily been going down for a hundred years and into which we have to infuse new life, new principles and new methods of doing things.''

The attempt to discredit independence was surpassed only by the effort to deprecate its advocates. Independence was as unworthy an ideal as its proponents were unfit to govern. Only the ''ignorant masses,'' the ''unruly rabble,'' the ''trouble makers''—''the element,'' in General Wood's words, ''absolutely without any conception of its responsibilities or duties as citizens''—advocated independence. ''The only people who are howling for [self-government],'' he concluded with undisguised contempt, ''are those whose antecedents and actions demonstrate the impossibility of self-government at present.''

The ideal of independence, however, persisted as a powerful force during the early years of the occupation. The popular appeal of those Cubans who opposed Spanish rule or defended national sovereignty was irresistible. Most North Americans in Cuba conceded, if only in private, that a majority of Cubans were devoted to the ideal of independence. But numbers alone, they were quick to counter, could not be permitted to determine the fate of Cuba—particularly when the sentiment of the majority was identified with disruption, disorder, and chaos. That Cubans in large numbers opposed annexation was cause enough to distrust and reason sufficient to discredit independence sentiment. If there were people who opposed United States rule, they probably knew no better or were led by wicked men. In either case, Cuban incapacity for self-government was confirmed. Over time, North Americans insisted, under the protection and patronage of the United States, the call for annexation would rise above the clamor for independence. There existed in Cuba a yet unrevealed majority, U.S. officials thought, that was silent in its preference but steadfast in its desire for annexation. ''The real voice of the people of Cuba,'' General Wood reassured the White House in late 1899, ''has not been heard because they have not spoken and, unless I am entirely mistaken, when they do speak there will be many more voices for annexation than there is at present any idea of.''

In the meantime, if the United States found no support in the anti-annexation majority, it derived some consolation in the quality of the pro-annexation minority. The ''better classes,'' the propertied, the educated, the white—those sectors, in short, most deserving of North American solicitude—wanted close and permanent ties with the United States. This offered North Americans some hope, for the purpose of the intervention was to foreclose more than the rise of a new political force; it was also to forestall the fall of an old social system. Propertied elites greeted U.S. intervention as nothing less than the providential deliverance from expropriation and extinction. It was to this group that the United States looked for political leaders and local allies. North Americans early detected in the shattered ranks of the creole property owners natural allies in its pursuit of control over Cuba. Both opposed Cuban independence. Both opposed Cuban government. Policymakers needed supporters, property owners needed security. The United States searched for a substitute for independence; *peninsular* and creole elites sought a substitute for colonialism. The logic of collaboration was compelling. There was an inexorable choicelessness about this collaboration, wholly improvised but as pragmatic as it was politically opportune. The old colonial elites in need of protection and the new colonial rulers in need of allies arrived at an understanding. United States efforts during the occupation centered on enrolling the services of the propertied elites as political surrogates in opposition to the *independentista* polity. The ascendency of a political coalition organized around colonial elites promised not only to obstruct the rise of *independentismo* but also to institutionalize United States influence at the point of maximum effectiveness—from within. It would matter slightly less, then, if Cuba were to become independent, if that independence were under the auspices of a client political elite whose own social salvation was a function of United States control.

One certain way to foreclose the rise of the unruly masses, North American authorities believed, was to deny the *independentista* leaders the opportunity to mobilize the vast political force of Cuban nationalism. And the surest way to promote the ascendency of the "better classes," was to exclude the "rabble" from the electorate. Secretary of War Elihu Root proposed limited suffrage, one that would exclude the "mass of ignorant and incompetent," and "avoid the kind of control which leads to perpetual revolutions of Central America and other West India islands." All voters were required to be Cuban males over the age of twenty and in possession in one of the following: real or personal property worth $250, or an ability to read and write, or honorable service in the Liberation Army. All Cuban women and two-thirds of all adult Cuban men were excluded from the franchise. Suffrage restrictions reduced the Cuban electorate to 105,000 males, approximately 5 percent of the total population.

But early elections revealed the power of the *independentistas'* appeal. They prevailed in the municipal elections of 1900, and again in the constituent assembly elections later that year. General Wood lamented: "The men whom I had hoped to see take leadership have been forced into the background by the absolutely irresponsible and unreliable element. . . . The only fear in Cuba to-day is not that we shall stay, but that we shall leave too soon. The elements desiring our immediate departure are the men whose only capacity will be demonstrated as a capacity for destroying all hopes for the future." And to the point: "I do not mean to say that the people are not capable of good government; but I do mean to say, and emphasize it, that the class to whom we must look for the stable government in Cuba are not as yet sufficiently well represented to give us that security and confidence which we desire."

Wood shared his despair with Elihu Root. "I am disappointed in the composition of the Convention," Wood wrote in March 1901. The responsibility of framing a new constitution had fallen to some of the "worst agitators and political radicals in Cuba." Wood questioned again the wisdom of proceeding with plans for evacuation. "None of the more intelligent men claim that the people are yet ready for self-government," Wood insisted. "In case we withdraw," he warned, the convention represented "the class to whom Cuba would have to be turned over . . . for the highly intelligent Cubans of the land owning, industrial and commercial classes are not in politics." Two-thirds of the convention delegates were "adventurers pure and simple," not "representatives of Cuba," and "not safe leaders."

X

By late 1900 the United States faced the unsettling prospect of evacuation without having established the internal structures of hegemony. Time was running out. So were justifications for continued military occupation. An anomalous situation arose. In 1900, the United States found itself in possession of an island that it could neither fully retain nor completely release. By 1900, too, the United States confronted the imminent ascendancy of the very political coalition that the intervention had been designed to thwart.

The outcome of the 1900 elections served to underscore the perils attending independence. By failing to elect the candidates approved by the

United States, Cubans had demonstrated themselves ill-suited to assume the responsibility of self-government. Cubans could simply not be trusted, United States officials contended, to elect the "best men." Some conclusions, hence, seemed in order. The elections revealed Cubans to lack political maturity. They were swayed easily by emotions and led readily by demagogues. All of which pointed to one last moral: Cubans were still not ready for independence. And a corollary: the United States could not release Cuba into the family of nations so palpably ill-prepared to discharge the responsibilities of sovereignty. One member of the McKinley cabinet asserted bluntly that the United States did not intend to expel Spain only to turn the island "over to the insurgents or to any other particular class or faction." The United States purpose in Cuba was not to be guided by the political issue of independence but by the moral necessity to establish a "stable government for and by all the people." "When the Spanish-American war was declared," Wood argued, "the United States took a step forward, and assumed a position as protector of the interests of Cuba. It became responsible for the welfare of the people, politically, mentally and morally." This was the position of the administration in Washington. "This nation has assumed before the world a grave responsibility for the future of good government in Cuba," President McKinley proclaimed in his 1899 message to Congress. He continued:

> We have accepted a trust the fulfillment of which calls for the sternest integrity of purpose and the exercise of the highest wisdom. The new Cuba yet to arise from the ashes of the past must be bound to us by ties of singular intimacy and strength if its enduring welfare is to be assured. . . . Our mission, to accomplish when we took up the wager of battle, is not to be fulfilled by turning adrift any loosely framed commonwealth to face the vicissitudes which too often attend weaker states.

The McKinley administration faced a policy dilemma: how to respect the congressional resolution without relenting to Cuban demands—when both called for independence. If the principle of the Teller Amendment could not be repudiated, its premises would be refuted. It was first necessary to devise a substitute for immediate independence that did not foreclose ultimate annexation, an arrangement, too, that neither defied the purpose of the congressional commitment nor disregarded the policy of the president. Not that Washington abandoned century-old designs on Cuba. Indeed, many in the administration persisted in the belief that an-

nexation remained Cuba's ultimate destiny, if not at the immediate conclusion of the intervention or as the consummation of the occupation,
then as the inevitable culmination of a future if still yet unresolved policy
design. Annexation was a probability that could be temporarily postponed
as long as its possibility was not definitively precluded.

Certainly the Teller Amendment had the immediate effect of obstructing annexation either as a deliberate outcome of the war with Spain or as
a direct outgrowth of the occupation of Cuba. But it is untenable to sup-
pose that the United States would suddenly renounce nearly a century of
national policy, one based on the inevitability of the annexation of Cuba,
solely as the result of a self-denying clause adopted by, many felt, an
over-zealous Congress in a moment of well-meaning but ill-placed fervor.
The administration's position was clear: formal annexation was proscribed, but complete independence was preposterous. A way had to be
found to reconcile presidential resolve with the congressional resolution—a way to exercise sovereignty, if not permanently then provision-
ally, a means through which to exercise the substance of sovereignty
without the necessity for the structures of sovereignty.

XI

In early 1901 the United States moved to resolve the dilemma. The "better classes" had shown themselves to be of limited political value. They
had not fared well at the polls, and no amount of United States backing,
it seemed, was adequate for the task of elevating them into power. In
Washington, the administration was coming under increasing political
pressure to comply with the Joint Resolution. In January, Secretary of
War Root outlined the administration's views to General Wood in Cuba.
The occupation was entering its third year, and had become, Root explained, a "burden and annoyance," and was expensive, too—half a
million dollars a month, Root estimated. The administration was prepared, and even anxious, to end the occupation, but not without first
securing guarantees necessary to United States interests. Root sought to
give United States hegemony legal form, something in the way of binding
political relations based on the Monroe Doctrine.

In January 1901 Root proposed to Secretary of State John Hay four
provisions he deemed essential to United States interests. First, that "in
transferring the control of Cuba to the Government established under the

new constitution the United States reserves and retains the right of intervention for the preservation of Cuban independence and the maintenance
of a stable Government adequately protecting life, property and individual liberty.'' Second, that ''no Government organized under the constitution shall be deemed to have authority to enter into any treaty or engagement with any foreign power which may tend to impair or interfere
with the independence of Cuba.'' Root also insisted that to perform ''such
duties as may devolve upon her under the foregoing provisions and for
her own defense,'' the United States ''may acquire and hold the title to
land, and maintain naval stations at certain specified points.'' Lastly, that
''all the acts of the Military Government, and all rights acquired there-
under, shall be valid and be maintained and protected.'' Root entrusted a
draft of the proposed relations to Senator Orville H. Platt. During a meeting of the Republican senators to prepare the final language of the proposed legislation, two additional clauses were attached. One prescribed
continuation of sanitary improvements undertaken by the military government. The other prohibited the Cuban government from contracting a
debt for which the ordinary public revenues were inadequate. Together,
the provisions became known as the Platt Amendment, enacted by Congress in 1901.

In its essential features, the Platt Amendment addressed the central
elements of United States objectives in Cuba as determined over the course
of the nineteenth century, something of an adequate if imperfect substitute for annexation. It served to transform the substance of Cuban sovereignty into an extension of the United States national system. The restrictions imposed upon the conduct of foreign relations, specifically the
denial of treaty authority and debt restrictions, as well as the prohibition
against the cession of national territory, were designed to minimize the
possibility of Cuban international entanglements.

But restraints on Cuban foreign relations did not satisfy all United States
needs. North American authorities could not contemplate Cuban independence without a presentiment of disaster. Self-government promised misgovernment, officials warned freely, and the mismanagement of domestic
and foreign affairs could have potentially calamitous repercussions on
United States interests. If the United States would not permit the sovereignty of government to be challenged from abroad, it could not allow
the solvency of government to be threatened from within. Elections had
underscored the uncertainty if not inefficacy of democratic process. If
extenuating circumstances prohibited immediate annexation, political

considerations precluded complete independence. The Platt Amendment rested on the central if not fully stated premise that the principal danger to United States interests in Cuba originated with Cubans themselves, or at least those Cubans with antecedents in the revolution. Whether in the direction of foreign affairs, or in the management of public funds, or in the conduct or national politics, government by Cubans remained always a dubious proposition, an enterprise as unsound in its premises as it was uncertain in its permanence. Root was blunt. The proposed relations represented "the extreme limit of this country's indulgence in the matter of the independence of Cuba." Simply stated, the political leadership emerging in Havana did not inspire confidence in the United States. "The character of the ruling class," Root acknowledged, "is such that their administration of the affairs of the island will require the restraining influence of the United States government for many years to come, even if it does not eventually become necessary for this government to take direct and absolute control of Cuban affairs." "The welfare of the Cuban people," Senator Albert Beveridge warned, "was still open to attack from another enemy and at their weakest point. That point was within and that enemy themselves. . . . If it is our business to see that the Cubans are not destroyed by any foreign power, is it not our duty to see that they are not destroyed by themselves?" Senator Platt agreed. U.S. policy required "a stable republican government which the United States will assist in maintaining against foreign aggression or domestic disorder." He added: "We cannot permit disturbances there which threaten the overthrow of the government. We cannot tolerate a condition in which life and property shall be insecure."

News of the proposed relations stunned Cubans and precipitated protests and anti-U.S. demonstrations across the island. On the evening of March 2, a torchlight demonstration converged on Wood's residence to protest the Platt Amendment. In Santiago, speakers at public rallies alluded to the necessity of returning to arms to redeem national honor. Across the island, municipalities, civic associations, and veterans' organizations cabled protests to Havana.

The administration in Washington stood firm. There would be neither compromise nor concession to Cuban independence, Washington warned, until Cubans ratified the proposed relations. Either the Cubans would accept the Platt Amendment or there would be no end to the military occupation. Root was adamant. "No constitution can be put into effect in Cuba," Root warned, "and no government can be elected under it, no electoral law by the Convention can be put into effect, and no election held under it until they have acted upon this question of relations in conformity with this act of Congress." Continued resistance to United States demands, Root threatened, would have dire consequences. "If they continue to exhibit ingratitude and entire lack of appreciation of the expenditure of blood and treasure of the United States to secure their freedom from Spain, the public sentiment of this country will be more unfavorable to them." In early June the Cuban constituent convention acquiesced and by a margin of one vote accepted the Platt Amendment as an appendix to the new 1901 constitution. Two years later, the Platt Amendment was incorporated into the Permanent Treaty of 1903.

8

The Structure of the Republic

I

The war ended in 1898, and no part of Cuba had escaped its ravages: in the eastern mountains, on the central plains, in the western valleys—the scenes of devastation were everywhere the same. It had been a brutal war, a war of excesses, at every turn disruptive and destructive, a war in which the opposing armies seemed determined more to punish the land than each other. For almost four years, contending forces had laid siege to the largesse of the land, preying upon the bounty of its resources, practicing pillage as the normal method of warfare.

And when it was over, in 1898, the toll of Cuban independence had reached frightful proportions. The price of independence was incalculable. The war may have delivered redemption, but it had also brought ruin. Cuba had been reduced to a wasteland. Travelers to the island that first autumn of peace were appalled by the extent of destruction. "I saw neither a house, nor a cow, calf, sheep or goat, and only two chickens," one journalist reported from Camagüey. "The country is wilderness," a "desert," another correspondent wrote from Las Villas. "The desolation is scarcely conceivable," General James H. Wilson wrote of Matanzas and Las Villas provinces. He went on:

> It has been shown that substantially every small farmhouse in the two provinces, as well as a large number of the sugar mills, were burned; that the growing crops were destroyed, the agricultural implements broken up, the poultry nearly all killed, and the farming population driven into the fortified towns and villages to starve. From the foregoing it will be perceived that nearly all the instruments of production in the hands of the poorer people have been swept away, and that production, outside of that carried on by the larger and richer sugar 'ingenios,' had entirely ceased. The people were rapidly dying of starvation and disease.

189

The people had dispersed, some to the cities, some to the interior, and some to no one knew where. The reconcentration policy aimed to depopulate the countryside, and almost succeeded. Hundreds of thousands of Cubans had perished, and only a fortunate few could comprehend that they had survived a population disaster of frightful proportions. A population of nearly 1.8 million had declined to less than a million and a half. In 1899, Cuba had the highest proportion of widowed to married persons in the Western Hemisphere: 35 per hundred. There was one widower for every five husbands and one widow for every two wives. The proportion of widows was highest among women of color: nearly three widows for every five wives and in Havana four widows for every five wives.

It was not only that hundreds of thousands died. Tens of thousands were never born. Births between 1890 and 1893 had increased steadily, averaging 32,000 births per year. But the annual number of births through the war years plummeted to just over 17,000. If the prewar birth rate had not been interrupted, an estimated 60,000 more children would have been born between 1895 and 1898. The combined effects of high child mortality and low fertility produced a skewed population structure in postwar Cuba: children under five made up only 8.3 percent of the total population. No country in the world for which data was available in 1899 had so small a proportion of children under five. The total loss of children dead and unborn was estimated conservatively at 100,000.

The toll of the war was everywhere visible, and was everywhere bleak. Houses throughout the interior were the same: roofless and in ruins, uninhabited and untended. Roads, bridges, and railroads had fallen into disuse and disrepair. Mines had closed. Commerce was at a standstill and manufacturing suspended. Where towns and villages once stood, there remained only scattered piles of rubble and charred wood. What were previously lush farming zones were now scenes of scorched earth and singed brush. Livestock had been scattered, or slain. Of nearly three million head of cattle grazing on Cuban pastures in 1895, less than 200,000 remained in 1898. In some districts the loss of breeding stock and work cattle was almost complete. Horned cattle in Matanzas declined from approximately 300,000 to 9,000 and in Las Villas from 967,000 to 66,000. The 50,000 cattle in Matanzas and the 150,000 in Las Villas were reduced to 5,500 and 15,000 respectively.

Agriculture was in desperate crisis in an economy predominantly agricultural. The fields were blighted, the pastures were barren, and the fruit trees bare. Of the 1.4 millions acres under cultivation in 1895, only some

TABLE 22.   Cuban Population, Ages 0–4 (1899, 1907)

Province	1899	1907	Percentage Increase
Pinar del Río	15,814	47,047	197.5
Havana	30,897	74,379	140.7
Matanzas	16,068	38,421	139.1
Las Villas	26,101	79,763	205.5
Camagüey	9,842	18,704	90.0
Oriente	32,156	84,338	162.2
Total	130,878	342,652	155.8

Source: United States War Department, *Informe sobre el censo de Cuba, 1899* (Washington, D.C. 1900) and United States War Department, *Censo de la republica de Cuba, 1907* (Washington, D.C., 1908).

900,000 acres returned to production after the war. Over 100,000 small farms, 3,000 livestock ranches, 800 tobacco *vegas,* and 700 coffee *fincas* were destroyed during the conflict.

After 1898, Cubans made an effort to return to the ordinary and the normal, to resume their lives at the point of interruption in 1895. Peace restored hope, and hope was expressed immediately in rising fertility levels. Men were released from the army and returned home. Families were reunited. Political prisoners were freed, émigrés returned, and peasants were discharged from reconcentration camps. Birth rates soared. Between 1899 and 1907, the population under five years of age increased from 8 percent of the total to almost 20 percent. The postwar baby boom affected all of Cuba (Table 22).

II

But all was not right in postwar Cuba. The military occupation ended on May 20, 1902, with an appropriate balance of ceremony and celebration, and much was made of the successful transition from colony to republic. It was not entirely clear, however, whether this notion of transition had much relevance to the Cuban social reality. Just how much was new was difficult to ascertain. Some things had changed, of course, but much had not. And therein lay the problem, for much of what had not changed was precisely what Cubans had set out to change in 1895. The U.S. military occupation deprived Cubans of the opportunity to reorder the economy and reorganize property relations to accommodate their own interests. The means through which to redistribute loyalist property and assets, of both *peninsular* and creoles alike, remained beyond the reach of the victorious Cubans. Expropriations would have offered Cubans the opportunity to recover lost property, expand control over production, and establish claim over the economy. Indeed, this was a covenant transacted earlier in the name of *Cuba Libre,* formally proclaimed and solemnly promised in the land reform decree of 1896. The U.S. intervention made this impossible. On the contrary, the presence of the United States, first directly by way of the military occupation and later implicity through the Platt Amendment, served to guarantee existing property relations and make a redistribution of property all but impossible. Cubans who had earlier lost property through the punitive Spanish expropriation decrees were denied the opportunity of recovering their assets through similar measures against their defeated adversaries.

Many contradictions of colonial society remained unresolved, giving renewed vitality to the historic sources of Cuban discontent. Cubans had been summoned to dramatic action but failed to produce dramatic change. The Platt Amendment complicated matters, for henceforth Cuban attempts to eliminate the continuing inequities of the colonial system would involve confrontation with the United States. The real significance and the lasting effects of the intervention passed virtually unnoticed. The United States had not only rescued and revived the moribund colonial order, it had also assumed responsibility for its protection and preservation. In all its essential features and in its principal functions, the republic gave new political form to the socio-economic infrastructure of the old colony. When independence finally arrived, in 1902, Cubans discovered that old grievances had assumed new forms. Cubans had achieved self-government without self-determination and independence without sovereignty.

There were also new grievances. Exactly how Cubans were beneficiary to their success remained unclear. In the weeks and months following the peace, across the bleak and devastated countryside, thousands of impoverished veterans wandered about, asking themselves "What have we gained by this war?" The Cuban war had been long and ruinous. It succeeded as a means, but failed in its ends. Peace was an anticlimax, for separation from Spain did not signify independence for Cuba. Foreigners again ruled Cuba, again in the name of Cubans, but, as before, for their own ends.

Cuba entered nationhood with its social order in complete disarray and its class structure totally skewed. The first permanent casualty of the war was the creole bourgeoisie. Disintegration began at the top, and it began early. Planters failed to survive the transition from colony to republic as the dominant social class. By the end of the nineteenth century, the colonial bourgeoisie was everywhere on the defensive and in disarray. The war sealed the planters' fate. This was a process so sweeping in scope and enduring in effect as to constitute effectively nothing less than the overthrow of the dominant social class. The war had set the stage for the demise of the planter bourgeoisie, and this was arguably one of the principal social consequences of the revolution.

In fact, the planter class had entered the war in crisis. The prospect of privileged access to U.S. markets as a result of the Fostor-Cánovas agreement had stimulated the expansion of sugar production and modernization of the mills. But most of all it encouraged a new round of indebtedness as planters rushed to borrow in response to what appeared to be unlimited opportunities for prosperity. The lapse of reciprocal trade agreements between the United States and Spain in 1894 found Cuban sugar planters with record crops but without adequate markets. A very much overextended planter class had reached the historic one-million-ton mark in 1894, only to lose access to the only market with the capacity to absorb the expanded production.

The outbreak of the war a year later dealt planters one more blow. Most did not survive. Everywhere sugar production was in disarray. The rich provinces of Havana and Matanzas were each cultivating fully less than one-half of the area in 1899 than in the year before the war. Of the 70 sugar mills in Pinar del Río, only 7 survived the war. Sugar mills across the island ceased operations during the war, and most did not resume production afterwards. In all, of the 1,100 sugar mills in operation in 1894, only 207 survived the war.

Property owners emerged from the war hopelessly in debt, and at the brink of ruin. The total urban indebtedness of some $100 million represented more than three-quarters of the declared property value of $139 million. The value of rural property *(fincas rústicas)* was set at some $185 million, on which rested a mortgage indebtedness of $107 million. Planters had borrowed at inflated interest rates, with loans at 20 to 40 percent interest not at all uncommon. After 1898 planters were anxious to revive the estates and resume production, but lacked capital or affordable credit. Warehouses had been demolished and machinery destroyed.

Private narrow-gauge railroads used for hauling cane were in disrepair, as were locomotives and cane cars. Repair and machine shops had been sacked and plundered during the war, and spare parts were difficult if not impossible to obtain. In other instances, mills survived the war more or less intact, but the destruction of cane fields and the dispersal of labor precluded the resumption of production. Without cane, the factories remained idle, and without funds, the fields stood barren.

Capital requirements in postwar Cuba were extraordinarily high. The war had taken a devastating toll, and the cost of reconstruction was incalculable. Virtually all machinery and equipment had to be imported, adding the cost of shipping to the cost of manufacture. Livestock was replaced from abroad. Large inventories were required in the absence of a network of industrial supplies. These needs, in turn, raised the requirement for working capital in addition to fixed capital.

The disruption of production at a time of indebtedness, and indebtedness at a time of the destruction of property, announced the demise of the Cuban planter class. North American rule confirmed what planters had always known: they needed a political position to defend their interests. And they were still without power in 1898, when it mattered most. That the United States seized control of government, appropriated the means of policy formulation and enforcement, controlled the collection of revenues, and determined the disbursement of public funds meant that the only source capable of providing the financial support sufficient to save the planter class was beyond the control of the creole bourgeoisie. The state was separated from the dominant social class. Without favorable state policy in any number of forms, including extended moratorium on debt collection, tax exemptions, cash subsidies, and long-term low-interest loans, the Cuban planter class moved ineluctably toward extinction.

These conditions worked their way down the social scale. Conditions that were difficult for planters were disastrous for peasants. Cuba's peasants had been transformed into partisans in the insurgent camps or made prisoners in reconcentration camps. In either case, they lost their homes, crops, livestock, and tools. When the war ended, it was not quite clear how, or where, they would begin again. Without agrarian reform there was no prospect of raising the standards of living of tens of thousands of rural families. The war had reduced the number of farms to some 60,107 *fincas*. Of the total 900,000 acres back in production in 1899, half was worked by renters. A destructive war had been followed by a difficult peace. Between 1898 and 1900, *fincas* were changing hands at the rate of some 3700 a year. Small farmers had neither the capital to revive agriculture nor the credit to return to work, and lacked collateral to obtain either. Families headed by widows often lacked even sufficient labor power to scratch subsistence out of the soil.

Across the island, the reports were the same: farmers in distress, peasants in despair, and agriculture in depression. The mayor of San Cristobal, Pinar del Río, complained that the municipality had "only 5 estates and 33 small farms out of 206 in ante bellum days. The owners are exceedingly poor. Their need is oxen and agricultural implements." Of the 395 *fincas* in Placetas, Santa Clara, 391 were destroyed during the war. Of the 219 farms in Ceiba del Agua, Havana, 171 were abandoned. Only 50 of the 466 farms in San Nicolás, Havana, were in production in 1899, while 111 of 175 *fincas* in Rodas, Santa Clara, were abandoned. All of the 169 *fincas* in Bauta, Havana, were destroyed. "No assistance has been received in this district from the Government," protested the mayor of Consolación del Sur, Pinar del Río, "not in work animals or in agricultural equipment. . . . There are 693 farms in this district, 630 of which were destroyed during the war."

Agricultural production, the source of livelihood and the means of subsistence for a population largely rural, was in crisis. It was not only a matter of restoring the land to production but reviving production to retain the land. The prospects for either were not good.

III

The beneficiaries of North American rule were North Americans. They descended upon the war-ravaged island by the shipload, a new generation of carpetbaggers: land-dealers and speculators of all types, agents for corporations and small homesteaders, all in search of opportunity.

During the occupation, and continuing through the early years of the republic, U.S. control over sugar production expanded. In 1899, the Cuban-American Sugar Company acquired possession of the seven-thousand-acre Tinguaro estate in Matanzas and the Merceditas mill in Pinar del Río. In that same year, Cuban-American organized the Chaparra sugar mill around 70,000 acres of land in northern Oriente. In 1899 a group of North American investors acquired the old Manuel Rionda estate of Tuinucú and purchased the 80,000-acre Francisco estate in southern Camagüey province. At about this time, too, the Constancia estate in Las Villas passed wholly under North American control. The American Sugar Company acquired several damaged estates in Matanzas. In 1901, the United Fruit Company purchased some 200,000 acres in Banes on the north Oriente coast, a vast tract of land that included scores of partially destroyed and defunct estates. That same year, the Nipe Bay Company, a United Fruit subsidiary, acquired title to 40,000 acres of sugar land near Puerto Padre. Between 1900 and 1901, the Cuba Company completed the construction of the Cuban Railway through the eastern end of the island, acquiring in the process some 50,000 acres of land for rail stations, construction sites, towns and depots, and a right-of-way 350 miles long. The Cuban Central Railway purchased the Caracas estate in Cienfuegos from Tomás Terry. During these years, the Cape Cruz Company acquired a total of 16,000 acres near Manzanillo. Joseph Rigney, an investment partner with United Fruit, acquired the estates San Juan, San Joaquín, and Teresa, all in the region around Manzanillo.

United States land speculators and real estate companies acquired title to vast tracts of land and ownership of countless estates. Most were similar to the Taco Bay Commercial Land Company. Incorporated in Boston, the syndicate bought vast expanses of land in Oriente. In 1904, the Taco Bay Company purchased the Juraguá plantation. Consisting of some 20,000 acres of banana, coconut, and sugar land west of Baracoa, the Juraguá estate had been one of the most successful plantations in Oriente. Juraguá had been devastated by the war and never returned to prewar production levels. Typical of other victims of the insurrection, the owners of Juraguá were heavily in debt and lacked the capital to restore the damaged estate to production.

Land companies from the United States multiplied during the early years of the republic and accounted for a large share of North American purchases. One New York company purchased 180,000 acres along the banks of the Cauto River in Oriente. Another syndicate acquired 50,000 acres on Nipe Bay for the purpose of establishing a winter resort. Illinois Cuban Land Company acquired Paso Estancia, a 10,000-acre estate in central Oriente. The Herradura Land Company acquired title to some 23,000 acres of land in Pinar del Río. The Cuban Land Company brought up defunct estates in Las Villas, Matanzas, Pinar del Río, and Camagüey. The Carlson Investment Company of Los Angeles acquired 150,000 acres in the region of Nuevitas Bay. The Cuba Colonial Company, incorporated in Chicago, acquired some 40,000 acres in Camagüey. The Canada

Land and Fruit Company purchased some 23,000 acres of land in Las Villas and the Isle of Pines. The Cuban Land and Steamship Company, incorporated in New Jersey, purchased 55,000 acres in the vicinity of Nuevitas. The Cuban Development Company, based in Detroit, purchased the 12,500-acre Vista Alegre estate in the region of Las Tunas in Oriente. The Cuban Agricultural and Development Company of Pittsburgh purchased over 135,000 acres of land around the region of Guantánamo. The Cuban Realty Company from New Jersey purchased 25,000 acres in western Oriente.

By 1905, some 13,000 North Americans had acquired title to land in Cuba, and these purchases had passed over the $50 million mark. A estimated 60 percent of all rural property in Cuba was owned by individuals and corporations from the United States, with another 15 percent controlled by resident Spaniards. Cubans were reduced to ownership of 25 percent of the land. Irene Wright wrote from Cuba in 1910, "I have heard their [foreigners'] real estate holdings estimated, by an office whose official business it is to know conditions here, at 90 or 95 percent of the whole. Foreigners (Americans and Europeans of many nationalities) are the owners of the far-reaching sugar fields, of the tobacco *vegas* of account, of the bristling ruby pineapple fields, of the scattered green citrus fruit orchards."

Cubans faced exclusion from more than the land. In a capital-starved and credit-hungry economy, they were all but overwhelmed by foreign capital in almost every sector. Foreigners expanded control over tobacco production and cigar manufacturing. In 1899, the newly organized Havana Commercial Company, under New York promoter H. B. Hollins, acquired twelve cigar factories, one cigarette factory, and scores of tobacco *vegas*. Even before the military occupation came to an end, the newly organized Tobacco Trust in the United States had established control of some 90 percent of the export trade of Havana cigars. By 1906, the Tobacco Trust acquired possession of some 225,000 acres of tobacco land in Pinar del Río.

Foreigners also controlled mining. The iron mines of Oriente were almost entirely owned by U.S. investors. During the occupation, the military government issued some 218 mining concessions, largely to North Americans. The Juraguá Iron Company controlled more than twenty separate claims around the region of Caney. The Spanish-American Iron Company, a subsidiary of Pennsylvania Steel, obtained claims to Oriente iron mines. Smaller enterprises included the Sigua Iron Company (Pennsylvania Steel and Bethlehem), Cuban Steel Ore Company (Pennsylvania Steel), and Ponupo Manganese Company (Bethlehem). Copper mines around Cobre were owned by British and United States investors.

The railroad system was dominated almost wholly by foreign capital. The United Railways Company, the Western Railway Company, the Matanzas Railway Company, and Marianao Railway were controlled by the British. The Cárdenas-Júcaro and Matanzas-Sabanilla systems were owned by Spaniards. The Cuban Eastern Railway and the Guantánamo Railroad were controlled by U.S. investors. The Havana Electric Railway Company, a New Jersey Corporation, established control of the capital's electric transportation system during the occupation.

Foreign capital controlled utility concessions as well. The Spanish American Light and Power Company of New York provided gas service to major Cuban cities. Electricity was controlled by two American corporations, the Havana Central and Havana Electric. United States contracting companies established branch offices in Havana and competed for government projects. The Havana Subway Company had sole right to install underground cables and electrical wires. United States capital controlled telephone service, the Cardenas City Water Works, and the Cardenas Railway and Terminal Company.

Banking remained under the control of Spanish capital, with England, France, and the United States participating. The two principal Spanish banking institutions, the Banco Español and the Banco de Comercio, dominated island finances. The Banco Nacional de Cuba and the Banco de La Habana were formed with United States capital. North American capital held some $2.5 million in mortgages.

Foreign capital dominated the Cuban economy. Total British investments reached some $60 million, largely in railways, port works, sugar, and communications. The French share accounted for an estimated $12 million, principally in railroads, banks, and sugar. German investments reached some $4.5 million, divided between factories and utilities. But it was United States capital that overwhelmed the local economy. By 1911, the total United States capital stake in Cuba passed over $200 million, distributed as shown in Table 23.

The reciprocity treaty of 1903, whereby Cuba received lower tariff rates for select exports in return for reducing duties on certain U.S. imports, delivered still another setback to Cuban enterprise and local entrepreneurs. Preferential access to U.S. markets for Cuban agricultural products served at once to encourage Cuban dependency on sugar and increase

TABLE 23. Distribution of U.S. Capital in Cuba

Sugar	$50,000,000
Other Land	15,000,000
Agriculture	10,000,000
Railway	25,000,000
Mines, Mercantile, and Manufacture	25,000,000
Shipping	5,000,000
Banking	5,000,000
Mortgages and credits	20,000,000
Public utilities	20,000,000
Public debt	30,000,000

Source: Leland Hamilton Jenks, *Our Cuban Colony* (New York, 1928), 164–65.

foreign control over this vital sector of the economy. Reciprocity also discouraged economic diversification by promoting the consolidation of land and the concentration of ownership.

The effects of reciprocity were not, however, confined to agriculture. The reduction of Cuban duties, in some instances as high as 40 percent, opened the island to United States imports on highly favorable items. The privileged access granted to United States manufactures created a wholly inauspicious investment climate for Cuban capital. Even before 1903, the dearth of local capital and depressed economic conditions combined to prevent development of national industry. After the reciprocity treaty, prospects for local enterprise diminished further. Undercapitalized small-scale industry and local manufacture were simply too weak to compete on the basis of prices and quality. The few owners of capital in Cuba had little inducement to invest in industry in the absence of a strong and protected market. U.S. goods quickly saturated the Cuban market.

IV

For members of the creole petite bourgeoisie who had enrolled in the separatist cause the transition from colony to republic was especially difficult. They faced insurmountable obstacles in finding a place in the postwar economy. They were bested, once again, by Spaniards. *Peninsulares*

TABLE 24. Male Occupational Groupings by Nationality and Race (1899)
(15 years and older)

	Total Males	White Foreign Males	Percent	White Cuban Males	Percent	Colored Males	Percent
Agriculture, fisheries and mining	255,724	30,893	12.1	140,569	55.0	84,262	32.9
Trade and transportation	76,289	41,697	54.6	27,482	36.1	7,110	9.3
Industry and manufacturing	77,979	14,263	18.3	33,146	42.5	30.570	39.2
Professions	7,076	1,932	27.3	4,675	66.1	479	6.6
Domestic services	87,870	21,339	24.3	34,654	39.4	31,877	36.3
Without gainful employment	17,178	2,482	14.4	11,129	64.8	3,567	20.8

Source: United States War Department, *Informe sobre el censo de Cuba, 1899* (Washington, D.C., 1900), 448–49.

not only remained in Cuba after the war but they increased their numbers and continued to expand their control over key sectors of the economy. The Spanish population in 1899 approached some 130,000 out of a total population of 1.6 million residents. There were vastly more Spanish men (108,000) than Spanish women (22,000), with the largest single concentration of *peninsulares* located in the province of Havana (62,000) and the majority of these in the capital city (47,000).

The census data of 1899 reveals a striking Spanish presence in postwar Cuba. The total population of males fifteen years of age and older numbered at some 523,000, 20 percent of which were white foreign-born. Some 252,000 white males were identified as Cuban *(nativos)*. Another 158,000 residents were identified as men of color, without mention of nationality, but presumably largely Afro-Cuban. Similarly, 113,000 men were identified as white foreigners, also without reference to nationality, but presumably mostly Spaniards. The distribution of male workers fifteen years of age and over reveals a significant Spanish presence in almost every occupational sector, particularly commerce, manufacturing, and the professions. (See Table 24.)

Spaniards were strategically located in the Cuban economy, most noticeably in commerce, retail trade, and industry. More than half the merchants on the island were Spaniards. Through the early decades of the republic, Spaniards persisted as a preponderant force in retail commerce. As late as 1927, some two-thirds of all general stores *(bodegas)* were foreign-owned, mostly by Spaniards. *Peninsular* prominence in retail commerce contributed, in turn, to Spanish preponderance in sales positions: two-thirds of all sales personnel were Spaniards.

Spanish dominance remained fairly constant through the early years of the republic, and in some instances increased slightly. The 1907 census listed some 22,000 Cuban merchants as against 24,000 Spaniards. Spanish personnel in sales neared 21,000 while Cubans numbered 10,000. Spaniards were also strongly represented in the professions, education, the press, and publishing. The Catholic church remained substantially Spanish. The census of 1907 listed some 106 Cubans and 202 Spaniards in the clergy. By 1919, the number of Cubans in the clergy had risen to 156 while the *peninsular* priests had increased to 426. The metropolis had relinquished political power, but its citizens had not relinquished their place in the economy.

V

The circumstances of war and the conditions of peace also caused havoc within the Cuban working class, for many of the same reasons. For the thousands of urban workers who served the patriotic cause in exile as well as the thousands of rural laborers who defended *Cuba Libre* in arms, the dream of *patria* turned quickly into a nightmare. The Cuban proletariat discovered that, for them, the transition from colony to republic meant a descent into destitution. They left the service of *Cuba Libre* only to discover they had been displaced from the farms and replaced in the factories, and were out of place everywhere else. Certainly, depressed economic conditions made the transition to peace difficult for Cuban workers. The problem, however, was not solely a depressed postwar economy. Rather, the problem was compounded by competition from cheap labor in the form of immigration.

Outsiders had long rivaled Cubans for control over the labor market. At one time the source had been principally African slaves, followed by contract labor from China. Spaniards also displaced Cubans, as did immigrants from the Middle East, Europe, the United States, and Latin

America. Immigration, particularly in the latter half of the nineteenth century, served to depress wages and create conditions in which Cuban wage workers could not compete.

The trend of immigration did not substantially change after 1898. On the contrary, new waves of immigrants continued to augment the ranks of foreign workers in Cuba. For the three-year period ending in 1901, the total immigration into Cuba reached some 70,000, of whom 55,000 were Spaniards, 2,000 Chinese, and the balance distributed among Europeans, North Americans, and Latin Americans. In 1901 alone some 23,000 immigrants arrived in Cuba, including 17,000 Spaniards, 1,000 Chinese, 1,000 Puerto Ricans, and 1,000 North Americans.

Immigration continued to increase through the early decades of the republic. Between 1902 and 1907, some 155,000 immigrants came to Cuba, of whom 98,000 were classified as unskilled. Between 1912 and 1916, another 182,300 immigrants arrived, 85 percent of whom were males and 66 percent illiterate. In total, some 700,000 immigrated to Cuba between 1902 and 1919.

It was Spaniards, again, who arrived in overwhelming numbers. Young, ambitious, impoverished, and driven, Spaniards arrived in Cuba disposed to work hard at almost any job, at almost any wage, for almost any hours. They were in the main Galicians, Asturians, and Canary Islanders, and they overwhelmed the local labor market. While in much of Latin America the *peninsular* population had been expelled after independence, in Cuba the *peninsular* population expanded, significantly and steadily. *Peninsulares* arrived in waves, seemingly inexhaustible and irreversible: over 400,000 between the years 1902 and 1916. Many were illiterate, and many arrived with less than thirty pesos on their person.

Not all Spaniards remained in Cuba. Migration tended to flow in both directions, in varying degrees, year to year. But arrivals always outnumbered departures, often by a margin of two to one. Almost 40 percent of the half a million Spaniards who emigrated to Cuba during the first two decades of the republic remained on the island.

That Spaniards in great numbers remained in Cuba after the war, and that they in large part retained control of key sectors of trade and commerce, did much to encourage *peninsular* immigration. Ties of kin and culture continued to favor Spanish workers among Spanish employers. But it was also true that employers in Cuba of all nationalities, most of whom were non-Cuban, preferred Spaniards as workers. One U.S. Department of Labor report indicated as early as 1902 that ''all [employers] agree that for manual labor the Spaniard excels the native Cuban. This is true of factory as well as field occupation.'' The report continued:

> The Spanish immigrants are reported to be steady, industrious, and reg-
> ular workers. Some American employers consider them the best un-
> skilled laborers of Europe. They are physically robust and not addicted
> to many of the vices of laborers of the same class in the United States.
> They are more docile than the latter, and fully as intelligent for many
> kinds of service. Unlike the Cuban, they are frugal, seldom gamble,
> and often allow their savings to accumulate in the hands of their em-
> ployers.

The steady influx of immigrant workers arriving in Cuba during these years competed with Cuban labor in all occupations—in the fields and factories, in mines and manufacturing, as artisans and apprentices. Some 30 percent of all immigrants remained in the city of Havana, creating a highly congested urban labor market. Spanish men soon displaced Cuban women in domestic services. In Oriente, the iron mines employed some 4,000 workers, most of whom were Spanish. Foreigners accounted for more than half of the mercantile work force, sailors, and miners, and for over one-quarter of bakers, tailors, blacksmiths, machinists, and cabinet-makers. Spaniards dominated the carting business. Foreigners filled the jobs created by the expansion of railroad construction during the early 1900s. Sixty percent of the 11,000 workers employed by the Central Railway in 1902 were Spaniards. The majority of foremen and engineers in the railroads were North American and British. United States construction companies contracted North American workers; bricklayers, for example, were hired in the United States. During the occupation, plumbers contracted in the United States organized a local trade union in Havana, and proceeded to exclude Cubans.

These patterns continued into the early years of the republic. The national census of 1907 suggests that the share of Cuban artisans and job-workers had not materially improved over foreign labor. As Table 25 indicates, some 20 to 30 percent of shoemakers, tailors, bakers, mechanics, machinists, day laborers, carpenters, potters, boilermakers, and masons were foreigners. Some 50 percent of sailors, railroad workers, servants, and charcoal vendors were non-Cuban, and 96 percent of all miners were foreigners.

When foreign capital opened the new canefields in Camagüey and Oriente after 1910, there was a new influx of immigrant labor in the form

TABLE 25.   Select·Occupations in Cuba (1907)

	Total	Cuban	Foreign
Day laborers	41,767	30,319	11,448
Servants	15,934	8,389	7,445
Carpenters	21,420	16,510	4,910
Sailors	6,446	2,935	3,510
Masons/bricklayers	12,161	9,321	2,840
Cigarworkers	24,161	22,085	2,076
Mechanics	7,917	6,227	1,690
Miners	1,662	71	1,591
Bakers	6,161	4,848	1,313
Charcoal venders	2,511	1,209	1,302
Shoemakers	6,829	5,551	1,278
Tailors	5,095	3,841	1,254
Barbers	5,011	4,324	687
Railroad workers	948	428	520
Stonecutters	715	259	456
Machinists	1,498	1,067	431
Boilermakers	888	606	282
Potters	555	421	134
Apprentices	1,130	1,104	24

Source: United States Department of War, *Censo de la república de Cuba, 1907*
(Washington, D.C. 1908), 572–74.

of cheap contract labor from Haiti and Jamaica. West Indian workers
arrived in increasing numbers: 4,000 in 1915, 12,000 in 1916, 18,000 in
1917, 20,000 in 1918, and 34,000 in 1919.

These conditions gave a distinctive character to the Cuban working
class during the early republic. The struggle to redeem the nation had
hardly ended when a new one to recover the national workplace began.
Unemployment, underemployment, and depressed wages became the central
features of the Cuban labor market. Local unions in Cienfuegos reported
in 1902 that one-third of their members were without work or working
only part-time. In Matanzas, sugar-mill mechanics and engineers who
previously earned four to five dollars a day during the harvest were earn-

ing one dollar a day. Cane cutters who earlier made a dollar a day were working for thirty-six cents.

The stirrings of Cuban workers in the early twentieth century were new forms of old discontents, grievances with antecedents in the nineteenth century. Indeed, the issues that drove Cuban labor to the picket lines in the republic were not unlike the ones that had propelled workers to the battle lines in the colony. Workers had sacrificed selflessly and unstintingly for *Cuba Libre,* only to find the republic to be the old colonial social system with a new political carapace.

Labor shared the fate of the separatist coalition in which it played such a decisive part. The circumstances that perpetuated colonial property relations also preserved colonial class relationships. Workers were divided by trade, nationality, and culture. Wages were depressed by immigration. Workers in Cuba remained weak as a class and Cubans were weak within that class. These were different facets of the same phenomenon, namely the incomplete triumph of nationality. Everywhere Cubans encountered obstacles to their integration into the republic they had sacrificed to create.

Of the tens of thousands of immigrants who arrived in Cuba during these years, many did not remain, working instead only for the duration of a season or the length of a contract. These conditions created havoc in the Cuban labor movement, and served to hinder early efforts at organizing. Cuban labor, hence, remained disorganized, divided, and in disarray. Even the most wholly Cuban-dominated trade, the cigarworkers, where over 90 percent of the labor force was Cuban, was a work force divided against itself, with one sector in Havana in competition with the other in Key West and Tampa.

Because so many foreigners were seasonal workers, they had little incentive to participate in local trade union politics. Because they were needy and without recourse, and because they were aliens and subject to deportation, many were loath to engage in activities which could arouse the wrath of local authorities. It was for all these reasons, and because their labor was cheap, that immigrants were so popular among employers. It was also for these reasons that the Cuban labor movement was set back almost two decades. Because, finally, foreign capital controlled property, production, and commerce, direct attempts by Cuban labor to ameliorate working conditions necessarily involved confrontation with foreign governments.

VI

Within the postwar population of Cuba, women faced a special set of limitations and obstacles. Women enjoyed few civil and political rights. By the terms of the 1901 constitution, women were denied the ballot. Women more than men suffered from a lack of educational opportunity. Illiteracy for males over ten years of age stood at 55 percent, while more than 58 percent of all women this age were illiterate. Greater differences existed between white women and women of color. Whereas 52 percent of all white females were unable to read and write, more than 70 percent of women of color were illiterate. The condition of women in cities was generally better, but the gap between white and colored women remained wide. Almost 62 percent of all women in Matanzas were literate—an average of 82 percent literacy for white Cuban women and 43 percent for women of color. Similarly, in Cienfuegos, with a female literacy rate of 60 percent, literacy for whites was 73 percent and for colored 42 percent. Only in Santiago, where opportunities for people of color had been historically greater, did a majority of Afro-Cuban women know how to read and write. White-colored disparities nevertheless persisted. An average of 63 percent of all women in the city were literate: 85 percent of the native white and 53 percent of those classified as colored.

Few women received formal education, and fewer still completed it. By 1899, only 3,830 women in Cuba had completed higher education, 64 percent of whom resided in the five cities of Havana, Matanzas, Cienfuegos, Puerto Príncipe, and Santiago.

Educational patterns were at once cause and effect of the low-status occupational status of women. In 1899, women made up 10.6 percent of total wage labor over the age of fifteen (66,356 out of 622,330). A majority of all women over the age of fifteen (412,495), more than six times the number of female wage earners, were classified as "without gainful employment"; presumably, these were housewives and older women. Most women worked in domestic services (63 percent), followed by manufacturing (16 percent), agriculture (10 percent), professions (2.4 percent), and trade and transportation (1 percent).

Distinctions existed between white and colored: white Cuban women were over-represented in the professions and in the category "without gainful employment," while women of color were dominant in agriculture and domestic services. Indeed, the difference between white and colored in the category "without gainful employment" is striking—more than a 2 to 1 ratio. This distinction in a category presumed to consist largely of housewives was related to several factors. It was indeed more likely that a greater number of women of color were obliged to earn wages rather than depend on a spouse's earnings. A larger proportion of the female Afro-Cuban population consisted of widows. No doubt, too, the legacy of slavery had contributed to all but eliminating the attitudinal constraints against female employment outside the home. Among whites, aversion to employment of women had served to stigmatize female wage labor. Only 3.6 percent of white women were employed wage earners, as compared with 18 percent of colored women. Stated in slightly different terms, nearly three-quarters of all female wage earners (48,767 out of 66,356) were colored. As might be expected, there were striking disparities in the large number of colored domestics as compared with whites. (See Table 26.)

Female employment patterns at the end of the nineteenth century revealed several general trends. Men prevailed in almost every occupation except dressmaker, seamstress, and teacher. White women tended to concentrate in professional and skilled positions, while women of color predominated in stitchery and low-status jobs. (See Table 27.) Approximately 9 percent of all women (66,356 out of 757,592) were classified as gainfully employed, as compared with 68 percent of all males (555,974 out of 815,205). Female wage earners were more numerous in the cities than in the countryside. The province with the highest proportion of female wage earners was Matanzas at 14 percent (13,575 out of 98,718) and Havana, at 12 percent (24,347 women out of 202,814). The highest proportion of women working in the cities was in Pinar del Río (25 percent), due to large numbers of cigar factories in the provincial capital.

Prostitution continued as another, unrecorded female occupation. At the turn of the century Havana had 338 brothels, most of which were located in the "zone of tolerance" in Old Havana along the waterfront and industrial sectors. At least 2,440 women worked as prostitutes, making prostitution the fourth largest source of female employment in Cuba. A survey of 585 prostitutes in 1904 indicated that most were Cuban-born, and more than half originated from outside the capital. There were also considerable numbers of foreigners, principally Spaniards, Mexicans, and Puerto Ricans. More than 425 of these women were white and over 300 were illiterate. Most had previously worked as servants; a few had been employed as launderers and seamstresses. Most were between 18 and 25.

TABLE 26. Occupational Groupings by Sex and Race (1899)
(15 years and older)

	Total	Males	Percent	Females	Percent	White Cuban Females	Percent	Colored Females	Percent
Agriculture, fisheries and mining	262,123	255,724	97.6	6,399	2.4	504	7.8	5,840	91.2
Trade and transportation	76,936	76,289	99.1	647	0.9	210	32.4	198	30.6
Industry and manufacturing	88,365	77,979	88.3	10,386	11.7	4,300	41.4	5,735	55.2
Professions	8,704	7,076	81.3	1,628	18.7	1,259	77.3	75	4.6
Domestic services	129,960	87,870	67.7	42,090	32.3	6,933	16.4	33,442	79.4
Without gainful employment	429,673	17,178	4.0	412,495	96.0	261,336	63.3	129,331	31.3

Source: United States War Department, *Informe sobre el censo de Cuba, 1899* (Washington, D.C., 1900), 448–49.

TABLE 27.   Selected Occupations by Race and Sex (1899)

	Total Males	Total Females	White Females	Colored Females
Attorneys	1,406	—	—	—
Bankers	219	—	—	—
Cigarworkers	22,589	1,580	1,250	330
Clerks	2,248	—	—	—
Dentists	354	—	—	—
Dressmakers	—	419	168	251
Government	473	—	—	—
Hotel & restaurant	69	4	2	2
Launderers	1,238	20,980	3,425	17,555
Merchants	46,851	414	323	91
Nurses	239	284	214	70
Physicians	1,223	—	—	—
Printers	1,481	18	17	1
Sales personnel	14,533	36	34	2
Seamstresses	—	8,329	3,043	5,286
Servants	18,657	22,807	5,417	17,390
Teachers	1,206	1,502	1,431	71
Telecommunications	406	5	5	—

Source: United States War Department, *Informe sobre el censo de Cuba, 1899* (Washington, D.C., 1900), 485–86.

Prostitutes were recruited almost entirely from the unskilled sectors of the female labor force: the poor, the illiterate, and otherwise marginalized sector of the population. They tended to concentrate principally in Havana, finding customers in the bustling maritime traffic of the capital as well as among soldiers and the tens of thousands of new male immigrants who arrived in Cuba without women. Most were recently arrived from the provinces. Many had been expelled from the countryside by the war and the reconcentration policy during the late 1890s. Unemployed and without the support of families, they moved into unskilled work, and some eventually to brothels.

The correlates of female occupations in the early republic were compelling. Certainly one was education, and across the island the lack of

educational opportunities for women was reflected in female preponderance in low-status employment. But restricted access to education was
itself symptomatic of other forces, some historic, some institutional. Racial and gender ideologies combined to define very narrowly the options
available to women. The persistence of patterns of slavery no doubt contributed to the concentration of almost 90 percent of women of color in
domestic service and agriculture. Of the 4,308 women engaged in agricultural labor in Matanzas province, 4,160 were women of color. Of a
total of 20,980 laundresses and 22,807 female servants, 17,555 and 17,390
respectively were women of color.

No less coercive, the ideology of appropriate roles and behavior in the
family and the community served to restrict employment opportunities
for white women. A proportionally larger number of white women remained at home, and of those white women who worked for wages, more
were in the professional ranks. Of the 733 professional women in the
province of Havana, 714 were white. Teaching was the most acceptable
of the professions generally open to females. It was seen as intellectual
labor, easy and light, whose principal clients were children and whose
principal responsibilities were a natural extension of the woman's maternal role. Thus of the 733 women in the professions in Havana province,
646 were teachers.

Employment outside the home, however, in whatever form, was still
generally seen as outside the proper purview of married women. Traditional cultural values served to exclude women from many occupations,
particularly those jobs that required contact with men. The ranks of employed women, hence, were filled largely with single women who could—
and often had to—work for wages. Of the 646 teachers in Havana province, 518 were single or widowed. This pattern, further, appears to have
cut across lines of race and class. In those occupations where women of
color predominated, such as laundresses and servants, 15,388 out of 20,980
and 19,970 out of 22,807 were single or widowed. Of 1,580 female
cigarworkers, 1,362 were single or widowed, as were 342 out of 419
seamstresses.

VII

Those Cubans who had emerged from slavery to freedom in the last decades of the colony, and those who, though long free, were of visible

African ancestry, faced a special set of obstacles in the early republic. The promises of independence fell far short. The separatist summons to black Cubans to serve the cause of *Cuba Libre* had raised hopes of social justice, political freedom, and racial equality. Afro-Cubans responded as much to the promise of a new society as they did to the prospects of a new country. And, in fact, the war itself provided Afro-Cubans with opportunity for rapid advance and mobility. They registered impressive gains within the separatist polity during these years. In every sector of the separatist amalgam, on the island and abroad—in the army, in the party, in mutual aid societies and revolutionary clubs, and in the government—Cubans of color occupied positions of distinction and power.

Conditions for Afro-Cubans took a turn for the worse after the war. The dissolution of the Cuban Revolutionary Party, the disbanding of the provisional government, and the demobilization of the army effectively suppressed the institutional structures in which Afro-Cubans had achieved the most conspicuous success. Nor were these organizations replaced by any other agencies in which they enjoyed as significant a representation. Gains registered by vast numbers of poor and propertyless Cubans of color, particularly within the officer corps of the old army, were thus immediately nullified.

Like white veterans, black soldiers suffered destitution and displacement. But Afro-Cubans confronted one additional obstacle: racism. And very early in the occupation, this difference had telling consequences. Black veterans were victims of discriminatory hiring practices; they were routinely excluded from the police and Rural Guard. Where it was not a casual practice, it was formal policy. When establishing the Artillery Corps in early 1902, U.S. military advisors stipulated that "all officers will be white."

Conditions for Afro-Cubans did not improve with the establishment of the republic. In fact, for many, conditions had actually deteriorated. Their contribution to the cause of *Cuba Libre* had been on a scale well out of proportion to their numbers. Their compensation from free Cuba was well below the scope of their contributions. They had been promised political equality and social justice. They received neither. "Many Cuban Negroes curse the dawn of the Republic," Arthur A. Schomburg wrote during a visit to Cuba in 1905. He continued:

> Negroes were welcomed in the time of oppression, in the time of hardship, during the days of the revolution, but in the days of peace . . .

they are deprived of positions, ostracized and made political outcasts. The Negro has done much for Cuba, Cuba has done nothing for the Negro.

Illiteracy rates of the population of color at the end of the colony were staggering. More than 72 percent of all Afro-Cubans over the age of 10 (290,235 out of 402,835) could neither read nor write, as compared with a 49 percent illiteracy rate of the total white population (400,330 out of 812,975). The figure was higher among the colored male population, where almost 76 percent of the voting-age population (96,463 out of 127,298) was illiterate, as compared with 41.5 percent of the comparable white cohort (120,899 out of 290,695). Conditions improved slightly after the inauguration of the republic, but Afro-Cubans still lagged behind whites. By 1919, almost 49 percent of the total population of color over the age of ten (271,544 out of 578,962) was illiterate, as compared with 37 percent among whites (448,479 out of 1.2 million). Among colored males 21 and over, the illiteracy rate was more than 48 percent, as compared with 37 percent illiteracy of their white counterparts. No less telling, by 1919, a total of 10,123 Cuban white males over 21 years of age had received professional or academic degrees, as compared with only 429 Afro-Cubans.

A disproportionate illiteracy rate among Afro-Cubans also meant that Afro-Cubans in disproportionate numbers were excluded from the franchise. Out of a total population of 106,000 Cuban males of color, only 30,000 met suffrage requirements. Lack of suffrage contributed to a loss of access to certain job sectors. Nowhere perhaps did the discrimination against Afro-Cubans stand out as sharply as it did in the public administration sector of the republic. Opportunities that blacks had hoped would open up in government simply did not materialize. Of a population of a million and a half people, Cubans of color represented some 33 percent, approximately 520,400. In the two categories of occupations listed in the 1907 census identified wholly as public service—teaching and the armed forces—blacks were under-represented: 440 out of 5,524 teachers and 1,718 out of 6,520 soldiers and policemen. "After the war ended," recalled former slave Esteban Montejo, ". . . the Negroes found themselves out in the streets—men brave as lions, out in the streets. It was unjust, but that's what happened. There wasn't even one percent of Negroes in the police force."

VIII

Almost everything turned out different from the way it was supposed to have been. Independence was a crushing disappointment for many patriotic leaders, a disastrous dénouement for thirty years of patriotic labor. Dedication to *Cuba Libre* was more than a duty to a cause, it was devotion to a faith. And for the faithful, no sacrifice was too great, no loss was too much in behalf of free Cuba. Between 1868 and 1898, two generations of Cubans had served the cause of *Cuba Libre*. They had derived purpose and defined politics around the quest for nationality. Many had devoted the better part of their adulthood to the pursuit of independence. But the pursuit of *patria* had disastrous consequences: all emerged from the war in various conditions of indigence and impoverishment. Households had been shattered and families dispersed. Almost all had deferred earnings, had depleted their assets, and had delayed their educations. Cubans of means emerged from the war humble, Cubans of humble origins were reduced to destitution. The ranks of *independentismo* were crowded with Cubans who had sacrificed personal fortunes, lost private property, and abandoned professional practices to make Cuba free. Many more peasants and wage earners had been expelled from the land and displaced from the workplace.

Rather than expressing the economic interest of any one class, the separatist movement was expected to open up opportunities for a heterogeneous social amalgam. The separatist appeal summoned Cubans from all classes; all expected independence to produce a new society: land would be restored, property returned, and economic opportunity assured. Instead, they discovered that during their toil for independence, the control over resources, property, production, and the professions had passed irretrievably into the hands of others. Sources of material security and economic well-being had slipped beyond the grasp of those who had reached for independence.

These conditions excluded Cubans from agriculture and mining, utilities and transportation, trade and commerce, industry and manufacture, banking and finance. Opportunities were few, jobs fewer. Cubans lacked the resources to restore their farms and estates to production; they lacked the means to revive businesses and return to their professions. They lacked capital, as well as the means through which to accumulate it. They were without collateral for credit, without funds to invest, and without the

capacity to borrow. Everywhere Cubans faced declining opportunity to
engage in production, diminishing access to property, and decreasing
prospects for employment. The striking feature of the early republic was
the under-representation of Cubans as property owners, as merchants and
managers, as shopkeepers and landowners, and as salaried personnel and
wage workers. They were undercut by immigration from abroad and
overwhelmed by capital from without. Cubans had succeeded in creating
a nation in which they controlled neither property nor production.

It was during the postwar years that the old separatist coalition acquired its definitive characteristics, organizing not around the pursuit of
property or the expansion of economic power but around the quest for
political power. These circumstances transfigured the very nature of the
separatist polity. Public office became an urgent issue, one with far-reaching
economic implications, the control of which offered a hedge against total
impoverishment in a wholly impoverished environment. Means became
ends. Moments of desperate want began immediately after the war. "My
family has been with me for a month," General Carlos Roloff lamented
in April 1899, "and I have to find work to support it. If I had money, I
would pursue any job other than public office; but today I am obligated
to find employment." Two months later, General Alejandro Rodríguez
wrote in similar despair: "I who have served my country, for which I
have sacrificed everything, cannot even have my family at my side for a
lack of means to support; I cannot embark upon any business nor recon-
struct my farm for lack of funds. I see myself perhaps forced to emigrate
to search for bread in a strange land, when here there are individuals in
high office who were indifferent or hostile to Cuba and always remained
on the side of Spain."

These circumstances served to shape the social content and economic
purpose of politics in the early republic. Public administration in general,
and politics in particular, acquired a special economic significance. It was
to government that Cubans looked for economic security. State revenues
became the principal source of economic solvency as Cubans came to
define their material well-being in political terms. Public office, patronage appointments, and civil service became ends; politics and electoral
competition were the means. And it was around both that separatist amalgam assumed definitive form. Vast sectors of the old separatist leadership
assumed fully the form of a class given principally to the quest of political office as a function of its social character and economic cohesion.
This development underscored the emerging social reality of the early

republic: the origins of a new elite organized around the control of the state and dependent upon control of public administration as the principal source of wealth and a means to property. Herein was one of the more anomalous features of the republic. Economic power did not produce political power. Rather, political power created the opportunity for enrichment and offered the basis for the emergence of a new elite. The state thus served at once as a source and instrument of economic power. The principal configurations of the republic took form early: foreigners prevailed over production and property, Cubans preoccupied themselves with politics. Wrote social commentator Miguel de Carrión in 1921:

> We had to pursue an abnormal course in the building of our country: instead of bringing to public power a proportional representation of wealth, we brought wealth to the hands of representatives of public power. . . . We made politics our only industry and administrative fraud the only course open to wealth for our compatriots. . . . This political industry . . . is stronger than the sugar industry, which is no longer ours; more lucrative than the railroads, which are managed by foreigners; safer than the banks, than maritime transportation and commercial trade, which also do not belong to us. It frees many Cubans from poverty, carrying them to the edge of a future middle class, which is still in an embryonic period, but that will necessarily form.

Public office came to symbolize opportunity in an economy where opportunity was limited to outsiders with capital or insiders with power. The overwhelming presence of foreign capital in Cuba had far-reaching effects. With so much of national wealth beyond the immediate reach of Cubans, public administration and political position guaranteed officeholders, their families, and supporters access to the levers of resource and benefit allocation in the only enterprise wholly Cuban—government.

Public administration provided many Cubans with an opportunity for economic well-being, a way to cross the threshold from public office to private enterprise. Either through appropriations from the public purse or expropriation of public lands, or both, officeholders guaranteed themselves a measure of social mobility and came eventually to serve as a nucleus of an emergent entrepreneurial bourgeoisie. They passed the bills and enforced the laws, and in the process created for themselves vast opportunities for enrichment. They secured the concessions, the franchises, the licenses, and the contracts that enabled officeholders to pass into the ranks of property owners. In this sense, the political class possessed the means of its own transfiguration and the potential to expand control over property and production. Public office promised to transform officeholders into a new social class, capable of expanding control over property and production even as they retained control over the state. Political positions provided the opportunity to acquire interests in areas that were otherwise immediately inaccessible to Cubans: commerce, industry, transportation, utilities, manufacturing, and agriculture.

The expansion of government development programs and extensive public works projects, no less than the distribution of franchises, licenses, and concessions, served to stimulate Cuban enterprise. The state possessed vast purchasing power through taxation, customs, and borrowing, and used this power to employ local enterprises to implement policy. It used taxes, subsidies, penalties, and loans to divert resources and promote development. Much of the capital used to stimulate local entrepreneurial activity originated from government sources. Indeed, many Cuban enterprises initiated in the early decades of the republic were essentially concessionary in character and dependent in one fashion or another upon continued support by public revenues. Cubans organized the public monopolies, awarded state subsidies, established legal quotas, distributed government contracts, and endeavored mightily to derive principal benefits of these policies. This was state intervention on massive proportions, providing employment, creating jobs, but most of all providing direct subsidy to national enterprise. A new entrepreneurial sector, largely Cuban, formed around government contracts—printers, clothing manufacturers, builders, and shoe manufacturers among the most prominent.

But inevitably—and a corollary of distributive politics in a socially truncated and economically skewed system—corruption followed and flourished. The drive for wealth was reinforced by a sense of impermanence, particularly at the upper reaches of government, where members who had four-year terms raced against the clock. Individual enrichment at the top did not emanate only from official salaries. Public administration created lucrative possibilities through bribery and appropriations of state funds. The sale of public concessions such as public works contracts—specifically the construction of new roads, bridges, and government buildings—provided ample opportunity for lucrative profits for officeholders. Through the 1910s, an estimated 25 percent of customs revenue, approximately $8 million, was lost annually through corruption. Political corruption was, in fact, an effective method of capital accumulation in a capital-scarce economic environment.

Certainly, much of the wealth obtained from public office through corruption did not go into the local economy but was expended on consumption and investments abroad, with no material contribution to national development. But much was applied to local enterprises, many of which delivered a net accretion to the stock of Cuban capital goods. Operating in an economic environment in which access to capital was limited, political corruption provided a way for Cubans to accumulate resources, a method of funneling capital from established property holders to subsidize the formation of a new entrepreneurial class either with political antecedents or political connections. Corruption, in the form of graft, bribery, and embezzlement, developed into an important method of capital formation. Some bribes originated with foreign sources of capital who were anxious to obtain local franchises, concessions, licenses, and titles. One immediate effect of this collaboration, to be sure, was to facilitate the penetration of foreign capital. But corruption also permitted Cubans to accumulate capital and thereby expand local control over property and production.

Corruption developed into a pervasive presence in Cuban public life. Graft, bribery, and embezzlement served as the medium of political exchange. Periodically, public officials were prosecuted for misconduct and malfeasance. Indictments were often partisan affairs, especially during a turnover of administrations, for criminal prosecution was one method of forcing out of office incumbent functionaries otherwise protected by civil service regulations, and thereby creating new employment opportunities for the incoming government. During the administrations of José Miguel Gómez (1908–12) and Mario G. Menocal (1912–20), a total of some 372 indictments were brought against public officials, dealing with a wide range of offenses, including embezzlement, fraud, homocide, infraction of postal regulations, violations of lottery law, misappropriation of funds, and violation of electoral laws. By 1923, the number of indictments had increased to 483.

But indictments were typically empty gestures, and even when convictions were obtained, sentences were rarely served. Most legislators enjoyed constitutional immunity from criminal prosecution. When that failed, there were ample alternative devices through which to elude prosecution and escape punishment. No type of bill was more popular with Cuban officeholders than congressional amnesty measures, for officeholders were especially mindful of the need to defend themselves and their interests. Amnesty bills served two purposes: to set aside convictions for past criminal wrongdoing and to absolve officials of crimes committed while in office, thereby foreclosing future prosecution. Six sweeping amnesty bills were passed during the administration of Tomás Estrada Palma (1902–6). The Gómez government enacted twenty-nine measures, while another thirty were passed under Menocal. The Alfredo Zayas administration (1920–24) passed a total of thirty-three. One of the last amnesty laws enacted under Zayas awarded immunity from prosecution to the former mayor of Havana and the city council for corruption, to the former governors of Matanzas and Oriente for graft, and to Alfredo Zayas, Jr., the son of the president, for fraud while he served as director of the lottery.

Amnesty bills were not the only means available to set aside indictments and dismiss convictions. Presidential pardons served the same purpose, and through the first four presidential administrations of the republic, successful prosecution of misconduct by public officials was an increasingly rare event. Estrada Palma and Zayas each issued hundreds of pardons; Gómez and Mendocal, thousands.

It was thus not uncommon for Cuban officeholders to have been, at one time or another, under criminal investigation and indictment. Indeed, fully one-fifth of all candidates for political office in the 1922 elections had criminal antecedents.

All public agencies involved in the collection and management of revenues were objects of special interest, but none more than the Bureau of the National Lottery. Established in 1909, the lottery was transformed immediately into a source of political pressure and personal enrichment. The lottery was organized into some 2,000 *colecturías,* collectorships that conferred on each owner the privilege of selling sixteen tickets for each of the three monthly drawings. Each ticket was purchased at discounted costs from the lottery administration and resold to the public at inflated prices. Of the approximately 2,000 *colecturías,* some 800 were reserved for direct sale by the director general of the lottery, acting in behalf of the president. Through this means, an incumbent administration generated some $250,000 each month for personal and political use. Another 500 *colecturías* were distributed among senators and representatives. While the number assigned to any one legislator varied, the average allocation was ten *colecturías* to each senator and five to each representative. Thus a senator holding ten collectorships stood to supplement his salary by as much as $54,000 during good economic times.

The balance of the *colecturías* was distributed by the administration as a function of favor and pay-off. Recipients included family and friends of the president, cabinet members, ranking officials of government, army and police officers, members of the judiciary, and newspaper editors.

Estimates concerning the total sums of revenue raised by each lottery drawing varied, but all agreed the total was staggering. The sum of $11 million is the figure most commonly cited.

Control of an agency capable of generating such vast sums of money placed a powerful political weapon in the hands of the president. Nor was the lottery without a socially useful purpose, particularly in a political system eminently distributive in function. The lottery provided employment for thousands of Cubans in the form of sellers and vendorships. These were positions typically reserved for the aged and infirm as well as for retired civil servants and pensioners.

All of this spoke to a larger social dimension of public expenditures. Patronage and the expansion of the public rolls affected more than the upper reaches of the political elites. An extensive network linked tens of thousands of state employees across the island in a common endeavor. Political sinecures and patronage were possessed of their own internal logic, with historically determined and functionally defined roles. Some antecedents reached deep into the colonial experience. Under Spain public office symbolized the joining of position, status, and power. But in the main, developments in Cuba conformed specifically to social conditions of the early republic. During the early years of the republic, government continuously absorbed onto state payrolls growing numbers of administrators, clerks, technicians, professionals, and workers, principally through the expansion of public administration, social services, and public works programs. These were requisite economic functions of the state, the minimum condition for political order and social peace. Patronage and public employment integrated into the national system the expanding ranks of the middle and working class that otherwise would face exclusion from economic livelihood. These mechanisms were, in short, a source of political stability and social order and a deterrent to politically motivated disorder.

State employment in all its forms, at all levels, served as the source of salaries, status, and security. Tens of thousands of functionaries and workers served in government departments, on boards, in education, health, construction, and maintenance.

As early as 1903, the public payroll, including municipal, provincial, and national government, had expanded to an estimated 20,000 public employees, with some 8,000 in the city of Havana. The state payroll continued to expand as both a cause and an effect of the expansion of state services and the increase in state revenues. In 1911, some 35,000 Cubans were on the payroll of the national and municipal government. This total did not include the employees of provincial government, or day laborers employed in the departments of public works and sanitation, or workers hired by private contractors engaged in government work, for which no reliable statistics exist. As much as two-thirds of total government expenditures were in the form of personnel salaries. In fiscal year 1914–15 the public payroll carried 32,000 full-time employees, an additional 7,000 day laborers, 1,000 lottery employees, and 5,000 temporary workers. Out of a total national budget of $38 million, some $21 million went toward the payment of salaries and wages. By 1924, the size of the national government payroll increased to 42,000 employees. The executive branch accounted for the vast part of public positions and personnel payrolls—a total of some 39,000, from cabinet officers to clerks to construction workers, distributed among ten government ministries and departments. Two years later, the payroll had increased again—mostly in the executive branch—reaching 48,000 and accounting for a total of some $38.5 million in salaries.

Politics, hence, was a matter of economic and social urgency. Political demand on public administration was the price paid for chronic unemployment and persisting underemployment. But most of all, it was a product of a political economy unable to accommodate national needs. The distribution of political sinecures and the disbursement of public revenues to create public jobs functioned like a social welfare system. The swelling civil service rolls were the most visible indication of the social cost to an economy dominated by foreign capital and a labor market depressed by vast numbers of cheap foreign workers. Public administration served to disguise unemployment, for it created jobs for the otherwise unemployed and unemployable, and in the process provided social equilibrium to an otherwise skewed political economy. It served to mute social conflict and reduce political tension. From contractors to cabinet ministers, from pieceworkers to the president, tens of thousands of Cubans, together with hundreds of thousands of dependents, relied on the state for their livelihood and well-being. Public positions multiplied and government spending increased, and any interference with or interruption of this process threatened the republic with social unrest. This was nothing less than improvisation institutionalized—not particularly stable, not especially efficient, but eminently functional. It was possessed of its own internal logic, and even if it offended the sensibilities of those outside the government, the system worked more or less, most of the time. But it was also true that the system had to work. The alternatives were so palpably few, and these so limited, as to make distributive politics one of the principal sources of stability in the republic.

On the one occasion in the early republic that the system failed, it plunged the island into political turmoil. Afro-Cuban discontent had continued to deepen during the early years of the republic. Repeatedly, Cubans of color protested their shabby treatment, and especially their continued exclusion from government position and public office. In 1907, many Afro-Cubans abandoned hope of obtaining redress within existing political structures and began to organize politically, outside the established party system, first in the Agrupación Independiente de Color in 1907, and later into a full-fledged political party, the Partido Independiente de Color. The new party offered immediately a full slate of candidates for national, provincial, and municipal office. In its first effort at electoral politics in the 1908 elections, the Agrupación fared poorly. But it persisted, and expanded the size of its organization and scope of its activities.

The *independientes* represented Afro-Cuban politicians originating largely from the officer corps of the old Liberation Army, men who before the war formed that part of the free population of color that included professionals, farmers, skilled artisans, and small property owners. They were generally representatives of the black petite bourgeoisie, Cubans who aspired to gain entrée into the expanding state bureaucracy, either through elected positions or appointed posts. They failed at both. The *independientes* directed their complaints against institutional racism and the systematic discrimination that obstructed their participation in the public life of the republic they had contributed to establishing. The party charter addressed itself almost exclusively to political matters, and specifically to government authorities and the leaders of the ruling parties. The *independientes* advocated better government, improved working conditions, and free university education. But the principal concerns centered on combating racial discrimination, especially in public office and appointive positions, including the armed forces, the diplomatic corps, the judiciary, and all civil departments of government.

The *Partido Independiente de Color* posed an immediate threat to the ruling Liberal Party, for it challenged the Liberals' traditional hold over the Afro-Cuban electorate. Indeed, the challenge was sufficiently formidable to prompt President José Miguel Gómez to move against the new party. In 1911, the government enacted the Morúa Law, prohibiting the organization of political parties along racial lines.

The Morúa Law was the first in a series of measures designed to force the *independientes* to dissolve. Party leaders were harassed and arrested. Party newspapers were banned.

In May 1912, the *Partido Independiente de Color* despaired of a political settlement and resorted to armed rebellion. The government responded swiftly and ruthlessly. Fighting lasted several months, mostly in Oriente, and when it was over thousands of Afro-Cubans had been slain in the conflict and in the ensuing repression.

The Afro-Cuban rebellion revealed in dramatic form one source of social tensions in the early republic. The rebellion was precipitated by the failure to incorporate an important segment of the population into republican structures. The failure of the state to function adequately in its distributive capacity set the socio-economic deficiencies of the republic in sharp relief. Rebellion was the inevitable recourse of a population unable to find sufficient opportunity as field hands or factory workers or functionaries in public administration. The rebellion served as an example of what could happen, and what would happen, when the state failed to accommodate the needs of a significant sector of the population.

IX

These circumstances served to confer a tenor of urgency and, on occasion, ferocity to Cuban public life. Control of resources and revenues was the central if unstated issue of politics at all levels of the republic. The forms of conventional electoral competition disguised the urgent nonpolitical issues of Cuban politics. At stake was the livelihood of hundreds of political contenders and the many more thousands of dependents and supporters who, in varying degrees, relied on political patronage and public office for their well-being. The peculiar distributive quality of Cuban politics served as the mechanism for resource allocation, a system whereby equitable access to the levers of benefit distribution served to mitigate the social consequences of scarce resources.

Republican politics organized around competition between the Liberal and Conservative parties, reflecting the two competing tendencies within the nineteenth-century separatist polity. The Liberal party had its origins in the populist military sector, and was largely composed of officers and enlisted men of the Liberation Army, many of modest social origins, committed to the most exalted version of *independentismo*. The Conservatives tended to originate from the bureaucratic civilian wing, mostly former officials of the expatriate diplomatic corps and the functionaries of the provisional government, many of whom were white men of comfortable social origins, some with Autonomist antecedents. Certainly there were areas of overlap, but in the main these two tendencies delineated the key distinctions that characterized politics in the early republic.

Both parties understood the urgency of politics, and demanded circulation of public office. Perhaps nothing was more politically explosive than the issue of presidential re-election. Monopolization of public office by one party, or one faction of a party, threatened to block access to the sinecures of state for others. Insofar as the state served as one of the principal means of economic well-being, elections institutionalized a process among political contenders by which all participants shared access to public administration. Re-election designs, in which incumbent access to the machinery of state all but guaranteed a second term, violated the informal intra-elite understanding by threatening to withdraw from circulation the principal source of economic well-being. This was an understood protocol among political contenders. Incumbency offered monopoly use of the apparatus of state through which to pursue re-election. The electoral agencies, the courts, and the armed forces, mobilized in behalf of partisan objectives, conferred on the incumbent advantages well beyond the reach of the opposition party.

No incumbent seeking a second term ever lost an election. Twice in as many decades, re-election of incumbents provoked armed rebellion and U.S. intervention. The re-election bid of President Tomás Estrada Palma provoked a Liberal armed uprising in August 1906, and subsequently a three-year U.S. military occupation of the island (1906–9). The re-election of Conservative President Mario G. Menocal provoked another Liberal uprising in February 1971, and again a U.S. armed intervention led to the deployment of armed forces in Camagüey and Oriente between 1917 and 1922.

Armed rebellion to protest re-election gave powerful expression to the urgency of politics in the republic. There was much at stake in these proceedings. Politics was serious business, at least serious enough to go to war for. If political means failed to dislodge incumbent authorities according to prescribed electoral methods, the nature of the stakes required the opposition to resort to military methods to restore parity of access to the distributive mechanisms of state.

X

The year 1920 was a presidential election year, and although the issue was not re-election, it did involve an incumbent effort to retain power for the government party. Political controversy again edged the republic toward armed strife. Both sides charged fraud and coercion, both sides claimed victory. Government candidate Alfredo Zayas prepared for his inauguration; the Liberal opposition candidate José Miguel Gómez plotted revolution.

The year 1920 was also a time of severe economic dislocation. Cuba had enjoyed extraordinary prosperity during and immediately after World War I. Sugar production expanded. Prices increased steadily during the war years—1.9 cents per pound in 1914, 3.3 cents in 1915, 4.4 in 1916, 4.6 in 1917—and soared dramatically after the war: 9.2 cents per pound in 1918 and 1919. In 1920, the year of the "dance of the millions," during the period of dazzling prosperity, the increase in prices was stunning: 10 cents per pound in March, 13 cents on April 1, 18 cents on April 15, and reaching the dizzying height of 22.5 cents a pound on May 19. The value of the sugar crop in mid-1920, at the peak of the boom, was more than double that of the previous year, rising from $455 million in 1919 to $1 billion. Increasingly, too, the value of sugar exports expanded as a share of Cuban total export values. (See Table 28.)

The increase of sugar production on this scale at this value, and at this speed, required a large volume of financing. Sugar producers and speculators accounted for much of this credit. In fact, all values became inflated during the "dance of the millions" and property changed ownership in rapid succession. Speculation was rampant. New enterprises were launched, construction projects expanded, and banks extended operations and opened new branches across the island. For example, the Banco Nacional managed 130 branches across the island and in 1920 claimed total deposits approaching $200 million. As the Cuban economy expanded between 1915 and 1920, older North American banks also increased operations. The Canadian Bank of Commerce opened an office in Havana. The National City Bank followed suit in 1915 and quickly established

TABLE 28.   Production and Value of Cuban Sugar (1913–20)

Year	Production (tons)	Value (millions)	Percentage of Total Export Value
1913	2,442,000	$ 115.8	72
1914	2,615,000	163.4	77
1915	2,609,000	202.4	84
1916	3,034,000	308.5	85
1917	3,063,000	332.2	86
1918	3,473,000	347.1	85
1919	4,012,000	472.1	89
1920	3,742,000	1,016.8	92

Source: Susan Schroeder, *Cuba: A Handbook of Historical Statistics* (Boston, 1982), 143.

branches across the island. The Mercantile Bank of the Americas and the American Foreign Banking Corporation, a Chase subsidiary, followed. As sugar production increased and prices soared, competition among lenders grew fierce. Credit to mill owners and farmers was cheap, and virtually unlimited. Some fifty mills, or around one-quarter of the 198 *centrales* in operation, were acquired by new owners between 1919 and 1920. Every banking house owned portfolios thick with notes of mortgaged sugar property, notes on standing and future crops, and liens on the bagged sugar that in 1919 already began to accumulate ominously in Cuban warehouses. By late summer of 1920, there was some $80 million in loans on sugar originally made at a valuation of 22 cents a pound.

Prosperity ended as quickly as it began, and with less warning. Producers overexpanded and prices plummeted. Sugar that sold for 22.5 cents a pound in May 1920 fell to 8 cents in September and 3.8 cents in December. Commodity imports ordered during the peak of the sugar boom arrived in Havana as prices collapsed, and were left unclaimed at Havana shipyards. The docks became congested. Trade and commerce came to a halt. Sugar surpluses increased as prices decreased, and across the island planters and mill owners found themselves with sugar that could not be sold and debts that could not be serviced. Bankers who had advanced loans to planters with abandon during the sugar boom found themselves over-extended and under-capitalized, facing ruin. In early October 1920 a run on the principal banks, including the Banco Nacional, the Banco Español, and the Banco Internacional, threatened Cuba's principal lend-ing institutions with collapse. The very solvency of the republic appeared at stake as the government fiscal agent, the Banco Nacional, struggled to stave off bankruptcy. In mid-October the government proclaimed a moratorium through December, renewed again through February 1921.

The collapse of sugar prices followed by the crash in Cuban banking announced calamity for all of Cuba. The cycle of boom and bust had again taken its toll on the island. Discontent was on the rise everywhere. Unemployment spread and shortages of consumer goods and foodstuffs increased. Prices rose for the provisions that were still available. Strikes increased and public demonstrations became commonplace.

Against this background, the unresolved elections in 1920 threatened to plunge the island into civil war. Government had come to a standstill, at the brink of a political collapse to follow the economic one. Periodically, during the previous two decades, the United States had conveyed displeasure at Cuban conduct of public affairs. Washington had, after all, assumed formal responsibility for the stability and solvency of the republic through the Platt Amendment. On three earlier occasions—1906–9, 1912, and 1917—the United States had invoked the intervention clause to land armed forces on the island to end political disorders. On numerous occasions, Washington had protested Cuban policies, sometimes privately through diplomatic channels, sometimes publicly through press releases, but most of the time to no avail. In 1920, there was an abiding conviction in Washington that it was precisely because Cubans had for so long disregarded U.S. counsel that the island was again approaching crisis.

The United States reacted quickly, and unilaterally. Invoking the Platt Amendment, the State Department appointed General Enoch H. Crowder as "Special Representative of the President" in Cuba. He arrived in late 1920 to settle the disputed presidential elections, which he did within two months, but stayed two more years as "Special Representative" to reorganize Cuban public administration.

Alfredo Zayas inherited an empty treasury. The collapse of sugar prices and the dislocation of the economy had combined to curtail drastically government receipts. New investments had all but ceased. The government was straining to meet salaries and failing. As much as $24 million of the government's money was hopelessly tied up in the insolvent Banco Nacional. The necessity of meeting interest and amortization payments of past debts added pressure of another sort. This alone amounted to $2 million in the first two months of the new government. Zayas was also obliged to remit $200,000 a month to New York bankers under the terms of a previous loan agreement. The government did not default. Instead, it issued treasury checks and continued to fall hopelessly in arrears: some $2 million by June 1921 on the internal debt, and some $4.5 million by June 1922. Government receipts for fiscal year 1920–21 amounted to $108 million and expenditures surpassed $182 million.

The Zayas government was in desperate need of new loans. Neither Crowder nor the State Department disputed the need. But a new loan, the State Department feared, would serve only to ease Cuba temporarily through difficult times without offering permanent remedy of what Washington believed to be the root cause of Cuban problems. Certainly one source of distress originated with the uncertain world price of sugar, over which Cuba had little control. But many of Cuba's problems, Washington insisted, were wholly of local origin, the cumulative result of nearly two decades of maladministration and misgovernment.

The occasion was auspicious for Washington to exact from Cuban authorities widescale concessions for reform and reorganization. U.S. approval of a new loan, Crowder informed the Cuban government, was contingent on the adoption of a series of far-reaching reforms. Zayas complied. In March 1922, Crowder dictated the first in a series of memoranda—fifteen in all—ultimatums directed to the Cuban government demanding reorganization of virtually every key aspect of national, provincial, and municipal administration. Several called for the reform of commercial structures, others called for the reorganization of municipal government and the reform of the electoral code. Others insisted upon various constitutional amendments to reform administrative procedures. Two demanding sweeping reorganization of the administration designed to end graft and corruption, suppress sinecures *(botellas)* and *colecturías,* and eliminate corrupt officials.

Washington called for more than the dismissal of dishonest public servants. It demanded, too, the appointment of honest ones, and claimed authority to appoint them. In June 1922, Crowder concluded that members of the Zayas cabinet could neither inspire confidence in or induce compliance with the reform program. He insisted upon a cabinet reorganization and proceeded to appoint new government ministers in key positions. The "honest cabinet," as it became known, included Crowder appointees Ricardo Lancis *(Gobernación),* Carlos Manuel de Céspedes

228 CUBA

(Foreign Relations), Demetrio Castillo (Public Works), Arístides Agramonte (Sanitation), and Manuel Despaigne (Treasury). Zayas complied on all counts, and in late 1922 Cuba was authorized to submit its loan application for $50 million to J. P. Morgan and Company.

9

Reform and Revolution in the Republic

I

The year 1923 was a good one for Cuba. The Zayas government received the coveted $50 million loan. It was also a good harvest year, and a good sugar harvest in a year of good sugar prices. Government receipts increased, unmistakable evidence of economic recovery. Seventy-three million dollars were collected in fiscal year 1922–23. And conditions improved the following year, a year in which the government collected an additional $90 million in new revenues. In one year the surplus in the national treasury increased from $3 million to $34 million.

Gone were the chronic deficits of the early 1920s. Gone, too, was the specter of uncertainty under which the Cuban economy had languished. But gone most of all was the need for Alfredo Zayas to continue to acquiesce to policy directives from the United States. He seized the opportunity. Within weeks of the completed loan transaction, he reorganized his cabinet and dismissed Agramonte, Castillo, Despaigne, and Lancis, the four ministers most closely associated with Crowder and the "honest cabinet." Members of the Zayas family—no less than fourteen relatives—returned to government payrolls. A flurry of legislative resolutions announced the resumption of government spending, including new public works programs, supplemental budget allocations, the award of new franchises, and a series of salary increments. A new lottery law was enacted, and the president's son was appointed director general of the lottery.

The intent was clear—to return things to normal, to the way they used to be. But too much had changed in Cuba. Things could never be the way they were before.

II

The skewed class structure of the early republic meant that in the exercise of local hegemony the officeholders had faced neither social challenge from below nor political competition from without. For two decades, they had enjoyed virtual monopolization of political power—without opposition from outside their own ranks. An economically dominant Cuban social class did not exist at the time of the establishment of the republic. What remained of the old planter class was absorbed into or eclipsed by nonresident foreign capital. In either case, the interests of the surviving creole bourgeoisie became intimately identified with United States interests; the creole bourgeoisie was incapable of articulating and defending its own needs. The old colonial commercial and industrial bourgeoisie that survived in the republic, made up principally of Spaniards, never developed into a rival internal political force. They may have had political preferences to promote and economic interests to protect, but they did not pursue either objective by organizing separate political parties or sponsoring candidates within existing parties. They remained politically unengaged. Neither the surviving sector of the planter class nor the commercial and industrial bourgeoisie was capable of exercising political power directly. At the same time, the working class remained weak and divided. Labor activity during the early years of the republic was confined largely to local trade unions—workers in a single trade, often at the same workplace, with specific grievances against a local management. In the early republic, attempts by labor to organize politically produced short-lived parties with few members.

It was within the interstices of the skewed social structure that the representatives of the old separatist polity came to exercise considerable freedom of action during the early decades of the republic. They ruled without pressure either to share power internally or accommodate state policy to the needs of other national groups. They were typically not recruited from the dominant landed, industrial, and commercial classes, and the separation of officeholders from the propertied classes of the republic and their dependence on control of government promoted the development of relatively autonomous state structures. Only on the occasion of the organization of the Partido Independiente de Color and the Afro-Cuban rebellion of 1912 was this hegemony challenged, and the thoroughness with which the Partido Independiente de Color was dissolved and the uprising defeated ended this threat to the political class.

III

But those were the early years of the republic, and times were simpler then. By the 1920s, the contradictions of this anomaly were rapidly overtaking Cuban society. These were years of economic growth and expansion in Cuba—uneven, to be sure, and not without moments of floundering and an occasional reversal. The prosperity of the war years and recovery after the war, however, stimulated new economic development and released new social forces out of which emerged a more complicated social order. A new Cuban entrepreneurial bourgeoisie took form during these years. The opportunities created during World War I provided a powerful incentive for the expansion of the Cuban economy. The decline of trade with Europe during the war created conditions favorable to the rapid development of import substitution of consumer goods. Local manufacture and light industry expanded during the war years, providing new opportunities for local capital. These developments were stimulated further when imports from the United States dropped from $404 million in 1920 to $120 million two years later. By the mid-1920s, Cuban capital dominated some 1,000 factories and businesses across the island. National ownership prevailed in such enterprises as confectionery shops; ice plants; shoe manufacturing; soap production; furniture construction; paper, perfume, and match factories; beer breweries; glass and bottling plants; distilleries; simple pharmaceuticals and drugs; cigarette factories; tanneries; soda and water bottlers; and a variety of food processing plants. Land speculation and a building boom in Havana, moreover, provided a boost to Cuban construction-related enterprise. Local capital expanded into building-materials such as cement, tiles, brick, metal, riggings, and limestone blocks.

By 1919, Cuban males over the age of fifteen had registered important gains in the economy, overtaking foreigners in all major occupational categories. (See Table 29.) For the first time, Cubans surpassed foreigners in industry and manufacture, while enhancing considerably their majority in commerce and professional services.

The new entrepreneurial class was of diverse origins. In part it drew

TABLE 29. Male Occupational Groupings by Nationality and Race (1919)
(15 years and older)

	Total Males	White Foreign Males	Percent	White Cuban Males	Percent	Colored Males	Percent
Agriculture, fisheries, and mining	433,197	67,178	15.5	239,215	55.2	126,804	29.3
Trade and transportation	141,546	59,058	41.7	63,840	45.1	18,648	13.2
Industry and manufacturing	157,871	35,694	22.7	63,425	40.1	58,752	37.2
Professions	24,542	3,818	15.6	18,175	74.0	2,549	10.4
Domestic	71,544	18,304	25.6	31,559	44.1	21,681	30.3
Without gainful employment	80,222	8,915	11.1	47,581	59.3	23,726	29.6

Source: Cuba, *Census of the Republic of Cuba, 1919* (Havana, 1920), 632–34.

its members from what remained of the old planter class, a group whose decomposition was accelerated by World War I. Many small investors had obtained short-term credit, which was vital to the organization of new enterprises. Capital was readily available during the boom years, and together with the opportunities of local market conditions provided powerful incentive for the expansion of Cuban industry and manufacturing. Representatives of the political elite, both in and out of office, came to constitute another sector of this new entrepreneurial bourgeoisie. With capital accumulated through public office, officeholders were themselves being transformed into property owners, and they participated in growing numbers in the steady expansion of Cuban control over sugar, mining interests, urban real estate, manufacturing, industry, and commerce. These were the men who prospered from controls, revenue policies, public credit facilities, and government franchises and grants. One last development that added to the apparent expansion of national control over property and production was the rise of second-generation immigrants who identified themselves as Cuban. These were the children of foreigners, mainly Spaniards, who had reached maturity in the republic and began moving into family businesses.

Admittedly tenuous and tentative, the emergence of this Cuban entrepreneurial bourgeoisie served to give shape to a new political constituency, representing capital largely local, advocating goals entirely national, but most of all demanding state support of interests wholly Cuban. This was a class, too, that was increasingly susceptible to the appeal of economic nationalism and to whom the officeholders' deference to foreign capital was becoming increasingly noxious and unacceptable. These were private men with an agenda for the public men, collectively a source of political pressure with which the officeholding class would have to contend and, ultimately, accommodate. No longer were officeholders free of internal pressure. New forces were stirring from below and within, stirrings characterized by mounting impatience with government inattention and official indifference to national economic interests.

The 1920–21 economic crisis served to galvanize the nascent entrepreneurial bourgeoisie into political action. Cuban property owners became alive to the necessity for greater political involvement in public affairs in defense of local economic interests. This new advocacy reflected growing concern with uncertainty and a desire to expand control over local resources and national markets. The postwar crisis served also to expose the magnitude of officeholders' indifference to local interests, for, in fact, there existed neither institutional forms nor political forums through which the new entrepreneurs could influence the course of government policies.

By the early 1920s, Cuban property owners, increasing in number and growing in strength, found themselves reduced to onlookers of political events over which they had little control. Certainly bribery and corruption offered one obvious avenue of influence, but even in the endeavor of graft local entrepreneurs could not hope to compete successfully with foreign capital. Nor could Cubans reasonably expect to obtain influence and secure favor through campaign donations and political contributions. These practices were inconsequential if not irrelevant in Cuban politics. Widescale corruption and coercion against the electorate, a growing trend of political violence and assassination, and the wholesale practice of electoral fraud, ballot stuffing, and falsification of returns served to underscore the degree to which political elites depended on the manipulation of state structures to perpetuate themselves rather than on the financial subsidy from local property interests. The routine rigging of elections meant, too, that even the value of the ballot and the worth of the franchise were themselves in question, and certainly of limited utility as a means of political change. The deepening involvement of the United States in Cuban internal affairs, moreover, in large part a response to charges of political malfeasance and public misconduct of officeholders, meant also that state policy would perforce continue to favor foreign interests. Only government indifference to the defense of national economic interests irked the entrepreneurial bourgeoisie more than did United States intervention, and the relationship between the two was manifest.

The spectacle of republican politics was played before an incredulous national audience. There seemed no limit to political abuses, no end to revelations of spectacular graft and accounts of official corruption in all branches of the Zayas government. A reading of the Havana press during the early 1920s provides powerful testimony of corruption in almost every division of public administration. Smuggling was rampant in custom houses and among port police officials. Allegations of corruption in the post office were routine. The Treasury Department was rocked by several scandals at once, including the disappearance of retirement pensions, misappropriation of tax revenues, and padded payrolls. One incident of misappropriation of funds almost forced a suspension of services by the Department of Communications. Corruption was especially rampant in the Department of Public Works, in which kickbacks and rake-offs were all normal aspects of awarding government contracts. So were bidding irregularities, misappropriation of funds, and cost overruns. Vast expanses of state lands were illegally transferred from the public patrimony to private possession.

By the early 1920s, many within the new entrepreneurial bourgeoisie had reached the limit of their patience with the political class. The new entrepreneurs demanded a greater voice in public affairs, and were prepared for it. They were stronger numerically, they were more solvent economically, and they intended to use their newfound strength to defend their interests, which increasingly they came to understand to be one and the same with national interests.

During the early 1920s, key sectors of the local bourgeoisie organized into associations to defend what they identified as national interests, and in so doing took the first step to challenge officeholders for control of the state. The emergence of interest groups created new political pressure for policies on the defense of local interests, currency stability, fiscal reform, tax and tariff reorganization, administrative integrity, and political stability. In January 1920, Havana merchants organized into the Asociación de Comerciantes de La Habana to demand improved trade conditions. Their principal concerns centered on improving port conditions and negotiating a more favorable trade relationship with the United States. In 1922, the prestigious Committee of One Hundred was established. Made up of young businessmen led by Porfirio Franca, the Committee called for an end to political misconduct and public malfeasance and the adoption of a merit system in government. In late 1922, industrialists organized in the Asociación Nacional de Industriales de Cuba, joining key sectors of national industry in one organization. Under the direction of Ramón F. Crusellas, a leading soap manufacturer, the Asociación Nacional de Industriales urged the adoption of strong protectionist policies to defend national industry. At about the same time, merchants across the island organized into the Federación Nacional de Detallistas and added their voice to the growing clamor for favorable government policies, including the establishment of a merchants bank and the abolition of the monopoly enjoyed by company stores on the large sugar estates. In 1923, Cuban producers and property owners established the Federación Nacional de Corporaciones Económicas de Cuba. Representatives from the new associations joined with members of older organizations, such as the Sociedad Económica de Amigos del País and Cámara de Comercio, Industria y Navegación de la Isla de Cuba, to promote cooperation among agricultural, commercial, and industrial sectors of the island.

The new associations represented first and foremost pressure groups committed to the defense of local economic interests. More than this, however, they provided the basis of a national constituency for a new political movement, one that challenged the power of the political elites and the position of the officeholders. The first tentative steps toward political organization occurred in January 1922 with the establishment of the Asociación de Buen Gobierno in Havana. Made up of young professionals and businessmen, the organization launched a campaign against corruption and graft in public office. Later that year, the Asociación made its debut in the field of electoral politics, joining with a dissident faction of the Conservative party to sponsor a candidate for the Havana mayoralty election of 1922. The new Republican party candidate, José Eliseo Cartaya, a founder of the Asociación Nacional de Industriales de Cuba, finished inauspiciously, a distant third in a field of five.

Defeated but undaunted, reformist elements continued to pursue political change through alternative political channels. Within a year, reformism surfaced again, this time in the newly organized Junta Cubana de Renovación Nacional. Under the direction of University of Havana professor Fernando Ortiz, the Junta issued a lengthy manifesto denouncing the accumulated ills of two decades of republican misgovernment. In economic matters, the Junta called for protection of Cuban industry, commerce, and agriculture and the renegotiation of reciprocal trade relations with the United States as a means to promote balanced national economic development. It drew up a social agenda that demanded labor reform, expansion of health services, and prison reform. On political matters the Junta called for an end to graft and corruption, judicial reorganization, and electoral reform. The Junta also gave expression to early nationalist stirrings by protesting "with alarm" the growing domination of Cuba by the United States. "The Cuban people," the Junta proclaimed, "want to be free as much from the foreigners who abuse the flag as from the citizens who violate it and will end up burying it."

The summons to national renovation united representatives from virtually all sectors of commerce, industry, finance, and professions. Among professionals represented were physicians, pharmacists, architects, lawyers, notaries, primary and normal school teachers, university professors, journalists, historians, editors, and artists. Represented also were feminist organizations, Afro-Cuban associations, and Catholic groups.

IV

Reform was in the air, and it was a presence that offered the prospect of nothing less than a total regeneration of the republic. Its appeal was irresistible, and its possibilities seemed unlimited. It quickly reached the university campus. In January 1922 students at the University of Havana led by Julio Antonio Mella seized control of several buildings and demanded university reforms, including the dismissal of incompetent faculty, free higher education, and autonomy for the University. The newly organized Federación de Estudiantes de la Universidad de La Habana (FEU) convoked the first National Student Congress, bringing to Havana 138 delegates representing 49 educational institutions across the island. Among the resolutions passed were demands for student participation in school governance, establishment of high professional standards for faculty, and increased government support of education. But not all resolutions were confined to matters of education. The FEU also demanded the abrogation of the Platt Amendment, decried United States intervention in Cuban internal affairs, and denounced corruption in government.

The dissent on campus had its antecedents in intellectual circles. During the early 1920s, and initially at the margins of the national debate, intellectuals explored the possibilities of revival in national literature and art. At the Café Martí near Central Park in Havana, writers and artists under the leadership of Rubén Martínez Villena engaged in passionate discussions on the essential form and function of national literature. The debate on form would persist unresolved for another decade, but on the matter of function, the consensus was striking and immediate. More than advocates of cultural revival, writers assumed for themselves the role of agents of national rejuvenation. In extolling things Cuban, they added content to the emerging nationalist revival; by denouncing corruption in Cuba, they added conscience to national reform.

By 1923 intellectuals had joined the reform swell. In March, a group of writers led by Martínez Villena walked out of a literary function to protest the participation of a Zayas cabinet minister. The "Protest of the Thirteen," as the incident became known, soon generalized to a blanket indictment against malfeasance in government. In a subsequent manifesto, the writers denounced corruption in the Zayas administration and solicited the support of all Cubans who "feel indignant against those who mistreat the Republic . . . and who believe that the time has arrived to react vigorously and punish in some manner the delinquent rulers." A month later, Martínez Villena organized the Falange de Acción Cubana, a political action group intended to organize opposition to the government. Later that year intellectuals organized the Grupo Minorista. *Minorismo* united the republican generation of intellectuals around the goal of cultural renewal and national redemption. Calling for a re-examination of national values, the Grupo Minorista identified itself with educational reform and university autonomy. *Minorismo* also denounced United States imperialism, called for labor and agrarian reform, and demanded an end to political corruption and electoral fraud.

During the later 1910s and early 1920s women were also expanding their participation in the economy and organizing for political, social, and economic reform. They too added their voice to the growing swell for change in the republic. The size of the female wage labor force had increased by more than 35 percent in twenty years (from 66,356 in 1899 to 89,656 in 1919), although the female share of the total labor market had declined from 10.6 to 9.4 percent and the total portion of women working for pay dropped from 8.8 to 6.6 percent. The decline, however, coincided with other significant developments. Urban employment opportunities for women, especially in Havana, had increased. Indeed, the percentage of female employment in the capital was more than twice the national average. More than 15 percent of all women in Havana were wage earners. In the seven largest cities of the island, more than 13 percent of all women formed part of the wage labor force. No less significant, the number of white women in the paid labor force more than doubled, going from 17,589 to 44,198, while the number of wage-earning women of color decreased from 48,767 to 44,728.

The increase in the number of white women workers in the cities since 1899 reflected other changes. The percentage of wage-earning women in domestic services declined to 46 percent (from 69.6 percent in 1899), while in manufacturing it almost doubled to 32 percent (from 12 percent), in agriculture declined to 8.5 (down from 10.4 percent), in the professions rose almost fourfold to 9.9 (from 2.5 percent), and in trade and transportation went up to 3.8 percent (from 1 percent). By 1919, more than one-quarter of the ranks of the professions were filled by women (see Table 30).The increases in key occupational groups were striking (see Table 31). Educational opportunities had expanded considerably for women during the first two decades of the republic. Illiteracy of females over the age of ten had declined from 58 percent in 1899 to 39 percent in 1919. In the cities, female literacy rates had increased even more substantially: to 84 percent in Havana, 80 percent in Matanzas, 83 percent in Cienfuegos, 85 percent in Santiago.

These conditions converged to make it possible for women to become increasingly active in public affairs. During the late 1910s and early 1920s, a number of feminist organizations were formed to press for the right to vote, for equality of educational opportunity, and for improved employment prospects. The goal of the electoral franchise in particular assumed a special significance to the growing numbers of professional middle-class women who were deprived of basic civil and political rights. They added their voices to the growing clamor for reform and regeneration of the republic. As early as 1915, the Partido Nacional Sufragista organized to secure the vote for women. Three years later, the Club Femenino de Cuba was established to assist in educational projects for women and to press for civil and social rights. These were followed by the creation of the Comité Pro Igualdad de la Mujer, a Cuban chapter of the Woman's National Party, and a host of women's professional groups, including teachers, writers, and artists dedicated to the elimination of employment discrimination. In 1921, women organized into the Federación Nacional de Asociaciones Femeninas, made up of five principal organizations: Club Femenino de Cuba, Congreso Nacional de Madres, Asociación de Católicas Cubanas, Asociación Nacional de Enfermeras, and the Comité de la

TABLE 30. Occupational Groupings by Sex and Race (1919)
(15 years and older)

	Total	Males	Percent	Total Females	Percent	White Cuban Females	Percent	Colored Females	Percent
Agriculture, fisheries, and mining	440,120	433,197	98.4	6,923	1.6	2,518	36.3	4,096	59.1
Trade and transportation	144,842	141,546	97.7	3,296	2.3	2,307	69.9	375	11.8
Manufacturing	185,439	157,871	85.1	27,560	14.9	10,031	36.4	15,849	57.5
Professions	33,368	24,542	73.5	8,826	26.5	6,359	72.0	1,317	14.9
Domestic service	110,776	71,544	64.6	39,232	35.4	10,564	26.9	21,262	54.2
Without gainful employment	750,420	80,222	10.7	670,198	89.3	436,801	65.2	184,394	27.5

Source: Cuba, *Census of the Republic of Cuba, 1919* (Havana, 1920), 632–34

TABLE 31. Selected Occupations by Race and Sex (1919)

	Total Males	Total Females	White Females	Colored Females
Attorneys	1,572	6	6	—
Bankers	2,460	31	31	—
Cigarworkers	20,484	4,905	2,767	2,138
Clerks	6,334	901	820	81
Dentists	303	11	11	—
Dressmakers	140	1,865	734	1,131
Employees in manufacturing	5,354	420	367	53
Employees of banks and offices	6,808	740	681	59
Government	9,730	1,274	1,174	100
Hotel and restaurant	2,906	366	341	25
Launderers	4,251	8,680	2,068	6,612
Merchants	66,704	779	643	136
Nurses	245	727	587	147
Physicians	1,736	35	32	3
Printers	10,225	204	196	8
Sales Personnel	15,749	235	204	31
Seamstresses	99	9,317	4,370	4,947
Servants	43,478	39,676	17,543	22,136
Teachers	1,911	5,122	4,465	657
Telecommunication	3,197	321	304	17

Source: Cuba, *Census of the Republic of Cuba, 1919* (Havana, 1920), 666–67.

Creche de La Habana Nueva. Under the auspices of the Federación Nacional de Asociaciones Femeninas, the first National Congress of Women was convened in Havana in 1923. Among the resolutions passed were the right to vote, the demand for equal rights under the law, an expansion of educational opportunities for women, and the protection of the family.

V

During the early 1920s, the working class also organized and expanded, to emerge as one more force for change and one more contender for power. Early labor organizing proceeded haltingly, in fits and starts, mainly in the larger provincial cities such as Havana. During the early decades of the republic, most crafts and trades had organized into local unions, including cigarworkers, typesetters, construction workers, bakers, stevedores, and railroad employees. During these years, too, labor moved toward the establishment of regional and national federations of local unions. In Havana, some thirty unions representing the principal crafts and trades merged into a local syndicate. Most of the twenty unions in Cienfuegos and the ten unions in Matanzas established local federations. In 1914, the first National Workers Congress met in Havana. An estimated 1700 delegates approved a variety of resolutions demanding preference to the hiring of Cuban workers, an eight-hour workday, a reduction of the cost of living, and the establishment of a government ministry to support labor demands. More important, however, the occasion encouraged the organization of new craft unions and gave impetus to the establishment of a national federation.

Economic conditions in Cuba after World War I contributed to the rising militancy among Cuban workers. For many workers, economic hard times arrived even before the postwar recession. The European war had caused cancellations of imports of Cuban tobacco products, resulting in the closing of cigar factories and unemployment for the thousands of workers engaged both in the production of tobacco and in the manufacture of cigars. But even for workers who enjoyed continued employment through the war years, the economic boom was a mixed blessing. The cost of living increased. The price of basic commodities soared, and workers' wages failed to keep pace.

The postwar depression transformed a difficult situation into an impossible one. Unemployment struck suddenly and spread swiftly. Shops closed, factories ceased production, and construction stopped. The bank moratorium meant that employers could not draw on more than 10 percent of cash reserves, a sum wholly inadequate for many to meet full payroll requirements. The result was mass layoffs. In the building trades alone, some 5,000 workers were immediately without jobs. By late 1920, some 10,000 workers were without employment, and observers predicted that the number would quickly increase to 50,000.

But even as external conditions accelerated workers' militancy, changes within the proletariat itself facilitated labor organizing. Over the preceding two decades, the size of the working class had increased in strategic sectors of the economy. More important, by 1919, Cuban workers had made significant advances over foreign workers in those sectors. Population growth accounted for much of these gains, as the first of the post-1898 baby-boom generation entered the wage force. Diminished Spanish immigration, especially during the war years, also allowed Cubans to expand their presence in the workplace. The 1919 census revealed that, for the first time, Cubans represented a majority among railroad workers and maritime employees. The total number of mechanics, machinists, bricklayers, masons, and printers almost doubled, and in this expansion Cubans increased their numbers significantly. The net effect was increased stability for workers, greater continuity at the workplace, and more homogeneity in the composition of the working class. And by the early 1920s, the effects of these developments were beginning to tell.

Not unlike bourgeois interest groups, workers organized initially in pursuit of improved working conditions and living standards. The principal demands were for an eight-hour workday, wage increases, improved working conditions, and miscellaneous social benefits. The economic crisis of 1920–21 served to accelerate labor organizing and broaden labor demands. Caught between declining employment and rising living costs, workers responded with renewed militancy. The ranks of organized labor increased in membership. So did work stoppages and boycotts, all of which announced the expanding power of Cuban trade unions. During 1917 and 1918, strikes reverberated across the island. Between January and February 1919, there was a strike somewhere in Cuba almost daily: stevedores in Cárdenas, ceramic workers in Rancho Boyeros, construction workers in Havana, cigarworkers in Matanzas, United Railway workers in Santa Clara, carpenters in Havana, miners in Oriente, bakers in Cienfuegos, textile workers in Havana. A strike in 1920 in Havana harbor paralyzed maritime traffic. A typographers' strike the same year brought

Havana presses to a halt. Strikes in sugar *centrales* closed mills in Las Villas, Camagüey, and Oriente. A railroad stoppage in August 1920 interrupted rail transportation across the island. Resistance to labor demands and repression of labor demonstrations added to workers' grievances as they called for the right to organize and strike, for freedom for imprisoned workers, and for an end to deportation of foreign labor leaders. Increasingly, strikes and boycotts were transforming labor into a political force of formidable proportions.

Against this backdrop, the second National Labor Congress convened in Havana in 1920. Representing some 102 unions and an estimated 90,000 workers, the assembled labor delegates passed a variety of resolutions calling for government assistance programs, the development of public housing, the adoption of an eight-hour workday, price controls on basic commodity staples, equal pay for men and women, the abolition of piecework, and the denunciation of United States imperialism.

Through the early 1920s workers continued to organize. Unions increased in size and strength. In late 1920, some eighteen unions in Havana consolidated into the anarcho-syndicalist Federación Obrera de La Habana (FOH). The movement toward federation gained momentum. Workers in similar trades and industries across the island organized into national unions. In February 1924, railroad workers organized into the Hermandad Ferroviaria de Cuba, the first organization to bring together in one national union all workers of a single industry. A year later, port workers followed the lead of the Hermandad Ferroviaria and organized nationally into the Federación Nacional Marítima de los Puertos de Cuba.

At the third National Labor Congress in 1925, resolutions called for preferential employment for Cuban workers, affirmed the right to strike and the use of boycott and sabotage in defense of workers' interests, and adopted an anti-imperialist plank. By far the most important accomplishment of the third congress, however, was the consolidation of Cuban trade unions into a single national organization. Delegations from eighty-two trade unions attending the congress, with the endorsement of forty-six others not present—in total representing some 200,000 workers—consolidated into one national labor federation, the Confederación Nacional Obrera de Cuba (CNOC).

Workers also organized politically. As early as 1920, the newly formed Partido Socialista Radical called for the socialization of property, equality for women, the construction of public housing, improvement of work conditions for women and children, amnesty for workers arrested in strikes,

244 CUBA

and government regulation of strategic national industries, including sugar, mining, railroads, and shipping. In March 1923, José Peña Vilabod, founder and secretary general of the FOH, and its treasurer, Alejandro Barreiro, joined with Carlos Baliño and Julio Antonio Mella to establish the Agrupación Comunista de La Habana. In the following two years, new communist groupings *(agrupaciones)* were established in San Antonio de los Baños, Guanabacoa, Manzanillo, and Media Luna. In August 1925, within weeks of the founding of CNOC, the *agrupaciones* met in Havana and consolidated into the Partido Comunista de Cuba (PCC). That same year, the PCC formally applied for membership in the Comintern. The PCC developed strategies for organizing political support among unions, rejected electoral politics, established educational programs for workers, and organized a youth movement. During the late 1920s, the PCC expanded its influence into the CNOC and established leadership over many constituent unions.

VI

These were also years of rising nationalism in Cuba. Much of the surge of Cuban nationalism during the 1920s derived directly from an abiding abhorrence of the Platt Amendment—a sentiment that translated quickly into revilement of the political elites and a revulsion for their U.S. backers, setting in sharp relief the feebleness with which the officeholders defended national sovereignty. For the first time since the debates at the Constituent Assembly of 1901, the Platt Amendment had become the object of national discontent and the subject of political debate. A vast corpus of literature—some of it polemical, much of it scholarly—detailed the Cuban case against it. Cubans of all political persuasions agreed on one proposition: the abrogation of the Platt Amendment. Nothing aroused as much collective Cuban indignation as the amendment did. A source of enduring injury to Cuban national sensibilities, it quickly became the focal point of growing nationalist sentiment. In 1926, the League Against the Platt Amendment was organized in Havana to mobilize public opinion. Two years later, the founding of the Anti-Imperialist League took up the same call.

Cubans carried their protests beyond the national arena. Opponents of the Platt Amendment appealed for international support. In 1922, University of Havana law professor Luis Machado urged Cuba to submit its case against the Platt Amendment to an arbitration commission of the League of Nations. In that same year, the Platt Amendment was the subject at the annual meeting of the Association of International Law of Cuba. Pressure also mounted for placing the amendment on the agenda of the Sixth Pan American conference, scheduled to convene in 1928 in Havana.

Through the 1920s, attacks against the Platt Amendment increased in virulence and frequency. On few other issues had Cuban public opinion arrived at such unanimity of purpose. The amendment had become a source of passionate debate. Political elites could neither dismiss rising nationalist sentiment nor remain neutral in the national debate. Nor could they acquiesce to continued United States intervention without impairing their ability to govern. These developments increasingly forced office-holders to adopt a stronger nationalist position, if only to undercut the rising nationalist surge. The Liberal party platform in the 1924 presidential election called for a "revision of the Permanent Treaty, eliminating the appendix to the Constitution, and winning Cuba an independent place in the world"—the first time a major party had formally demanded the abrogation of the Platt Amendment.

VII

Simultaneously the political class confronted a threat to its continued rule from a newly organized bourgeoisie and a newly mobilized proletariat. Suddenly the premises upon which the officeholders had traditionally presided over the polity passed into desuetude. Their power was no longer incontestable, their position no longer unassailable. New social groups aspired to hegemony, and they could not be ignored.

These were currents swirling about the republic in the early 1920s, and when flowing in the same direction they formed a tide that was nearly irresistible. The organization of sectors of the new entrepreneurial bourgeoisie into economic interest groups and the articulation of political and social dissent in the form of women's activism and workers' militancy announced the emergence of new social forces in the republic. The immediate effect of these developments was to subject officeholders to pressure from below in the form of the entrepreneurial bourgeoisie and the working class, and from everywhere in the form of a rising tide of nationalism. Officeholders now faced pressure to share political power and accommodate policy to the needs of a new constituency.

The national mood was in flux during the early 1920s—uncertain, uneasy, and unsettled. The murmurs of discontent were everywhere audible, the auguries of change were everywhere visible. Zayas could not have chosen a more inauspicious moment to reorganize his cabinet. The unabashed purposefulness with which the president and his family subsequently pursued the amassing of personal fortunes from public funds, the manifest cynicism with which legislators passed special interest bills, and the magnitude of corruption that returned to government generally, offended the sensibilities even of those long inured to the excesses of public officials. This was too much, too fast, too public—irrefutable evidence that the officeholders remained incorrigibly corrupt.

This most recent display of official misconduct helped consolidate the advocates of reform and summoned them to participate more actively in politics. Reform had become a political issue, but it was not at all certain that traditional politics could accommodate it. Reformist groups could not reasonably rely on the traditional political parties and ordinary electoral mechanisms to displace incumbent officeholders from power. They needed an alternative political vehicle for power. In 1923, the opportunity presented itself.

In August 1923, the prestigious and powerful Veterans Association met in Havana to protest rumored pension cuts. Made up principally of the veterans of the nineteenth-century wars for independence, the association was generally identified as a national repository of civic virtues and patriotic sentiment. The veterans' protest expanded and quickly became a general indictment of all aspects of public life in Cuba. They called for the regeneration of Cuba and adopted a twelve-point resolution, including the repeal of the lottery law, honest collection of taxes, the abolition of *botellas,* honest elections, competitive public bidding for government contracts, the establishment of an independent judiciary, legal accountability in the disbursement of public funds, limitations on congressional immunity from criminal prosecution, laws favoring Cuban workers over foreigners, abolition of presidential re-election, political rights for women, and defense of national industry and commerce. The veterans organized into the National Association of Veterans and Patriots to coordinate political action and press for their demands.

The Veterans and Patriots movement gave political expression to national stirrings of reform. It received the endorsement of scores of organizations, including the Federación Nacional de Corporaciones Económicas, the Asociación de Industriales, the Asociación de Buen Gobierno, the FEU, the Falange de Acción Cubana, the Federación de Asociaciones Femeninas, as well as local veterans groups, professional organizations, and a variety of civic clubs. General Carlos García Velez, a ranking veteran leader, assumed the presidency of the association. The six active vice presidents included Alejo Carreño, president of the Asociación de Hacendados y Colonos, Carlos Alzugaray, head of the Asociación de Comerciantes de La Habana, Lorenzo Nieto, historian Manuel Sanguily, and philosopher Enrique José Varona. Also included among the "honorary presidents" were Enrique Hernández Cartaya, a member of the "honest cabinet," Porfirio Franca, Julio Antonio Mella, Antonio G. Mendoza, Vicente Soler, Fernando González, Manuel Enrique, and Carlos Zaldo. Manual Despaigne, the secretary of the treasury in the "honest cabinet," became treasurer. Oscar Soto and Gustavo Gutiérrez of the Asociación de Buen Gobierno served as secretaries and Rubén Martínez Villena directed propaganda. Signatories to subsequent pronouncements in 1923 included representation from the full spectrum of the reform surge of the early 1920s: Manual Despaigne, Hortensia Lamar, Federico Laredo Bru, Alejo Carreño, Carlos Alzugaray, Aníbal Escalante, Rubén Martínez Villena, and Juan Marinello.

The establishment of a formal organization with duly elected officers and a publicly ratified program underscored the central feature of the Veterans and Patriots Association. It was more than a passing protest. This was a political movement in the making, one that quickly captured popular imagination and public support. By September there was growing sentiment to transform the Veterans and Patriots Association formally into a political party. Behind its official slogan—"For the Regeneration of Cuba"—the Veterans and Patriots movement gained momentum and gathered supporters. Provincial delegations were organized, municipal committees established, and neighborhood councils created. Public endorsements came from across the island. So did financial donations. In all but name, a new political party had arisen to challenge the incumbent officeholders.

By early autumn the Zayas government had arrived at some understanding of the magnitude of threat posed by the Veterans and Patriots movement. The president did not hesitate. Leaders were harassed and meetings were disrupted. Printing shops publishing propaganda for the association were closed. In October 1923, Zayas issued a presidential order prohibiting the Veterans and Patriots Association from holding public meetings. When the association defied the executive decree, government authorities moved quickly to arrest the leadership. Some twenty officials were immediately imprisoned and others fled into hiding. In late autumn, at one of its last public meetings, the Veterans and Patriots Association governing council proclaimed itself frankly revolutionary and vowed to take whatever steps necessary for the regeneration of Cuba.

The Veterans and Patriots movement now plotted the overthrow of the Zayas government, but it was too late. Many of the ranking leaders had been imprisoned, others had fled abroad. Still, reform was an issue that would not go away, and the Veterans and Patriots movement remained popular. In April 1924, what remained of the leadership of the Veterans and Patriots movement made good on its threat to rebel. The long-awaited summons to rebellion was issued in the form of a *pronunciamiento* in Las Villas province. With key reformist leaders in prison or exile, the Veterans and Patriots uprising collapsed within days.

It was almost a stillborn effort—but not quite. The reform surge had been contained, at least for the time being. In the course of the next decade the tide of pressure for political change would be channeled into different currents, and Cuba would not be the same. Officeholders had survived a serious challenge to their power. This was the first threat to incumbent officeholders to originate outside their ranks since the short-lived uprising by the Partido Independiente de Color. Both threats had been driven to the fringes of the law, and both were ultimately crushed by force.

The year 1924 was a presidential election year in Cuba. Zayas stepped down, considerably wealthier than when he stepped in. The Conservative party nominated Mario G. Menocal and the Liberals chose Gerardo Machado. No one doubted that the Liberals would win. No one was disappointed.

VIII

Gerardo Machado stood in 1924 at the threshold of the presidency, the apogee of an undistinguished career in politics. He had held the rank of brigadier general at the conclusion of the war and was active in Liberal politics in Las Villas province. He had occupied a number of political positions in the early republic, including mayor of Santa Clara, inspector general of the army, and secretary of *gobernación*. But Machado was different—different if only because the times were different. Reform was in the air, an ethereal presence to be sure, programmatically formless and politically leaderless. Machado the candidate intuitively adopted the rhetoric of reform and instinctively assumed the role of redeemer. Reformism entered mainstream politics in the form of the program of the Liberal party and in the platform of the Liberal candidate.

Machado called it the "Platform of Regeneration" and summoned all Cubans to participate in what he proclaimed as nothing less than a crusade for national revival. He pledged an end to political corruption. He repudiated re-election. Candidate Machado committed himself to new schools, new roads, new social services. The army was to be professionalized and the civil service modernized. The candidate favored the development of new local industry, the protection of existing industry, and the diversification of the economy. Throughout the campaign Machado invoked nationalism, defended the integrity of the republic, and repeatedly called for a revision of treaty relations and the abrogation of the Platt Amendment.

These themes struck a responsive chord in 1924. Many who only twelve months earlier had seen no prospect for reform except through revolt returned enthusiastically to electoral politics and endorsed the Liberal candidate. Machado won endorsements from Fernando Ortiz, organizer of the Junta Cubana de Renovación Nacional, historian Ramiro Guerra, the Federación Nacional de Corporaciones Economicas, and the FEU. Several members of the Supreme National Council of the Veterans and Patriots Movement joined the new Machado government, including Rogelio Zayas Bazán, as secretary of the *gobernación,* and Enrique Hernández Cartaya, as secretary of the treasury.

Not a few rushed to proclaim the victory of Machado as vindication of reform—a view not entirely without merit. Many persuaded themselves, at least during the early years of the new administration, that in Machado they had found redemption of reformism. Certainly Machado played the part deftly. By necessity, incrementally and without comprehensive design, Machado appropriated the symbols and substance of reform. He recognized the symptoms of national discontent, and by adopting the role of proponent of reform and protector of national sovereignty, Machado successfully brought a measure of political legitimacy to the goals of a movement outlawed only months earlier.

Machado's advocacy of national interests was neither wholly specious nor entirely cynical. Machado differed from his predecessors in one last respect. In the course of three decades of politics, he had amassed a personal fortune of considerable proportions. He entered the presidency as a wealthy man. Machado represented a success story, a member of the old separatist amalgam passing into the ranks of the new entrepreneurial bourgeoisie. Machado owned the Santa Marta sugar mill, a construction company, a paint factory, newspapers *(El País* and *Excelsior),* a bank (Banco del Comercio), a shoe company, a contracting business, a market, and interests in several other local enterprises, including a soap factory and a beer brewery.

Those sectors of the bourgeoisie that only twenty-four months earlier had organized to demand state support for national interests now looked to the Machado government for implementation of these goals. They were not disappointed. During the first two years of his administration, Machado continued to extoll the virtues of national industrial development and the need for economic diversification. He encouraged the development of new industry and diversification of agriculture. He committed the government to the support of economic growth in the form of communication and transportation facilities (most notably the Central Highway), agricultural credit, and, most important, tariff reform. In 1927, the government enacted the Customs-Tariff Law, arguably one of the most important pieces of economic legislation of the early republic. For the better part of a decade, Cuban industrialists had clamored for protectionist measures. Machado delivered. The Customs-Tariff Law provided state support and government subsidy for the expansion of national industry and agriculture. Duties on raw materials decreased to promote local manufacturing activity. The tariff on crude oil was reduced to encourage the expansion of refining facilities. Sisal was exempted from duties to promote local rope and cordage manufacturing. Duty on cotton was lowered to encourage textiles. Lower duties on the import of machinery and heavy equipment stimulated the expansion of industrial facilities. Tariffs on manufactured goods were raised to stimulate local production. A variety of new manufacturing enterprises developed behind the tariff shield, including cheese, condensed milk, butter, shoes, starch, paint, paper, clothing, knitting yarns, hosieries, and glass containers. Among the existing industries that expanded were soap, beer, lubricants, furniture, and cement. By 1929, permits for fifty new industries had been issued by the government.

Livestock and agricultural production diversified and expanded: production of meat and milk increased, and under tariff protection tannery facilities expanded operations. The production of salted meat increased and reduced meat imports; imports of fowl and eggs also declined. Duties on cacao and coffee remained set at high levels to protect and promote national producers. A new tariff rate on rice provided direct stimulus to national rice production, and the use of rice flour and yucca flour increased over more expensive wheat flour imports. Fruit and vegetable production expanded, as did the production of textile fibers. In 1928, the government created a national commission for the protection and promotion of tobacco. The construction of the Central Highway provided an alternative to the largely foreign-owned railroad system, and facilitated the distribution of locally produced fruits and vegetables.

IX

The alliance was sound in its design and, at moments, even compelling in its function. But the structure was faulty, largely because the premises were flawed. Machado's attempt to balance the increasingly diverse socio-economic forces during the 1920s represented an ingenious effort to resolve the outstanding contradictions of the Cuban political economy. But in a larger sense, it was an experiment conceived at a time of prosperity, one that required continued economic growth of sufficient vigor to permit both foreign and national capital the opportunity to expand. Cuban capital expanded tentatively, always under the shadow of dominant foreign interests and dependent on favorable state policies. As long as the economy continued to grow, foreign investors and local interests enjoyed a reasonably felicitous coexistence. It was a short-lived experiment, however.

The depression came early to Cuba. Starting in the mid-1920s, the price of sugar began to drop, a decline that would not end until the following decade. The government responded to the crisis with the Verdeja Act, an attempt to halt declining world prices by decreasing Cuban exports. The 1926 crop was fixed at 4.5 million tons, a 10 percent reduction from the 1925 harvest, and the length of the *zafra* was shortened from 136 to 87 days. Subsequent decrees imposed a moratorium on new planting and fixed the start of the harvest for January 1927, a month later than usual.

Efforts proved futile. Instead of stabilizing world prices on reduced supplies, the curtailment of Cuban production stimulated increased sugar exports elsewhere. Prices continued to drop. The 1924 price of 4.2 cents a pound fell to 2.6 cents in 1926 and 2.5 cents in 1928.

The economy faltered and floundered. All sectors suffered from the drop of sugar prices and the decline of sugar production. Hardest hit were sugar workers. The shortened *zafra* meant less work for tens of thousands of Cubans already suffering from chronic unemployment. Distress spread upward and outward. The harvest began later and ended earlier, so workers were without work longer. Higher unemployment and lower wages meant also a drop in consumption. Inventories began to pile up as sales declined. Retailers and importers found themselves without customers. A decline in import and retail trade, in turn, resulted in the discharge of employees in those sectors. Professionals lost clients, merchants lost customers, and white-collar employees lost jobs. Government employees faced salary cuts and, increasingly, discharge. These were especially troubling developments, for the expansion of the state payroll had traditionally absorbed the expanding ranks of the middle class. This signified nothing less than a breakdown of the mechanism by which the officeholders had traditionally underwritten political order and social stability.

In a deteriorating economic environment, Machado prepared for re-election. Re-election was arguably a hazardous enterprise, one not to be undertaken lightly. The year 1928, moreover, was not the best of times for an incumbent president to seek re-election. The administration that appeared incapable of resolving the economic crisis of the previous two years could hardly be expected to win a mandate for another six. Machado understood this, and through a combination of intimidation, coercion, and bribery secured from the traditional parties the joint nomination of his bid for a second term. *Cooperativismo,* as the arrangement became known, joined the Liberal, Conservative, and Popular parties behind Machado's candidacy for re-election. On November 1, 1928, as the *candidato único,* Machado secured uncontested re-election to a new six-year term.

Machado had hardly been inaugurated for a second term in 1929 when the full impact of the world-wide depression hit the already ailing Cuban economy. A second blow was not long in coming. A year later, the United States passed the Hawley-Smoot Tariff Act, which increased the duty on Cuban sugar. Domestic producers and island possessions gained an increasing share of the U.S. market at the expense of Cuban sugar. The Cuban share of the market declined from 49 percent in 1930 to 25 percent in 1933. In 1931 Cuba joined six other sugar producing countries in signing the Chadbourne Plan, a strategy designed to raise floundering prices by restricting supplies for five years.

The cumulative effect of these developments was devastating. Sugar production, the fulcrum upon which the entire economy balanced, dropped 60 percent. All at once sugar producers found themselves with surplus sugar, in search of new markets, at a time of declining prices. The volume of all Cuban exports declined by 80 percent, while the price of the principal export, sugar, fell over 60 percent. Producers struggled to remain solvent by lowering wages and cutting production through layoffs. The length of the *zafra* was reduced again, this time to a sixty-two-day harvest—that is, only two months' work for tens of thousands of sugar workers. The value of tobacco, the island's second largest export, declined from $43 million in 1929 to $13 million in 1933.

Salaries and wages were reduced, workers laid off, and businesses and factories closed. Unemployment soared. Some 250,000 heads of families, representing approximately one million people out of a total population of 3.9 million, found themselves totally unemployed. Those fortunate enough to escape total unemployment found temporary work difficult to come by and wages depressed. Pay for agricultural workers declined by 75 percent. In the sugar zones, wages fell as low as twenty cents for a twelve-hour workday. On one large estate, workers received ten cents a day—five in cash and five in credit at the company store. In some districts, laborers received only food and lodging for their work. "Wages paid . . . in 1932," one wage survey reported grimly, "are reported to have been the lowest since the days of slavery." Wages for the urban proletariat decreased by 50 percent. As wages fell in absolute terms, the value of the peso decreased in purchasing power. The peso was worth 28 centavos less in 1928 than in 1913. By 1933, 60 percent of the population lived at submarginal levels of under $300 in annual real income; another 30 percent earned marginal wages between $300 and $600.

Profits plummetted everywhere. Commerce came to a standstill. Local industry and manufacturing reduced production in response to reduced purchasing power of the population; this, in turn, caused a new round of unemployment and wage cuts. The cycle seemed to have no end. Commercial, banking, and manufacturing failures reached record proportions. Business failures produced another spiral of unemployment and new rounds of shortages and price rises. Local business sectors called for government subsidies, relief programs, and economic supports. Under Machado, during the worse moments of the depression when national need was the greatest, government revenues that long had served as the major source of both subsidy of the entrepreneurial bourgeoisie and the solvency of officeholders were transferred into foreign hands in the form of servicing the government's debt.

Between 1930 and 1931 the government inaugurated a policy of drastic salary cuts for all public employees except the armed forces. Pay reductions of as much as 60 percent were not uncommon. A year later, budget cuts resulted in the first of a series of sweeping layoffs of civil servants. Highway construction projects that had previously employed some 15,000 workers in 1928 were suspended, creating immediate hardships in thousands of households. In the second half of 1931 alone, the government closed two hundred post offices, nine diplomatic legations, seven public hospitals, and several nurseries, schools, and agricultural stations. In desperation, civil servants turned on each other. As early as 1928, pressure mounted on Machado to enforce the constitutional requirement that only voters occupy government positions, a move designed to fire women employees. And for most who remained on state payrolls, public employment offered diminishing consolation. Salaries of public employees were cut, and soon the reduced salaries themselves fell hopelessly in arrears. By 1932, the salaries of the vast majority of civil servants had fallen six months behind. A year later, the total salary arrears for government personnel approached $19 million. Almost all government agencies moved to a half-day at half-pay work schedule. Thousands of government employees, traditionally secure in civil service and public administration, were among the newest arrivals to augment the swelling ranks of the unemployed.

These conditions set the stage for political confrontation and social conflict on a scale unprecedented in the republic. Political opposition spread. Much of it originated with members of the old-line parties, for whom Machado had violated the standing political injunction against re-electionism. Some opposition came from the president's own party. In 1927, Liberal Carlos Mendieta broke with Machado and organized a new political party, La Asociación Unión Nacionalista. This was a significant development, for Mendieta had been one of the central figures of the Veterans and Patriots movement and brought to his cause many of the old reformist elements. Other Liberal leaders included Federico Laredo Bru and Roberto Méndez Peñate. Former Conservative president Mario G. Menocal also denounced re-electionism.

Labor continued to organize, union membership expanded, and the number and frequency of strikes increased. The economic crisis led to national labor militancy. In 1927 cigarworkers organized the Federación Nacional de Torcedores, uniting some 30,000 workers in all six provinces. In 1928, electrical workers organized nationally into the Unión de Obreros y Empleados de Plantas Eléctricas. In 1932, sugar workers established the first national union, the Sindicato Nacional de Obreros de la Industria Azucarera (SNOIA). By 1929 the Cuban Communist Party (PCC) had expanded control over large sectors of organized labor. Mass demonstrations and hunger marches increased. Between 1929 and 1932, strikes halted production in a number of industries, including sugar, cigar manufacturing, railroads, metallurgy, construction, and textiles. In March 1930, the CNOC, now outlawed, organized a stunning general strike. Directed by Martínez Villena and involving some 200,000 workers, the strike paralyzed the island. It ended only after a wave of government violence and repression. A month later, workers and soldiers clashed again. The occasion was the May 1 celebration in Regla, and in the ensuing confrontation scores of demonstrators were killed and injured. Several weeks later, railroad workers struck and paralyzed national rail transportation. Strike organizers were arrested and trains resumed operations under army direction. Encouraged by the events of mid-1930, the PCC and CNOC established provincial committees and expanded into the countryside to organize agricultural workers and peasants.

Clashes increased, too, between the government and its political opponents. In May 1930, the Unión Nacionalista organized a political rally in Artemisa. Even before speakers addressed the assembled thousands, the army opened fire and moved in to disperse the panic-stricken crowd by force. The attack resulted in eight deaths and hundreds of wounded, including children. Within twenty-four hours, virtually all ranking Unión Nacionalista leaders were either in jail or in exile. The following September, a student demonstration in Havana led to another armed confrontation that left one student dead and scores of others injured. In October Machado suspended constitutional guarantees in the province of Havana. Students outside Havana reacted immediately and demonstrations in Santiago de Cuba, Santa Clara, and Pinar del Río produced a new wave of clashes with the police. Classes were suspended and the university closed. Across the island, normal schools closed one by one.

A kind of desultory warfare broke out in the countryside. The torching of canefields became commonplace, and millions of *arrobas* of cane went up in smoke. Armed bands operated throughout the interior, ambushing trains, cutting telephone and telegraph wires, destroying rail bridges and tunnels, and attacking isolated Rural Guard posts. Military escorts became a permanent and necessary feature of railroad traffic between Havana and Santiago de Cuba. In November 1930, constitutional guarantees were lifted throughout the island and a state of siege proclaimed. Army units in full combat dress assumed police functions throughout provincial cities and towns. Military supervisors displaced civilian governors in Pinar del Río, Matanzas, Las Villas, Camagüey, and Oriente. Army tribunals superseded civilian courts. Constitutional guarantees were restored on December 1, but suspended again ten days later. In January 1931, Machado invoked an old colonial law of public order, never before used in the republic, to suspend the publication of some fifteen newspapers and periodicals and ordered the arrest of the editors. Military censors supervised editorial boards of newspapers and magazines.

Repression on such a scale summoned into existence an extensive police apparatus penetrating every aspect of Cuban social life, not only to arrest, torture, and execute but to maintain surveillance over Cubans not in prison and over the countless thousands who were. A secret police was organized. The Sección de Expertos was formed—"experts" in the method of torture. The Partida de la Porra served as a government death squad. Cuba assumed the appearance of an armed camp, and terror became the principal means of government. The government physically eliminated opposition, real and suspected. Arrests, torture, and assassination became commonplace. Government opponents were kidnapped, and most were never heard from again. This was a regime that eliminated critics in anticipation of opposition, and struck at people willing to conform on the suspicion that they might eventually cease to be willing. Neutrality was suspect, criticism was subversive.

X

Both the character and composition of the opposition changed during the early 1930s. New political forces were summoned to the struggle against Machado. A new republican generation had emerged, one that rejected traditional politics as unacceptable and repudiated traditional methods of opposition as unworkable. As early as 1927, a new student organization, the Directorio Estudiantil Universitario (DEU), was organized to oppose

Machado. The ABC Revolutionary Society was founded four years later, made up mainly of young men and women, intellectuals, professionals, and students, organized around underground cells. The ABC embraced armed struggle and responded to government violence with reprisal, committing itself to creating conditions of revolution through systematic use of force against the government. The Organización Celular Radical Revolucionaria (OCRR) also adopted a cellular structure and used armed struggle and sabotage as the means to overthrow Machado. Other new anti-government groups joined the swelling ranks of the opposition. Women's resistance groups, university professors, and normal school teachers and students became part of a vast clandestine network dedicated to armed struggle against Machado.

These were, in the main, representatives of the vast body of new professionals, men and women, lawyers, teachers, engineers, and accountants, as well as many of those discharged from public service, who emerged to challenge the old political class for control of the state. This first-born republican generation faced problems not unlike those of the last-born colonial generation: finding a place in Cuba. Politics was serious business, if only because politics remained the principal means of access to that most Cuban of all businesses—government. To the ordinary urgency normally associated with politics was added a new immediacy, for if there were few economic opportunities for Cubans outside government before the late 1920s, there were fewer afterwards.

There was, further, one additional if not immediately apparent demographic dimension to the depression in Cuba. What made the collapse of the Cuban economy between the late 1920s and early 1930s especially devastating was timing: it occurred just at the moment that the vast post-1898 baby-boom population was reaching the age of peak economic productivity. Nearly three-quarters of a million young Cubans, between the ages of late twenties and early thirties, had recently entered the labor force, many with newly established families of their own, and most could not find work. In 1931, the baby-boom generation constituted 20 percent of the population and children under nine years of age made up another 30 percent of the total. The economic dimensions of Cuban politics assumed a new demographic urgency.

Throughout the early decades of the republic, government had continued to expand its activities and seemed possessed of an infinite capacity to absorb and accommodate the needs of middle-class Cubans. Education was the obvious preparation for such a career, and the preponderance of graduating lawyers, teachers, and engineers suggested that Cubans in vast numbers had early committed themselves to the pursuit of careers in public office. Government was the most available outlet for the talents of the middle-class republican generation. Their claim was based on education, and they had every reason to believe that their credentials would provide them with entrée into public administration. But by the early 1930s the collapse of the economy prevented most of the educated and talented middle-class Cubans from achieving their aspirations. They were not slow to hold the old political class responsible. "Many of Cuba's ills," the ABC proclaimed in 1931, "derive from the fact that the generation of '95 has kept for itself the governmental posts, systematically excluding those Cubans who came of age under the republic."

Open warfare broke out in Cuba after 1931. Repression by the regime increased, but so did reprisals by the opposition. Government opponents were murdered and the murderers were assassinated. Every member of the Machado government was a potential target. Assassinations, bombings, and sabotage became the principal expression of opposition. But the price for opposition was dear. The government responded with mounting fury and indiscriminate violence. Jails filled with government opponents, and they were the fortunate ones. More often, suspects were executed summarily at the site of capture.

Once the state lost the capacity to finance itself and to underwrite social peace, contradictions long in the making appeared in sharp relief. Labor militancy continued. Strikes increased. Local manufacturers, industrialists, and landowners also abandoned the government. They recognized, too, that as economic conditions worsened and political opposition intensified, Machado himself had become the issue. The political opposition despaired of a political settlement to the crisis. A revolt in 1931 led by mainstream political leaders, and the subsequent imprisonment of the moderate opposition—some four hundred arrests in all—served to polarize opponents even further. The elimination of the moderate opposition set the stage for confrontation between the embattled extremities of the Cuban polity. As economic conditions deteriorated and social unrest spread, the struggle against Machado was transforming daily into a movement seeking to overthrow the system along with the president.

The collapse of the moderate opposition, particularly the Unión Nacionalista, left the Cuban bourgeoisie without political representation in the conflict. Local manufacturers, industrialists, merchants, and landowners, as well as members of the moderate old-line opposition, found themselves economically insolvent and politically impotent, facing repression from above and revolution from below. At the same time, the struggle against Machado assumed fully the character of revolutionary upheaval. As the prospects of a moderate settlement decreased, the possibilities of a radical solution increased.

By the early 1930s, many members of the beleaguered bourgeoisie had concluded that only intervention by the United States could offer redemption from Machado and rescue from revolution. These were frustrating times for members of the moderate opposition, a period of deepening despair. The Unión Nacionalista seemed destined for dissolution. Most moderate leaders were in prison, or in exile, or dead. Machado seemed stronger, not weaker. Government confidence increased, and with it repression. In the years that followed, as the crisis deepened, appeals for U.S. intervention increased. Some anti-government elements who had earlier denounced the Platt Amendment and decried North American intervention in Cuban internal affairs now insisted that treaty obligations imposed on the United States responsibility for ending the Cuban crisis. As early as 1927, Fernando Ortiz, the former leader of the Junta de Renovación in 1923, appealed to the State Department for "moral intervention." Ortiz insisted that the United States had the "obligation" to guarantee "good government," one based on the right of intervention—a right that could not "exist without a corresponding obligation." Two years later, Octavio Seigle, a cofounder of the Unión Nacionalista, struck a similar tone. "The United States," he insisted, "is duty bound to see that Cuba does not continue in the hands of a dictator. Under the Platt Amendment, which is the law in such matters, the United States is obliged to see to it that a government is maintained . . . 'capable of protecting life, property and individual liberty.' . . . There is a direct obligation to protect the Cubans' right to vote for a government of their own choosing and under which their lives and liberties will be safe." In 1930, several ranking leaders of the moderate opposition visited the U.S. embassy to urge privately the adoption of a "preventive intervention policy" to unseat Machado. A year later, Mendieta urged the United States to pressure Machado to resign and call new elections. In fact, so frequent were opposition calls for U.S. intervention that the pro-Machado congress proposed amending the penal code to provide a penalty of long-term or life imprisonment for "any Cuban who seeks the intervention or interference of a foreign power in the internal or external development of national life"—in the name of defending national sovereignty.

Through the early 1930s the conflict deepened and confrontations increased. War had broken out across Cuba, in the cities and in the countryside, a war without quarter, in which neither the regime nor its opponents flinched from escalating deeds of violence and blood. A political solution became increasingly elusive and daily more improbable. Political repression and economic depression had transformed the Cuban conflict into a social crisis, and into a source of concern in the United States.

XI

As during the Cuban crisis in 1920, Washington responded quickly. In May 1933, the new Franklin D. Roosevelt administration appointed Assistant Secretary of State Sumner Welles as ambassador to Cuba. Welles was instructed to offer "the friendly mediation" of the United States government to Machado and the political opposition and to obtain "a definite, detailed, and binding understanding between the present Cuban Government and the responsible leaders of the factions opposed to it."

Welles arrived in Havana with a specific charge: mediate "in any form most suitable" an end to the Cuban crisis. Both sides believed themselves the beneficiary of the Welles mission. The government believed that the proposed mediation represented a clever form of continued U.S. support and a guarantee that Machado would serve the full length of his term. The opposition believed that the mediation was an ingenious method by which the United States planned to remove Machado.

Both sides were right. To Machado, Welles promised a new commercial treaty to relieve economic distress if he reached a political settlement with the opposition. To opposition leaders, Welles promised a change of government and participation in the subsequent administration if they joined the mediations and supported an orderly transfer of power.

The mediations provided the United States the means with which to pursue several policy objectives at once. They offered a way to obtain Machado's retirement by creating the constitutional basis for presidential succession, and thus end the revolutionary threat created by Machado's continued incumbency. Machado had outlived his usefulness. The order and stability that he had so deftly provided during his first term, the basis upon which he had previously received United States support, had disintegrated in his second term. Neither the application of repression nor attempts at reconciliation seemed capable of diminishing the intransigence of the opposition. After five years of sustained political strife and unrelieved economic stress, it had become apparent that Machado could not end disorder. His continued presence was now the central issue for the political opposition, and was easily the greatest single obstacle to the restoration of political stability. The impossibility of attaining political reform increased the probability of social revolution.

The mediations also provided the forum through which to return opposition groups, specifically the "responsible leaders" referred to in Welles's instructions, from the fringes of illegality to the fold of legality. This signified a repudiation of revolution, and a way to relieve mounting revolutionary pressure by diverting the opposition away from a conspiratorial solution and toward a constitutional settlement. The mediations provided, too, the means through which opposition groups could obtain their objectives and join the political process in an orderly, institutional fashion. Just as important as easing Machado out was the necessity of easing new political elements in. The mediations conferred on sectors of the outlawed opposition a measure of political legitimacy, providing them with a vested interest in a settlement sanctioned and supported by the United States. This served as a recruitment process, a method by which the United States determined which groups were "responsible" and which were not. Through United States political intervention in the form of mediation, select opposition groups would secure access to power, and they would be linked to the United States by ties of gratitude and indebtedness. United States influence over the new government would be preserved, and the place of the United States as a powerbroker among political contenders would be preserved.

Not all sectors of the opposition were compatible with U.S. interests, and hence not all were invited to participate. Students in the DEU denounced the mediations, as did the PCC and the CNOC. Groups opposing mediations protested foreign intermeddling in Cuban internal affairs, and vowed to seek a Cuban solution independent of the United States.

Representatives from the mainstream opposition, including the Unión Nacionalista, agreed to participate. So did the ABC, the OCRR, university professors, women's opposition groups, and normal school teachers. The government representatives included leaders of the Liberal, Conservative, and Popular parties, and Secretary of War General Alberto Herrera representing the administration.

The mediations began on July 1, and pressure on the government for reform began immediately. Methodically, and patiently, Welles edged the unsuspecting Machado closer to his expulsion. The president acquiesced in succession to pressure for constitutional reform, restoration of the vice presidency, freedom of the press, release of political prisoners, and revision of the electoral code. In mid-July, Welles prepared to deliver the final blow: a suggestion that Machado appoint a vice president satisfactory to all parties and forthwith resign, thereby shortening his term by one year.

Machado responded first with incredulity, and then rage. He convened a special session of congress to repudiate publicly the proposal, vowing to remain in power through his full term of office. Machado reiterated his commitment to "any fair solution proposed," but, he added, he would not be "thrown into the street." He denounced United States intermeddling, vowed to defend national sovereignty, and exhorted Cubans to defend the homeland against armed aggression from the United States. Machado defied the United States to intervene. "Inform the President of the United States," Machado taunted Welles, "that [I] would prefer armed intervention to the acceptance of any such proposal." Privately he informed Welles that he would repel with arms the landing of foreign troops on national territory. As a last resort, Machado appealed to the court of Latin American public opinion, asking the Western Hemisphere republics to condemn United States intervention in Cuba.

In late July both Welles and Machado faced a new problem. Striking bus drivers in Havana clashed with the police, leading to an outbreak of sympathy strikes. Under the direction of the PCC and the CNOC, the strike quickly spread to other sectors and within days all movement of people and goods came to a halt. The strike had become general, and Havana was paralyzed. On August 7, a clash between demonstrators and police resulted in scores of deaths and injuries. The crisis deepened. By the end of the first week of August, the general strike had acquired the full proportions of a revolutionary offensive.

Machado and Welles recognized the gravity of the strike and turned immediately to defuse the deepening revolutionary situation. Each responded in a manner designed at once to end the strike and establish advantage over the other. Machado conferred with the leadership of the PCC and CNOC and offered the party legality and the union recognition in exchange for their support to end the strike. It was an opportunity seized by the Communist party. By the terms of the agreement, the government released labor leaders and communists from prison and pledged to legalize the PCC upon the end of the strike. The party, in return, promised to order workers back to their jobs. In fact, both Machado and the PCC misjudged conditions. The government believed the party to have more control over the strike than it had; the PCC believed the government to be stronger than it was. But the strike had expanded beyond communist control, and the government was beyond salvation.

Welles, too, took extraordinary measures. The source of the new urgency was self-evident. If Machado could not be persuaded to relinquish the presidency, then the general strike would sweep aside the whole government, an eventuality, Welles predicted grimly, with catastrophic consequences that would inevitably require United States armed intervention. Tensions mounted. The *New York Times* correspondent described conditions as "a race between mediation by the United States Ambassador and open revolution." The moment was critical, and Welles was desperate. "The ominous signs provided by a paralyzing general strike," he later wrote, "wholly political in character, made it doubly clear that only some radical solution could forestall the cataclysm which otherwise was inevitable." Welles recommended that if Machado insisted on remaining in power, that the United States withdraw recognition of the Cuban government. And if after the expiration of this time Machado still refused to resign, Welles proposed meeting with the government parties and opposition groups to prepare for the installation of a new government. Welles was certain that withdrawal of recognition would persuade Machado's supporters, specifically the traditional political parties, the congress, the cabinet, and the armed forces, to abandon the doomed president.

Welles's calculations were not without effect. The first defections occurred among the *machadista* parties. Pro-government parties viewed Machado's defiance with foreboding, sensing uneasily that this was a contest the president could not win. And what, then, would become of them? Leaders of the Liberal, Conservative, and Popular parties, determined to preserve their positions, recognized the necessity of participating in the solution proposed by the United States. If the Machado government fell solely through U.S. pressure, the traditional parties faced the prospect of drastic reorganization under the best of circumstances, or complete dissolution—as many opposition factions demanded. Alternatively, the success of a revolution against Machado also threatened the old parties with extinction and party leaders with reprisals at the hands of their foes. Endorsement of the U.S. proposal, however, and a timely defection from a president facing an uncertain future, had the virtue of aligning the old parties with the new politics, thereby assuring their survival in post-Machado Cuba. If the new opposition factions could obtain legitimacy by participation in the mediations, the old political parties would guarantee their own survival by supporting the mediator. In early August, leaders of the Liberal, Conservative, and Popular parties endorsed the proposed early retirement of Machado and turned to the task of framing the legislation necessary to expedite the president's departure.

On August 12 the army moved against the president. As the balance of power tipped against the government, the armed forces had found themselves increasingly vulnerable. Throughout the summer, the army leadership had viewed the mediations with mounting misgivings. Participation in the mediation had conferred legitimacy on the formerly outlawed opposition groups, guaranteeing the sectors which the armed forces had persecuted in the preceding years positions of political authority in post-Machado Cuba. It was essential for the army command to participate at some point in the settlement, if only as a means to protect its interests. But it was, in the end, growing fear of U.S. armed intervention that finally moved the army to act. Welles had calculated correctly. Army leaders shrank in horror when Machado, seeking to arouse the population to defend the island against U.S. armed intervention, defied the United States and appealed to Latin American public opinion to condemn the United States. The "sole purpose" of the military coup, one army representative later explained, "was the avoidance of American intervention." On August 12, Machado boarded a plane and departed for the Bahamas.

XII

Carlos Manuel de Céspedes was selected to be the new president. The choice of Ambassador Welles, he emerged from political obscurity. Apart from a historic family name, Céspedes's principal virtue consisted in his lack of affiliation with any political party or political tendency. He was something of a political nonentity—a "statesman," he described himself loftily, above partisan passions, lacking a public personality—and as such he represented an inoffensive compromise candidate to the embattled extremes of the Cuban polity. He was without popularity, without a party, and without a program, and all at once he inherited a cabinet, a constituency, and a country in collapse.

The inauguration of the Céspedes government did little to diminish the contradictions that had accumulated during the *machadato*. Congress remained virtually unchanged, the bureaucracy untouched, the army unaffected. The mediations had served to legitimize the new political groups and guarantee their inclusion in the new government. The timely desertion of Machado by the government parties, moreover, had assured the old-line parties a place in the new administration. Participation in the mediations had created the conditions whereby diverse and ideologically irreconcilable groups obtained legitimacy in post-Machado Cuba, and on August 12, these groups were assimilated into the Céspedes government. The distribution of cabinet portfolios to representatives of such diverse groups as the ABC, the Liberal party, the Unión Nacionalista, the Conservative party, the OCRR, and the Popular party served to give institutional form to the unresolved ambiguities and persisting contradictions of the *machadato*.

The difficulties confronting the new government were not confined to internal contradictions, however. To be sure, the departure of Machado ended the most repressive features of government. Certainly, too, the change of governments served to reduce political tension and armed conflict. But Cuba remained in the throes of depression, and the economic stagnation and social unrest that had plunged the *machadato* into crisis continued unrelieved after August 12. Strikes spread. The labor militancy that precipitated the fall of Machado continued unabated. Unions in Santiago threatened a general strike. Tobacco workers in Pinar del Río, stevedores in Havana, railroad workers in Camagüey, and coffee workers in Oriente remained on strike. Sugar production came to a virtual halt. Workers seized sugar mills, organized "workers' soviets," and called for revolution. Those opposition groups that earlier had boycotted the mediations, principally those sectors of the opposition that aspired to something more than simply a change of presidents, found the Céspedes succession wholly unsatisfactory. Many of these groups, including labor organizations, the DEU, and the PCC, had toiled too long in the pursuit of revolution to settle for a palace coup.

There were other problems for Céspedes. Beset by contradictions from within and beseiged by opposition from without, the authority of the new government deteriorated. Old-line political parties maneuvered to recover lost prestige and authority while new political groups intrigued to expand power and influence. Reports that former *machadista* officials had returned to their old jobs served to weaken the moral authority of the Céspedes government. That the new government had permitted the flight of large numbers of officials responsible for atrocities offended public sensibilities. Legislators could not meet for fear of precipitating a mob attack against congress. Many provincial governors and municipal mayors and their staffs had gone into hiding, leaving local government unattended. Public order had collapsed. The rioting produced by Machado's flight continued intermittently through August. Angry mobs stalked Havana streets and outlying suburbs bent on dispensing revolutionary justice to suspended *machadista* officials. Government offices were gutted, stores looted, and homes sacked. Suspected Machado supporters were lynched. Army and police authorities moved to restrain civilian excesses tentatively, if at all. Too many officers feared that strict enforcement of public order would serve to revive anti-military sentiment among their former opponents now in power.

The Céspedes government was an administration without a mandate. It was formed largely to facilitate Machado's succession and to accommodate political debts incurred to the groups participating in the mediations. It was a government made up of discredited political parties that had functioned under the pall of unconstitutionality, and dissident clandestine factions that had operated on the fringes of illegality. It neither possessed popularity nor promised a program. This was a government summoned into existence largely in response to U.S. needs. And because it was so patently artificial in origins and palpably superfluous in function, and because it recognized the sources of its origins and the constituency it served, the government proceeded haltingly and indecisively.

XIII

The end of the Céspedes government came from the most improbable source. On the evening of September 3, sergeants, corporals, and enlisted men of Camp Columbia in Havana met to discuss a backlog of grievances. Deliberations concluded late at night with the preparation of a list of demands to be submitted to the army command. The officers on duty, however, declined to discuss the demands of the aroused soldiery and, instead, retired from regimental headquarters. Suddenly, and unexpectedly, the troops found themselves in control of Camp Columbia—and in mutiny. The army protesters, under the leadership of Sergeant Fulgencio Batista, exhorted the troops to hold the post until the officers agreed to negotiate their demands.

Anti-government groups immediately rallied around the mutinous troops. In the early morning hours of September 4, leaders of the DEU arrived at Camp Columbia and persuaded the sergeants to expand the objectives of their movement. The intervention of civilians changed radically the nature of the army protest, transforming a mutiny into a putsch.

The "Sergeants' Revolt," as the mutiny became known, began with modest objectives. The sergeants planned a demonstration to protest deteriorating conditions in the army—specifically, poor pay, inadequate housing facilities, and rumored cuts in enlisted ranks—not to overthrow Céspedes or oust the officer corps. Having unexpectedly found themselves in a state of mutiny, however, and thereby effectively in rebellion against the Céspedes government, the sergeant leaders faced the certain prospect of severe disciplinary action, including court martial and imprisonment. For many there was no going back, although during some anxious moments on the morning of September 4, they were not quite certain how to proceed forward.

The anti-government opposition provided the means. Civilians transformed an act of insubordination into a full-fledged military coup and proceeded to use the mutiny as an instrument of political change. It was a coalition of convenience, to be sure, an improvisation not without flaws but one that offered rebellious soldiers pardon, and dissident civilians power. Out of this tentative civil-military arrangement emerged a revolutionary junta organized around a pentarchy of Ramón Grau San Martín, Porfirio Franca, Guillermo Portela, José Miguel Irisarri, and Sergio Carbó. On September 5, 1933, a political manifesto announced the establishment of a new provisional revolutionary government and proclaimed the affirmation of national sovereignty, the establishment of a modern democracy, and the "march toward the creation of a new Cuba." Within a week, the pentarchy dissolved in favor of an executive form of government under Grau San Martín.

XIV

The new government was the fulfillment of the reformist movement that began fully ten years earlier. The organizer of the Junta Cubana de Renovación Nacional, Fernando Ortiz, never wavered in his public support of the new government. Many members of the provisional government in 1933 had been first active in the reformist projects of 1923. Of the pentarchy, Professor Grau San Martín, banker Porfiro Franca, and attorney José Miguel Irisarri had participated in the Veterans and Patriots movement. The members of the subsequent cabinet included physicians, attorneys, academics, and an engineer, all representatives of the liberal professions. The new cabinet included Carlos Finlay (health), Manuel Costales Latatu (education), Julio Aguado (defense), Antonio Guiteras *(gobernación)*, Gustavo Moreno (public works), Ramiro Capablanca (presidency), Joaquín del Río Balmaseda (justice), and Manuel Márquez Sterling (state). Manuel Despaigne came out of retirement to assume the portfolio of treasury, the position he had previously held as a member of the "honest cabinet."

For one hundred days the provisional government devoted itself to the task of transforming Cuba with exalted purposefulness. The demands of 1923 became the decrees of 1933. This was the first government of the republic formed without the sanction and support of the United States. Under the injunction of "Cuba for Cubans," the new government proceeded to enact reform laws at a dizzying pace. Organizing its program along the "lines of modern democracy and . . . upon the pure principles of national sovereignty," the provisional government committed itself to economic reconstruction, social reform, and political reorganization. On the day of his inauguration as president, Grau unilaterally proclaimed the abrogation of the Platt Amendment. Reforms followed rapidly. The traditional political parties were dissolved. The government lowered utility rates by 40 percent and reduced interest rates. Women received the vote and the university secured autonomy. In labor matters, government reforms included a minimum wage for sugar cane cutters, compulsory labor arbitration, an eight-hour workday, workers' compensation, the establishment of a Ministry of Labor, a Nationalization of Labor decree requiring Cuban nationality for 50 percent of all employees in industry, commerce, and agriculture, and the cancellation of existing contract labor arrangements with Haiti and Jamaica. In agricultural matters, the government sponsored the creation of a sugar farmer *(colono)* association, guaranteed farmers permanent right over the land under cultivation, and inaugurated a program of land reform.

The rhetoric of revolution notwithstanding, this was pre-eminently a reformist regime. It chose regulation over expropriation, the distribution of public lands over the redistribution of private property, the defense of trade union objectives over those of the workers' parties. This was not a government without opposition, however. The forces of old Cuba responded to the change of governments with unrestrained indignation. This was the ouster of the old political class, and it came at a singularly inopportune moment. The *cooperativista* parties that had deserted Machado as a means to survive the discredited regime once again faced persecution and extinction. So, too, did the ousted army officers who, for all their efforts to secure immunity from post-Machado reprisals, now found themselves vulnerable to prosecution and imprisonment. Representatives of foreign capital recoiled in horror at the new laws that regulated and restricted the freedom they had traditionally enjoyed under previous governments.

Nor was it only old Cuba that opposed the provisional government. New political groups, including the ABC, OCRR, and the Unión Nacionalista, organizations that earlier had paid dearly to acquire political legitimacy in post-Machado Cuba, were not reconciled to this abrupt and inglorious end to their debut in national politics.

If the factions that had made up the Céspedes government denounced the Grau regime as too radical, the PCC and CNOC condemned the new reformist government as too moderate. The communist party and labor organizations continued to pressure the Grau government throughout the autumn. Under ordinary circumstances, labor reforms might have met long-standing worker demands. But these were not ordinary times. Neither setting minimum wages and maximum hours nor compulsory arbitration and workers' compensation addressed the immediate and fundamental issue: there was no work. Labor demonstrations continued. By the end of September, workers had seized control of thirty-six sugar mills, representing some 30 percent of the national sugar production. Workers' militias organized, and in several instances, engaged army units in combat.

But the United States was implacable in its opposition. More than constitutionality had perished. The overthrow of the pro-United States government, the suppression of the traditional political parties, and the removal of the officer corps represented nothing less than the dismantling of the internal structures that had underwritten and institutionalized U.S. hegemony. And in repudiating the Platt Amendment, the new government had abolished the formal source of U.S. control over Cuba. The long-term implications of the policies of the new government were not lost on Washington. The defense of Cuban interests jeopardized U.S. interests. Labor legislation affected North American employers. Agrarian reform concerned U.S. landowners. The reduction of utility rates affected the Electric Bond and Share Company. In fact, so thoroughly had the United States penetrated Cuba that it was hardly possible for any social or economic legislation to not affect U.S. capital adversely.

The tempo and tenor of the reform measures persuaded Welles that the provisional government aspired to nothing less than the elimination of United States interests and influence in Cuba. "It is . . . within the bounds of possibility," Welles wrote with alarm two weeks after the coup, "that the social revolution which is under way cannot be checked. American properties and interests are being gravely prejudiced and the material damage to such properties will in all probability be very great." Many of the government decrees, he protested, were outright "confiscatory" in nature and enormously prejudicial to U.S. property interests. "Our own commercial and export interests in Cuba," Welles asserted flatly, "cannot be revived under this government." When the government announced in October an agreement with Mexico to train Cuban army officers, Welles drew immediate conclusions: "In view of the existing situation here and particularly in view of the fact that since the independence of the Republic of Cuba the training of Cuban officers had been undertaken solely in the United States or under the direction of American officers this step can only be construed as a deliberate effort by the present Government to show its intention of minimizing any form of American influence in Cuba."

Welles was neither slow nor unequivocal in his response. He deliberately characterized the new government in terms calculated to promote suspicion and provoke opposition in Washington. The army had fallen under "ultra-radical control," Welles charged, and the new government was "frankly communistic." He described Irisarri as a "radical of the extreme type" and Grau and Portela as "extreme radicals." Welles conceded that Franca was a "conservative businessman of good reputation," but insisted that he served merely as "window dressing."

For the remainder of his stay in Havana, Welles pursued a policy calculated to isolate the government abroad and weaken at home. He turned immediately to unifying the opposition. Welles sought to bolster the resolve of the ousted political groups and the dispossessed army officers to prevent either a diminution of anti-government activity or, worse still, defections to the provisional regime. He accomplished this in several ways. He assured civilian and military groups that Washington would respond decisively. With the traditional political parties divested of influence in government councils and the old officers deprived of command over the army, the United States had lost direct access to and influence over local government. Armed intervention offered one means to recover lost authority. On the day of the formation of the pentarchy, Welles summoned the ousted political groups and army commanders to plot the restoration of the Céspedes government. The dispossessed groups looked to the United States for help. Welles urged Washington to land "a certain number of troops," ostensibly to guard the U.S. embassy and protect lives and property. In fact, he acknowledged, Céspedes could not be restored without the "aid of an American guard." Two days later, he proposed his most ambitious intervention proposal, recommending a "strictly limited intervention" entailing "the landing of a considerable force at Habana and lesser forces in certain of the most important ports of the Republic." This "strictly limited intervention" would provide the "police force to the legitimate Government of Cuba for a comparatively brief period," thereby enabling the Céspedes government to function as it had prior to its fall.

But requests for intervention received no support in Washington. On the contrary, Roosevelt moved immediately to sanction intervention only for the purpose of protecting property. Secretary of State Cordell Hull also shrank from intervention. "Despite the legal right we possessed," Hull later recalled, "such an act would further embitter our relations with all Latin America." Armed intervention in Cuba, Hull feared, would have undone "all our protestations of nonintervention and noninterference."

But the disinclination in Washington to act militarily did not suggest an inclination to acquiesce politically. If the United States would not overthrow the government from without, it would seek to undermine it from within. And nothing was as central to this policy as promoting conditions of continued instability and disorder. Three decades of policy imperatives were suddenly reversed: stability and order were now inimical to U.S. interests in Cuba.

Destabilization required first and foremost the denial of U.S. recognition. Welles had earlier threatened to withdraw recognition to force Machado out of office. The withholding of recognition from the Grau government had a similar end, if the means differed somewhat. Optimally, nonrecognition would eventually produce the collapse of the government. But failing that, it would force the government into moderation, a way of exacting concessions from Havana in exchange for normalization of relations. Nonrecognition was also indispensable to encourage continued anti-government opposition in Cuba. This was a deliberate orchestration of chaos, designed to maintain pressure on both the government and the opposition. Nonrecognition obstructed government efforts to reach reconciliation with its opponents precisely because nonrecognition offered the opposition incentive to resist the government. Those who otherwise might have supported the government demurred; those who opposed the government were encouraged to participate in active conspiracy and armed resistance.

With the government thus thrown on the defensive, the United States was free to pursue subversion. To the deposed political groups, Welles urged continued resistance. To the displaced officers, he counseled a continued boycott of the army. Nonrecognition exercised a particularly powerful restraint on the officers, encouraging army leaders to remain away from their command in the belief that the Grau government could not long survive without U.S. support. On September 9 Welles reported that the officers had entered into a "definite compact" not to support "any government except a legitimate government." Several days later, Horacio Ferrer, secretary of war under Céspedes, asserted flatly that the officers would never serve under any government not recognized in Washington.

The prospect of armed intervention further encouraged the officers to remain away from their commands. Indeed, in the days immediately following the coup, U.S. intervention seemed imminent. These were compelling circumstances, certainly sufficient to persuade the officers of the logic of their decision and the legitimacy of their deed. Few army leaders were disposed to jeopardize their careers by breaking ranks to join a government expected momentarily to fall to U.S. troops. The continued boycott was essential, for it served to corroborate the charge that the new government lacked support and authority. The officers who only three weeks earlier had led the army against Machado to prevent intervention now refused to lead the army under Grau to provoke intervention.

On September 7 the government summoned an officer's delegation to the Presidential Palace to discuss the means through which to reunite the armed forces. The government proposed organizing a junta of five officers and Sergeant Batista to supervise a reorganization of the armed forces and oversee the reintegration of the military. The officers declined the government offer, refusing to sanction in any form the legitimacy of the sergeants' mutiny. In late September, the Grau government ordered the officers to return to their command, an order rejected by the army chiefs. The officers were proclaimed deserters and ordered arrested.

A second blow to anti-government forces was not long in coming. In early November, a combined force of the ABC and Unión Nacionalista joined a rebellion of dissident army elements. After several days of fighting in Havana, government forces overcame resistance and ended the revolt.

The arrest of the former officers and the defeat of the ABC and Unión Nacionalista had several effects. Most immediately, these developments signaled the collapse of organized opposition. Resistance continued, to be sure, largely in the form of sporadic acts of sabotage and terrorism. But the principal opposition groups that had formed the previous government, and around which Welles had hoped to reconstitute the "legitimate government," had been dispersed and demoralized. The purge of the former officer corps also paved the way for a sweeping reorganization of the armed forces. Some four hundred sergeants, corporals, and enlisted men received commissions and filled the newly created vacancies in the army command. Batista was formally promoted to the rank of colonel and ratified in his position as chief of the army.

XV

The arrest of the former officers, to be sure, strengthened the position of the provisional government. But more than the prestige and power of the government increased. The defeat of the ABC and the Unión Nacionalista and, in particular, the ouster of the old officer corps were political triumphs for the army and a personal victory for Fulgencio Batista. Government successes eased political pressure, but in so doing also revealed the contradictions within the ruling coalition. In fact, the civilians and the soldiers had gone separate ways shortly after September 4. This was not so much the result of new disagreements as it was the product of old differences. To be sure, both remained joined together by a common transgression against duly constituted authority. They shared a mutual concern in the success of the provisional government, if only because they shared a common fate if it failed.

Nevertheless, the gap between civilians and soldiers continued to widen through the early autumn. The civilians had carried Cuba deep into the uncertain realm of experimental government. As the civilians continued to advance on their "march to create a new Cuba," the army became an increasingly reluctant escort. Military support of the provisional government was always more practical than political, more a form of self-interest than a function of solidarity. This was the government that had initially sanctioned the sedition and subsequently validated four hundred new commissions. This was the government, in short, from which the new army command derived legitimacy. But the military leaders were also anxious for a political settlement, if for no other reason than to legitimize their recent promotions. The army command saw little to be gained by social experimentation except a prolongation of the political uncertainty. Indeed, many commanders feared that the government policies would result inevitably in visiting grief on the new officer corps. It had been from the start only a coalition of convenience, and by midautumn the soldiers found themselves increasingly inconvenienced by civilian policies. The new army command perceived the reform projects as hazardous ventures, ill-conceived programs by a government upon whose continued solvency they depended to underwrite their ill-gotten commissions. Only another source of authority, capable of constituting itself into a legitimate government willing to underwrite the new order in the army, or, alternatively, evidence that the provisional government no longer possessed the will or means to uphold the new commissions, could persuade Batista to abandon the government that had originally infused political life into a military sedition.

These were the stress lines perceived by Welles. By mid-fall, the emphasis of U.S. policy shifted away from promoting unity among government opponents to encouraging disunity among its supporters. Welles understood the inherent cross-purposes that separated the civilians from the soldiers, and played upon them with great skill. The September army mutiny, he reminded Washington only days after the arrests of the old officers, did "not take place in order to place Grau San Martín in power." He noted, correctly, that the "divergence between the Army and civilian elements in the government is fast becoming daily more marked" as Batista's authority and influence increased. Two weeks later Welles reiterated his contention: "The mutiny was not directed against Céspedes or his cabinet; it was not political in its origin and it was not . . . in any sense responsive to a social movement."

These conditions had important implications for the shaping of U.S. policy, for they suggested the absence of unanimity within the provisional government and the presence of mutual suspicions to play upon. These were insights, too, into the character of the ruling coalition, and, after the fall of the old officer corps, they gave direction to U.S. policy.

Throughout the autumn months Welles maintained close, and increasingly cordial, contact with Batista. On October 4, only days after the arrest of the former officers, Welles reported having held a "protracted and very frank discussion" with Batista. Welles informed the army chief that he was the "only individual in Cuba today who represented authority." He explained that his leadership of the army had earned him the support of "the very great majority of the commercial and financial interests in Cuba who are looking for protection and who could only find such protection in himself." Political factions that only weeks earlier had openly opposed him, Welles disclosed, were now "in accord that his control of the Army as Chief of Staff should be continued as the only possible solution and were willing to support him in that capacity." However, the only obstacle to an equitable political settlement, and presumably U.S. recognition and a return to conditions of normality, the ambassador suggested, "was the unpatriotic and futile obstinacy of a small group of young men who should be studying in the university instead of playing politics and of a few individuals who had joined with them for selfish motives." In a thinly veiled warning, Welles reminded Batista of the tenuous position in which his continued affiliation with the government had placed him. "Should the present government go down in disaster," Welles warned, "that disaster would necessarily inextricably involve not only himself but the safety of the Republic, which he has publicly pledged himself to maintain."

Welles's comments could not have been interpreted by Batista in any other fashion than as an invitation to create a new government. By the end of October, Batista had arrived at the conclusion that "a change in government is imperative." Welles had forged a coalition consisting of some of the anti-Machado political groups, the traditional political parties, foreign capital, and the United States State Department in which Batista could find an authority that would at once ratify the new army command and organize a government consistent with United States policy needs. In January 1934, Batista transferred army support from Grau to Unión Nacionalista leader Carlos Mendieta. Within five days, the United States recognized the new government.

10

The Eclipse of Old Cuba

I

The forces for change released during the *machadato* did not all subside
with the passing of the Grau government—many assumed new forms.
The *ancien régime* had found new life in the Mendieta-Batista government, but also faced renewed challenge. The reform program of the short-
lived provisional government acquired institutional form with the organization of a new political party, the Partido Revolucionario Cubano (Auténtico) in 1934. The provisional government gave rise to one additional
political group. Under the leadership of Antonio Guiteras, formerly Grau's
minister of government, radicals organized a clandestine revolutionary
organization, Joven Cuba. Eschewing electoral politics, Joven Cuba adopted
armed struggle as the principal means to combat the Mendieta-Batista
government. Student opposition resumed in 1934 with the reopening of
the University of Havana. Assassination, bombings, and sabotage again
became the dominant mode of political opposition. Anti-government
demonstrations became commonplace, as did labor protests. Between 1934
and 1935, more than one hundred strikes flared up across the island. In
March 1935, momentum for revolutionary change assumed formidable
proportions when a general strike again brought the government to the
brink of collapse. Unlike the August 1933 strike, however, authorities
were neither willing to negotiate with labor nor reluctant to suppress the
strike. Proclamation of martial law announced a reign of terror that lasted
through late spring. Unions were outlawed and the university was occupied anew. Many were arrested, tortured, and killed; others fled into exile. In the weeks that followed, military firing squads executed political
prisoners. In May 1935, the army killed Antonio Guiteras.

The general strike in 1935 was the last revolutionary surge of the first
republican generation. It collapsed in days, but its effects lasted through
the decade. The severity of military repression caused dissension in and
ultimately dissolution of the ruling coalition. By the end of March, Men-

dieta found his support reduced to the military and a small faction within the Unión Nacionalista. Within months, he too resigned.

The strike had achieved its desired effect but did not accomplish its principal objective. The Mendieta government did indeed collapse, but creating a political vacuum filled immediately by Batista and the armed forces. Virtually every branch of government passed under army control. Military supervisors replaced provincial and municipal officials. The military command purged striking civil servants and established control over every division of public administration. In the process, Batista emerged as the single most dominant political force on the island.

Batista's authority increased throughout the 1930s. He restored order and tranquility. As the new incarnation of stability, Batista won the support of foreign capital. Washington found in the Pax Batistiana sufficient cause for diplomatic support. For the rest of the decade, Batista ruled Cuba through puppet presidents and shadow governments: José A. Barnet (1935–36), Miguel Mariano Gómez (1936), and Federico Laredo Bru (1936–40).

Batista's opponents never recovered. The tempest of the decade had spent itself. A respite from revolutionary activity settled over the island, due principally to the exhaustion of the passions and depletion in the ranks. Many of the most prominent opponents of the Mendieta-Batista regime had lost their lives in 1935. Others sought security in exile. Still others departed Cuba to carry the banner of revolution to other lands, most notably, Spain. Revolutionary groups had been shattered and crushed. The university reopened in 1937 and classes resumed uneventfully. The Auténticos turned to electoral politics and devoted themselves to the arduous work of constructing a new party infrastructure and developing grass-roots support. In 1937, the Communist party reorganized itself as the Partido Unión Revolucionaria (PUR), made peace with Batista, and turned to the task of developing an electoral apparatus. After 1938, the party adopted a reformist and openly collaborationist posture. It acquired legality and permission to organize labor and in return pledged to support Batista. In May 1938, the party newspaper *Hoy* was published and distributed openly. By the late 1930s, communist candidates appeared on the electoral rolls and party leaders campaigned for public office. In 1939 the party convened its third national congress. The 350 delegates representing an estimated 24,000 members passed a number of resolutions, the most important of which led to the reorganization of the national labor federation (CNOC). After a series of local and provincial elections, and with the support of the government, an estimated 1500 delegates representing 576 unions convened to establish the new Confederación de Trabajadores de Cuba (CTC). Boasting a membership of 350,000 by the end of the decade, the CTC emerged as a source of enormous political influence, henceforth the object of special government attention.

The restoration of social tranquility during the 1930s was due in part to social programs enacted by Batista. Repression was followed by reform. After 1935, with the defeat and dispersal of most revolutionary groups and the return to electoral politics of others, Batista adopted increasingly the role of populist reformer. He spoke more and more of *"los humildes,"* the humble ones, and increasingly identified himself with the dispossessed, the workers and peasants everywhere in Cuba who had suffered the most during the depression. At the same time, Batista moved toward rapprochement with the Communist party, the largest mass-based political organization in Cuba. In 1937 the government proclaimed a general amnesty, the principal effects of which were to release political prisoners and prepare the way for political reconciliation between Batista and many of his opponents. In that same year Batista announced an ambitious three-year plan for the social and economic reconstruction of Cuba. The plan called for a workers' health insurance system, state-sponsored health programs, the establishment of consumer cooperatives, and the reorganization of tax structures. In early 1938, the army chief announced an agrarian reform program. Recipients received state lands, up to a maximum grant of thirty-three acres of arable land, upon which they were required to construct a home to be occupied for a minimum of six years. Such grants could change ownership only by inheritance. In 1939, the government enacted a rent control law, reducing rents to pre-1937 levels and granting tax exemptions up to ten years to owners of newly constructed houses. Boarding houses were ordered to reduce rates by 25 percent and water taxes were lowered by one-third. Batista urged the enactment of easy mortgage credits, a way to allow *"los humildes"* to purchase a home on reasonable terms. By the mid-1930s, too, Batista had met a long-standing reformist demand by supporting extension of the suffrage for women.

Batista also used the army to implement reform programs in the countryside. In 1936, the armed forces established the Civic-Military Institute to oversee the implementation of a number of social enterprises, including health programs, support for public and private welfare agencies, care for the aged, and protection of orphans. By far the most ambitious army-sponsored program, the Civic-Military Institute undertook a vast educational program for rural Cuba. Sergeants served as teachers and spread out across the interior, providing many rural communities their first experience with formal schooling. The *misiones educativas* were designed to provide basic learning skills as well as information concerning agriculture, hygiene, and nutrition. By the late 1930s, the army was operating more than a thousand schools where children and adults (at night) were instructed. By the end of the decade, an estimated 100,000 people had been served.

Batista was also beneficiary of the readjustment of Cuba's international relations. In 1934, the Platt Amendment, the bane of the republic's existence, was abrogated. With the exception of the clause regarding the Guantánamo naval station, a new treaty abolished the odious amendment. Henceforth, Cuba-U.S. relations would be conducted formally between "independent though friendly states." The abrogation of the Platt Amendment helped Batista to assume the mantle of defender of national sovereignty and protector of national honor.

Liberal middle-class political leaders reacted to developments of the 1930s with a mixture of dismay and distain. They denounced communists for their cooperation with Batista, they denounced Batista for his collaboration with the communists—ample evidence that neither could be trusted. In fact, Batista and the communists had appropriated and implemented many of the key reformist objectives of 1923–33. By the late 1930s, liberals sensed correctly, Batista had developed a considerable popular following among the urban working class and the peasantry. For a second time, reformism had been pre-empted—first by Machado in the mid-1920s after the events of 1923 and now again by Batista in the wake of 1933. Liberal reformists in the republic, like their counterparts in the colony, continued to be outmaneuvered by rival social groups.

Economic conditions improved through the 1930s. Gradually Cuban sugar recovered a larger share of the North American market, although it would never again attain the prominence it had enjoyed during the late 1910s and early 1920s. By the terms of the Jones-Costigan Act (1934), the United States lowered protectionist tariffs on sugar imports. Cuba benefited from this measure, but only slightly. The Jones-Costigan bill substituted quotas for tariff protection as the means to protect domestic sugar producers. By the terms of the law, the U.S. secretary of agriculture was empowered to determine national sugar needs, whereupon all sugar producing regions, domestic and foreign, were assigned an annual quota of the total, based on the participation of sugar producers in the

U.S. market for the years 1931–33. The selection of these three years was unfortunate for Cuban producers, for it was precisely this period—the years of Hawley-Smoot—during which the Cuban share of the U.S. market was the smallest.

Nevertheless, Cuban participation in the U.S. market improved gradually through the 1930s, increasing from 25.4 percent in 1933 to 31.4 in 1937. These were years, moreover, in which overall sugar production expanded, and the value of the expanded production increased. Between 1933 and 1938, Cuban sugar output increased from 1.9 million to 2.9 million tons, with the corresponding value increasing from $53.7 million to $120.2 million.

Much of this increase was due to the readjustment of Cuban trade relations. Under the Mendieta government a new reciprocal trade agreement was negotiated with the United States. The 1934 treaty assured Cuba of a guaranteed market for its agricultural exports. In return, Havana conceded to tariff reductions on a large variety of commodities and the reduction of internal taxes on North American products. Concessions granted by the United States covered 35 articles; Cuban concessions affected 400 items. Tariff reductions on both sides ranged from 20 to 60 percent. The new agreement also specified that the enumerated tariff schedule could not be altered as a result of changing money and currency values.

The new reciprocity treaty, to be sure, contributed to Cuban revival, but not without a price. Cuba's principal export, sugar, was the item most favored by the 1934 amendment. The U.S. tariff on Cuban raw sugar was reduced from 1.50 cents to 0.90 cents per pound. Reductions were also made on tobacco leaf, cigars and cigarettes, honey, fish products, citrus, pineapples, and other agricultural products. At the same time, however, the 1934 treaty dealt a body blow to Cuban efforts at economic diversification. Cuban entrepreneurs had not yet recovered from the effects of the depression when they were dealt a new reversal, this in the form of increased competition from North American producers. Reciprocity sealed their fate. Scores of agricultural and manufacturing enterprises, many of which had arisen in the aftermath of the 1927 Customs-Tariff Law, were adversely and permanently affected. In a larger sense, the new treaty allowed U.S. producers to adjust to changing market conditions in Cuba, and ultimately re-established North American primacy in the Cuban economy. Cuba was again linked closely to the United States, thereby returning the island to the patterns of pre-depression dependency. The total value of North American imports increased from $22.6 million in 1933 to $81 million in 1940; the U.S. portion of Cuban imports for the same period increased from 54 percent to 77 percent.

II

The decade that began under the pall of constitutional illegality ended with a call for constitutional renovation. The passing of the economic crisis and the return of political tranquility created a climate favorable to constitutional reform. Batista's political position was firmly established and could only be enhanced further by identifying himself with a new constitution, one incorporating the reform measures of the previous decade. The old 1901 constitution, further, remained permanently stigmatized among Cubans, for it contained as an organic part the now defunct Platt Amendment. A new constitution promised to make a break with the past and institutionalize the gains of post-Machado Cuba.

A constituent assembly representing the full spectrum of political affiliation, from old *machadistas* to the Auténticos and communists, convened in 1939 to draft a new constitution. Rivals of the previous decade again did political battle. The 1940 constitution provided the forum for renewed debate over virtually all the key issues of republican politics. Nor did political alignments alone determine the direction of the debates. The pro-government coalition included discredited Liberals and the declining Unión Nacionalistas, as well as the PUR. The opposition was led by the Auténticos and included the ABC and reform liberals. On any given issue, however, ideology tended to transcend partisan affiliation. Left-liberal delegates frequently joined forces to form voting majorities against conservatives, without regard to affiliation with government or opposition blocs.

The net result was the promulgation of a remarkably progressive constitution. The document provided for universal suffrage, free elections, and referenda, and sanctioned a wide range of political and civil liberties. Equally important were the social provisions, which included maximum hours and minimum wages, pensions, workers' compensation, and the right to strike.

For all its enlightened clauses, however, the constitution of 1940 remained substantially a statement of goals, an agenda for future achievement. The absence of enforcement provisions meant that the new constitution would remain a dormant document. Nevertheless, it immediately occupied a place of central importance in national politics, for it served alternately as the banner through which to mobilize political support and the standard by which to measure political performance. The new constitution brought both synthesis and closure to the revolutionary stirrings of the previous decade. Many of the reform objectives of the 1930s found vindication, if not implementation, in the new constitution. But more than this, the constitution of 1940 provided the foundations for legitimacy and consensus politics for the next two decades. Success in Cuban politics would henceforth turn on which political group promised to interpret most faithfully and implement most vigorously the principal clauses of the constitution.

The promulgation of the new constitution also set the stage for presidential elections in 1940. Fulgencio Batista stepped out of uniform and Ramón Grau San Martín returned from exile, and once more the two rivals did political battle. And again Grau was bested. The campaign was vigorously waged, and by all accounts the election was fairly conducted, certainly among the most honest in the nearly four decades of the republic's history. Batista obtained more than 800,000 votes, Grau, 575,000.

The Batista presidency (1940–44) had the good fortune to coincide with the war years. Cuban entry into World War II in December 1941 served to facilitate trade agreements and loan and credit programs with the United States. The decline of sugar production in war-torn Asia and Europe spurred Cuban producers. Output increased, and so did world prices. Between 1940 and 1944 the Cuban crop increased from 2.7 million to 4.2 million tons, the largest harvest since 1930. The value of Cuban raw sugar production for the same period also increased, from $110 million to $251 million. During the early 1940s, Cuba was also beneficiary to several large trade deals with the United States. In 1941, both countries signed a lend-lease agreement whereby Cuba received arms shipments in exchange for North American use of Cuban military facilities. In the same year, the United States agreed to purchase the full 1942 sugar crop at 2.65 cents per pound. A second agreement the following year similarly disposed of the 1943 crop. With the continued revival of sugar production, the economy moved out of a state of lethargy. Prosperity returned, public works programs grew, and the government bureaucracy resumed its expansion.

But the war was not an unmixed blessing, for the effects of prosperity were not evenly distributed. Some sectors of the economy suffered during the war. Shortages of all kinds became commonplace. The lack of ocean transportation facilities, and the risk attending the trans-Atlantic shipping that did exist, severely restricted Cuban trade with Europe. Cuban exports to Great Britain and Spain declined and those with Germany and Italy ended altogether. After the German occupation of France in 1941, Cuba also lost the French market. Cigar manufacturers suffered the most from the loss of the luxury markets of Europe, and no increase in the amount of leaf tobacco exports to the United States could compensate Cuban producers for the decline of their cigar exports. Cigar factories began to close. Fruit and vegetable growers also suffered. They lost between one-half to three-quarters of their customary export tonnage to the United States due to a lack of available sea vessels. Fruit exports halved from 32.8 million tons in 1940 to 16.5 million tons in 1943, while vegetables fell from 8.1 million to 1.1 million tons. Raw materials declined, merchandise inventories fell, and the lack of steel and iron disrupted the construction industry, causing widespread unemployment in building trades. Railroad traffic, on the other hand, increased, and, indeed, rail transportation may have been one of the most buoyant sectors of the Cuban economy during the war. The threat of German submarines forced sugar producers to haul their sugar by rail to Havana for shipment under convoy. But the effects of these measures on other regions of the island were severe. The twelve major ports from which sugar had previously been shipped all but suspended operations, creating vast unemployment among dockworkers across the island. During the war years, further, tourism declined markedly: from 127,000 visitors in 1940 to 12,000 in 1943. Hotels closed, restaurants reduced services. Wages rose, but not as quickly as prices. New taxes were imposed, old ones were raised: luxury taxes increased; there was a new income tax; and a 20 percent surcharge was added to all existing taxes.

There was discontent in Cuba as the war entered its fourth year in 1944, enough to generate lively political debate. It was also a presidential election year. Batista's Prime Minister Carlos Saladrigas campaigned with the support of the government. He was opposed by Ramón Grau San Martín. It was a spirited contest: Saladrigas extolling the previous four years of the Batista administration, Grau recalling nostalgically his one hundred days in 1933. Indeed, the mystique of Grau, no less than the source of the Auténtico appeal, was very much derived from those heady and exalted days of 1933. In 1944, Grau promised much of the same, and more of it.

The electorate responded in overwhelming numbers. In June 1944, Grau obtained more than one million votes, sweeping five out of six provinces, losing only in Pinar del Río. After more than a decade of repeated and unsuccessful bids for political power, Grau San Martín, now almost sixty years old, had finally won a presidential election.

The Auténtico victory raised enormous popular expectations that the reform program that had served as both the legacy and promise of the PRC had at last found fulfillment. Neither the Grau government (1944–48) nor that of his successor, Carlos Prío Socarrás (1948–52), however, met Cuban expectations.

Most leading Auténticos had spent the better part of their adult lives as political prisoners or victims of political persecution, alternating with periods of exile. From the earliest political stirrings against Machado in the 1920s, through the revolutionary tumult of the 1930s and the disappointing electoral setbacks of the early 1940s, reformists had been banished to a political wilderness, there to suffer a bitter mixture of disillusionment and hard times. Their debut in Cuban politics was inauspicious. By the mid-1940s, idealism had given way to cynicism, and public office no longer offered the opportunity to pursue collective improvement so much as it provided the occasion to promote individual enrichment.

Government fell under a siege of a new generation of hungry office-seekers, and their appetite was voracious. For the first time, Auténticos acquired control over lucrative posts and privileges. The opportunity was not lost. Embezzlement, graft, corruption, and malfeasance of public office permeated every branch of national, provincial, and municipal government. The public trust was transformed into a private till. Politics passed under the control of party thugs, and a new word entered the Cuban political lexicon: *gangsterismo*. Violence and terror became extensions of party politics and the hallmark of Auténtico rule.

The ranks of civil service became bloated. The number of persons on the government payroll more than doubled, from 60,000 in 1943 to 131,000 in 1949. By 1950, some 186,000 persons, fully 11 percent of the working population, occupied active public positions at national, provincial, and municipal levels of government; another 30,000 retired employees were on the state payrolls. An estimated 80 percent of the 1949–50 budget was used to pay the salaries of public officials. Pensions accounted for another 8 percent of national expenditures.

Auténticos approached their success with considerable uncertainty, fearful that their tenure would be brief and their rule temporary. These circumstances served to distinguish Auténtico corruption from the practices of its predecessors and shaped its defining characteristics. Indeed, the boom-bust mentality had worked its way into politics, as public officials at all levels of Auténtico administration enjoyed the dazzling prosperity offered by control of the government. The emphasis fell on immediate returns and spectacular graft. Pension funds were looted, the national treasury was sacked, public funds were misappropriated. Grau himself was formally charged with embezzling $174 million. The outgoing Minister of Education in 1948 was accused of having stolen $20 million. The Minister of Finance in the Prío government was accused of misappropriating millions of old bank notes scheduled for destruction.

That these conditions prevailed, and indeed so permeated the institutional fabric of the republic during the Auténtico years, was in no small way a result of the postwar prosperity enjoyed by the island. The economies of cane producers in Asia and beet growers in Europe were in ruins. During World War II, world sugar production declined by almost 60 percent, from a combined cane and beet production of 28.6 million tons in 1940 to 18.1 million tons in 1946. It was not until 1950 that world production overtook earlier prewar levels, and just when it appeared that rival producers were about to threaten Cuban prosperity, the Korean war gave renewed life to high prices. World production was decreasing, consumption was increasing, and prices were rising: a familiar series of circumstances that always brought profits and prosperity to Cuban producers. The boom years after 1945 never quite reached the proportions of the "dance of the millions" following World War I, but they brought a level of prosperity not known since those years. Between 1944 and 1948, Cuban sugar production increased almost 40 percent, from 4.2 million to 5.8 million tons. By 1948, sugar had come to constitute a record 90 percent of the island's total exports by value.

Good times arrived in spectacular form. Sugar exports accounted for nearly a 40 percent increase in national income between 1939 and 1947. Record sugar exports and simultaneous import scarcities caused by the war produced a large balance-of-payment surplus, averaging more than $120 million annually between 1943 and 1947. Through the 1940s, domestic industrial and commercial activity increased. Government revenues also increased through taxation, rising from $75.7 million in fiscal year 1937–38 to $244 million in 1949–50.

But not all enjoyed the new prosperity. Food prices increased almost threefold between 1939 and 1948, while the cost of living more than doubled from the 1939 level. Inflation would have been more acute had it not been for the wartime import scarcities and the willingness of many individuals and institutions to keep the better part of their savings in idle balances. The money supply increased 500 percent between 1939 and 1950, while the cost of living rose only 145 percent. For approximately the same period, the dollar, gold, and silver holdings of the national treasury rose from $25 million to $402 million, the net balance abroad from $6 million to more than $200 million, and the public's dollar holding from $14 million to $205 million.

Postwar economic opportunities were squandered. Funds available were used irrationally. Corruption and graft contributed no small part to these missed opportunities, but so did mismanagement and miscalculation. Few structural changes were made in the economy, thus leaving unattended chronic problems of unemployment, underemployment, and a flawed agrarian order. The economy began to decline by the late 1940s, and only the temporary reprieve of high sugar prices occasioned by the Korean war delayed the inevitable reckoning. The problem of inflation increased through the decade. Opportunities to enhance the productive capabilities of the economy during a period of favorable economic circumstances were lost. Capital generated by the postwar prosperity was either invested abroad or mismanaged at home. "Much of the savings of Cubans," wrote the International Bank for Reconstruction and Development of these years, "has gone abroad, been hoarded or used for real estate construction and for speculation." Between 1946 and 1952, the Cuban gross fixed investment as a percentage of gross income was only 9.3 percent, while in Argentina it reached 18.7 percent, Colombia, 18.6 percent, Brazil, 15.7 percent, Mexico, 13.4 percent, and Chile, 13.1 percent.

These developments, of course, were not entirely new. They had long been associated with the boom-bust cycle of the island export economy. But in the late 1940s and early 1950s, these conditions had far-reaching implications. In fact, the Cuban economy was approaching stagnation, a condition partially obscured by a dazzling postwar prosperity. Sugar continued to dominate the Cuban economy. This led potential investors to retain large portions of their assets in liquid form in anticipation of an increase in the price of sugar and the possibility of quick and large profits. Most of all, sugar production tended to discourage new investment and economic diversification. Cuba found itself continuing to depend upon an export product in which market conditions were uncertain and competition was intense. The decline of rival producers as a result of World War II lulled Cubans into a false sense of security. The most dynamic development of the economy had been achieved prior to 1925, during the expansion of the agricultural and industrial phase of sugar production. After the mid-1920s, the Cuban economy made relatively little progress. The symptoms of stagnation were momentarily obscured by the booms of World War II and the Korean war. However, the structures of stagnation had already been formed. The Cuban economy was not growing fast enough to accommodate the new jobs required to meet the growing numbers of people entering the labor market.

These problems would have challenged even the most enlightened administration. They were historical and structural, and defied easy solution. And Auténticos were far from enlightened. Two years after Grau's election in 1944, Auténticos controlled both houses of the legislature, and the party ruled Cuba with reckless abandon.

Auténtico scandals were played before an incredulous national audience. But not all Auténticos succumbed. The apparent indifference with which the Auténtico leadership viewed the historical mandate of 1933 and the electoral triumph of 1944 created dissent and tension within the party. In 1947, Auténtico misgovernment resulted in an open rupture in the ruling party when Senator Eduardo Chibás, a prominent student leader in 1933, broke with the administration and organized a new party, the Partido del Pueblo Cubano (Ortodoxo). In claiming to uphold the ideals of the 1930s, the Ortodoxos became generally associated in the popular imagination with economic reform, political freedom, social justice, and public honesty. Perhaps the most gifted orator of the era, Chibás articulated public grievances against the incumbent Auténticos, in a campaign that thrived on spectacular accusations and disclosures of high-level government corruption. Chibás contributed powerfully to a final discrediting of the Auténtico administration, undermining what little remained of public confidence in government leadership. Chibás's campaign aroused political emotions and heightened hopes of a new political order devoted to public integrity, administrative honesty, and national reform. In 1951, however, Chibás committed suicide. His dramatic self-destruction delivered one more blow to a political system held in varying degrees of suspicion and scorn. The mass disillusionment that followed his death found expression in cynicism, resignation, and indifference. But the Prío government remained substantially weaker after its three-year bout with the fallen Ortodoxo leader. Thoroughly disgraced, politically weak, morally bankrupt, the Auténticos presided over a discredited government and a demoralized body politic.

The communist party also experienced difficult times during these years. Reorganized in 1944 as the Partido Socialista Popular (PSP), the party had flourished during its collaboration with Batista. It had gained access to the cabinet, and in the 1944 elections the PSP obtained three seats in the senate and ten in the lower house. In the 1948 elections, the PSP claimed some 160,000 supporters. But PSP fortunes declined markedly during the Auténtico years. The Cold War bode ill for PSP influence in Cuba, and the Auténticos lost no opportunity to expand their power at the expense of all political rivals. They moved against the communist-controlled trade unions, and by the late 1940s had established control over key labor organizations. Communist labor organizers were killed, including Jesús Menéndez, the sugar workers' leader, and Aracelio Iglesias Díaz, of the Maritime Workers Union. The government confiscated the PSP radio station and continually harassed the party newspaper. But even as PSP influence declined, the party remained an effective political contender. At the time of the Batista coup in March 1952, the PSP held nine seats in the lower house.

III

Batista would later derive enormous satisfaction from recounting the details of his return to power in 1952. Within one hour and seventeen minutes, he boasted, the military conspirators had overturned the Auténtico government. And, indeed, the March 10 coup unquestionably owed much of its success to the organizational prowess of its planners. All principal army posts in Havana were seized at 2:40 a.m., from which military units moved into the city to garrison strategic positions. Bus and rail stations, airports, docks, electricity plants, radio transmitters, banks, and offices of government ministries passed under army control. Military roadblocks sealed access to and from the capital. Army units occupied local radio stations and continued normal programming without, however, broadcasting news. Later that morning city residents awoke amidst rumors of a coup; when they turned to radio broadcasts, they heard only uninterrupted music. Telecommunication service to the interior was interrupted. Sites of potential protest demonstrations against the coup passed under military control. Opposition press offices were closed. Local headquarters of various unions and the communist party were occupied, and union leaders and political opponents were detained and arrested. The university was closed. Constitutional guarantees were suspended; congress was dissolved.

The ease with which Batista and the army seized power, however, reflected considerably more than the adroit application of conspiratorial talents. The effects of nearly a decade of graft, corruption, and scandal at all levels of civilian government had more than adequately paved the way for the return of military rule in 1952.

The demise of the Auténticos caused little mourning. Indeed, the general indifference to the coup underscored the depth and breadth of national cynicism with politics. The discredited Auténtico government possessed neither the popular confidence nor the moral credibility to justify an appeal for popular support. On the contrary, for many the coup was a welcome and long overdue end to an intolerable state of affairs. And even those who did not support Batista were not sorry to see the Auténticos ousted. To the business community Batista pledged order, stability, and labor tranquility. To the United States he promised respect for foreign capital. To political parties he promised new elections in 1954.

Political reactions to the coup acquired several notable characteristics. Most immediately, the Auténtico and Ortodoxo parties, disoriented by the coup and disorganized as a result of the arrest and exile of their leaders, proved incapable of responding effectively to Batista's takeover. The Ortodoxos were leaderless and the Auténticos could not lead. After 1952, Cuba's two principal parties became increasingly irrelevant to a solution of the political crisis. In much the same way that the crisis of the 1930s had been both the doing and downfall of the Liberal and Conservative parties, events in the 1950s contributed to the decline of the Auténticos and Ortodoxos. Both parties, to be sure, duly condemned and properly protested the violation of the 1940 constitution. But neither party responded to the military coup with either a comprehensive program or a compelling plan of action. On the contrary, both the Auténticos and Ortodoxos were thrown into disarray and confusion. The established political leadership appealed for a peaceful settlement of the crisis, exhorting party rank and file to begin preparations for the 1954 elections. The little opposition that did arise originated largely from outside the organized political parties, principally from ousted military officers, splinter political groups, and personalistic factions of the major parties.

The early challenges to the *batistato* failed, and failed without much fanfare. An abortive plot, the routine arrest of café conspirators, the quiet retirement of dissident army officers—all indications of anti-government activity, certainly, but not the stuff to arouse the national conscience or inspire national resistance. On July 26, 1953, a young Ortodoxo, Fidel Castro, led a nearly suicidal attack on the second largest army installation of Moncada in Santiago de Cuba. The attacked failed, but the dimensions of the failure distinguished it from all others: the plan was as daring as its failure was spectacular. It served to catapult Fidel Castro into contention for leadership over anti-Batista forces and reaffirmed armed struggle as the principal means of opposition. Once again a new generation of Cubans responded to political crisis and filled the political vacuum.

The strategy of arms gained new adherents throughout the mid-1950s. The much anticipated elections of 1954 offended all but the most cynical *batistianos*. Even major political parties, in the end, refused to participate. The leading opposite candidate withdrew. Running unopposed, obtaining a majority of a mere 40 percent of the electorate, Batista won a new term. Those moderate political forces that had counted on elections to settle national tensions found themselves after 1954 isolated and without alternatives. Re-electionism again brought the island to the edge of a precipice. One last effort to negotiate a political settlement of the deepening crisis occurred in 1955 when representatives of the moderate opposition arranged a series of conferences with Batista. The Civic Dialogue, as the discussions became known, sought to secure from Batista the promise of new elections with guarantees for all participants. He refused. The stage was now set for armed confrontation.

The first response was not long in coming. In late 1955, student demonstrations resulted in clashes with the army and the police. Government repression compelled student leaders to organize a clandestine revolutionary movement, the Directorio Revolucionario. A year later, an insurgent sector of Auténticos took up arms and attacked the Goicuría army barracks in Matanzas. In 1957, after an unsuccessful assassination attempt against Batista, the Directorio Revolucionario also turned to rural insurgency and organized a guerrilla front in Las Villas province known as the II Frente Nacional del Escambray. But it was in the Sierra Maestra mountains of Oriente province that the fate of the Batista regime was being determined.

Within three years of Moncada, Fidel Castro had organized another uprising in Santiago, this one timed with his return from Mexico aboard the small yacht *Granma*. The Santiago uprising of November 30, 1956, was crushed well before the *Granma* crew set foot on Cuban soil. Alerted to the arrival of the expeditionaries, government forces ambushed the landing party in southern Oriente, reducing the force of some eighty men to a band of eighteen. The *Granma* survivors, near defeat, without arms, ammunition, or supplies, retreated into the wilderness of the Sierra Maestra mountains in southeastern Oriente. The 26 July Movement had made a second inauspicious and disastrous attempt to overthrow Batista.

Fidel Castro and his followers found themselves in a wilderness both geographic and political, fortunate to be alive, distant from their base of support in Havana and Santiago, and without the apparent means to continue their opposition to the regime. Confined to remote southeastern Oriente, the *sierra* combatants began military operations at the periphery of the national order. The insurgents soon discovered that in the Sierra Maestra the politico-military symbols of the government they were committed to overthrowing were reduced to isolated Rural Guard outposts. In waging war against the Rural Guard, however, the rebels attacked at once the local underpinnings of the Batista regime and the symbolic expression of Havana's presence in the Sierra Maestra region. For decades, arbitrary Rural Guard commanders had terrorized rural communities. And however modest rebel successes against the rural constabulary may have seemed, they did, in fact, strike at one source of Havana's authority.

The insurgent force expanded irregularly. The *fidelistas* attracted recruits from the mountain population. And with a slightly augmented force, the insurgents mounted their early offensives. By January 1957, the rebel force was sufficiently strong to overpower the Rural Guard post at La Plata; in May the guerrillas defeated the Rural Guard station at El Uvero. News of insurgent victories served to keep the nation alive to the struggle unfolding in the Sierra Maestra, thereby attracting new recruits to the guerrilla camp. Rebel operations also forced government forces to leave the security of the cities to give chase to the rural insurgents. In the process, the arbitrary manner in which the army conducted field operations served further to alienate the rural population and generate additional support for the guerrilla force. In late 1957, the government responded to insurgency with indiscriminate terror. Vast regions of the Sierra Maestra were transformed into proscribed military zones. The armed forces scoured the countryside, forcing peasant families to relocate into hastily constructed detention camps in Santiago and Bayamo. An estimated two thousand families, together with their livestock, supplies, and personal possessions, were evacuated from the highlands. Peasants remaining in the cleared zones, the army command warned, were presumed guilty of aiding the guerrillas, and were to be treated accordingly.

The forced relocation of peasants alienated a large portion of the mountain population. The government campaign revived memories of Spanish re-concentration policies nearly sixty years earlier, and the effects were similar. Many peasants refused to leave and instead fled deeper into the interior to join the guerrilla columns.

The success of the guerrillas in the Sierra Maestra, however, was only in part due to the excesses of the regime. Much more was due to social conditions there. The region was home to an estimated 50,000 peasants, living in varying degrees of indigence and impoverishment: part-time itinerant workers on large estates, part-time indigent cultivators on marginal land. They occupied the worst of both worlds: low-paid laborers, low-producing farmers. Thousands had retreated into the impenetrable folds of the mountain ranges that rimmed the outer perimeter of southern Oriente. Thousands of others moved onto untended tracts of land, and within several decades the problem of squatters *(precaristas)* assumed major proportions. An estimated 14,000 squatters occupied almost 9 percent of the total farms of the republic, almost 3 percent of the total farm area. Of the total number of squatters, some 84 percent were located in Oriente province. One-fifth of the farms in Oriente were occupied by *precaristas*. Evictions escalated, and were frequently accompanied by violence. These conditions set the stage for continuing conflict between *precaristas* on one side and landowners and the armed forces on the other.

These conditions were historic, and persisted through the 1950s. When Fidel Castro and his followers arrived in the Sierra Maestra in 1956, they stepped into a tradition of rebellion, however vague and ill-defined. They came upon armed struggle, they did not introduce it. The *fidelistas* discovered communities of outcasts, peasants surviving at precarious levels of subsistence, by whatever means necessary. Almost half the Sierra Maestra population lived as squatters. They continued to exist at the margins of criminality, as fugitives, outlaws, and bandits, in the inhospitable and impenetrable mountain ranges of Oriente, communities in more or less an intermittent state of rebellion.

They were also among the earliest recruits in the emerging Rebel Army. As the armed struggle spread across the Oriente mountain system, the expanding guerrilla columns discovered the existence of peasant fugitives at almost every new site of operations. These were mostly poorly armed peasant outlaws and bandits, many of whom were integrated directly into the Rebel Army. When Raúl Castro established the Second Front "Frank País" in early 1958 in the areas of Guantánamo, Alto Songo, San Luis, Baracoa, Sagua, and Mayarí, he encountered hundreds of fugitives operating in the region. By the end of 1958, the Second Front had recruited a thousand peasants into the guerrilla army. Peasants soon assumed command positions in the guerrilla columns, among them Cresencio Pérez, Víctor Mora, and Guillermo García. An estimated seven thousand guerrillas were engaged at various levels of military operations in late 1958, direct evidence of extensive involvement of rural people in the guerrilla movement.

Throughout the insurgency, guerrilla bands were the beneficiaries of the sympathy and support of local peasant communities. "Support from the peasants is almost absolute," Castro wrote in July 1957, and again a month later: "Among the people—the peasants—our control is absolute, our support unconditional and unanimous. I cannot remember having had so very many courageous collaborators. The entire Sierra is up in arms." The tradition of rural unrest had transformed itself into an ending enmity against the sugar latifundia, the foreigners who owned them, and the Rural Guards who protected them. Nowhere else on the island was land as impassioned an issue and as powerful a longing as it was among the displaced and dispossessed *montuno* families of eastern Cuba. The first territory occupied by the Rebel Army, Ernesto Che Guevara later recalled, was "inhabited by a class of peasants different in its social and cultural roots from those that inhabit the regions of extensive, semi-mechanized Cuban agriculture. In fact, the Sierra Maestra, locale of the first revolutionary column, is a place that serves as a refuge to all the peasants who struggle daily against the landlord. They go there as squatters on the land belonging to the state or some rapacious landlord, searching for a new piece of land that will yield them some small wealth. They struggled continuously against the exactions of the soldiers, always allied with the landowning power. . . . The soldiers who made up our first guerrilla army of rural people came from that part of this social class which was most aggressive in demonstrating its love for the land and its possession."

Insurgent victories forced the government to concede rebel-occupied zones to the guerrillas in the Sierra Maestra, creating enclaves of liberated territory throughout Oriente. Throughout 1957 and early 1958, the size of the insurgent force increased and field operations expanded. By mid-1958, guerrilla columns had expanded the zones that were more or less under the authority of the Rebel Army command. Raúl Castro operated a second front in the north. Juan Almeida opened a third front around Santiago de Cuba. In April 1958 a column under Camilo Cienfuegos left the Sierra stronghold for the Holguín plains, while another guerrilla force under Ernesto Che Guevara operated east of Turquino peak.

The expanding struggle in the countryside was accompanied by growing resistance in the cities. The urban underground organized by the 26 of July Civic Resistance coordinated acts of sabotage and subversion in the cities. Bombs were set, incendiary fires started. Power lines were cut and trains derailed. Kidnappings and assassinations increased. The regime responded in kind, and with increasing ferocity. Indiscriminate violence and widespread murder served to increase further the isolation of the government.

By the mid-1950s, anti-government opposition had worked its way into the armed forces. Batista's return to power in 1952 had produced a wholesale transformation of the army command. Officers previously retired by the Auténticos returned to positions of command. Politics and nepotism determined new commissions, promotions, and command positions in the early 1950s. Batista virtually dismantled the professional officer corps. The return of old Batista cronies, many with antecedents in the sergeants' revolt of 1933, produced widespread demoralization among younger commanders. Many professional officers, irked by the unabashed partisan manipulation of promotions and appointments, grew increasingly restive in a command structure so politically given to the incumbent regime. Proud of their academy preparation and professional training, younger officers took umbrage at appointments that made a mockery of career standards and placed the old sergeants in positions of command.

In April 1956, the first of a series of army conspiracies jolted the government. Led by Colonel Ramón Barquín, the anti-government plot implicated some of the most distinguished field grade officers of the army. Over two hundred officers were directly implicated in the conspiracy. In the subsequent reorganization of the army, some four thousand officers and men were removed, reassigned, and retired. In September 1957, another conspiracy, this one in the navy, resulted in a mutiny at the Cienfuegos naval station. Subsequent investigation revealed that the Cienfuegos uprising was part of a larger conspiracy involving the principal naval installations across the island. In the same year, conspiracies were uncovered in the air force, the army medical corps, and the national police. By the late 1950s, Batista was facing mounting popular opposition and an army that was increasingly unreliable.

IV

The Cuban crisis during the 1950s went far beyond a conflict between Batista and his political opponents. To be sure, many participants in the anti-Batista struggle defined the conflict principally in political terms, a struggle in which the central issues turned wholly on the elimination of the iniquitous Batista and the restoration of the constitution of 1940.

But Cuban discontent during the decade was as much a function of deepening socio-economic frustration as it was the result of growing political grievances. Through the 1950s, Cuba was experiencing economic dislocation. Cubans continued to suffer from the vagaries of an export economy, and relief was nowhere in sight. Vulnerability to the effects of price fluctuations in the international sugar market and the boom-bust cycles continued to play havoc with all sectors of the Cuban economy. By the 1950s sugar had ceased to be a source of economic growth and could not sustain continued economic development.

The class structure of Cuba during the 1950s reflected several fundamental elements of continuity with the late nineteenth century, and some notable differences. In 1953 the Cuban population had reached 3 million males and 2.8 million females. An estimated 220,000 Cubans made up the peasantry, 70 percent of whom were engaged in small-scale subsistence *(minifundista)* farming as owners, renters, and squatters. Most lived in desperate conditions, without access to minimum educational, health, and housing facilities. Another 575,000 Cubans were employed as paid agricultural workers, half of whom were cane cutters. The urban proletariat included another 500,000 Cubans, distributed in manufacturing, commerce, and transportation. Almost 200,000 Cubans were engaged in various service sectors, including domestics, waiters, entertainers, and street vendors. The Cuban middle class numbered approximately 621,000, a category that consisted almost entirely of salaried personnel, a span that ranged from corporate executives to sales people and clerks. The 1953 census categorized 85,909 Cubans as "professionals and technicians," of whom 42,571 were teachers, 10,577 were medical personnel, 7,858 attorneys, 9,914 artists, and 2,184 clerics. The ranks of the middle class also included 90,000 managers and administrators of companies and another 260,000 office workers and sales personnel. An estimated 185,000 Cubans, approximately 11 percent of the total labor force, were employed by national, provincial, and municipal governments.

Despite this appearance of well-being, the Cuban middle class was in crisis. The decade of the 1950s was a period of mounting instability and growing uncertainty. Middle-class expectations that the return of Batista in 1952 would end political turmoil proved short-lived and illusory. By the mid-1950s, Cuba was again in the grip of political violence and personal insecurity. The malaise went deeper, however, than unsettled political conditions. To be sure, by prevailing measurements of economic development Cuba boasted of one of the highest standards of living in Latin America. In 1957, Cuba enjoyed among the highest per capita income in Latin America, ranked second at $374 after Venezuela ($857). Only Mexico and Brazil exceeded Cuba in the number of radios owned by individuals (one for every 6.5 inhabitants). The island ranked first in television sets (one per 25 inhabitants). Daily average food consumption was surpassed only by Argentina and Uruguay. Cuba was first in telephones (1 to 38), newspapers (1 copy per 8 inhabitants), private motor vehicles (1 to 40), and rail mileage per square mile (1 to 4). An estimated 58 percent of all housing units had electricity. By 1953, 76 percent of the population was literate, the fourth highest literacy rate in Latin America after Argentina (86 percent), Chile (79.5 percent), and Costa Rica (79.4 percent).

The apparent affluence enjoyed by Cuba, however, concealed tensions and frustrations that extended both vertically and horizontally through Cuban society. The fluctuations of the export economy continued to create conditions of apprehension that affected all classes. The deepening political crisis of the 1950s exacerbated this uncertainty and, together with an uncertain economy, contributed to eroding the security of middle-class Cubans. They found little comfort in statistical tallies that touted their high level of material consumption and placed the island near the top of the scale of per capita income in Latin America. The social reality was quite different. Cuba was integrated directly into the larger United States economic system and the concomitant consumption patterns. While Cubans enjoyed a remarkably high per capita income in Latin American terms, they lived within a North American cost of living index. Cuba enjoyed a material culture underwritten principally by imports from the United States. While Cuban currency and wages remained comparatively stable through the 1950s, consumption of foreign imports, in the main

North American products, increased dramatically from $515 million in 1950 to $649 million in 1956 to $777 million in 1958. Cubans paid North American prices at a time when the purchasing power of the U.S. dollar was declining and the U.S. consumer price index was rising. The United States, not Latin America, served as the frame of reference for Cubans. And against this measure, the Cuban per capita income of $374 paled against the United States per capita of $2,000, or even that of Mississippi, the poorest state, at $1,000. Life in Havana, further, was considerably more expensive than in any North American city. Havana ranked among the world's most expensive cities—fourth after Caracas, Ankara, and Manila. In 1954, Havana had the largest number of Cadillacs per capita of any city in the world.

Cubans participated directly in and depended entirely on the North American economic system in very much the same fashion as U.S. citizens, but without access to U.S. social service programs and at employment and wage levels substantially lower than their North American counterparts. It was a disparity keenly felt in Cuba, a source of much frustration and anxiety. Middle-class Cubans in 1950s perceived their standard of living in decline as they fell behind the income advances in the United States. These perceptions were not without substance, for even the much-acclaimed Cuban per capita income represented a standard of living in stagnation. Between 1952 and 1954, the decline in the international sugar market precipitated the first in a series of recessions in the Cuban economy during the decade. Per capita income declined by 18 percent, neutralizing the slow gains made during the postwar period. In 1958, the Cuban per capita income was at about the same level as it had been in 1947. Increasingly, middle-class Cubans were losing ground, losing the ability to sustain the consumption patterns to which they had become accustomed.

No amount of favorable comparisons with per capita income in Latin America could reduce Cuban resentment over their predicament. Economist Levi Marrero expressed dismay in 1954 that while Cuba's per capita income was twice as high as Latin America, it was five times lower than U.S. levels, and he asked rhetorically: "Why this Cuban poverty?" Three years later, writer Antonio Llanes Montes expressed a similar complaint: "Although one hears daily of the prosperity that Cuba is now experiencing, the fact is that the workers and the middle class find it more difficult each day to subsist owing to the scarcity of articles of basic necessity."

The mid-1950s were years of mounting inflation in Cuba. The cost of

TABLE 32.   Food Prices in Havana (1956–57)
(per lb. unit)

Product	April 1956	April 1957	Percentage Increase
Lard	$0.20	$0.23	15
Olive oil	.56	.72	29
Black beans	.11	.12	10
Sausage	.15	.27	70
Bacon	.03	.06	100
Malanga	.05	.08	60
Yuca	.04	.06	50
Plátano	.05	.08	60
Codfish	.45	.50	11

Source: Oscar Pino Santos, "El alza del costo de la vida," *Carteles* XXXVIII (April 14, 1957), 38–40.

basic foodstuffs was rising, in some regions of the island by as much as 40 percent. Price increases in Havana between 1956 and 1957 were significant (see Table 32). Real estate values in Havana were soaring. Land in Vedado selling in 1941 for $12 a meter had increased in 1957 to $200 a meter. The prospects of home ownership were diminishing for increasing numbers of middle-class Cubans.

Through the 1950s, further, the long-term effects of the 1934 reciprocity treaty were taking their toll. The industrial development that characterized other Latin American countries during these years did not occur in Cuba. That local industry had to face strong foreign competition with little or no tariff protection discouraged the establishment of new enterprises. There was little incentive to expand manufactures beyond light consumer goods, largely food and textiles.

Cuban investment patterns were at once a cause and effect of these conditions, symptomatic of the larger malaise of the economy—and of a state of mind. The uncertain sugar economy and the specter of a sudden end to prosperity loomed over the upper reaches of the economy. Few Cuban capitalists were unaffected by this insecurity, and it figured prominently in their investment strategies. The emphasis fell on the distribution of existing wealth and unemployment rather than on the creation of new wealth. Investment in industry did not keep up with the availability of domestic savings. Instead, considerable sums of capital were transferred abroad, by way of profits on foreign investments in Cuba and through Cuban investments outside the island. Cubans rarely invested in government securities or long-term stocks. Cubans preferred liquidity, principally in short-term funds in banks abroad or hoarded in safety deposit boxes at home. They preferred ventures promising rapid and spectacular returns, high profits on small turnovers—all as a hedge against future market contraction. Thus, prices remained high and the market was restricted, which in turn limited Cuban investments, reduced income, and curtailed employment opportunities. This attitude was reciprocated by organized labor, who matched management's penchant for quick profit with demands for immediate concessions, and this created added problems for investors. The long-term investments Cubans did make were principally in U.S. stocks. By the mid-1950s, the U.S. Department of Commerce estimated the combined Cuban short-term assets and long-term investments in the United States at $312 million, of which $265 million was in the form of short-term assets. During the 1950s, Cubans invested primarily in real estate, in Havana and, especially, New York and Florida. By 1955, Cuban real estate investments totaled over $150 million, mostly in south Florida.

All of this bode ill for Cuban workers. Significant distinctions existed within the labor force. Rural workers received low wages and few social services; they were poorly housed and poorly educated. Agricultural workers typically earned less than $80 a month. Urban workers were comparatively better off—with higher wages, greater job security, and better access to health and educational facilities. This was particularly true if workers were employed by major companies or members of strong union organizations. The average industrial wage was approximately $120 a month, to which was typically added pension allowances and other fringe benefits.

Unemployment and underemployment continued to cast a dark shadow over the entire Cuban working class. An estimated 475,000 sugar workers, approximately 25 percent of the total labor force, averaged less than one hundred days of employment annually. The seasonality of the sugar economy, in turn, affected transportation, retail trade, and other sectors linked to the central activities of the export economy. Beyond the problem of seasonality was that of unpredictability. Cuban workers lived precariously, dependent on the vagaries of invisible market forces over which they had little control. Nearly 60 percent of the total labor force lan-

TABLE 33.   Weeks Worked by Population 14 Years and Over (1953)

Weeks Worked	Total Number	Percent of Total	Percent of Male	Percent of Female
10 or less	1,863,014	48.7	16.5	82.5
10–19	87,422	2.3	4.0	.4
20–29	165,819	4.3	7.8	.7
30–39	134,954	3.5	6.0	.9
40–49	169,388	4.4	7.6	1.1
50–52	1,407,867	36.8	58.1	14.4
Total	3,828,464	100.0	100.0	100.0

Source: Cuba, Tribunal Superior Electoral, *Censos de población, viviendas y electoral* (Havana, 1953), 176.

guished permanently in conditions between unemployment and under-employment. (Table 33.)

Cuban workers were in desperate need of immediate relief and long-term remedy, but none was forthcoming. Unemployment/underemployment was taking its toll on both the morale and material condition of the Cuban working class. In a survey of living conditions among rural workers in 1958, almost all of whom suffered from seasonal unemployment, more than 73 percent identified greater employment opportunities as their most pressing need. To the question "From whom do you expect a solution of your problem?" 69 percent answered "the government."

The deteriorating condition of the Cuban labor force was expressed in other forms. Between 1953 and 1954, labor's share of net income declined from 70 percent to 66 percent. During this same period, the wages of sugar workers were declining. A worker who earned $5 daily in 1951 was earning $4.35 per day in 1955. Over a hundred-day harvest, this represented a wage decrease from $500 to $348. Workers in transportation, tobacco, henequen, and manufacturing similarly experienced an approximate 20 percent loss of wages during these years.

The repercussions of pervasive unemployment/underemployment, further, had adverse effects on other sectors of the economy. As unemployment increased so too did labor resistance to measures for raising productivity. Sugar workers successfully opposed mechanized cutting and bulk loading. Cigarworkers were successful in limiting mechanization. The attempt to introduce mechanical devices in Cuban port facilities met strong resistance from dock workers. One results of these conditions was to reduce the ability of Cuban exports to compete successfully on international markets.

The problems ran deep, and in a circle. Unions realized the implications of workers' opposition to mechanization. Indeed, many union leaders believed workers would benefit by higher production, the expansion of industry, and new job opportunities. Few were convinced, however, that employers would use labor concessions and the subsequent savings in a productive manner.

For related reasons, further, Cuban labor was not cheap. Successive labor laws through the 1940s and 1950s made the dismissal of workers in many industries all but impossible. In this environment, job security became a question of paramount importance and ultimately a volatile political issue. Labor disputes typically were settled by government intervention, rarely by collective bargaining agreements. These circumstances served to discourage the development of new industries and deter the expansion of old ones. "The legal causes for dismissal of unsatisfactory employees are reasonable and ample in theory," the U.S. Department of Commerce cautioned prospective investors in Cuba in 1956, "but the difficulties of proving cause and the delays in administrative proceedings make the system unsatisfactory from the employer's standpoint."

Conditions were exacerbated by a steady growth in the Cuban population, expanding at an annual rate of 2.5 percent. An estimated 50,000 young men reached working age every year, vast numbers of whom entered an economy in which there were no new jobs. Between 1955 and 1958 only 8,000 new jobs were created in industry, a period in which an estimated 150,000 young men joined the wage labor force. Anxiety mounted as the result of instability, economic stagnation, chronic unemployment/underemployment, and the lack of new job opportunities. A recurring cycle was thus set in motion: organized labor became increasingly rigid in pressing for new political and economic benefits advantages and holding old ones. New investment was discouraged, and industrial expansion did not keep up with population growth. "Unless this vicious cycle can be broken," the International Bank for Reconstruction and Development warned in 1951, "all efforts at economic betterment in Cuba will be severely handicapped. Then Cubans of all classes will suffer by lower incomes, by few and inferior job opportunities, and perhaps even by internal dangers to their cherished political freedoms."

Inequities existed too in land tenure structures. Vast areas of rural Cuba

TABLE 34.   Distribution of Land per Farms (1946)

Size of Farm (hectares)	Number of Farms	Percentage of Total Number of Farms	Total Area of Farms	Percentage of Total Area
0.1–9.9	62,500	39.1	296,739	3.2
10–24.9	48,778	30.5	725,071	8.0
25–74.9	32,058	20.0	1,278,362	14.1
75–499.9	14,286	8.9	2,523,281	27.7
500–4,999.9	2,222	1.4	2,436,031	26.9
5,000+	114	0.1	1,817,602	20.1
Total	159,958	100	9,077,086	100

Source: Vladimir Akulai and Domingo Rodríguez Fragaso. "La situación socioeconómica del campesinado cubano antes de la revolución," *Islas* LIV (May–Aug. 1976), 67.

were held in latifundia form. Almost three-quarters of all land in production was held by only 8 percent of the farms (numbering 16,622); into the remaining quarter were squeezed 143,336 *fincas* (Table 34). Of all land devoted to agriculture, one-fifth was run by large sugar companies (22 in all). The vast proportion of large holdings were devoted to ranching (480,412 *caballerías*) and sugar (203,000 *caballerías*. In the case of sugar, less than one-half were in actual production, the balance held in reserve for the prospective cyclical boom that producers so eagerly awaited.

Cuban society, moreover, showed sharp regional disparities. Statistical averages tended to ignore distinctions in distribution between urban and rural Cuba, between west and east. Thus, the 58 percent of housing units with electricity actually signified that 87 percent of all urban units and only 9 percent of rural homes had electricity. So too with literacy rates. Rural illiteracy was four times greater than that of the cities. The illiteracy rate in the countryside stood at 42 percent and in the historically deprived and depressed regions of the east it was almost 50 percent.

Rural Cuba enjoyed few of the amenities and services that characterized urban Cuba. On the contrary, the rural population suffered abject poverty and persistent neglect. Only 15 percent of rural inhabitants possessed running water as compared with 80 percent of the urban residents. Health and educational services rarely reached the countryside. Medical and dental personnel as well as hospitals and clinics tended to concentrate around the cities. In Havana, the doctor to population ratio was 1 to 227;

in Oriente it was 1 to 2,423. Out of every peso spent to support hospitals, 55 centavos was spent in Havana and 5 centavos in Camagüey. The per capita distribution of the Ministry of Public Health allocated $2.69 to Havana and $0.88 to Oriente. The capital received a disproportionate share of national revenues. Almost 20 percent of the population living on 0.5 percent of national territory accounted for 80 percent of all construction, 70 percent of the consumption of electricity, 62 percent of salaries and wages, 73 percent of all telephones, and 60 percent of all automobiles.

Social undercurrents ran deep during the late 1950s and contributed to transforming the struggle against Batista from a political contest between elite power contenders into a more ambiguous movement for socioeconomic change. Cubans looked upon their condition during the 1950s with a mixture of incredulity and incomprehension. In many ways, they were worse off in the 1950s than they had been in the 1920s. Cuba's share of the vital U.S. sugar market had decreased. In real terms, Cuban incomes had increased little. The purchasing power of Cuban exports between 1952 and 1956 was no more than it had been thirty years earlier, while between 1902 and 1926 it had doubled. Illiteracy was on the rise. Indeed, the proportion of children attending primary school in the late 1950s was lower than in the 1920s. By the late 1950s, protest and unrest among different classes had given the anti-Batista struggle the character of a protest movement drawing on social frustration, economic loss, and political anger.

V

The year 1958 began on a note of uncertainty and anguish. Indiscriminate government terror and repression left few households unvisited by grief. Middle-class impatience increased. On May 26, 1957, the weekly news magazine *Carteles* had disclosed that no less than twenty members of the Batista government owned numbered Swiss bank accounts, each with deposits over $1 million. Batista used proceeds from the lottery in ways that his predecessors could only have dreamed out. He lavished funds on potential sources of political opposition. Few resisted the president's generosity. To the Catholic church he donated $1.6 million, to labor unions he gave $1.3 million outright and gave another $3.7 million for social security funds. He lavished funds on newspaper editors and reporters. Government bribes to the press were paid at the rate of $1 million monthly.

The failure of the Cuban economy to sustain expansion and accommodate the growing expectations of the upwardly mobile middle class served to disillusion the class initially most disposed to support Batista. But in 1958 it was no longer simply an issue of economic disarray—the economy was approaching collapse. Public works programs came to a halt, and inevitably unemployment increased. Organized labor began to desert the government. The unemployment rate rose from 8.9 percent in January to 18 percent in December, approaching desperate proportions. Out of a total labor force of 2.7 million, 365,000 people were totally without employment. Another 150,000 people were underemployed. An additional 150,000 people worked without pay for families. Provincial unemployment patterns stated the problem in slightly different terms, with stark implications. Oriente accounted for almost 30 percent of national unemployment (108,000), accounting in part for the popular support of the rebellion against Batista in the east. Las Villas followed with 82,000, then Havana (78,000), Camagüey (48,000), Matanzas (32,000), and Pinar del Río (17,000). It was not only that there were more people in search of fewer jobs, but also that vast numbers of Cubans with work were receiving marginal wages. Of approximately the 892,000 people fully employed, a total of 62 percent of the population with work earned under $75 monthly.

The effects of these developments were visible everywhere in Havana. Urban slums ringed the capital. The neighborhoods of Luyano, Jesús del Monte, and Las Yaguas were crowded with tens of thousands of poor, unemployed, and unemployable, living in squalor and destitution, eight to a room in hovels of tin sheeting and cardboard without sanitary facilities, garbage collection, sidewalks, or street lighting, and increasingly without hope. Many wandered about aimlessly, without work and some without motivation, many crippled, maimed, and ill, living off public welfare and private charity. Many were petty criminals, peddlers, and panhandlers, or, at best, bootblacks, newspaper vendors, car washers, and dishwashers. More than five thousand beggars walked the streets of Havana in 1958, many of whom were homeless women with children. Wrote sociologist Lowry Nelson of Cuba in the early 1950s: "It would be impossible to give even a rough estimate of the beggar population of Cuba, but it is considerable, as anyone who has visited Cuban cities can testify. Large numbers of them are women. . . . They are found at the gates and on the steps of the churches on a Sunday morning, begging alms of the churchgoers.''

Signs of social stress appeared in other ways. Havana was transformed into a center of commercialized vice of all sorts, underwritten by organized crime from the United States and protected by Batista's police officials. Illegal drugs were plentiful. Gambling casinos emerged as a major industry. In 1957, receipts reached $500,000 a month. Pornographic theaters and clubs were expanding everywhere in the capital. Brothels multiplied through the early 1950s; by the end of the decade, 270 brothels were in full operation. By 1958, an estimated 11,500 women earned their living as prostitutes in Havana. Arthur Schlesinger, Jr., later recalled a visit to Havana during these years: "I was enchanted by Havana—and appalled by the way that lovely city was being debased into a great casino and brothel for American businessmen over for a big weekend from Miami. My fellow countrymen reeled through the streets, picking up fourteen-year-old Cuban girls and tossing coins to make men scramble in the gutter. One wondered how any Cuban—on the basis of this evidence—could regard the United States with anything but hatred.''

Crime was on the rise, so was juvenile delinquency. In 1957, almost 70 percent of all children entering public orphanages had been abandoned as infants in hospitals. By the mid-1950s, more than 1,000 Cubans a year committed suicide—400 of whom were women—and more than 3,000 others attempted it, an increase from 844 in 1945 and 849 in 1951.

Female mendicancy, prostitution, and suicide were only the most visible manifestations of the deteriorating condition of women in Cuba. Out of a female population of 1.8 million over age fourteen in 1953, approximately 20 percent (362,000) had joined the ranks of the labor force. However, not all women worked full-time or even year-round, and not all women who worked earned wages. Almost 21,000 were totally without employment and looking for work. Another 7,400 were employed but not working the week prior to the 1953 census. Still another 77,500 women worked for a relative without pay. The total number of women employed for wages in 1953 was approximately 256,000, approximately 12 percent of the working labor force. An estimated 83 percent of all employed women worked less than ten weeks a year. Only 14 percent worked year-round.

The traditional concentration of women in the service sector persisted through the 1950s. Nearly 65 percent of all women employed in 1953 were engaged in the service sector (see Table 35). Women tended to

TABLE 35.　Occupational Distribution by Sex (1953)

	Total	Male	Percentage	Female	Percentage
Agriculture	818,706	804,106	98.2	14,600	1.8
Mining	9,618	9,345	97.2	273	2.8
Manufacturing	327,208	278,332	85.0	48,876	15.0
Construction	65,292	64,350	99.0	942	1.0
Utilities	8,439	7,828	92.8	611	7.2
Commerce	232,323	212,177	91.3	20,146	8.7
Transportation	104,003	99,689	95.9	4,314	4.1
Service	395,904	229,986	58.0	165,918	42.0
Misc.	10,773	10,013	92.9	760	7.1

Source: Cuba, Tribunal Superior Electoral, *Censos de población, viviendas y electoral* (Havana, 1953), 185.

occupy the extremities of the Cuban occupational structure. On one hand, they represented almost half of domestic servants (87,522 out of 178,504). On the other hand, in a 1952 occupational survey, women accounted for more than 55 percent of professional and technical occupations (38,616 out of 70,018). They were most strongly represented in the teaching profession, where women numbered 34,769: 51 percent of university teachers, 90 percent of secondary instructors, and 84 percent of primary school teachers. Women also dominated the field of pharmacy (1,275 out of 1,866). Occupational data confirmed educational patterns. Two out of every three women in Cuba was literate; almost one-third of all Cubans with a college education were women (17,500 out of 53,400).

Similar conditions characterized the condition of the Afro-Cuban population during the 1950s. In 1953, people of color made up 27 percent of the total population, approximately 1.6 million out of 5.8 million residents, and constituted approximately the same percentage of the labor force. Afro-Cubans tended to be over-represented in entertainment, construction, and domestic services and under-represented in banking and finance, professional and technical occupations, and government. Few Cubans of color reached the upper levels of public administration, and were under-represented in elected office. Out of 54 senators in 1945, only five were Afro-Cubans. The house of representatives included twelve Afro-Cubans out of 127 members. The 1943 census, the last pre-revolutionary census to identify occupations by race, provided an approximation of

TABLE 36. Occupational Percentages by Color (1943)

	Colored Percent	White Percent
Agriculture	23.0	77.0
Mining	33.0	67.0
Construction	44.2	55.8
Manufacturing	35.9	64.1
Transportation and Communication	22.9	77.1
Commerce	15.9	84.1
Banking and Finance	9.2	90.8
Domestic and Personal Service	46.9	53.1
Recreation	39.7	60.3
Profession	14.5	85.5
Government	19.3	80.7
Misc.	28.0	72.8
Industry	26.5	73.5

Source: Lowry Nelson, "The Social Class Structure in Cuba," in Theo R. Crevenna, ed., *Materiales para el estudio de la clase media en la América Latina* (6 vols., Washington, D.C., 1950–51), II, p. 63, and Benigno E. Aguirre, "Differential Migration of Cuban Social Races," *Latin America Research Review* XI (1976), 107–9.

Afro-Cuban employment patterns (Table 36). Afro-Cuban leadership was expressed most significantly in organized labor, where the class-color correlates of Cuban discontent were most dramatically joined. Cubans of color emerged among the most prominent leaders of organized labor and the PSP during the 1940s and 1950s: Lázaro Peña of the CTC, Aracelio Iglesias Díaz, who represented dock workers, and Jesús Menéndez, sugar workers.

In the main Afro-Cubans occupied the lower end of the socio-economic order. Almost 30 percent of the population of color over twenty years of age was illiterate. Blacks tended to constitute a majority in the crowded tenement dwellings of Havana. They suffered greater job insecurity, more unemployment/underemployment, poorer health care, and constituted a proportionally larger part of the prison population. They generally earned lower wages than whites, even in the same industries. Afro-Cubans were subjected to systematic discrimination, barred from hotels, resorts, clubs, and restaurants.

VI

The expanding anti-Batista rebellion during the late 1950s transformed an unsatisfactory situation into an intolerable one. Batista's continuation in power compounded the crisis by creating political conditions that made renewed economic growth impossible. He was now perceived by many to be the largest single obstacle to the restoration of political stability and a return of economic good times. The political conflict was playing havoc with the economy. Tourism declined. The insurgency had halted the flow of dairy, vegetable, and meat products from the countryside to the cities. Prices of basic staples soared. Many products disappeared altogether from grocery shelves. Sabotage and the destruction of property further contributed to economic dislocation. Sugar production dropped. Indeed, in 1958 the insurgency had reached its most advanced stage in three eastern provinces—the region making up more than 80 percent of the total sugar land and accounting for more than 75 percent of the annual crop. Shortages of gasoline and oil brought railroads, trucking, and sugar mills to a standstill. Telephone and telegraph service across the island was paralyzed. Transportation between Havana and the three eastern provinces was all but totally suspended. Large sections of highway and railroads had been destroyed. Bridges were out of service. Manufacturers' inventories began to pile up at the plants. Wholesale dealers were unable to move medicines, supplies, machines, and foodstuffs across the island, making life in the eastern provinces intolerable.

In 1958, further, the 26 of July Movement opened a new front against the regime—a war against property and production across the island as a means to isolate Batista from the support of economic elites, both foreign and domestic. The message was clear: conditions of normality would not return until Batista departed. In February 1958, the 26 of July leadership announced its intention to wage war against the economy—sugar mills, tobacco factories, public utilities, railroads, and oil refineries. The destruction of the sugar harvest once again emerged as the principal goal of insurgent strategy. "Either Batista without the *zafra* or the *zafra* without Batista," the Movement intoned again and again. By March 1958, the rebel army command reported having applied a torch to every cane-producing province on the island, destroying an estimated two million tons of sugar.

Insurgent operations against property cost millions of dollars. As early as September 1957, the resident *New York Times* correspondent in Havana cabled that commerce, industry, and capital, "which have wholeheartedly supported President Batista since he took over the Government in 1952, are growing impatient with the continued violence in the island." By 1958, this impatience had turned to exasperation.

Batista's supporters outside of government had come to the understanding that the president had to leave, and quickly. In no other way could they envision an end to the civil war. And because the regime was perceived to defend no interests other than its own, through illegal and corrupt means, it could be removed and replaced without risk to others. Its principal *raison d'être* had been its ability to maintain political order and social peace. When it failed in this minimum mission, it was expendable.

In 1958 Cuba approached a revolutionary situation. In July representatives of the leading opposition groups met in Caracas to organize a united front and develop a strategy against Batista. The Pact of Caracas established Fidel Castro as the principal leader of the anti-Batista movement and the Rebel Army as the main arm of the revolution.

Even as the conference in Caracas convened, the final act of the Cuban drama was approaching its climax. In mid-1958, Batista launched his most formidable offensive against the guerrillas in the Sierra Maestra. Every branch of the armed forces participated in the offensive. An estimated 12,000 troops moved on the Sierra Maestra. Air force squadrons bombed and strafed suspected rebel-held regions. Naval offshore units pounded the southeastern mountain range. By the end of the summer, the government offensive collapsed. The army simply ceased to fight. Desertions and defections reached epidemic proportions. Retreating units became easy prey for advancing guerrilla columns. Demoralization turned to fear and ultimately panic; retreat became a rout.

In the late summer, the 26 of July launched its counteroffensive. Within weeks, government forces in the eastern half of the island found themselves engulfed by the swelling tide of the armed opposition, isolated and cut off from relief and reinforcements. Provincial towns and cities fell to guerrilla columns. Local military commands surrendered, often without firing a shot. Some defected and joined the opposition. Loyal troops sought desperately to return west in advance of the revolutionary current that moved inexorably toward Havana from the east.

By late 1958, it did not require the gift of prophecy to realize that the Batista regime was doomed, and that the 26 of July under Fidel Castro had established clear hegemony over all the revolutionary factions. In the summer of 1958, the communist party, proscribed during the years of the second Batista regime, allied itself with the 26 of July Movement as part of the revolutionary coalition against Batista. This conversion to *fidelismo* won the PSP several key positions within the 26 of July, most notably within the Rebel Army columns of Raúl Castro and Ernesto Che Guevara, positions later to serve as the basis of expanding PSP authority in post-revolutionary Cuba.

By 1958 Batista had acquired one more adversary: the United States government. The year began inauspiciously for the Cuban government when in March Washington imposed an arms embargo on Cuba. The move was tantamount to a withdrawal of support. The suspension of arms shipments helped weaken Batista's hold over his supporters, both civil and military. Coming as it did on the eve of the government spring offensive, the embargo dealt a blow to army morale. For the better part of the 1950s, Batista had been assured of unqualified support from Washington. After March 1958, the army command was no longer sure. Intimation that Washington no longer backed Batista, Ambassador Earl E. T. Smith later wrote, "had a devastating psychological effect" on the army and "was the most effective step taken by the Department of State in bringing about the downfall of Batista."

The year 1958 was also an election year, an opportunity for Batista to demonstrate to Washington that democratic processes were still capable of functioning, civil war notwithstanding. But to the surprise of few, government candidate Andrés Rivero Agüero triumphed. The 1958 electoral hoax contributed further to weakening Batista's position both at home and abroad. The victory of the official candidate disillusioned the few who still hoped for a political end to the armed insurrection. It now became apparent that the regime would not make even the slightest concession to the moderate opposition, and the revolutionary opposition would not accept anything less than the complete removal of the president and president-elect. Army officers loyal to Batista, moreover, disheartened by the prospect of a transfer of executive power, lost their enthusiasm for defending a lame duck president. Washington rejected outright the rigged presidential succession and announced in advance plans to withhold diplomatic recognition of Rivero Agüero. The refusal of the U.S. to endorse the Rivero Agüero government further undermined political and military support of a regime whose future appeared bleak.

In fact, Washington had already determined to ease Batista out of of-

fice. The crisis in 1958 recalled the one of 1933. The incumbency of an
unpopular president threatened to plunge the island into political turmoil
and social upheaval. Once again Washington sought to remove the source
of Cuban tensions as a means to defuse a revolutionary situation. In early
December, the State Department dispatched financier William D. Pawley
to Havana to undertake a covert mission as a personal representative of
the president. The United States, Pawley later recalled, urged Batista "to
capitulate to a caretaker government unfriendly to him, but satisfactory
to us, whom we could immediately recognize and give military assistance
to in order that Fidel Castro not come to power." On December 9, Pawley held a three-hour conference with Batista, offering him an opportunity
to retire unmolested to Florida with his family. The North American envoy informed the Cuban president that the United States "would make
an effort to stop Fidel Castro from coming into power as a Communist,
but that the caretaker government would be men who were enemies of
his, otherwise it would not work anyway, and Fidel Castro would otherwise have to lay down his arms or admit he was a revolutionary fighting
against everybody only because he wanted power, not because he was
against Batista." Batista refused.

Even as the United States sought to ease Batista out of office, the
revolutionary momentum had sealed the fate of the regime. Failure of the
government offensive and the success of the guerrilla counter-offensive
had a galvanizing effect on Cubans. Government reversals were the signal for spontaneous uprisings across Cuba. Vast quantities of arms and
equipment fell into the control of civilians in the wake of the army's
retreat, including artillery, tanks, and small weapons of every type. In
the closing weeks of 1958, revolutionary ranks, both the urban resistance
and the guerrilla columns, increased rapidly. By December 1958, the
batistiano army command in Santiago reported that fully 90 percent of
the population supported guerrilla actions. At about the same time, spontaneous uprisings in Camagüey overwhelmed local army detachments. In
the decisive battle of Santa Clara, Guevara's column received critical
assistance from the local population. The guerrilla columns expanded rapidly
during the counter-offensive, and by January 1959, the Rebel Army numbered some 50,000 officers, troops, and hangers-on.

Batista's expendability was the signal for military intrigue. The army
that had ceased to fight in the countryside had become the focal point of
political intrigue in the cities. By December, no fewer than half a dozen
conspiracies were brewing in the armed forces. During the early morning

hours of January 1, 1959, as guerrilla columns marched across the plains of central Cuba, the generals seized power. The 26 of July rejected the coup and demanded unconditional surrender to the Rebel Army. Pledging to continue the armed struggle, Fidel Castro called for a nationwide general strike.

With the news of Batista's flight, army units throughout the island simply ceased to resist further rebel advances. The new military junta complained to the U.S. embassy that it had inherited the command of a "dead army." Seeking to revive the moribund government war effort, the imprisoned Colonel Ramón Barquín was summoned by the junta to head a new provisional government. He agreed, and immediately ordered a cease-fire, saluted the insurgent "Army of Liberation," and surrendered command of Camp Columbia and the military fortress at La Cabaña to Ernesto Che Guevara and Camilo Cienfuegos. A week later, Fidel Castro arrived in Havana.

11

Between the Old and the New

I

The end of the Batista regime came amidst a revolutionary general strike on January 1, 1959, summoning hundreds of thousands of Cubans to a final offensive against the old order, demanding nothing less than unconditional surrender to the new. But it was not immediately apparent that the resulting transition of power signified anything more than a turnover of personnel. The new provisional revolutionary government was unremarkable enough: a loose coalition made up of representatives of the established political parties, largely from the ranks of the Auténticos and Ortodoxos, mostly men from liberal professions who either in person or in kind had long governed Cuba.

But it was also increasingly clear that authority in Cuba after January 1959 did not come from the new provisional revolutionary government or the old political parties, but originated in the 26 of July Movement, in its armed forces, and most of all in its leader, Fidel Castro. And herein lay the difference between what was new in this transition and what was old. The movement was led by a new generation—the "generation of the *centenario*," they called themselves: on the centennial of José Martí's birth (1853), Moncada was attacked (1953). For a new movement to proclaim itself charged with a mission of deliverance was not an unfamiliar phenomenon in Cuba. This was not the first time that youth had aspired to power in the name of the people, justice, and freedom and stepped forward to claim responsibility for redemption. The leader of the new generation was different, however. To be sure, he, like others before him, aspired to the role of redeemer, in behalf of the people and, of course, in the name of justice and liberty. But he also invoked history. It was to history that Fidel Castro appealed for absolution during his trial in 1953. It was from history that he sought the mandate and sanction for revolution—a self-conscious effort to represent this new generation and

313

this new movement as the fulfillment of unmet aspirations and unkept promises of the past.

Revolutionaries were conscious of their role as liberators, and they played the part with alacrity. They declined to shed the trappings of armed struggle, so that to be revolutionary was often as much a function of one's appearance as it was of one's politics. Beards, long hair, and olive fatigues assumed powerful symbolic value, another way of distinguishing the new from the old, another way of saying that the struggle for redemption was not yet over.

From the outset the 26 of July Movement contained elements that defined the purpose of armed struggle less in terms of destroying the old order and more in terms of creating a new one. These tendencies were politically inchoate and programmatically incomplete. But if this ambiguity was a cause of potential weakness, it was also the source of actual strength, for it permitted improvisation in response to rapidly changing circumstances. The success of Cuban arms carried the island over a threshold never before crossed. Not since the nineteenth century had Cubans employed arms with such effect, and never before had the effects of Cuban arms been so complete. They had challenged a repressive regime on its own terms, and succeeded—unconditionally and unassisted. The armed struggle announced the rise of a generation that owed its success to its own resources and resolve. An unpopular government was displaced, its political allies discredited, and its armed forces defeated.

But it was not clear that the traditional political opposition to the fallen regime, principally in the form of the Auténticos and Ortodoxos, stood to benefit from this triumph. Certainly, they had contributed to the fall of Batista, and in some instances at great sacrifice. In a larger sense, however, they also had contributed to the rise of Batista. Their years in power during the 1940s and early 1950s had ended in disgrace, and their years in opposition could not erase the memory of their years in office. In some fashion or other almost all political leaders after 1933, of all political parties, were implicated in misgovernment and malfeasance. Thus, an indictment of the accumulated ills of Cuban society was no less an indictment of past politicians in the aggregate, irrespective of their part in the struggle against the Batista government. And there was more, for the principal institutions of the republic, by virtue of association, had also failed and fallen into discredit: the presidency, congress, the courts, the army and police, the old political parties, the press, the church.

The new provisional government, a mix of mostly liberals and some revolutionaries, understood the implications of these conditions, and took immediate steps to make a substantive and symbolic break with past politics. The Batista congress was dissolved. Property owned by *batistianos* was confiscated, their safe deposit boxes seized, and their bank accounts frozen. The old political parties were abolished. All candidates who participated in the elections of 1954 and 1958 were proscribed from all future political activity.

II

Distinctions between the past and the present were drawn without difficulty, with almost celebratory unanimity. In 1959, Fidel Castro stood at the head of a movement of enormous popularity. Much of this was derived from his personal appeal. A gifted orator and charismatic personality, Castro emerged as a leader virtually without rival. He displayed almost unlimited energy, delivering spellbinding speeches hours in length, daily it seemed. Making full use of an extensive radio and television system, addressing mass rallies often numbering in the hundreds of thousands of people, Fidel Castro was a ubiquitous presence through the early months of 1959. He exhorted his followers and excoriated his foes; he explained his policies and expounded on his philosophies. He appealed directly to the Cuban people, raising revolutionary morale and summoning Cubans to heroic action.

However great the part played by Fidel Castro in the triumph and consolidation of the revolution during the early years, it was also apparent that the source of his appeal and the success of his authority were in a larger sense a function of conditions both historic and actual. Social structures were in disarray, the political system was in crisis, the economy was in distress. National institutions were in varying degrees of disintegration and disrepute, and because they had not served Cubans well, if at all, they were vulnerable. By attacking the past that had created these hardships, the revolutionary leadership struck a responsive chord that initially cut across lines of class and race and served to unite Cubans of almost all political persuasions. It aroused extraordinary enthusiasm for *"la revolución,"* and as ambiguously defined as it was, it could mean all things to all people. Aroused too was a powerful surge of nationalism, one summoned by the revolution and soon indistinguishable from it.

Revolutionary leaders reached ascendency in spectacular fashion, and en route were endowed with proportions larger than life. Already in 1959 the leaders of the revolution had become the stuff of legends and lore, the subject of books and songs, of poems and film. Revolutionaries were celebrities, folk heroes, and the hope of the hopeful. There was, during the early months, no creditable opposition, and what opposition did exist was either out of the country or out of favor, or both.

But power of this magnitude, confined on this scale to the leadership of one revolutionary organization, did not long stay unchallenged. Those appointed to the provisional government believed themselves endowed with the authority to rule, and when they sought to exercise that authority, they clashed directly with the shadow authority of Fidel Castro. In early 1959, Prime Minister José Miró Cardona protested and resigned. Fidel Castro was his replacement. Some months later, President Manuel Urrutia resigned, and no longer was there any doubt about where real authority rested. Through 1959, moderates and liberals found themselves increasingly isolated, alienated and ultimately pushed aside by forces they could not comprehend, much less control. In part, the conflict was one of a clash of approaches. Liberals and moderates were appalled by what appeared to them as a flagrant disregard for due process, the fashion in which Fidel Castro and his supporters spurned legal forms and juridical procedures. When forty-four Batista air force pilots were acquitted on charges of bombing civilian centers, widespread popular indignation prompted Castro to denounce the verdict and demand a new trial. In a second trial the pilots were convicted and sentenced to long prison terms. Liberals and moderates were exasperated, and had growing doubts and suspicions about the intentions of the *fidelistas*. Those who defended law and legal form conflicted with those who demanded immediate justice. Liberals expected the state to uphold the rule of law and defend individual rights and private ownership. Castro insisted that the state dispense justice and defend the collective over the individual, the public over the private. Fidel found sanction in the moral imperatives of the revolution. "Revolutionary justice," Castro insisted on the occasion of the pilots' acquittal, "is based not on legal precepts, but on moral conviction."

But the source of the dispute was deeper than a disagreement over means. It was also about ends. Already in early 1959, Fidel Castro, among others in the 26 of July, spoke increasingly of the revolution as a *"proceso"*—a historical, process that was underway, inalterable, and invincible. From the outset these metaphors were an essential part of the ideological baggage the *fidelistas* carried into Havana. They were in part historic—revolution as continuity with 1895 and 1933. These concerns had been addressed in the speech and in its expanded, published form, "History Will Absolve Me." Again and again, during the revolutionary war, promises of the new Cuba—of social justice, economic security, political freedom—were made. And the promises did not end with the victory. On the contrary, they increased, if only because it was easy— perhaps necessary—to be revolutionary in early 1959. The language of revolution filled the airwaves and the news columns—moderates, liberals, and radicals alike dipped freely, and frequently, into the wellspring of revolutionary rhetoric. Revolution was in the air, and the atmosphere was rarified indeed. It was intoxicating and seemed to thrive on its own excesses. This was redemption by revolution, and conversions proceeded apace. Under the circumstance, it could hardly be otherwise.

The problem with these developments was that many of the political leaders who invoked the language of revolution were, in fact, either ill-prepared to be revolutionaries or ill-disposed toward the revolutionaries. This did not deter them from playing the part, however, or assuming supporting roles, so that they too contributed to creating an atmosphere that was at once revolutionary and could be calmed only by more revolution. The rhetoric of revolution awakened the imagination of hundreds of thousands of Cubans, creating a vast constituency for radical change. It raised expectations of revolution, and not since 1933 had Cuban hopes for change reached such levels. Pressure for immediate, deep, sweeping change was building from below and the invocation of revolution encouraged it to rise to the top. Organized labor mobilized to press demands on a wide variety of issues. The Confederación de Trabajadores de Cuba (CTC) demanded outright a flat 20 percent wage increase for all workers. Strikes increased in number and frequency. Six thousand workers of the Cuban Electric Company staged a slow-down strike to dramatize their demands for a wage increase. Unemployed electrical workers demonstrated at the presidential palace. Unemployed railway workers proclaimed a hunger strike, as did former employees of a Havana paper mill. Construction workers called a wildcat strike at the Moa Bay Mining Company. Restaurant workers threatened to strike. Cane cutters marched. Labor protests disrupted sugar production in twenty-one mills.

The pressure for dramatic action mounted. It originated from the sectors of the population most immediately mobilized, with the most to gain: an urban proletariat numbering approximately 500,000; a rural proletariat almost 600,000 strong; a peasantry numbering 220,000; and the vast le-

gions of the unemployed/underemployed, who by the end of 1958 numbered as many as 665,000 men and women. This constituency for change
made up almost 70 percent of the total labor force, a marginalized population of nearly 2 million people out of an employable labor force of
2.7 million.

This was the social landscape confronting the new government. The
revolution had the masses as its foundations, new populists as its leaders,
and a charismatic authority as *jefe máximo*. A mobilized population,
hundreds of thousands of people, demanded redress and relief at a speed
and scope that could not be reasonably accommodated within the ideological framework and legal structures the liberal provisional government
sought to preserve. The situation was not unlike that of 1933, when the
provisional government of Ramón Grau San Martín, confronted with
mounting pressure for radical change, had balked and collapsed. That
marginalized groups would experience a rise in expectations after 1959
was not at all surprising. The revolution, they were given to understand,
was made in their behalf, for their interests. This revolution was for all
Cubans who suffered, Fidel Castro proclaimed as early as 1953, and repeated with regularity thereafter: for the unemployed "who desire to earn
their daily bread honestly without having to emigrate in search of livelihood"; for rural workers who inhabited "miserable shacks, who work
four months of the year and starve for the rest of the year"; for industrial
workers "whose retirement funds have been embezzled, whose benefits
are being taken away, whose homes are wretched quarters"; for peasants
who "live and die working on land that is not theirs." And to the young
men and women of the beleaguered middle class, Fidel invoked a familiar
and recurring theme—he promised employment for the "ten thousand
young professionals . . . who come forth from school with their degrees,
anxious to work and full of hope, only to find themselves at a dead end
with all doors closed, and where no ear hears their clamor or supplica-
tion."

Vast numbers of Cubans projected their aspirations for social and economic change onto the one person they believed was endowed with unlimited power. Fidel had vast opportunities for manipulation, and indeed
there was no small amount of circumlocution during the early months of
the revolution. However, while he channeled popular hopes for change,
he did not create them. Having once raised hopes for dramatic and substantive change, he could not risk alienating his source of power, which

by the end of 1959 was also the principal source of the support for the revolution.

Fidel became the object of popular importuning, both cause and effect of a style of *personalismo* that fostered direct dialogue between the leader and his followers. He listened to grievances, received petitions, considered complaints. Fidel's effectiveness increased in direct proportion to rising popular confidence in it. As the belief took hold that Fidel could provide redress, immediately and easily, so too did his ability to do so. At every turn individuals and groups urged him to intervene on behalf of one demand or another. Fidel played the part deftly, and in so doing all but undercut the authority of the provisional government by depriving it of popular sanction. Fidel was becoming the government. More and more he responded directly to popular calls for action. It was a symbiotic relationship of enormous vitality. Fidel propounded the goals of the revolution, the people demanded deeds of the revolution. This interplay gathered momentum, and soon assumed a logic of its own. There was much spontaneity in all this—improvisation from an exhilarated Fidel and impatience from an aroused population. These forces converged in powerful combination during the heady months of 1959, with predictable if not inevitable results. Fidel became the point of first appeal and the place of last resort.

These convictions appeared confirmed almost immediately when Fidel Castro joined the government as prime minister. Reform decrees provided immediate material relief to vast numbers of people. In March, the government enacted the first Urban Reform Law. One of the more popular early reform decrees, the law sought to discourage investments in real estate and construction of private dwellings, to which a considerable portion of national savings had been devoted. The law decreed a 50 percent reduction of rents under $100 monthly, 40 percent reduction of rents between $100 and $200 and 30 percent reduction in rents over $200. The newly established National Savings and Housing Institute (INAV) acquired vacant lots upon which it pledged to construct inexpensive public housing.

Other measures soon followed. In the first nine months of 1959, an estimated 1500 decrees, laws, and edicts were enacted. The government intervened in the telephone company and reduced its rates. Electricity rates were cut drastically. Virtually all labor contracts were renegotiated and wages raised. Cane cutters' wages were increased by a flat 15 percent. Health reforms, educational reforms, and unemployment relief followed in quick order. Property owned by all past government officials, senior army officers, mayors and governors, and members of both houses of congress during 1954–58 was seized. The government restricted the importation of more than two hundred luxury items through higher sales taxes and special licensing requirements. It was a symbolic gesture, certainly, but also substantive, for in one year, Cuba saved as much as $70 million in foreign exchange. Television imports decreased from $3 million to $150,000. Automobile imports fell from $25 million in 1958 to $3.4 million in 1960. Few new Cadillacs were entering Havana.

By far the most sweeping measure enacted in the first year was the Agrarian Reform Law of May 1959. By the terms of the new law, all real estate holdings were restricted in size to 1,000 acres, with the exception of land engaged in the production of sugar, rice, and livestock, where maximum limits were fixed at 3,333 acres. Land exceeding these limits was nationalized, with compensation provided in the form of twenty-year bonds bearing an annual interest rate of 4.5 percent. Payments would be based on the assessed value of land used for tax purposes. Expropriated lands were to be reorganized into state cooperatives or distributed into individual holdings of sixty-seven acres, with squatters, sharecroppers, and renters receiving first claim to the land which they were working. The law also created the Agrarian Reform Institute (INRA) designed initially to supervise the reorganization of land systems and the transfer of land. In fact, the role of INRA expanded rapidly through 1959, and soon came to include responsibility for most programs in rural Cuba, including road construction, health facilities, credit enterprises, educational projects, and housing programs.

III

These were euphoric times in Cuba. Expectations ran high, were met, and then raised higher again. Cuba had become an aroused nation. Everywhere and, it seemed, continually, Cubans were marching in protest, meeting in mass rallies, dramatizing demands in public demonstrations. And somehow, Fidel seemed always in the thick of it.

The early reform measures won the revolutionary government widespread popular support, instantly. Workers, peasants, the unemployed received benefits that were immediate and direct. Labor received wage increases, the unemployed received jobs. The urban proletariat received rent and utility rate reductions. Peasants received land and credit. That Afro-Cubans made up a disproportionate share of the uneducated, unskilled, and unemployed meant that they were among the principal and immediate beneficiaries of the early distributive policies of the revolution. Moreover, in March 1959, the revolutionary government abolished legal discrimination, and scores of hotels, beaches, night clubs, resorts, and restaurants were opened to blacks. The reform measures were dramatic and historic, and all provided immediate relief to those sectors of Cuban society that demanded relief immediately. The effects were visible. A significant redistribution of income had taken place. Real wages increased approximately 15 percent through a corresponding decline in the income of landlords and entrepreneurs. In the short space of six months, hundreds of thousands of Cubans developed an immediate and lasting stake in the success of the revolution.

But support was not unanimous. Apprehension and misgivings increased among liberals in and out of government and among property owners in and out of Cuba. Cuba was seen moving toward government by decree and rule by one man. Many were growing increasingly suspicious of the phenomenon of *fidelismo*, which smacked of demagoguery and over which, they sensed correctly, they could exercise little restraint. Concern increased over the arbitrariness of government. On the matter of national elections, the revolutionary leadership was increasingly vague and noncommital and, on occasion, even hostile, as if mere inquiry into the subject suggested lack of confidence in the direction of the revolution. Elections had originally been scheduled to occur within a year. By March, elections had become more problematical, when Fidel Castro insisted upon the completion of the agrarian reform first, including the elimination of rural illiteracy and the establishment of health facilities in the countryside. "Elections will be held at the appropriate time," Ernesto Che Guevara promised ambiguously in April 1959; "now the people want revolution first and elections later." Nor was this rendering entirely a dissimulation. Recalled former President Manuel Urrutia: "The first time I heard the promise of elections repudiated was when Castro and I attended the opening of the library at Marta Abreu University at Las Villas. At the end of the meeting, Castro mentioned elections and a large number of his listeners shouted against them. After his speech, Castro asked me,

'Did you notice how they opposed elections?' '' By the end of the summer, elections were deferred for two more years, and then pushed back
further to some undetermined point in the future.

Discontent increased also among property owners. Large urban landlords denounced the reduction of rents. So did middle-class small property owners, many of whom had invested years of savings into small
apartment houses, most of which were mortgaged. Rent reductions
threatened these properties, for mortgages were based on higher rental
income. Landowners protested the agrarian reform decree. The National
Association of Cattle Ranchers freely predicted economic ruin as a result
of the limitation on land ownership. The Sugar Mill Owners Association
and the Association of Tobacco Planters agreed, and vigorously attacked
the Agrarian Reform Law. Implementation of the decree, sugar mill owners warned, threatened to cripple national production. Newspaper edito-
rials and radio commentaries also registered their disapproval. The church
moved openly into opposition.

By this time, too, alarm had reached official circles in the United States.
In fact, the breach began early in 1959. That so many *batistianos* had
found safe haven in the United States, beyond the reach of the revolutionary tribunals, and that some of these ex-officials were already engaged openly in counter-revolutionary activity, aroused no small ire in
Havana. The work of the tribunals, in turn, including the execution of
former Batista officials, led to diplomatic protests from the United States.
Inevitably, too, given the magnitude of North American investments in
Cuba, Washington reacted with a mixture of concern and consternation
at the enactment of each new revolutionary decree. International Telephone and Telegraph protested the reduction of its rates, as did the Cuban
Electric Company. The Agrarian Reform Law strained relations even further. North American sugar companies and cattle enterprises denounced
the measure as confiscatory. The 3,333-acre limit reduced the Pingree
ranch in Oriente to one-sixteenth of its size. The King ranch in Camagüey
lost nine-tenths of its holdings. By the end of the summer, an estimated
2.5 million acres of ranch land had been nationalized. The State Department expressed its ''concern'' at the rush of events in Cuba and insisted
upon ''prompt, adequate, and effective compensation'' for all property
nationalized by the Cuban government. In late 1959, U.S. officials alluded to the possibility of cutting the Cuban sugar quota in retaliation.

Into this highly charged setting was introduced one more volatile issue.
Members of the Cuban communist party, the Partido Socialista Popular

(PSP), were moving in increasing numbers, into government positions, not high ones but certainly visible ones: in the armed forces, in the administration of INRA, at sub-cabinet levels, and in the provinces and municipalities.

IV

A critical threshold was crossed in the autumn of 1959. Despair spread among liberals who were, in any case, already disoriented and on the defensive. The emerging prominence of the PSP did nothing to calm their misgivings. For property owners in Cuba and the United States, the participation of the PSP in the government confirmed their worst fears. Opposition to government programs, in part spontaneous, in part organized, began to have a sobering effect on Fidel Castro and his closest advisors. Resistance to the agrarian reform program in particular, both within Cuba and from the United States, served to draw sharply the ideological battle lines. Revolutionary leaders stood at a crossroad. "The great landowners," Ernesto Che Guevara recalled later, "many of them North Americans, immediately sabotaged the law of Agrarian Reform. We were therefore face-to-face with a choice . . . : a situation in which, once embarked, it is difficult to return to shore. But it would have been still more dangerous to recoil since that would have meant the death of the Revolution. . . . The more just and the more dangerous course was to press ahead . . . and what we supposed to have been an agrarian reform with a bourgeois character was transformed into a violent struggle." The revolution had reached the limits of what it could accomplish through collaboration with liberals and countenance from the United States. To advance further required a fundamental realignment of social forces, no less than a reordering of Cuban international relations. For this, Fidel Castro needed the Cuban communist party, an organization of singular discipline and preparation, with historic ties to mass organizations and political connections to the socialist bloc. The PSP, Fidel Castro acknowledged to Herbert Matthews years later, "had men who were truly revolutionary, loyal, honest and trained. I needed them."

The effects were immediate. To domestic critics Fidel Castro vowed to proceed with full implementation of agrarian reform, adding that opponents to the law were traitors to the revolution. He also rejected outright North American demands for "prompt" compensation, reiterating the Cuban decision to compensate landowners in the form of twenty-year bonds. Personnel turnovers in the government, in part voluntary, in part forced, increased quickly thereafter. Liberals and moderates resigned, or were forced out, their places taken by loyal *fidelistas* and members of the PSP. The breach deepened, and the pace of liberal resignations and radical replacements quickened. Through 1959 the leadership of trade unions passed under the control of the PSP. At the same time, senior administrative positions in the Ministry of Labor were filled by the PSP. The presence of the PSP in the armed forces also increased. Party members received teaching appointments at various Rebel Army posts in Havana and Las Villas. The appearance of the PSP in the armed forces, in turn, led to wholesale resignation and, in some cases, arrest of anti-communist officers. In October Raúl Castro assumed charge of the Ministry of the Revolutionary Armed Forces (MINFAR), and forthwith launched a thorough reorganization of the military, distributing key commands to only trustworthy officers.

By the end of the year, anti-communism had become synonymous with counter-revolution. By the end of the year, too, opposition took new forms. Sabotage was on the rise. Organized resistance by exiles in the United States increased. These developments, in turn, had far-reaching consequences, for increasingly political opposition was transformed into armed opposition, much of which originated from abroad. Defense of the nation became indistinguishable from defense of the revolution and, in fact, at once accelerated and facilitated the centralization of power, curtailment of civil liberties, and elimination of opposition, all in the name of national security. Opposition was portrayed as tantamount to subversion. "To be a traitor to the Revolution is to be a traitor to the country," Fidel Castro proclaimed in 1960. "The destiny of our sovereignty is at stake. . . . We have decided that either we are or we are not a free country and we are and want to be a free country." And if opposition was subversion, then neutrality was suspect. It was time again in Cuba to choose sides, and no one could remain impartial. "In a revolutionary process," Fidel Castro announced, "there are no neutrals, there are only partisans of the revolution or enemies of it." In this climate, opposition newspapers and radio stations, one by one, were seized by the government, or closed down altogether. In early January 1960, *Avance* was closed. Several weeks later *El Mundo* was seized. In March the government took over the CMQ station, the most important television network in Havana. In May, the last of the opposition press, *Diario de la Marina* and *Prensa Libre,* were seized. And in increasing numbers, opponents of the regime emigrated. Relations with the United States continued to deteriorate. Attacks against Cuba from exiles in the United States prompted denunciations from Havana. In February 1960, a Soviet trade delegation headed by Deputy Premier Anastas Mikoyan arrived in Havana. This was followed several days later by the visit of an East German trade mission. In late March, Poland signed a trade agreement with Cuba. Several weeks later, Cuba and the Soviet Union resumed diplomatic relations, suspended since 1952.

The guarantee of alternative markets for sugar exports, no less than the promise of economic assistance, undoubtedly strengthened the government's position against internal opponents and foreign opposition. Cubans were assured at least of the capacity to survive economic warfare with the United States. The North American threat to cut the sugar quota now lost some of its potency. At the same time, these developments also increased the vulnerability of liberals and moderates, for as the influence of the United States waned in Cuba, the U.S. lost the capacity to protect and promote the interests of those social groups who had long been the beneficiaries of its hegemony. On the other hand, the shift increased the importance of PSP, which had direct and institutional contacts with Cuba's new patron. The commercial agreements with the socialist bloc introduced the Soviet Union into the dispute, a development that Cubans were able to exploit with great effect.

Events moved rapidly thereafter, in Cuba as well as in the United States and the Soviet Union. According to the terms of the 1960 economic agreement, the Soviets agreed to purchase 425,000 tons of sugar immediately, and one million tons in each of the following four years. The Soviet Union offered Cuba $100 million in the form of credits, technical assistance, and crude and refined petroleum. In March 1960, President Dwight D. Eisenhower authorized the Central Intelligence Agency to proceed with the arming and training of Cuban exiles. In April 1960, the Soviet Union agreed to sell Cuba crude oil at prices considerably lower than those charged by foreign oil companies, thereby providing immediate foreign exchange savings for the island.

The Cuban-Soviet oil agreement had immediate consequences. In May, Cuban authorities ordered Standard Oil, Texaco, and Shell to refine Soviet petroleum. On June 7 the companies refused. Three weeks later Cuba nationalized foreign refineries. Up to this point, Cuban expropriations had been confined principally to sugar and cattle land, within the larger

framework of the agrarian reform law. More than one year had lapsed
between these two expropriation decrees. After June 1960, there was no
going back. The United States retaliated. On July 5, Eisenhower cut Cuban sugar imports by 700,000 tons, the balance of the quota for 1960.
The quota was thereafter fixed at zero.

The Cuban reaction was not long in coming. On August 5 Cuba expropriated additional North American properties on the island, including two
utilities, 36 sugar mills, and petroleum assets. A month later, the government nationalized the Cuban branches of North American banks. On October 13, the United States responded with an economic embargo on Cuba,
a ban of all U.S. exports except medicines and some foodstuff. Cuba
reacted the same day, now in almost predictable fashion: the nationalization of additional properties. What distinguished the October 13 expropriations from previous state seizures, however, was that the government
nationalized a broad range of private enterprises irrespective of national
ownership. For the first time since the confiscation of *bastistiano* property, the state moved against non-agricultural Cuban-owned interests. A
total of 382 private enterprises were expropriated, including sugar mills,
rice mills, Cuban-owned banks, railroads, textile factories, distilleries,
department stores, and cinemas. A second Urban Reform Law in October
prohibited ownership of more than one residence. Lessees of confiscated
property became tenants of the state and former owners received compensation at a maximum rate of $350 a month. Later that month, Cuba na-
tionalized another 166 North American enterprises, including insurance
companies, import firms, hotels, casinos, textile firms, metal plants, tobacco export firms, chemical companies, and food processing plants, all
but eliminating U.S. investments in Cuba. In January 1961, the United
States severed diplomatic relations with Cuba.

The North American attempt to use economic coercion first to force
Fidel Castro into moderation and subsequently to remove him from power
failed to achieve the desired results. On the contrary, the internal strength
of the government increased and its relations with the socialist bloc expanded. On July 9, four days after the United States had suspended the
quota, the Soviet Union announced its decision to purchase 700,000 tons
of Cuban sugar, the full quantity cut by the United States. This was
followed shortly thereafter by an announcement from the People's Republic of China to purchase annually 500,000 tons of Cuban sugar for
the following five years. In December 1960 the Soviet Union and several
eastern bloc countries agreed to take the balance of Cuban sugar. By the

end of the year, the bulk of Cuba's sugar exports was purchased by the socialist bloc.

V

Cuba was in transition again. Far-reaching changes were transforming the island, in large part, as in the past, the result of Cuban attempts to read-just on its own terms the nature of hegemonial relationships. This read-justment, in turn, served to shape the internal dynamic of transformation. The confrontation with the United States could not but accelerate the radicalization of the revolution. It aroused powerful nationalist senti-ments, revived long historic grievances, created a national unanimity of purpose perhaps unattainable by any other means, all of which was mas-terfully directed by Fidel Castro. Cuba's initial alignment with the Soviet Union was a response to this confrontation. In the end, confrontation with the United States necessitated realignment, and the realignment further deepened the confrontation. The revolution had challenged the fundamen-tal premises of U.S. hegemony in Cuba, and as the Cuban leadership moved implacably to eliminate U.S. influence in Cuba, the United States moved with equal determination to remove the Cuban leadership. It is not certain that any one could have anticipated where this would all end, not the Cubans, not the North Americans. However, it required no pro-phetic gift for Cubans to realize that this was a confrontation they could not hope to win, at least not alone.

The affirmation of the socialist character of the Cuban revolution and Fidel's subsequent embrace of Marxism-Leninism must be seen as part political, in part programmatic, but above all pragmatic. It was a way to obtain protection and support without which the revolution would have eventually faltered and inevitably collapsed. It also presented the Soviet Union with a fait accompli, one that probably surprised the Soviets as much as the United States. Cuba had made a socialist revolution with only marginal participation by the communist party. The PSP had not led the revolution, it did not control the government, it did not even have a single member at ministerial rank in a government that proclaimed itself socialist, and the head of state did not originate from the party ranks— all in all, anomalies that could not have escaped the attention of the Soviet leadership. At the same time, however, the Soviets could hardly refuse to assist a government that proclaimed membership in the socialist camp, not, at least, without suffering a blow to its prestige among Third World nations.

The confrontation with the United States, further, had important internal consequences for which Cubans had neither planned nor prepared. So central was the presence of North American property in the national economy that its expropriation suddenly thrust upon Cubans responsibility for managing production, resources, and distribution on a vast scale. The Cuban government found itself assuming an increasingly larger role in the management of the economy. Once this process was underway, it was all but impossible to arrest and reverse.

Efficient and rational economic planning henceforth required greater control of production, resources, and distribution, and not just in those sectors controlled by U.S. capital, however large that control may have been. The state subsequently consolidated control over virtually all key sectors of private enterprise, Cuban as well as North American. New, substantive investments had all but ceased, due in large measure to conditions of uncertainty during the late 1950s and early 1960s. Under these circumstances, it was not reasonable to expect private owners to take decisive initiatives to stimulate the economy. On the contrary, under the political conditions prevailing between 1959 and 1961, it was easy to see that private enterprise might contemplate action damaging to national economic interests. In seizing private enterprise, the state acquired liquid assets estimated at hundreds of millions of dollars, thereby allowing government agencies to allocate vital resources to other sectors of the economy, as well as plan production and direct investments in a rational way. By late 1961, approximately 85 percent of the total productive value of Cuban industry was under state control. The crisis with the United States, moreover, climaxing in the trade embargo, increased the importance of state planning to reorganize Cuban industry around Soviet exports and facilitate the integration of Cuban trade with the socialist bloc.

The confiscation of North American property resulted in more than the elimination of the United States from the Cuban economy. It facilitated too the seizure of Cuban property. Cuban landowners, cattle ranchers, and property owners were dislodged with relative ease. Moreover, the rupture shattered the basis of collaboration between the Cuban middle classes and the United States. For the nearly 150,000 Cuban employees of North American enterprises, including managers, clerks, technicians, accountants, and attorneys, the expropriations were traumatic. Many suffered immediately a decline in their standard of living, for Cubans in the employ of foreigners had traditionally enjoyed higher salaries. Foreign enterprise had also served to insulate them from the vagaries of the deepening political dispute. Middle-class Cubans working for foreign enterprises could oppose government policies without necessarily endangering their material well-being or job security. As state control over the private sector expanded, however, and government functionaries moved into ranking administrative and managerial positions, political loyalties acquired new importance and now determined employment or dismissal.

Nationalization transformed the state into employer and landlord and made middle-class Cubans associated with private enterprise and foreign interest subject to new scrutiny. Those Cubans who opposed the revolution, no less than those who showed insufficient ardor for the revolution, were now enormously vulnerable. One Cuban refugee who had sought to remain uninvolved later recalled to Richard Fagen: "Life there was impossible. You had to be with them, or they would drive you crazy." They were dismissed by the thousands, and their positions filled by loyal supporters of the revolution. Almost seven hundred employers of the Cuban Electric Company were fired and placed by militants. By 1961, every senior administrator of the 161 sugar mills was a revolutionary. Indeed, between 1959 and 1961, that was the case in nearly 75 percent of the administrative positions of all sugar mills.

At the same time, entire sectors of the old economy became superfluous and disappeared, and with them the jobs of thousands of middle-class Cubans. Insurance services, real estate agencies, law firms, rent collectors, travel agencies, gambling casinos, and middlemen and brokers of all types were abolished. Thousands of opponents of the regime lost at once the positions with which to support themselves and the material basis on which to sustain opposition to the government. Countless thousands of other Cubans, largely members of the liberal professions, faced similar situations and resigned or were removed from positions in government. Once the elimination of the United States presence was underway, and its influence as an economic force and political powerbroker inside Cuba began to wane, those classes economically dependent on and ideologically allied to the United States all but collapsed. Those groups with the greatest resources and resolve to oppose the radicalization of the revolution found themselves vulnerable, without the institutional position or economic base from which to oppose the regime.

The radicalization of the revolution quickly assumed an internal logic of its own. As *fidelista* policies lost favor among liberals and moderates, it became necessary to find new political allies. This need was, in part, fulfilled by the support of the PSP. But the needs of the leadership were greater. As sectors of the middle class passed from political support to armed opposition, it became necessary to broaden the social base of support. This is precisely what the radicalization of revolutionary programs and policies accomplished: the incorporation and mobilization of vast sectors of the population, including the poor, dispossessed, and unemployed. But it was also true that the mobilization of this population to defend the revolution added new pressures within the revolution. The broader the social base of the revolution, the greater the demand for radical change. It was a process that thrived on its own determination to survive, and that once started could not be reversed easily.

The control of mass organizations was achieved within the first year. The University Students' Federation (FEU) passed under *fidelista* control. The CTC was under the PSP. After late 1959 the government embarked on the creation of new mass organizations designed specifically for the purpose of defense and political mobilization. In the autumn of 1959, the MINFAR created a civilian militia, a popular armed force that increased from 100,000 in 1960 to almost 300,000 in 1961. In August 1960, the Federation of Cuban Women (FMC) was organized in direct response to a call from Fidel Castro for women to join the revolution. A month later, the government formed the Committees for the Defense of the Revolution (CDRs) for the purpose of combating internal subversion and sabotage. By the end of the first year, the CDRs claimed a membership of almost 800,000, with committees organized block by block, in every large factory, at all work centers. The CDRs were joined by the Association of Young Rebels (AJR), designed to mobilize and organize youths between the ages of 14 and 27. In May 1961, an estimated 100,000 farmers and peasants were organized into the National Organization of Small Agriculturalists (ANAP). At about the same time, the government launched a massive literacy campaign. Thousands of Cubans, men and women, were mobilized in a national campaign to eradicate illiteracy across the island and generate in still another form a revolutionary spirit during the critical period of its consolidation. By mid-1961, the proliferation of mass organizations had created a need for central coordination. In July, the government created one more organization, the Integrated Revolutionary Organization (ORI), which formed the nucleus for the formation of the new Cuban Communist Party (PCC) in 1965.

VI

These were critical times in Cuba. The revolution was under attack from both within and without. By late 1960, political disaffection had found increasing expression in armed conflict. Anti-government elements armed themselves and launched new guerrilla operations. Urban sabotage again became commonplace. In the United States, the Central Intelligence Agency was organizing Cuban exiles for an invasion of the island, and when it arrived in April 1961 at the Bay of Pigs (Playa Girón), the only surprise was the ease and speed with which it was crushed. The survival of the revolution was all but guaranteed a year later, when the United States, as part of the negotiations to remove Soviet missiles from Cuba, agreed not to invade the island.

These developments had far-reaching consequences. Attacks against a government that enjoyed wide support among vast numbers of Cubans had the effect of facilitating further political centralization. Under siege at home, under attack from abroad, the government moved quickly to eliminate all opposition. The Bay of Pigs brought matters to a climax. The government moved against anyone suspected of opposition to the regime, including priests, foreigners, and ordinary men and women, in and out of government. By the end of April an estimated 100,000 persons were imprisoned or otherwise detained. Virtually no suspected opponent of the government remained free in Cuba after that time. Prisons filled with political enemies. Most were released after the Cuban victory at Girón, but by then all organized opposition had been effectively eliminated. Thereafter, planeload after planeload of Cubans left the island.

Within days of crushing the invasion, on the occasion of May Day 1961 Fidel Castro reiterated the socialist character of the revolution. The 1940 constitution was proclaimed "too old and outdated." "That constitution," Fidel announced, "has been left behind by this revolution, which, as we have said, is a socialist revolution." There would be no further discussion of elections. "The Revolution has no time to waste in such foolishness." Castro proclaimed that the revolution had "exchanged the conception of pseudo-democracy for direct government by the people." And again stressed: "This is a socialist regime." In November 1961, Fidel Castro proclaimed: "I am a Marxist-Leninist, and I shall be one until the last day of my life."

VII

The revolution established itself in a remarkably short space of time. Its socialist character was apparently neither intrinsic to its original ideological content nor essential to its initial political ascendancy. There was no plan. That Fidel Castro was not from the outset a communist, that leadership was based on charismatic authority and in part legitimized by a rising swell of nationalism, served to obscure the implications of Cuban radicalism. The sequence of events that brought the socialist revolution to Cuba was more improvised than calculated, more reaction than intention—up to a point. And after that point, Cubans moved deliberately, with design and dispatch. There was perhaps something inevitable about these turns of events. The North Americans responded predictably, but this time the Cubans did not. History had prepared Cubans for North American reactions. There was nothing to prepare the United States for the Cuban response. In this sense, the Cubans had the advantage. Once initial reforms encountered foreign resistance, the alternatives facing Cubans were reduced to a stark two: do nothing or do everything. What they could not do was anything in between. There was no social base of support for moderate reform that would be, as in times past, too radical for property owners and too conservative for workers and peasants.

Cuba had stood at this threshold several times before in its history, but never before had crossed it. The situation in 1959 was significantly different from that of 1898 or 1933. One difference was the spellbinding presence of Fidel Castro: indefatigable, passionate, pragmatic, calculating. This time the charismatic leader had survived the armed struggle and remained to defend his vision from corruption and compromise. Another difference was the role of the communist party. In 1933, it had adopted a posture of frank opposition to reform. Now the PSP collaborated. Another difference was the Soviet Union. There was no doubt more swagger than substance to Nikita Khrushchev's threat in July 1960 to defend the Cuban people with Soviet "rocket fire if the aggressive forces in the Pentagon dare to launch an intervention against Cuba." It nevertheless served to add one more consideration into U.S. policy calculations. There was, in fact, no telling if, or how, or where, the Soviets would react to an attack against Cuba, and this uncertainty introduced an element of caution with which U.S. policy in the Caribbean had never before had to contend.

At the same time, it would be excessively facile to attribute the internal success of the Cuban revolution to Soviet assistance. Certainly the regime derived strength through support from the socialist bloc. But it was no less true that the regime was able to obtain outside support because it was strong from within. It had dismantled the old army and replaced it with a new one. It had organized a vast popular militia. It had demonstrated its capacity for mass mobilization. On its own it had stood up to U.S. authority and seized North American property, and survived. Its internal opponents were in disarray. Thus, well before the Soviets committed themselves, the Cuban regime was internally secure. This was the incentive for Soviet involvement, not the outcome. National strength begot international strength.

The revolutionary government was driven to adopt socialist structures by the logic of its reform agenda, especially the requirements of the Agrarian Reform Law. The nationalization of sugar properties involved the state directly in the organization and management of a strategic sectory of the economy in varying degrees of decline, the revival of which, Cubans were convinced, required central planning and state-sponsored development. Cuban leadership employed socialist mechanisms early, not in reaction to hostility from the United States but as a response to national economic needs. These were strategies designed to implement reforms as fully and as quickly as possible and at the same time guarantee the political ascendancy of revolutionary elements. The Cuban embrace of Marxism-Leninism, however, no less than the decision to ally the island with the Soviet bloc, was a different kind of strategy, and must be seen as a function of North American policy. Faced with the threat of extinction from a vastly superior adversary, Cuban leaders took the steps necessary to guarantee their survival.

What was especially striking about the sequence of events between 1959 and 1961 was the comparative ease with which the essential character of the revolution was transformed. No national institutions, no internal structures, no person seemed capable of containing the radicalization of the revolution. Much of this, certainly, was the result of the central role played by Fidel Castro. But no less important were the specific historical conditions in which the revolution unfolded in mid-twentieth-century Cuba. National institutions were in varying degrees of disrepute. There was no outcry against the suppression of old political parties, for the old political parties had served few other than the professional politicians, who were, in any case, already discredited. There was little protest against the seizures of opposition newspapers. They had more than adequately prepared the way for their own destruction. Their credibility was suspect and their integrity doubted, for it was commonly known that they had long accepted subsidies from previous, corrupt regimes. Few Cubans mourned their passing. The old armed forces had been defeated and de-mobilized. A new army was formed out of the victorious guerrilla col-umns, commanded by loyal *fidelistas*. The army command underwent ideological transformation and thereby served as a defender of and not a deterrent to radical change. Nor was the church effective in restraining revolution. In fact, the Catholic church was a negligible factor in national life. A total of 725 priests, one for every 7,850 parishioners, exercised only limited influence on the island. Priests were mainly Spaniards, lo-cated largely in the cities, ministering mostly to white, middle-class con-gregations. The church had little national credibility, and when it warned against the perils of communism, its influence was limited to those sec-tors of the population already on the defensive. By the early 1960s, fur-ther, the sector of the population over which the church had the greatest influence was already in exile.

The skewed social order in Cuba rendered least effective the classes with the most to lose. There were few bourgeois institutions and less class affinity. This disarticulation had begun in the late nineteenth century with the collapse of the planter bourgeoisie and continued through the 1930s with the demise of the entrepreneurial bourgeoisie. Both were sub-sequently integrated directly into the structures of North American capi-talism. The eclipse of an independent Cuban national bourgeoisie all but precluded the emergence of an effective and autonomous defense of class interests. Bourgeois class institutions and class cooperation had failed to develop fully. Instead, sectors of the bourgeoisie had pursued their own narrow interests independently and often in conflict. Industrialists and manufacturers resented the prominence of the sugar industry. Small sugar producers were unhappy with large sugar producers. *Colonos* resented the control of mill owners. Small ranchers turned against big ranchers. Cu-bans employed by North American firms were suspicious of the economic nationalism of Cuban-owned enterprises. Rice growers resented sugar producers, and both distrusted cattle ranchers. Light industry was in con-flict with heavy industry. They all tended to function independently, un-interested in coordination and cooperation, and hence were eminently vulnerable. Sugar producers were indifferent to urban reform measures. Many manufacturers and industrialists initially approved the Agrarian Reform Law. In a surge of economic nationalism many Cuban property owners denounced foreign control of the economy. Local manufacturers welcomed restrictions on foreign imports, and in similar fashion national producers did not initially lament the expropriation of North American property.

When their demise became imminent, large sectors of the middle class discovered they lacked the effective political institutions, ideology, and experience with which to defend their interests. This, in turn, set the stage for one of the developments critical to the consolidation of the revolution. Unable to oppose the revolution, disaffected Cubans emigrated by the tens of thousands. The loss of population in the early years was stunning: 62,000 in 1960, 67,000 in 1961, 66,000 in 1962.

Middle-class flight between 1959 and 1962 was in part spontaneous, in part sponsored. For the Cuban government, emigration was a relatively cost-effective means through which to eliminate vast sectors of the opposition, and it therefore facilitated their departure. For the United States, the spectacle of tens of thousands of Cubans fleeing the island was the stuff of good propaganda, and it too encouraged their flight. That the emigration happened to include a disproportionate number of technicians and professionals provided the United States with an opportunity to cause Havana hardship of another kind by draining the island of trained personnel. Washington eased visa requirements, and subsequently dropped them altogether. Cubans were henceforth free to enter the United States in unlimited numbers.

Departing Cubans, for their part, were themselves acting out the final scene of a century-long drama. For almost three generations, Cubans of means, owners of property, holders of positions, had looked to the United States for protection against the forces of radical change that periodically challenged the status quo. Cuban elites had historically shown themselves ill-prepared to defend their interests on their own. This was not the first time that local elites were challenged by popular forces—it had happened in 1895–98 and again in 1931–33. On both occasions, they were saved by U.S. intervention. Few Cubans who departed between 1959 and 1962 could have remotely anticipated that their expatriation would become permanent. Many believed their absence would be a short one, a period during which the United States would step into the breach and return them and the island to the way it used to be. There was no need to be unduly exercise or overly alarmed, emigrating Cubans reassured themselves. The United States would not tolerate a communist government

ninety miles from its shores. "I waited for one more year," one Cuban
refugee explained, "thinking when the North American properties were
nationalized the U.S. Government would step in to prevent this action.
The moment came, and nothing happened." "The passivity of the former
possessing classes was startling," commented Philip W. Bonsal, the U.S.
ambassador to Cuba during these months. "The Revolution was vastly
encouraged by the demonstrated impotence of the old order. The dispossessed and their friends believed that the United States would soon set
things in order again." Bonsal made another point: "A conviction that
the U.S. would take care of the situation sapped the activism of much of
the opposition."

The exportation of counter-revolution foreclosed any possibility of a
sustained and extensive internal challenge to the revolution. The flight of
the opposition served also to strengthen the revolutionary consensus within
the island, thereby contributing in another fashion to the further consolidation of the government. Henceforth, organized opposition to the revolution developed outside of Cuba, largely in the United States. But even
in this instance, the possibilities of Cubans organizing independent and
autonomous opposition capabilities were severely limited by the circumstances of their expatriation. Almost entirely dependent on funding and
support from the Central Intelligence Agency, Cuban exiles became instruments of North American policy, without the means of organizing
into a genuine opposition force, unable to articular autonomous strategies, and incapable of developing objectives independent of U.S. policy
needs. Their ultimate demise was nothing less than a function of their
original ascendancy.

12

Socialist Cuba

I

The Cuban transition from capitalism to communism after 1961 was characterized by many noteworthy achievements and some notable disappointments, some immediately apparent, others emerging over time. Much of old Cuba was changed totally; some things stayed the same. Three decades of revolution in Cuba can be characterized as a combination of success and failure, change and continuity.

Nowhere perhaps did the balance stand as sharply in relief as in the evolution of Cuban developmental strategies. To overcome the conditions of underdevelopment, during the early 1960s emphasis fell on planning, universally understood in Cuba to require the reduction of the historic dependence on sugar exports. The aversion to sugar was palpable. It symbolized the source of old oppression, slavery in the colony, and subservience to foreigners in the republic, and always uncertainty and unpredictability. For sound economic reasons, Cubans argued, no less than psychological ones, it was necessary to reduce the importance of sugar. This was to be achieved through two means: industrialization and agricultural diversification. These strategies were expected to reduce Cuban susceptibility to the vagaries of the world sugar market, reduce the need for foreign imports through internal production, improve Cuban balance of trade, and create new employment opportunities. Agricultural diversification promised to reduce agricultural imports, increase national production, and promote new exports. The idea was quite simple. Too much emphasis had been given to sugar. Foreign exchange was being spent on goods that could be produced in Cuba, such as rice, cotton, and potatoes. For example, Cuban economists calculated that an estimated $25 million were spent annually on lard imports that could be produced on the island for much less. The objectives of import substitution and diversification required the organization of new industrial and manufacturing units which, in turn, depended on substantial investments in industry, capital goods,

338   CUBA

TABLE 37.   Cuban Agricultural Production (1960–65)
(millions of pounds)

Year	Coffee	Corn	Rice	Potatoes	Malanga	Boniato	Yuca
1960	42.0	212	323	97.4	157.0	230.5	255.0
1961	48.0	198	207	88.4	77.0	117.0	155.0
1962	39.0	159	231	92.4	61.0	181.0	152.0
1963	28.5	173	237	86.0	45.0	81.7	230
1964	36.0	200	123	75.0	43.2	89.3	180.0
1965	23.0	210	55	83.0	46.6	80.7	200.0

Source: Susan Schroeder, *Cuba: A Handbook of Historical Statistics* (Boston, 1982), 253, 268–69.

and technology. Consumption was curtailed to divert investments into industrialization and rapid economic growth.

Efforts to reduce dependency on sugar did not signify a total abandonment of sugar production, but rather an attempt to pursue lower production at stable and predictable levels of output. At the same time, greater emphasis was given to non-sugar exports to reduce the percentage of total sugar exports. Cuban planners also hoped to achieve self-sufficiency in food production. Industrial objectives included the development of new import substitution industries, specifically, metallurgy, chemicals, heavy machinery, and transportation equipment. Hopes ran high that the discovery of large new reserves of petroleum would assist in balance of payments and boost industrial expansion. The investment component of this strategy, Cuba expected, was to originate from credits from socialist countries.

Within four years, Cuban efforts at industrialization and diversification were abandoned. The failures were evident everywhere. Agricultural production declined, and in some sectors the decline was disastrous (see Table 37). Nowhere was the decline of agriculture more conspicuous or more catastrophic than in the output of sugar. Production dropped from 6.7 million tons in 1961 to 4.8 million tons in 1962 and 3.8 million tons in 1963. Not in twenty years had Cuban sugar production been so low. The effects reverberated across all sectors of the economy. Foreign earnings declined and in some sectors disappeared altogether. Domestic shortages increased. Food supplies dwindled, and basic consumer goods of all kinds grew scarce. By early 1962, shortages spread and became more severe. In March, the government responded to increasing scarcity and imposed a general food rationing that soon came to include consumer goods of all types. Cuban dependence on foreign imports actually increased, as did Cuban reliance on sugar exports. As a proportion of total exports, sugar increased from 78 to 86 percent. The balance of trade deficits increased from $14 million in 1961 to $238 million in 1962, to $323 million in 1963, almost all of which was incurred with socialist bloc nations, $297 million with the Soviet Union alone.

During the mid-1960s conventional economic wisdom proclaimed anew the efficacy of sugar production. Cubans had come to the sober realization that the strategies of the early 1960s had failed to meet even their most modest objectives. On the contrary, efforts at import substitution and industrialization had resulted in widespread social distress and economic dislocation. New strategies after 1965 involved increased emphasis on all sectors of agricultural production, particularly sugar but also dairy products, beef, citrus fruits, tropical agricultural products, coffee, and tobacco, as a means of generating foreign exchange and a way to increase imports of machinery and equipment, which in turn would increase the production of agriculture and agricultural commodities. Industrial planning shifted to the development of those sectors that utilized Cuban natural resources most efficiently, with special attention to those industries that supported agricultural production. The renewed emphasis on sugar offered an obvious and relatively cost-effective method of reversing the mounting balance of trade deficits by mobilizing efforts around a sector in which Cuba possessed adequate personnel and sufficient experience. The rise of the world price of sugar in 1963, moreover, served to confirm the wisdom and timeliness of once again promoting the expansion of sugar production.

After the mid-1960s, sugar production received preference and priority. Indeed, Cubans became transfixed on sugar production. Output was expected to increase steadily, climaxing dramatically in 1970 with a predicted ten-million-ton crop. This was not simply an objective—it became an obsession. Acreage planted in cane expanded. The duration of the harvest was lengthened. The pursuit of the ten-million-ton crop assumed the dimensions of a national campaign in which all Cubans were exhorted to participate. The very prestige of the revolution was placed at stake in this endeavor. "The question of a sugar harvest of ten million tons," Fidel Castro exhorted in March 1968, "has become something more than an economic goal; it is something that has been converted into a point of honor for this Revolution, it has become a yardstick by which to judge the capability of the Revolution . . . and, if a yardstick is put up to the Revolution, there is no doubt about the Revolution meeting the mark.'' Virtually all national resources and collective resolve were diverted to the making of the ten-million-ton crop. ''What are you doing towards the ten million?'' billboards everywhere in Cuba asked sternly.

The campaign implied more than a commitment to forming a new economy. It involved also dedication to forging a new consciousness. Mobilization strategies after 1965 were based on appeals to selflessness and sacrifice. Cubans were exhorted to subscribe to a new code, nothing less than a new morality. Emphasis was given to *conciencia,* the creation of a new consciousness that would lead to a new revolutionary ethic. The goal was the making of a new man *(hombre nuevo),* motivated not by expectation of personal gain but by the prospects of collective advancement. The *hombre nuevo* was disciplined, highly motivated, and hardworking. Work was an end unto itself, the means by which to purge persisting bourgeois vices and complete the transformation into the *hombre nuevo.*

Cubans announced their intention to construct socialism and communism at one and the same time, and more: the use of moral incentives to construct socialism and communism simultaneously was a way to use consciousness to create wealth. The appeal to consciousness, with emphasis on sacrifice and solidarity, would suffice to raise levels of production. The revolutionary leadership repudiated prolonged use of material incentives in the form of wage differentials, administrative bonuses, and salary scales as the means through which to attain abundance. The use of material incentives and individual self-interest to construct communism, the Cubans insisted, served to delay if not discourage altogether the formation of communist virtues. They argued that communism required the creation of a new consciousness as a function of economic development. The development of the *hombre nuevo* and the attainment of economic growth were proclaimed to be one and the same process.

Central to this approach was a greater emphasis on moral incentives. Workers were exhorted to greater efforts as part of the new morality: it was the right thing to do. That there were comparatively few material goods available to distribute no doubt also influenced the decision to emphasize moral rewards. Material incentives were proclaimed incompatible with the goals of the revolution. Workers were no longer paid for quality of production or for meeting—or surpassing—production quotas. Overtime pay was eliminated. Production achievements were acknowledged in a non-monetary way with badges, medallions, scrolls, and awards, frequently distributed by Castro himself. Exemplary workers were recognized and celebrated at rallies, parades, and mass meetings, and awarded titles such as "National Work Hero," "Vanguard Worker," and "Heroes of the 1970 Sugar Crop." Through the system of socialist emulation, workers or groups of workers competed for such prizes as flags and banners. Emphasis fell on voluntarism, the subjective over the objective—will, discipline, and dedication would prevail. It was guerrilla war all over again, a time for individual sacrifice and collective abnegation. Production metaphors borrowed freely from guerrilla vernacular. The harvest was conceived in military terms, of "combat" and "campaign." Cane cutters were organized into "brigades." In 1968, the government launched the "revolutionary offensive" in which the remaining 57,000 private enterprises—principally small retail shops, handicrafts, service and repair centers, bars, and cafés—were nationalized. In one stroke, Cuba was transformed into one of the most socialized societies in the world.

Efforts were also made to expand the distribution of free goods and services. No fees were charged for health services, day-care facilities, education, funeral services, utilities, sports events, local bus transportation, and local telephone service. Rents were fixed at a maximum of 10 percent of income. In many units, rent was not collected at all. By 1969, an estimated 268,000 households paid no rent, and the government contemplated the eventual abolition of all rent. Cuban officials spoke freely and frequently of the abolition of money altogether.

The 1970 harvest produced a record crop, but not ten million tons. An 8.5-million-ton harvest was a spectacular accomplishment, but it fell short of the much exalted goal. A historic achievement was transformed into a failure, and a powerful blow against the national esprit. The casualty list included more than revolutionary morale, however. In fact, the entire economy had suffered, and in 1970 Cuba faced serious trouble. The ten-million-ton effort had been made at the expense of all other sectors of the economy, and even the 8.5-million-ton harvest could not adequately compensate for the damage inflicted everywhere else in the economy. Industrial planning had been oriented entirely toward complementing harvest goals. Priority was given to plants and equipment in the sugar industry and the transportation system serving sugar production. Industries producing agricultural supplies such as farm machinery, equipment, and fertilizers received special attention. Investments were diverted to transportation equipment, most notably tractors, wagons, and rolling stock.

Attention was given to road maintenance and repairs along the principal sugar transportation routes. Port installations and harbor facilities designated to handle increased production were expanded, to the detriment of others. Mills were overhauled and emphasis given to the manufacture of mill equipment. Labor needs of the harvest were met by massive mobilization of the population. An estimated 1.2 million workers from all sectors of the economy, as well as 100,000 members of the armed forces and 300,000 sugar workers, had participated in the harvest.

The effects of an effort of this magnitude on other sectors of the economy were immediate, and almost everywhere disastrous. Production of consumer goods declined. Basic foodstuffs of every type—milk, vegetables, fruits, meat, poultry—were in short supply across the island. The goods that were produced often encountered shipping difficulties, for much of the rail and road transportation was diverted to sugar. Once more Cuba had experimented with a new developmental strategy, and found it wanting.

II

The Cuban economy performed erratically through the 1960s and early 1970s. Small gains were offset by large reversals. Many of the problems were caused by overzealous and overconfident planners, dedicated revolutionaries who devised impractical if not impossible goals. In large measure, the setbacks of the 1960s, and especially the disarray resulting from the ill-starred ten-million-ton crop, underscored the effects of excessive centralization of planning. The leadership had devised programs and developed policies without clear understanding of local conditions, which in turn led to the setting of unrealistic goals and inefficient utilization of resources. At the local level, too, ineptitude and ignorance led to negligence, and sometimes squandering of resources. Directives were poorly conceived and badly implemented. The expansion of state control over newly nationalized property was characterized by chaos and frightful wastefulness. Some were errors of enthusiasm, some were errors of incompetence. Occasionally local administrators slaughtered valuable breeding stock for food even as scarce foreign exchange was being used to import additional animals. When the Pingree ranch in Oriente was converted into a cooperative, a $20,000 breeding bull was killed by local army officials for a barbeque. A farming cooperative produced a bumper tomato crop for export, only to discover that the materials necessary for packaging were not available.

The havoc caused by inexperienced planners and inept administrators became more serious as centralization increased. Unions declined and party cadres were drawn away from political tasks into administrative chores. Bureaucratic isolation increased as administrators lost contact with their constituency. These were heady times in Cuba, when fervor was an acceptable substitute for fitness, when political commitment was valued more than professional capability. Inexperience was compounded by incompetence, and the results were predictable. That many new administrators of state enterprises were selected more for their allegiance than for their ability was perhaps inevitable, maybe even necessary, particularly during the early years as the government sought to contain counterrevolutionary activity. But the toll was high.

These problems, in turn, served to underscore the conditions of adversity under which the Cuban economy reorganized during the 1960s. Certainly the flight of hundreds of thousands of opponents of the regime was of inestimable political advantage, but it came at an incalculable economic cost. The departure of professionals, technicians, administrators, and managers in vast numbers created a desperate shortage of skilled personnel for which there was neither easy nor immediate remedy. An estimated 81 percent of the economically active population reaching Florida through 1962 were professional, managerial, clerical, and skilled workers. In the United States these occupational sectors were represented well out of proportion to their distribution in the Cuban population at large (Table 38). Of the 300 agronomists working in Cuba in 1959, 270 departed. Approximately half of all teachers emigrated. Of an estimated total 85,000 professionals and technicians in Cuba, approximately 20,000 emigrated. More than 3,000 physicians out of a total 6,000 and 700 dentists out of almost 2,000 departed. The senior medical faculty at the University of Havana was reduced from 200 to 17. Only one trained engineer stayed at the vast Ariguanabo textile factory. One mechanic was all that remained of a large staff trained to run a newly constructed automated glass factory. The adverse effects of emigration were not confined to the departure of Cubans. No less important was the flight of almost all of the 6,500 North American residents, many of whom had worked in important technical and managerial capacities in both U.S. and Cuban enterprises. Foreigners directed the oil refineries, operated the Nicaro nickel plant and the Matahambre copper mine, supervised the sugar mills, serviced the

TABLE 38.   Percentage Distribution of Occupations of Cuban Émigrés

Occupation Sector	Cuban Emigration (1959–62)	General Population (1953 Census)
Professional, semi-professional, and managerial	37.0	9.5
Clerical and sales	31.0	14.0
Skilled, Semi-skilled and un-skilled	20.0	27.0
Services and armed forces	9.0	8.0
Agriculture, mining, and fishing	3.0	41.5

Source: Adapted from Richard R. Fagen et al., *Cubans in Exile: Disaffection and the Revolution* (Stanford, 1968), 19, 115, and Benigno E. Aguirre, "Differential Migration of Cuban Social Races," *Latin American Research Review* XI (1976), 105.

airline industry, and otherwise occupied an assortment of strategic positions in manufacturing, industry, agriculture, transportation, and communications.

The nationalization of 57,000 small businesses in 1968 also had adverse and unforeseen circumstances. Large numbers of businesses were consolidated into larger operations, or eliminated altogether. Almost half of the operations nationalized in Pinar del Río (934 out of 1,834) were suppressed. The efficiency of the 9,600 small manufacturers and 14,100 service enterprises that remained deteriorated markedly. State enterprises simply could not adequately replace the goods and services eliminated. The suppression of 3,700 street vendors in urban centers, for example, effectively destroyed informal food distribution networks across the island. Already overburdened state stores were unable to make up the difference. Food queues at stores and restaurants lengthened, and absenteeism increased as workers took time off to wait on line. Absenteeism increased also as the incentive to work waned. A scarcity of consumer goods and services and the abolition of wage differentials caused widespread demoralization.

In some cases, the consequences were even more serious. After 1968, another 50,000 businessmen joined the ranks of the disaffected; a new wave of discontent rippled across the island, leading to new emigration and a new loss of managerial personnel. Bottlenecks in distribution followed, exacerbating old shortages and scarcities. Crimes against property increased. Almost a hundred acts of sabotage against industries, warehouses, and government buildings were reported, most of which were not committed by counter-revolutionaries from abroad but by disgruntled citizens at home.

But it was not only a shortage of trained personnel and skilled labor that contributed to Cuban problems. Appeals to self-sacrifice and moral incentives failed to sustain high productivity levels consistently. Certainly the summons to heroic production efforts through the use of moral persuasion and socialist emulation increased output in key sectors of the economy, and indeed prevented setbacks from assuming even larger proportions. As a method for mobilizing the entire labor force over long periods of time, however, the emphasis on moral incentives proved unsatisfactory. Morale declined, and the problem of motivation assumed serious proportions. Absenteeism increased and reached alarming levels. In some industrial sectors it approached 15 percent. Tardiness increased too. Workers who dropped out of the labor force found little difficulty in obtaining all rationed goods allocated to them through the income of a spouse or relative. Across the island productivity declined in the factories as well as in the fields. Low productivity was exacerbated by poor performance. In many sectors quality was sacrificed to assure savings and meet production quotas. Poor quality was also due to the absence of adequate raw materials and poor manufacturing.

The weather, too, contributed to the disruption of the economy. In 1961 a record low rainfall created one of the most severe droughts in Cuban history. All sectors of agriculture were affected. Two years later, hurricane Flora struck Cuba with devastating results. More than four thousand lost their lives. The total damage, concentrated in Camagüey and Oriente, was estimated at $500 million. A year later, another hurricane destroyed the tobacco crop. In 1966 hurricane Inez destroyed a large portion of the eastern sugar crop.

The disengagement of the Cuban economy from North American capitalism was itself a source of no small amount of disruption and dislocation. It was a disengagement, moreover, to which the United States refused to acquiesce. Yet Cubans were determined to achieve it at whatever costs, and the costs were considerable. After 1961, one of the key elements of U.S. policy against Cuba was to isolate Cuba economically as a way to disrupt the Cuban economy, increase domestic distress, and encourage internal discontent—all designed to weaken the regime from within. Cuba was especially vulnerable to this policy. For the better part of the previous sixty years, virtually all the machinery, equipment, and supplies used in Cuban industry, agriculture, mining, transportation, communications, and utilities—more than 70 percent of total Cuban imports—had come from the United States. Cuban dependence on North American spare parts was almost total, a corollary of dependence on North American capital-stock and the proximity of North American suppliers. The economy had long operated on the basis of quick supply and low inventory. Orders were placed by telephone, thereby obviating the necessity of developing large inventories of spare parts and replacement stock. Inventories of most spare parts were traditionally low. Shipments were frequently small. Replacement goods were purchased as needed, often directly out of catalogues, over the telephone, and delivered within days.

The U.S. trade embargo after 1961 had jolting effects. By the early 1960s, conditions in many industries had become critical due to the lack of replacement parts. Virtually all industrial structures were dependent on supplies and parts now denied to Cuba. Many plants were paralyzed. Havoc followed. Transportation was especially hard hit: the ministry was reporting more than seven thousand breakdowns a month. Nearly one-quarter of all buses were inoperable by the end of 1961. One-half of the 1,400 passenger rail cars were out of service in 1962. Almost three-quarters of the caterpillar tractors stood idle due to a lack of replacement parts.

Across the island, improvisation became the hallmark of early Cuban developmental efforts—sometimes with remarkable successes, other times with disastrous setbacks. Many small and inefficient plants were closed and their operations transferred to larger and more efficient factories, thereby pooling desperately needed equipment. By 1965, nine sugar mills had been dismantled to provide an inventory of spare parts for other mills. The 106 pharmaceutical factories were reduced to 18. Textile plants declined from 153 to 63, and less than half of the paper factories were functioning.

Cuban dependence on raw materials imports from the U.S. also created vulnerability. Without access to vital supplies, Cuban production slowed, and in some instances stopped altogether. Denied rubber and petrochemicals, the manufacture of automobile tires halted; without ready access to pancreatic enzymes and tannin, Cuban tanneries suffered; paint factories depended on imports of oils, pigments, and solvents; pharmaceuticals on imported serums and antibiotics; the manufacture of soaps and detergents on imported caustic soda and tallow. A newly constructed $4 million factory for the production of synthetic fiber could not operate for lack of cellulose acetate.

The reorientation of Cuban trade with eastern Europe created problems of a different sort. The distance of Cuba's new trading partners required new investment in infrastructure facilities, including the expansion of port facilities to accommodate long-haul trade and the construction of new warehouses and storage facilities. The Cuban port system, including the design of the docks, the depth of water at dockside, and the nature of the unloading equipment and facilities, had been originally designed to accommodate short-haul trade from the United States by ferries and sea trains, not oceangoing freighters. Storage facilities were also designed for short-haul traffic. There was little warehouse space either at the ports or in the interior. The arrival of large freighters carrying huge shipments of supplies created monumental unloading and storage problems. A 5,000-ton shipment of soybean oil from China in 1961 created a small crisis. Never before had Cuba received shipments of fats and oil on this scale. Similarly, a Japanese freighter with a cargo of fresh fish found Cuba without adequate refrigeration facilities. A shipment of onions from Egypt could not be properly stored for lack of appropriate temperature-control warehouse facilities. Ports were congested, distribution was slow, and, inevitably, losses were considerable. The substitution of socialist bloc replacement parts was further complicated because old machinery had to be adapted to metric system parts and new equipment had to be converted to U.S. electrical currents. Language and cultural obstacles further hindered the preparation of import orders. During Cuba's conversion to new spare parts, new machinery, and new production techniques, large sectors of Cuban industry remained underutilized or idle altogether.

These were years, too, during which Cuba suffered the greatest effects from U.S. covert operations. Through the 1960s, the Central Intelligence Agency conducted punitive economic sabotage operations against Cuba, the principal aim of which was to foster popular disaffection with government policies. Paramilitary missions were organized to destroy sugar mills, sugar and tobacco plantations, farm machinery, mines, oil refineries, lumber yards, water systems, warehouses, and chemical plants. Communication facilities were attacked; railroad bridges were destroyed and trains derailed. The United States was also successful in disrupting

Cuban trade initiatives with western Europe, by blocking credit to Cuba, thwarting the sale of sugar products, and contaminating Cuban agricultural exports. European manufacturers were discouraged from trading with Cuba. Cargoes were sabotaged: corrosive chemicals were added to lubricating fluids, ball bearings were manufactured deliberately off-center, and defective wheel gears were manufactured. More sophisticated operations included the seeding of rain clouds before they arrived over Cuba as a means to induce drought. These activities were apparently intensified between 1969 and 1970 as a way to foil the ten-million-ton crop. The C.I.A. was also charged with having been instrumental in the outbreak of African swine fever in Cuba in 1970–71, requiring the slaughter of 500,000 pigs.

Security and defense requirements, moreover, peaking in April 1961 during the Bay of Pigs and October 1962 at the time of the missile crisis, also disrupted planning and development. Military expenditures continued to receive high priority. At the same time, vital equipment of all kinds—construction, transportation, maintenance—was diverted to defense. The expansion of the army and militia meant that tens of thousands of people were intermittently removed from productive activity. By 1962, the shortage of field labor assumed serious proportions.

III

The economic reversals of the 1960s had a sobering impact on the Cuban leadership. The prevalence of absenteeism, low worker morale, low productivity, and poor product quality all suggested that something had gone very much awry. Developmental strategies were again re-evaluated and revised, and a new course charted for the 1970s and 1980s. Cubans moved to deal with two problems at once, both believed to be at the source of the unsatisfactory performance of the economy: over-centralization and ineffective incentives. The remedy for the former required the development of new mechanisms for widening participation in decision-making. The solution to the latter necessitated partial restoration of material incentives.

The new strategies reflected not only a rejection of old policies but also a recognition of new conditions. Cuba had weathered the tumult and hardship of the 1960s with a great deal of goodwill for revolution still intact. Part of this was due to Fidel Castro—indefatigable and unwavering, the leader as teacher and conscience, constantly exhorting, enjoining, importuning. He was aided in this role by the actions of the United States. Rather than promoting internal discontent and dissent, U.S. policy served to forge a unanimity and resolve among the Cuban people almost impossible to create any other way. Cubans responded to seige with solidarity. Certainly opposition developed, and by the late 1960s an estimated 20,000 political opponents of the government languished in prison. In 1965, the government established the Military Units to Aid Production (UMAP), designed principally to draft dissidents and "social deviants" into the army for "rehabilitation." The UMAP was disbanded in 1967, but during its two-year existence was known to have routinely used torture and corporal punishment on draftees. During this period discontent continued to find expression through emigration. Between 1966 and 1971, another 200,000 Cubans left the island. By the end of the decade, more than half a million Cubans had resettled in the United States, Latin America, and Europe. By the 1970s, hence, the stability and security of the revolution had been established. While the U.S. trade embargo continued in full force, its impact was having increasingly diminishing effects. The Cuban disengagement from the North American economic system was almost complete. United States covert operations had dwindled. The political foundations of the revolution were sufficiently secure to permit the development of new forms of political participation; the economy was in such disarray as to require the development of new ways of economic planning.

Throughout the early 1970s, Fidel Castro made repeated speeches critizing excessive centralization of administration, the bureaucratization of decision-making, the usurpation of administrative functions by the communist party (PCC), the expansion of state authority at the expense of the mass organizations, the inflated authority of the manager system of state enterprises at the expense of worker participation, and the apparent lethargy into which mass organizations had fallen. These criticisms announced far-reaching changes. Ministries were reorganized, a process already underway, in fact, with the reorganization of the Ministry of Industries into new ministries for sugar, food production, basic industry, light industry, and mining. The reorganization drive continued through the early 1970s with the restructuring of the Ministry of Construction into four separate agencies according to the nature of construction (construction materials, social and agricultural construction, agriculture livestock, and industrial construction). A new ministry of Merchant Marine and Ports

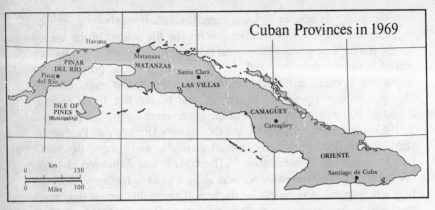

Cuban Provinces in 1969

was established. The finance ministry was reorganized and a new
ministerial-rank committee on prices and supplies established. To facilitate coordination among the new agencies, an Executive Committee of
the Council of Ministers was created in 1972. The ten-member committee
consisted of the prime minister as chairman and nine deputy prime ministers responsible for the coordination of several ministries and state agencies
organized by sector, including basic industry and energy, consumer goods
and domestic trade, sugar, non-sugar agriculture, construction, transportation and communication, labor, education and culture, foreign relations,
and foreign trade.

In 1976 the reform and reorganization culminated in the promulgation
of a new constitution. The provisions of the Constitution of 1976 established a presidential system of government. Power was concentrated in
the executive, who presided over the Council of State and the Council of
Ministers. The constitution provided for the creation of a National Assembly and the election of provincial and local government officials across
the island. The National Assembly assumed the legislative authority previously exercised by the Council of Ministers. The new constitution also
reorganized the politico-administrative units of the island. Local government was consolidated into 169 municipalities. The former six provinces
were reorganized into fourteen. Pinar de Río and Matanzas remained substantially intact. Havana was divided into the city and the rest of the
province. Las Villas was organized into three provinces (Cienfuegos, Villa
Clara, and Sancti Spíritus). Camagüey was divided into Ciego de Avila

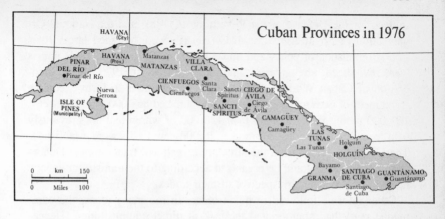

and Camagüey. Oriente was organized into five provinces (Las Tunas, Holguín, Granma, Guantánamo, and Santiago de Cuba).

As part of the continuing democratization process, and institutionalized in the Constitution of 1976, Cuba inaugurated a new system of political organization. *Poder popular* (people's power) established the mechanism for the popular election of municipal assemblies, which in turn elected the provincial assemblies and chose the deputies that made up the National Assembly. For the 1981–86 five-year term, the National Assembly consisted of 499 deputies, approximately one representative for every 20,000 inhabitants. *Poder popular* expanded during the 1970s as part of the new emphasis on mass participation. This represented an attempt to decentralize decision-making and advance the process of institutionalization, which in turn was related to economic functions and political organization. Municipal assemblies of *poder popular* assumed responsibility over local enterprises, including retail operations, consumer services, and factories producing for local consumption. Municipal assemblies also exercised authority over all schools, health services, cinema and sports facilities, and transportation enterprises within the municipal boundaries. The assemblies were charged with the responsibility for the selection of three lay judges and two professional judges who presided over the municipal people's court.

The democratization process also resulted in the revival of mass organizations and the expansion of their role in decision-making at all levels and in all spheres. The Federation of Cuban Women (FMC), the Committees for the Defense of the Revolution (CDRs), and the National Organization of Small Agriculturalists (ANAP) were assigned larger roles in the formulation of policy and implementation of programs. Trade unions were revitalized, strengthened, and democratized. In 1970, the Confederation of Cuban Workers (CTC) organized elections to form executive committees of each trade union local. An estimated 867,000 workers elected 164,000 union officials, more than 130,000 of whom had not previously held leadership positions. More than 26,000 new locals were established. The CTC also reorganized the structure of national trade unions. Henceforth, all workers would be organized according to the ministry or agency of their employment, irrespective of their trades.

Other reforms followed in quick order. In too many areas, the communist party had appropriated the task of direct administration. Henceforth, the role of the PCC was restricted to the coordination and supervision of administrative functions. The party set policy, but was enjoined to refrain from interfering in the daily aspects of administration. The one-person management system of state enterprises was replaced by management councils, consisting typically of a senior administrator, management assistants, and elected representatives from the local party organization, trade union, and Communist Youth Organization. Factory workshops elected delegates who met on a quarterly basis with the management council to discuss production decisions, policy, and labor issues.

The drive to democratize decision-making and increase mass participation, finally, was accompanied by the convocation of national meetings of mass organizations; the ANAP and the CDRs met in 1971, the CTC in 1973, and the FMC in 1974. In 1975 the First Party Congress was convoked.

IV

During the early 1970s, further, material incentives were reintroduced into the economy. Wages were linked more to productivity and prices more to scarcity. The reintroduction of material incentives was supported by the thirteenth labor congress in 1973, which ratified several resolutions calling variously for the revision of wage scales per quality and quantity of production, a maximum forty-four-hour work week, except in vital industries, and overtime pay.

The government moved quickly to organize a new system of incentives. Labor norms, the system whereby work quotas fixed output levels for a specific time period (hour, day, week, and month), were reinstated during the early 1970s as a way to measure and regulate labor productivity. Production norms were established by labor commissions made up of managerial personnel, party members, technicians, and skilled workers. Wages henceforth were linked with established labor norms. Workers fulfilling the assigned quota received the full fixed wage. Failure to meet norms resulted in a commensurate percentage of wage reduction. Conversely, a worker surpassing the assigned quota was rewarded with an appropriate percentage increase. Overtime bonuses were reintroduced. Consumer goods became available in increasing quantities and were distributed directly through the workplace. Exemplary workers received preferential access to durables such as automobiles, televisions, washing machines, and refrigerators. In 1973, 100,000 television sets were distributed to vanguard workers through labor assemblies on the recommendation of party and union officials. Overtime bonuses were offered to workers who exceeded the normal work week. Preferential access to the rationing system was used as an incentive to increase individual productivity. In 1974, Fidel Castro announced the allocation of $132 million for wage increases for managerial and technical workers.

In an effort to increase productivity, the government moved against absenteeism. An anti-loafing act enacted in 1971, subsequently incorporated into the 1976 constitution, required all males between the ages of seventeen and sixty to perform productive labor. As a result of the law, more than 100,000 persons joined the labor force, more than half of whom had never before worked.

Adjustments were also made in the distribution of free goods and services, as the government announced a new "policy of prices." Fees were restored for the use of telephone service, local bus transportation, and sporting events. Day-care centers instituted enrollment fees based on family income. Plans for the total elimination of rents were abandoned. No further talk was heard about abolishing money.

The move away from non-market distribution was not total, however. Health care remained free. So did education. Employment and old-age pensions were preserved. Housing rents were maintained at 10 percent of income or less. Many food items were still rationed.

The new Cuban purchasing power, together with an emphasis on material incentives, stimulated the supply of consumer goods. A rise in wages held little appeal without a commensurate increase in consumer items.

Many rationed items became available on the free market at costs higher than their rationed prices. A larger variety of manufactured goods were removed from the ration list, some at inflated prices, and included cameras, phonographs, appliances, bicycles, jewelry, cosmetics, and perfumes. Other products were periodically offered on a non-rationed basis for brief intervals, including furniture, clothing, and kitchenware.

Plans to increase labor productivity were accompanied by policies to improve capital efficiency. Planning techniques improved; so did data collection. A system analogous to cost accounting was adopted. Skilled managers and technicians replaced old revolutionary administrators. Administrative and technical work were systematized. At the end of 1970, a new Center for National Computation and Applied Mathematics (CEMACC) was in operation. Through the 1970s and 1980s, Cuban investment in computer technology increased steadily. New attention was given to the training of technicians, economists, systems analysts, and business administrators.

The sweeping reorganization efforts of the decade had salutary effects on the Cuban economy, which responded by sustained growth during the 1970s. Productivity expanded, exports increased. The decline in sugar production in the years after the 1970 high of 8.5 million tons was partially offset by favorable world prices. In 1974, Cuba registered its first balance of trade surplus since the triumph of the revolution in 1959. Productivity increased in virtually every sector. Output in non-sugar agriculture increased and the livestock sector expanded. Between 1971 and 1980, the economy grew at an estimated annual rate of 5.7 percent. Industrial activity enjoyed vigorous growth through the 1970s: manufacturing expanded at a rate of 7 percent annually, the capital goods industry at 16 percent, and the construction industry at 14 percent.

Through the 1970s and 1980s, Cuba continued to pursue a program of export diversification and import substitution as a means through which to reduce dependency on sugar, and had some success. The share of sugar in the total value of Cuban exports declined from 90 percent in 1975 to 65 percent in 1985. By 1983, the value of non-sugar exports increased by 60 percent. During the Five-Year Plan for 1980–85, Cuba experienced an annual growth rate of 5 percent. Renewed effort was also given to production and trade in convertible currency. Resources were diverted to heavy industry to diminish foreign dependency. Priority was also given to investments in those sectors which reduced imports from capitalist countries or increased exports to capitalist countries. Attention continued to center on traditional exports—sugar, tobacco, rum, nickel, citrus, sea products—and tourism, but also extended to the development of new exports such as textiles, clothing, shoes, cement, steel products, and construction materials.

V

No small part of Cuban achievements between the 1960s and 1980s, many of which were formidable and accomplished under difficult circumstances, was due to sustained support and subsidies from the Soviet Union and other socialist countries. Soviet participation in the Cuban economy took two principal forms after the early 1960s: trade and aid. From the early 1960s, when the Soviets first agreed to purchase the unsold portion of the former U.S. sugar quota, through the 1970s, especially in the aftermath of the debacle of the ten-million-ton crop, the Soviet Union played an increasingly greater role in the Cuban economy. Trade between Cuba and the socialist bloc expanded dramatically after 1959. Between 1959 and 1961, Cuban exports to socialist countries increased from 2.2 percent to 74 percent, while imports expanded from 0.3 percent to 70 percent. The Soviet Union alone accounted for almost half of these exports and 40 percent of the imports. Between 1959 and 1970, exports to the Soviet Union increased from 12.9 million pesos to 529 million, and imports went from zero to 686 million pesos. These were the critical years of the revolution, and it is probable that the revolution would have been thwarted had not the socialist bloc purchased Cuban sugar and provided vital imports.

The trade pattern established in the early 1960s remained comparatively stable through the mid-1970s. The Soviet share averaged about 40 percent of exports and 50 percent of imports. By the mid-1980s, Cuban export dependence on the Soviet Union had increased to 64 percent, while import dependence reached 62 percent. The Soviet share of Cuban trade, even at its highest levels, never matched the United State's share before the revolution, which during the 1950s averaged 75 percent of imports and 69 percent of imports.

Trade deficits mounted erratically and almost immediately upon the reorientation of Cuban commerce after 1961: from 237 million pesos in 1962 to 322 million in 1963, down to 294 million pesos in 1967 and up to 451 million one year later, down to 314 million in 1973. Trade with socialist countries other than the Soviet Union after 1970 produced a surplus. It was with the Soviets that Cuba incurred the larger portion of its trade deficits. During the 1970s and early 1980s, the Soviet share of the deficit accounted for approximately 85 percent of the total.

These conditions underscored still another vital role the Soviet Union played in the Cuban economy. Soviet willingness to finance Cuban trade deficits, which by the mid-1980s approached $30 billion, served effectively as grants in aid and underwrote Cuban economic development. Repeatedly the Soviets postponed debt payment schedules, extended new lines of credit, and increased the price paid for Cuban exports. These gestures were not, to be sure, entirely unconditional. In the aftermath of the ten-million-ton crop, desperately needed assistance arrived only after Cubans agreed to reorganize planning policies and production procedures according to Soviet recommendations. In 1972, Cuba and the Soviet Union signed a series of agreements under which Cuban repayment of previous credits was postponed until 1985. Interest-free credit was extended through 1975, scheduled for repayment in 1986. Under the terms of a new trade agreement negotiated in 1986, Cuba received Soviet credits of $3 billion for the period 1986–90.

The Soviet Union supported Cuban economic development in other ways. Cuban sugar was purchased at prices higher than prevailing world levels. The Soviets provided technical assistance and material support for the construction of a variety of industrial enterprises. As many as seven thousand Soviet advisors worked in Cuba during the 1970s and 1980s, participating in construction, oil exploration, mining, telecommunications, and transportation. Soviet assistance was instrumental in building and modernizing an estimated 160 industrial enterprises, including the modernization of over a hundred sugar mills and the construction of an electrical plant and two fertilizer factories. In addition, tens of thousands of Cubans availed themselves of educational opportunities in the Soviet Union in such fields as engineering, computer science, agriculture, construction, and food processing.

VI

The combination of sustained economic growth and political stability, backed by Soviet economic support and credit subsidies, allowed Cuba to fulfill many of the most ambitious programs of the revolution. In the pursuit of egalitarianism, the government implemented a series of redistributive economic policies with determination and effect. Objectives were set early, initially as a means of gaining political support and later as the social basis of government. Land was redistributed, rents were reduced. The rationing of food and vital goods, indicative certainly of scarcity and setbacks, nevertheless guaranteed a just distribution of limited resources. Available goods were shared more equitablly; the absence of goods was borne more equally. Private beaches, clubs, and schools were eliminated, and resorts and luxury hotels were opened to all Cubans. The social security law of 1963 extended illness benefits to all workers, including cash payments to the ill and retirement to the totally incapacitated. Wages increased, especially agricultural wages. Income of sugar workers rose from 272 million pesos in 1958 to 481 million in 1968.

With the restoration of material incentives after 1970, the momentum toward egalitarianism faltered. During the early 1960s, Cubans had made considerable progress in narrowing income differentials. Wages ranged from 64 pesos per month paid to agricultural workers to 844 pesos paid to senior government officials. Efforts to achieve wage equalization, one of the priorities during the 1960s, and in part achieved through the elimination of bonuses and overtime pay, ended in 1970 without substantial modification of the prevailing income distribution. The monthly minimum wage increased to 85 pesos, but the upper end also expanded, to 900 pesos. The gap in earnings was greater in the 1970s than in the late 1960s, but was still lower than in the mid-1960s and considerably less than during the 1950s.

A striking overall redistribution of income, however, did occur during the first two decades of the revolution. The per capita income of the poorest 40 percent of the population increased enormously between 1958 and 1978 (from $182 to $865), while the per capita income of the richest 5 percent declined (from $5,947 to $3,068).

The implementation of non-wage policies, including free health care, education, and social security, also served to reduce somewhat the significance of money income as an adequate indicator of material well-being in Cuba. Moreover, the constraints imposed on market forces also changed the importance of income in determining economic welfare and security. The living standards of the lower 40 percent of the population could thus increase even as the national consumption levels declined.

After 1970, however, with the restoration of consumer policies, disparities of another type emerged. The practice of awarding productive workers privileged access to the purchase of televisions, washing machines, and refrigerators created a new type of differentiation related less to income than to the labor sector. Since each work center received only limited quantities of coveted consumer durables, access to these goods became as important as actual wages. At a higher level, this practice stood in sharp relief as the government made available to high-level technicians, labor union leaders, and ranking state functionaries valued goods and services, including automobiles, better housing, and access to vacations abroad. By the late 1970s and through the 1980s, new inequities had surfaced.

VII

Perhaps the most notable achievements of the revolution occurred in the areas of education, nutrition, and health services. Indeed, nowhere was the quest for an egalitarian society more fully attained than in the area of education. No longer was education restricted to Cubans of means, no longer was the opportunity for education confined to Cubans in urban areas. Cuban education strategy served at once as a means and an end: the diffusion of new values and development of new skills as a way to ensure political support and promote economic growth.

The government committed itself early and earnestly to the elimination of illiteracy and the development of educational facilities across the island. At the time of the triumph of the revolution, the illiteracy rate in the population ten years or older stood at 24 percent, a figure that concealed a telling dichotomy of illiteracy rates between urban dwellers and rural residents. In 1958, almost half of all Cuban children aged six to fourteen years had received no education. Only a quarter of the population fifteen years or older had ever attended school. Three-quarters were either illiterate or had failed to complete primary education.

The inauguration of the literacy campaign in 1961—the "Year of Education"—mobilized Cubans in a national crusade to eliminate illiteracy. An estimated 271,000 people were organized into four instructional groupings. The "Conrado Benítez" brigade consisted of almost 100,000 student volunteers who received intensive training courses and were distributed into the interior countryside. The brigadistas worked and lived with rural families for the duration of the campaign. The second group were known as the alfabetizadores populares, numbering about 121,000 men and women, who volunteered part-time in urban regions. The "Patria o Muerte" brigade was organized by the CTC, made up of 15,000 workers who received paid leaves of absence to participate in the program. The fourth group consisted of 35,000 salaried professional school teachers, virtually all the teachers in Cuba, serving as administrators and technical advisors.

The literacy campaign was the first in a series of educational programs, and sought to raise functional literacy to the first-grade level. By 1962, the revolutionary government reported the adult literacy rate to be 96 percent, the highest in Latin America and one of the highest in the world. The accomplishments of the literacy campaign, even if less than reported in official sources, were nevertheless recognized as a triumph of considerable magnitude for the revolution.

The government launched a second educational campaign a year later, designed to expand schooling among adult Cubans without previous formal education. The "Third Grade Campaign" organized evening classes at local work centers. At its peak, the program enrolled an estimated 500,000 adults. This was followed by the "Battle of the Sixth Grade," designed to expand adult educational levels. Shortly thereafter, the government inaugurated the Worker-Peasant Educational program, equivalent to secondary education, completion of which allowed graduates to continue their education in vocational schools or at universities. During the mid-1960s, more than 800,000 adults were enrolled in the Worker-Peasant program. A decade later, almost 530,000 adults had successfully completed the sixth-grade program, and another 578,000 completed the Worker-Peasant program.

Comparable success was achieved in other areas of education. Full-time school enrollment increased from 800,000 in academic year 1958–59 to 3.3 million in 1982–83, with notable increases registered in elementary school enrollments (from 626,000 to 1.4 million) and secondary school attendance (88,000 to 1.1 million). The number of elementary schools increased from 7,600 to 11,200; secondary schools expanded from 80 to 1,900. The total number of teachers expanded from 20,000 after the flight of the middle class to 60,000. The percentage of children between the ages of 6 and 12 years enrolled in schools increased from 56 percent in 1953 to 88 percent in 1970 to almost 100 percent in 1986. An estimated 86 percent of youth between the ages of 13 to 16 years attended school. The percentage of the population completing sixth grade increased from 20 in 1953 to 32 in 1970 and 61 in 1981.

The revolution also transformed the character and content of higher
education. The number of university centers increased from three in 1959
to forty in the 1980s; enrollments expanded tenfold. Nowhere else did
the institutional distortion of pre-revolutionary Cuba stand in sharper relief than in the structure of the university curriculum. Previously, programs most relevant to the national economy were inadequately subsidized and poorly studied. Cuba had developed a dependence on foreign
technicians and specialists to assist in the management of the most strategic sectors of the national economy. University students typically enrolled in the humanities, social sciences, and law, all preparation principally for positions in government and public administration. The total
budget of the School of Agronomical Engineering and Sugar and the
university farm program in 1950 totaled less than 4 percent of the total
university budget. In 1952, the 6,560 lawyers represented ten times the
total number of agricultural engineers and technicians. Of the 17,527
students enrolled in the University of Havana in 1953–54, only 1,500
were enrolled in civil engineering, agricultural studies, and pure science
and mathematics. "Among the major obstacles to Cuban economic progress," reported a U.S. Department of Commerce study in 1956, "is the
lack . . . of adequate industrial research, agricultural extension, and education in trades, technology, and business. . . . The inadequacy of educational facilities in the trade, technical, and business fields has long
been recognized, but few remedial measures have thus far been taken."
    Conditions changed radically after the revolution. Significant program-
matic and curriculum changes were introduced during the 1960s and 1970s.
Greater emphasis was given to technological programs, and many of these
were linked directly to national planning programs. Through appeals to
conciencia and commitment, and if that failed, through the use of enrollment quotas, the curriculum was restructured during the 1960s. Between
1959 and 1967, enrollments in the humanities declined by 50 percent, in
the social sciences by 72 percent, in law by 93 percent. Enrollments
increased in education by 32 percent, in natural sciences by 51 percent,
in medicine by 34 percent, in engineering and architecture by 82 percent,
and in agricultural sciences by 128 percent. The overall percentage of
students enrolled in technical programs increased from 59 percent in 1959
to 90 percent in 1967. Between 1902 and 1959, the University of Havana
had graduated a total of 3,000 architects and civil and mechanical engineers; by the mid-1970s, an average total of 1,500 were graduating annually. The distribution of 3,951 degrees awarded to the graduating class

of 1975 at the University of Havana reflected the structure of the new curriculum: 30 percent in medicine, 17 percent in technology, 12 percent each in science, economics, and the humanities, 10 percent in agronomy, and 7 percent in pedagogy. National priorities had reshaped the character of post-secondary education.

VIII

Significant advances were also registered in the areas of nutrition and health care. The most dramatic and immediate effect of the early distributive policies occurred in the consumption and allocation of vital foodstuffs. Higher wages and reduced unemployment increased the buying power of most Cuban households. The reduction of costs of many goods and services, no less than the elimination of all costs in others, contributed immediately to an improvement in the quality of diet. The imposition of rationing in the early 1960s guaranteed every household a minimum allocation of vital foodstuffs. In this fashion, the revolution achieved one of its most dramatic achievements: the elimination of malnutrition. The rationing system sought to guarantee every Cuban a minimum intake of 1,900 calories a day. The standard fixed allocation for average households were adjusted to meet the specific conditions of each household, including the number of children under seven and adults over sixty-five, those on special diets prescribed by physicians, and pregnant women. The food ration was supplemented by a variety of sources. Workers obtained meals at work center canteens at nominal fees and without charge to ration cards. During the early 1970s, more than 800,0000 workers were regular patrons of work center cafeterias. Similarly, children at public schools received free luncheons and at secondary boarding schools received all their meals at no cost. During the early 1980s, an estimated 2 million Cubans, approximately one-fifth of the population, received at least one hot meal at work canteens, school cafeterias, and hospitals.

The production and availability of foodstuffs generally improved during the 1970s and 1980s, with several notable exceptions. Meat and rice production floundered, and supplies declined. Fruit and vegetable output, on the other hand, expanded, as did milk production. The effects were threefold. Most immediately, the allotment of rationed foodstuffs (*por la libreta*) increased. At the same time, the number of foods sold both on and off the ration increased, differentiated by price. A liter of milk that cost 25 centavos on the ration sold for 80 centavos off; a package of coffee that sold for 30 centavos on the ration cost 3 pesos off. An increasing number of food staples, finally, were "liberated" *(por la libre)* from the rationing system. The commodities thus *liberado* included bread, eggs, fish, butter, sugar and spaghetti. Beer and rum became more available.

The official ration system and the liberated markets were supplemented by other allocation mechanisms. The "gray market" and black market served as auxiliary channels of food distribution. Gray market transactions involved families and individuals exchanging goods obtained through the ration. One household would thus trade its excess egg allotment for another's unneeded milk quota. Black market activities expanded rapidly during the 1960s as Cuban purchasing power increased without a commensurate increase in consumer goods.

Cuban nutritional needs were all but fully met by the 1970s—not, to be sure, with any great quantity or with great variety, but with certainty, regularity, and sufficiency. Malnutrition was all but eliminated. By the early 1980s, the United Nations Food and Agriculture Organization estimated the Cuban daily per capita calorie intake at 2,705, considerably above most Latin American countries and above the generally recognized minimum daily requirement of 2,500 calories.

These developments also reflected the expansion of health services across the island. The Cuban revolution inherited a fairly advanced if skewed health service network. Health care before the revolution was distributed unequally and favored Cubans of means and especially those living in Havana and provincial capitals. The medical needs of vast sectors of the population went unattended. The initial effects of the revolution on health care were almost all pernicious. During the early 1960s, the number of infectious diseases increased, including polio, diptheria, tuberculosis, measles, syphilis, typhoid fever, and hepatitis. General death rates increased from 6.3 per 1,000 inhabitants in 1957 to 7.3 in 1963; infant mortality rose from 32.3 to 39.6 per 1,000 babies born.

The deterioration of health services resulted largely from the dislocation caused by the revolution. Among the nearly half a million Cubans who emigrated during the 1960s were large numbers of physicians and other health personnel. More than half the total number of practicing physicians, nearly as many dentists, and virtually the entire senior medical faculty at the University of Havana departed. Private practices disappeared and were not replaced. Medical services and facilities, clinics, and hospitals were disrupted. Medical studies at the university were in disarray. The break of diplomatic relations with the United States resulted in a shortage of medicines, pharmaceutical supplies, and medical equipment that Cuban production could not meet. The government moved with haste to train new health service personnel, but the reduction of the years required for study and preparation often resulted in the certification of professional personnel less than fully competent.

From these inauspicious beginnings, Cuban health services expanded haltingly during the 1960s. The revolutionary government found itself at a deficit, from which it spent the first decade attempting to recover. Indeed, it required fully ten years to return to the condition at the time of the triumph of the revolution. By 1969, the doctor/population ratio had returned to the pre-revolutionary level (approximately one per 1,000 persons). By the early 1960s, medical and dental care was extended to all Cubans, free of charge. The number of health facility beds increased from 38,791 in 1962 to 49,224 in 1974. The pre-revolutionary urban-rural imbalance was gradually redressed. Inequalities persisted, but in declining proportions. The construction of new health facilities favored the countryside over the cities. In 1959, Havana, with 22 percent of the population, accounted for 62 percent of all hospital beds. By 1973, the ratio had been reversed, with 44 percent in Havana and 56 percent in the countryside. Oriente, with 35 percent of the population, accounted for 16 percent of all beds in 1959; this had increased to 23 percent in the early 1970s. The rate of increase of hospital construction was 8 percent in Havana as compared with 184 percent in Camagüey and 147 percent in Oriente. The proportion of physicians practicing in Havana declined from 62 percent of the total in 1955 to 42 percent in 1972. The budget of rural hospitals increased from 0.3 percent in 1958 to 8.1 percent in 1962 and 9.7 percent in 1974.

Health service expanded steadily across the island. Budgetary appropriations increased from 25 million pesos in 1959 to 236 million in 1969. Between 1959 and 1976, the total number of hospitals increased from 58 to 257—148 general medical-surgical hospitals, 25 maternity, 22 pediatric, 31 maternal-infant care, and 19 psychiatric hospitals. The number of polyclinics increased from 161 in 1962 to 397 in 1983. By the 1980s, polyclinics served as the basis of a nationwide primary health care system. In addition, 183 medical outposts were established in the remote regions. By 1976, a total of 115 dental clinics were in operation across the island. Geriatric facilities were nonexistent in 1958; by 1974, a total of 47 centers served the elderly. By the early 1980s, Cuba produced 83 percent of its own pharmaceutical and medical supplies. Still, shortages persisted through the 1980s, particularly of those medicines patented and distributed in the United States.

The number of trained health personnel increased steadily. By 1984, physicians numbered 20,500—making for an estimated doctor-population ratio of one to 490. During the 1980s, moreover, Cuba was graduating an average of 1,100 physicians annually, with a goal of 50,000 practicing doctors set for the 1990s. The number of nurses increased from 6,724 in 1962 to 31,702 twenty years later. Professional training programs of ancillary health personnel, rare before 1959, increased, and included X-ray technicians, laboratory technicians, dental assistants, rehabilitation specialists, nutritionists, technical sanitarians, and anesthetists.

Increased effectiveness of preventive medicine led to improved health conditions, a declining mortality rate, and a rising life expectancy. During the 1970s, in collaboration with the World Health Organization and the Pan American Health Organization, Cuba inaugurated a campaign to reduce mortality associated with communicable diseases, such as tuberculosis, polio, tetanus, diphtheria, whooping cough, measles, and infectious hepatitis. The campaign reduced the ratio of incidence from 39 cases per 1,000 inhabitants in 1962 to 16 in 1973. The death rate from contagious diseases as a proportion of all deaths declined from 13 in 1964 to 4.7 in 1974. In 1962 the malarial morbidity rate was 50 per 1,000. Eleven years later, the World Health Organization proclaimed the island malaria-free. As a result of a massive immunization program polio was virtually eliminated. Similarly, a large inoculation campaign reduced the incidence of tuberculosis from 39 cases per 100,000 population in 1962 to 2.7 in 1976. The total number of cases reported in 1982 was less than 100, and deaths from the disease all but ended. Vaccination programs were also effective in reducing the number of diphtheria cases from 1,400 in 1962 to a total of two during 1971–74. Death associated with diarrheal diseases declined from 58 per 100,000 inhabitants in 1962 to 18 per 100,000 in 1971.

The reduction of infant mortality rates also reflected improvements in the Cuban health system. Overall infant mortality declined sharply from 39.6 per 1,000 live births in 1963 to 16 in 1984. (In 1985, however, infant mortality rates increased somewhat to 16.5) Gastroenteritis, previously the leading cause of infant mortality, was reduced from six cases per 1,000 live births to two. Life expectancy increased from 57 years during the 1950s to 74 by the mid-1980s—by which time, too, Cuba had joined the ranks of industrialized nations in which the principal causes of death were heart disease, cancer, and stroke.

IX

Improved nutrition and better health services had a generally salutary effect on population growth. Notwithstanding the loss of nearly one million residents as a result of the massive outflow of refugees between 1959 and the Mariel emigration of 1980, the population experienced uninterrupted growth. Between the census of 1953 and that of 1970, the population increased from 5.8 million to 8.5 million. By 1984, the total population of the island had reached ten million. During the 1950s, Cuban population growth rate averaged 1.9 percent annually. Growth increased to 3 percent during the 1960s. One of the more notable features of Cuban population was the dramatic increase in fertility during the early 1960s. Birth rates climbed from 27 per 1,000 inhabitants in 1958 to 37 in 1962. Fertility rates increased after the political disorders of the late 1950s and during the return of optimism and euphoria during the early period of the revolution. Marriage rates also reflected this new confidence, rising from 4.5 per 1,000 in 1958 to 10 in 1961. Early mobilization campaigns brought large numbers of young women from the cities into the countryside, where men far outnumbered women. The birth surge of the early 1960s, lastly, was also the result of the recurring thirty-year echo of the baby boom between 1899 and 1904.

As conditions stabilized, the initial increases subsided. The number of births and marriages dropped during the inter-census period 1970–80. In 1978, birth rates declined to a new low of 15 per 1,000 inhabitants. Overall, the population growth slowed to an annual average of 1.1 percent, the lowest in the twentieth century. Marriages declined to 6.2 per 1,000, and in 1974 30 percent of all marriages ended in divorce, compared with 8.5 percent in 1959.

Population growth continued to favor urban centers. By the 1970s more than 60 percent of the population resided in urban centers. Although population growth of Havana slowed considerably between 1970 and 1981, the capital approached a population of 2 million. A significantly larger proportion of all women resided in the cities: 62 percent of the female population and 58 percent of males were urban residents. With the decline in birth rate between 1970 and 1981, the average age of the population increased from 17 to 29.5 years. By the mid-1980s, more than half the population had been born after the triumph of revolution.

Cuban population growth and demographic shifts had far-reaching implications for government planners. As early as the 1970s, population growth had created considerable stress in housing. The problems did not originate with the revolution. Housing shared many of same skewed features characteristic of all institutional structures in pre-revolutionary Cuba. An estimated 63 percent of all dwellings were located in urban areas for 57 percent of the total population, requiring the balance of 43 percent of the rural population to occupy the remaining 37 percent of housing units. The 1953 census classified 15 percent of all dwellings as *malo* (bad), averaged from 6 percent *malo* in Havana and 24 percent in Oriente. At the same time, 62 percent of all housing in Havana was classified as *bueno* (good), compared with 26 percent in Oriente. The vast majority of the 143,000 housing units constructed between 1943 and 1958 were located in urban centers, and a large portion of these during the Havana building boom in the form of luxury and semi-luxury units.

The basic urban/rural imbalance was not altered during the early years of the revolution. Certainly the first Urban Reform Law of March 1959 provided tenants with immediate relief. So too did the second Urban Reform Law of October 1960, which in a three-stage program proclaimed the right of all families to decent housing. In the first stage, the state assumed responsibility for assuring each tenant household full amortization of the occupied dwelling through payments made in lieu of rents. The second stage fixed the rental fees of all new, state-built housing at no more than 10 percent of family income. The third stage, abandoned in the 1970s, was to have ceded permanent usufruct of dwellings free of charge to the occupants.

While these measures improved conditions for rental residents, they accomplished little in the way of adding to the aggregate supply of housing units. Partial relief arrived another way—not by constructing new dwellings but by redistributing old ones. The emigration of vast numbers of Cubans placed into circulation large numbers of additional dwellings. Between 1959 and 1975, emigration made available an estimated total of 135,000 housing units.

But neither the reduction of rents mandated by reform laws nor the reallocation of housing made possible by emigration eliminated shortages. Nor did these developments address the crisis in its most acute manifestation, in the countryside. On the contrary, rural housing was hardly affected. According to the 1953 census, rental dwellings were largely urban. Almost 59 percent of all urban households and 75 percent of all Havana residents rented their homes. The proportion of rural households occupying rental quarters was a negligible 8.6 percent. Nor did the countryside reap any benefits from emigration, for the vast majority of housing units made available by the exodus were located in cities.

Attempts to remedy these conditions began early. Housing construction expanded at a brisk pace, averaging an annual 17,000 new units between 1959 and 1963, most of which were located in the countryside. One of the enduring aspects of the new housing program—priority of the countryside over the cities, and the provinces over the capital—was established early and sustained throughout. "A modern city has many expenses," Fidel Castro explained in 1965; "to maintain Havana at the same level as before would be detrimental to what has to be done in the interior of the country. For that reason, for some time Havana must necessarily suffer a little this process of disuse, of deterioration, until enough resources can be provided."

But, in fact, by the mid-1960s there were not sufficient resources for the construction of new housing anywhere. Housing starts languished. The number of units completed through the late 1960s declined to an annual average of 7,000. The decline in construction was due in part to the flight of architects, engineers, and building technicians and in part to the U.S. trade embargo. Mostly, however, it reflected the priority given to construction programs in other sectors. Limited funds, scarce construction labor, and low inventories of building materials were diverted to enterprises deemed more important, such as hydroelectric dams, industrial plants, port and storage facilities, hospitals, roads, and schools.

During the 1970s, housing construction received renewed emphasis. Greater quantities of building materials were available, much of it produced by the very factories constructed in the 1960s. The organization of the microbrigades, construction teams of thirty-three factory workers detached from normal work assignments and under the supervision of Ministry of Construction engineers and technicians, accelerated the completion of new dwellings. Vast new housing projects were completed, including Ciudad José Martí in Santiago de Cuba, housing 50,000 residents, and Alamar East outside of Havana, accommodating more than 100,000 residents. Other projects included the construction of low-cost one- and two-story housing in rural communities, sugar mill towns, government farms, small towns and villages, and the suburban areas of larger cities. Urban projects concentrated on four- and five-story walk-ups and high-rise elevator buildings. By the 1970s, housing construction had again reached an annual level of 17,000 new units.

The expansion of units notwithstanding, Cuba entered a period in which housing shortages were approaching desperate conditions. New construction did not keep pace with population growth. Thousands of dwellings, especially in Havana, had passed into varying conditions of disrepair and decay. The priority given to construction in the countryside exacerbated conditions in the cities. Havana suffered most from the new parity in expenditures with the provinces. In Old Havana, the housing problem approached calamity. Increasing numbers of dwellings were proclaimed structurally unsound and abandoned, thereby worsening an already critical situation. In 1979 alone, a total of 25,000 houses across the island collapsed. Demolition of entire neighborhoods was not uncommon, requiring the relocation of thousands of families in temporary shelters that often had a way of becoming permanent. Cuba was straining to construct 17,000 new units annually at a time it actually needed to provide almost 40,000 units. By the end of the 1970s, the shortage reached one million units.

The conditions became particularly acute during the late 1970s and early 1980s. As the baby-boom generation of 1960–62 prepared to establish separate households, new demands were placed on an overtaxed system. Crowding increased. The effects of the housing crisis reverberated across the island. One manifestation of the crisis was the Mariel exodus of 1980. At the same time, young couples were obliged to delay marriage, often for as long as two or three years at a time, waiting for apartments to become available. This explains in part the decline of the marriage rate during the late 1970s. Young couples who did marry were often required to live with parents for an indefinite period. In 1979, 40 percent of all households in Cuba, and nearly 50 percent of all urban households, consisted of extended families. A vicious cycle ensued. The doubling-up of families, and the inevitable overcrowding and loss of privacy, contributed to declining births and rising divorces. Divorce, in turn, broke up households, thereby creating new demands for housing. Not infrequently, divorced people were obliged to continue living with former spouses.

The government responded in a number of ways. New industries and factories were purposely located in the interior in an effort to redistribute the population and relieve the housing pressures of the large cities. During the 1980s, moreover, efforts to expand the construction of housing units increased, with some success. An estimated 30,000 new dwellings were completed in 1980, a marked increase from the 1970s, but still short of the optimum level of construction. In fact, the government all but conceded that it lacked the means to reduce the housing shortage through construction of new dwellings alone. In 1984, the National Assembly passed a sweeping housing law designed to create new dwellings in addition to those established through state construction projects. The new law permitted free market sales of land and housing and authorized extensions of existing dwellings. Individuals and cooperatives were encouraged to construct multifamily housing, for which the government provided low-interest loans to defray the cost of building materials and the purchase of land. Short-term private rental housing was restored, based on a maximum six-month renewable lease. Two years later, in response to government charges of abuse, the 1984 housing law was restricted, and again housing sales were limited.

The acute housing shortage continued through the 1980s as population growth continued to cancel the expansion of housing construction. Government efforts, including partial restoration of market mechanisms, failed to meet fully the housing needs of the population.

X

The socio-demographic trends of the late 1970s reflected considerably more than a deficit in housing. At work too were forces transforming the role of women in Cuban society and redefining the responsibility of women in production and reproduction.

From the early years and through the later years, at every critical point in the transition to socialism, Cuban women participated decisively in the revolution. Women were mobilized to combat the threat of counter-revolution in 1960–61. The establishment of the Federation of Cuban Women (FMC) integrated women directly into an important mass organization in defense of the revolution. From its original membership of 17,000 in 1961, the FMC expanded to 2.6 million in 1985, representing approximately 82 percent of all women over the age of fourteen years. Women joined the militia and by 1963 constituted fully 44 percent of the 1.5 million members of the CDRs. More than half of 100,000 *brigadistas* of the "Conrado Benítez" Brigade during the 1961 campaign against illiteracy were women.

It was not until the late 1960s, however, the years during which Cuba mounted the "revolutionary offensive," that women in significant numbers participated directly in production. The urgent needs of the economy, and especially the year of the "decisive effort" to harvest the ten-million-ton sugar crop, required the mobilization of women into the labor force. In response to the exhortations of the revolutionary leadership, almost 200,000 new female workers volunteered for sugar production and other agricultural activities. Employment opportunities were not confined to agriculture, however. Women also worked part-time at factories, filling in for workers participating in the "Patria o Muerte" Brigade. The nationalization of small service and retail enterprises in 1968 created new administrative and managerial positions. Of the 4,000 new administrators appointed by the Ministry of Domestic Commerce, 90 percent were women.

Many of the effects of the first decade of mobilization were permanent. Women who had previously never worked outside the home traveled across the interior countryside as teachers, agricultural workers, and administrators. For many, it was their first experience in positions previously reserved for men, in the factories, in the fields, on construction sites, as operators of machinery, and as managers of state enterprises.

The changes occurring in the workplace were accompanied by changes in educational centers. Even as women in greater numbers were being incorporated into the economy, they were also incorporated into the educational system at every level. More than 56 percent of those who learned to read and write during the literacy campaign were women. By the early 1970s, 73 percent of all Cuban women had reached the sixth-grade level. During these years, females composed 49 percent of elementary school students and 55 percent of secondary school enrollment. They made up 46 percent of university enrollments and 50 percent of medical students, one-half the enrollments in the natural sciences, and 42 percent of the enrollments in economics. Enrollments in technical training programs increased. Women made up more than one-third of all engineering students at the University of Oriente. Women received half the degrees awarded in geology, mineralogy, and metallurgy, and outnumbered men at the Forestry Technical Institute and the Technological Institute of Industrial Electronics.

The results of political mobilization and educational opportunities were telling. During the early 1970s, women entered the wage labor force in growing numbers, increasing from 256,000 in 1953 to more than one million in 1985, from 14 percent of adult females to 37 percent. Women constituted 60 percent of those employed in education, 64 percent in public health, 41 percent in light industry, 38 percent of all physicians, and 37 percent in trade and commerce.

The integration of women in such large numbers into the labor force led to other changes. To meet the needs of working women with children, day-care centers expanded across the island, numbering almost 1,000 in 1985 and serving an estimated 96,000 households. In 1974 the government enacted the law on the "Maternity of the Working Woman." Under its provisions, pregnant women received an eighteen-week paid leave of absence—six weeks prior to delivery and twelve weeks after, with guaranteed job security for one year. To meet the needs of women who did not desire children, the government made contraceptive devices available. Abortion was available on demand during the first twelve weeks and upon physician's advice thereafter.

The integration of women into the revolution had other consequences, not all of them foreseen, not all of them felicitous. The new role of women in the paid labor force of the economy clashed with their unpaid labor function in the household. At a time when Cuban women were exhorted to participate in political activity, to join the labor force, to volunteer their services to the revolution, they were also expected to continue their traditional roles as wives, mothers, and housekeepers. Government efforts to ease the pressures created by women working the double shift outside the home *(calle)* and at home *(casa)* provided some relief. Day-care facilities were restricted to children of working mothers. Stores extended their business hours to allow women to shop after work. Plans were devised to give working women priority at food markets.

These measures did not, however, fundamentally reduce the tensions or minimize the consequences of the double shift. Indeed, the requirements of the *casa,* which women were expected to meet, were in conflict with the demands of the *calle,* which they were exhorted to fulfill. Without relief from the former, women were experiencing difficulty in the latter. Women who were required to pick up children at day-care centers and to do household chores at the end of the day could not remain at the workplace to attend assemblies and participate in volunteer activity, both of which were vital for advancement. Domestic conflicts mounted. Men generally refused to share housework or assume larger responsibility in child-rearing. Husbands often resented the deepening involvement of their wives in activities outside the home and the commensurate and de facto decline of their traditional household functions. Pressures of family and home took their toll. An estimated 76 percent of the women who entered the labor force in 1969 dropped out within one year.

During the early 1970s, pressure from women, exerted largely through the FMC, mounted for measures equalizing sex roles. "If they're going to incorporate us into the work force," one FMC member demanded, "they're going to have to incorporate themselves into the home, and that's all there is to it." Traditional patriarchal norms were obstructing efforts to incorporate women into the labor force, an objective that had been placed high on the list of revolutionary priorities.

In 1974 the government responded and enacted a new Family Code, an elaborate legal framework governing family relations. The comprehensive law superseded all other laws regulating the family, marriage, and divorce. Among the most debated features of the code were those clauses addressing the responsibilities of married couples. The Family Code acknowledged that the expectation that women would both be fully integrated into the revolution as workers and fully responsible for households was unrealistic and unreasonable. The code further stipulated that both marriage partners possessed the right to pursue careers and improve their education. Divorce procedures were simplified. The Family Code further mandated shared housework: "Both partners must care for the family they have created and each must cooperate with the other in the education, upbringing and guidance of the children. . . . They must participate to the extent of their capacity or possibilities in the running of the home."

The enactment of the Family Code put the full moral and legal force of the revolution behind the long-standing demands of working women. And, indeed, through the 1970s and 1980s, women entered the labor force in increasing numbers and at all levels. More than 30 percent of the female labor force consisted of technicians, professionals, and managers.

Problems persisted, however. Male accommodation to changing sex roles came slowly, when it came at all. The Family Code remained more a statement of goals than a reality. Conjugal tensions provided the central themes for contemporary Cuban cinema—*Lucía* (1969), *De cierta manera* (1974), and *Retrato de Teresa* (1979): each chronicling women taking the revolution at its word in the promise of self-actualization, and men resisting. Increasing numbers of marriages ended in divorce, in part a reflection of male resistance to the new ways. During the mid-1970s, the PCC joined the debate and committed itself to "an ideological effort designed to eliminate the holdovers of the old society," but acknowledged ruefully that the attitudes necessary "to ease the burden of housework" had not advanced much: "Unfortunately, in practice, not everyone displays such an awareness . . . [and] in many homes these tasks are still not shared."

Women also continued to encounter hiring discrimination, for new as well as old reasons. The new emphasis after the 1970s on cost accounting procedures added pressures on state administrators to show profit, and worked to the detriment of women job-seekers. The cost of absenteeism related to maternity leave was borne by employing enterprises. Additional disruption was caused if a new mother exercised her option to remain on the full year leave. "Managers sometimes refused to employ female labor," the FMC complained in 1974, "because this forces them to increase the number of substitutes with the consequent growth of staff, which affects the evaluation of production."

Women were also underrepresented at supervisory and executive levels in both state enterprises and political positions. In the mid-1970s, the CTC conducted a nationwide survey to determine the cause of the limited participation of women in leadership positions. The poll involved 211 workplaces and 5,168 men and women in all sectors of the economy. More than 85 percent mentioned housework as the limiting factor; 83 percent cited caring for children as the obstacle; 59 percent indicated that added responsibility meant staying at work for greater periods of time; 23 percent indicated that management believed that housework and children would adversely affect their performance; 26 percent believed that added responsibility would lead to problems with husbands. In municipal elections in Matanzas in 1974, women constituted a mere 7.6 percent of the total nominees and only 3 percent of candidates elected. In a postelection survey to determine the lack of participation of women, a majority of females polled cited responsibility "for housework and care for the children and husband." One year later, the First Party Congress criticized the persisting tendency to discriminate against women: "When, in deciding who is to be promoted to a political or administrative responsibility, women are denied this right to avoid possible future difficulties arising from limitations connected with taking care of the home and the family."

The patterns of female underrepresentation persisted through the 1980s. Women made up more than half the membership of the CDRs, and 32 percent of the leadership, 27 percent of the leadership of the Young Communist League, 18 percent of the leadership in the CTC, and only 11 percent of ANAP. Women made up 12 percent of the municipal assemblies, 20 percent of the provincial councils and 24 percent of the National Assembly. Of the 29 members of the Council of State in 1984, only two were women; of the 32 ministers of state, one was a woman; of the 100 Cuban ambassadors abroad, six were women. The representation of women in the party membership increased slightly through the three party congresses, rising from 13 percent in 1975 to 22 percent in 1986. The 41 women in the 1986 Central Committee represented 19 percent of the total membership.

The Cuban revolution, in fits and starts, had confronted the issue of women's equality at the highest levels, and sought through state policy to increase female participation in the economy. The results, in terms of both the representation of women in the paid labor force and the transformations in patterns of life, were impressive. But the struggle for equality was at the same time hampered by two structural features of Cuban revolutionary society. First, a severe scarcity of resources prevented the state from doing as much as was necessary in the provision of child care and in the lightening of household burdens. The persistence of *machista* attitudes did not make these shortcomings any easier to bear. On the contrary, the gains made outside the home were often threatened by demands from within the home. Second, it had become virtually impossible within an all-encompassing revolutionary ideology to develop an autonomous feminist movement, one capable of articulating and pressing for its own conception of women's rights. Attempts to deal with sexism had to be integrative, not divisive; changes in sex roles were required to show a net benefit to the revolutionary effort. Thus the FMC was from the outset, as its leaders were wont to describe it, an *organización femenina,* not an *organización feminista.*

XI

No less than domestic policy, Cuban foreign policy passed through a number of distinct phases after 1959, each reflecting a convergence of changing national conditions and shifting international circumstances. The revolution transformed more than the content and conduct of Cuban foreign relations. It changed too its scope—a shift from bilateral to regional to global. For almost three decades, Cuba conducted a foreign policy of international proportions committed principally and, when possible, simultaneously to the consolidation of the revolution at home and the support of the revolution abroad—always with a mixture of revolutionary zeal and pragmatic calculation.

Cuba's turbulent disengagement from the United States during the early 1960s was followed by an only slightly less turbulent alignment with the Soviet Union in the late 1960s. Both experiences served to define the essential features of Cuban internationalism. For Cuban leaders, events between 1961 and 1962 served to set in relief the precariousness of their position. The Bay of Pigs in 1961 gave form to the North American determination to destroy the revolution; the missile crisis in 1962 revealed the Soviet disinclination to defend the revolution. There were limits to socialist solidarity, the Cubans learned. That the Soviets withdrew their missiles, and did so without even so much as a pretense of consultation with Havana, served to remind Cubans of their continuing vulnerability. The North Americans were implacable adversaries, the Soviets were unreliable allies. Cuban efforts thereafter centered on the creation of new security arrangements: principally, to reduce its politico-economic isolation while reducing the threat of the United States on one hand, and to enhance its effectiveness in negotiating the terms of its relationship with the Soviet Union on the other. In pursuit of both objectives at the same time, Cuba sought to reduce its vulnerability in the East-West context by increasing its influence within the North-South alignment.

Efforts by Cuba to establish itself in a position of leadership in the Third World were confined initially to the Western Hemisphere, for reasons both practical and ideological. North American policy to isolate Cuba culminated during the early 1960s, first with a trade embargo and later with a rupture of diplomatic relations. Under pressure from the United States, the Organization of American States (OAS) voted in 1962 to suspend Cuban membership. Two years later, all member nations of the OAS except Mexico severed diplomatic and commercial relations with Cuba.

Cuba countered in kind. Throughout the early 1960s, Havana exhorted Latin Americans to emulate the Cuban example and transform the Andes into the Sierra Maestra of South America. "The duty of every revolutionary," Fidel Castro proclaimed in the Second Declaration of Havana in 1962, "is to make the revolution." In exhorting Latin Americans to revolution, Cuba was pursuing several objectives. Most immediately, it sought to replace hostile governments with friendly ones, and thereby reduce Cuban isolation. No less important, Cuba advanced a rival claim for leadership in the Western Hemisphere, with the ambitious objective of isolating the United States. The Cuban summons to revolution was no less a challenge to the Soviet claim of leadership over world revolution. Still smarting from their humiliation during the missile crisis, Cubans were openly critical of Soviet strategies; they scorned the notion of peaceful coexistence and rejected "the peaceful road to revolution." The world was divided into two camps, Cuba insisted: revolutionaries and everybody else. And the only acceptable strategy for true revolutionaries was armed struggle, in the form of guerrilla movements (*focos*).

The Cuban challenge, hence, was directed at both the United States and the Soviet Union. For the better part of the 1960s, Cuba sought to maintain a balance between both countries, trying at one and the same time to create distance from the United States without developing dependency on the Soviet Union. The Soviet connection enabled the Cubans to achieve the former. But as long as the United States maintained military pressure and economic sanctions, Cuba faced an increasingly diminished capacity to resist Soviet influence. Domestic policies underscored Cuban efforts at establishing autonomy from Moscow. In 1968, pro-Soviet party personnel were purged from the PCC, a move followed by a series of arrests and additional expulsions and resignations. The ten-million-ton crop was likewise an effort to reduce Cuban dependence on Soviet assistance by generating increased foreign exchange.

Cuban foreign policy had similar objectives. By emerging as a force in Third World politics, Cuba sought to acquire an independent position of influence that could in turn serve as a source of leverage to obtain a more equitable relationship with the Soviets. After 1962, Cuba pursued an ambitious foreign policy. It extended moral and material support to guerrilla movements across Latin America—in Guatemala, Colombia, Venezuela, Peru, and Bolivia. In the mid-1960s activities broadened significantly. In 1966, Havana hosted the first Tricontinental Conference at which the Organization for the Solidarity of the Peoples of Asia, Africa, and Latin America (OSPAAAL) was founded. The Tricontinental provided an even larger forum from which Cuba pressed its claim for leadership in the Third World. Cuban militancy peaked the following year, with the establishment in Havana of the Organization of Latin American Solidarity (OLAS). Fidel Castro excoriated the traditional communist parties of Latin America, describing them variously as "opportunistic," "reformist," and "serving the interests of imperialism." Soviet foreign policy was attacked, particularly Soviet diplomatic and commercial relations with Latin American countries in which Cubans were supporting active guerrilla movements. "The least we expect of any state of the socialist camp," Fidel Castro proclaimed, "is that it will lend no financial or technical assistance of any type to those governments." And in a thinly veiled reproach to the Soviet Union: "And whoever, no matter who, aids those oligarchies where guerrillas are fighting will be helping to suppress the revolution, for repressive wars are carried on not only with weapons but also with the millions of dollars used for purchasing the weapons and for paying the mercenary armies."

Cuba also expanded its contacts in Africa. In 1963, Havana provided military support to Algeria in a border dispute with Morocco. Increasingly, Cuba was drawn deeper into the anti-colonial wars in Africa. Cubans actively supported the Popular Movement for the Liberation of Angola (MPLA), the African Party for the Liberation of Portuguese Guinea and Cape Verde Islands (PAIGC), and the Front for the Liberation of Mozambique (FRELIMO). In 1965 a Cuban military detachment under the command of Ernesto Che Guevara arrived in Congo-Brazzaville to fight against the government of Moise Tshombe. In the same year, Cuba established a formal military mission in Congo-Brazzaville, followed a year later by one in Guinea.

Cuban activism in the Third World waned toward the end of the decade. Guerrilla movements in Latin America were on the defensive and in decline. The most serious setback to the *vía insurreccional* occurred in October 1967 with the defeat and death of Che Guevara in Bolivia. The Soviets, too, for their part, did not let Cuba's insubordination pass unchallenged. In 1967 Moscow withheld from Cuba 20 percent of its scheduled petroleum allotment, causing a serious depletion of Cuban oil reserves and a new round of fuel and gasoline rationing. And just in case Havana missed the moral of the message, the Soviets announced plans to increase oil exports to Brazil and Chile, two countries with which Cuba had bitter disputes. Moderation was also induced by the deterioration of the Cuban economy, culminating in the debacle of the ten-million-ton crop, after which Cubans became increasingly preoccupied with domestic reorganization and economic recovery. The results were the exact opposite of what Cuba had set out to accomplish. Cuban dependency on the Soviet Union increased. These were not the times to engage the Soviets in ideological polemics or impugn Soviet revolutionary credentials. On the contrary, it was now necessary to make common cause with Moscow.

In 1968, Cuba grudgingly endorsed the Soviet invasion of Czechoslovakia. Rapprochement had begun, and culminated in 1972 when Cuba became one of the first non-European nations to gain membership status in
the Soviet bloc Council for Mutual Economic Assistance.

Conditions had changed in Latin America, too, and increasingly Cuban
economic and diplomatic isolation was diminishing. In 1968, Chile and
Cuba established commercial relations. The election of Salvador Allende
two years later provided Cuba with an ally in South America. Equally
important, the Allende victory provided Cubans with the opportunity to
endorse the strategy of the nonviolent road to power. Relations with other
Latin American governments resumed thereafter: in 1972 with Peru, Barbados, Jamaica, Guyana, and Trinidad and Tobago, followed by Argentina in 1973, Panama and the Bahamas in 1974, and Colombia and Venezuela in 1975. In 1975, belatedly, the OAS passed a resolution allowing
members to normalize relations with Cuba.

Diplomatic reconciliation with Latin American nations did not, however, involve a repudiation of Cuba's internationalist policies in Africa
and the Middle East. Cuba continued to expand its influence in the Nonaligned Movement. Between 1972 and 1973, Fidel Castro undertook extensive tours abroad. In 19773, he led the Cuban delegation to the Fourth
Nonaligned Movement summit in Algeria. During these years, moreover,
Cuba continued to expand military aid programs to Africa and the Middle
East. Military missions were established in Sierra Leone (1972), South
Yemen (1973), Equatorial Guinea (1973), and Somalia (1974). Cuba also
dispatched combat troops to Syria in 1973 during the Yom Kippur War.

Relations with the United States improved, if only briefly. An anti-
hijacking accord was signed in 1973. Cuba accepted the possibility of
detente, thereby coming around to the Soviet position on peaceful coexistence. In 1974, high-level secret meetings between the United States
and Cuba explored the potential for normalization of relations. Washington abruptly suspended negotiations in 1975, however, when Cuba dispatched combat troops to Angola.

Cuban participation in the Angolan war for national liberation on the
side of the Popular Movement for the Liberation of Angola proved decisive. An estimated 36,000 Cuban combat troops assisted the MPLA in
consolidating power in 1975–76 during the ensuing civil war, where it
faced forces backed by the United States, South Africa, and China. Two
years later, at the request of Mengistu Haile Mariam, another 15,000
Cuban troops aided Ethiopia against a Somalian invasion.

Cuban assistance to Third World countries was not limited to military aid. Indeed, the larger part of Cuban commitments consisted of a wide range of socio-economic programs. With the improvement of economic conditions on the island during the 1970s, Cubans were in a position to increase their aid to other countries. An estimated 20,000 civilian internationalists, largely construction workers, physicians, technicians, engineers, agronomists, and teachers, served in nearly forty countries on three continents. By far the largest activity centered on civil construction projects in the form of technical advice, planning, and organization and involved approximately 8,000 Cuban workers. Educational and medical assistance programs represented the another key area of Cuban overseas activities, accounting for an estimated 3,500 teachers and 2,000 medical personnel. At the same time, a large number of Cuban specialists and technicians served abroad as advisors in agriculture, mining, livestock, industry, transportation, and fishing. In addition, more than 10,000 foreign students, largely from Africa and Latin America, were enrolled in Cuban health programs and technical and vocational schools.

Cuban military involvement in Africa during the 1970s and 1980s, and especially support of the MPLA, received general approval among Third World nations. The 1976 Nonaligned Movement conference in Sri Lanka applauded Cuban internationalism. "The Conference . . . commends the Republic of Cuba and other States," the Final Declaration of the Nonaligned Summit proclaimed, "which assisted the people of Angola in frustrating the expansionist and colonialist strategy of South Africa's racist regime and its allies." And as a gesture of its approval of Third World policies,the Nonaligned Movement unanimously selected Havana as the site of the 1979 summit. The decision meant, too, that as head of the Cuban government, Fidel Castro would serve as the Nonaligned Movement organizational chair and the international spokesperson until the next meeting in 1983.

The Sixth Nonaligned Summit in Havana in September 1979 marked the high point of Cuban prestige among Third World nations. With Fidel Castro serving as chair of the conference, the Cuban position on many important issues prevailed. Indeed, Cuban leadership in the Nonaligned Movement appeared secure and strengthening.

Cuban ascendancy was short-lived, however. In December 1979, only months after the conclusion of the Havana summit, the Soviet Union invaded Afghanistan, a member state of the Nonaligned Movement. In January 1980, the majority of the Nonaligned members voted 56 to 9 (with 26 abstaining or absent) on a United Nations resolution to condemn the Soviet invasion. Cuba faced an impossible situation. On one hand, Havana was indebted to the Soviet Union for two decades of aid and obliged to reciprocate with political support in the United Nations. At the same time, the Nonaligned members expected Cuba, and especially the incumbent chair of the organization, to defend the interests of an aggrieved member. Cubans responded feebly in the General Assembly, arguing that the resolution was a divisive machination of U.S. imperialism, and voted against passage.

The vote against the resolution weakened Cuban claim to nonaligned status. It opened Cuba to charges that it was little more than a surrogate of Soviet foreign policy and that Cuban military-developmental projects were, in fact, instruments of Soviet expansionism.

The effects were immediate. Cuba's bid for membership in the UN Security Council, requiring a two-thirds' majority in the General Assembly, failed. Cuban prestige suffered irreparable harm. For the duration of the Cuban tenure of leadership of the Nonaligned Movement (1979–83), Fidel Castro assumed an uncharacteristically low-key caretaker role. At the 1983 Nonaligned Movement Summit, leadership passed uneventfully to the moderates led by Indira Gandhi.

The decline of Cuban global influence occurred at the same time of renewed ascendancy of Cuba in regional affairs. Once more, changing circumstances created an atmosphere conducive to Cuban participation. The triumph of the Sandinistas in Nicaragua in 1979 provided Cuba a new ally in the region. So too did the emergence in 1980 of the Maurice Bishop government in Grenada. An armed insurgency in El Salvador showed every sign of expanding. At the same time, Cuba won new friends through its defense of Latin American interests. Havana supported Panama's demands for control over the canal. Cuba's support of Argentina during the Falklands/Malvinas war led ultimately to strengthened ties between both countries. For a brief period, U.S.-Cuban relations had improved in 1977, as Washington and Havana resumed limited diplomatic relations through the establishment of interests sections: North American diplomats handling U.S. interests as a section of the Swiss embassy in Havana and Cuban diplomats managing Cuba's interests as a section of the Czechoslovak embassy in Washington. However, in 1978, the United States again suspended further negotiations in retaliation for Cuba's involvement in the Ethiopian-Somalian war.

Tensions increased in the 1980s. The Reagan administration appeared to pose new threats to Cuba. Rumors that the United States was preparing to attack led to full-scale mobilizations on the island. A new round of diplomatic ruptures increased Cuban isolation again. A new government in Jamaica severed ties with Cuba in 1981. The U.S. invasion of Grenada in 1983 eliminated another ally. Economic and military pressure increased against Nicaragua.

Cuban policy objectives during the 1980s remained substantially similar to those of the 1960s, for in a very real sense, conditions were similar to those of the sixties. The United States remained a security threat. Problems of diplomatic and economic isolation persisted. Nor were Cuban efforts to influence the terms of their relationship with the Soviet Union successful. On the contrary, the repercussions of the invasion of Afghanistan suggested that the Cuban position had actually weakened.

Cuban efforts to create security from the United States and autonomy from the Soviet Union faltered. Havana was unwilling to sacrifice its relationship with the Soviet Union for a larger international role, but neither was it willing to forgo internationalism to improve relations with the United States. "Principles are not negotiable," Fidel Castro proclaimed in 1980. And in defense of principles, Cubans were prepared to return to the beginning of their history. "They will see that they will never bring us to our knees," Fidel continued, "that we can resist for one, ten or as many years as necessary, even if we have to live like the Indians that Christopher Columbus found here when he landed 500 years ago."

Political Chronology

1000 B.C.:   Ciboney Indians (Guayabo Blanco) migrate to central-western regions of Cuba.

1000 A.D.:   Ciboney Indians (Cayo Redondo) settle eastern third of Cuba.

1100–1450:   Successive migration waves of Arawak Indians (Sub-Taíno and Taíno) disperse across Cuba and displace Ciboney from all areas of the island except the western extremities.

1492:   Christopher Columbus reconnoiters the northeastern coast of Cuba, establishing Spain's claim of possession.

1508:   Sebastián de Ocampo completes the first circumnavigation of Cuba, thereby establishing definitively its insularity. The information gathered by Ocampo about Cuban coastlines and harbors is used in preparation for Spanish occupation of the island.

1511–15:   An expeditionary force under the leadership of Diego de Velásquez departs from Española and enters eastern Cuba at Maisí. The Spanish conquest of Cuba is completed within four years. The seven original towns *(villas)* are established: Baracoa (1512), Bayamo (1513), Trinidad (1514), Sancti Spíritus (1514), Puerto Príncipe (1514), and Santiago de Cuba (1515).

1519:   Havana is relocated from its original site on the Gulf of Batabanó to its present location on the north coast.

1519–40:   Migration from Cuba to Mexico, Central America, South America, and Florida threatens the island with depopulation. The last significant Indian uprisings against Spanish rule occur.

1538:   Santiago de Cuba is formally selected as the capital of Cuba.

1538–60:   Cuba is subjected to attacks by French and English corsairs. Smaller coastal settlements are sacked and plundered. In 1555, Jacques de Sores destroys Havana, raising concern among Spanish authorities for the future security of the island. Plans are completed to construct fortifications for the protection of Havana. The trans-Atlantic fleet convoy system *(flota)* is inaugurated.

1594:   The status of Havana is elevated from town *(villa)* to city *(ciudad)*.

1602–7:   Government efforts to curtail contraband in Bayamo lead to the first successful colonial rebellion against Spanish authority.

1607:   In an effort to reduce contraband and improve coastal surveillance, insular administration of Cuba is reorganized into two governing units. Havana is formally established as the capital of the island under the authority of a captain-general and exercising juridical authority over all the colony and administrative responsibility for Mariel, Cabaña, Bahía Honda, Matanzas, and 50 leagues into the eastern interior, coast to coast. The administrative authority of Santiago de Cuba is restricted to Bayamo, Baracoa, and Puerto Príncipe.

1700:   Bourbons claim Spanish crown and place Philip V on the throne, precipitating the War of Spanish Succession (1700–1714).

1715–30:   Political administration is centralized across the island. Local town councils *(cabildos)* are deprived of the authority to distribute land to settlers. Position of *teniente de rey* is established to substitute for the captain-general upon the death of an incumbent. The measure reduces insular initiative in selecting a replacement from local government officials.

1717–23:   Spain establishes a tobacco monopoly *(Factoría)*, provoking a series of popular armed rebellions among tobacco farmers.

1728:   University of Havana founded.

1733:   The authority of Havana is expanded. Henceforth all administrative units on the island are placed under the jurisdiction of the capital. The division of authority between Havana and Santiago de Cuba ends in favor of the former.

1740:   The Real Compañía de Comercio is chartered for the purpose of consolidating Cuban trade and commerce into one monopoly enterprise.

1752–63:   The English seize and occupy Havana for ten months, opening the port to world trade.

1764:   The intendancy system is introduced into Cuba as a means to improve efficiency in administration and increase centralization of authority.

1776:   North American colonies rebel against England, thereby encouraging increased commerce between the newly independent nation and Cuba.

1778:   A free trade decree provides a score of Cuban cities with direct commercial access to Spain and its colonies in the New World.

1789:   The island is divided into two ecclesiastical jurisdictions: the eastern half of Cuba is placed under the authority of the Bishop of Santiago de Cuba; the western half of the island, together with Louisiana and Florida, are placed under the jurisdiction of the newly established bishopric of Havana.

1789:   A royal decree authorizes free trade in slaves.

1791:   Slave rebellion in the French colony of St. Domingue precipitates the migration of French coffee and sugar planters to Cuba. The destruction of St. Domingue's vast agricultural wealth provides Cuba with the opportunity to expand sugar and coffee production.

1792:   The Sociedad Económica de Amigos del País is chartered.

1800:   As a result of the Haitian invasion of Santo Domingo, the *audiencia* is transferred to Cuba, conferring on the island supreme judicial authority over Puerto Rico, Louisiana, and Florida.

1808:   Napoleon invades Spain and establishes his brother Joseph Bonaparte on the throne. Colonists in Cuba proclaim their loyalty to the deposed Ferdinand VII.

1809–10:   A conspiracy is organized by attorneys Román de la Luz and Joaquín Infante. The plan joins creoles and free people of color in an effort to establish an independent republic.

1810–26:   The wars of independence spread among Spain's mainland colonists. With the end of Spanish rule, thousands of loyalists, clerics, and soldiers migrate to Cuba, thereby reinforcing the presence of pro-Spanish elements on the island and contributing to the Cuban loyalty to Spain. Henceforth, Cuba is recognized officially as the "Ever-Faithful Isle."

1811–12:   José Antonio Aponte, a free black carpenter, leads an uprising that involves whites, free people of color, and slaves. Designed to put an end to slavery, the rebellion secures supporters across the island.

1817:   Spain and England sign a treaty proclaiming the end of legal slave trade in Spanish colonies, effective May 1820.

1818:   A royal decree opens Cuban ports to free international trade.

1821–23:   A conspiratorial movement is organized by poet José María Heredia and creole army officer José Francisco de Lemus. Known as the "Soles y Rayos de Bolívar," the movement aspired to the abolition of slavery and the establishment of the independent "Republic of Cubanacán."

1824:   Creole ensign Gaspar A. Rodríguez launches an ill-fated rebellion for independence.

1826:   Manuel Andrés Sánchez and Francisco de Agüero Velasco organized a short-lived separatist rebellion in Puerto Príncipe.

1837–38:   The first railroad in Cuba, and the first railroad in Latin America, commences operation, linking Havana with Bejucal and Güines. The subsequent expansion of the rail system in Cuba reduces substantially the transportation cost associated with sugar production.

1844:   La Escalera conspiracy is uncovered.

1847:   Club de La Habana is founded. The Club emerges as the center of creole conspiracy seeking annexation to the United States. Membership includes many of the most prestigious creole sugar planters, including Count of Pozos Dulces, Miguel Aldama, Cristobal Madán, and José María Sánchez.

A government decree formally authorizes the importation of Asian indentured laborers into Cuba.

1848–51:   Three abortive filibustering expeditions are organized by Narciso López.

1851:   Annexationist uprising led by Joaquín de Agüero in Camagüey province is suppressed in May. Another rebellion led by Isidoro Armenteros in Trinidad is put down in July.

1853:   José Martí is born.

1865:   The Reformist party is founded. Representing the interests of creole property owners, the new party adopts a program urging modification of tax and tariff regulations, separation of military and civil functions in the office of governor general, and Cuban representation in the Spanish parliament.

1866:   The first trade union of Cuba, the Asociación de Tabaqueros de La Habana, is founded.

1866–67:   Elections are held in Cuba for the position of sixteen delegates in the Junta de Información, in which fourteen creoles from the Reformist party are elected. The Junta was expected to negotiate with the Spanish government a series of insular reforms. Upon arrival in Spain, the Junta is dissolved. The Reformist program subsequently flounders.

1868–78:   On October 10, 1868, the "Grito de Yara" announces the outbreak of the Ten Years' War in Oriente province. In 1869, insurgent representatives convoke an assembly at Guáimaro in Camagüey province to establish a unified provisional government under a new constitution. The republic in arms is headed by President Carlos Manuel de Céspedes. The insurrection expands across Oriente and Camagüey and briefly into the province of Las Villas. The inability of the insurgents to carry the war to the western provinces dooms the rebellion.

1870:   Spanish government enacts the Moret law, whereby Madrid commits itself to the emancipation of slaves on a gradual basis.

1878:   Pact of Zanjón in February brings Ten Years' War to an end. According to the terms of the peace settlement negotiated by Spanish General Arsenio Martínez Campos and the insurgent command, Spain pledges to institute a program of political and administrative reform and extends amnesty to insurgents. Asian contract workers and African slaves who participated in the rebellion receive guaranteed unconditional freedom. A month after the negotiations, Cuban General Antonio Maceo denounces the pact (the "Protest of Baraguá") and renews Cuban commitment to armed struggle. In May, all insurgents lay down their arms.

A new political party, the Liberal party (Autonomist) is founded. Reviving the old creole reformist program of the 1860s, the Autonomist party urges gradual emancipation of slavery with indemnification to owners, juridical equality with Spanish provinces, and tax and tariff reforms. In the same year, pro-Spanish elements also form a new party, the Partido Unión Constitucional. The *peninsular* party demands the retention of traditional colonial relationships in favor Spanish interests.

The island is reorganized into six civil provinces, each taking the name of its respective capital: Pinar del Río, Havana, Matanzas, Santa Clara, Puerto Príncipe, and Santiago de Cuba.

1879–80: A new separatist war breaks out in Oriente in August 1879. "La Guerra Chiquita" is led by General Calixto García and involves many of the ranking veterans of the Ten Years' War. After nine months of desultory armed conflict, the rebellion is crushed.

1880–86: Spain enacts a new law abolishing slavery, whereby emancipation is planned on a gradual basis over the course of an eight-year transition period of tutelage *(patronato)*. Two years before the scheduled expiration of the *patronato,* a Spanish decree totally abolishes slavery.

1885: The first labor federation of Cuba, the Círculo de Trabajadores de La Habana, is founded, joining into one union cigarworkers, shoemakers, bakers, lithographers, and carpenters.

1891: Spain and the United States sign the Foster-Cánovas Treaty, whereby Cuban agricultural products receive tariff concessions in the U.S. market in return for reciprocal duty reductions for North American imports.

1892: Under the leadership of José Martí, a new party is founded in Tampa, Florida. The Cuban Revolutionary Party (PRC) proclaims its commitment to the independence of Cuba and renews the Cuban determination to win independence by armed struggle. José Martí is elected chief delegate of the PRC.

Cuba produces the first one-million-ton sugar harvest.

The first National Labor Congress convenes in Havana.

1894: The Foster-Cánovas Treaty lapses, and old tariff rates are reinstituted.

1895: The Cuban war for independence begins on February 24. José Martí is killed in battle in May. The following September, insurgent Cubans meet at Jimaguayú (Puerto Príncipe) to establish a provisional government under a new constitution. Salvador Cisneros Betancourt is elected president of the republic in arms. In October Antonio Maceo and Máximo Gómez launch the invasion of the western provinces.

1896:   In January, Maceo completes the westward march into
             Mantua (Pinar del Río) while Gómez commences mili-
             tary operations in Havana province. General Valeriano
             Weyler arrives in Cuba and launches the "war with war"
             strategy. In October, the reconcentration policy is inau-
             gurated. Antonio Maceo is killed in battle in December.

1897:   In October, Weyler is recalled. The following month au-
             tonomy is granted to the island.

1898:   In July the United States intervenes in the Cuban war.
             One month later, Spain capitulates to the United States.
             In December, Spain and the United States sign the Treaty
             of Paris, whereby sovereignty of Cuba is transferred to
             the United States.

1899–1902:   The formal military occupation of Cuba by the United
             States commences on January 1, 1899. In 1900 a con-
             stituent assembly convenes to prepare a new constitu-
             tion. In February 1901 the United States enacts the Platt
             Amendment and requires the Cuban constituent assem-
             bly to incorporate the statute into the new constitution.
             In June, the constituent assembly adopts the Platt
             Amendment by a vote of 16 to 11, with four absten-
             tions. In national elections in December 1901, Tomás
             Estrada Palma is elected president. On May 20, 1902,
             the United States ends the military occupation of Cuba,
             formally inaugurating the Cuban republic.

1903:   The United States and Cuba sign three treaties. The Per-
             manent Treaty enacts the Platt Amendment into a formal
             treaty relationship. A second accord, the Reciprocity
             Treaty, concedes a 20 percent concession to Cuban ag-
             ricultural products entering the U.S. market in exchange
             for reductions between 20 to 40 percent on U.S. im-
             ports. In the third agreement, Cuba leases the sites of
             Bahía Honda and Guantánamo to the United States. A
             naval base is constructed in Guantánamo.

1905: President Estrada Palma obtains a second presidential term by defeating Liberal candidate José Miguel Gómez in a disputed election.

1906: In the "August Revolution" disgruntled Liberals rebel against Estrada Palma. The Cuban government is unable to defeat the insurgents and requests U.S. military intervention.

1906–9: The United States military occupies Cuba and governs the island through a provisional government.

1907: The Agrupación de Color is founded by Afro-Cubans protesting racism in the republic.

1908: In national elections held under U.S. supervision, Liberal candidate José Miguel Gómez wins election to a four-year presidential term (1908–12).

1912: The United States cedes its rights over Bahía Honda in exchange for larger facilities at Guantánamo Bay.

Armed rebellion by Afro-Cubans protesting political, social, and economic conditions. The revolt is brutally repressed. The United States military intervenes at the site of the conflict in oriente province to protect North American property.

1912–20: Conservative Mario G. Menocal is elected president in 1912 for a four-year term. After a disputed presidential election in November 1916, in which Menocal won a second term, disaffected Liberals organized a rebellion in 1917, the "February Revolution." The U.S. undertakes an armed intervention in the regions of the political disorders and maintains a military presence in the eastern third of Cuba until 1922.

1917: Cuba declares war on Germany.

1920–24:   Liberal President Alfredo Zayas governs Cuba. Due to political and economic problems, the first three years of the Zayas administration were under the direct control of U.S. special envoy General Enoch H. Crowder.

1920:   Second National Labor Congress convenes in Havana.

             "Dance of the Millions." Between February and May, the price of sugar reaches the extraordinary price of 22.5 cents per pound, only to collapse to 3.7 cents in December. The Cuban economy plunges into disarray and depression.

1923:   The Veterans and Patriots Movement organizes to protest social, economic, and political conditions in the republic.

             The first National Congress of Women meets in Havana.

             Under the leadership of Julio Antonio Mella, the first National Congress of Students convenes in Havana.

1924:   Gerardo Machado elected to his first term as president (1924–28).

1925:   At the third National Labor Congress, union delegates establish the first national labor federation, the Confederación National Obrera de Cuba (CNOC). This same year, the Cuban Communist Party (PCC) is founded.

1927:   The Customs-Tariff law is enacted, providing Cuban manufacturers and industrialists substantive protectionist relief.

             Opposition to Machado increases. Carlos Mendieta leads disaffected Liberals out of the party to organize the new Asociación Unión Nacionalista. University of Havana students establish the Directorio Estudiantil Universitario (DEU).

1928:   Through unconstitutional means, Machado is elected un-opposed to a new and extended six-year term of office.

1930:   The U.S. Hawley-Smoot Tariff Act reduces the Cuban share of the U.S. sugar market, exacerbating economic conditions on the island.

          The CNOC, led by Rubén Martínez Villena, organizes a general strike in March against the Machado government. In September, student demonstrations result in the death of Rafael Trejo.

1931:   Old-line political chieftains led by former Conservative president Mario G. Menocal and ex-Liberal Carlos Mendieta launch an abortive armed uprising against Machado.

1932:   The first national union of sugar workers, the Sindicato Nacional de Obreros de la Industria Azucarera (SNOIA) is founded.

1933:   The worsening political crisis in Cuba prompts the United States to dispatch Ambassador Sumner Welles to organize mediations between the Machado government and the opposition. The mediations commence in July. A general strike in August brings the brewing political crisis to a climax with a military coup ousting Machado and installing Carlos Manuel de Céspedes as president. In September, the "Sergeants' Revolt" led by Fulgencio Batista overthrows the Céspedes administration and aids the establishment of a new provisional government headed by Ramón Grau San Martín. Known as the "government of 100 days," the Grau regime inaugurates a wide range of social, economic, and political reforms.

1934:   In January, Batista overthrows the Grau government and installs Carlos Mendieta as president. In May the United States abrogates the Platt Amendment.

Ramón Grau San Martín and others organize the first new post-Machado political party, the Partido Revolucionario Cubano (Auténtico).

1935: A general strike forces the resignation of President Mendieta, who is replaced by José A. Barnet.

1936: Miguel Mariano Gómez is inaugurated president and within twelve months is ousted by Batista. Batista replaces him with Federico Laredo Bru, who serves the balance of the four-year term.

1938: The communist party obtains recognition as a legal political organization.

1939: The CNOC is reorganized as the Confederación de Trabajadores de Cuba (CTC).

1940: The constitution of Cuba is promulgated.

Fulgencio Batista is elected president for a four-year term.

1942: Cuba declares war on Germany, Italy, and Japan.

1944: Ramón Grau San Martín elected president for a four-year term and carries the Auténtico party into power.

Communist party is reorganized and changes its name to the Partido Socialista Popular (PSP).

1947: Eduardo Chibás breaks with the Auténtico party to organize a new opposition party, Partido del Pueblo Cubano (Ortodoxo).

1948: Carlos Prío Socarrás is elected president for a four-year term.

1951: Eduardo Chibás commits suicide.

1952: Fulgencio Batista seizes power through a military coup and ousts the Prío administration, thereby ending constitutional government in Cuba.

1953: Fidel Castro attacks the Moncada barracks in Santiago de Cuba. The attack fails and survivors are sentenced to fifteen-year prison terms.

1954: Running unopposed, Batista is elected to another four-year term as president.

1955: Batista proclaims a general amnesty in which Fidel Castro and other participants in the Moncada attack are released from prison. The leader of the newly organized 26 of July Movement departs for Mexico to organize armed resistance against the Batista government.

1956: Fidel Castro returns to Cuba aboard the *Granma* yacht and establishes guerrilla operations in the Sierra Maestra mountains of southeastern Cuba.

       Colonel Ramón Barquín is arrested for organizing an antigovernment plot within the armed forces. More than 200 officers are implicated in the conspiracy.

1957: In January, Fidel Castro leads the first successful guerrilla operation against the Rural Guard post at La Plata in the Sierra Maestra foothills. In March the Directorio Revolucionario led by José Antonio Echeverría attacks the Presidential Palace in an effort to assassinate Batista. The assault fails and Echeverría is killed. In September a naval uprising in Cienfuegos leads to the temporary seizure of the local naval station.

1958: In March, Raúl Castro establishes guerrilla operations on a second front in the Sierra Cristal mountains in northern Oriente province. In the same month, the United States imposes an arms embargo against the Batista government. The attempt by the 26 of July Movement in

April to topple the Batista government through a general strike fails. In May the government launches a major offensive against guerrilla forces in the Sierra Maestra. Government military operations fail, and the guerrilla columns mount a counter-offensive. In late December, a military coup led by General Eulogio Cantillo ousts Batista.

1959:   A general strike in early January forces the military government to relinquish power to the 26 of July Movement. On January 8, Fidel Castro arrives in Havana. The following month, Castro becomes Prime Minister. In May the government enacts the agrarian reform bill.

1960:   In May, Cuba and the Soviet Union re-establish diplomatic relations. The following month, the Cuban government nationalizes U.S. petroleum properties. In July, the United States cuts the Cuban quota. Between August and October, additional North American properties are seized, including utilities, sugar mills, banks, railroads, hotels, and factories. In mid-October, the United States imposes a trade embargo on Cuba. In the course of the year, a number of mass organizations are founded, including the militia, the Committees for the Defense of the Revolution (CDRs), the Federation of Cuban Women (FMC), the Association of Young Rebels (AJR), and the National Organization of Small Peasants (ANAP).

1961:   In January the United States and Cuba sever diplomatic relations. In April the Bay of Pigs (Playa Girón) invasion fails, with some 1,200 expeditionaries taken prisoner.

The Cuban government proclaims the "Year of Education," inaugurating a national campaign to eliminate illiteracy.

1962:   October 22–28: the missile crisis.

1965:   The PSP is reorganized as the Communist Party of Cuba (PCC).

1967:   Ernesto Che Guevara is killed in Bolivia, thereby dealing Cuban advocacy of armed struggle *(foquismo)* a serious and irrevocable blow.

1968:   Fidel Castro tacitly endorses the Soviet invasion of Czechoslovakia, announcing the beginning of Cuban reconciliation with the Soviet Union.

          The Cuban government launches the "revolutionary offensive," leading immediately to the nationalization of the remaining 57,000 small businesses and preparing for the ten-million-ton crop of 1970.

1970:   The sugar harvest totals 8.5 million tons, short of the much heralded and symbolic target of ten million tons. The economy falls into serious disarray.

1971:   Poet Herberto Padilla is arrested and charged with writing counter-revolutionary literature.

1974:   *Poder Popular* (People's Power) inaugurated in Matanzas province, establishing local elections for municipal assemblies.

1975:   The Family Code is promulgated, establishing a comprehensive body of law regulating family, marriage, and divorce.

          The First Party Congress convenes.

          Cuban combat troops participate in the Angolan war for national liberation against Portugal.

1976:   The new socialist constitution is promulgated. The government is reorganized around a Council of Ministers headed by the president. The administrative units of the island are reorganized into fourteen new provinces: Pinar del Río, Havana, the city of Havana, Matanzas, Cienfuegos, Villa Clara, Sancti Spíritus, Ciego de Avila, Camagüey, Las Tunas, Holguín, Granma, Santiago, and Guantánamo.

1977:   The United States and Cuba establish limited diplomatic relations by opening interests sections in Washington and Havana.

1978:   Cuba inaugurates family reunification program, whereby Cuban exiles are permitted to return to the island for brief family visits.

1979:   At the sixth Non-Aligned Movement summit in Havana, Fidel Castro is elected president of the organization. The Soviet invasion of Afghanistan later in the year effectively neutralizes Cuban leadership of the Non-Aligned Movement.

1980:   The Mariel boatlift results in the emigration of 125,000 Cubans to Florida.

         The Second Party Congress is convened.

1983:   The U.S. armed intervention in Grenada results in the capture and arrest of Cuban construction workers and soldiers.

1985:   The United States inaugurates Radio Martí broadcasts to Cuba. Havana responds by suspending family visits to Cuba.

1986:   Limited family travel to Cuba is re-established.

         The Third party Congress is held.

1987:   Cuba and the United States sign a pact whereby Cuba agrees to accept the return of 2,000 "undesirables" who arrived during the 1980 Mariel boatlift. In return, the United States agrees to accept 20,000 new Cuban immigrants annually. News of accord sparks riots among Cuban inmates in U.S. detention centers.

Selective Guide to the
Literature

Introduction

The reader with an interest in Cuba has available a vast and varied body of literature from which to select additional reading materials. Since the century of Spanish conquest and colonization, Cuba has attracted considerable interest and study. That the island occupied a place of strategic importance in the New World balance of power made it immediately an object of political attention. Almost all modern world powers, at one time or another, in one form or another, have had interests at stake in Cuba. Successively, Spain, England, France, the United States, and the Soviet Union found themselves involved in Cuban affairs. Cuba's position at the maritime crossroads of the New World had one other effect: the island became something of an obligatory port of call for untold numbers of travelers and tourists visiting the Western Hemisphere, out of which emerged an extensive travel literature. In Cuba, a rich literary tradition took form during the eighteenth century, and expanded during the nineteenth and twentieth centuries into one of the principal forms of Cuban erudition and learning. The Cuban literature is vast, and has been especially noteworthy in such fields as history, philosophy, jurisprudence, and political economy. The Cuban revolution after 1959, lastly, brought the island renewed attention, and on an international scale. For the last three decades, the literary output on Cuba has been nothing less than prodigious.

This bibliographical essay covers a wide range of subjects and includes titles useful for further reading and research. It does not intend to be comprehensive but suggestive. Accordingly, in pursuit of these objectives, a number of criteria were employed. The material included is designed to provide a thorough treatment of the subject that is representative at once of the field and/or genre and the "state of the art." Effort has also been made to include materials that will themselves, either by way of notes or bibliography, serve as a guide to additional literature in the field. A guide to general bibliographical guides appears first, followed by general titles in English. Subsequent sections deal with more specialized works.

I. Bibliographies and Research Guides

A considerable number of general bibliographical aids are available to readers. The more specialized bibliographies have been included in the appropriate subject categories that follow. Fermín Peraza Sarausa, ed., *Bibliografías cubanas* (Washington, D.C., 1945), and Tomás Fernández Robaina, ed., *Bibliografía de bibliografías cubanas* (Havana, 1973), are comprehensive compilations of Cuban bibliographies, arranged as general bibliographies, specialized guides, library catalogues, and guides to newspapers. Carlos Manuel Trelles y Govín, ed., *Bibliografía cubana de los siglos XVII y XVIII* (2nd ed., Havana, 1927), is a comprehensive bibliographical guide to materials published during the colonial period arranged in five categories: materials written by Cubans in or out of the island; the colonial press; manuscript collections; materials written by foreigners; and cartography. Carlos Manuel Trelles y Govín, ed., *Bibliografía cubana del siglo XIX* (8 vols., Matanzas, 1911–15), is unparalleled in its completeness, organizing the nineteenth century into eight periods, with a volume for each. Each volume has annotations, notes, and brief biographical sketches. Carlos Manuel Trelles y Govín, ed., *Bibliografía cubana del siglo XX* (2 vols., Matanzas, 1916–17), is similar to the titles cited above for 1900 to 1916. Fermín Peraza Sarausa, ed., *Anuario bibliográfico cubano: bibiografía cubana* (30 vols., Havana, 1937–66), is a massive bibliographical series published on an annual basis and especially useful for the social sciences and humanities. David S. Zubatsky, ed., "United States Doctoral Dissertations on Cuban Studies in the Twentieth Century," *Cuban Studies Newsletter* IV (June 1974), 35–55, provides a compilation of dissertations on Cuba with information to assist ordering through University Microfilm, Inc.

Perhaps the best single research guide is found in Earl J. Pariseau, *Cuban Acquisitions and Bibliography* (Washington, D.C., 1970). The volume is an indispensable guide to books, manuscripts, and archives in various depositories in the United States, the United Kingdom, Spain, and Germany. Also surveyed are the strong Cuba holdings of major research libraries in the United States and Europe. Louis A. Pérez, Jr., "Record Collections at the Cuban National Archives: A Descriptive Survey," *Latin American Research Review* XII (1984), 142–56, serves as a general inventory of the principal manuscript collections, record groups, and published holdings of the National Archives of Cuba. Fermín Peraza Sarausa, ed., *Directorio de archivos y museos de Cuba* (Havana, 1945), is a brief guide to the archives and museums of Cuba. George S. Ulibarri and John P. Harrison, *Guide to Materials on Latin America in the National Archives of the United States* (Washington, D.C., 1974), is an invaluable research guide to records relating to Latin America in the U.S. National Archives. The Cuba materials are well described and elaborately discussed. Somewhat dated but still useful is the guide by Seymour Pomrenze, *Materials in the National Archives Relating to Cuba* (Washington, D.C., 1948). Louis A. Pérez, Jr., "Cuba Materials in the Bureau of Insular Affairs Library," *Latin American Research Review* XIII (1978), 182–88, is a compilation of materials in the BIA Library in the U.S. National Archives. The listing includes newspaper, unpublished manuscripts, and rare books. A.P.C. Griffin and P. Lee Phillips, eds., *List of Books Relating to Cuba with Bibliography of Maps* (Washington, D.C., 1898), is a compilation of materials housed in the Library of Congress. Lisandro Pérez, "The Holdings of the Library of Congress on the Population of Cuba," *Cuban Studies/Estudios Cubanos* XIII (Winter 1983), 69–76, provides an inventory of Library of Congress holdings relating to demography. The essays include titles for the colonial period, the period 1899–1958, and the post-revolutionary years. University of Miami Library, *Catalog of the Cuban and Caribbean Library* (6 vols., Boston, 1977), serves as a guide to one of the larger and most complete Cuba collections in the United States. Eduardo Lozano, ed., *Cuban Periodicals in the University of Pittsburgh Libraries* (Pittsburgh, 1976), serves as a useful guide to the serials collection of a library with an extensive Cuba holding.

II. Selected General Studies in English

One of the more comprehensive single volumes is Wyatt MacGaffey and Clifford R. Barnett, *Cuba* (New Haven, Conn., 1962), which deals expertly with a wide variety of subjects including history, art and literature, politics, economics, education, foreign relations, and banking and finance. A similar format is used in the Foreign Area Studies of American University under the direction of Jan Knippers Black et al., *Area Handbook for Cuba* (2nd ed., Washington, D.C., 1976). Robert Freeman Smith, *Background to Revolution* (New York, 1966), provides a useful introduction to Cuba in a collection of 26 essays designed to provide a historico-cultural context for the Cuban revolution. The essays deal with nationalism, historiography, U.S.-Cuban relations, economic development, race and slavery, political parties, labor, agriculture, and class structures. The collection also includes translations of excerpted Cuban materials otherwise unavailable in English. Waldo Frank, *Cuba, Prophetic Island* (New York, 1961), is a well-written, evocative portrayal of Cuba in the twentieth century. The account is unabashedly sympathetic with the Cuban struggle for social justice and self-determination, concerns that lead Frank to look sympathetically upon the early years of the Cuban revolution. Reginald Lloyd et al., *Twentieth Century Impressions of Cuba: Its History, People, Commerce, Industries, and Resources* (London, 1913), is a comprehensive, over-sized book dealing with virtually all aspects of early twentieth-century Cuba. Among the subjects examined are climate, economy, history, fauna and flora, mining, music, sports, literature, agriculture, mass media, and public health. José Alvarez Díaz et al., *A Study on Cuba* (Coral Gables, 1965), provides useful economic, political, administrative, and geographic data spanning the period of conquest and colonization through the early years of the revolution.

III. Travel Accounts

The travel literature provides one of the most versatile and often most insightful sources for the study of Cuba, past and present. In the hands of a discerning reader, travel accounts can yield a wealth of useful information often unavailable anywhere else. For a detailed bibliographical guide to the Cuba travel literature see Rodolfo Tro, *Cuba, viages y descripciones, 1493–1949* (Havana, 1950). Perhaps the most frequently cited work is that of Alexander von Humboldt, published in English as *The Island of Cuba*, trans. J.S. Thrasher (New York, 1856). Humboldt traveled through Cuba early in the nineteenth century, when Cuban society was in a state of transition. He was a shrewd observer of local conditions and a serious collector of statistics and data. His commentary includes observations on politics, economy, administration, population, race, slavery, commerce, and sugar production. In the 1856 English-language edition, editor/translator J.S. Thrasher updates many of Humboldt's statistics. Robert Francis Jameson, *Letters from Havana, During the Year 1820* (London, 1821), is a compilation of correspondence written during travels in Cuba. The letters provide a useful account of slavery and the slave trade. Abiel Abbot, *Letters Written in the Interior of Cuba* (Boston, 1829), is a collection of 65 letters written by Reverend Abbot in the course of an 1829 visit. The correspondence provides a wealth of information on plantation life on the eve of the transition to steam power. Similarly, David Turnbull, *Travels in the West. Cuba: With Notices of Porto Rico, and the Slave Trade* (London, 1840), is a detailed account of Cuba, with particular emphasis on the conditions of blacks, both free and slave. The Countess of Merlin (María de la Mercedes), *Viaje a La Habana* (Havana, 1974), traveled to Cuba during the 1840s. This 1974 reprint of her collected correspondence written during a visit to Havana contains perceptive comments on the private and public life of *habaneros*. She writes on such diverse themes as family life, street scenes, religion, theater, funerals, social customs, commerce, and architecture. John G.F. Wurdemann's *Notes on Cuba* (Boston, 1844) has descriptive vignettes on life in mid-nineteenth Cuba. Wurdemann was a physician and hence particularly sensitive to social conditions, health, and occupations. Richard R. Madden's *The Island of Cuba* (London, 1849) is a general account of society, the economy, commerce, religion, and education. The principal focus of Madden's account is slavery and slave conditions in mid-nineteenth century. Richard Burleigh Kimball, *Cuba and the Cubans* (New York, 1850), recounts in detail the abortive 1844 uprising in Matanzas province. It is anti-Spanish and pro-annexation in outlook. Alexander Jones, *Cuba in 1851* (New York, 1851), deals principally with agriculture, commerce, and politics. Jones was attentive to political disturbances in Cuba during the late 1840s and early 1850s. Also traveling in Cuba at that time was Scandinavian novelist Fredrika Bremer, whose *Cartas desde Cuba* (Havana, 1981) serves as a useful source of life in Havana and its suburbs. Richard Henry Dana, *To Cuba and Back* (Boston, 1859), is a vivid and detailed description of social, economic, and political conditions in western Cuba, principally Havana and Matanzas. The book has especially good descriptions of life on the estates in rural Cuba. Writer Julia Ward Howe, *A Trip to Cuba* (Boston, 1860), records details about women in colonial education, social customs, and politics. Howe's strong abolitionist sentiment made her a particularly astute and critical commentator of slavery in Cuba. Samuel Hazard, *Cuba with Pen and Pencil* (Hartford, Conn., 1871), is a richly detailed and elaborately illustrated first-hand survey of Cuban life. Half of the book deals with conditions in Havana, the other half consists of vignettes of conditions in rural Cuba and the provincial capitals. Antonio Carlo Napoleoni Gallenga, *The Pearl of the Antilles* (London, 1873), is one of the more important journalistic accounts for these years. Gallenga was a careful observer, who was visiting the island as a correspondent for the London *Times* during the Ten Years' War. His accounts deal with the character of the war, conditions of the slaves, and the world of the slaveowners. James J. O'Kelly, *The Mambí-land, or Adventures of a 'Herald' Correspondent in Cuba* (Philadelphia, 1874), is also a first-person account of Cuba during the Ten Years' War. Kelly's narrative is especially useful, for he wrote from behind the insurgent lines and lived among the Cuban rebel forces. James W. Steele, *Cuban Sketches* (New York, 1881), is a valuable memoir by a former U.S. consul in Cuba who lived on the island during and immediately following the Ten Years' War. Maturin Murray Ballou, *Due South; or, Cuba Past and Present* (2nd ed., Boston, 1886), is a perceptive and detailed account of Cuba during the latter part of the nineteenth century. It is one of the best contemporary accounts of the 1880s economic depression and the attending dislocation across the island. While not strictly a travel account, Edwin F. Atkins, *Sixty Years in Cuba* (Cambridge, Mass., 1926), nevertheless is one of the more important first-person accounts for Cuba between the 1860s through the 1910s. Atkins owned considerable sugar property in central Cuba and moved freely among the Spanish officialdom and creole planters while Cuba was a colony, among North American authorities during the U.S. occupation, and among Cuban politicians in the early republic. The memoir is an invaluable source for the study of the sugar system, plantation life, banking and finance, and the penetration of foreign capital in Cuba. Tesifonte Gallego García, *Cuba por fuera* (Havana, 1890), is an account of social and economic conditions in Cuba by a Spaniard. Critical of Cubans, the narrative is valuable for the insight into prevailing *peninsular* attitudes toward creoles. A travel account of unusual historical value is Eva Canel's *Album de la trocha* (Havana, 1897). Canel visited the battle zones during the war for independence (1895–98), recording impressions that are especially useful in the study of this period.

The Cuban war for independence (1895–98) and the U.S. war with Spain (1898) in Cuba attracted scores of travelers to the island—some of whom participated, others who simply reported. Among the better first-person accounts of the struggle by foreigners are Jean Antomarchi, *Life with the Cubans* (New York, 1898); John Black Atkins, *The War in Cuba* (London, 1899); Mario Carrillo, *In the Saddle with Gómez* (London, 1898); Grover Flint, *Marching with Gómez* (Boston, 1898); N.G. Gonzales, *In Darkest Cuba* (Columbia, S.C., 1922); and Frank R.E. Woodward, *With Maceo in Cuba* (Minneapolis, 1896). Accounts of the U.S. war with Spain include Stephen Bonsal, *The Fight for Santiago* (New York, 1899); Stephen Crane, *Wounds in the Rain* (New York, 1900); Richard Harding Davis, *The Cuban and Porto Rican Campaign* (New York, 1898); Irving Hancock, *What One Man Saw, Being the Personal Impressions of a War Correspondent in Cuba* (New York, 1898); George Kennan, *Compaigning in Cuba* (New York, 1899); John D. Miley, *In Cuba with Shafter* (New York, 1899); Kirk Munroe, *Forward March. A Tale of the Spanish-American War* (New York, 1899); George S. Musgrave, *Under Three Flags in Cuba* (Boston, 1899); and Thomas J. Vivian, *The Fall of Santiago* (New York, 1898).

The conclusion of the war and the subsequent U.S. military occupation (1899–1902) provided the occasion for a new surge of travelers to Cuba. Some were journalists who remained in Cuba after the war, some were entrepreneurs looking for investment opportunities, some were former government officials, others were simply curious tourists. This literature is especially rich and in the aggregate provides an enormously useful corpus of information about conditions in Cuba during the years after the war. Pulaski F. Hyatt and John T. Hyatt, *Cuba: Its Resources and Opportunities* (New York, 1898), is important for two reasons. First, it provides a detailed account of post-war social and economic conditions in Cuba, including agriculture, mining, forestry, trade, labor, and transportation. Second, written by two U.S. Consular agents, the book provides insight into official North American views on Cuba, for in a very real sense, this is an exhortatory work, seeking to encourage U.S. investment on the island. Franklin Matthews, *The New-Born Cuba* (New York, 1899), is a comprehensive account of the land and people at the end of the war. Charles M. Pepper, *Tomorrow in Cuba* (New York, 1899), is one of the better journalistic accounts of Cuba during the late 1890s. Richard Davey, *Cuba Past and Present* (London, 1898), is a detailed account of the conditions in Havana and the provincial capitals at the end of the war. Robert Thomas Hill, *Cuba and Porto Rico; With the Other Islands of the West*

Indies (London, 1898), has a hundred pages devoted to economic conditions in Cuba in 1898.

After the establishment of the republic in 1902, travel to Cuba increased. Tourists, vacationers, and sight-seers of all types flocked to the island. The literature is voluminous and provides insight and into changing conditions in twentieth-century Cuba. E. Ralph Estep, *El Toro: A Motor Car Story of Interior Cuba* (Detroit, 1909), is a colorful account of an early automobile journey across the island. Along the way Estep makes passing but discerning observations about conditions in rural Cuba. Charles Berchoz, *A Través de Cuba* (Sceaux, 1910), is an informative account by a geographer who traveled across the island east to west. His observations include commentaries on climate, agriculture, mining, fauna and flora, and economic conditions. Francisco González Díaz, *Un canario en Cuba* (Havana, 1916), offers a detailed account of social, economic, political, and cultural conditions in Cuba. What makes this memoir particularly useful is the running commentary on life in Cuba for immigrants, especially Spaniards and Canary Islanders *(Isleños)*. Carlos Martí, *El país de la riqueza* (Madrid, 1918), provides information on conditions in Cuba during the years of World War I, a period of rapid economic expansion and dazzling prosperity. His itinerary included all six provinces and most of the large cities; he comments on sugar, labor, immigration, politics, agriculture, and transportation. A. Hyatt Verrill, in *Cuba, Past and Present* (New York, 1920), is similarly concerned with the 1910s, with particular attention to conditions in Havana. Basil W. Wood comments on leisure, amusements, sports, and recreation in *When It's Cocktail Time in Cuba* (New York, 1928). At the same time, it offers a fascinating look into the lifestyles of the North American expatriate community in Cuba during the 1920s. Charles H. A. Forbes-Lindsay, *Cuba and Her People of Today* (Boston, 1928), is a general account politics, natural resources, and climate, designed, in the author's words, "to aid the prospective investor or settler." Olive G. Gibson's *The Isle of a Hundred Harbors* (Boston, 1940) and Sydney A. Clark's *Cuban Tapestry* (New York, 1939) are among the better travel accounts of Cuba during the 1930s. Attention is given to the varieties of Cuban culture—in the large cities, in small provincial towns, and in the interior countryside. They provide perceptive commentaries on social and economic conditions in Cuba in the wake of the depression and political tumult of the 1930s. Erna Fergusson, *Cuba* (New York, 1946), is a well-written and thoughtful account of conditions immediately after World War II. Fergusson is especially good in recording conversation and dialogue with Cubans across the island.

The triumph of the Cuban revolution in 1959 and the subsequent development of socialism produced a new wave of foreign travelers, mostly the committed, some just curious, a few critical. The literature of travel and description was particularly popular during the 1960s and 1970s, when travel to Cuba was proscribed for most. The accounts provided a steady if uneven flow of impressionistic views of life in socialist Cuba during some of the most difficult moments of the revolution. These first-person accounts are generally sympathetic, for during these years travel to Cuba was restricted largely to outsiders known for their sympathy— or, at least, lack of hostility—toward the Revolution. This caveat notwithstanding, however, many travelogues offer useful perspectives of Cuba in the throes of revolutionary change and stand as important sources of information for these years. Among the better early accounts are Warren Miller, *90 Miles from Home: the Face of Cuba Today* (Boston, 1961); Victor Franco, *The Morning After: A French Journalist's Impressions of Cuba Under Castro* (New York, 1963); and Elizabeth Sutherland, *The Youngest Revolution: A Personal Report on Cuba* (New York, 1969). Ernesto Cardenal, *In Cuba* (New York, 1974), is the result of two trips to Cuba betweeen 1970 and 1971, at the time of the ten-million-ton sugar harvest. Much of the book is in the form of recorded conversations with writers, priests, bureaucrats, workers, farmers, teachers, and senior government officials, including Fidel Castro. Sandra Levinson and Carol Brightman edited a collection of essays, memoirs, letters, poems, interviews, in *Venceremos Brigade* (New York, 1971). The collection contains detailed impressions by the young men and women who traveled to Cuba to participate in the ten-million-ton harvest. Enrique Raab, *Cuba, vida cotidiana y revolución* (Buenos Aires, 1974), is a collection of journalistic vignettes of life in socialist Cuba. Among the scenes portrayed are a wedding, the Committees for the Defense of the Revolution, popular culture, cinema, and the visit of North American volunteer workers. Joe Nicholson, Jr., *Inside Cuba* (New York, 1974), is an impressionistic account of conditions in Cuba during a six-week visit in 1972. Lee Chadwick, *Cuba Today* (Westport, Conn., 1976), is an account based on two visits to Cuba in 1971 and 1975. The author comments about life in the countryside, education, the arts, farming, and religion. Fred Ward, *Inside Cuba Today* (New York, 1978), provides an account of socialist Cuba based on seven different visits to the island. Ward traveled across the island and conducted interviews throughout his travels. The result is a detailed commentary on the economy, public health, home life, education, arts, sports, tourism, mass organizations, agriculture, and Cuban foreign policy. The volume is richly illustrated with photographs.

IV. Geography, Maps, and Atlases

Interest in Cuban geography began with Columbus, and has continued since then. For a general bibliographical guide to the older geographic literature, see Carlos Manuel Trelles y Govín, *Biblioteca geográfica cubana* (Matanzas, 1920). One of the better general geographic surveys written in the nineteenth century is Esteban Pichardo y Tapia, *Geografía de la isla de Cuba* (4 vols., Havana, 1854–55), offering a detailed geographical survey of the island. The multi-volume study provides a wealth of statistical data and detailed information about water resources, mining, climate, soil, and topography. Jacobo de la Pezuela, *Diccionario geográfico, estadístico, histórico de la isla de Cuba* (4 vols., Madrid, 1863–66), stands as a classic and indispensable work on colonial Cuba of the mid-nineteenth century. The encyclopedic study provides a wealth of information about geography, agriculture, fauna and flora, population, and trade and commerce. Pedro José Imbernó, *Guía geográfica y administrativa de la isla de Cuba* (Havana, 1891), is also an indispensable reference work for nineteenth-century Cuba. It provides information on all aspects of insular geography, municipal and provincial administration, and the economy. The book includes a discussion of provinces, cities, villages, and municipal districts as well as a description of natural resources, rivers, mountains, and lakes.

Twentieth-century geography surveys include Salvador Massip and Sarah A. Ysalque de Massip, *Introducción a la geografía de Cuba* (Havana, 1942); Levi Marrero, *Geografía de Cuba* (Havana, 1951); Antonio Núñez Jiménez, *Geografía de Cuba* (Havana, 1959); and Delia Díaz de Villar, *Geografía de Cuba* (Miami, 1965). All the aforementioned surveys share more or less a common format in their approach to the geography of the island. They deal variously with physical geography, natural resources, economic geography, climate, coasts, cartography, geology, topography, water resources, soil, and population. They also examine the specific geographic characteristics of each province. José de Jesús Márquez, *Dic-*

cionario geográfico de la isla de Cuba (Havana, 1926), provides a compilation of the island's principal geographical features, with specific attention to geological developments, natural resources, fauna and flora, and geographical sites. José Alvarez Conde, *Historia de la geografía de Cuba* (Havana, 1961), is one of the better histories of geography in Cuba, stressing ethnology, archaeology, and natural history. The volume also includes brief biographies of the most prominent Cuban geographers. José López Fernández, *Indicador-guía de la isla de Cuba, geografía política* (Havana, 1949), is somewhat dated but still a useful guide to the administrative and geo-political divisions of the island. Antonio Núñez Jiménez, *La liberación de las islas* (Havana, 1959), is a collection of essays dealing with the geographic aspects of the early agrarian reform programs of the revolution. Ernesto de los Ríos, *Nomenclatura geográfico y toponímico de Cuba* (Havana, 1970), is a catalogue of Cuban geographic names and places and geological features. Francisco A. Pardeiro, *Geografía económica de Cuba* (3 vols., Havana, 1957), is a study of the regional economy of the island with specific attention to natural resources, topography, population, and climate of all of the provinces. Yuri M. Puscharosky edited a collection of essays in *Contribución a la geología de Cuba* (Havana, 1974) dealing with geology, mines, and mineral resources of Cuba. English summaries are provided in each chapter. Gustavo Furrazola-Bermúdez, *Geología de Cuba* (Havana, 1964), is one of the more comprehensive geological surveys of Cuba, including discussions on mineral resources, land formation, and water management.

Some of the better English-language material is dated but still generally useful. A thorough treatment of Cuban geology is found in Hugh H. Bennettt and Robert V. Allison, *The Soils of Cuba* (Washington, D.C., 1928). J. W. Spencer, "Geographical Evolution of Cuba," *Bulletin of the Geological Society of America* VII (Dec. 12, 1895), 67–94, provides a good overview of the physical aspects of the island. A detailed and technical discussion can be found in R. H. Palmer, "Outline of the Geology of Cuba," *Journal of Geology* LIII (Jan. 1945), 1–34.

A number of useful atlas collections are available, each having distinctive attributes. Gerardo A. Canet Alvarez, *Atlas de Cuba* (Cambridge, Mass., 1949), is a general atlas richly illustrated with photographs, charts, graphs, and maps. Among the themes covered include history, oceanography, geology, climate, population, social structures, government, industry, mining, communications, trade, and tourism. The text is in both Spanish and English. The volume published by Cuba, Oficina Nacional de los Censos Demográfico y Electoral, *Atlas censo 1953* (Havana, 1958), provides a collection of maps based on the 1953 census, emphasizing population and demographic trends. It includes maps portraying political shifts, economic development, local natural resources, and geographic patterns. The most recent atlas was published by the Instituto Cubano de Geodesia y Cartografía, *Atlas de Cuba* (Havana, 1978). It contains a collection of 462 maps, clearly and colorfully produced. Maps dealing with physical features treat separately such diverse topics as geology, minerals, soils, climate, precipitation, forests, wildlife, and atmospheric pressure. Also included are economic, population, historical, and a variety of political and administrative maps. Salvador Massip, "Cartografía cubana. Catálogo de mapas, 1435–1820," *Revista Bimestre Cubana* XXXII (July–Dec. 1933), 90–102, 256–70, provides an annotated guide to Cuban maps, compiled from books, atlases, and manuscripts. The Cuban National Archives published *Exposición de cartografía, numismática y grabados antiguos de Cuba* (Havana, 1944), which serves as a guide to the maps, engravings, and medals available in the Cuban National Archives.

V. General Historical Surveys and Historiography

The general historical literature is enormous, and continues to expand. The standard general reference work on Cuban history is Ramiro Guerra y Sánchez et al., *Historia de la nación cubana* (10 vols., Havana, 1952). This stands as one of the most comprehensive and detailed historical works on Cuba. It is a collaborative effort of the principal Cuban historians of the period, brought together to contribute chapters on their respective areas of expertise. The work deals chronologically with prehistory, the colonial period, the independence struggles, and the republic, and thematically with literature, art, theater, foreign policy, economics, education, constitutional law, architecture, and labor. The one-volume work edited by Emilio Roig de Leuchsenring, *Curso de introducción a la historia de Cuba* (Havana, 1938), is also a collaborative project but on a more modest scale. The essays deal with selected aspects of Cuban history, including prehistory, conquest and colonization, trade and commerce, the wars for independence, and the early republic. One of the most ambitious recent undertakings, and still in progress, is Levi Marrero, *Cuba, economía y sociedad* (12 vols., Madrid, 1972–86). The most recently published volume reached the end of the eighteenth century. The completed set is projected to continue through to the present. It is a mix of historical narrative, published archival documents, statistical charts, facsimile reproductions, and bibliography. Upon completion, this massive work will no doubt stand as one of the principal reference works on Cuban history. Emeterio S. Santovenia and Raúl Shelton, *Cuba y su historia* (2nd ed., 3 vols., Miami, 1966), provides a useful survey of Cuban history that is especially good for its treatment of the nineteenth century. José Duarte Oropesa, *Historiología cubana* (5 vols., n.p., 1969–70) is a lively interpretative historical survey with emphasis on the twentieth century.

Among the better one-volume histories of Cuba are Ramiro Guerra y Sánchez, *Manual de historia de Cuba* (Havana, 1925); Calixto C. Masó, *Historia de Cuba* (Miami, 1976); Fernando Portuondo, *Historia de Cuba* (6th ed., Havana, 1965); Carlos Márquez Sterling, *Historia de Cuba, desde Colón hasta Castro* (New York, 1963); and Juan and Verena Martínez-Alier, *Cuba: economía y sociedad* (Paris, 1972). Mario Riera Hernández, *Cuba política, 1899–1955* (Havana, 1955), is a vast compendium of republican politics. The volume contains an account of every election in Cuba—national, provincial, and municipal—between 1898 and 1955, with the names of the candidates (victors and losers), for all elective offices, including the presidency, senate, house of representatives, governors, mayors, and municipal councils. The book also examines elections for constitutent assemblies (1901, 1928, and 1940), political party histories, and military coups (1933 and 1952).

Also useful are the historical surveys written in Cuba after the revolution. These include Dirección Política de las Fuerzas Armadas Revolucionarias, *Historia de Cuba* (3rd ed., Havana, 1971); Oscar Pino Santos, *Historia de Cuba: aspectos fundamentales* (2nd ed., Havana, 1964); Julio LeRiverend, *Breve historia de Cuba* (Havana, 1981); and Francisco López Segrera, *Raíces históricas de la revolución cubana (1868–1959)* (Havana, 1981).

Several important historical surveys have been published in English. Hugh Thomas, *Cuba, the Pursuit of Freedom* (New York, 1971), stands as a work of singular value. This encyclopedic tome serves as the principal English-language reference work on Cuba between 1762 and the early 1960s. Jaimes Suchlicki, *Cuba, from Columbus to Castro* (2nd. ed., Washington, D.C., 1986), provides a useful historical survey, with emphasis given to twentieth-century developments. Ramón Eduardo Ruiz,

Cuba: The Making of a Revolution (Amherst, Mass., 1968), is an interpretative account of Cuban history spanning the latter part of the nineteenth century through the first years of the Cuban revolution. Robert Freeman Smith, *What Happened in Cuba?* (New York, 1963), is a collection of documentary sources for the study of Cuban history between 1783 and 1962. The materials tend to favor U.S.-Cuban diplomatic history, but also included are documents bearing on economic development, politics, and military affairs. Federico G. Gil, "Antecedents of the Cuban Revolution," *Centennial Review of Arts and Science* VI (Summer 1972), 373–93, offers a general historical survey of twentieth-century Cuba, focusing on those factors believed to have contributed to the revolution. Somewhat dated but still useful is Walter Fletcher Johnson, *The History of Cuba* (5 vols., New York, 1920). A handy reference work is Susan Schroeder, *Cuba: A Handbook of Historical Statistics* (Boston, 1982), providing a wide range of historical data on virtually all aspects of Cuban society and economy from the sixteeenth century to the 1970s.

Other general works of interest are those that reprint previously published essays by many of Cuba's most prominent historians. Fernando Portuondo, *Estudios de historia de Cuba* (Havana, 1972), is a collection of thirty-two essays written by one of Cuba's most prolific scholars. The reprinted essays were originally published betweeen 1943 and 1972; eleven appear for the first time. The essays deal with such diverse themes as conquest and colonization, the wars for independence, education, historiography, and biographical portraits of José Martí, Antonio Maceo, and Julio Antonio Mella. José Luciano Franco, *Ensayos históricos* (Havana, 1974), is similar in format. It presents in one volume some of the more important essays published by one of Cuba's premier historians. The subjects include precursor independence movements, pirates and corsairs, slavery, Afro-Cuban conspiracies, the Ten Years' War, and a short biography of José Maceo. Some of the most important historiographical advances made in the last twenty-five years by social historian Pedro Deschamps Chapeaux were republished in *Contribución a la historia de la gente sin historia* (Havana, 1974). The essays deal variously with African slaves, Chinese coolies, and fugitive slave communities. A similar approach is used in the reprinted essays of historian-demographer Juan Pérez de la Riva, *El barracón y otros ensayos* (Havana, 1975). The subjects include population, Chinese coolies, immigration, slavery, and plantation culture.

The historiographical literature has expanded rapidly in recent years.

The revolution produced a re-examination of the principal issues of Cuban history by a new generation of historians trained in new methodologies, and concerned with new theoretical issues. Indeed, more than Cuba's future changed on January 1, 1959. So did its past. Not only did the revolution overturn Cuban society as it has previously existed—it also overturned Cuban history as it had been previously known. It created immediately the need for new information, and new interpretation of old information. These developments, in turn, served to promote the discourse on historiography on a scale never before known. Some of the most important historiographical essays include Jorge Ibarra, "Algunos problemas teóricos y metodológicos de la historiografía cubana," *Santiago* II (June 1971), 185–93; Jorge Ibarra, Manuel Moreno Fraginals, and Oscar Pino Santos, "Historiografía y revolución," *Casa de las Américas* IX (Nov. 1968–Feb. 1969), 101–15; José Antonio Portuondo, "Hacia una nueva historia de Cuba," *Cuba Socialista*, III (Aug. 1963), 24–39; and Jorge Ibarra, "Sobre las posibilidades de una síntesis histórica en Cuba," *Revista de la Biblioteca Nacional "José Martí"* XI (May–Aug. 1960), 73–103. A useful summary of early historiographical trends in Cuba can be found in Aleida Plasencia Moro, "Panorama de la historiografía cubana de 1959 a 1967," *Universidad de La Habana*, no. 186–88 (July–Dec. 1967), 91–98. For a discussion of the demographic dimensions in recent Cuban historiography see Guy Bourde, "Fuentes y métodos de la historia demográfica en Cuba (siglos XVIII y XIX)," *Revista de la Biblioteca Nacional "José Martí"* XVI (Jan.–April 1974), 21–68, and Juan Pérez de la Riva, "Estudios y estadística demográfica: tradición y realidad," *Revista de la Biblioteca Nacional "José Martí"* IX (Jan.–March 1967), 101–10. José Manuel Pérez Cabrera, *Historiografía de Cuba* (México, 1962), is a detailed discussion of the principal works dealing with Cuban history. Almost all the materials examined are from before the twentieth century. For its coverage of the historiography of the colonial period, it is unrivalled and stands as one of the standard reference works in the field.

The principal historiographical trends during the first twenty years of the revolution served as the theme of a special issue of the *Revista de la Biblioteca Nacional "José Martí"* XXVII (Jan.–April 1985). Some of the more significant aspects in the development of the new social history in Cuba are discussed in Oscar Zanetti Lecuona, "La historiografía de temática social (1959–1984)," pp. 5–17. Mildred de la Torre, "Apuntes sobre la historiografía del pensamiento cubano del siglo XIX (1959–

1984)," pp. 19–39, examines the treatment of nineteenth-century Cuban historians in post-revolutionary scholarship. Similarly, Francisco Pérez Guzmán, "La historiografía de las guerras de independencia en veinticinco años de revolución," pp. 41–61, discusses the treatment of the nineteenth-century wars of independence in the hands of a generation of Marxist scholars. Ibrahim Hidalgo Paz, "Notas acerca de la historiografía martiana en el período 1959–1983," pp. 63–78, examines the major currents of the study of José Martí, paying specific attention to the thematic content of recent literature. Alina Pérez Menéndez and Lilián Vizcaíno González, "Breve estudio historiográfico sobre el movimiento juvenil cubano (1959–1983)," pp. 79–89, is a survey of the historical literature dealing with the student movements from the 1920s through the 1950s. Ana Cairo, "La revolución del 30: una aproximación historiográfica," pp. 91–105, provides a useful discussion of the literature dealing with the revolutionary upheavals of the 1930s. Olga Portuondo Zúñiga, "La historiografía cubana acerca del período 1510–1868 en XXV anos de revolucion," pp. 119–39, provides a summary discussion of the treatment of colonial themes with specific attention to conquest and colonization, slavery, and economic development.

The historiographical reviews in English are principally article-length essays. Duvon C. Corbitt, "Cuban Revisionist Interpretations of Cuba's Struggle for Independence," *Hispanic American Historical Review* XLIII (Aug. 1963), 395–404, examines the changing interpretations in Cuba concerning the war for independence (1895–98) and the role of the U.S. armed intervention. Robert Freeman Smith, "Twentieth Century Cuba Historiography," *Hispanic American Historical Review* XLIV (Feb. 1964), 44–73, is a thorough analysis of the principal historical works and trends of Cuban historiography. The essay examines the literature within the following periodization schema: colonial history to 1800, the nineteenth century, the independence war of 1895, and the U.S. intervention, the republic, and cultural history. Louis A. Pérez, Jr., "In the Service of the Revolution: Two Decades of Cuban Historiography, 1959–1979," *Hispanic American Historical Review* LX (Feb. 1980), 79–89, is a survey of the literature written during the first twenty years of the revolution. Louis A. Pérez, Jr., *Historiography in the Revolution: A Bibliography of Cuban Scholarship, 1959–1979* (New York, 1979), is a compilation of books and articles written by Cubans during the first twenty years of the revolution.

VI. Regional and Local History

Provincial and municipal history occupies a time-honored place in Cuban historiography. Much of this genre, to be sure, consists of little more than sentimental paeans to a home province or municipality. Regional and local histories at the hands of a competent historian, however, provide a useful antidote to the more general national surveys. Julio J. LeRiverend, "De la historia provincial y local en sus relaciones con la historia de Cuba," *Santiago,* no. 46 (June 1982), 121–36, develops a well-argued essay underscoring the relationship between provincial and local history and the larger national history. Ricardo V. Rousset, *Historial de Cuba* (3 vols., Havana, 1918), is a historical survey of all six provinces, two per volume—on a *municipio* by *municipio* basis.

All provinces have been the subject of historical studies. Emeterio S. Santovenia, *Pinar de Río* (México, 1946), surveys the history of the westernmost province through the 1940s. Emphasis is given to economic developments, with particular attention to the cultivation of tobacco and the participation of Pinar del Río in the war for independence. Gloria García, *Historia de Santa Cruz del Norte* (Havana, 1971), is the history of a municipality in Pinar del Río. Francisco J. Ponte Domínguez, *Matanzas (Biografía de una provincia)* (Havana, 1959), surveys Matanzas history from prehistoric times through the twentieth century. Attention is given to a variety of themes, including economic development, slavery, colonial administration, and the struggle for independence. Carlos M. Trelles y Govín, *Matanzas en la independencia de Cuba* (Havana, 1928) provides a chronological account of the role of Matanzas province in the wars for independence between 1868 and 1898. More than half the book is of published correspondence of leading provincial figures who participated in the independence struggle. José Ramón González Pérez, *Santa Ana-Cidra: apuntes para la historia de una comunidad* (Havana, 1975), is a model study of a small town in Matanzas province.

By far the subject of greatest interest both in and out of Cuba has been the history of Havana. Julio J. LeRiverend, *La Habana (Biografía de una provincia)* (Havana, 1960), stands as one of the outstanding provincial histories. It gives a balanced treatment of political, social, economic, administrative, and cultural developments from the pre-Columbian period to the early twentieth century. Among other useful works dealing with the early history of the capital are Irene A. Wright, "The Beginnings of Havana," *Hispanic American Historical Review* V (Aug. 1922), 498–503, and Calixto E. Masó, "La Habana en el siglo XVI," *Cuba Contemporánea* XXXII (June 1923), 97–125, and July 1923, pp. 201– 25. Eduardo Anillo Rodríguez, *Cuatro siglos de vida* (Havana, 1919), traces the history of Havana from its founding in 1514 to 1919, emphasizing key developments on a yearly basis. Emilio Roig de Leuchsenring, *La Habana, apuntes históricos* (3 vols., 2nd ed., Havana, 1964), provides a comprehensive historical survey of the city and its suburbs from the early sixteenth century through the early years of the revolution. Domingo Rosain, *Necrópolis de La Habana. Historia de los cementerios de esta ciudad* (Havana, 1875), is a detailed historical account of the cemeteries of the capital, with special attention to ethnic and burial sites of various population groups in Havana. Among historical accounts of other cities and towns in Havana province are José Rivero Muñiz, *Vereda Nueva* (Havana, 1964); Elpidio de la Guardia, *Historia de Guanabacoa* (Guanabacoa, 1946); and Francisco Fina García, *Historia de Santiago de Las Vegas* (Santiago de Las Vegas, 1954).

The standard reference work for the history of Las Villas province is Rafael Rodríguez Altunaga, *Las Villas (Biografía de una provincia)* (Havana, 1955). The work is a general historical survey from conquest and colonization through the early twentieth century. Attention is given principally to politics, particularly in the nineteenth century. The two cities that have received the greatest attention in Las Villas provinces are Cienfuegos and Trinidad. Enrique Edo, *Memoria histórica de Cienfuegos y su jurisdicción* (Havana, 1943), provides a detailed study of Cienfuegos and its suburbs from the 1520s through the end of the 1880s. Emphasis is given to the nineteenth century. It is encyclopedic in proportions, and deals with almost all aspects of politics, economy, administration, church, society, culture, and education. Another valuable study of Cienfuegos is Orlando García Martínez, "Estudio de la economía cienfueguera desde la fundación de la colonia Fernandina de Jagua hasta mediados del siglo XIX," *Islas,* nos. 55–56 (Sep. 1976–April 1977), 117–70.

The city of Trinidad has also been the subject of several useful historical surveys. Francisco Marín Villafuerte, *Historia de Trinidad* (Havana, 1945), examines the history of Trinidad with special concentration on the period between the seventeenth and nineteenth centuries. Among the themes discussed include early settlement, ecclesiastical history, the wars for independence (1868–98), and social and cultural developments. The two essays by Alicia García Santana, "De la historia de Trinidad," *Islas,* no.

13 (Sep.–Dec. 1972), 51–63, and "Trinidad: arquitectura de la primera mitad del siglo XIX," *Islas,* no. 42 (May–Aug. 1972), 151–216, together with Carlos J. Zerquera, "La villa india de Trinidad en el siglo XVI," *Revista de la Biblioteca Nacional "José Martí"* XIX (May–Aug. 1977), 71–94, provide useful accounts of the history of Trinidad. Hernán Venegas Delgado, "Apuntes sobre la decadencia trinitaria en el siglo XIX," *Islas,* no. 46 (Sep.–Dec. 1973), 159–251, is a detailed account of the collapse of sugar production in the Trinidad region and the consequences of the ensuing economic depression.

Studies of other Las Villas cities include Manuel Martínez–Moles, *Epítome de la historia de Sancti Spíritus* (Havana, 1936), which offers a survey history between the year 1554 and 1934. The book is organized into several sections, including historical chronology, biography, and documents. Manuel Martínez Escobar, *Historia de Remedios* (Havana, 1944), is a comprehensive historical narrative examining politics, public administration, the local economy, and the wars of independence. The study concentrates on the colonial period through the end of the nineteenth century. Also dealing with Remedios is Hernán Venegas Delgado, "Acerca del proceso de concentración y centralización de la industria azucarera en la región remediana a fines del siglo XIX," *Islas,* no. 60 (Sep.–Dec. 1982), 63–119.

The province of Camagüey has been the subject of several noteworthy studies. Mary Cruz del Pino, *Camagüey (Biografía de una provincia)* (Havana, 1955), surveys the history of Camagüey from the period of Spanish colonization to the early 1950s. The study is well balanced, treating politics, military affairs, culture, economic development, and cultural trends. Antonio Perpina, *El Camagüey: viajes pintorescos por el interior de Cuba y por sus costas* (Barcelona, 1889), provides a first-person account of conditions in Camagüey in the latter part of the nineteenth century. Angela Pérez de la Lama, *El Camagüey legendario* (Camagüey, 1944), is a survey of local history, with particular attention to provincial folklore.

The province of Oriente and its capital, Santiago de Cuba, have also received considerable attention. Juan Jerez Villarreal, *Oriente (Biografía de una provincia)* (Havana, 1960), surveys the history of Oriente from pre-Columbian times to the 1930s, with particular emphasis on the nineteenth century and the struggle for independence. Rafael Gutiérrez, *Oriente heroico* (Santiago de Cuba, 1915) provides a detailed account of political developments during the 1880s through the early part of the war for independence. It was the first of a projected two-volume work, but the second volume was never completed. Robert B. Hoernel, "Sugar and Social Change in Oriente, Cuba, 1898–1946," *Journal of Latin American Studies* VIII (Nov. 1976), 215–49, is an excellent survey of socio-economic changes affecting the eastern province over a fifty-year span. The essay focuses on the impact of the sugar system on local communities and culture. José María Callejas, *Historia de Santiago de Cuba* (Havana, 1911), is a narrative history of the province spanning the years 1492 to 1823. César García del Pino, "Corsarios, piratas y Santiago de Cuba," *Santiago*, nos. 26–27 (June–Sep. 1977), 101–78, examines the impact of foreign attacks and the emergence of the contraband trade. Francisco Pérez Guzmán deals with the same subject from a slightly different perspective in "Documentos sobre las fortalezas militares de Santiago de Cuba," *Santiago*, nos. 26–27 (June–Sep. 1977), 181–200. Emilio Bacardí y Moreau, *Crónicas de Santiago de Cuba* (10 vols., Madrid, 1972), is a detailed chronology of the major events in the history of the eastern capital. The work spans the early years of conquest through 1898. José Ignacio Castro, *Baracoa, apuntes para su historia* (Havana, 1977), is a narrative history of the oldest Spanish settlement in Cuba, with an emphasis on the nineteenth century. G. Pelayo Yero Martínez, *Baracoa: cuna de historia y tradición* (Baracoa, n.d.), surveys the social, political, cultural, and religious aspects of Baracoa history. Regino E. Boti, *Guantánamo* (Guantánamo, 1912), provides a historical survey of the origins and development of Guantánamo with particular emphasis on political and administrative developments. José Yglesias, *In the Fist of the Revolution: Life in a Cuban Country Town* (New York, 1968), is a well written and informative account of the impact of the revolution in the town of Mayarí. Yglesias lived in the town for three months in 1967 and made detailed observations on the private and public lives of the residents. Other works dealing with local history include "Historia de Bayamo," *Universidad de La Habana*, no. 191 (July–Sep. 1968), 37–74; Juan Albanes Martínez, *Historia breve de la ciudad de Holguín* (Holguín, 1947); Ernesto de la Cueva, *Narraciones históricas de Baracoa* (3 vols., Baracoa, 1920); José A. García Castañeda, *La municipalidad holguinera. (Comentario histórico) 1898–1953* (Holguín, 1955); Ariel James, *Banes: imperialismo y nación en una plantación azucarera* (Havana, 1976); Enrique Orlando Lacalle y Zauquest, *Cuarto siglos de historia de Bayamo*

(Bayamo, 1947); Nemesio Lavie Vera, *Bayate* (Manzanillo, 1951); Antonio Núñez Jimínez, *Mayarí* (Havana, 1948); and Ricardo Varona Pupo, *Banes (Crónicas)* (Santiago de Cuba, 1930).

VII. Prehistory and Archaeology

For decades, the study of pre-Columbian Cuba was more actively pursued from outside the island than from within. This changed after the revolution, but some of the better studies are still the older works undertaken by foreigners. Daniel G. Brinton, "The Archaeology of Cuba," *American Archaeologist* II (Oct. 1898), 17–21, provides a general summary of the known sites in Cuba. Cornelius Osgood, *The Ciboney Culture of Cayo Redondo, Cuba* (New Haven, 1942), is one of the most thorough treatments of early Ciboney culture in Cuba. The most comprehensive English-language account of pre-Columbian cultures in Cuba is found in Mark Raymond Harrington, *Cuba Before Columbus* (2 vols., New York, 1921). The text is accompanied with illustrations, plates, and maps.

Among the older Cuban studies still of value are Manuel Rivero de la Calle, *Las culturas aborígines de Cuba* (Havana, 1866), and Antonio Bachiller y Morales, *Cuba primitiva* (2nd ed., Havana, 1883). José Alvarez Conde, *Arqueología indocubana* (Havana, 1956), and Rafael Azacarate Rosell, *Historia de los indios de Cuba* (Havana, 1937), provide useful general surveys of pre-Columbian cultures on the island, with particular attention to the Taíno. Ernesto E. Tabio, *Culturas más primitivas de Cuba precolombiana* (Havana, 1951), is a treatment of the Ciboney and Guanahatabey Indians. Fanny Azcuy Alón, *Psicografía y supervivencia de los aborígines de Cuba* (Havana, 1941), is a general treatment of Cuban prehistory with particular emphasis on the Taíno Indians. The author is especially concerned with the surviving contributions of Indian culture to Cuban society. Also useful as summary surveys of pre-Columbian cultures are Fernando Ortiz, *Las cautro culturas indias de Cuba* (Havana, 1943), and Felipe Pichardo Moya, *Caverna, costa y meseta. Intrepretaciones de arqueología indocubana* (Havana, 1945). One of the more recent and comprehensive studies is Ernesto E. Tabio and Estrella Rey, *Prehistoria de Cuba* (Havana, 1966). The work is an excellent summary of what is currently known about pre-Columbian cultures on the island. The authors provide a balanced treatment of the Ciboney-Guayabo Blanco, Ciboney-Cayo Redondo, the Mayarí, Sub-Taíno, and Taíno. The monograph is both a useful guide to previous research and an expression of current thinking in socialist Cuba about the island's prehistory. The essays by Estrella Rey, *Las peculiaridades de la desintegración de las comunidades primitivas cubanas* (Havana, 1969), and Juan Pérez de la Riva, "Desaparición de la población indígena cubana, "*Universidad de La Habana*, nos. 196–97 (1972), 61–84, provide the most current information concerning population, demography, and demise of the Indian cultures through the first half of the sixteenth century. Antonio Núñez Jiménez, *Cuba, dibujos rupestres* (Havana, 1975) is a study of cave drawings and paintings. Each site is examined in detail and accompanied by illustrations. Among the better regional studies are Ramón Dacal and Ernesto Navarro, *El ídolo de Bayamo* (Havana, 1972), examining pre-Columbian culture in the eastern regions of the island, and José Alvarez Conde, *Revisión indoarqueológica de la provincia de Las Villas* (Havana, 1961), which is a comprehensive treatment of the archaeology of central Cuba. José M. Guarch, *La cerámica taína de Cuba* (Havana, 1972), is a detailed account of Taíno pottery based on archaeological work in eastern Cuba. Two lengthy studies examine the contribution of Indian languages to the Spanish vernacular of Cuba: Juan L. Martín, "Sobre el dialecto cubano y el origen de las razas primitivas de América," *Revista Bimestre Cubana* XXII (Jan.–Feb. 1927), 43–62, and Juliano Vivanco y Díaz, *Las raíces de la lingüística indígena de Cuba* (Havana, 1953). Fernando Ortiz, "Historia de la arqueología cubana," *Cuba Contemporánea* XXX (Sep. 1922), 5–35, and Oct. 1922, pp. 126–64, remains one of the best overall accounts of the development of archaeology on the island from the early colonial period through the beginning of the twentieth century. The essay discusses the findings of the principal investigators, Cuban and non-Cuban alike, as well as their principal published works. The latter essay deals with museums, philology, and general Antillean archaeology.

VIII. Colonial Cuba (1512–1868)

The study of the colonial period has produced a rich and extensive literature. A number of general interpretive works provide a useful overview of the principal themes of colonial history. Gerardo Brown Castillo, *Cuba colonial: ensayo histórico social de la sociedad cubana* (Havana, 1952), is a thought-provoking work examining the origins and sources of Cuban nationality, with particular attention to the socio-economic determinants of national character. Francisco Figueras, *Cuba y su evolución colonial* (Havana, 1959), provides a general survey of colonial Cuba, stressing such themes as religion, demography, education, health, and women. One of the better works dealing with the early colonial period is Nicasio Silverio Sainz, *Cuba y la casa de Austria* (Miami, 1972), which examines Cuba under the Hapsburgs (1521–1700). Emphasis is given to administration and policy. Isabel Macías Domínguez, *Cuba en la primer mitad del siglo XVII* (Seville, 1978), is arguably the definitive work on much of the seventeenth century. The focus of the monograph is on social, economic, and commercial aspects of Cuban development, with particular attention to the rise of Havana. Cuba, Ministerio de las Fuerzas Armadas Revolucionarias, *Historia militar de Cuba: conquista de Cuba* (Havana, n.d.), is a discussion of the military aspects of the Spanish conquest through the early part of the sixteenth century. The study examines the role of artillery, the importance of cavalry units, the social origins of the *conquistadores,* and the Indian response to Spanish colonization efforts. One of the few English-language studies dealing with the early phase of colonial Cuba is Irene A. Wright, *The Early History of Cuba, 1492–1586* (New York, 1916). Based on original archival research, this study remains—more than seventy years after its appearance—one of the standard reference works for the period. Emphasis is given to political development, public administration, and international rivalries.

The subject of the international dimensions of Cuban development has long been a central theme in the Cuba historiography. Irene A. Wright, "'Rescates': With Special Reference to Cuba, 1599–1610," *Hispanic American Historical Review* III (Aug. 1920), 333–61, is a study of the illegitimate trade, largely in the eastern regions of the island, and Spanish efforts to combat it. Wright returns to this theme with a narrower focus in "The Dutch and Cuba, 1609–1643," *Hispanic American Historical Review* IX (Nov. 1921), 597–634, in which she examines the impact of Dutch traders and corsairs on Cuban economic development. Two general works dealing with contraband and corsairs are Saturnino Ullivarri, *Piratas y corsarios en Cuba* (Havana, 1931), and Kenneth R. Andrews, *The Spanish Caribbean: Trade and Plunder, 1530–1630* (New York, 1978). David Syrett edited *The Siege and Capture of Havana, 1762* (London, 1970), which provides a collection of the principal English documents pertaining to the planning, preparation, and assault against Havana. Materials include correspondence, naval communiques, official orders, and ledgers detailing the sequence of events. Francis Russell Hart, *The Siege of Havana* (Boston, 1931), provides a readable account of the English capture of the Cuban capital, with detailed attention to naval and military tactics and the strategies employed by both the English attackers and the Spanish defenders. William R. Lux, "French Colonization in Cuba, 1791–1809," *The Americas* XXIX (July 1972), 57–61, provides an overview of the French contribution to Cuban economic development in the aftermath of the Haitian revolution. Allan J. Kuethe, *Cuba, 1753–1815: Crown, Military, and Society* (Knoxville, 1986), provides an excellent study detailing the aftermath of the English occupation of Havana. This account of the Bourbon reforms in Cuba is one of the most complete studies available in English.

The history of the Catholic Church during the colonial period has been the subject of several important studies. Pedro Agustín Morell de Santa Cruz, *Historia de la isla y catedral de Cuba* (Havana, 1929), is a survey account of the general history of the Catholic church, and particularly the development of the Cathedral of Havana. Juan Martín Leiseca, *Apuntes para la historia eclesiástica de Cuba* (Havana, 1938), examines church activities from the early missionaries during the century of conquest and colonization through the early twentieth century. Ismael Teste, *Historia eclesiástica de Cuba* (4 vols., Burgos, 1969), is a comprehensive historical account of the church in Cuba. The work tends to be largely institutional in nature, concentrating on the biographies of the most prominent prelates, the workings of the religious orders, and the procedures used in formal governance and administration. The study spans the years between early colonization through the 1950s.

The development of education and the emergence of national culture during the colonial epoch have long been important themes in Cuban historiography. Antonio Bachiller y Morales, *Apuntes para la historia de las letras y de la instrucción pública en la isla de Cuba* (3 vols., Havana, 1859–61), chronicles the origins and development of the principal educational institutions in colonial Cuba. The three volumes deal separately with primary education, secondary and professional training, and university education. Pelayo González de los Ríos, *Ensayo histórico-estadístico de la instrucción pública de la isla de Cuba* (Havana, 1864), is an invaluable source for the study of public education during the colonial period. The work provides a vast amount of useful data concerning the number of schools and children in school, regional distribution of schools, and educational finances. Among the better surveys of the history of education in the colony are Arturo Montori, "La educación en Cuba," *Cuba Contemporánea* XXXVIII (May 1905), 19–60, and June 1905, pp. 121–64, and Edward D. Fitchen, "Primary Education in Colonial Cuba: Spanish Tool for Retaining 'La Isla Siempre Leal'?" *Caribbean Studies* XIV (April 1974), 105–20. Juan Manuel Dihigo y Mestre, *Influencia de la Universidad de La Habana en la cultura nacional* (Havana, 1924), is a historical survey of the educational role and development of the University of Havana, with particular emphasis on the role of the University in the development of national character. Hortensia Pichardo, *Biografía del Colegio de San Cristobal de La Habana* (Havana 1979), investigates the role and influence of one of the more important institutions of higher learning during the nineteenth century.

Cuban historiography has been concerned also with the making and makers of national culture during the colonial period. José Manuel Carbonell y Rivero, *Evolución de la cultura cubana, 1608–1927* (18 vols., Havana, 1928), is a comprehensive treatment of all aspects of Cuban cultural developments. The volumes deal variously with lyrical poetry, science, oratory, revolutionary poetry, and essays. Carlos Chain Soler, *Formación de la nación cubana* (Havana, 1968), provides an interpretive account of the development of national culture from the early sixteenth through the end of the nineteenth century. The study examines elements considered decisive in shaping Cuban nationality, including race relations, sugar production, plantation economy, and the wars for independence. Raimundo Menocal y Cueto, *Origen y desarrollo del pensamiento cubano* (Havana, 1945), is a sweeping survey of Cuban intellectual history, beginning with the early years of the colonial regime through the twentieth century. The author skillfully places the development of Cuban thought within a broader socio-economic context, stressing slavery and sugar as the vital determinants of Cuban national character. Rafael María Merchán, *Patria y cultura* (Havana, 1948), offers an account of the intellectual and artistic currents in the nineteenth century and their impact on the emergence of a national culture and nationalism. Medardo Vitier, *Las ideas en Cuba y la filosofía en Cuba* (Havana, 1970), provides one of the most complete studies examining Cuban intellectual currents in the nineteenth century. While most of the study is devoted to a discussion of political philosophies, attention is also given to economic thought, literary criticism, philosophical currents, and pedagogy. The material is given thematic unity by an analysis of the role of various schools of thought in shaping Cuban nationality. The Ateneo de La Habana published *Los maestros de la cultura cubana* (Havana, 1941), a collection of essays examining the role of several outstanding Cubans in shaping national culture, including José Agustín Caballero, Félix Varela, José Antonio Saco, Conde de Pozos Dulces, Rafael María Mendive, and José Martí. A similar format was used in Carlos M. Alvarez, *Grandes hombres de Cuba; estudio histórico-biográfico de la vida de cubanos ilustres* (Matanzas, 1928), and Emeterio S. Santovenia and Raúl M. Shelton, *Fundadores de la nación cubana* (Miami, 1967).

The subject of slavery looms large over the historiography of the colony. Some of the older works still of value are Hubert H. S. Aimes, *A History of Slavery in Cuba, 1511–1868* (New York, 1907), and Fernando Ortiz, *Los esclavos negros* (Havana, 1916). David Murray, *Odious Commerce: Britain, Spain and the Abolition of the Cuban Slave Trade* (London, 1980), provides a detailed account of the slave trade in Cuba from 1762 to its final suppression during the 1860s. The work is meticulously documented and provides one of the most detailed accounts of the slave traffic. Herbert S. Klein, *Slavery in the Americas: A Comparative Study of Cuba and Virginia* (Chicago, 1967) offers a balanced comparative study of slave conditions in both societies. The emphasis is on legal systems, education, religion, role of government, and the comparative status of free people of color. Also comparative in approach is Gwendolyn Midlo Hall, *Social Control in Slave Plantation Societies: A Comparison of St. Domingue and Cuba* (Baltimore, 1971). Hall examines the policies on slaves in both societies, with particular attention to religion, education, law, and manumission. Racism is examined as an ideological instrument of social and political control. Arthur F. Corwin, *Spain and the Abolition of Slavery in Cuba, 1817–1886* (Austin, 1967), is a detailed account of the evolution of policies that led eventually to the suppression of slavery. Franklin W. Knight, *Slave Society in Cuba During the Nineteenth Century* (Madison, 1970), provides a broad socio-economic context to his study of the emergence, expansion, and decline of the Cuban slave system. The relationship between sugar and slavery, on one hand, and politics, culture and economic development, on the other, is developed in compelling fashion. Rebecca J. Scott, *Slave Emancipation in Cuba* (Princeton, 1985), is one of the better accounts dealing with the interaction among slaves and slaveowners, merchants, government officials, and Cuban insurgents, out of which emerged the conditions leading to the abolition of slavery. Based on Cuban archival sources, the study examines the process of emancipation as it affected individual slaves and as it

occurred on individual estates. C. Stanley Urban, "The Africanization of
Cuba Scare, 1853–1855," *Hispanic American Historical Review* XXXVII
(Feb. 1957), 27–45, examines fears in the United States concerning the
modification and ultimate extinction of slavery in Cuba, which gave rise
to apprehension about racial strife and massacre of whites. Esteban Montejo, *The Autobiography of a Runaway Slave,* ed. Miguel Barnet (London, 1968), is an invaluable source on the plantation economy and slave
system in nineteenth-century Cuba. The memoir offers a first-person account of the condition of slaves, life as a fugitive slave, the impact of
abolition, and participation of Afro-Cubans in the wars for independence.
Raúl Cepero Bonilla, *Azúcar y abolición* (Havana, 1971), is a landmaark
study of the sugar system slavery and the process of emancipation. The
work examines the interaction of the class structures, the sugar economy,
slavery, and the Ten Years' War as providing the determining factors
leading to emancipation. Kenneth F. Kiple, *Blacks in Colonial Cuba,
1774–1899* (Gainesville, Fla., 1976), is a rich compilation of census data
dealing with blacks, both free and slave, through the end of the colonial
period.

IX. Wars for Independence (1868–98) and U.S. Intervention (1898–1902)

With the possible exception of the years following the triumph of the
Cuban revolution in 1959, no other period in Cuban history has attracted
and sustained such a great interest as the years between 1868 and 1902.
These were the crucial years of the development of Cuban nationality and
nationalism, heroic struggle and sacrifice, and of the very making of the
Cuban nation. Because of the involvement of the United States in these
developments, moreover, the period has attracted considerable attention
from North American scholars. The literature is voluminous. Effort here
is simply to indicate some of the most useful works. Three bibliographical compilations provide the most complete guide to this vast literature:
Aleida Plasencia, ed., *Bibliografía de la guerra de los diez años* (Havana, 1968); Miriam Hernández Soler, ed., *Bibliografía de la guerra
chiquita, 1879–1880* (Havana, 1975); and Araceli García Carranza, ed.,
Bibliografía de la guerra de independencia, 1895–1898 (Havana, 1976).
    The survey works dealing generally with the period include Ramiro
Guerra y Sánchez, *En el camino de la independencia* (Havana, 1974),

and Emilio Roig de Leuchsenring, *La guerra libertadora cubana de los treinta años: 1868–1898; razón de su victoria* (Havana, 1952). Several important works have been published examining various aspects of the Ten Years' War. Enrique Collazo, *Desde Yara hasta Zanjón* (Havana, 1967), is a reprint of the 1893 edition. The study examines the Ten Years' War from its outbreak through the final peace negotiations. The work is a compilation of essays dealing with the personalities and politics of the separatist conflict. Particular attention is given to the military aspects of the war, the role of the expatriate communities, and the process of peace negotiations. Ramiro Guerra y Sánchez, *Guerra de los diez años, 1868–1878* (2 vols., Havana, 1972), stands as one of the better accounts of the conflict. Emphasis is given to the war's socio-economic context and politico-military developments. Francisco J. Ponte Domínguez, *Historia de la guerra de los diez años* (Havana, 1958), is a detailed account of the war. The work concentrates on the political conflicts within the separatist polity, the organization of the military command, constitutional developments, foreign relations, and the ultimate collapse of the Cuban effort. Fernando Figueredo, *La revolución de Yara* (2 vols., Havana, 1969), is a reprint of the classic 1902 study. The Figueredo account is one of the more detailed accounts of the military and political aspects of the conflict. María Cristina Llerena edited *Sobre la guerra de los 10 años, 1868–1878* (Havana, 1973), a collection of more than fifty articles ranging over a wide variety of aspects of the war. The essays treat military strategy, international relations, political developments, culture, slavery, labor, economic development, and social structures. The volume is representative of current historiographical treatment of the Ten Years' War. Richard H. Bradford, *The "Virginius" Affair* (Boulder, Colo., 1980), provides a readable and scholarly account of the Spanish seizure of the ship *Virginius* in 1873 and the execution of most of its crew. Set against the backdrop of the Ten Years' War, the maritime incident increased diplomatic tensions between the United States and Spain, adding pressure for U.S. intervention in the war.

The Ten Years' War also produced a vast corpus of autobiographies, memoirs, reminiscences, and correspondence from both sides of the conflict. Some of the most important Cuban sources include Eva Ada de Rodríguez, *Hojas de recuerdos* (Havana, 1935); Francisco R. Argilagos, *Patria, páginas para la historia de Cuba, 1868–1895* (Santiago de Cuba, 1912); Francisco de Arredondo y Miranda, *Recuerdos de la guerra de Cuba (Diario de campaña, 1868–1871)* (Havana, 1962); Manuel Cruz,

Episodios de la revolución cubana (Havana, 1967); José María Izaguirre, *Recuerdos de la guerra* (Havana, 1941); and Ramón Mauricio Roa, *Con la pluma y el machete* (Havana, 1950). The Spanish accounts include Ramón Domingo Ibarra, *Cuentos históricos, recuerdos de la primera campaña de Cuba, 1868–1878* (Santa Cruz de Tenerife, 1905); Antonio del Rosal y Vázquez, *Los mambises, memorias de un prisionero* (Madrid, 1874); Antonio Rosal y Vázquez, *En la manigua, diario de mi cautivero* (Madrid, 1876); and Antonio Serra Orts, *Recuerdos de las guerras de Cuba, 1868–1898* (Santa Cruz de Tenerife, 1906).

The literature dealing with the inter-war years of 1878 to 1895 concentrates on economic conditions and Cuban preparations for a new separatist war. Luis Estévez Romero, *Desde el Zanjón hasta Baire* (2 vols., Havana, 1975), is a compilation of essays dealing with economic developments, politics, and social conditions. Earl R. Beck, "The Martínez Campos Government of 1879: Spain's Last Chance in Cuba," *Hispanic American Historical Review* LVI (May 1976), 268–89, examines short-lived efforts by Spanish reformists to make concessions to Cuba in the aftermath of the Ten Years' War. Spanish failure at reform, the author argues convincingly, set the stage for the next war and the ultimate loss of the colony. For a useful summary of economic conditions during these years, see Julio E. LeRiverend, "Raíces del 24 de febrero: la economía y la sociedad cubana de 1878 a 1895," *Cuba Socialista* V (Feb. 1965), 1–17. Two essays by Louis A. Pérez, Jr., "Toward Dependency and Revolution: The Political Economy of Cuba Between Wars, 1878–1895," *Latin American Research Review* XVIII (Spring 1883), 127–42, and "Vagrants, Beggars, and Bandits: The Social Origins of Cuban Separatism, 1878–1895," *American Historical Review* XC (Dec. 1985), 1092–121, deal with socio-economic developments.

The study of the war for independence (1895–98) has resulted in an enormously diverse and rich literature. Ramón de Armas, *La revolución pospuesta* (Havana, 1975) argues that the separatist struggle sought as much to change fundamental political, economic, and social relationships within the colony as to end colonial relationships. Philip S. Foner, *The Spanish-Cuban-American War and the Birth of American Imperialism* (2 vols., New York, 1972), is one of the more comprehensive accounts of the war for independence, carrying the account through the U.S. military occupation. Louis A. Pérez, Jr., *Cuba Between Empires, 1878–1902* (Pittsburgh, 1983), similarly examines the war for independence through the period of U.S. occupation. Emilio Roig de Leuchsenring, *Cuba no debe su independencia a los Estados Unidos* (3rd ed., Havana, 1960), is one of the earliest works to argue that Cubans had already defeated Spain at the time of the U.S. intervention in 1898. Enrique José N. Piñeyro, *Como acabó la dominación de España en América* (Paris, 1908), is a useful general survey of the war for independence through the peace negotiations culminating in the Treaty of Paris (1899). Enrique Collazo, *Cuba independiente* (Havana, 1900), examines the origins of the war, with particular emphasis on the support provided by the expatriate communities. Horatio S. Rubens, *Liberty, the Story of Cuba* (New York, 1932), is a valuable first-person account of the conflict from the vantage point of the Cuban North American legal counsel in New York. Joseph E. Wisan, *The Cuban Crisis as Reflected in the New York Press, 1895–1898* (New York, 1934), is a reliable study of the Cuban war as portrayed in New York newspapers and their role in precipitating U.S. intervention. Other useful accounts of the war include Evelio Rodríguez Lendián, *La revolución de 1895* (Havana, 1926); Miguel Angel Varona Guerrero, *La guerra de independencia de Cuba, 1895–1898* (3 vols., Havana, 1946); Herminio Portell Vilá, *Historia de la guerra de Cuba y los Estados Unidos contra España* (Havana, 1949); and René E. Reyna Cossío, *Estudios histórico-militares sobre la guerra de independencia de Cuba* (Havana, 1954).

Like the Ten Years' War, the 1895–98 conflict produced a large number of first-person accounts. Some of the better Cuban memoirs include Luis de Radillo y Rodríguez, *Autobiografía o episodios de su vida histórico-político-revolucionaria, desde el 24 de febrero de 1895 hasta el 1° de enero de 1899* (Havana, 1899); Ricardo Batrell Oviedo, *Para la historia; apuntes autobiográficos de la vida de Ricardo Batrell Oviedo* (Havana, 1912); Rodolfo Bergés, *Cuba y Santo Domingo. Apuntes de la guerra de Cuba, de mi diario en campaña, 1895–96–97–98* (Havana, 1905); Bernabé Boza, *Mi diario de la guerra, desde Baire hasta la intervención americana* (2 vols., Havana, 1900–1904); José Castillo y Zúñiga, *Autobiografía* (Havana, 1910); Wilfredo Ibrahim Consuegra, *Diario de campaña; guerra de independencia, 1895–1898* (Havana, 1928); Horacio Ferrer, *Con el rifle al hombro* (Havana, 1950); Máximo Gómez, *Diario de campaña* (Havana, 1940); Orestes Ferrara, *Mis relaciones con Máximo Gómez* (2nd ed., Havana, 1942); José Isabel Herrera, *Impresiones de la guerra de independencia* (Havana, 1948); Eduardo F. Lores y Llorens, *Relatos históricos de la guerra del 95* (Havana, 1955); Luis Rodolfo Miranda, *Diario de la campaña del comandante Luis Rodolfo Miranda* (Havana, 1954); Santiago C. Rey, *Recuerdos de la guerra, 1895–*

1898 (Havana, 1931); Manuel Piedra Martell, *Memorias de un mambí* (Havana, 1966); Juan Pedro de la Rosa Quijano, *Diario de la guerra del año 1895 al 1898* (Havana, 1953); Eduardo Rosell y Malpica, *Diario del teniente coronel Eduardo Rosell y Malpica (1895–1897)* (2 vols., Havana, 1949–50); Avelino Sanjenís, *Memorias de la revolución de 1895 por la independencia de Cuba* (Havana, 1913), Luis Lagomasino Alvarez, *Reminiscencias patriotas* (Manzanillo, 1902); José Silviera Llorens y Maceo, *Con Maceo en la invasión* (Havana, 1928); and Fermín Valdés Domínguez, *Diario de soldado* (4 vols., Havana, 1972–74).

Spanish accounts include Manuel Corral, *El desastre; memorias de un voluntario en la campaña de Cuba* (Barcelona, 1899); Ricardo Burguete, *¡La guerra! Cuba. (Diario de un testigo)* (Barcelona, 1902); Valeriano Weyler, *Mi mando en Cuba* (5 vols., Madrid, 1910–11); Manuel Bueno y Javaloyes, *El 1er batallón de María Cristina en el Camagüey* (Matanzas, 1897); El Capitán Verdades, *Historia negra: relato de los escándalos ocurridos en nuestra ex-colonias durante las últimas guerras* (Barcelona, 1899); Antonio Díaz Benzo, *Pequeñeces de la guerra de Cuba por un español* (Madrid, 1897); and Antonio Vesa y Fillart, *Voluntarios de la Isla de Cuba. Historial del Regimiento Caballería de Jaruco y de su estandarte* (Barcelona, 1908).

In many ways, Cuban events of 1878–98 are inseparable from the lives of the principal revolutionary leaders, most notably José Martí, Antonio Maceo, Máximo Gómez, and Calixto García. The literature on Martí alone reaches vast proportions, and the works mentioned here are intended only to introduce the reader to the principal English language titles. The best overall bibliographical guide to this voluminous literature is found in the *Anuario del Centro de Estudios Martianos,* an annual publication by the Biblioteca Nacional "José Martí" in Havana. The standard English-language Martí biographies include Félix Lizaso, *Martí, Martyr of Cuban Independence* (Albuquerque, 1953), and Jorge Mañach, *Martí, Apostle of Freedom* (New York, 1950). Among the better critical studies are Richard Butler Gray, *José Martí, Cuban Patriot* (Gainesville, Fla., 1962); John M. Kirk, *José Martí, Mentor of the Cuban Nation* (Gainesville, Fla., 1983); Manuel Pedro González, *José Martí, Epic Chronicler of the U.S. in the Eighties* (Chapel Hill, 1986); Peter Turton, *José Martí, Architect of Cuba's Freedom* (London, 1986); and Christopher Abel and Nissa Torrents, eds., *José Martí, Revolutionary Democrat* (Durham, N.C., 1986). Some of Martí's writings appear in several English translations: Juan de Onis, ed., *The America of José Martí: Selected Writings* (New York,

1953); Philip S. Foner, ed., *Inside the Monster: Writings on the United States and American Imperialism* (New York, 1975), and by the same editor, *Our America: Writings on Latin America and the Struggle for Cuban Independence* (New York, 1977); and Luis A. Baralt, ed., *Martí on the U.S.A.* (Carbondale, Ill., 1966).

The better biographies of Antonio Maceo are José Luciano Franco, *Antonio Maceo: apuntes para una historia de su vida* (3 vols., Havana, 1975); Raúl Aparicio, *Hombradía de Antonio Maceo* (Havana, 1967); Daniel Corzi Pi, *Historia de Antonio Maceo; el Aníbal cubano* (Havana, 1943); and José Antonio Portuondo, *El pensamiento vivo de Maceo* (Havana, 1960). In English, Philip S. Foner, *Antonio Maceo: The 'Bronze Titan' of Cuba's Struggle for Independence* (New York, 1977), provides a useful biography of Maceo, with emphasis on the years between 1895 and 1896. Magdalen M. Pando, *Cuba's Freedom Fighter, Antonio Maceo; 1845–1896* (Gainesville, Fla., 1980), is a sympathetic account dealing principally with the latter years of Maceo's life.

Several biographies of Máximo Gómez include Leonardo Griñán Peralta, *El carácter de Máximo Gómez* (Havana, 1946); Leopoldo Horrego Estuch, *Máximo Gómez, libertador y ciudadano* (Havana, 1948); Ramón Infiesta, *Máximo Gómez* (Havana, 1937); and Benigno Souza, *Máximo Gómez, el generalísimo* (Havana, 1936). The better Calixto García biographies are Juan José E. Casasús, *Calixto García (el estratega)* (Havana, 1942), and Aníbal Escalante Beatón, *Calixto García, su campaña en el 95* (Havana, 1946).

The years of the United States occupation of Cuba have been examined from several different perspectives. One of the better overall accounts of these years is found in David F. Healy, *The United States in Cuba, 1898-1902* (Madison, 1963). This study emphasizes the dynamics of policy formulation, the means by which U.S. policy was determined, and the interaction between U.S. officials and Cuban authorities. James H. Hitchman, *Leonard Wood and Cuban Independence, 1898–1902* (The Hague, 1971), and Rafael Martínez Ortiz, *General Leonard Wood's Government in Cuba* (Paris, 1920), provide generally sympathetic accounts of the U.S. military occupation under the administration of Leonard Wood. Enrique Collazo, *Los americanos en Cuba* (2nd., Havana, 1972), is a reprint of the 1905 critical study of U.S. administration. Emilio Roig de Leuchsenring, *La lucha cubana por la república, contra la anexión y la Enmienda Platt, 1899–1902* (Havana, 1952), deals with Cuban efforts to establish self-determination during the occupation and resist the imposition of the

Platt Amendment. Jack C. Lane, "Instrument for Empire: The American Military Government in Cuba, 1899–1902," *Science and Society* XXXVI (Fall 1972), 314–30, argues that the period of U.S. occupation was utilized to prepare the way for future control of the island. Louis A. Pérez, Jr., "Insurrection, Intervention, and the Transformation of Land Tenure Systems in Cuba, 1895–1902," *Hispanic American Historical Review* LXV (May 1985), 229–54, examines the combined effects of the war for independence and the agrarian policies of the U.S. military government on Cuban land tenure forms. Two essays deal with the education policies of the military government: Edward D. Fitchen, "The United States Military Government: Alexis E. Frye and Cuban Education, 1898–1902," *Revista/Review Interamericana* II (Summer 1972), 123–49, and Louis A. Pérez, Jr. "The Imperial Design: Politics and Pedagogy in Occupied Cuba, 1899–1902," *Cuban Studies/Estudios Cubanos* XII (Summer 1982), 1–19.

X. The Plattist Republic, 1902–34

A number of general works provide a useful overview to this period. Somewhat dated but still useful is Charles E. Chapman, *A History of the Cuban Republic* (New York, 1927). This study concentrates largely on Cuban political developments and foreign policy issues. Similarly, Russell H. Fitzgibbon, *Cuba and the United States, 1900–1935* (Menasha, Wis. 1935), is also still useful. Contrary to its title, the Fitzgibbon work is devoted more to internal political developments than foreign policy issues. Historian Irene A. Wright's *Cuba* (New York, 1910) provides useful if perhaps somewhat jaded commentary on conditions on the island during the early years of the republic. As a permanent resident in Cuba, Wright served at once as chronicler of her time and scholar of the past, often with effective results. Louis A. Pérez, Jr., *Cuba Under the Platt Amendment, 1902–1934* (Pittsburgh, 1986), examines the impact of the Platt Amendment on the class formations, state structures, and political culture. Julio E. LeRiverend, *La república: dependencia y revolución* (3rd ed., Havana, 1973), provides a survey of the early republican period. Jorge Ibarra, *Un análisis psicosocial del cubano: 1898–1925* (Havana, 1985), is a psycho-cultural study of the early republican years. A collection of nine essays deal with such diverse and different topics as culture and folklore, the social content of national poetry, pathogenesis in the republic, and plastic arts as a function of political culture. Carleton Beals, *The Crime of Cuba* (Philadelphia, 1933), is a critical study of Cuban politics, U.S. policies, and, in particular, the Machado regime. Extremely useful for its perceptive analysis of the major issues of the early decades of the republic is Rafael Martínez Ortiz, *Cuba, los primeros años de independencia* (2 vols., Paris, 1921). A two-volume anthology published under the auspices of the Grupo de Estudios Cubanos at the University of Havana, *La república neocolonial* (Havana, 1975–79) deals expertly with a variety of themes, including labor, population and demography, economic development, the armed forces, and the opposition to Machado.

Some of the more specialized studies for this period include David A. Lockmiller, *Magoon in Cuba: A History of the Second Intervention, 1906–1909* (Chapel Hill, 1938), Allan Reed Millett, *The Politics of Intervention: the Military Occupation of Cuba, 1906–1909* (Columbus, Ohio, 1968), and Teresita Yglesias Martínez, *Cuba: primera república, segunda ocupación* (Havana, 1977), all of which deal variously with the government of Tomás Estrada Palma (1902–6), the August 1906 rebellion, and the U.S. occupation (1906–9). Bernardo Merino and F. de Ibarzabal, *La revolución de febrero. Datos para la historia* (Havana, 1918), is a detailed account of the Liberal party uprising of 1917. The study examines the disputed election of 1916 that led to the rebellion, the development of conspiracy, the outbreak of the conflict, and the eventual government victory. Along similar lines, Louis A. Pérez, Jr., *Intervention, Revolution, and Politics in Cuba, 1913–1921* (Pittsburgh, 1978), examines the years of the government of President Mario G. Menocal, with particular attention to the 1917 revolution, the U.S. intervention, and economic development during the years of World War I. The two volumes by León Primelles, *Crónica cubana, 1915–1918* (Havana, 1955) and *Crónica cubana, 1919–1922* (Havana, 1957), are indispensable reference works for these years. All aspects of Cuban society are treated, including politics, economics, labor, education, sports, religion, jurisprudence, crime, and foreign policy. Included too are lengthy bibliographical listings for each topic.

The years between 1923 and 1933 witnessed rapid social, economic, political, and intellectual change on the island, culminating ultimately in the revolutionary tumult of the early 1930s. Among the more comprehensive accounts of these years are Lionel Soto, *La revolución del 33* (3 vols., Havana, 1977), and Luis E. Aguilar, *Cuba 1933: Prologue to Rev-*

olution (Ithaca, NY, 1972). Harry Swan, "The Nineteen Twenties: A Decade of Intellectual Change in Cuba," *Revista/Review Interamericana* VIII (Summer 1978), 275–88, is an informed discussion of the artistic and cultural regeneration in Cuba and its impact on national politics. Dealing with similar themes but in greater detail are the two works by Ana Cairo Ballester, *El Grupo Minorista y su tiempo* (Havana, 1978) and *El Movimiento de Veteranos y Patriotas* (Havana, 1976). A useful overview of these years is found in Carlos Ripoll, *La generación de 23 en Cuba* (New York, 1968).

Dictatorship, economic depression, and rising nationalism converged in fateful fashion in Cuba during the late 1920s and early 1930s. The revolutionary upheavals of the period are examined from a variety of vantage points by scholars both in the United States and in Cuba. Jules R. Benjamin, "The 'Machadato' and Cuban Nationalism, 1928–1932," *Hispanic American Historical Review* LV (Feb. 1975), 66–91, traces the development of Cuban nationalist sentiment during the second Machado term. The essay discusses the role of labor, students, intellectuals, communists, and middle-class reformers in the shaping of the new nationalism. Olga Cabrera and Carmen Almododar edited *Las luchas estudiantiles universitarias, 1923–1934* (Havana, 1975), bringing together in one volume a collection of documents, newspaper articles, manifestos, and excerpts from university publications relating to student political activism of the decade. Also useful for explaining aspects of student politics during these years is Jaime Sucklicki, *University Students and Revolution in Cuba, 1920–1968* (Coral Gables, 1969), and Ladislao González Carbajal, *Mella y el movimiento estudiantil* (Havana, 1977).

A substantial literature exists dealing with the succession of governments under Gerardo Machado, Carlos Manuel de Céspedes, and Ramón Grau San Martín. Alberto Lamar Schweyer, *Como cayó el presidente Machado* (Madrid, 1934), is a critical study of U.S. policy toward Machado. Lamar Schweyer was a Machado advisor, and hence in a position to observe and record the events leading to the president's downfall. One of the more interesting accounts of this period, but one also to be used with circumspection, is the chronicle by President Gerardo Machado himself, *Memorias: ocho años de lucha* (Miami, 1982). M. Franco Varona, *La revolución del 4 de septiembre* (Havana, 1934), is an informed journalistic account of the events of 1933, with particular emphasis on the sergeants' revolt and the Grau government. Ricardo Adam y Silva, *La gran mentira. 4 de septiembre de 1933* (Havana, 1947), is a detailed chronicle of the sergeants' revolt told by a former officer of the Cuban army. Other useful accounts of these events include Enrique Lumen, *La revolución cubana, 1902–1934* (Mexico, 1934); Carlos Manuel de la Cruz, *Proceso histórico del machadato* (Havana, 1935); and Gonzalo de Quesada y Miranda, *¡En Cuba Libre! Historia documentada y anecdótica del machadato* (2 vols., Havana, 1938).

A sizable body of literature exists on the Platt Amendment. The best guide to this material is found in James H. Hitchman, "The Platt Amendment Revisited: A Bibliographical Survey," *The Americas* XXIII (April 1967), 343–69. Useful discussions dealing with the origins, formulation, and intent of the Platt Amendment are James E. Scott, "The Origin and Purpose of the Platt Amendment," *American Journal of International Law* III (July 1914), 585–91, and Lejenue Cummins, "The Formulation of the 'Platt Amendment,'" *The Americas* (April 1967), 370–89. Ambrosio López Hidalgo, *Cuba y la enmienda Platt* (Havana, 1921), M. Márquez Sterling, *Proceso histórico de la enmienda Platt (1897–1934)* (Havana, 1941), and Luis Machado y Ortega, *La enmienda Platt, estudio de su alcance e interpretación y doctrina sobre su aplicación* (Havana, 1922), are Cuban critiques of the interpretation and application of the Platt Amendment. Emilio Roig de Leuchsenring, *Historia de la enmienda Platt* (2nd ed., 2 vols., Havana, 1961), is a critical and detailed examination of United States-Cuban relations under the aegis of the Platt Amendment. The study analyzes the evolution and the changing interpretations of the amendment through its abrogation in 1934.

XI. Cuba, 1934–58

The literature for these years reveals several skewed patterns. Scholarly interest continued in the late 1930s. The period between 1940 and 1952, however, represents a lacuna of serious proportions. Comparatively little research has been undertaken for these years. Conversely, the literature for the period of the 1950s, particularly the revolutionary struggle against Batista government, approaches vast proportions. The subsiding passions of the revolutionary espirit of the 1930s is well chronicled in José A. Tabares del Real, *La revolución del 30: sus dos últimos años* (3rd ed., Havana, 1975). Niurka Pérez Rojas, *El movimiento estudiantil universitario de 1934 a 1940* (Havana, 1975), is one of the better accounts of student politics for these years. Samuel Farber, *Revolution and Reaction in Cuba, 1933–1960* (Middletown, Conn., 1976), provides one of the more comprehensive studies of these years. Farber examines in depth the development and evolution of political and social groupings that emerged from the revolutionary experience of the 1930s and their part in the events of the 1950s. Diego de Pereda, *El nuevo pensamiento político de Cuba* (Havana, 1943), is a collection of political speeches, proclamations, and policy statements made by nearly one hundred leading political figures the years 1930s and early 1940s. R. Hart Phillips, *Cuba, Island of Paradox* (New York, 1959), provides a perceptive and insightful first-person account of years between the early 1930s through the triumph of the Cuban revolution. Phillips served as the resident *New York Times* correspondent in Havana for most of these years, a position that provided a unique vantage point from which to observe and record conditions across the island. Raymond Leslie Buell et al., *Problems of the New Cuba* (New York, 1935), is one of the most comprehensive appraisals of conditions in Cuba in the aftermath of economic depression, political upheavals, and social dislocation. The study treats virtually all aspects of Cuban national life, including economic development, politics, population, family, public health, social welfare, education, banking and finance, labor, agriculture, commerce, and transportation. E. Vignier and G. Alonso, *La corrupción política y administrativa en Cuba, 1944–1952* (Havana, 1963), is an indictment of the Auténtico administrations of Ramón Grau San Martín (1944–48) and Carlos Prío Socarrás (1948–52), based on a reprinting of news articles from these years.

The literature of the revolutionary struggle during the 1950s is as vast as it is varied. For a general guide to the literature on the revolutionary war, see Louis A. Pérez, Jr., *The Cuban Revolutionary War, 1953–1958: A Bibliography* (Metuchen, N.J., 1976). Ovidio García Reguero, *Cuba: raíces y frutos de una revolución* (Madrid, 1970), provides a historical survey of the years immediately preceding the triumph of the Cuban revolution. Robert Taber, *M-26, the Biography of a Revolution* (New York, 1961), is one of earliest accounts of the revolutionary war. Taber served as a correspondent in Cuba who lived among the guerrillas of the 26 of July movement. Ramón L. Bonachea and Marta San Martín, *The Cuban Insurrection, 1952–1959* (New Brunswick, N.J., 1973), examines in detail the role and participation of a number of revolutionary organizations and the part played by several revolutionary leaders. The study argues that the victory over Batista was as much the result of the urban resistance as it was the rural guerrillas. Andrés Suárez, "The Cuban Revolution: the Road to Power," *Latin American Research Review* VII (Fall 1972), 5–29, is an analysis of the varieties of interpretations concerning the triumph of the 26 of July. Among the subjects examined include the attack on Moncada barracks, the landing of *Granma*, the origins and expansion of the guerrilla movement, the 1958 general strike, the role of the communist party, and the impact of Fidel Castro. Mario Llerena, *The Unsuspected Revolution: The Birth and Rise of Castroism* (Ithaca, N.Y., 1978), is a political memoir of the anti-Batista struggle by an early supporter—and later opponent—of Fidel Castro. Charles D. Ameringer, "The Auténtico Party and the Political Opposition in Cuba, 1952–1957," *Hispanic American Historical Review* LXV (May 1985), 327–51, provides an account of the mainstream opposition to the Batista government. Alfred L. Padula, Jr., "Financing Castro's Revolution, 1956–1958," *Revista/ Review Interamericana* VIII (Summer 1978), 234–46, is a detailed analysis of the means employed to finance the cost of the armed struggle against Batista. Padula argues that the larger share of donations originated with the middle class. John Dorschner and Roberto Fabricio, *The Winds of December* (East Rutherford, N.J., 1980), is perhaps the most complete and certainly most multifaceted account of the last month of the armed struggle against Batista in 1958. Based on published materials, State Department records, and 200 interviews with eyewitnesses and participants from all sides, the authors provide a compelling chronicle of the political, diplomatic, and military aspects of the final days of the Batista regime. Other useful accounts of the revolutionary war are Merle Kling, "Cuba: A Case Study of a Successful Attempt to Seize Political Power by the Application of Unconventional Warfare," *The Annals of the American Academy of Political and Social Science* CCCXLI (May 1962), 42–52; Special Operations Research Office, *Cast Study in Insurgency and Revolutionary Warfare: Cuba, 1953–1959* (Washington, D.C., 1963); Armando Giménez, *Sierra Maestra. La revolución de Fidel Castro* (Buenos Aires, 1959); Rafael Otero Echeverría, *Reportaje a una revolución. De Batista a Fidel Castro* (2nd ed., Santiage de Chile, 1959); and Rafael San Martín, *El grito de la Sierra Maestra* (Buenos Aires, 1960).

XII. The Cuban Revolution, 1959–Present

In the nearly three decades since the triumph of the revolution, developments in Cuba have inspired a literature of truly vast proportions. So

prodigious, in fact, has this scholarship become, that it, in turn, has served
to summon into existence an equally vast body of bibliographical compilations and research guides. Indeed, the publication of bibliographical
aids has itself become an enterprise of no small scope, without which
research on the Cuban revolution would be a daunting proposition indeed.
Among the more useful general guides to this literature include Edwin
Lieuwen and Nelson P. Valdés, eds., *The Cuban Revolution: A Research
Guide, 1959–1969* (Albuquerque, 1971); Jaime Suchlicki, ed., *The Cuban Revolution: A Documentary Bibliography, 1952–1968* (Coral Gables, 1968); Research Institute for Cuba and the Caribbean, University of
Miami, *Revolutionary Cuba: A Bibliography* (Coral Gables, Fla., 1959);
Gilbert V. Fort, ed., *The Cuban Revolution of Fidel Castro Viewed from
Abroad* (Lawrence, Kansas, 1969); Fermín Peraza Sarausa, ed., *Revolu-
tionary Cuba: A Bibliographical Guide* (3 vols., Coral Gables, Fla., 1966–
1968); Irving Louis Horowitz, "Cuba Libre? Social Science Writings on
Postrevolutionary Cuba, 1959–1975," *Studies in Comparative International Development* X (Fall 1975), 101–23; and Ronald Chilcote, ed.,
Cuba, 1953–1978: A Bibliographical Guide to the Literature (2 vols.,
White Plains, N.Y., 1986). By far the most complete and continually
current biographical guide to the Cuba literature is *Cuban Studies/Estu-
dios Cubanos,* published annually by the Center for Latin American Studies at the University of Pittsburgh.

Perhaps no other aspect of the literature is as extensive as the works
dealing with the politics and performance of the Cuban revolution in the
nearly three decades since the seizure of power. No other period has so
closely and continuously engaged the attention of writers and researchers.
Several early surveys of these years are still useful for the general reader.
These works deal generally with the period immediately prior to and after
the triumph of the revolution. Andrés Suárez, *Cuba: Castroism and Communism* (Cambridge, Mass., 1967), discusses the radicalization of the
revolution and the early transition period to socialism. Loree Wilkerson,
Fidel Castro's Political Programs from Reformism to 'Marxism-Leninism'
(Gainesville, 1965), studies the ideological transformation of the Cuban
revolution with attention to three themes: the early political influences on
Fidel Castro, the original reform programs of the revolution, and the
radicalization of the revolution. K. S. Karol, *Guerrillas in Power. The
Course of the Cuban Revolution* (New York, 1970), is a detailed account
of the political antecedents of the revolution through the years of the ten-
million-ton crop. James O'Connor, *The Origins of Cuban Socialism* (Ith-

aca, 1970), surveys more than a decade of socio-economic achievements of the revolution. Leo Huberman and Paul M. Sweezy's *Socialism in Cuba* (New York, 1969) provides a sympathetic general account of conditions in Cuba after 1959, with attention to health, education, and economic development strategies. Richard R. Fagen, *The Transformation of Political Culture in Cuba* (Stanford, 1969), is an important study of the early years of the Cuban transition to socialism, focusing on the literacy campaign of 1961, the schools of revolutionary instruction, and the establishment of the Committees for the Defense of the Revolution (CDRs). The early role of the communist party is examined in Samuel Farber, "The Cuban Communists in the Early Stages of the Cuban Revolution: Revolutionaries or Reformists?" *Latin American Research Review* XVIII (1983), 59–84. Farber argues that the PSP was overtaken by the radicalism of the revolutionary leadership and that it was the bold leadership of Fidel Castro and not the strategically and tactically conservative PSP, that accounts for the success of communism in Cuba. Along similar lines, Edward González, "Castro's Revolution, Cuban Communist Appeals, the Soviet Response," *World Politics* XXI (Oct. 1968), 39–68, examines the early period of the revolution with emphasis on shifting coalitions between the PSP and the 26 July Movement. Maurice Zeitlin and Robert Scheer, *Cuba: Tragedy in Our Hemisphere* (New York, 1963), is a well-written overview of Cuban developments through the early 1960s set against a larger historical context. Claude Julien, *La revolución cubana* (Montevideo, 1961), examines the years immediately preceding and following the triumph of the revolution. The study is particularly useful in its account of the armed struggle. Luis Emiro Valencia, *Realidad y perspectivas de la revolución cubana* (Havana, 1961), and Silvio Frondizi, *La revolución cubana; su significación histórica* (Montevideo, 1960), are surveys of political, social, and economic conditions in pre-revolutionary Cuba set against the programs through which the revolution sought to change these conditions.

Almost from the outset of the revolution, the literature acquired several notable characteristics. During the early years, the period in which the revolution evolved from its humanist origins to its Marxist-Leninist destination, the principal themes of the literature reflected the policy debate and political dispute prevailing in the United States and Cuba. As the revolution radicalized, it polarized, and produced a literature that was largely polemical in format and policy-oriented in function. Sides were quickly chosen, and almost from the outset the Cuba literature became possessed of one of its most enduring qualities—engagement. Defenders and detractors participated in lengthy, often passionate, disputation over the virtues and vices of revolutionary developments in Cuba. An extensive literature resulted to exonerate one side or excoriate the other. Among English-language works, the defenders included C. Wright Mills, *Listen, Yankee: The Revolution in Cuba* (New York, 1960); Jean-Paul Sartre, *Sartre on Cuba* (New York, 1961); Herbert L. Matthews, *The Cuban Story* (New York, 1961); William Appleman Williams, *The United States, Cuba, and Castro* (New York, 1961); Leo Huberman and Paul Sweezy, *Cuba, Anatomy of a Revolution* (New York, 1961); J. P. Morray, "Cuba and Communism," *Monthly Review* XIII (July-Aug. 1961), 3–55; and J. P. Morray, *The Second Revolution in Cuba* (New York, 1962). The detractors included Nathaniel Weyl, *Red Star Over Cuba* (New York, 1972); Daniel James, *Cuba, the First Soviet Satellite in the Americas* (New York, 1961); Irving P. Pflaum, *Tragic Island: How Communism Came to Cuba* (Englewood Cliff, N.J., 1961); and Edwin C. Stein, *Cuba, Castro, and Communism* (New York, 1962). A useful orientation to the early debate about the Cuban revolution is found in the books written by Theodore Draper, *Castro's Revolution: Myths and Realities* (New York, 1962) and *Castroism: Theory and Practice* (New York, 1965).

A part of this polemic, but largely independent of the policy debate, were the writings produced by Cuban exiles. A vast émigré literature emerged in the months and years following the fall of Fulgencio Batista and the radicalization of the revolution, and was itself divided into two distinct categories. One body of writing consisted almost entirely of the books and articles produced by the first group of political refugees from Cuba, principally *batistianos*—Cubans who had supported Fulgencio Batista and/or were members of the discredited government. They constituted the first wave of exiles during the early part of 1959. The writings of this group represented a polemic within a polemic. The literature was certainly anti-revolutionary. But it also tended toward rancor and recrimination, as this first wave of displaced and dispossessed Cubans sought to locate responsibility for the calamity that had overtaken them. Some blamed the army command for military defeat. Some blamed Batista for political incompetence. Some accused the United States of abandoning loyal allies. But all agreed that something had gone terribly wrong, and that someone was responsible. It became a highly charged atmosphere as Cubans in exile engaged in a spirited exchange of epithets. It was an intense debate, often in public and always acrimonious, one that occurred entirely within the community of exiled *batistianos*. This environment provided special incentive for former public officials to set down for the record the part they played in the last crucial months and years of the Batista government. Personal accounts came to constitute in quantity and quality an impressive part of the early literature dealing with the revolution. Key political and military leaders during the Batista years chronicled their accounts, often in great detail, as a means of vindicating their part in the ill-starred regime. They surfaced in the form of books, tracts, and articles. But it was on the pages of the exile press and periodicals that the debate acquired its most formidable proportions. So extensive is the literature published in this fashion that it is perhaps not an undue exaggeration to suggest that through research on the closing years of the Batista government would be impossible without consultation with this material. Regrettably, however, there are no bibliographical guides to this extensive literature, making its use a task of no small amount of effort and enterprise. This literature includes Alberto Baeza Flores, *Las cadenas vienen de lejos* (Mexico, 1959); Florentino Rosell Leyva, *La verdad* (Miami, 1960); José Suárez Núñez, *El gran culpable* (Caracas, 1963); and Orestes Ferrara, *Memorias: una mirada sobre tres siglos* (Madrid, 1975). Fulgencio Batista, *Cuba Betrayed* (New York, 1962), is an important source for the study of the political conflict during 1950s. In this work, the former president provides valuable insight into government political policies, military operations, and foreign relations. The volume also contains large numbers of excerpts of personnel correspondence, official memoranda, and military communiques. Some of the periodical and newspaper literature includes Pedro A. Barrera Pérez, "Por qué el ejército no derrotó a Castro," *Bohemia Libre* LIII (July 9, 1961–Sept. 3, 1961); Rafael Guás Inclán, "Todos erramos," *Cuba Libre* (Miami) II (Oct. 28, 1960); and Florentino E. Rosell Leyva, "Confirme el acerdo Batista-Cantillo," *La Crónica* (Aug. 16, 1960).

Shortly thereafter, a second wave of political refugees augmented the swelling ranks of Cubans in exile, and the émigré literature took a slightly different turn. The newest group included early supporters of the revolution, many who subsequently became disaffected and disenchanted during the period of radicalization and thereupon defected. Many had been active in the anti-Batista struggle, either in the 26 of July Movement or other revolutionary organizations. Some had served briefly in various positions of government. A few were high ranking colleagues and collaborators of Fidel Castro. This literature was only slightly less acrimonious than *batistiano* writing. It directed its ire toward the leadership of the revolution, stressing ideological questions and leveling charges of the revolution betrayed. This literature is represented by Teresa Casuso, *Cuba and Castro* (New York, 1964); Manuel Urrutia Lleo, *Fidel Castro and Company, Inc.* (New York, 1984).

Together, these two categories of exile literature serve as important sources for the study of the final years of the Batista government and the early years of the revolution. In a very real sense, these writings fall within a broader genre of literature, that of memoirs and reminiscences. Almost all key actors in the Cuban drama have written a memoir in some form, and in the aggregate, these first-person accounts serve as an important source of information for the early years of the Cuban revolution.

A third source of the first-person narrative, and perhaps the most extensive body of writings, is the literature published in Cuba. Indeed, nowhere do memoirs provide as much and diverse a source of information as in the scores of published accounts of the revolutionary war between 1956 and 1958. Virtually all key Rebel Army commanders and urban resistance leaders penned their recollections and memoirs of the revolutionary struggle in the period following immediately the triumph of the revolution. Perhaps among the most well known is Ernesto Che Guevara, *Reminiscences of the Cuban Revolutionary War* (New York, 1969). The memoir provides insight into the organization, leadership, and strategy of the rebel army between 1956 and 1958. Neill Macaulay, *A Rebel in Cuba: An American's Memoir* (Chicago, 1970), is a first-person account of the revolutionary war in Pinar del Río. Luis Pavón, eds., *Días de combate* (Havana, 1970), is an anthology of first-person accounts by participants in various anti-government movements. Other autobiographical accounts of the armed struggle include Faure Chomón, *La verdadera historia del asalto al Palacio Presidencial* (Havana, 1959); Camilio Cienfuegos, *Páginas del diario de campaña* (Havana, 1962); José Quevedo Pérez, *La batalla del Jigüe* (Havana, 1973); José Pardo Llada, *Memoria de la Sierra Maestra* (Havana, 1960). Like the exile literature, the vast proportion of first-person accounts of the revolutionary war appeared principally in periodicals and newspapers. Numerous memoirs were serialized in *Bohemia*, *Verde Olivo*, *Juventud Rebelde*, *Granma*, *El Mundo*, and *Revolución*.

Perhaps no other single aspect of the Cuban revolution looms as large as the presence of Fidel Castro. From the earliest days of the guerrilla struggle, Fidel Castro has been the object of enormous curiosity and the subject of large numbers of biographies. Few heads of state have been the subject of more biographies during their lifetime—something all the more remarkable considering that the state over which Fidel Castro presides is hardly the size of Florida, with barely a population of 10 million. After thirty years, interest in Fidel Castro remains high, and biographies continue to appear. Indeed, so extensive is this literary output as to constitute itself a genre of the literature of the revolution. Biographies of Fidel Castro typically conform to three types: panegyrics and polemics, which exalt or excoriate; scholarly studies, which also exalt or excoriate; and accounts by former insiders, who especially exalt or excoriate. Some of the early biographies were printed during the early weeks and months of the revolution, when Cuban euphoria was at its peak and opinion about Fidel Castro was neither unfavorable nor unequivocal. He was everyone's hero. Some of the early biographies include Luis Conte Agüero, *Fidel Castro, vida y obra* (Havana, 1959); Gerardo Rodríguez Morejón, *Fidel Castro, biografía,* (Havana, 1959); Jules Dubois, *Fidel Castro, Rebel-liberator or Dictator?* (Indianapolis, 1959); and Giuliano Ferrieri, *Fidel Castro* (Milan, 1961). Critical biographies followed, and include Miguel A. G. Colzadilla, *The Fidel Castro I Knew* (New York, 1971), and José D. Cabús, *Castro ante la historia* (México, 1963). Maurice Halperin, *The Rise and Decline of Fidel Castro* (Berkeley, 1972), examines the period of the consolidation of the revolution between 1959 and 1964. Herbert L. Matthews, *Fidel Castro* (New York, 1969), provides a sympathetic political biography, chronicling the emergence of Fidel Castro from an aspiring officeseeker in the early 1950s to the consolidation of the revolution a decade later. Enrique Meneses, *Fidel Castro* (New York, 1968), concentrates on the period during the late 1950s and early 1960s. Lionel Martin, *The Early Fidel: Roots of Castro's Communism* (Secaucus, N.J., 1978), concentrates on Fidel Castro's youth, up to the triumph of the insurgency. One of the more recent biographies is Peter G. Bourne, *Fidel: A Biography of Fidel Castro* (New York, 1986). Bourne's training as a psychiatrist has him emphasizing Fidel Castro's "psychological characteristics." By far the most ambitious recent biography is Tad Szulc, *Fidel: A Critical Portrait* (New York, 1986). The volume was completed with the collaboration of Cuban officials themselves, including Fidel Castro, and provides one of the most detailed works available in English.

Translations of Fidel Castro's work are available in several publications. Rolando E. Bonachea and Nelson P. Valdés, eds., *Revolutionary Struggle, 1947–1958. Selected Works of Fidel Castro* (Cambridge, Mass.,

1972), provides an invaluable collection of the translated materials by Fidel Castro from his early days at the University of Havana through the triumph of the revolution. The materials include speeches, manifestos, newspaper and magazine articles, letters, messages, and interviews. The introductory essay serves as an excellent biographical sketch of this early period in the life of Fidel Castro. Martin Kenner and James Petras, eds., *Fidel Castro Speaks* (New York, 1969), includes translations of major speeches between 1960 and 1968. A complete guide to the early published literature by Fidel Castro is found in Nelson P. Valdés and Rolando E. Bonachea, "The Making of a Revolutionary: A Fidel Castro Bibliography," *Latin American Research Review* V (Summer 1970), 83–88.

Interviews and oral histories serve as important sources of information about Cuba. The formal interview technique has found extensive use with Cuban leaders, past and present, in and out of Cuba. It is a format, too, that lends itself well to the style of Fidel Castro. Indeed, several book-length interviews have been published in recent years that provide interesting personal and political portraits of the *Jefe Máximo*. Lee Lockwood, *Castro's Cuba, Cuba's Fidel* (New York, 1969), is based on extensive interviews covering a wide range of subjects, including Cuban relations with the United States and the Soviet Union, land reform, industrialization, education, censorship, and political prisoners, human rights, and the revolutionary struggle against Batista. Frank Mankiewicz and Kirby Jones, *With Fidel: A Portrait of Castro and Cuba* (New York, 1975), is the product of thirteen hours of interviews over the course of three visits to Cuba between 1974 and 1975. Subjects include foreign policy, the armed forces, the relationship between the party and the state, and the missile crisis. The most recent work of this type is Frei Betto, *Fidel y religión* (Havana, 1985). While dealing principally with Fidel's view of religion and church-state relations, the Betto interview provides considerable insight into the childhood and the early adulthood of the Cuban head of state.

During the late 1960s and the 1970s, the scholarship on the Cuban revolution underwent several significant changes. Increasingly, the literature moved toward specialized research. This is not to suggest that the polemical tide of the early years abated. It did not. Nor did the prevailing partisanship end. Indeed, much of the scholarship on Cuba has been unabashedly hostile toward the revolution.

These changes themselves foretold of other developments. The failure

of the United States to overthrow the Cuban government in April 1961 at
the Bay of Pigs, followed by the North American promise to not invade
Cuba after the missile crisis seemed to guarantee the permanence of the
revolution. These were years, too, in which the consolidation of power
in Cuba was complete. With a measure of security guaranteed from without and with the revolution uncontested from within, other changes followed. Cuban willingness to permit foreign scholars to travel to the island
served to stimulate new research.

The revolution appeared to have acquired something of permanence,
and the socialist experiment if not entirely flourishing was nevertheless
still functioning. Research shifted to the study of the consolidation of
political power and the Cuban transition from capitalism to communism.
This literature stressed such diverse aspects as political mobilization,
leadership—specifically the role of Fidel Castro—and domestic developmental policies. Several new trends characterized the Cuba literature. On
one hand, larger, scholarly syntheses began to appear. The revolution
was completing its second decade and a sufficient body of data had accumulated to permit a broad, narrative approach to Cuban developments.
These works typically adopted a historical format, tracing the origins of
the revolution to the colonial past and/or the early twentieth-century republic. The narrative was carried through the early 1970s and tended to
focus upon political, economic, and social aspects of the revolutionary
change in Cuba. Several English-language surveys of socialist Cuba provide useful overviews for these years. Jorge I. Domínguez, *Cuba: Order
and Revolution* (Cambridge, Mass., 1978), provides a sweeping panorama of Cuban developments during the twentieth century, with emphasis
on conditions in Cuba after 1959. Edward González, *Cuba Under Castro:
The Limits of Charisma* (New York, 1974), concentrates on the evolution
of the Cuban revolution beginning with antecedents of the late nineteenth
century. Carmelo Mesa-Lago, *Cuba in the 1970s: Pragmaticism and Institutionalization* (Albuquerque, N.M., 1974), examines the social and
economic policies of the revolution through the 1970s. Lowry Nelson,
Cuba: The Measure of a Revolution (Minneapolis, 1972), is a general
discussion of the impact of the revolution on agriculture, economic diversification, labor, education, religion, and social services. Juan M. del
Aguila, *Cuba: Dilemmas of a Revolution* (Boulder, Colo., 1984), is a
general survey discussion of Cuba before and after the revolution. Particularly useful for these years are the oral histories produced by Oscar
Lewis, Ruth Lewis, and Susan Rigdon. *Four Men: Living the Revolution.*

An Oral History of Contemporary Cuba (Urbana, Ill., 1977), has autobiographical accounts by four men of different ages, occupations, races,
and social origins; in *Neighbors: Living the Revolution. An Oral History
of Contemporary Cuba* (Urbana, Ill., 1978), the same authors present
oral histories of tenants of an apartment complex in Havana. Men and
women, white and black, young and old, all neighbors at the time of the
interviews, provide a rich and textured series of reminiscences. Through
their lives emerges a compelling view of pre- and post-revolutionary Cuba.
Among the many aspects of daily life in Cuba discussed are male/female
relations, religion, politics, race and class antagonisms, family life, work,
and recreation. Also useful in this regard is Douglas Butterworth, *The
People of Buena Ventura: Relocation of Slum Dwellers in Post-
Revolutionary Cuba* (Urbana, Ill., 1980), which is an ethnographic study
of a working-class community in Havana, providing insight into the private and public aspects of family life in socialist Cuba.

By the late 1970s, the literature shifted its attention Cuban efforts at
institutionalization in the aftermath of the 1970 debacle. J. David Ed-
wards, "The Consolidation of the Cuban Political System," *World Affairs* CXXIX (Summer 1976), 10–16, examines the institutionalization of
the revolution from the standpoint of revolutionary zeal, ideology, and
leadership. Attention is given to the character of the 1976 constitution,
people's power, and the expanding role of the party and the armed forces.
William M. LeoGrande, "Continuity and Change in the Cuban Political
Elite," *Cuban Studies/Estudios Cubanos* VIII (July 1978), 1–31, concentrates on the shifting patterns of political elites through the membership of the Central Committee of the Cuban Communist Party (PCC).
Nelson P. Valdés, "Revolution and Institutionalization in Cuba," *Cuban
Studies/Estudios Cubanos* VI (Jan. 1976), 1–37, examines the process
by which the revolutionary leaders seized political power, consolidated
control, and subsequently directed the revolution toward the path of institutionalization. Max Azicri, "The 'Institucionalización' of Cuba's
Revolution," *Revista/Review Interamericana* VIII (Summer 1978), 247–
62, discusses the conditions and consequences of Cuban institutionalization strategies. Marifeli Pérez-Stable, "Institutionalization and Workers
Response," *Cuban Studies/Estudios Cubanos* VI (July 1976), 31–54,
discusses labor's response to the process of institutionalization. Other works
treating various aspects of the institutionalization include Irving Louis
Horowitz, "Institutionalization as Integration: the Cuban Revolution at
the Age of Twenty," *Cuban Studies/Estudios Cubanos* IX (July 1979),

84–90; Edward González, "The Party Congress and Poder Popular: Orthodoxy, Democratization, and the Leader's Dominance," *Cuban Studies/Estudios Cubanos* VI (July 1976), 39–65.

Several aspects of socialist Cuba have been the subject of specialized interest over the years. A large body of literature has emerged dealing with the various aspects of the Cuban health care system during the last twenty-five years. A useful point of departure is Roberto E. Hernández, "La atención médica en Cuban hasta 1958," *Journal of Inter-American Affairs* XI (Oct. 1969), 533–57. Hernández argues that the pre-revolutionary medical system, while deficient in some areas, was basically providing adequate attention to the population at large. Emphasis is on hospital care, infant mortality, number and distribution of physicians, and the training of medical personnel. Ross Danielson, *Cuban Medicine* (New Brunswick, N.J., 1979), is one of the more complete surveys of medicine in Cuba. Beginning with the colonial period, the work examines the development of medical practice in Cuba, with emphasis on health care after the revolution. Sergio Díaz-Riquets, *The Health Revolution in Cuba* (Austin, 1983), studies health conditions in the twentieth century, with emphasis on mortality rate. Z. Stein and M. Susser, "The Cuban Health System: A Trial of a Comprehensive Service in a Poor Country," *International Journal of Health Services* II (Fall 1972), 551–66, is a generally favorable assessment of Cuban health programs, with attention to the training of health personnel, preventive medicine, and the development of comprehensive health care. Nelson P. Valdés, "Health and Revolution in Cuba," *Science and Society* XXXV (Fall 1971), 311–31, examines health care and health delivery systems in Cuba, comparing developments in post-revolutionary Cuba with the pre-revolutionary period. Topics examined include nutrition, infant mortality, the training of health personnel, and the prevention and treatment of disease. Two essays by Vicente Navarro, "Health, Health Planning, and Health Services in Cuba," *International Journal of Health Services* II (Summer 1972), 397–432, and "Health Services in Cuba: An Initial Approach," *The New England Journal of Medicine* CCIIC (Nov. 9, 1972), 954–59, examine the manner in which equality in the distribution of health resources has affected mortality and morbidity patterns. Particular attention is given to Cuban efforts to minimize inequalities in the availability and consumption of health resources through the following means: centralization of in-patient services, a decentralization of ambulatory services, and increased use and training of paramedical and auxiliary personnel within the health services system.

Robert N. Ubell, "High-Tech Medicine in the Caribbean: 25 Years of Cuban Health Care," *The New England Journal of Medicine* CCCIX (Dec. 8, 1983), 1468–472, surveys health conditions and health delivery systems in Cuba after 1959. The focus of the essay is on polyclinics, provincial hospitals, medical education, and clinical research. Willis P. Butler, "The Undergraduate Education of Physicians in Cuba," *Journal of Medical Education* IIL (Sept. 1973), 846–57, examines the ideological orientation of undergraduate physician training in Cuba, including such issues as the social context of medical education, the dissemination of health care, and the reduction of professional elitism. Willy de Geyndt, "The Cuban Hospital System," *World Hospitals* VIII (July 1972), 279–84, examines the Cuban hospital network, including its theoretical basis, rural hospitals, hospital management, and maternal and childrens' hospitals. "A Promise Kept: Health Care in Cuba," *Cuba Review* VIII (March 1978), 3–38, is a special issue devoted entirely to aspects of the health delivery system in Cuba. Among the topics examined are mental health, occupational illness, hospital administration, polyclinic organization, dental clinics, and government health policies. Antonio M. Gordon, Jr., "The Nutriture of Cubans: Historical Perspective and Nutritional Analysis,"*Cuban Studies/Estudios Cubanos* XIII (Summer 1983), 1–34, compares Cuban nutriture with other Third World countries. The essay examines food production efficiency of local food industries and the character of the Cuban diet. Along similar lines, Howard Handelman, "Cuban Food Policy and Popular Nutritional Levels," *Cuban Studies/Estudios Cubanos* XI–XII (July 1981–Jan. 1982), 127–46, discusses nutrition policy and consumption patterns after the revolution. The essay traces government efforts to redistribute available food supplies equitably as a means to guarantee all citizens an adequate diet.

An equal amount of attention has been directed to the Cuban educational system. A useful bibliographical guide to this literature is found in Larry R. Oberg, *Contemporary Cuban Education: An Annotated Bibliography* (Stanford, 1980). Carl J. Dahlman, *The Nation-Wide Learning Sytem in Cuba* (Princeton, N.J., 1973), is a comprehensive examination of education in Cuba with emphasis on pre-revolutionary education, the development of education policy after 1959, informal education (literacy campaign, adult education), formal education (primary, secondary, vocational, professional, and university), and an evaluation of overall performance. Jonathan Kozol, *Children of the Revolution* (New York, 1978), is a first-person account of educational programs in Cuba, with attention to anti-illiteracy campaigns, adult education, and the administration of the public school system. Marvin Leiner, *Children Are the Revolution: Day Care in Cuba* (New York, 1974), is a thorough study of pre-school centers in Cuba, with attention to social goals of day care, organization, nutrition and health care, instruction, and the physical setting. Karen Wald, *Children of Che: Childcare and Education in Cuba* (New York, 1977), provides a comprehensive account of day care and primary education. Max Figueroa, Abel Prieto, and Raúl Gutiérrez, *The Basic Secondary School in the Country: An Education Innovation in Cuba* (Paris, 1974), examines the secondary rural school programs, with emphasis on curriculum, administration, and teacher training. Samuel Bowles, "Cuban Education and the Revolutionary Ideal," *Harvard Educational Review* XLI (Nov. 1971), 472–500, analyzes the means used to transmit new social values through education, with particular emphasis on four basic objectives: economic growth, elimination of U.S. hegemony, attainment of egalitarian norms, and the creation of the "new man." Gerald H. Read, "The Cuban Revolutionary Offensive in Education," *Comparative Education Review* XIV (June 1970), 131–43, discusses the development of Cuban education in the first ten years of the revolution. Attention is given to the larger design of revolutionary education, particularly its efforts to universalize schooling and disseminate Marxist-Leninist values, and to the relationship between pedagogical theory and practice. Rolland G. Paulston, "Cultural Revitalization and Educational Change in Cuba," *Comparative Education Review* XVI (Oct. 1972), 474–85, discusses the theoretical determinants of Cuban educational policy. Jonathan Kozol, "A New Look at the Literacy Campaign in Cuba," *Harvard Educational Review* II (Aug. 1978), 341–77, examines the historical development of the literacy campaign during the early 1960s. Emphasis is given to the logistical aspects of the program, the recruitment and training of volunteer teachers, and the development of institutional methods that were deemed both pedagogically appropriate and politically correct. Eugene F. Provenzo, Jr., and Concepción García, "Exiled Teachers and the Cuban Revolution," *Cuban Studies/Estudios Cubanos* XIII (Winter 1983), 1–15, is a study of Cuban teachers in exile and their attitudes toward the educational system during the early years of the revolution, thereby providing a useful view of the transition in education between the late 1950s and early 1960s. Lisandro Pérez, "The Demographical Dimensions of the Educational Problems in Socialist Cuba," *Cuban Studies/Estudios Cubanos* VII (Jan. 1977), 33–57, examines the relationship between population growth, primary school enrollment since 1959, and the development of Cuban educational strategies.

Religion in socialist Cuba has been addressed by several scholars. Alice L. Hageman and Philip E. Wheaton, eds., *Religion in Cuba: A New Church in a New Society* (New York 1971), presents a series of essays and interviews dealing variously with the impact of the revolution on church institutions, the changing role of the church under socialism, the impact of socialism on theology, and historical perspectives. Margaret E. Crahan, "Salvation Through Christ: Religion in Revolutionary Cuba," in Daniel H. Levine, ed., *Churches and Politics in Latin America* (Beverly Hills, Calif., 1980), 238–66, examines religion in Cuba both before and after the revolution, arguing that the weakness of religion after 1959 was as much a function of its weakness before 1959 as it was of government policy. "Church, Theology, and Revolution," *Cuba Review* V (Sept. 1975), 3–34, is a special issue devoted almost exclusively to religion, treating such topics as changes in theology, the condition of Presbyterian and Methodist churches, and the changing role of the Catholic clergy in Cuba. Mateo Jover, "The Cuban Church in a Revolutionary Society," *LADOC* IV (April 1974), 17–36, examines the changing relationship between state and church, with focus on the interaction between church hierarchy, lay leaders, Catholic organizations, practicing Catholics, and various state agencies. Donna Katzin, "Cuban Jews: Continuity and Change," *Cuba Resource Center Newsletter* III (Dec. 1973), 25–28, reports on condition of the Jewish community in Cuba and how it has fared since the revolution.

Human rights in post-revolutionary Cuba is the subject of several publications. Lars Schoultz, *Human Rights and United States Policy Toward Latin America* (Princeton, 1981), provides a general appraisal of the impact of U.S. policy on human rights. Discussion of Cuba is within the larger, hemispheric context, assessing pre- and post-revolutionary conditions. The International Commission of Jurists, *Cuba and the Rule of Law* (Geneva, 1962), is an early critical study of conditions in Cuba three years immediately after the triumph of the revolution, dealing with such themes as constitutional law, criminal legislation, offenses against property, and infringement of freedom of the press, freedom of travel, and religious freedom. Inter-American Commission on Human Rights, *Report on the Situation of Political Prisoners and Their Relatives in Cuba* (Washington, D.C., 1963), is a general indictment of the Cuban revolutionary government for violation of civil liberties. The central focus of the report is on the condition of political prisoners and the situation of women in prison. The General Secretariat, Organization of American States, *The Situation of Human Rights in Cuba* (Washington, D.C., 1983), is critical of Cuban policy toward political rights, personal security, right to life, religious freedom, right of residence and movement, and right to work. United States Congress, House of Representatives, *Human Rights in Cuba* (Washington, D.C., 1984), is the transcript of House hearings held in June 1984 discussing human rights conditions in Cuba. The generally critical testimony was provided by representatives of the State Department, Cuban exiles, and representatives from Amnesty International and Americas Watch.

Anthologies on the Cuban revolution have also flourished. Indeed, the anthology has offered one of the most versatile and valuable formats through which to publish new research and report the findings of works in progress. One of the better general anthologies, if now somewhat dated, is Carmelo Mesa-Lago, ed., *Revolutionary Change in Cuba* (Pittsburgh, 1971), which presents a collection of eighteen essays arranged in three parts: policy, economy, and society. Among the themes examined in policy include the role of the communist party, consolidation of political power, and the influence of foreign countries. The section on the economy treats central planning, labor, international economic relations, and strategies of development. The essays on society deal with education, religion, art, theater, cinema, and literature. Jaime Suchlicki, ed., *Cuba, Castro, and Revolution* (Coral Gables, 1972), includes essays dealing with the historical antecedents of the revolution, pre-revolutionary social structures, politics, Cuban-Soviet-Latin American relations, and Cuban ties with Latin American communist parties. Jorge I. Domínguez, *Cuba: Internal and International Affairs* (Beverly Hills, Calif., 1982), is a collection of five essays dealing with politics, revolutionary elites, mass media, economic planning, foreign policy, and U.S.-Cuba relations. Rolando E. Bonachea and Nelson P. Valdés, eds., *Cuba in Revolution* (Garden City, N.Y., 1972), gives attention to the revolutionary war, bureaucracy, mobilization strategies, economic policy, sugar production, labor, health, education, and culture. Irving Louis Horowitz, ed., *Cuban Communism* (New Brunswick, N.J., 1977), is a collection of sixteen essays dealing with race and class, education, military, agriculture, urban planning, economic policy, and foreign relations. Sandor Halebsky and John M. Kirk, eds., *Cuba: Twenty-Five Years of Revolution, 1959–1984* (New York, 1985), is a quarter-century retrospect on the Cuban revolution, examining education, social programs, women, religion, popular culture, cinema, literature, economic planning, labor, historiography, foreign policy, and U.S.-Cuban relations. Ronald Radosh, ed., *The New Cuba: Paradoxes and Potentials* (New York, 1976), includes essays examining the role of the communist party, culture, U.S.-Cuba relations, and economic development. James Nelson Goodsell, ed., *Fidel Castro's Personal Revolution in Cuba, 1959–1973* (New York, 1975), reprints essays and excerpts dealing with various aspects of the revolution, including politics, economic development, culture, and foreign policy. Bertram Silverman, ed., *Man and Socialism in Cuba: The Great Debate* (New York, 1971), examines the debate over the efficacy of moral incentives through a variety of viewpoints including those of the Cuban officals, European economists, and North American academics.

Current information on recent developments in Cuba can be obtained from a variety of sources. *Cuba Update* (New York) is a bi-monthly newsletter published by the Center for Cuban Studies, providing translations of major speeches and news summaries from Cuba. The *U.S.-Cuba Bulletin* (Washington, D.C.) is a quarterly publication concentrating on U.S.-Cuban relations and matters relative to the Cuban émigré community in the United States. The Cuba Resource Center publishes the *Cuba Times* bi-monthly, providing a digest of news stories and longer feature articles dealing with current social, economic, and political developments in Cuba.

The most useful Cuban publication is the weekly *Bohemia* (Havana) dealing with current events, sports, art, entertainment, and international news. *Cuba Internacional* (Havana) is a monthly devoted to current developments in culture, education, politics, and the economy. *Verde Olivo* (Havana) is a weekly magazine published by the Ministry of the Revolutionary Armed Forces (MINFAR) and devoted to issues relevant to the education and training of the Cuban military, including weaponry, culture, news, and history. Issues relating to labor are discussed in bi-weekly *Trabajo* (Havana). The Writers and Artists Union publishes the quarterly *Unión* (Havana), dealing with current issues in Cuban literature and art. The two principal daily newspapers are *Juventud Rebelde* (Havana) and *Granma* (Havana). *Granma* also publishes an English-language summary edition on a weekly basis.

XIII. Immigration and Emigration

Immigration has developed into an expanding field of research and writing. Older studies tend to concentrate on Spanish immigration to Cuba. Carlos Martí, *Los catalanes en América: Cuba* (Barcelona, 1920), surveys Catalan immigration to Cuba during the late colonial period and the eary republic. José M. Alvarez Acevedo, *La colonia española en la economía cubana* (Havana, 1936), is a detailed analysis of the economic impact of the Spanish community in Cuba between 1899 and 1933. Duvon C. Corbitt, "Immigration in Cuba," *Hispanic American Historical Review* XXII (May 1942), 280–88, examines Spanish efforts in the nineteenth century to promote white immigration to counterbalance the increasing number of African slaves. A general study of immigration in late nineteenth- and early twentieth-century Cuba is provided in José Sixto de Sola, "Los extranjeros en Cuba," *Cuba Contemporánea* VIII (June 1915), 105–28. Francisco Carrera y Justiz, *El municipio y los extranjeros. Los españoles en Cuba* (Havana, 1904), examines the Spanish predominance in local political affairs during the course of the nineteenth century. Francisco Federico Falco, *La inmigración italiana y la colonización en Cuba* (Turin, Italy, 1912), is a general study of Italian immigration in the nineteenth century, with particular attention to the role of Italians in the Cuban wars of independence. Chinese and East Indian migration has been the subject of several studies. Duvon C. Corbitt, *A Study of the Chinese in Cuba, 1847–1947* (Wilmore, Ky. 1971), provides a general overview of Chinese immigration, tracing the transformation from coolie labor in the nineteenth century to successful merchants and professionals in the twentieth. Denise Helly, *Idéologue et ethnicitié: Les Chinois Macao à Cuba, 1847–1886* (Montreal, 1979), is a survey of Chinese contract laborers through abolition. Mary Turner, "Chinese Contract Labour in Cuba, 1847–1874," *Caribbean Studies* XIV (July 1974), 66–81, examines the presence of Chinese laborers in sugar production with emphasis on population and demographic trends. Two studies examine the role of the Chinese in the Cuban struggles for independence: Juan Pastrana Jiménez, *Los chinos en las luchas por liberación cubana (1847–1930)* (Havana, 1963), and Gonzalo de Quesada, *The Chinese and Cuban Independence* (Leipzig, Germany, 1925). Some of the more recent research on Asian migration to Cuba includes Rafael López Valdés, "La inmigración indostana a Cuba y sus antecedentes en las Antillas," *Santiago* XXV (March 1977), 161–92, and the essays by Juan Pérez de la Riva: "Aspectos económicos del trafico de culíes chinos a Cuba, 1853–1873," *Universidad de La Habana,* no. 173 (May–June 1965), 95–116; "Los culíes chinos y los comienzos de la inmigración contratados en Cuba (1844–1847)," *Revista de la Biblioteca Nacional "José Martí,"* (Jan.–Dec. 1963), 57–86; "Demografia de los culíes chinos (1853–1874)," *Revista de la Biblioteca Nacional "José Martí"* XVII (May –Aug. 1975), 74–88; and "El tráfico de culíes chinos," *Revista de la Biblioteca Nacional "José Martí"* VI (July–Dec. 1964), 47–57.

The study of immigration into Cuba during the twentieth century has concentrated on the influx of West Indian contract labor through the early 1930s. Two excellent surveys provide an overview of this aspect of Caribbean migration: Juan Pérez de la Riva, "La inmigración antillana en Cuba durante el primer tercio del siglo XX," *Revista de la Biblioteca Nacional "José Martí"* XVII (May–Aug. 1975), 74–88, and Franklin W. Knight, "Jamaican Migrants and the Cuban Sugar Industry, 1900–1934," in Manuel Moreno Fraginals, Frank Moya Pons, and Stanley L. Engerman, eds., *Between Slavery and Free Labor: The Spanish-Speaking Caribbean in the Nineteenth Century* (Baltimore, Md., 1985), 84–114. Mats Lundahl, "A Note on Haitian Migration to Cuba, 1890–1934," *Cuban Studies/Estudios Cubanos* XII (July 1982), 21–36, examines economic pressures in Haiti and the need for cheap agricultural labor in Cuba as the crucial factors in Haitian migration to Cuba.

The subject of Cuban emigration from the island has a long tradition in Cuban studies. The first significant Cuban emigrations occurred during the nineteenth century. José Rivero Muñiz, "Los cubanos en Tampa," *Revista Bimestre Cubana* LXXI (First Semester 1958), 5–140, is an extensive historical survey dealing with the origins and development of the Cuban cigarworkers' communities in central Florida and their contribution to the independence struggles. The Rivero Muñiz study was translated into English by Eustasio Fernández and H. Beltrán and published under the title of *The Ybor City Story, 1885–1954* (Tampa, 1976). Juan José E. Casasús, *La emigración cubana y la independencia de la patria* (Havana, 1953), is one of the most complete histories of Cuban emigration in the nineteenth century, examining the relationship between the expatriate communities in the United States and the independence movements in Cuba. The study spans the latter half of the century, with attention to fundraising activities, propaganda efforts, and politico-military contributions. Manuel Deulofeu, *Heroes del destierro* (Cienfuegos, 1904), examines the émigré communities in Florida, with particular emphasis on the 1890s. Wen Gálvez, *Tampa, impresiones de emigrado* (Tampa, 1897), is a useful first-person account of the Cuban community in Tampa. Louis A. Pérez, Jr., "Cubans in Tampa: From Exiles to Immigrants, 1892–1901," *Florida Historical Quarterly* LVII (Oct. 1978), 129–40, examines the transformation of the Cuban expatriate community in Tampa from political exiles to permanent residents. Susan D. Greenbaum, "Afro-Cubans in Exile: Tampa, Florida, 1886–1984," *Cuban Studies/Estudios Cubanos* XV (Winter 1985), 59–72, discusses black Cubans in exile by focusing on the history of the Afro-Cuban club "La Unión Martí-Maceo." Two essays by Durward Long, "Labor Relations in the Tampa Cigar Industry, 1885–1911," *Labor History* XII (Fall 1971), 551–59, and " 'La Resistencia': Tampa's Immigrant Labor Union," *Labor History* VI (Fall 1965), 193–210, examine the labor activities of Cuban cigarworkers, with emphasis on immigrant radicalism and strikes. Two essays by Gerald Poyo also examine the role of émigrés both in Cuba's independence struggles and in Florida politics: "Cuban Revolutionaries and Monroe County Reconstruction Politics," *Florida Historical Quarterly* LV (April 1977), 407–22, and "Key West and the Ten Years War," *Florida Historical Quarterly* LVII (Jan. 1979), 289–307. José Luciano Franco, "Panamá: refugio de la rebeldía cubana en el siglo XIX," *Casa de las Américas* XV (July–Aug. 1974), 16–26, analyzes the Cuban expatriate community in Panama during the last third of the nineteenth century, with particular attention to émigré political activities. Rodolfo Ruz Menéndez, *La primera emigración cubana a Yucatán* (Mérida, 1969), examines Cuba migration to the Yucatan during the early nineteenth century, climaxing in the Ten Years' War. Paul Estrade, "L'emigration cubaine de Paris (1895–1898)," *Caravelle* XVI (1971), 33–53, discusses the émigré community of Paris, made up principally of creole elites, during the war for independence.

The second principal period of Cuban emigration occurred after 1959, and on this subject the literature reaches voluminous proportions. Several bibliographical guides are of considerable use: Lourdes Casal and Andrés R. Hernández, "Cubans in the United States: A Survey of the Literature," *Cuban Studies/Estudios Cubanos* V (July 1975), 25–51; Lourdes Casal, "An Annotated Bibliography on Cuban Exiles," in *The Cuban Minority in the U.S.* (Boca Raton, Fla., 1973), 179–99; Esther B. González, *Annotated Bibliography on Cubans in the United States 1960–1976* (Miami, 1977); and Lyn MacCorkle, *Cubans in the United States*

(Westport, Conn., 1984). Effort will be made to cite some of the more general and thematic representative material of this vast literature. Richard R. Fagen, Richard M. Brody, and Thomas J. O'Leary, *Cubans in Exile: Disaffection and Revolution* (Stanford, Calif., 1968), stands as one of the better early studies of the sources of Cuban emigration after 1959. It provides a survey of social origins, professional training and education, racial composition, and income distribution of Cubans who migrated between 1959 and the mid-1960s. Eleanor R. Rogg, *The Assimilation of Cuban Exiles: the Role of Community and Class* (New York, 1974), is a sociological study of the adjustment of Cuban exiles in West New York, New Jersey, to North American norms. José Llanes, *Cuban Americans: Masters of Survival* (Cambridge, Mass., 1982), seeks to develop specific types of Cuban exiles through the use of 58 composite characters created out of extensive interviews. Lynn Darrell Bender, "The Cuban Exiles: An Analytical Study," *Journal of Latin American Studies* V (Nov. 1973), 271–78, deals with various phases of Cuban immigration to the United States and the occupational/professional strata represented during each phase. Silvia Pedraza-Bailey, "Cubans and Mexicans in the United States: The Function of Political and Economic Migration," *Cuban Studies/Estudios Cubanos* XI/XII (July 1981–Jan. 1982), 79–97, is a comparative study of Cuban and Mexican migration, with attention to the causes of migration, the role of public assistance, the impact of ideology, and the class origins of émigrés. Benigno Aguirre, "Differential Migration of Cuban Social Race," *Latim American Research Review* XI (1976), 103–24, analyzes race as a determinant of Cuban immigration to the United States. The essay evaluates Afro-Cuban migration from a comparative perspective, examing factors that account for differences in immigration between pre- and post-revolutionary Cuba. Alejandro Portes, Juan M. Clark, and Robert L. Bach, "The New Wave: A Statistical Profile of Cuban Exiles to the United States," *Cuban Studies/Estudios Cubanos* VII (Jan. 1977), 1–32, develops a statistical profile of Cuban émigrés coming to the United States during the mid-1970s with attention to age, education, occupation, and patterns of adjustment in the United States. Myra Max Ferree, "Employment Without Liberation—Cuban Women in the United States," *Social Science Quarterly* LX (June 1979), 35–50, examines the employment of émigré women in the United States. The essay deals with the economic realities confronting Cubans and the effect of these conditions on attitudes toward women's participation in the paid labor force. Geoffrey E. Fox, "Working Class Emigrés from Cuba: A

Study of Counter-Revolutionary Consciousness'' (unpublished Ph.D. dissertation, Northwestern University, 1975), is a compilation of personal histories and political attitudes of 47 Cubans of working-class origins interviewed in Chicago in 1969. Juan M. Clark, ''The Exodus from Revolutionary Cuba (1959–1974): A Sociological Analysis'' (unpublished Ph.D. dissertation, Univ. of Florida, 1975), examines the character of Cuban immigration, the causes of emigration, the successive phases of emigration, and the conditions of exile. Studies of the Mariel boatlift in 1980 include Sergio Díaz Briquets, ''Demographic and Related Determinants of the Recent Cuban Emigration,'' *International Migration Review* XVII (April 1983), 59–119; Robert L. Bach, Jennifer Bach, and Timothy Triplett, ''The Flotilla 'Entrants': Latest and Most Controversial,'' *Cuban Studies/Estudios Cubanos* XI–XII (July 1981–Jan. 1982), 29–48; and Robert L. Bach, ''The New Cuban Exodus: Political and Economic Motivations,'' *Caribbean Review* XI (Winter 1982), 22–25, 58–60.

XIV. Population and Demography

Researchers on Cuba are especially fortunate in having a rich corpus of population data. Comprehensive census compilations began in 1774 and continued through 1981. The early census data, to be sure, must be used with circumspection and care. Older census material does, however, provide at least a suggestive portrait of Cuban society during the last one hundred years of the colonial regime. The censuses of 1774 and 1792 are contained in Ramón de la Sagra, *Historia económico-política estadística de la isla de Cuba* (Havana, 1831). The census of 1817 is found in Cuba, *Estado general de la población de la isla de Cuba, dispuesto por el excmo. Sr. D. José Cienfuegos y acuerdo para que sirviera de base a las elecciones de 1821* (Havana, 1821). The census of 1828 was published as Cuba, *Cuba, año de 1828. Censo de la siempre fidelísima ciudad de La Habana* (Havana, 1829). The 1841 census appeared as Cuba, *Cuba, resumen del censo de población de Cuba a fin del año de 1841* (Havana, 1842). Five years later another census was taken and appeared as Cuba, Comisión de Estadística, *Cuadro estadístico de la siempre fiel Isla de Cuba, correspondiente al año de 1846* (Havana, 1847). The census of 1861 was released as Cuba, Centro de Estadística, *Noticias estadísticas de la Isla de Cuba, en 1861* (Havana, 1864). The 1877 census was published as Spain, Instituto Geográfico y Estadístico, *Censo de la población de España, segun el empadronamiento hecho en 31 de diciembre de 1877* (2 vols., Madrid, 1883–84). Ten years later the last colonial census was published as Spain, Instituto Geográfico y Estadístico, *Censo de la población de España, segun el empradonamiento hecho en 31 diciembre de 1887* (2 vols., Madrid, 1891–92).

The first census after Cuba's independence from Spain appeared as United States War Department, *Informe sobre el censo de Cuba, 1899* (Washington, D.C., 1900). The next census was completed in 1907 and published as Cuba, Oficina del Censo, *Censo de la república de Cuba, 1907* (Washington, D.C., 1908). Twelve years later, a new census was completed and released as Cuba, Dirección General del Censo, *Censo de la República de Cuba, 1919* (Havana, 1919). The censuses of 1899, 1907, and 1919 were completed under U.S. auspices and published simultaneously in English-language editions. Political factors prevented the 1931 census from appearing in any form other than an abbreviated 93-page pamphlet, Cuba, Dirección General del Censo, *Censo de 1931: estados de habitantes y electores* (Havana, 1932), which was little more than an enumeration of the number of eligible voters in each province and *municipio*. The full 1931 census, including demographic and economic data, was subsequently published in 1978 as Cuba, Dirección de Demografía del Comité Estatal de Estadística, *Memorias inéditas del censo de 1931* (Havana, 1978). The 1953 census appeared as Cuba, Oficina Nacional de los Censos Demográficos y Electoral, *Censos de población, viviendas y electoral. Enero 28 de 1953* (Havana, 1955). The next complete censos was undertaken at the close of the 1960s and appeared as Cuba, Junta Central de Planificación, *Censo de población y viviendas, 1970* (Havana, 1975). The most recent census was completed in 1981 and published as Cuba, Comité Estatal de Estadísticas, *Censos de población y viviendas, 1981* (16 vols., Havana, 1984).

A number of general works provide interpretation and analyses of Cuban censuses. Lisandro Pérez, "The Political Contexts of Cuban Population Censuses, 1899–1981," *Latin American Research Review* XIX (1984), 143–61, discusses the political conditions during which censuses were completed and how those factors may have affected the organization and interpretation of the data. Victor Olmstead and Henry Gannet, *Cuba: Population, History and Resources, 1907* (Washington, D.C., 1909), was prepared by the two North American directors of the 1907 census. This volume serves as a useful summary of the 1907 census, concentrating specifically on population, demography, the economy, climate, and transportation. Gustavo Gutiérrez y Sánchez, *Urgencia de los censos y estadísticas nacionales* (Havana, 1949), is a study of the census data from the colonial period through the 1940s. It reproduces a wide array of statistical information published by various government agencies interpreting the previous censuses. Lowry Nelson, "Cuban population estimates, 1953–1970," *Journal of Inter-American Studies and World Affairs* XII (July 1970), 392–400, provides a general discussion of Cuban population growth with emphasis on fertility and emigration. Niurka Pérez Rojas, *Características sociodemográficas de la familia cubana, 1953–1970* (Havana, 1979), examines the changing form of Cuban family structures. The study is especially useful in its assessment of the transformation of the family in the years following the revolution. Junta Central de Planificación, *Densidad de población y urbanización* (Havana, 1975), is based on the 1970 census. The study stresses two aspects of population: density and urbanization. The material dealing with population density emphasizes comparative urban-rural densities, comparison with past censuses, and projection of future growth. The section dealing with urbanization examines historical developments, growth rate, size of urban centers, and projected trends. The Centro de Estudios Demográficos, *La población de Cuba* (Havana, 1976), is a comprehensive work examining the major demographic trends, including population growth, fertility, mortality, migration, labor force characteristics, race, and population projections. Intended principally for the general reader, this volume is one of the more complete and readily accessible studies in Cuban demography. Two essays by Sergio Díaz-Briquets and Lisandro Pérez, "Cuba: the Demography of Revolution," *Population Bulletin* XXXVI (April 1981), 1–43, and "Fertility Decline in Cuba: A Socioeconomic Interpretation," *Population and Development Review* X (Sept. 1982), evaluate the causes and consequences of the demographical changes in Cuba after 1959.

XV. Class

The subject of class structures in Cuba has long been a topic of interest, in and out of Cuba, before but especially after the revolution. Several useful surveys provide a large overview of the class structures in the colony and through the republic. The papers presented at a special seminar organized by the Cuban communist party in 1976 were published by the Editorial de Ciencial Sociales as *Las clases y lucha de clases en la sociedad neocolonial cubana* (4 vols., Havana, 1980). Among the many themes examined are working-class politics in the early republic, the peasantry in the twentieth century, the armed forces, and aspects of U.S. hegemony. Dennis B. Wood, "The Long Revolution: Class Relations and Political Conflict in Cuba, 1868–1968," *Science and Society* XXXIV (Spring 1970), 1–41, traces the interplay of social formations and political developments over one hundred years. The essay examines politics, the nature of Cuban class structures, and the evolution of the local economy during the late nineteenth and early twentieth century. Nelson Amaro Victoria, "Mass and Class in the Origins of the Cuban Revolution," in Irving Louis Horowitz, ed., *Masses in Latin America* (New York, 1970), 547–76, deals with the dynamics of twentieth-century class relations, examining the various roles played by peasants, workers, and the middle class in the overthrow of the Batista government and the consolidation of the revolution. Wyatt MacGaffey, "Social Structure and Mobility in Cuba," *Anthropological Quarterly* XXXIV (Jan. 1961), 94–109, examines Cuban class structures on the eve of the revolution. Along similar lines, the essay by Jorge L. Martí, "Class Attitudes in Cuba on the Eve of the Revolution, 1952–1958," *Specialia* (Carbondale, Ill.) III (Aug. 1971), 28–35, provides a useful overview of class relations in pre-revolutionary Cuba. Several studies deal extensively with the nature of the Cuban middle class. Theo R. Crevenna edited a six-volume study, *Materiales para el estudio de la clase media en América Latina* (Washington, D.C., 1950–51), in which appeared the following essays on Cuba: Juan F. Carvajal, "Observaciones sobre la clase media en Cuba," II, pp. 30–44; Lowry Nelson, "The Social Class Structure in Cuba," II, pp. 45–72; and Carlos Manuel Raggi Ageo, "Contribución al estudio de las clases medias en Cuba," II, pp. 73–89. A general examination of the middle class in found in Fergo Arregui, *La class media en Cuba* (Havana, 1958). Hugh Thomas, "Middle-Class Politics and the Cuban Revolution," in Claudio Veliz, ed., *The Politics of Conformity in Latin America* (New York, 1967), 249–77, evaluates the class origins of the Cuban revolution. Thomas disputes the commonly held view that the revolution was primarily a middle-class phenomenon, arguing instead that working-class participation was significant during the early phase of the armed struggle. Lino Novás Calvo, "La tragedia de la clase media cubana," *Bohemia Libre* LIII (Jan. 1, 1961), chronicles the antecedents and collapse of the middle class during the first eighteen months of the Cuban revolution. The most detailed study of the demise of the Cuban bourgeoisie is found in Alfred L. Padula, Jr., "The Fall of the Bouregoisie: Cuba, 1959–1961" (unpublished Ph.D. dissertation, Univ. of New Mexico, 1974), a revised portion of which appeared as "The Ruin of the Cuban Bourgeoisie, 1959–1961", *SECOLAS Annals* XI (March 1980), 5–21.

The literature dealing with working-class politics has long occupied a place of importance in the Cuba historiography. During the last three decades, research on workers has expanded rapidly. A useful guide to these materials is found in Biblioteca Central Rubén Martínez Villena, *Historia del movimiento obrero en Cuba: bibliografía* (Havana, 1973). Several general surveys provide useful overviews of labor history. Mario Riera Hernández, *Historical obrero cubano, 1574–1965* (Miami, 1965), is a general account with emphasis on the period between the 1930s through the early 1960s. Hobart A. Spalding, Jr., "The Workers' Struggle: 1850–1961," *Cuba Review* IV (July 1974), 3–10, surveys labor history, emphasizing the participation of workers in the revolutionary struggles of the 1930s and 1950s and the part labor played in the consolidation of the revolution. Adrián García Hernández, "Movimiento obrero y liberación nacional," *Trabajo* I (June 1960), 38–43, and Gaspar Jorge, "Influencia del tabaquero en la trayectoría revolucionaria de Cuba," *Revista Bimestre Cubana* XXXIX (First Semester, 1937), 100–121, examine the participation of Cuban workers in the nineteenth-century struggles for independence. This is also the central theme of Orlando Castañeda, *Martí, los tabaqueros y la revolución de 1895* (Havana, 1973), provides a detailed discussion of all labor congresses during the nineteenth and twentieth century. Among other useful general labor histories are Joaquín Ordoqui, *Elementos para la historia del movimiento obrero en Cuba* (Havana, 1960), and Esteban Rito, *Lucha de clases y movimiento obrero* (Havana, 1961). The development of the origins of the labor press in Cuba is examined in José Antonio Portuondo, *'La Aurora' y los comienzos de la prensa y de la organización obrera en Cuba* (Havana, 1961), and José Rivero Muñiz, "Las orígines de la prensa obrera en Cuba," *Revista de la Biblioteca Nacional "José Martí"* II (Jan.–Dec. 1960), 67–89. Among the better monographic treatments of labor during the early twentieth century are the works of José Rivero Muñiz: *El movimiento obrero durante la primera intervención* (Havana, 1961) and *El movimiento laboral cubano durante el período 1906–1911* (Santa Clara, 1962). John Dumoulin, *Azúcar y lucha de clases: 1917* (Havana, 1980), examines the expansion of sugar production during the years of World War I and the concurrent movement by sugar workers to organize. The volume contains several documentary appendices. The Dumoulin study should be ready in conjunction with Olga Cabrera, *El movimiento obrero cubano en 1920* (Havana, 1970), which continues the study of labor organizing and the increasingly important role played by the communist organizations. Fabio Grobart, "The Cuban Working Class Movement from 1925–1933," *Science and Society* XXXIX (Spring 1975), 73–102, surveys the development of the National Confederation of Cuban Workers (CNOC) and the role labor played in the struggle against the Machado regime. Also useful for the study of labor during the 1930s is Ursinio Rojas, *Las luchas obreras en el Central Tacajo* (Havana, 1979). The most comprehensive account of labor activity during these years is found in Mirta Rosell, ed., *Luchas obreras contra Machado* (Havana, 1973), a compilation of documents, manifestos, speeches, and resolutions relating to labor activities during the late 1920s and early 1930s. Harold D. Sims, "Cuban Labor and the Communist Party, 1937–1958: An Interpretation," *Cuban Studies/Estudios Cubanos* XV (Winter 1985), 43–58, evaluates the relations between organized labor and the Cuban communist party during the Batista years. Jean Stubbs, *Tobacco in the Periphery: A Case Study in Cuban Labour History, 1860–1958* (London, 1985), is an examination of the emergence of the cigar industry and the development of cigarworkers' unions and the part they played in the overall labor movement. Maurice Zeitlin, *Revolutionary Politics and the Cuban Working Class* (Princeton, 1967), surveys working-class attitudes toward the revolution based on more than 200 interviews. The book is a useful source for the years between the 1930s and 1950s. Several collections of oral histories serve as important source material for the study of Cuban workers. Among the better collections are Francisco García Moreira, *Tiempo muerto: memorias de un trabajador azucarero* (Havana, 1969); Roberto Branly, *MINAZ-608: coloquios en el despegue* (Havana, 1973); Andrés D. García Suárez, *Los fundidores relatan su historia* (Havana, 1975); Salvadore Morales et al., *Matahambre: empresa y movimiento obrero* (Havana, 1971); Ana Núñez Machín, *Memoria amarga del azúcar* (Havana, 1981); and Comisión Nacional de Activistas de Historia, Departamento de Orientación Revolucionaria del Comité Central del Partido Comunista de Cuba, *Los obreros hacen y escriben su historia* (Havana, 1976).

The literature treating the Cuban peasantry tends to concentrate almost entirely on the twentieth century, with particular attention to the immediate pre-revolutionary period. In part, this is very much a function of the debate over the nature of the Cuban revolution and its class origins, and specifically the discourse on the part peasants played in the armed struggle. For general guide to the literature on peasants see Aleida de los Santos Quilez, *El campesinado cubano: Breve bibliografía* (Havana, 1980). Antero Regalado, *Las luchas campesinas en Cuba* (Havana, 1973), is a historical survey of peasant resistance to land expropriations and expulsion. While the early chapters deal with the colonial period, most of the book concentrates on the twentieth century. Lowry Nelson, *Rural Cuba* (Minneapolis, 1950), is one of the better studies of class structures in Cuba, with particular emphasis on conditions in the countryside. Much of this material appears in summary form in Lowry Nelson, "Cuban Paradoxes," in A. Curtis Wilgus, ed., *The Caribbean at Mid-Century* (Gainesville, Fla., 1951), 136–48. Many of these themes are re-examined by Lowry Nelson in *Cuba: The Measure of a Revolution* (Minneapolis, 1972). Brian Pollitt, "Some Problems of Enumerating the 'Peasantry' in Cuba," *Journal of Peasant Studies* IV (Jan. 1977), 162–80, examines the principal censuses of pre-revolutionary Cuba and the data used to classify Cubans as peasants. The author argues that flaws in methodologies, data collecting, and interpretation of data obscure as much as they reveal. Vladimir Akulai and Domingo Rodríguez Fragaso, "La situación socio-económica del campesinado cubano antes de la revolución," *Islas,* no. 54 (May–Aug. 1976), 55–80, is a detailed examination of conditions of the peasantry during the 1940s and 1950s. Another useful survey of rural conditions is found in Dennys Moreno, "La vivienda del campesinado cubano," *Etnología y Folklore* VI (July–Dec. 1968), 27–76.

The nature of peasant participation in the revolution has generated considerable controversy. For a general overview of the peasantry in the revolutionary war see the chapter on Cuba in Eric R. Wolf, *Peasant Wars of the Twentieth Century* (New York, 1969). Bert Useem, "Peasant Involvement in the Cuban Revolution," *Journal of Peasant Studies* V (Oct. 1977), 99–111, argues that local landlord-squatter conflicts fused with state-guerrilla conflict and facilitated the incorporation of peasants into insurgent ranks. Neill Macaulay, "The Rebel Army: A Numerical Survey," *Hispanic American Historical Review* LVIII (May 1978), 284–95, examines the growth of the size of the rebel army between 1957 and 1958, concluding the peasant participation in the armed struggle was larger than previously believed. Other studies examining the part played by peasants in the insurrection include the two essays by Gil Carl Alroy, "The Meaning of 'Peasant Revolution': The Cuba Case," *International*

Review of History and Political Science II (Dec. 1965), 87–96, and "The Peasantry in the Cuban Revolution," *Review of Politics* XXIX (Jan. 1967), 87–99; Víctor Alba, "Cuba: A Peasant Revolution," *The World Today* XV (May 1959), 183–95; Carlos Rafael Rodríguez, "The Cuban Revolution and the Peasantry," *World Marxist Review* VIII (Oct. 1965), 62–71. Two oral histories dealing with peasants include Ramiro Guerra y Sánchez, *Mudos testigos* (2nd ed., Havana, 1974), and Julián Sánchez, *Julián Sánchez cuenta su vida,* ed. Erasmo Dumpierre (Havana, 1970).

XVI. Race

The literature on race in Cuba is voluminous. The subject has attracted the attention of historians, sociologists, ethnologists, linguists, and economists. The presence of Afro-Cubans is pervasive, and there are few aspects of Cuban national culture unaffected by the African influence. Three published bibliographies are available to guide the reader through the general literature. Carlos M. Trelles y Govín, "Bibliografía de autores de la raza de color en Cuba," *Cuba Contemporánea* XLIII (Jan. 1927), 30–78, is a compilation of references to literary works by and about Afro-Cubans. The bibliography is arranged in sections dealing with slavery and emancipation, Afro-Cuban newspapers, works by white authors dealing with blacks, and materials dealing with Afro-Americans in the Western Hemisphere. Rafael Fermoselle-López, "The Blacks in Cuba: a Bibliography," *Caribbean Studies* XII (Oct. 1972), 103–12, is a compilation of citations organized the following topics: general themes, slavery and abolition, race relations, folklore, literature, and language. By far the most comprehensive and current available guide to the literature on Afro-Cubans is Tomás Fernández Robaina, ed., *Bibliografía de temas afrocubanas* (Havana, 1985).

Several general studies serve as useful overviews of race and race relations. Kenneth F. Kiple, *Blacks in Colonial Cuba, 1774–1899* (Gainesville, Fla., 1976), provides commentaries and compilations of population census data dealing with Africans and Afro-Cubans, both free and slave. The data is derived from the principal population censuses between 1774 and 1899. Lawrence Smallwood, "African Cultural Dimensions in Cuba," *Journal of Black Studies* VI (Dec. 1975), 191–99, surveys the African impact on language, literature, music, and the formation of Cuban nationalism. A similar approach is used by Rosa Valdez-Cruz, "The Black

Man's Contribution to Cuban Culture," *The Americas* XXXIV (Oct. 1977), 244–51, with attention given to religion, music, medicine, plastic arts, and literature. Marianne Masferrer and Carmelo Mesa-Lago, "The Gradual Integration of the Black in Cuba: Under the Colony, the Republic, and the Revolution," in Robert Brent Toplin, ed., *Slavery and Race in Latin America* (Westport, Conn., 1974), 348–84, surveys the condition of Afro-Cubans from 1500 to the early 1970s. The essay examines population growth, education, slavery, and employment. Argelier León, "Presencia del africano en la cultura cubana," *Islas,* no. 41 (Jan.–April 1972), 155–69, surveys the acculturation process and the attending effects on whites and blacks during a colonial period. Specific subjects studied include religion, literature, music, dance, and musical instruments. Alberto Arredondo, *El negro en Cuba* (Havana, 1939), is an eloquent account of the conditions of Afro-Cubans and the state of race relations from the colonial regime through the early republic. The study examines Afro-Cuban cultural contributions and documents the part played by blacks in the struggles for independence. Pascual B. Marcos Veguer, *El negro en Cuba* (Havana, 1955), is a thoughtful discussion of the condition of Afro-Cubans in the republic. The author examines the promise of social justice made to blacks in the nineteenth century against the achievement of the twentieth, and concludes that much had remained undone. Elias José Entralgo, *La liberación étnica cubana* (Havana, 1953), is a comprehensive account of the role of race in the development of Cuban nationality, with emphasis on the Afro-Cuban participation in the independence movements and the racial dimensions of Cuban political thought in the nineteenth century. Franklin W. Knight, "Slavery, Race, and Social Structure in Cuba During the Nineteenth Century," in Robert Brent Toplin, ed., *Slavery and Race in Latin America* (Westport, Conn., 1974), 204–27, treats the impact of the expansion of slavery on attitudes toward race. Juan F. Risquet, *Rectificaciones, La cuestión político-social en la isla de Cuba* (Havana, 1900), deals with the condition of Afro-Cubans in the nineteenth century. The study is especially useful for documenting the role of blacks in the struggle for independence, particularly Afro-Cubans in exile. The volume contains biographical sketches of leading Afro-Cuban patriots. Donna M. Wolf, "The Cuban 'Gente de Color' and the Independence Movement, 1879–1895," *Revista/Review Interamericana* V (Fall 1975), 403–21, examines the role of Afro-Cubans in shaping the course and content of the separatist movement during the years between the wars. Erwin H. Epstein, "Social Structure, Race Relations, and Political Stability Under U.S. Administration," *Revista/Review Interamericana* VIII (Summer 1978), 192–203, assesses the impact of the policies of the two U.S. military occupations (1899–1902 and 1906–9) with specific attention to race relations.

Much of the literature dealing with Afro-Cubans during the twentieth century focuses on the first decade of the republic, a period of immense political importance that culminated in the Afro-Cuban uprising of 1912. Perhaps the best single work dealing with Afro-Cuban politics during the early republic is Thomas T. Orum, "The Politics of Color: The Racial Dimension of Cuban Politics During the Early Republican Years, 1900–1912" (unpublished Ph.D. dissertation, New York Univ., 1975). The study is a richly detailed account of the racial politics at the close of the colony and at the outset of the republic. It is an indispensable reference work for the subject of race and politics for the early twentieth century. Also useful for this period is the more general survey Rafael Fermoselle-López, *Política y color en Cuba: la guerrita de 1912* (Montevideo, 1974). The account traces the development of the Independent Party of Color and the events leading to the 1912 rebellion. Martha Verónica Alvarez Mola and Pedro Martínez Pérez, "Algo acerca del problema negro en Cuba hasta 1912," *Universidad de La Habana,* no. 179 (May–June 1966), 79–93, examines the status and situation of blacks during the period of emancipation of the 1880s, through the organization of the Independent Party of Color and the 1912 uprising. The most thorough discussion of the Independent Party of Color is Serafín Portuondo Linares, *Los independientes de color. Historia del Partido Independiente de Color* (Havana, 1950). The work is a sympathetic account of the organization of Afro-Cuban political parties and the events of 1912. Louis A. Pérez, Jr., "Politics, Peasants, and People of Color: The 1912 'Race' War in Cuba Reconsidered," *Hispanic American Historical Review* LVI (Aug. 1986), 509–39, examines the socioeconomic aspects of the 1912 rebellion. Carlos de Velasco, "El problema negro," *Cuba Contemporánea* I (Feb. 1913), 73–79, is a general discussion of the social and political conditions of Afro-Cubans in the aftermath of the 1912 revolt. John Clytus, *Black Man in Red Cuba* (Coral Gables, 1970), is a critical account of social conditions in post-revolutionary Cuba. The author lived on the island for several years during the mid-1960s and concluded that racial intolerance in socialist Cuba continued to obstruct the attainment of social justice for Afro-Cubans.

An equally large body of literature deals specifically with the Afro-

Cuban influence in literature, music, and folklore. José Fernández de Castro, "El aporte negro en las letras de Cuba en el siglo XIX," *Revista Bimestre Cubana* XXXVIII (July–Dec. 1936), 71–88, surveys the contribution of Africans and Afro-Cubans to literary forms of the nineteenth century. Sergio Valdés, "Las lenguas africanas y el español coloquia de Cuba," *Santiago,* no. 31 (Sept. 1978), 81–107, analyzes the impact of African languages on Cuban Spanish. Distinctions are drawn between language in rural and urban Cuba. The essay includes a lengthy bibliography. Rose Teresa Amor, "Afro-Cuban Folk Tales as Incorporated into the Literary Tradition of Cuba" (unpublished Ph.D. dissertation, Columbia Univ., 1969) deals with the impact of Afro-Cuban themes in the development of national literature. Among the topics explored include Afro-Cuban themes as a subject of white writers, Afro-Cuban folklore, religion, and the technical and stylistic aspects of the Afro-Cuban literary tradition.

Antonio Olliz-Boyd, "Race Relations in Cuba: A Literary Perspective," *Revista/Review Interamericana* VIII (Summer 1978), 225–53, examines Cuban authors and their definition of the Afro-Cuban social reality. The works of fiction examined span the nineteenth and twentieth centuries. Pedro Barreda, *The Black Protagonist in the Cuban Novel* (Amherst, Mass., 1979), examines the evolution of the Afro-Cuban as the central figure in Cuban fiction, from the early abolitionist works of the early nineteenth century to the avant-garde literature of the 1930s. Edward J. Mullen, ed., *The Life and Poems of a Cuban Slave: Juan Francisco Manzano, 1797–1854* (Hamden, Conn., 1981), is a collection of Manzano poetry set against the larger context of the Afro-American slave narrative and the Afro-Hispanic literary tradition. An excellent introductory biographical essay provides a detailed picture of the life and time of the slave poet. Leslie N. Wilson, *La poesía afroantillana* (Miami, 1979), is a general discussion of Afro-Caribbean poetry, with particular emphasis on Cuban poems and poets. Ildefonso Pereda Valdés, *Lo negro y lo mulato en la poesía cubana* (Montevideo, 1970), is a book in which the first half is devoted to a critical study of the Afro-Cuban influence on national poetry, and the second half is an anthology of Cuban poetry representative of the Afro-Cuban genre. Constance S. de García Barrio, "The Black in Post-Revolutionary Cuban Literature," *Revista/Review Interamericana* VIII (Summer 1978), 263–70, examines the presence of Afro-Cuban themes in the literature of socialist Cuba. Among the authors discussed are Nicolás Guillén, Manuel Grandos, Miguel Barnet, Severo

Sarduy, Alejo Carpentier, Edmundo Desnoes, and Humberto Arenal. Roberto Márquez, "Racism, Culture, and Revolution: Ideology and Politics in the Prose of Nicolás Guillén," *Latin American Research Review* XVII (1982), 43–68, provides a critical study of the poetry of Nicolás Guillén as it addresses the issues of the Afro-Cuban experience and the process of social change. Julio Matas, "Revolución, literatura y religión afro-cubana," *Cuban Studies/Estudios Cubanos* XIII (Winter 1983), 17–23, examines the persistence of Afro-Cuban cults and the problem they pose to the revolution interpreted through the fiction of Antonio Benítez Rojo.

Much work has also been done on Afro-Cuban folklore. Ramón Guirao, ed., *Cuentos y leyendas negras de Cuba* (Havana, 1942), is a compilation of Afro-Cuban folk tales, myths, parables, and legends. Julia Cuervo Hewitt, "Ifa: orácula Yoruba y Lucumé," *Cuban Studies/Estudios Cubanos* XIII (Winter 1983), 24–40, examines Afro-Cuban traditions through the place of Ifa, a mythical figure in Yoruba tradition. Lydia Cabrera, *El monte* (Miami, 1975), is one of the more complete studies of Cuban folklore and Africanisms in Cuba. The book examines the relationship between Afro-Cuban culture and religion and magic. Fernando Ortiz, *Los negros brujos* (2nd ed., Miami, 1973), is a study of Afro-Cuban witchcraft. The work examines the African sources of religious beliefs and practices, the development of witches and warlocks, and the Cubanization of African traditions and rituals. Jorge Duany, "Stones, Trees, and Blood: An Examination of a Cuban Santero Ritual," *Cuban Studies/Estudios Cubanos* XII (July 1982), 37–53, is an analysis of an Afro-Cuban religious ceremony as a system of symbolic communication. The essay deals with Afro-Cuban religious beliefs and customs as syncretic cultural responses to the social environment of the nineteenth-century plantation system. Mercedes Cros Sandoval, *La religión afrocubana* (Madrid, 1975), is a detailed account of the practices, rituals, and symbolisms, of Afro-Cuban religions.

Several studies examine the Afro-Cuban contribution in the performing arts. Fernando Ortiz, *La africanía de la música folklórica de Cuba* (Havana, 1950), is a comprehensive study of the African sources of Cuban music, with particular emphasis on form, structure, and function. Similarly, Odilio Urfe, "Music and Dance in Cuba," in Manuel Moreno Fraginals, ed., *Africa in Latin America* (New York, 1977), 170–88, examines the African contribution to music and dance. Emphasis is given to the impact of African rhythms, instruments, and lyrics in both religious and popular music.

XVII. Women

The study of women in Cuba has expanded rapidly in the last several decades. Two bibliographical guides compiled by Nelson P. Valdés provide a useful introduction to this literature. "A Bibliography on Cuban Women in the Twentieth Century," *Cuban Studies Newsletter* IV (June 1974), 1–31, is a detailed guide to the pre- and post-revolutionary literature. "A Bibliography of Cuban Periodicals Related to Women," *Cuban Studies/Estudios Cubanos* XII (July 1982), 73–80, is an inventory of 56 different periodicals and magazines dealing with women published in Cuba between the 1880s and 1980s. The bibliography includes information concerning the location of the serials and the run of each collection.

There exists no general historical survey of women in Cuba. Medardo Vitier, "La vida civil de la mujer cubana en su relación con la historia de Cuba," *Cuba Contemporánea* XIV (Aug. 1914), 323–40, is a general discussion of the legal status of women. The essay gives attention to the role and participation of women in all aspects of national development and the means through which that involvement shaped the juridical status of women. The situation of women during the colonial period is examined Rolando Alvarez Estévez, *La 'reeducación' de la mujer cubana en la colonia* (Havana, 1976), which concentrates on the establishment of the women's house of correction in Havana in 1746. The study provides an overview of the 150-year history of the institution which served to impose the prevailing patriarchal ideologies of the colonial regime.

Prostitution in the colonial period is discussed by Benjamín de Céspedes, *La prostitución en la ciudad de La Habana* (Havana, 1888). Cuba, Comisión de Higiene Especial, *La prostitución en Cuba especialmente in La Habana* (2 vols., Havana, 1903), provides a general discussion of prostitution during the latter half of the nineteenth and the early years of the twentieth century. The work is organized into several sections dealing with the antecedents of prostitution, the medical aspects, and social backgrounds of prostitutes. The study also contains useful statistics dealing with age, race, nationality, and demography. Tomás Fernández Robaina, ed., *Recuerdos secretos de dos mujeres públicas* (Havana, 1984), is an oral history of two former prostitutes of Havana. Verena Martínez-Alier, *Marriage, Class and Colour in Nineteenth Century Cuba: A Study of Racial Attitudes and Sexual Values in a Slave Society* (London, 1974), is a landmark study of the interplay of racial attitudes, marriage norms, and the control of women in the late colonial period. Similar themes are treated in Verena Martínez-Alier, "El honor de la mujer en Cuba en el siglo XIX," *Revista de la Biblioteca Nacional "José Martí"* XIII (May–Aug. 1971), 29–62. *Mujeres ejemplares* (Havana, 1977) is a collection of 33 biographical essays dealing with women prominent in revolutionary struggle. While some of the essays deal with women outside of Cuba, most deal with the Cuban experience ranging from the mid-nineteenth century to the twentieth. Armando O. Caballero, *La mujer en el 68* (Havana, 1978) is a general account of the participation of women in the Ten Years' War. Much of the work is organized around individual biographies of the most prominent women. Francisco J. Ponte Domínguez, "La mujer en la revolución de Cuba," *Revista Bimeste Cubana* XXXIII (Jan.–June 1933), 276–300, is an examination of the role of women in the struggle for independence, with special emphasis on the Ten Years' War. Women and the emerging labor movement in the nineteenth century is examined in Mariana Serra, "La mujer y su emancipación social en la prensa de los trabajadores del siglo XIX," *Santiago* XX (Dec. 1975), 139–53. The participation of women in the patriotic efforts of the 1890s is discussed in Luis Toledo Sandé, "José Martí hacia la emancipación de la mujer," *Casa de las Américas* XI (May–June, 1975), 25–41.

The literature on women in the early republic tends to concentrate on the struggle for civil rights and political equality. Among the better such studies are Lynn Stoner Wheeler, "In Defense of Motherhood: Divorce Law in Cuba During the Early Republic," *Studies in Third World Societies* XV (March 1982), 1–32, and "From House to the Streets: The Woman's Movement for Legal Change in Cuba, 1898–1958" (unpublished Ph.D. dissertation, Indiana Univ. 1983). Eduardo LeRiverend, *El derecho de la mujer casada* (Havana, 1945), provides a detailed exposition of the legal rights of Cuban women as defined in the 1940 constitution. Ramiro Pavón, "El empleo femenino en Cuba," *Santiago* XXII (Dec. 1975), 97–137, is a detailed analysis of the role and impact of women on the labor force for the years spanning 1953 and 1970. Analysis includes data on age, marital status, occupation, and education.

Several works deal with the role and participation of women in the revolutionary struggles of the 1950s: Vilma Espín, "La mujer en la revolución cubana," *Cuba Socialista* I (Dec. 1961), 59–67; M. Hernández Vidaurreta, "La mujer en la revolución," *Humanismo* VII (Jan.–April, 1959), 383–87; and Aurelia Restano, *Las mujeres en la revolución cubana* (Havana, 1960).

Much of the recent literature examines the impact of the revolution on the lives of the Cuban women. Ana Ramos, "La mujer y la revolución en Cuba," *Casa de las Américas* XI (March–June 1971), 56–74, and Chris Camarano, "On Cuban Women," *Science and Society* XXV (Spring 1971), 48–57, provide general discussions on the status of women in socialist Cuba. Margaret Randall, *Cuban Women Now* (Toronto, 1974), is based on twenty interviews and provides a representative cross-section of women in socialist Cuba, each recounting the impact of the revolution upon their professional and personal lives. Along similar lines, Oscar Lewis, Ruth Lewis, and Susan Rigdon, *Four Women: Living the Revolution. An Oral History of Contemporary Cuba* (Urbana, Ill., 1977), provides a collection of lengthy oral histories of four Cuban women: a single woman living with her parents and formerly a counter-revolutionary, an educated married woman and member of the Cuban communist party, a housewife who was formerly a domestic servant, and a former prostitute. *La mujer en Cuba socialista* (Havana, 1977) and Elizabeth Stone, ed., *Women and the Cuban Revolution* (New York, 1981), provide a collection of documents and speeches dealing with women in Cuba after 1959. Materials include speeches made by Fidel Castro on women's issues; pronouncements by Vilma Espín, president of the Federation of Cuban Women; legal codes, the maternity law, and the Family Code. Susan Kaufman Purcell, "Modernizing Women for a Modern Society: The Cuban Case," in Ann Pescatello, ed., *Female and Male in Latin America* (Pittsburgh, 1973), 257–71, analyzes the Cuban transition from a traditional to a modern polity and the attending changes occurring in the status and role of women. Linda Gordon, "Speculation on Women's Liberation in Cuba," *Women: A Journal of Liberation* I (Summer 1970), is a sympathetic account of both the success and failures of the revolution. Joan Berman, "Women in Cuba," *Women: A Journal of Liberation* I (Summer 1970), 10–14, examines the changing status and condition of women in Cuba since the revolution. Inger Holt-Seeland, *Women of Cuba* (New York, 1982), deals principally with women after the revolution. The work includes a series of interviews with women of different social origins, occupational positions, and educational backgrounds, including a farm worker, a brigade leader, a student, a housewife, and a factory worker. Johnetta B. Cole, "Women in Cuba: The Revolution within the Revolution," in Beverly Lindsay, ed., *Comparative Perspectives of Third World Women* (New York, 1980), 162–78, evaluates the status and situation of women in Cuba before and after the revolution, focusing on health, education, employment, housing, and culture. Virginia Olesen, "Confluence in Social Change: Cuban Women and Health Care," *Journal of Interamerican Studies and World Affairs* XVII (Nov. 1975), 398–411, examines the relationship between the changing roles of women and the attending transformation of the health care system. Emphasis is on health care and formal health structures. The essay gives attention to the changing participation of women in economic spheres and social roles and the manner in which developments in the health care system have facilitated these changes.

The contribution of women to Cuban fiction is highlighted in Antonio González Curquejo, ed., *Florilegio de escritoras cubans* (3 vols., Havana, 1910), a collection of major lyric poems, essays, and works of fiction by women writers. The large part of the material is drawn from the nineteenth century. Beth K. Miller, "Avellaneda, Nineteenth Century Feminist," *Revista/Review Interamericana* IV (Summer 1974), 177–83, examines the feminist aspects of the work of Gertrudis Gómez de Avellaneda as expressed in her themes, plots, and autobiographical works. Polly F. Harrison, "Images and Exile: The Cuban Woman and Her Poetry," *Revista/Review Interamericana* IV (Summer 1974), 184–219, reviews the principal work of female poets in Cuba. The essay evaluates the conflicts and tensions in the work of women poets as expressed in key symbols, themes, and values. The essay spans the colonial period to post-revolutionary Cuba.

XVIII. Economy

This section includes both general economic surveys and specialized monographs. The literature is voluminous, and unfortunately is without adequate bibliographical and research aids. Several historical surveys provide useful overviews with which to approach Cuban economic development. H. E. Friedlaender, *Historia económica de Cuba* (Havana, 1944), is the standard economic history text. This comprehensive survey examines chronologically and by sector Cuban economic development in sugar, tobacco, coffee, commerce, banking, and finance. Levi Marrero,

Historia económica de Cuba (Havana, 1956), provides a readable and balanced survey of economic history of Cuba from the pre-Columbian period to the seventeenth century. Roland T. Ely, *La economía cubana entre las dos Isabelas, 1492–1832* (Bogotá, 1962) is an overview of Cuban economic development with particular attention to sugar. Julio Le-Riverend, *Economic History of Cuba* (Havana, 1967), is the English translation of one of the standard economic histories of Cuba. The study arranges Cuban economy history into six stages: pre-Columbian and Iberian economic organizations; conquest and colonization; the early colonial economy (1510–1659); the development and demise of the slave economy (1659–1886); the imperialist phase (1886–1958); and socialism. Each section contains separate bibliographical entries. Alberto Arrendondo, *Cuba: tierra indefensa* (Havana, 1945), spans the period between pre-Columbian cultures and the revolutionary upheavals of the 1930s. The book examines key sectors of Cuban economic development: sugar, tobacco, livestock, coffee, banking and monetary institutions, and finance. Francisco López Segrera, *Cuba: capitalismo dependiente y subdesarrollo (1510–1959)* (Havana, 1981), is a survey of economic history with emphasis on the impact of the international system on the insular economy. Jorge Gilbert, *Cuba, from Primitive Accumulation of Capital to Socialism* (Toronto, 1981), examines the history of capitalism in Cuba, from the conquest and colonization to the triumph of the revolution. Felipe Pazos, "La economía cubana en el siglo XIX," *Revista Bimestre Cubana* XLVII (Jan.–Feb. 1941), 83–106, provides a balanced survey of economic developments in the nineteenth century. Ramiro Guerra y Sánchez, *Un cuarto de siglo de evolución cubana* (Havana, 1924), surveys social and economic gains achieved during the first twenty-five years of independence. Attention is given to employment, industry, commerce, and sugar production. Gustavo Gutiérrez y Sánchez, *El desarrollo económico de Cuba* (Havana, 1952), is a study of the first fifty years of the republic's economy, with emphasis on agriculture, mining, industry, banking and finance, and commerce. Julian Alienes y Urosa, *Características fundamentales de la economía cubana* (Havana, 1950), focuses principally on developments during the 1930s and 1940s, including sugar production, natural resources, capital accumulation, the import-export sector, and industrial infrastructure. Fernando Berenguer, *La riqueza de Cuba* (Havana, 1917), is a detailed account of the Cuban political-economy during the early twentieth century. Berenguer examines banking and finance, investment, agriculture, and industry against a backdrop of immigration, rural poverty, and declining standards of living. Julian Alienes y Urosa, *Economía de post-guerra y desempleo* (Havana, 1946), is an economic survey of Cuba between 1918 and 1945. Commissioned by the Cuban Chamber of Commerce principally to anticipate and prepare for postwar economic adjustment, it provides one of the most detailed examinations of Cuban economic development during World War II. Raúl Lorenzo, *El empleo en Cuba* (Havana, 1955), is a general treatment of employment, unemployment, and underemployment in a monoculture economy. The author deals extensively with such diverse issues as foreign trade, public finances, and monetary policies as they affect employment patterns. Henry Christopher Wallich, *Monetary Problems of an Export Economy: The Cuban Experience, 1917–1947* (Cambridge, Mass., 1950), is a detailed and comprehensive examination of fiscal issues during and between World War I and World War II. Francis Adams Truslow et al., *Report on Cuba* (Washington, D.C., 1951) is an encyclopedic study of the Cuban economy. It is a basic reference text for this period and is organized into ten "books": general economy, production, aids of production, human problems, administration, finance, international economic relations, economic development, technical questions, and policy recommendations.

The central element of Cuban economic development has been agriculture, specifically, sugar production. Roland T. Ely, *Cuando reinaba su majestad el azúcar* (Buenos Aires, 1963), is a detailed analysis of sugar production during the first half of the nineteenth century, with particular attention to the emergence of a monoculture economy. Manual Moreno Fraginals, *El ingenio: complejo económico-social cubano del azúcar* (3 vols., Havana, 1978), is an outstanding history of sugar production in all its multifaceted phases, including slavery, cane cultivation, production and manufacturing, and international trade. Fernando Ortiz, *Cuban Counterpoint: Tobacco and Sugar* (New York, 1947), is an interpretive essay of the socio-economic dynamics of the twin pillars of the Cuban economy. Ramiro Guerra y Sánchez, *La industria azucarera. Su importancia, su organización, sus mercados, su situación actual* (Havana, 1940), is a comprehensive analysis of sugar production. Set in a larger historical context, the study is concerned largely with twentieth-century issues, including cane cultivation, manufacture, labor, wage structures, trade and tariffs, and the role of government. Ramiro Guerra y Sánchez, *Sugar and Society in the Caribbean* (New Haven, 1964), is slightly dated, but nevertheless remains one of the classics on Cuban agriculture. Fernando Agete y Piñeiro, *La caña de azúcar* (2 vols., Havana, 1946), is a technical study of sugar cultivation in Cuba. Arnaldo Silva León, *Cuba y el mercado internacional azucarero* (Havana, 1975), examines the history of the relationship between Cuban sugar production and world market conditions, with emphasis on four periods: World War I, the Machado years and the depression, World War II, and the post-revolutionary period. The two best studies of coffee are Fernando Agete y Piñeiro, *El café* (Havana, 1937), and Francisco Pérez de la Riva, *El café. Historia de su cultivo y explotación en Cuba* (Havana, 1944).

No less voluminous—and controversial—a literature has developed in the last thirty years dealing with the economy and economic performance of socialist Cuba. Archibald R. M. Ritter, *The Economic Development of Revolutionary Cuba: Strategy and Performance* (New York, 1974), analyzes the phases of Cuban developmental strategies between 1959 and 1972, with specific attention to income distribution, employment, economic growth, and the reduction of economic dependence. Edward Boorstein, *The Economic Transformation of Cuba* (New York, 1968), is a sympathetic first-person account of the early economic policies of the revolution. Boorstein served in several advisory capacities and participated in the planning and execution of a number of decisions affecting various sectors of the economy. Dudley Seers, Andres Bianchi, Richard Jolly, and Max Nolff, *Cuba, the Economic and Social Revolution* (Chapel Hill, N.C., 1964), is a collection of four lengthy essays dealing with the economic and social background of the revolution, education, agriculture, and industry. José M. Illán González, *Cuba: datos sobre una economía en ruinas, 1902–1963* (Miami, 1964), is a critical study of the performance of the Cuban economy during the first five years of the revolution, concentrating on mismanagement, poor planning, and production shortfalls. Carmelo Mesa-Lago, *The Economy of Socialist Cuba: A Two-Decade Appraisal* (Albuquerque, N.M., 1981), is a comprehensive overview of the performance of the economy with attention to economic growth, diversification efforts, employment patterns, distribution of income, and social services. Claes Brundenius, *Revolutionary Cuba: The Challenge of Economic Growth with Equity* (Boulder, Colo., 1983), is a general analysis of income distribution, employment, and economic growth. Comparisons are made with Brazil and Peru for approximately the same period. Nelson P. Valdés, "The Cuban Revolution: Economic Organization and Bureaucracy," *Latin American Perspectives* VI (Winter 1979), 13–37, examines the various stages of economic organization between 1959 and 1979, including the model of moral incentives, the decentralized budgetary system, and institutionalization. Roberto M. Bernardo, *The Economics of Moral Incentives in Cuba* (University, Ala., 1971), is a detailed analysis of moral and material incentive systems, examining the use of moral rewards as the means to achieve production quotas, combat absenteeism, and promoting economic efficiency. Carmelo Mesa-Lago, "Ideological Radicalization and Economic Policy in Cuba," *Studies in Comparative International Development* V (1969–1970), 203–16, discusses the development of economic policies during the late 1960s as they affected capital accumulation and economic growth. Claes Brundenius, "Measuring Income Distribution in Pre- and Post-Revolutionary Cuba," *Cuban Studies/Estudios Cubanos* IX (July 1979), 29–44, assesses qualitative changes in standards of living in Cuba by concentrating on income distribution in the period immediately before and immediately after the revolution. William M. LeoGrande, "Cuban Dependency: A Comparison of Pre-Revolutionary and Post-Revolutionary International Economic Relations," *Cuban Studies/Estudios Cubanos* IX (July 1979), 1–28, compares patterns of dependency in capitalist Cuba with the conditions in socialist Cuba. The essay utilizes a number of economic indicators to measure levels of dependency, including export data, trading patterns, capital dependency, and external debt.

Agricultural and sugar policies in socialist Cuba are the topics of several specialized studies. René Dumont, *Cuba: Socialism and Development* (New York, 1970), is a critical first-person account of Cuban agricultural planning during the early years of the revolution. Oscar A. Echevarría Salvat, *La agricultura cubana, 1934–1966* (Miami, 1971), surveys Cuban agriculture with emphasis on workers' standard of living, income distribution, and the agrarian reform policies. James O'Connor, "Agrarian Reform in Cuba, 1959–1963," *Science and Society* XXXII (Spring 1968), 169–217, examines the early agrarian reform program, including policies affecting ranching, the expropriation of sugar lands, and the establishment of farm cooperatives. Cuban Economic Research Project, *Cuba, Agriculture and Planning* (Coral Gables, 1965), is a critical survey of agricultural production and state planning during the early years of the revolution, with emphasis on sugar, agrarian reform, ranching, and the relationship between rationing and production. Heinrich Brunner, *Cuban Sugar Policy from 1963 to 1970* (Pittsburgh, 1977), analyzes the planning policies and developmental strategies employed during the first decade of the revolution. Sergio Roca, *Cuban Economic Policy and Ideology: The Ten Million Ton Sugar Harvest* (Beverly Hills, Calif.,

1976), discusses the 1970 harvest from the viewpoint of planning and consequences. Charles Edquist, "Mechanization of Sugar Cane Harvesting in Cuba," *Cuban Studies/Estudios Cubanos* XIII (Summer 1983) 41–64, surveys Cuban efforts to mechanize the harvest between the 1950s and 1980s. Nancy Forster, "Cuban Agricultural Productivity: A Comparison of State and Private Farm Sectors," *Cuban Studies/Estudios Cubanos* XI–XII (July 1981–Jan. 1982), 106–25, is an analysis of comparative agricultural outputs between state and private farms in socialist Cuba on a crop-by-crop basis.

XIX. Foreign Relations

The literature on Cuban foreign relations falls broadly into two general categories: the pre-revolutionary phase, during which Cuban foreign relations were dominated almost entirely by the United States, to the virtual exclusion of the rest of the world, and the post-revolutionary period, during which Cuban foreign policy was concerned with the rest of the world, to the virtual exclusion of the United States. The literature on the former period is considerable, for which there exists a generally useful guide in David F. Trask, Michael C. Meyer, and Roger R. Trask, eds., *A Bibliography of United States-Latin American Relations Since 1810* (Lincoln, Neb., 1979). D. S. Whittlesey, "Geographical Factors in the Relations of the United States and Cuba," *Geographical Review* XII (April 1982), 241–56, argues that geography was the determining factor in the development of U.S.-Cuba relations. A useful general survey of U.S.-Cuba relations is found in Lester P. Langley, *The Cuban Policy of the United States* (New York, 1968). Philip Foner, *A History of Cuba and Its Relations with the United States* (2 vols., New York, 1962–65), surveys Cuban historical development against the backdrop of the U.S. presence. Herminio Portell Vilá, *Historia de Cuba en sus relaciones con los Estados Unidos y España* (4 vols., Havana, 1938–41), spans the years between the late eighteenth and early twentieth century and serves as one of the standard reference works for U.S.-Cuba relations during this period. Emilio Roig de Leuchsenring, *Cuba y los Estados Unidos, 1805–1898* (Havana, 1949), is a critical study of U.S. annexationist designs culminating in the 1898 intervention. Emeterio S. Santovenia, *El presidente Polk y Cuba* (Havana, 1936), provides a detailed account of U.S. policy during the 1840s, with particular attention to the variety of means employed by the United States to secure possession of the island. Jules R. Benjamin, *The United States and Cuba: Hegemony and Dependent Development* (Pittsburgh, 1977), examines the sources of U.S. hegemony in Cuba in a balanced treatment of politics, diplomacy, and economic development. Leland H. Jenks, *Our Cuban Colony* (New York, 1928), is a critical study of U.S. economic penetration of Cuba during the late nineteenth and early twentieth century. The book offers a wealth of data and information concerning U.S. investments in sugar, utilities, transportation, mining, and banks. Robert Freeman Smith, *The United States and Cuba: Business and Diplomacy, 1917–1960* (New Haven, Conn., 1960), chronicles the inter-relationship between the North American economic stake on the island and U.S. policy formulation. Emilio Roig de Leuchsenring, "Análisis y consecuencias de la intervención norteamericana en los asuntos interiores de Cuba," *Cuba Contemporánea* XXXII (June 1923), 138–53, examines the changing forms of U.S. intervention in Cuban internal affairs under the auspices of the Platt Amendment. Harry F. Guggenheim, *The United States and Cuba* (New York, 1934), is both a personal memoir and a historical narrative of U.S.-Cuba relations by a former ambassador to Cuba. Guggenheim served in Havana during the early 1930s and concluded that U.S. policy, and especially the Platt Amendment, had contributed significantly to the making of the Cuban political crisis. Irwin F. Gellman, *Roosevelt and Batista: Good Neighbor Diplomacy in Cuba, 1933–1945* (Albuquerque, N.M., 1973), is an account of U.S.-Cuba relations during the 1930s and early 1940s. The work examines the shifts in U.S. policy during these years, concluding that the exercise of North American hegemony, although modified, remained substantially unaffected, rhetoric notwithstanding. Morris H. Morley, "The U.S. Imperial State in Cuba, 1952–1958: Policymaking and Capitalist Interests," *Journal of Latin American Studies* XIV (May 1982), 143–70, is an analysis of U.S. hegemony in Cuba during the last Batista period, with attention to the relationship between U.S. capital and the Batista government.

The study of U.S.-Cuba relations after 1959 conforms to two general categories: the period between the triumph of the revolution in January 1959 and the rupture of diplomatic relations in January 1961, and all the rest. Earl E. T. Smith, *The Fourth Floor: An Account of the Castro Communist Revolution* (New York, 1962), is a personal memoir of U.S.-Cuba relations between 1957 and 1959 by a former ambassador. Smith is critical of State Department policy, arguing that ineptitude in Washington contributed to the triumph of communism in Cuba. Philip W. Bonsal,

Cuba, Castro, and the United States (Pittsburgh, 1971), is also a first-person account by the last U.S. ambassador to Cuba, chronicling the final months of formal diplomatic relations between the countries. Leland J. Johnson, "U.S. Business Interests in Cuba and the Rise of Castro," *World Politics* XVII (April 1965), 440–59, examines the relationship between U.S. investments and the course of political relations between Havana and Washington during the early 1960s, with specific attention to role of U.S. economic interests in contributing to the radicalization of the revolution. Richard E. Welch, Jr., *Response to Revolution: The United States and the Cuban Revolution, 1959–1961* (Chapel Hill, N.C., 1985), examines the last two years of diplomatic relations from four different perspectives: background to revolution, the Eisenhower-Kennedy policy, the role of North American public opinion, and U.S.-Cuba relations in the larger context of the Cold War. Donald Losman, "The Embargo of Cuba: An Economic Appraisal," *Caribbean Studies* XIV (Oct. 1974), 95–119, is a detailed examination of the economic dislocation and production disruptions caused by the U.S. trade embargo.

The Bay of Pigs (Playa Girón) invasion is detailed in several works. Haynes E. Johnson, *The Bay of Pigs* (New York, 1964), is a journalistic account of the 1961 invasion based principally on published materials and interviews with exile participants. Peter Wyden, *Bay of Pigs: The Untold Story* (New York, 1979), relies on interviews with participants both in Cuba and in the United States and on archival materials obtained through the Freedom of Information Act. Howard Hunt, *Give Us This Day* (New Rochelle, N.Y., 1973), provides a first-person account of the invasion as told by one of the C.I.A. organizers. A first-rate documentary collection is found in Paramilitary Study Group, *Operation Zapata: The "Ultrasensitive" Report and Testimony of the Board of Inquiry on the Bay of Pigs* (Frederick, Md., 1981). For Cuban accounts of the invasion see Justina Alvarez, *Heroes eternos de la patria* (Havana 1964); Rafael Pino, *Amanecer en Girón* (Havana, 1964); Raúl González, *Gente de Playa Girón* (Havana, 1962); and Lisandro Otero, *Playa Girón, derrota del imperialismo* (4 vols., Havana, 1961–62).

Several other studies chronicle the conduct of U.S. covert operations against Cuba during the 1960s and 1970s. Bradley Earl Ayers, *The War That Never Was: An Insider's Account of CIA Covert Operations Against Cuba* (Indianapolis, Ind., 1976), is a first-person account of sabotage against Cuba in the aftermath of the Bay of Pigs. Warren Hinckle and William W. Turner, *The Fish Is Red: The Story of the Secret War Against*

Castro (New York, 1981), examines covert activities against Cuba during the 1960s and 1970s, concentrating on U.S. efforts to sabotage Cuban industry, disrupt agricultural production, and assassinate Fidel Castro.

U.S.-Cuban relations, or non-relations, after 1961 is the subject of several studies. Lynn Darrell Bender, *The Politics of Hostility: Castro's Revolution and U.S. Policy* (Hato Rey, P.R., 1975), surveys U.S. policy and Cuban response. Attention is given to the effect of Soviet-Cuba relations on North American diplomacy. Lynn Darrell Bender, "U.S. Cuban Policy under the Nixon Administration: Subtle Modifications," *Revista/Review Interamericana* II (Fall 1972), 330–41, analyzes U.S. policy during the late 1960s and early 1970s, during which Bender argues that Washington adopted a "semi-conciliatory posture" toward Cuba. John Plank, ed., *Cuba and the United States: Long Range Perspectives* (Washington, D.C., 1967), is a collection of ten essays exploring various aspects of U.S.-Cuba relations. Among the themes discussed are historical antecedents, economic factors, U.S. response to the revolution, the Cold War, bilateral relations in a hemispheric context, and military-strategic considerations. Roger W. Fontaine, *On Negotiating with Cuba* (Washington, D.C., 1975), is based on the assumption that at some future date the United States and Cuba will normalize relations. The study discusses the principal issues before both countries, paying attention to historical dimensions of the conflict, problems of large power-small power relations, and the advantages to both countries in conducting normal political relations.

Cuban foreign policy after the revolution has been the subject of several anthologies and general studies. Martin Weinstein, ed., *Revolutionary Cuba in the World Arena* (Philadelphia, 1979), looks at Cuban relations with the Soviet Union; Cuba in Africa; military, ideological, and economic aspects of Cuban foreign policy; and the role of Cuban exiles in shaping the U.S.-Cuban policy. Cole Blasier and Carmelo Mesao-Lago, eds., *Cuba in the World* (Pittsburgh, 1979), is a collection of essays examining various aspects of Cuban foreign policy, including theoretical issues and relations with the United States, the Soviet Union, and Latin America. H. Michael Erisman, *Cuba's International Relations: The Anatomy of a Nationalistic Foreign Policy* (Boulder, Colo., 1985), examines the nationalist sources of Cuban foreign policy after 1959. Erisman argues that the nationalist aspects of Cuban global policies have been obscured by charges that Havana functions as a surrogate of the Soviet Union. Carla Anne Robbins, *The Cuban Threat* (New York, 1983), is a survey of Cuban foreign policy and North American responses between the early 1960s and the early 1980s. Jorge I. Domínguez, "Cuban Foreign Policy," *Foreign Affairs* LVII (Fall 1978), 83–108, traces Cuban foreign policy between the 1960s and 1970s as expressed in its policy toward Africa, Latin America, and the Soviet Union. Two books published in Havana, *Política internacional de la revolución cubana* (2 vols., Havana, 1966), and Juan J. Soto Valdespino, ed., *Proyección internacional de la revolución cubana* (Havana, 1975), contain the principal speeches, essays, and lectures of Cuban leaders dealing with the foreign policy of revolutionary government.

Cuban relations in Latin America is the subject of William E. Ratliff, *Castroism and Communism in Latin America, 1959–1976* (Stanford, Calif., 1976). The study analyzes the interaction of Soviet and Chinese communism and its effect on Cuban policy. Boris Goldenberg, *The Cuban Revolution and Latin America* (New York, 1965), is a two-part study: one devoted to a general account of the revolution and the other examining the impact of the revolution in Latin America. Along similar lines, Alfonso González, "Castro: Economic Effects on Latin America," *Journal of Inter-American Studies* XI (April 1969), 286–309, assesses the early impact of Cuban developments in Latin America, including the emergence of reformist regimes, increased foreign aid, and the expansion of U.S. markets for Latin American exports. Jorge I. Domínguez, "Cuba's Relations with Caribbean and Central American Countries," *Cuban Studies/Estudios Cubanos* XIII (Summer 1983), 79–112, analyzes Cuban policy in the region between 1979 and 1981, stressing objectives, means, and phases. A Cuban view is presented in Juan Valdés Paz, "Cuba and the Crisis in Central America," *Contemporary Marxism* X (1985), 38–67, arguing that Havana's foreign policy in the region must be understood in the context of U.S. policy initiatives in Central America. Barry Levine, ed., *The New Cuban Presence in the Caribbean* (Boulder, Colo., 1983), is a collection of essays examining geopolitical and cultural competition in the Caribbean and various aspects of Cuban relations with the Commonwealth Caribbean, Mexico, Venezuela, Panama, the United States, and the Soviet Union. Anthony P. Maingot, "Cuba and the Commonwealth Caribbean," *Caribbean Review* IX (Winter 1980), 7–10, 44–49, details the history of diplomatic relations between Cuba and the English-speaking West Indies, with special attention to Jamaica, Grenada, and Trinidad. Steve C. Ropp, "Cuba and Panama," *Caribbean Review* IX (Winter 1980), 15–20, is a brief review of diplomatic relations between

Cuba and Panama since 1959, with emphasis on the period of the Torrijos regime in Panama. William M. LeoGrande, "Cuba and Nicaragua: From the Somozas to the Sandinistas," *Caribbean Review* IX (Winter 1980), 11–14, surveys relations between Havana and Managua between 1959 and 1979. The essays deal with Somoza's opposition to the Cuban revolution, Cuban support of the anti-Somoza opposition, and the collaboration between the Sandinistas and Cuba. Olga Pellicer de Brody, *México y la revolución cubana* (México, 1972), is a general study of Mexico's foreign policy toward the Cuban revolution. Miles D. Wolpin, *Cuban Foreign Policy and Chilean Politics* (Lexington, Mass., 1972), examines the impact in Chile of the Cuban revolution and U.S. policy toward the revolution for the years between 1959 and 1970.

Cuban policy in Africa is surveyed in William LeoGrande, *Cuba's Policy in Africa, 1959–1980* (Berkeley, 1980). June Belkin and Carmelo Mesa-Lago, eds., *Cuba in Africa* (Pittsburgh, 1982), is a collection of essays dealing variously with overviews of Cuban policy in Angola, Ethiopia, and the Eritrean question. Gordon Adams and Michael Locker, "Cuba and Africa: The Politics of the Liberation Struggle," *Cuba Review* VIII (Oct. 1978), 3–9, examines Cuba's African policy in a larger context of African developments and U.S.-African policy. Nelson P. Valdés, "Cuban Foreign Policy in the Horn of Africa," *Cuban Studies/ Estudios Cubanos* X (Jan. 1980), 49–80, assesses Cuban relations with Somalia and Ethiopia as it impinged on the Eritrean question. William J. Durch, "The Cuban Military in Africa and the Middle East: from Algeria to Angola," *Studies in Comparative Communism* XI (Spring/Summer 1978), 34–74, examines Cuban policy toward Africa, Syria, and Iraq between 1959 and 1970 through a concise and detailed chronology of the development of Cuban armed forces in the region. Jiri Valenta, "The Soviet-Cuban Intervention in Angola, 1975," *Studies in Comparative Communism* XI (Spring/Summer 1978), 3–33, is an analysis of the decisive role played by Cuban military forces in the Angolan liberation movement. Jorge I. Domínguez, "Political and Military Limitations and Consequences of Cuban Policies in Africa," *Cuban Studies/Estudios Cubanos* X (July 1980), 1–35, examines the political and economic costs of Cuban military involvement in Africa and the Cuban role as a source of stability and restraint in the internal affairs of its African allies. Along similar lines, Sergio Roca, "Economic Aspects of Cuban Involvement in Africa," *Cuban Studies/Estudios Cubanos* X (July 1980), 55–90, provides a detailed cost-benefit analysis of Cuban policy in Africa during the 1970s.

A number of studies examine Cuban relations with the Soviet Union. Angel García and Piotr Mironchuk, *Esbozo histórico de las relaciones entre Cuba-Rusia y Cuba-URRS* (Havana, 1976), surveys relations between both countries beginning in the nineteenth century. Blanca Torres Ramírez, *Las relaciones cubano-soviéticos, 1959–1968* (Mexico, 1971), is a chronological study of Cuban-Soviet relations. The book deals successively in four chapters with the early period (1959–60), the integration of Cuba into the socialist bloc (1960–62), the period of conflict (1963–65), and the years of greatest tension (1966–68). W. Raymond Duncan, *The Soviet Union and Cuba: Interests and Influence* (New York, 1985), provides a comprehensive analysis of relations between both countries. The chronological study stresses the economic and international determinants of foreign policy. D. Bruce Jackson, *Castro, the Kremlin, and Communism in Latin America* (Baltimore, Md., 1969), is a study of Cuba-Soviet relations within the larger context of the socialist bloc for the years between 1964 and 1967. Cole Blasier, "The Cuban-U.S.-Soviet Triangle: Changing Angles," *Cuban Studies/Estudios Cubanos* VIII (January 1978), 1–9, surveys the interaction of relations among the Soviet Union, the United States, and Cuba, with particular attention to the Carter years. Jacques Levesque, *The USSR and the Cuban Revolution: Soviet Ideological and Strategical Imperatives, 1959–1977* (New York, 1978), is a detailed study of Soviet-Cuban relations, with emphasis on the Soviet perspective.

XX. Armed Forces

A number of studies examine the role of the armed forces in Cuba during the colonial period, in the republic, and after the revolution. Allan J. Kuethe, "The Development of the Cuban Military as a Socio-Political Elite, 1763–1783," *Hispanic American Historical Review* LXI (Nov. 1981), 695–705, provides an overview of the impact of the Bourbon military reforms in Cuban society. Louis A. Pérez, Jr., *Army Politics in Cuba, 1898–1958* (Pittsburgh, 1976), traces the development of the Cuban army from its inception in 1899 through its collapse in the late 1950s. Allan R. Millet, "The Rise and Fall of the Cuban Rural Guard, 1898–

1912," *The Americas* XXIX (Oct. 1972), 191–213, surveys U.S. efforts to organize the Rural Guard in the course of two armed interventions (1899–1902 and 1906–9). The essay examines the emergence of the Rural Guard as a political force under the Liberal government of José Miguel Gómez (1909–12). Maricela Mateo, "El ejército oligárquico en la política neocolonial cubana (1925–1952)," *Santiago*, no. 22 (June 1976), 87–120, surveys the role of the army from Machado to Batista. Emphasis falls on the relations between the armed forces and the Auténtico governments of 1933–34 and 1944–52. Federico Chang, *El ejército nacional de la república neocolonial, 1899–1933* (Havana, 1981) provides one of the most thorough studies of the armed forces during the early decades of the republic, to the collapse of the National Army in the wake of the sergeants' revolt. Emphasis is given to government military expenditures and the ideological formation of the officer corps. Jorge Mañach, *El militarismo en Cuba* (Havana, 1939), is a collection of essays generally critical of the expanding role of the army in national life during the late 1930s.

A number of studies have looked at the Cuban armed forces after the triumph of the revolution. Louis A. Pérez, Jr., "Army Politics in Socialist Cuba," *Journal of Latin American Studies* VIII (Nov. 1976), 251–71, traces the early origins and development of the Rebel Army and its emergence as a political force in the first decade of the revolution. Irving Louis Horowitz, "Military Origins of the Cuban Revolution," *Armed Forces and Society* I (Summer 1975), 402–18, suggests that the importance of the armed forces in Cuba after 1959 originated with the guerrilla war and that as political problems increased during the 1960s, it was a natural response for the leadership to rely on military solutions. C. Fred Judson, *Cuba and the Revolutionary Myth: The Political Education of the Cuban Rebel Army, 1953–1963* (Boulder, Colo., 1984), examines the historico-social sources of revolutionary esprit for the Rebel Army during the armed struggle of the 1950s. Judson assesses how the successes and victories of the Rebel Army during the 1950s themselves became part of the revolutionary myth that served for the political education of the new armed forces to emerge after 1959. Emilio T. González, "The Development of the Cuban Army," *Military Review* LXI (April 1981), 56–64, provides a general overview of the development of the armed forces from the early days of the guerrilla war to the organization of the Revolutionary Armed Forces (FAR). Particular treatment is given to the performance of Cuban army units in Angola and Ethiopia. William M. Leo-

Grande, "Civil-Military Relations in Cuba: Party Control and Political Socialization," *Studies in Comparative Communism* XI (Autumn 1978), 278–91, examines the relations between the FAR and various civil political organizations, culminating in the organization of the Cuban communist party (PCC).

XXI. Constitutional Developments

Several different volumes contain the full texts of nineteenth- and twentieth-century Cuban constitutions. Leonel Antonio de la Cuesta, ed., *Constituciones cubanas, desde 1812 hasta nuestros días* (New York, 1974), is a compilation of all constitutions beginning with the Spanish constitution of 1812, through the constitutions of the various insurgent provisional governments between 1868 and 1898, the 1901 and the 1940 constitutions, through the Fundamental Law of the Cuban revolution (1959). Included too are the amendments and legislative revisions made for the constitutions of 1901 and 1940. The volume contains an extensive annotated bibliography of Cuban constitutional law. Andrés M. Lazcano y Mazón, *Las constituciones de Cuba* (Madrid, 1952), provides a compilation of Cuban constitutions accompanied by extensive commentary dealing with constitutional law and history. Antonio Barrera y Martínez, ed., *Textos de las constituciones de Cuba (1812–1940)* (Havana, 1940), is a compilation of Cuban constitutions. Fernando Alvarez Tabio, *Teoría general de la constitución cubana* (Havana, 1946), provides a well-conceived study of the theory of constitutional law in Cuba. It is essential to all work dealing with Cuban jurisprudence and constitutional theory. Juan Clemente Zamora y López, *Derecho constitucional* (Havana, 1925), provides a collection of select documents for the study of Cuban constitutional history. Enrique Hernández Corujo, *Historia constitucional de Cuba* (2 vols., Havana, 1960), is a sweeping historical survey of constitutional law in Cuba through the nineteenth and twentieth century. Similarly, Ramón Infiesta, *Historial constitucional de Cuba* (Havana, 1942), provides a balanced constitutional history designed principally as an introduction to Cuban law. Antonio Bravo y Correoso, *Como se hizo la constitución de Cuba* (Havana, 1928) is an informative first-person account by a member of the 1901 Constituent Assembly. The memoir provides important insights into the discussions and debates preliminary to the ratification of the first republican constitution. José Clemente Vivanco, *Constitución de la república de Cuba* (Havana, 1902), is a detailed commentary on the 1901 constitution by a leading Cuban jurist. Enrique Gay Calbó, *Nuestro problema constitucional* (Havana, 1936), review changing conditions in Cuba during the 1930s, with emphasis on those politico-juridical issues that contributed to making the 1901 constitution obsolete. Enrique Hernández Corujo, *Los fundamentos históricos y filosóficos de la constitución de 1901* (Havana, 1953), provides a discussion of the nineteenth-century juridical antecedents and philosophical inspiration for the 1901 constitution. Gustavo Ramírez Olivella, *Jurisprudencia constitucional (1903–1944)* (Havana, 1944), analyzes cases and judicial reviews affecting the constitutionality of laws, statutes, and presidential decrees as settled by the Cuban supreme court *(Tribunal Supremo).* Angel C. Betancourt y Miranda, *Jurisprudencia cubana* (2 vols., Havana, 1912–29), provides a comprehensive discussion of the theory and practice of Cuban jurisprudence. The topics examined include criminal law, constitutional law, and the administration of justice. Marco Ortega y Díaz, *Nociones sobre la constitución de 1940* (Havana, 1947), serves a juridical treatise on the 1940 constitution. Emilio Menéndez Menéndez, *La nueva constitución cubana y jurisprudencia (1940–1941)* (Havana, 1945), provides the full text of the 1940 constitution and the acts and judgments passed under its auspices during the first four years of its promulgation. Juan B. Moré y Benítez, ed., *Leyes complementarias de la constitución* (Havana, 1941), is a compilation of articles of the 1940 constitution requiring additional legislation in the form of by-laws. Juan José Casasús, *La constitución a la luz de la doctrina magistral y de la jurisprudencia* (Havana, 1946), is a ranging study of the 1940 constitution, containing extensive commentary on the debates of the constituent assembly, discussion of the juridical antecedents of key portions of the constitution, and commentary on the impact of the new law of the land. Andrés M. Lazcano y Mazón, *Constitución de Cuba* (3 vols., Havana, 1941), is a compilation of the transcripts of the key debates and discussions of the 1940 constituent assembly, indispensable to understanding the juridical, philosophical, and ideological currents dominating the constituent assembly. Leonel Antonio de la Cuesta, ''The Cuban Socialist Constitution: Its Originality and Role in Institutionalization,'' *Cuban Studies/Estudios Cubanos* VI (July 1975), 15–30, examines the 1976 constitution with attention to the sources of the document and role of the new constitution in the larger process of institutionalization. Fernando Alvarez Tabio, *Comentarios a la constitución socialista* (Havana, 1981), provides an analysis of the 1976 constitution based on the central argument that the island's transition to Marxist-Leninist legality was consistent with Cuba's historico-juridical traditions. Julio Fernández Bulte, Gilberto Muñoz, Miguel A. D'Estefano, and Mercedes Rodríguez, *Derecho constitucional* (Havana, n.d.), is a comprehensive volume by four members of the University of Havana Law School examining the sources and origins of socialist constitutionality, beginning with the 1812 constitution and continuing through the subsequent magna cartas of the nineteenth and twentieth century.

XXII. Literature, Plastic Arts, and Performing Arts

Several bibliographical guides serve as useful research aids to the study of Cuban literature: David William Foster, *Cuban Literature: A Research Guide* (New York, 1984); Jeremiah D. M. Ford and Maxwell I. Raphael, eds. *A Bibliography of Cuban Belles-Lettres* (Cambridge, Mass., 1933); Lourdes Casal, ed., "The Cuban Novel, 1959–1969: An Annotated Bibliography," *Abraxas* I (Fall 1970), 77–92; Lourdes Casal, ed., "A Bibliography of Cuban Creative Literature, 1958–1971," *Cuban Studies/Estudios Cubanos* II (June 1972), 2–29; Terry J. Peavler, ed., "Prose Fiction Criticism and Theory in Cuban Journals: An Annotated Bibliography," *Cuban Studies/Estudios Cubanos* VII (Jan. 1977), 58–118; Matías Montes Huidobro and Yara González, eds., *Bilbiografía crítica de la poesía cubana* (New York, 1972); Bilbioteca Nacional "José Martí," Departamento Colección Cubana, *Bibliografía de poesía cubana en el siglo XIX* (Havana, 1965); and Roberto González Echeverría, and Klaus Muller-Bergh, eds., *Alejo Carpentier, Bibliographical Guide* (Westport, Conn., 1983).

Several surveys provide useful historical overviews of Cuban literature. Juan J. Remos y Rubio, *Historia de la literatura cubana* (3 vols., Havana, 1945), is a comprehensive chronological survey of Cuban literature, discussing the varieties of Cuban literature and their principal exponents. José Antonio Fernández de Castro, *Esquema histórico de las letras en Cuba, 1548–1902* (Havana, 1949), provides a general historical survey of Cuban literature, with particular emphasis on the literature of the struggle for independence. The work spans the period from conquest and colonization to the 1940s. Max Henríquez Ureña, *Panorama histórico de la literatura cubana* (2 vols., New York, 1963), examines Cuban literary developments from Spanish colonization through the 1950s. The two volumes examine virtually all principal literary forms, including novels, essays, journalism, drama, poetry, historical narrative, and literary criticism. Raimundo Lazo, *La literatura cubana. Esquema histórico desde sus orígenes hasta 1964* (Mexico, 1965), provides a historical survey of Cuban literature in chronological fashion in the following format: antecedents (1492–1790), the colony (1790–1834), the period of cultural transformation (1834–68), the struggle for independence (1868–1902), the early republic (1902–40), the bourgeois republic (1940–59), and the revolution (1959–64). Juan Remos y Rubio, *Proceso histórico de las letras cubanas* (Madrid, 1958), José Antonio Portuondo, *Bosquejo histórico de las letras cubanas* (Havana, 1960), and Salvador Bueno, *Historia de la literatura cubana* (3rd ed., Havana, 1963) survey the diverse forms of Cuban literature from the Spanish conquest and colonization to the early years of the revolution. Instituto de Literatura y Lingüística, Academia de Ciencias de Cuba, *Perfil histórico de las letras cubanas desde los orígenes hasta 1898* (Havana, 1983), places the pre-twentieth-century antecedents of national literature into three general categories: origins (1492–1790), formation of national consciousness (1790–1878), and crystallization (1879–98). Marguerite C. Suárez-Murias, "La novela en Cuba en el siglo XIX," *Revista Interamericana de Bibliografía* XI (June 1961), 125–36, surveys the development of the nineteenth-century novel, with particular emphasis on the works of Cirilo Villaverde, José Antonio Echeverría, Anselmo Suárez y Romero, José Zacarías González del Valle, Gertrudis Gómez de Avellaneda, and Ramón Pina. Raymond D. Souza, *Major Cuban Novelists: Innovation and Tradition* (Columbia, Mo., 1976), examines the evolution of the novel from the 1850s to the revolution. Souza argues that the development of the Cuban novel is closely related to the emergence of national consciousness and the creation of national identity. The *costumbrista* literature of the eighteenth and nineteenth centuries is examined in Roberta Day Corbitt, "A Survey of Cuban Costumbrismo," *Hispania* XXXIII (Feb. 1950), 41–45, and Emilo Roig de Leuchsenring, *La literatura costumbrista cubana de los siglos XVIII y XIX: los escritores* (Havana, 1962). Marcelo Pogolotti, *La república de Cuba al través de sus escritores* (Havana, 1958), reviews the varieties of Cuban literature during the twentieth century, with particular attention to the means by which national literature reflects both popular moods and political conditions in the republic. Salvador Bueno, *Temas y personajes de la literatura cubana* (Havana, 1964), surveys nineteenth- and twentieth-century literature, with specific emphasis on literary movements, individual writers, and the principal literary journals that influenced national trends.

Poetry is surveyed in Roberto Fernández Retamar, *La poesía contemporánea en Cuba (1927–1953)* (Havana, 1954), giving attention to social commentary, the influence of race, and vanguard poets. Martín González del Valle, *La poesía lírica en Cuba* (Barcelona, 1900), provides a critical discussion of Cuban lyric poetry of the nineteenth century. Marta Linares Pérez, *La poesía pura en Cuba y su evolución* (Madrid, 1975), examines the poets of the early twentieth century, particularly Mariano Brull, Emilio Ballagas, and Eugenio Floret. Samuel Feijóo, ed., *El movimiento de los romances cubanos del siglo XIX* (Santa Clara, 1964), is an anthology of Cuban romantic poetry of the nineteenth century, most of which serves as an affirmation of things Cuban and a rejection of Spanish rule. Cintio Vitier, ed., *Cincuenta años de poesía cubana (1902–1952)* (Havana, 1952), provides an anthology of Cuban poetry. The introductory essay is a useful summary of the development of national poetry in the republic. Nathaniel Tarn, *Con Cuba. An Anthology of Cuban Poetry of the Last Sixty Years* (London, 1969), is a collection of Cuban poems with English translations.

Interest in post-revolutionary Cuban literature has resulted in a number of important studies. Seymour Menton, *Prose Fiction of the Cuban Revolution* (Austin, Texas, 1975), provides a comprehensive overview of the historical and social forces shaping fiction in socialist Cuba, organizing a periodization schema of four distinct phases: 1959–60, the struggle against tyranny; 1961–65, exorcism and existentialism; 1966–1970, experimentation and escapism; and 1971–75, the ideological novel and short story. Joseph Pereira, "Towards a Theory of Literature in Revolutionary Cuba," *Caribbean Quarterly* XXI (March–June 1975), 62–73, discusses the theoretical context of Cuban literature after 1959 with attention to the role of political leadership in the development of a theory and the subsequent founding of various literary journals and agencies. Roberta Salper, "Literature and Revolution in Cuba," *Monthly Review* XXII (Oct. 1970), 15–30, is a general survey of the post-1959 literature as it reflected the changing course of the revolutionary policies. Roberto González-Echeverría, "Criticism and Literature in Revolutionary Cuba," *Cuban Studies/Estudios Cubanos* XI (Jan. 1981), 1–17, examines literary criticism in socialist Cuba with specific attention to academic criticism and journalistic criticism. Mario Benedetti, *Literatura y arte nuevo en Cuba* (Barcelona, 1977), provides a collection of essays dealing with post-1959 journalism,

Afro-Cuban poetry, social influences on the novel, and the role of intellectuals. Julio E. Miranda, *Nueva literatura cubana* (Madrid, 1971), surveys post-1959 literary forms, including poetry, historical narrative, literary criticism, essays, and drama. William L. Siemens, "Recent Developments in the Cuban Novel," *Revista/Review Interamericana* VIII (Summer 1978), 305–8, is a description of the condition of the novel in socialist Cuba with attention to Guillermo Cabrera Infante, José Lezama Lima, and Alejo Carpentier. Bell Gale Chevigny, "Running the Blockade: Six Cuban Writers," *Socialist Review* XI (Sept.–Oct. 1981), 83–112, provides informative profiles of six prominent Cuban writers based on extensive interviews: Pablo Armando Fernández, Humberto Arenal, Miguel Barnet, Reynaldo González, Nancy Morejón, and Manuel Pereira. J. M. Cohen, ed., *Writers in the New Cuba* (Baltimore, Md., 1967), is an anthology of authors representative of post-1959 trends. The collection contains short stories, poetry, and one-act plays.

Studies of the visual arts deal principally with painting, cinema, caricature, and poster art. José Manuel Carbonell y Rivero, *Las bellas artes en Cuba* (Miami, 1970), is a survey of Cuban art from 1519 to 1960s, including painting, architecture, and sculpture. Jorge Mañach, "La pintura en Cuba," *Cuba Contemporánea* XXXVI (Sept. 1924), 5–23 and Oct. 1924, pp. 105–25, examines the history of painting in Cuba from the early sixteenth to the early twentieth century. Juan Marinello "Nuestro arte y las circunstancias nacionales," *Cuba Contemporánea* XXXVII (April 1925), 298–304, comments on the emergence of a national style of painting and sculpture, arguing that plastic arts should serve to uplift national spirit and promote national pride. Adelaida de Juan, *Dos ensayos sobre plástica cubana* (Santiago de Chile, 1972), is a general survey of twentieth-century Cuban painting. Emilio C. Cueto, "A Short Guide to Old Cuban Prints," *Cuban Studies/Estudios Cubanos* XIV (Winter 1984), 27–42, is a discussion of the most important Cuban graphics made during the colonial period. Some 200 prints are identified in alphabetical order, indicating location of originals and availability of reproductions. The most comprehensive account of the history and development of Cuban cinema over the past century is Michael Chanan, *The Cuban Image* (London, 1985). The study establishes relationships between artistic achievements and technical advances on one hand, and socio-historical context on the other. Andrés R. Hernández, "Cinema and Politics: The Cuban Experience," *Cuba Resource Center Newsletter* III (Oct. 1973), 19–22, surveys the history of Cuban cinema from the end of the nineteenth century to the post-1959 period, with emphasis on the latter. Arturo Agramonte, *Cronología del cine cubano* (Havana, 1966), is a historical survey of Cuban film from the late nineteenth century to the mid-1960s. The varieties of Cuban film examined include melodramas, animation, and documentaries. Michael Myerson, ed., *Memories of Underdevelopment: The Revolutionary Films of Cuba* (New York, 1973), is a collection of essays examining the development of socialist cinema. The volume includes portions of movie scripts, interviews, and critical studies of several major films. Bernard G. Garros, "La caricatura en Cuba," *Cuba Contemporánea* V (July 1914), 313–25, and Aug. 1914, pp. 458–73, chronicles the history of this popular national art form, beginning with the early nineteenth century through the 1910s. The essay gives particular attention to the means by which caricature served as a form of political commentary. Dugald Stermer and Susan Sontag, *The Art of Revolution* (New York, 1970), is a richly illustrated over-sized volume containing reproductions of Cuban poster art. An introductory essay provides an informative treatment of the aesthetic and function of poster artist. Stephanie Rugoff, "Posters from and for the People," *Cuba Resource Center Newsletter* III (Oct. 1973), is a general discussion of poster art based on an interview with artist Félix Beltrán.

Several works deal with the development of theater in pre- and postrevolutionary Cuba. Yolanda Aguirre, *Apuntes sobre el teatro colonial (1790–1833)* (Havana, 1969), examines the development of theater during its formative period. Attention is given principally to theater in Havana and the administration and function of stage productions. Edwin Teurbe Tolón and José Antonio González, *Historia del teatro en La Habana* (Santa Clara, 1961), provides a historical survey of theater from the late eighteenth through the end of the nineteenth century, with attention to the varieties of theater performed in Havana, including Italian and French operas, comedy, drama, and ballet. Natividad González Freire, *Teatro cubano, 1927–1961* (Havana, 1961), studies three generations of Cuban playwrights. The work provides biographical notes on leading dramatists, summaries of the context and content of their works, and general commentary on the evolution of both the form and the function of Cuban theater. George W. Woodward, "Perspectives on Cuban Theater," *Revista/Review Interamericana* IX (Spring 1979), 42–49, surveys the development of drama in post-1959 Cuba, with attention to the role of state support of theater, the intellectual climate in which playwrights work, and policies governing productions. Paul Christoper Smith, "Theater and

Political Criteria in Cuba: Casa de las Américas Awards, 1960–1983,'' *Cuban Studies/Estudios Cubanos* XIV (Winter 1984), 43–47, analyzes the interaction between shifting ideological developments and shifting artistic modes of expression. "Transforming Theater," *Cuba Review* VII (Dec. 1977), 3–24, is a special issue dedicated to an assessment of developments in theater in socialist Cuba. Among the topics examined are children's theater, popular theater, rural theater, and interviews with several Cuban actors and playwrights.

Dance and music are examined in a number of studies. Aaron Segal, "Dance and Diplomacy: The Cuban National Ballet," *Caribbean Review* IX (Winter 1980), 30–32, examines the role of the Cuban National Ballet in projecting a favorable image of Cuba in the world. The essay traces the development of the dance company under Alicia Alonso from its origins in 1960 through the 1970s. Miguel Cabrera, *Orbita del Ballet Nacional de Cuba: 1958–1979* (Havana, 1979), examines the origins, development, and expansion of the National Ballet Company after the triumph of the revolution. The work documents the impact of foreign dancers, the development of the repertoire, accounts of past tours, and biographies of Cubans most prominently associated with the company. Aurora Bosch, "Desarrollo de la danza en Cuba," *Revista de la Biblioteca Nacional "José Martí"* XXI (May–Aug. 1979), 89–102, examines the development of dance in Cuba since the triumph of the revolution, with particular attention to the National Ballet Company, the National Folklore Group, and the Ballet of Camagüey Province. José Ardevol, *Introducción a Cuba: la música* (Havana, 1969), is a collection of essays dealing with a wide range of themes, all of which are united by common concern for the social function of music in revolutionary Cuba. The essays examine variously the development of classical music as well as folk music, national and foreign composers, the national symphony, and the question of nationalism in music. Alejo Carpentier, *La música en Cuba* (Havana, 1961), provides a balanced historical account of the evolution of music in Cuba. The work deals with the colonial origins of national music, church influences, the influence of romanticism and nationalism, the Afro-Cuban impact, and the varieties of popular music. Sergio Fernández Barroso, "La música en Cuba durante le etapa revolucionaria," *Revista de la Biblioteca Nacional "José Martí"* XXI (May–Aug. 1979), 119–31, discusses the condition of music after 1959, paying attention to the development of music education programs, the establishment of a national recording industry, the organization of the National Symphony, and the manufacturing of musical instruments.

Several good introductions to Cuban architecture are available. F. Prat Puig, *El pre-barroco en Cuba* (Havana, 1947), examines colonial architecture during the first two centuries of Spanish rule, with attention to churches, monuments, public buildings, and private homes. Joaquín E. Weiss y Sánchez, *La arquitectura cubana del siglo XIX* (Havana, 1960), surveys developments in the nineteenth century, while Roberto Segre, "Continuidad y renovación en la arquitectura cubana del siglo XX," *Santiago* IV (March 1981), 9–35, investigates trends in the twentieth century. A thoughtful essay linking architectural styles and social class during the 1950s is found in Roberto Segre, "Contenido de clase en la arquitectura cubana de los años 50," *Revista de la Biblioteca Nacional "José Martí"* XVII (Sept.–Dec. 1975), 97–129. Works examining architecture in post-revolutionary Cuba include Carmen María Cuevas and José Peláez, "Cuba arquitectura y revolucion, 1959–1963," *Areíto* I (Jan.–March, 1974), 16–22, and Roberto Segre, *Diez años de arquitectura en Cuba revolucionaria* (Havana, 1970).

Index

ABC Revolutionary Society, 258, 265; organized, 257; participate in mediations (1933), 261; opposed to Grau govenment (1933), 269, 273; and 1940 Constitution, 281
Adams, John Quincy, 108-109
Afghanistan, 379-380, 381
Agramonte, Arístides, 228, 229
Agramonte, Ignacio, 121
Agrarian Reform Institute (INRA), 320
Agrarian Reform Law, 320; opposition to, 322
Agriculture, 10, 42; during colonial period, 28, 43-44; effects of independence war (1985–98), 190-191, 194-196; and Reciprocity Treaty (1903), 198-199; and Customs-Tariff Law (1927), 250; during depression (1920s–30s), 251-252, 253-254; and Reciprocity Treaty (1934), 280; during 1950s, 301-302; and Agrarian Reform Law, 320; attempt to diversify after 1959, 337-338; and Cuban revolution, 337-343
Agrupación Comunista de La Habana, 244
Aguado, Julio, 268
Agüero, Joaquín de, 111
Agüero Velasco, Francisco de, 101
Aguilera, Francisco Vicente, 121
Aldama, Miguel, 110, 112
Alfonso, José Luis, 110, 112
Algeria, 377, 378
Allende, Salvador, 378
Almeida, Juan, 294
Alzugaray, Carlos, 247
American Sugar Company, 196
Angola, 377, 378
Annexationism, 106-107, 111-112; 19th-century annexationist movements, 110-111; and Ten Years' War, 124-125; during U.S. occupation (1899–1902), 186-187

Anti-Imperialist League, 244
Aponte, José Antonio, 99
Arango y Parreño, Francisco de, 66
Arawak Indians, 16-20
Argentina, 129, 286, 296, 380
Armenteros, Isidro, 111
Arrate, Martín Félix de, 68
Asociación de Buen Gobierno, 235, 247
Asociación de Católicas Cubanas, 238
Asociación de Comerciantes de La Habana, 234, 247
Asociación de Hacendados y Colonos, 247
Asociación Nacional de Enfermeras, 238
Asociación Nacional de Industriales de Cuba, 235, 247
Asociación de Tabaqueros de La Habana, 119
Asociación Unión Nacionalista, 254, 265; opposition to Machado government, 259; participate in mediations (1933), 261; opposition to Grau government (1933), 269, 273; and 1940 Constitution, 281
Atkins, Edwin F., 138
Aurora, La, 119
Auténtico party (Partido Revolucionario Cubano), 313, 314; organized, 276; and 1940 Constitution, 281; in power (1944–1952), 283–288; and corruption, 284-285, 286; and Communist party, 288; ousted by Batista (1952), 288-289; attack on Goicuría barracks, 290; and armed forces, 294
Automomist party (Liberal party), 154; organized, 140-141; and colonial reforms, 142; and failure in colonial politics, 152-155; oppose 1958 revolution, 157, 158; and Valeriano Weyer, 168-170; and U.S. intervention, 174-175
Avance, 324
Ayesterán, Joaquín de, 94

496   INDEX

Baliño, Carlos, 244
Banco de Comercio, 131
Banco Español, 225
Banco Industrial, 131
Banco Internacional, 225
Banco Nacional, 224, 225, 226
Bank of Santa Catalina, 131
Banking: and 1880s depression, 131; for-
eign investment, 198; and "Dance of the
Millions," 224-226; and depression
(1920s–30s), 253
Barbour, George M., 180
Barnet, José A., 277
Barquín, Ramón, 294, 312
Barreiro, Alejandro, 244
Batista, Fulgencio, 272, 277, 314, 315;
and sergeants' revolt, 266; promoted
army chief, 273; and Summer Welles,
273-275; ousts Grau (1933), 275; and
Communist party, 277-278; and political
support (1930s), 278-279; and 1940
Constitution, 281; presidency (1940–
1944), 282-283; returns to power (1952),
288-289; elected president (1954), 290;
and guerrilla war, 291-294; army oppo-
sition to, 294-295; and corruption, 303-
304; and political opposition, 308-309;
and the United States (1950s), 309-311;
and 1958 elections, 310; ousted, 311-
312, 313
Bay of Pigs, 331, 348, 375
Bermúdez, Anacleto, 110
Betancourt Cisneros, Gaspar, 110
Bethlehem Steel Company, 198
Beveridge, Albert, 187
Bishop, Maurice, 380
Blanco, Manuel, 138
Bobadilla, Francisco de, 24
Boletín Tipográfico, El, 119
Bolivia, 376, 377
Bonsal, Philip W., 336
Bourbon dynasty, 57, 58; ascends to Span-
ish throne, 49; and colonial reforms, 50-
56, 59-60; and Charles III, 59
Brazil, 286, 296, 377
Bremer, Fredrika, 96
Brodie, Alexander, 180
Brooke, John R., 180

Cabañas y Carvajal, 119
Caja de Ahorros, 131
Calatrava, José María, 103

Cámara de Comercio, Industria y Navega-
ción, 235
Canada Land and Fruit Company, 196-197
Canadian Bank of Commerce, 224
Capablanca, Ramiro, 268
Carbó, Sergio, 267
Cárdenas City Water Works, 198
Cárdenas Railway and Terminal Company,
198
Carlson Investment Company, 196
Carreño, Alejo, 247
Carrión, Miguel de, 215
Cartaya, Jose Eliseo, 235
Castillo, Demetrio, 228, 229
Castro, Fidel, 12, 313, 348-349, 367; attack on Moncada barracks, 290; returns
to Cuba from Mexico (1956), 290-291;
and guerrilla war, 291-294; and Pact of
Caracas, 309; U.S. opposition to, 311;
arrival to Havana, 312; early revolutionary government, 313-319; appointed
prime minister, 316; relations with Communist party, 323; and anti-communism,
323-324; relations with Soviet Union;
and expropriation of foreign property,
325-326; economic development, 339-
340, 348-349, 353; foreign policy, 375-
381; and Non-Aligned Movement, 379
Castro, Raúl, 393, 294; and Communist
party; 310; appointed head of armed
forces, 324
Central Intelligence Agency (CIA), 325,
336, 347-348
Central Railway Company, 203
Centro de Propietarios, 141
Céspedes, Carlos Manuel de (1819–1874),
121, 122, 125
Céspedes, Carlos Manuel de (1871–1939),
8, 269, 271, 272; appointed to "honest
cabinet," 227-228; chosen president,
264; policies, 264-266; ousted, 266-267
Chadbourne Plan, 253
Charles III, 59
Chibás, Eduardo, 287-288
Chile, 286, 296, 377, 278
China, 115-116, 201, 326, 378
Ciboney Indians, 14-17, 19-20
Cienfuegos, Camilo, 294, 321
Cimarrones, 12
Círculo de Abogados, 141
Círculo de Hacendados y Agricultores,
141, 150

A-1